FROMMER'S
WHERE TO STAY USA

COUNCIL ON INTERNATIONAL
EDUCATIONAL EXCHANGE

Written by Marjorie A. Cohen
Edited by Deborah S. Joost

1988–89 Edition

Published by the Council on International Educational Exchange
205 East 42nd Street
New York, NY 10017
and
Prentice Hall Press
A Division of Simon & Schuster, Inc.
One Gulf + Western Plaza
New York, New York 10023

PRENTICE HALL PRESS is a trademark of Simon & Schuster, Inc.

Maps by Mark Stein Studios

ISBN 0-13-957234-1

Manufactured in the United States of America

*Although every effort was made to ensure the accuracy of price information appearing in this book,
it should be kept in mind that prices can and do fluctuate in the course of time.*

Contents

About This Book

When we first sat down to write *Where to Stay USA* 15 years ago, our purpose was simple enough: We wanted as many people as possible to enjoy an American experience, and we wanted them to be able to do it even on a limited budget. We've done what we set out to do, judging from the letters of praise and encouragement that we've received from readers. Many of these readers have sent us suggestions for additions, and we've followed up on all of them. You'll notice italicized quotes all the way through the book—these are from our readers.

We now have sections on 15 of the most visited U.S. cities. We cover New York, Washington, D.C., Denver, Houston, Phoenix, Los Angeles, San Francisco, San Diego, Chicago, Boston, St. Louis, Seattle, Miami, New Orleans, and Atlanta. In these sections we've tried to put enough information to give travelers a good start in a new, sometimes overwhelming city. We've included information on how to get around, where to stay, where to eat, what to see and do, and where to go for help and information.

Where to Stay is meant to be carried with you and used on the road, although some of the introductory sections should be read before you begin your trip. See pages 23–24 for an explanation of how the accommodation listings are set up—and be sure to read Chapter 2 so that you know what to expect from some of the accommodation facilities.

We should probably explain how we at the Council on International Educational Exchange (CIEE) first came to write this book on low-cost travel in the U.S. CIEE was founded in 1947 as the Council on Student Travel (it became CIEE in 1967), and since then it has been actively involved in helping thousands of students and other travelers plan their trips both abroad and in the U.S. It is a membership organization made up of nearly 200 colleges, universities, secondary schools, national organizations, and youth-serving agencies. Since its founding, CIEE has been arranging transportation and providing information and advisory services for both educational groups and individual students. Any U.S. student planning to travel abroad or in North America will want to get a free copy of CIEE's *Student Travel Catalog,* which describes the services offered by CIEE to both students and non-students. These services include the International Student Identity Card (ISIC), which entitles eligible students to a number of travel-related discounts and services in the U.S. and abroad; budget flight information and travel services to Europe, Latin America, Asia, Africa, and the Middle East; scheduled transportation from the U.S. to all parts of the world and within the U.S.; student/youth flights connecting European cities with points in the Middle East, Africa, and Asia; worldwide educational tours; information and publications on international study, travel, and work opportunities—including *Work, Study, Travel Abroad: The Whole World*

Handbook; Volunteer! The Comprehensive Guide to Voluntary Service in the U.S. and Abroad; The Teenager's Guide to Study, Travel, and Adventure Abroad; and the 64-page *Student Travel Catalog;* work abroad programs in the United Kingdom, Ireland, Germany, France, Costa Rica, and New Zealand—a service that provides U.S. students with work authorization and information on how to find jobs; a student center and student hotel at the New York Student Center, William Sloane House, 356 West 34th St., New York, NY 10001.

Council Travel Offices

New York: 205 East 42nd St., New York, NY 10017 (tel. 212/661-1450).

New York: 35 West 8th St., New York, NY 10011 (tel. 212/254-2525).

San Francisco: 312 Sutter St., San Francisco, CA 94108 (tel. 415/421-3473).

San Francisco: 919 Irving St., San Francisco, CA 94122 (tel. 415/566-6222).

Berkeley: 2511 Channing Way, Berkeley, CA 94704 (tel. 415/848-8604).

Los Angeles: 1093 Broxton Ave., Los Angeles, CA 90024 (tel. 213/208-3551).

Sherman Oaks: 14515 Ventura Blvd., Suite 250, Sherman Oaks, CA 91403 (tel. 818/905-5777).

Long Beach: 5500 Atherton St., Suite 212, Long Beach, CA 90815 (tel. 213/598-3338).

San Diego: UCSD Student Center B-023, La Jolla, CA 92093 (tel. 619/452-0630.)

Pacific Beach: 4429 Cass St., San Diego, CA 92109 (tel. 619/270-6401).

Austin: 1904 Guadalupe, Suite 6, Austin, TX 78705 (tel. 512/472-4931).

Dallas: Executive Tower Office Center, 3300 West Mockingbird, Suite 101, Dallas, TX 75235 (tel. 214/350-6166).

Seattle: 1314 N.E. 43rd St., Suite 210, Seattle, WA 98105 (tel. 206/632-2448).

Portland: 715 S.W. Morrison St., Suite 600, Portland, OR 97205 (tel. 503/228-1900).

Boston: 729 Boylston St., Suite 201, Boston, MA 02116 (tel. 617/266-1926).

Amherst: 79 South Pleasant St., 2nd floor rear, Amherst, MA 01002 (tel. 413/256-1261).

Cambridge: 1384 Massachusetts Ave., Suite 206, Cambridge, MA 02138 (tel. 617/497-1497).

Providence: 171 Angell St., Suite 212, Providence, RI 02906 (tel. 401/331-5810).

Atlanta: 12 Park Place South, Atlanta, GA 30303 (tel. 404/577-1678).

Chicago: 29 East Delaware Place, Chicago, IL 60611 (tel. 312/951-0585).

Minneapolis: 1501 University Ave., SE, Room 300, Minneapolis, MN 55414 (tel. 612/379-2323).

New Haven: Yale Co-op, 77 Broadway, New Haven, CT 06520.

France: 31 rue St. Augustin, 75002, Paris (tel. 42-66-34-73).

Japan: Sanno Grand Building, Rm. 102, 14-2 Nagata-Cho, 2-Chome, Chiyoda-ku, Tokyo 100 (tel. 03/581-7581).

Acknowledgments

There are lots of people to thank for their help in putting together this ninth edition of *Where to Stay USA*—some on CIEE's staff and some from other organizations.

Our greatest debt of thanks is to Marjorie Cohen, author of the first eight editions of *Where to Stay,* who nurtured this guide from 1974 to 1986. Her thoughts and research fill its pages.

We want to thank, too, Mindy Naiman and Greg Posey for their help and encouragement from the beginning to the end of the project, and Michael Burke, who organized and compiled absolutely everything that's here.

Special thanks to the following people who helped us put the city sections together: Mara Abolins, Laura Basshardt, Steven Beaver, Marilyn Bouma, Elizabeth Brown, Lisa Hardy, Julia House, Sheila Johnson, Cindy Lake, Mary Lohre, William Munson, Teresa Rosen, Lorenda Schrader, and Connie Seldman.

This is also the best place to thank the people who answered the letters and questionnaires that we sent all over the U.S. in order to collect firsthand information on each area. Some of the people to whom we wrote filled in the questionnaires and returned them, and we are grateful for that. But others who went even further and offered encouragement and additional information deserve our collective and special thanks.

Finally, to everyone who helped in the process of putting together *Where to Stay USA,* our thanks.

DEBORAH S. JOOST

The International Student Identity Card

What Is the ISIC?

As soon as American students decide to make a trip abroad, they go out and buy an International Student I.D. Card (ISIC). For more than 20 years, young Americans have been setting out on their travels with the ISIC tucked carefully into their wallets. High school and university students have found the ISIC to be their passport to low-cost travel—it is proof to anyone who needs to know, anywhere in the world, that the holder is a student and is eligible for special student privileges, discounts, and travel bargains. In more than 62 countries, ISIC holders can obtain lower airfares, tours and accommodations, and reduced or free admission to many museums, theaters, cultural and historical sites. With an ISIC, students are eligible, too, for discounts of up to 50% on a special network of low-cost flights that crisscrosses Europe and connects Europe with cities in Africa, Asia, and the Middle East, and now ISIC holders are eligible for savings of up to 50% on many regular transatlantic and transpacific fares. Holders of the ISIC also receive an automatic accident and medical insurance. The card is valid for a period of 16 months beginning Spetember 1 through December 31 of the next year, and costs, as of this writing, $10.

The idea of the ISIC was initiated and is administered by the International Student Travel Conference (ISTC), a federation of national student travel bureaus representing more than 62 countries. The U.S. sponsor of the ISIC is the Council on International Educational Exchange (CIEE). For information on the ISIC and its discounts, contact any Council Travel Services office.

Please send me an application for the International Student Identity Card.

Name _____

Address _____

_____

Return to: **CIEE - WTS**
I.D. Department
205 East 42nd St.
New York, NY 10017

Where to Get the ISIC

Students may obtain their International Student Identity Card at one of the 400 college campuses across the U.S. (check to see whether your campus issues the ISIC—try the international studies office, student travel office, or modern languages department, for example). Or students may obtain the ISIC directly from any Council Travel Services office. We've included a reply coupon for you above in case you would like to order the ISIC directly from the Council.

Who Is Eligible

You are eligible to receive the ISIC if you are (1) at least 12 years of age or older; (2) a high school / vocational school / college or university student; and (3) able to provide documentation as to your current student status.

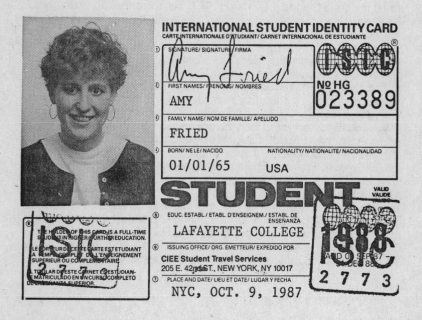

The International Teacher ID Card

This relatively new card offers some of the same benefits as the ISIC, such as the medical insurance, but not all. As a faculty member—elementary, secondary, vocational or college-level—you can receive 20% to 40% discounts on the flights between the U.S. and Latin America, Asia or Australia through Council Travel Services. Discounts of 10% are available on Eurocentre Teacher Refresher Language courses all over Western Europe. For the latest information on new discounts, cardholders should contact their nearest Council Travel Services office.

To get your International Teacher ID Card just send any Council Travel

Services office one 1½″ × 2″ photo of yourself, a letter from your school principal or college registrar stating your full-time teacher status during the current
academic year and a $10 application fee (certified check or money order payable
to Council Travel Services).

INTERNATIONAL STUDENT TRAVEL CONFERENCE
CARTE INTERNATIONALE DE PROFESSEUR / CARNET INTERNACIONAL DE PROFESOR

① SIGNATURE / SIGNATURE / FIRMA — № TD

Meredith Andrews 007464

② FIRST NAME / PRENOMS / NOMBRES

MEREDITH

③ FAMILY NAME / NOM DE FAMILLE / APELLIDO

ANDREWS

④ BORN / NE LE / NACIDO — NATIONALITY / NATIONALITE / NACIONALIDAD

07/02/58 — USA

TEACHER

⑤ TEACHING AT / ENSEIGNANT À / ENSEÑA EN

PITTSFORD HIGH SCHOOL

⑥ ISSUING OFFICE / ORG. EMETTEUR / EXPEDIDO POR

CIEE

⑦ PLACE AND DATE / LIEU ET DATE / LUGAR Y FECHA

NYC 10/02/87

VALID 01 SEP 87 –
31 DEC 88
2 7 9 4

CHAPTER 1

Getting Around

How are you going to get from one place to another in this enormous and fascinating country? Will you fly? Drive? Bicycle? What's best for you? What's the least expensive way to go? What kinds of "deals" are available?

In this first chapter we'll consider all of the possibilities, and then it's up to you. To make your decision you'll have to consider a number of variables. How much money you have to spend is important, of course, but so is understanding your own style. A little old-fashioned "know-thyself" is what's called for first of all. Because so many of our readers are from abroad, it's important, too, to emphasize the enormous size of this country. The distance from New York to California is over 3,000 miles or 5,100 kilometers; from New York to Florida it's over 1,000 miles or 1,700 kilometers. Many people forget about the expanse that is the U.S. when they set out to plan their visit, so they design an unrealistic itinerary that has them covering too much, too quickly.

An encyclopedia guide to all aspects of low-cost travel is *Cheap/Smart Travel*, by Theodore Fischer, published by M. Evans and Co., Inc., 216 East 49th St., New York, NY 10017 ($6.95). The section on air travel will give you everything you need to know on getting the best deal, including an evaluation of the pros and cons of each possibility. The chapters on ground transportation, lodging, and food will also help you save money as the author shares his vast knowledge of these systems.

Going by Air

Except on very short trips, the quickest way to travel between two points in the U.S. is by air. There are ways of saving money on airfares, but the airlines' policies and fare schedules are complicated and prices change regularly. This week's lowest fare may be replaced by another by next month. What we can tell you— and it's important—is that there are lots and lots of bargain fares around and finding out about them can be a bit tricky. In addition, new airlines have recently appeared and old ones have merged, causing even more rapid and dramatic change as established airlines alter their fares to compete. These new carriers generally offer low-cost service on short-haul routes and their lowest fares on an advance purchase, no refund policy. For the very latest in airfare bargains, we suggest contacting your nearest Council Travel Services office (see page 2 for a listing). The people there keep up with the subject and can advise you and book your flights, too.

If you plan to do a lot of air traveling, you may be interested in a handy little guide called *How to Get From the Airport to the City All Around the World*, from Crampton Associates, Airport to the City, P.O. Box 1214, Homewood, IL 60430 ($3.95). Taxi, limousine, and public transit options are described with prices and departure times where applicable. It even lists which car rental agencies rent there.

To illustrate the variety of fares that are available on any given route and how much money it's possible to save over the regular economy fare, we gathered the following information from one of the Council Travel Services office's computers: a flight from New York to Chicago via Pan Am is $290 one-way/regular coach, and from $59 to $109 one-way/SuperSaver fare (restrictions). Continental gave these prices on the same route: regular coach—$190 one-way, and 7-day advance purchase—$118 round trip.

The moral of the story: Be merciless in questioning the airline's reservation clerk or your travel agent in order to uncover the best fare for you.

"Night flights are sometimes cheap, it's true, but you arrive in a strange city at an ungodly hour in the morning."

Foreign visitors are entitled to some special discounts on domestic air fare arrangements. See Chapter 4 for details.

"Hitchhiking by small plane can be a quick, cheap way to get around the U.S. To do this, go to a small airport or the private hangar section of the larger airports. You may find a pilot who is willing to give you a lift in the direction you're going."

In a letter from a reader, we got some more interesting advice on how to save on airfare.

"I have found that great travel savings are possible on trips to some of the smaller U.S. cities if I fly to a major city nearby and then rent a car for the rest of the trip. For example, I had to go from Lubbock, Texas to Longview. My wife and I flew to Dallas and then rented a car for three days. The total cost of the car rental, including maximum insurance coverage, was less than the cost of one Dallas-Longview fare. We saved over $100 on airfare and we would have had to rent a car in Longview anyway."

Air-Courier Services: This is certainly one of the cheapest ways to fly, but it has its disadvantages too. As a courier you carry packages—completely legally—from one destination to another, nationally or overseas. Your airfare will be lower than any existing fare, your personal baggage will be limited to carry-on, you may have to take the last flight of the day or follow other restrictions, such as limited destinations. Look for these companies under "Air Courier Service" in the Yellow Pages or in the newspaper under "Travel," "Transportation," or "Tickets."

Fee-Based Travel Agencies: These companies charge you the list price on airline tickets, package tours, and cruises, minus the agents' commission, adding a flat per-transaction service fee. In exchange, you do your own research to find the lowest fare.

Going by Bus

"The bus is a terrific way to explore the U.S., especially for the first time. The bus goes everywhere and is on time. But you shouldn't spend too much time at the terminals, especially overnight. They're often not located in the best neighborhoods."

"Bus travel is usually a good thing, but sometimes you miss the small cities, which is a real pity."

Bus travel has always been inexpensive so it's no wonder that the bus is such a popular way (especially for young people) to travel around the U.S. Buses are almost always air-conditioned in the summer, well heated in the winter. Service is efficient, connecting most cities and towns of the U.S. no matter how small, and if you break your trip in several short trips, you won't be too uncomfortable.

Two of the largest bus companies, Greyhound and Trailways, have merged with Greyhound's acquisition of Trailways. Greyhound-Trailways offers various discounts and special rates for both the individual traveler and a family traveling together.

For years, the best bargains in bus travel have been the unlimited travel plans. Currently, Greyhound-Trailways is offering a $119 maximum one-way fare (good for 16 days, and unlimited stopovers, but you must declare your stopovers at the time you purchase your tickets), or $159 maximum round-trip rate (good for 30 days). Children aged 5 to 11 accompanied by a fare-paying adult ride for half-price. Children under five travel free. Greyhound-Trailways is also offering a $59 one-way ticket based on an advance purchase. There are also numerous discounts between specific city pairs around the country.

Greyhound-Trailways offers its "Money-Saver" fare: $59 maximum one-way fare, purchased 30 days in advance, with a $15 cancellation penalty. It's good for 30 days with unlimited stopovers. The round-trip fare is $118, good for 60 days with unlimited stopovers. For the handicapped, the "Helping Hand" program will allow a companion to ride for free. Check directly with Greyhound-Trailways for current specials.

We've talked to lots of people who have used discount bus fares and they're generally enthusiastic about them. One friend from Minnesota told us:

"In two months I made four separate round trips lasting 9 to 12 days each. During that time I covered thousands of miles, 39 states, three Canadian provinces, and one Mexican city. In general, bus travel is best if you're not in a hurry and you've never been that route before. It's an excellent way to see the country and to meet people along the way. Most of the bus drivers are friendly and helpful."

"Bus trips are such an easy way to meet people—for me that advantage outweighs any of the discomforts I felt."

Senior citizens are entitled to discounts of 10% to 15% on bus fares, and additional local discounts exist. Check with Greyhound-Trailways for details.

Don't overlook the fact that traveling by bus can also save you money on accommodations. If you travel at night, you can sleep on the bus and avoid paying for a place to stay. Ameripasses are available from Council Travel Services offices, and additional discount tickets may be purchased from travel agents or from the bus lines directly.

"For greater comfort on the bus, bring a battery-operated AM-FM transistor radio and tape-player with headphones, a Thermos bottle, and a pillow and earplugs for sound sleep."

An "alternative bus company," the Green Tortoise, calls itself a vacation/transportation service for budget travelers. "We use sleep-aboard, fuel-efficient diesel coaches and have frequent stops for hot springs, swimming, hiking, rafting, and sailing. Green Tortoise trips, including two delicious cookouts each day, cost between $20 and $30 a day." The Green Tortoise connects San Francisco, Los Angeles, Seattle, Boston, and New York. It goes to New Orleans every year from the East and West Coasts; and during Mardi Gras the buses remain in the French Quarter for up to one week in order to provide accommodations. The Green Tortoise also travels from the West Coast to Alaska and Mexico. At press time, a one-way, cross-country trip of 10 to 12 days was $199 to $249; the four-week Alaska trip was $850; and the trip between Seattle and Los Angeles was $69. For information, write to the Green Tortoise, P.O. Box 24459, San Francisco, CA 94124; or call: in Boston, 617/265-8533; in New York, 212/431-3348; and in San Francisco, 415/821-0803.

The Bus Traveler's Guide to the USA has clear advice for budget-conscious foreign visitors as well as Americans, with sections on cities, accommodation listings, and bus routes that crisscross the U.S. Many accommodations and restaurants offer discounts to travelers carrying this guide. Write to John Hensolt, Editor-in-Chief, On Our Way, Inc., P.O. Box 1972, Sedona, AZ 86336, 1986 ($12.95).

The USA by Bus and Train, Gary Hawkins, Pantheon Books ($9.95). As author Gary Hawkins states, "Bus and train travel . . . open up more of this country for you, in more detail and with more intimacy, than any other means available." His guide describes the transportation networks across the U.S., discusses trip planning and pricing, how to find places to stay and many more tips. It goes on to detail 16 bus and 11 train itineraries, giving "Where to stay" and "What to do" on your overnights. The author's essays of personal experiences while traveling are engaging and enliven this guide. It's quite complete.

Going by Train

"If a person wants to have a relaxed—though long—trip and still see the country, he or she should take the train. I was on Amtrak from New York to New Mexico and from Kansas to Boston. I was able to do what I wanted to do. I saw the country without feeling cramped and met many people and I didn't have to pay for overnight accommodations since the coaches had comfortable seats. I found it more economical to bring fruits, biscuits, etc., on board rather than to have meals on the train."

Amtrak—the National Railroad Passenger Corporation, which operates the nation's passenger trains—is trying to entice people away from planes, cars, and buses and on to trains.

A spokesman for Amtrak's public relations department said: "We have made a special effort to attract young people back to the trains and have succeeded in many parts of the country. If you ride our *Silver Meteor,* for instance, between New York and Orlando, you see many college students enjoying themselves enormously. Our *Coast Starlight,* which operates between Los Angeles and San Francisco and on to Seattle, is also heavily patronized by young people, who obviously are having a fine time. Our California *Zephyr* also attracts a lively crowd."

Unfortunately, Amtrak has stopped selling its unlimited travel USA Rail Pass to Americans—it is available now only to foreign visitors. But there is, at least at press time, the "All Aboard America" fare, which offers minimum coach fares for trips taken within a certain period of time. Under the plan, tickets must be reserved and purchased before boarding the train. The plan divides the country into three regions—Eastern, Central, and Western. Round-trip travel in one region is $159; in two, $239; and in three, $299. Passengers have 45 days to make their "All Aboard America" trips. There are also some family plans available whereby the head of household pays full fare and the spouse and children ages 12 to 21 pay only half fare; children 2 to 11 pay one-quarter fare, and children under 2 travel free. To qualify for family fares, travel can begin any day of the week.

You can save money if you take advantage of special peak and off-peak fares on certain routes between major cities, for instance, New York/Washington. There are usually some restrictions on dates when the fares are valid and the return trip must be made within a certain period of time. For example, along the Northeast Corridor between New York and Washington the round-trip excursion fares are good for travel anytime except between 1 p.m. and 7 p.m. on Friday and Sunday and some holiday periods. At press time, the excursion fare between New York and Washington was $62 round trip; the normal round-trip coach fare was $82 and the round-trip Metroliner was $108. Excursion travel must be completed within 45 days of the purchase of the ticket. Amtrak also offers a 25% discount on fares to people 65 and over and to those who are handicapped. (Amtrak recently renovated many of their passenger cars and stations to conform to the needs of the handicapped.)

From time to time, Amtrak offers special promotional deals, too. For instance, at press time, they were offering a round-trip Detroit/Chicago fare for $45.50. Call toll free 800/USA-RAIL for current Amtrak information.

If you want to take your car, Amtrak operates its Auto Train with daily service in both directions between Lorton, VA (near Washington, D.C.) and Sanford, FL (in Walt Disney World area). There are special one-way fares and round-trip excursion fares. Under the plan you take your car with you, save 900 miles of driving, and still save money.

Amtrak also offers a 96-page Travel Planner that describes routes, equipment, and services. It's free from your travel agent or by calling toll free 800/USA-RAIL.

"Traveling by train was an easy way to meet people and it was also comfortable. The only problem is that we were never on time."

If train is your choice, you may want to get a copy of *Train Trips: Exploring America by Rail,* by William Scheller, Globe Pequot Press, Box Q, Chester, CT 06412 ($9.95). The book is a guide to American passenger service and includes Canadian routes as well.

Going by Car

It's not cheap to maintain a car and all sorts of things can go wrong with a car en route, but if you want to be able to travel at your own pace and come and go as you please, travel by car is probably best for you. If you don't have your own car you can either rent one, buy a used one, take advantage of the driveaway system, or find someone to ride with—all possibilities that are discussed below. (Special information for foreign visitors who intend to drive in the U.S. can be found in Chapter 4.)

The American Automobile Association (AAA) offers many services to its members all over the U.S., Canada, and overseas. These include 24-hour emergency road service, free maps, personalized itinerary maps (triptiks), guidebooks to the states, camping guides, travel agency services, insurance, free American Express travelers checks, and more. If you're a member of your country's automobile association, find out if there's a reciprocal service arrangement with AAA. You may well be able to obtain the AAA services on your home country's automobile association membership. Yearly membership costs from $20 to $50, depending on the location of the home office.

DRIVEAWAYS: There are several agencies throughout the U.S. that arrange the transport of cars from one part of the country to another. This provides an excellent opportunity for students over 21 years of age—or sometimes over 25—to go long distances at minimal cost. The car owner usually pays for the tolls and occasionally for the gas. A direct route must be followed, since the agencies usually contract to get the car to its destination by a certain time. The time allotted is reasonable, though; no one expects you to drive day and night. It's typical for a company to require that you cover about 400 miles per day. Most large cities have driveaway companies. They are listed in the classified section of the telephone book—the Yellow Pages—usually under the heading "Automobile Transport and Driveaway Companies," or in the classified sections of the daily newspapers. Probably the most popular routes for driveaways are between New York and either Philadelphia or Boston, and between Florida and California.

The process of contracting with a driveaway company involves making a deposit of between $50 and $100 and being fingerprinted. If you get a choice of cars, take the smaller one so you can save on gasoline. Most cars are late models, privately owned, and are given to the driver with a full tank of gas.

If you're a foreign student interested in a driveaway, your English must be fluent before most companies will let you have a car, and you must have an International Driving Permit as well.

As with all things, before you sign on the dotted line for a driveaway you should be confident of the firm's reliability.

Other companies with offices throughout the U.S. are Auto Caravan, Auto Driveaway Company, and Dependable Car Travel Service, Inc.

CAR RENTALS: In some cities of the U.S., car rental companies require that you be 25 or over in order to rent one of their cars. Others will rent to anyone 21 or over. New York is one place that requires you to be 25, but if a friend who is over 25 actually rents the car you may go along as a driver even if you are younger. Also, if you have a major credit card companies will often adjust the minimum age requirement. Having a major credit card will make car rental easier—some companies won't rent to you without one, or if they do, they will require a deposit. (The situation for foreign visitors is a bit different. The minimum age is 18 as long as you have a valid International Driver's Permit and can show a return ticket and a passport.)

Most of you have heard of the major car-rental companies—National, Hertz, and Avis—but when you're thinking of renting a car, consider some of the smaller companies as well, such as Rent-a-Wreck ("Don't let the name fool you" is their motto). Their "stolen car" rate is $25 per day with a two-week minimum. Vehicles are clean, well-maintained new and used cars, trucks, and vans, contrary to the company's name. Although the larger companies, with offices all over the world, offer such advantages as allowing you to pick up a car in one city and leave it in another (often at a charge), the smaller companies usually charge less and may have more economy cars available than the larger ones.

The cost of car rental varies considerably not only from city to city but within any given area, depending on the location of the rental office, day of the week, size of the car, automatic or manual transmission, and gas and mileage policies. For instance, a one-week rental in Miami will cost much less than a car rented for the same period in New York. The difference can easily be $100.

To give you a general idea of how much it will cost to rent a car, consider that most of the companies have special one-week rates that usually provide unlimited mileage for approximately $100. This rate does not include the cost of gasoline. As for the "collision damage waiver," check if your own car insurance covers you in a rental vehicle before taking on this extra charge. The personal accident insurance can be avoided if you have your own health insurance. Check before assuming anything and ask for a confirmation number when you make your reservation. You can also get special weekday, weekend, and monthly rates that can make car rental an economical way to travel—especially if you have some friends along to share costs. Be sure to investigate all the possibilities.

"I don't know if two people can live cheaper than one, but they sure can travel cheaper. Three is even better when you're splitting the gas, motel bills, and driving. We found a fellow traveler on our way home and the added savings and companionship were most welcome."

USED CARS: If you're the kind who enjoys taking chances, you can buy yourself a used car and hope for the best. An American car that is only a few years old may sell for half its original price; a car five to ten years old may sell for under $800 and can usually be resold at a small loss, as long as you can keep it in one piece. It's best to buy used cars through ads in the newspapers rather than from used-car dealers. Here's one good suggestion we got from someone who has bought several used cars: check the tires, since their condition is a good measure of the care that the previous owner gave the car.

Exercise great caution, though, in buying a used car. We received a letter from a man in Switzerland telling us that, in response to an advertisement in a Swiss newspaper, he made arrangements to buy a used car in Florida for $1,200. He sent a deposit of $400 and paid the balance when he got to the U.S. The car turned out to be a mess and he was able to get only half his money back. Buying anything, especially a used car, sight unseen, is foolish.

Going by Bicycle

A lot of people are deciding that two wheels are better than four. There's been an incredible boom in bicycling in recent years, and that's a good thing both for the people who are doing the bicycling and for the ones who aren't, since they're being spared the pollution of another car.

There are lots of bicycle clubs and organizations in the U.S. One of the best-known organizations associated with bicycle travel is American Youth Hostels, Inc., which has been around since 1934. AYH was operating hostels throughout the U.S., and organizing bicycle tours for its members for years before the present bicycle boom began. Membership cards, available from any Council Travel Services office, from the AYH National Office, P.O. Box 37613, Washington, D.C. 20013-7613, or from any of AYH's more than 35 councils or over 500 pass-selling agents, cost $10 for anyone under 18 or over 60, and $20 for anyone 18 to 59. For all membership categories, include $1 for postage and handling. See Chapter 2 for more about AYH and its hostels.

Because of the recent bicycle boom, many communities are creating more bikeways. The word "bikeway" is a bit misleading—it is used to refer to a marked route on streets and roads that are considered suitable for bicycling; it does not mean a roadway set aside only for bicyclists. According to the International Bicycle Touring Society, 2115 Paseo Dorado, La Jolla, CA 92037, "Bikeways exist in hundreds of towns and cities, but they are of questionable value because they don't go anywhere." The average length of a bikeway in the U.S. is four miles. Only Wisconsin has a longer one. It stretches from Kenosha to La Crosse, a distance of 300 miles. IBTS runs tours in the U.S. and overseas at cost (about $30 to $50 per day). Membership dues are $25, individual or couple, and run from January 1 to December 31. You will receive three newsletters with tour announcements and tour reports, and may request several free informative reports on biking. For a copy of a newly revised set of bike maps showing 10,000 miles of routes in 72 counties, send $2.25 to Wisconsin Department of Transportation, Documents and Map Sales, 3617 Pierstorff Street, Madison, WI 53707.

One organization is Bikecentennial, which celebrated America's birthday by inaugurating a 4,500-mile Trans America Bicycle Trail. Besides running organized trips for bicyclists during the summer, Bikecentennial has 15,000 miles of researched bicycle routes. The newest is the California Coast Route from Crescent City to San Diego. The group's catalog, *Cyclosource,* which includes accessories, order forms for map routes, and books on cycling in the U.S. and abroad, is free from Bikecentennial, P.O. Box 8308, Missoula, MT 59807 (tel. 406/721-1776).

The League of American Wheelmen (L.A.W.) is a membership organization of, by, and for bicyclists in all 50 states with 20,000 individual members and about 500 affiliated bicycle clubs. L.A.W., Suite 209, 6707 Whitestone Rd., Baltimore, MD 21207 (tel. 301/944-3399), actively works to protect bicyclists' rights to the road, and it provides safety and touring information. *Bicycle USA,* a monthly magazine, contains an almanac and an extensive and timely listing of bicycle events in the U.S. A directory of 1,200 "Hospitality Homes," where people are willing to accommodate touring League cyclists for the night, costs $2. The "Bicycle USA Tourfinder" ($3) lists over 150 bike trip operators in the U.S. and abroad.

In general, bike books can be divided into two separate categories: the ones that tell you how to buy, maintain, and repair your bike; and the ones that tell you where you can go with your bike. One of the first type that is most often recommended is *The New Complete Book of Bicycling,* by Eugene A. Sloane, Simon and Schuster, 1981 ($12.95).

Globe Pequot publishes a host of the "where-to-go" genre, called *Short Bike Rides,* specializing in the New England states and Long Island, NY ($5.95 to $9.95). For guides to routes in the Northwest, try The Mountaineers, 306 2nd Ave. West, Seattle, WA 98119 (tel. 206/285-2665), with *Bicycling the Back Road around Puget Sound . . . Northwest Oregon . . . & Northwest Washington,* and *Bicycling the Pacific Coast* ($9.95 each). Their guide, *Freewheeling,* offers "practical solutions for long-distance touring, bike selection, route research, breakdowns," and more ($8.95).

Bicycling is a magazine published 10 times a year for the true enthusiast. Rodale Press, Inc., 33 East Minor St., Emmaus, PA 18049 (tel. 215/967-5171). Single copy: $2.50.

The Countryman Press publishes a series called "25 Bicycle Tours" on New Hampshire, Vermont, Maine, the Finger Lakes, New York City, and Eastern Pennsylvania. The Countryman Press, Backcountry Publications, P.O. Box 175, Woodstock, VT 05091 ($6.95 to $8.95).

Rules of the Road

From what people tell us, we sense a growing feeling of paranoia about hitchhiking-related crimes. Nowadays, it seems people are convinced that the potential danger is greater for the hitchhiker than for the driver. In the past it was the driver who felt threatened.

There are no nationwide laws regarding hitchhiking; individual cities and states make their own laws and regulations. Whether a law exists or not, the attitude of the police toward hitchhikers is something that can't be regulated and varies from area to area. Some police are cordial, even helpful, to hitchhikers, and others treat thumbers like escaped criminals. Although hitching is not illegal, there are personal safety considerations, so think twice before hitting the road.

Other road rules you should know regard drinking and the use of seatbelts. Drinking and driving don't mix, and the police are enforcing this more and more. If you are stopped, you may be tested for alcohol on your breath and taken in to the police station. You may even spend the night. Don't drink if you plan to drive.

As for seatbelts, many states require their use in the front seats and for children up to a certain age in the back seat. In certain states children under 12 are not allowed to sit in the front seat at all. Children under 40 pounds may be required to sit in a car seat, sometimes available at car-rental locations or from baby equipment rental companies.

Going on Foot

If you like to walk with a group, you might want to find out about the many clubs throughout the U.S. that promote hiking and sponsor organized outdoor trips —generally in the parks and wilderness areas. Most of these organizations are regional or statewide.

A listing of more than 32 key hiking clubs along the East Coast can be obtained by writing to the Appalachian Trail Conference, P.O. Box 807, Harper's Ferry, WV 25425. This conference of trail clubs manages the 2,000-mile Maine-to-Georgia Appalachian Trail, in conjunction with the National Park Service. For 50¢, they'll send you an information packet about the Trail, membership, etc. Be sure to ask specifically for the list of clubs, or you can ask for the names of clubs in a particular area.

One of the hiking clubs on the East Coast is the Adirondack Mountain Club, 174 Glen St., Glens Falls, NY 12801 (tel. 518/793-7737). The club sponsors hiking outings, does conservation work, and operates Adirondack High Peaks lodges year-round for hikers, as well as publishes trail guides and natural history books.

On the West Coast, there's the well-known Sierra Club, which has chapters in all 50 states throughout the U.S. If you write to their headquarters at 730 Polk St., San Francisco, CA 94109, they can direct you to the nearest chapter. Sierra Club books include guides to natural areas by region, adventure travel guides to the U.S., guides to the national parks, and outdoor activity guides. For details, write to Sierra Club Books, 730 Polk St., Dept. T-150, San Francisco, CA 94109 (tel. 800/852-5000).

The American Hiking Society looks for volunteers ages 16 and over for ten days of working on trail maintenance, bridge-building, and other work projects aimed at preserving our natural resources. The cost is a $30 tax-deductible registration fee. For more information, send a business-size, self-addressed, stamped envelope to AHS Volunteer Vacations, P.O. Box 86, Scituate, MA 02060.

The Mountaineers publishes its "100 Hikes" series: *North Cascades, Alpine Lakes,* and *South Cascades* ($9.95 each). Globe Pequot's series of "Short Walks" guides covers *Connecticut, Long Island,* and *Cape Cod and the Vineyard* ($5.95 each).

Southern Snow, by Randy Johnson, published by Appalachian Mountain Club Books ($12.95), is the first comprehensive guide to winter hiking and skiing in the southern Appalachian Mountains. Another in the collection of outdoor guides include *Hiking the Mountain States,* by Allen de Hart ($12.95). For the casual walker, they publish a "Country Walks" series for walks near Boston, Philadelphia, Baltimore, Washington, and New York ($7.95 each).

Globe Pequot has a variety of hiking and walking guides including *Rocky Mountain National Park Hiking Trails,* by Kent and Donna Dannem ($8.95); *Hiking Virginia's National Forests,* by Karin Wuertz-Schaefer ($7.95); *South Carolina Hiking Trails,* by Allen de Hart ($8.95); *Walks in the Catskills,* by John Bennett ($7.95); *Tennessee Trail,* by Evan Means ($8.95); and *Walks in the Great Smokies,* by Rodney and Priscilla Albright ($7.95).

The Countryman Press publishes a host of hiking guides: the "50 Hikes" series, covering much of the East Coast ($8.95 to $9.95 each), and *Walks and Rambles in Rhode Island* ($8.95) . . . *in Westchester and Fairfield Counties* ($7.95) . . . and *on the Delmarva Peninsula* ($8.95). *America's Greatest Walks,* Yanker and Tarlow, Addison-Wesley ($10.95) covers "100 scenic adventures" all around the U.S.

Going by Boat

Had you thought of this one? Paddlers can get all the information they need on canoes, kayaks, rafts, accessories, rentals, books, maps, and where to use them, from the Chicagoland Canoe Base, Inc., 4019 N. Narragansett Ave., Chicago, IL 60634. Send a stamped, self-addressed envelope for a copy of their book list, or visit if you're in the area.

The Countryman Press publishes *The Complete Boating Guide to the Connecticut River,* by Mark C. Borton ($9.95); *Canoeing Massachusetts, Rhode Island and Connecticut,* by Ken Webster ($7.95); *Camping Vermont and New Hampshire Rivers,* by Roioli Schweiker ($6.95); and *Canoeing Central New York,* by William P. Ehling ($9.95).

The Appalachian Mountain Club publishes seven books that would interest canoeists and kayakers: *AMC River Guide: Maine* ($8.95); *AMC River Guide: New Hampshire and Vermont* ($8.95); *The Wildest Country: A Guide to Thoreau's Maine* ($11.95); *AMC River Guide: Massachusetts, Connecticut, Rhode Island* ($8.95); *New England White Water River Guide,* by Ray Gabler ($8.95); *Whitewater Handbook,* by John Urban and T. Walley Williams ($6.95);

and *River Rescue,* by Les Bechdel and Slim Ray ($9.95). All are available by mail (add $1.50 shipping on orders for one book, 25¢ for each additional title) from AMC Books, 5 Joy St., Boston, MA 02108.

The Mountaineers publishes *Canoe Routes: Northwest Oregon,* by Phil Jones ($8.95). Globe Pequot offers *Canoeing in the Jersey Pine Barrens,* by Robert Parnes ($8.95). *Watertrips: A Guide to East Coast Cruise Ships, Ferryboats and Island Excursions* describes an interesting way of seeing the East. Write to Theodore Scull, International Marine Publishing Co., 21 Elm St., Camden, ME 04843 ($14.95). *Ferries of America* details hundreds of routes, long and short, all around the country. From Sarah Bird White, Peachtree, 494 Armour Circle, NE, Atlanta, GA 30324 ($12.95).

Some Books to Read

Here are some books that we can recommend for background on the places you're going to visit. To really get yourself in the mood for your trip, read novels about the areas you're going to be visiting and see movies set in the places you'll eventually see. But for practical information on getting around the various cities, where to eat cheaply and well, and for other advice, consult some of the guidebooks listed below.

Guides to bed and breakfasts are listed in Chapter 2 in the section on that topic. Guides specific to a particular state or city are listed with the respective destination. Some guides to special activities like hiking and biking, and special-interest groups like senior citizens, families, and the disabled, are listed in their separate sections in the introductory chapter, if general; and if specific to one destination, in the state introduction.

There are three series of guides, all published by Prentice Hall Press, that might interest you: Frommer guides on Hawaii, New York, and Washington, D.C., were once entitled "$5-a-Day," but with things the way they are, they are now *Hawaii on $50 a Day* ($11.95), *New York on $50 a Day* ($10.95), and *Washington, D.C., & Historic Virginia, on $40 a Day* ($11.95).

Also by Prentice Hall Press is the Frommer City Guide series, which includes guides to Washington, D.C., Boston, New York, New Orleans, Philadelphia, Atlantic City/Cape May, Las Vegas, Los Angeles, San Francisco, Orlando/Disney World/EPCOT, Minneapolis/St. Paul, and Hawaii. They cost $5.95 each. Recently Frommer has added seven guides to its Dollarwise series: *Florida, California and Las Vegas, New England, The Southeast and New Orleans, The Northwest, The Southwest,* and *Texas. New England* costs $12.95; the others cost $11.95 each. Frommer's *Beat the High Cost of Travel* ($4.95) tells how to save money on absolutely all travel-related items. *Marilyn Wood's Wonderful Weekends* ($11.95), covers trips in Connecticut, Massachusetts, Rhode Island, New York, Pennsylvania, New Jersey, and Vermont.

All Frommer Guides are available at bookstores or from Prentice Hall Press, Travel Books, One Gulf + Western Plaza, New York, NY 10023. Add $1.50 for shipping.

Another well-known series is by Fodor's. The following regional titles are available in bookstores or from Fodor's Travel Publishing, 201 East 50th Street, New York, NY 10022: *Fodor's American Cities on a Budget* ($12.95); *Fodor's Far West* ($12.95); *Fodor's New England* ($11.95); *Fodor's Pacific North Coast* ($9.95); *Fodor's South* ($12.95). The same people do guides to individual cities and states, for example, California, New Orleans, New York, Texas and on and on. The Fielding's series from William Morrow offers a couple of titles for us.

Spanish Trails in the Southwest covers the explorations of the Spanish conquistadors in New Mexico and Arizona with sights, accommodations, and restaurants. Another historically based guide of theirs is *Fielding's Lewis and Clark Trail* following these explorers from Missouri to Oregon. Both are $12.95.

The Mobil Travel Guides, published by Prentice Hall Press, are also popular with travelers. There are seven regional guides: *California and the West, Great Lakes Area, Middle Atlantic States, Northwest and Great Plains States, Southeastern States, Southwest and South Central States,* and *Northeastern States.* Each guide has about 300 pages and includes hotels, restaurants, and sightseeing information; the 1988 editions cost $8.95 each. Another Mobil guide is *The Major Cities,* which concentrates on the 53 most-visited U.S. cities; the 1988 edition costs $8.95.

Rand McNally publishes a collection of guides on camping and on national parks. *Camping America's Public Lands* ($5.95) covers eastern U.S. and eastern Canada; *National Park Guides* ($11.95); *Camping the National Parks* ($13.95); *Great National Park Vacations* ($10.95); *America's Favorite National Parks* ($5.95); *Camp for Under $10 a Day* ($5.95); eight regional *RV Park and Campground* directories ($5.95 to $12.95); two small directories, *Camp Texas* and *Camp California* ($2.95 each); a *Road Atlas and Vacation Guide* ($12.95); and a *Family Adventure Road Atlas* ($7.95).

For budget travel advice, we recommend *Let's Go: USA,* one of the excellent Harvard Student Agencies' travel series published by St. Martin's Press ($10.95).

For outdoorsy vacation suggestions, read the following books: *Farm, Ranch & Country Vacations,* by Pat Dickerman, is a 240-page listing of ranches, farms, and lodges in the U.S. and Canada where city people can go to enjoy some country living. Some of these places are working farms, but don't be alarmed: "At a working farm, ranch guests don't do the work—they *watch* it— unless, of course, they have a special hankering for pitching hay or moving cattle." The 1986 edition is available from Farm and Ranch Vacations, 36 East 57th St., New York, NY 10022 ($12.95 postpaid in the U.S. and $16 by check drawn on a U.S. bank for airmail delivery abroad).

For more "out west" trips, see *Budget Vacationers Guidebook—Western U.S.,* by Michael Studebaker, Glastonbury Press, 12816 East Rose Drive, Whittier, CA 90601 ($8.95). It's filled with tips on free and very inexpensive accommodations and attractions.

An unusual new guide for nature lovers is *Natural Attractions,* by John Thaxton (Warner Books, 666 Fifth Ave., New York, NY 10103, $8.95). Chapter by chapter, learn to find whales, bison, eagles, glaciers, and more, all over North America. Naturalist guides to all parts of the U.S. are published by the Sierra Club ($9.95).

One of the newer entries in the field of travel books is *United States 1987,* a "Get'em and Go Travel Guide" to the "finest in 44 cities," edited by Stephen Birnbaum, published by Houghton Mifflin ($12.95). It is revised and updated annually.

And there are more:

Adventure Travel North America, by Pat Dickerman, Adventure Guides, Inc., 1986 ($12.95). Who, what, where, when, and how much for outdoor vacations—scaling rock, backpacking, riding horseback into wilderness, river rafting and more. Send orders to Adventure Guides, Inc., 36 East 57th St., New York, NY 10022.

The following are all guides to the Northeast: *Guide to the Recommended Country Inns of New England,* by Elizabeth Squier, Globe Pequot Press, Old Chester Rd., Chester, CT 06412 ($10.95), a delightful book with the personal touch. Description of menus at each inn will make your mouth water.

Budget Dining and Lodging in New England, by Frank and Fran Sullivan, another Globe Pequot Press offering; this one is a guide to 400 places to eat and to spend a night or two. The authors must have had great fun researching this one—the result is a well-organized, homey kind of guide ($8.95).

Day Trips and Budget Vacations in New England, by Patricia and Robert Foulke, published by Globe Pequot Press ($8.95), is based on six recommended itineraries that go from the coast to the mountains, from busy cities to quiet colonial-style villages. By the same authors is their guide *Day Trips and Budget Vacations in the Mid-Atlantic States* ($10.95).

Countryman Press publishes *New England's Special Places: a Day Tripper's Guide,* by Michael Schuman ($10.95).

Harvard Common Press' *Best Places to Stay in New England,* by Christina Tree and Bruce Shaw ($9.95) divides accommodations into categories like "Beachside," "Village B & B's," and "Island Getaways."

The same Michelin that publishes guides for Europe, now has *New England* (and New York City) on its roster, in the same organized and informative format ($9.95).

Globe Pequot publishes a unique guide, *Special Museums of the Northeast,* by Nancy Frazier ($9.95), which will lead you to some fascinating and uncommon collections. For budget shoppers are the following: *Guide to the Recommended Thrift Shops of New England,* by L.A. Collins, Julie Hatfield, and Ruth Weinstein ($5.95); *Factory Store* guides to *All New York, Pennsylvania and New Jersey,* by A. Pennypincher and A. Tightwad, and *All New England* by A. Miser and A. Pennypincher ($5.95 each).

Michelin has recently released a *Green Guide to New England,* which we recommend, particularly for foreign visitors. Published by the Michelin Tire people, P.O. Box 3305, Spartanburg, SC 29304 ($9.95), it's crammed with interesting facts and includes an excellent tourist map.

Favorite Daytrips in New England, by Michael Schuman, Yankee Books, Dublin, NH 03444 ($9.95). Forty ways to get to know New England a little better; in its fourth edition.

Another great information source on New England is the New England Vacation Center, 630 5th Ave., Concourse Shop 2, New York, NY 10111 (tel. 212/307-5780), where you'll be provided with every kind of tourist material on these states.

And here are some guides that don't fit into the above categories:

There's a series of guides describing inns in various parts of the country published by Burt Franklin and Co., Inc., 235 East 44th St., New York, NY 10017 (tel. 212/687-5250, or toll free 800/223-0766 out of New York State). The titles in the series are *Country Inns of New England, Country Inns of the Mid-Atlantic States, Country Inns of the Midwest and the Rocky Mountains,* and *Country Inns of the South.* The 1987–88 editions of these books cost $8.95 each. Request the latest edition from the publisher.

Country Inns of the Mid-Atlantic States and Chesapeake Region features 146 full-service and bed-and-breakfast inns selected from hundreds visited and evaluated by the author, Brenda B. Chapin, Globe Pequot Press ($9.95).

Art Now/USA/The National Art Museum and Gallery Guide, published by

Art Now Inc., 320 Bonnie Burn Rd., Scotch Plains, NJ 07076 ($3 per copy; $22 for 11 issues). A monthly magazine which lists exhibits in over 1,300 galleries and museums from coast to coast.

Pilot Books publishes a host of handy and practical guides: *The National Directory of Budget Motels,* edited by Raymond Carlson ($3.95); *Directory of Low Cost Vacations with a Difference,* by J. Crawford ($4.95); *Directory of Free Vacation and Travel Information,* edited by Raymond Carlson ($3.95); *The Senior Citizen's Guide to Budget Travel in the U.S. and Canada,* by Paige Palmer ($3.95); *National Directory of Free Tourist Attractions,* edited by Raymond Carlson ($3.50); and *National Directory of Theme Parks and Amusement Areas,* edited by Raymond Carlson (new edition published in late 1987 costs $3.95). To order, add $1 for postage and handling to the price of the book or books you desire. You will receive a 25% discount when ordering three or more guides. Write to 100 Cooper St., Babylon, New York 11702 (tel. 516/422-2225).

And for those of you who want to keep informed, on a regular basis, of what's happening in the world of value travel—in the U.S. and everywhere else as well—you may want to consider a subscription to *Travel Smart,* a newsletter published monthly. Filled with news on the latest fares, hotel bargains, etc., it costs $39 for a one-year subscription, $69 for two years. Write to Communications House, Dobbs Ferry, NY 10522 to order.

An interesting little newspaper is *The Wonderful World of Budget Travel,* published by the $35-a-Day Travel Club, Prentice Hall Press, One Gulf + Western Plaza, 15th Floor, New York, NY 10023. Subscriptions are $18 a year and give you discounts on travel books as well as tips on budget travel all over the U.S. and the world.

CHAPTER 2

Staying Awhile

When we first began searching out inexpensive places to stay in the U.S., we were encouraged by what most people told us. However one of our favorite responses was a letter that said: "You must be kidding or out of your minds. For that amount of money you can't even get accommodations in a tent—you are wasting your time."

We are delighted to say that the person who wrote that was completely and absolutely wrong. We have uncovered hundreds of places to stay that are $35 and under per person per night, and frequently much less expensive than that. Some of the accommodations listed are spartan—room for a sleeping bag on a gymnasium floor for a few dollars a night—but we've also found luxurious rooms in a modern resort with just about every recreation facility imaginable and many charming bed and breakfasts and family-run motels for $35 or less a night. We list places suitable for people of all ages, although we do have some "students only" information. (In the larger cities, we've listed hotels where singles are more than $35 but doubles work out to $35 or less per person.) Needless to say, we haven't found everything that exists in this category. In some sections of the country nearly all accommodations fall into our price range, and we haven't the space to list them all. If you come across a good place to stay that's within our range, let us know; we'll contact the people who run it and try to list it in our next edition. Many of the additions to this year's listings have come via our readers, and we're pleased with their willingness to help. Write to us at 205 East 42nd Street, New York, NY 10017, and if we are able to use what you tell us in the next edition of *Where to Stay USA*, we'll send you a complimentary copy.

Accommodations are listed here alphabetically by city within each state chapter. In order to make it easier for you to find these cities we have provided a map at the beginning of each state section marking the cities where we have listings. Fifteen of the largest U.S. cities have expanded sections incorporated into the state-by-state listings. These sections include information not only on accommodations but also on places to eat, things to do, how to get around, etc.

In each accommodation listing we have included its name, address, telephone number, and, when helpful, the name of the person to ask for when calling for information. The individual properties of motel chains are listed by city. All details on the chains' facilities, rates, and discounts are in our newly amplified "Low-Cost Motel Chains" section (see page 27). Whenever a facility has agreed to offer a special discount rate to holders of the International Student Identity Card (ISIC), readers of *Where to Stay*, senior citizens, or has access facilities for the disabled, we have indicated this with the following symbols:

Ⓢ   ISIC discount
★   *Where to Stay* book discount
∨   Senior citizen discount
♿   Access facilities for the disabled

We have listed the rates (per room unless otherwise indicated) and have noted whether accommodations are for men or women only and whether children can be accommodated. If the facility is open only at a certain time of the year, the dates are given, and if reservations are necessary this is also indicated. Any other information that we thought was either interesting, helpful, or both, is also included. To help you understand the variety of accommodations in this book, we've described them below, detailing what to expect from them, and, in some cases, what they expect from you.

"Where did I stay? In motels, campgrounds, youth hostels, with friends and relatives, in a barn, a school bus, on a picnic table, in a cave, and in a university dorm."

American Youth Hostels

". . . Youth hostels were my salvation. Without fail, the houseparents were friendly and helpful, accommodation was good if sometimes basic, and prices were rock-bottom. I almost always found someone to travel with for a few days. Altogether, a really good deal."

There are about 250 youth hostels scattered throughout the U.S. that are operated by American Youth Hostels, Inc., a member of the International Youth Hostel Federation. Some AYH hostels are in private homes. Some are meant for people who travel under their own steam—hikers, bicyclists, canoeists, skiers, or horseback riders—and are often located in rural areas near parks, forests, or preserves. They are often in particularly beautiful settings, off the beaten path. There are now many AYH facilities in the larger cities as well—cities like Washington, D.C., Phoenix, Philadelphia, Boston, San Francisco, Los Angeles, San Diego, Chicago, Seattle, New Orleans, etc.

In order to use the hostel facilities of AYH, you may or may not be a member of the organization (members pay less). One year's membership costs $10 for anyone under 18 or over 60 years of age and $20 for anyone else. Membership passes are available from American Youth Hostels, National Office, P.O. Box 37613, Washington, D.C. 20013-7613 (tel. 202/783-6161), from AYH councils and agencies in certain metropolitan areas, or from any Council Travel Services office. Check the telephone directory for listings or call the AYH national office. Visiting foreign students should have a membership card from their own national youth hostel association; in emergencies they may obtain an International Guest Pass from AYH National Headquarters (see above address), Council Travel Services offices, and major hostels.

"A youth hostel card, bought either in the U.S. or in a foreign visitor's home country, is strongly recommended. Non-members are charged a higher fee, and if space is short, members are given preference."

Not all AYH facilities are the same; there are, in fact, three categories of hostels. By definition, a full hostel is a low-cost, supervised, overnight accommodation for people traveling. It has maximum fees established by AYH, Inc., resident houseparents, separate dormitories and washing/toilet facilities, a kitchen, a dining room, and a common room. A "home hostel" is someone's private residence and usually has all the basic elements of a hostel. The difference is size. A hostel usually has between 10 and 100 beds; a home hostel usually has only one to eight beds. Often the kitchen is the homeowner's private kitchen and, while meals may be provided, the hostelers cannot always expect to prepare their own meals. Home hostels always require advance reservations. Overnight rates vary from hostel to hostel and sometimes change with the seasons. Rates are usually from $4 to $10 per night; exact rates that were in effect at press time are given in the individual listings. Most hostels limit the number of nights you may stay—anywhere from three to seven consecutive days.

And finally, there are "supplemental accommodations" (indicated in this book by "AYH-SA" in parentheses after the name), which provide most of the facilities of a regular hostel but lack one or more of the basic elements—usually a kitchen or a houseparent, since the supplemental accommodations are often YMCAs, camps, etc. Rates at supplemental facilities are higher than standard hostel rates, and AYH membership is not usually required. Unless otherwise stated, the AYH-SA rates given in *Where to Stay*'s listings are for AYH members; non-members can expect a higher rate.

Reservations are generally recommended for overnight stays in hostels and should be made as far in advance as possible. To make a reservation, send the hostel a deposit equal to one night's accommodation. If reservations are absolutely required, the listings will indicate it.

International Advanced Booking Vouchers, whereby hostelers can make reservations at hostels all over the world before they set off on their trip, are available. Write to the AYH National Headquarters for details.

All hostels share a common set of "customs": cooking, cleaning, and general hostel duties must be shared by hostelers; drinking, smoking, and illegal drugs are not allowed; check-out time is 9:30 a.m., and hostels are usually closed between 10 a.m. and 4 p.m.

The *U.S. Hostel Handbook* is given free of charge with membership. Non-members may purchase a copy for $5 plus $2 postage and handling from the AYH National Office.

Other Hostels

As you read through the accommodation listings in *Where to Stay USA,* you will find some facilities that call themselves hostels but are not affiliated with American Youth Hostels and do not have AYH written after their names. These are independent accommodation facilities set up by a variety of people and groups but all with a common goal: to provide a cheap, relatively comfortable, and friendly place for people on the road to spend a night or two. Many of these hostels are in urban areas; often they have cooking facilities and sometimes even free kitchens. These independent hostels are operated by churches, community groups, and sometimes even by YMCAs.

Many of these hostels are open only a few hours a day for registration since they are often short-staffed, so we suggest that you call ahead to find out the best time to arrive. All of them are adamant about some basic rules: the prohibition of alcohol, drugs, or weapons on the premises. It is also common for the facilities to have a minimum-age requirement. This is because in some states sheltering anyone under 16, or even 18, may be defined legally as "housing a runaway." If you are under 18 and traveling, it may be wise to carry a letter from your parents stating that they know you are traveling and that you have their permission to do so.

Most of these independent hostels also limit the length of your stay to two or three nights. They are, after all, for people passing through, and you must leave room for others who need what is usually rather limited space. The cost is approximately $8 per night.

One organization is American Association of Independent Hostels, P.O. Box 28038, Washington, D.C. 20038, with members coast to coast.

YMCAs and YWCAs
Young Men's Christian Assocations (YMCAs) and Young Women's Christian Associations (YWCAs) are well known all over the world as organizations that will often provide inexpensive housing to travelers. Y's are completely non-denominational in spite of their name and provide, besides accommodations, many recreational facilities such as swimming pools, gymnasiums, ball courts, and various programmed activities.

Not all Y's have accommodation facilities, but we contacted the ones that do and have listed those that responded. There are certain generalizations that we can make about staying in Y facilities. Usually rooms in Y's do not have private baths or showers. Some YMCAs can accommodate both men and women, but most YWCAs can accommodate only women. This is indicated in the listings. Usually you may use the Y's recreational facilities at no extra cost when you spend the night there; sometimes if you are not a member of the YMCA or YWCA you will be required to pay a small membership fee along with the over-night rate. In well-traveled areas, Y's are popular places to stay, so it is usually wise to call ahead to see if there is room for you. Some Y's require reservations; our listing will indicate if this is the case. Reservations at YMCAs in the larger metropolitan areas may be made by contacting "Y's Way International" at 356 West 34th Street, New York, NY 10001 (tel. 212/760-5856). "The Y's Way International" is a central reservation service for over 130 YMCA's and accommodation centers located in 56 North American cities and 27 countries overseas. Particularly when you want accommodations in the more popular cities—New York, Montreal, Seattle, New Orleans, San Francisco, or Los Angeles—it's best to contact the "Y's Way International" as far in advance of your trip as possible.

Dormitories and Residence Halls
There are many dormitories and residence halls at large and small schools that will put up travelers. We received a positive response from the housing offices of many U.S. colleges and universities and would certainly recommend that whenever you are in the neighborhood of a campus, you investigate its accommodation facilities. Even if a campus is not listed here, call the housing office or ask at the student union about a place where you can spend the night. You will rarely be turned away.

Besides the dormitories and residence halls that are operated by colleges, there are residence halls that are operated privately to serve the local student population. Most of these residence halls are only a few years old and are quite luxurious. Usually they are divided into apartment-type areas with four single bedrooms, one kitchen, and one bathroom to each area. The buildings are often equipped with swimming pools, tennis courts, etc.

Try sorority and fraternity houses, too, when you're on a campus. They may have room for you.

"I traveled with another guy for most of my trip. We found the easiest places to crash were fraternity houses. We stayed in them at Northwestern (Chicago, IL), Washington University (St. Louis, Mo.), and at the University of Utah in Salt Lake City. The best thing about frats is they usually have kitchens. Bring a sleeping bag to use on the floor."

Hotels

Although many of the large groups of hotels charge rates far above our price limits, come the weekend and special seasons the prices may go down. For example, during the summer of 1987, Holiday Inns (tel. toll free 800/HOLIDAY) was offering "Great Summer Rates" of $29, $39, and $49 per room at selected Inns and Crowne Plaza hotels nation wide. The Potomac Hotel Group in Washington, D.C. offered weekend packages of 3 days/2 nights ranging from $22.50 to $30 per person based on double occupancy. *The New York Times'* Sunday travel section and other large city publications are good resources for discovering these deals.

All-Suite Hotels

Another new development in the world of hospitality is the all-suite hotel. If you're a small group or a family this may be a great choice. Most offer, at the least, more space than a normal hotel room and sometimes a kitchen and complimentary breakfast. When divided by the four who can sleep there, rates often fall into our price range. As of 1987, Residence Inns is offering special introductory rates as low as $49 for three to four persons and some special weekend rates, too. Call toll free 800/331-3131.

Off-season and weekend rates dip down towards $50 to $80 for up to four adults, and complimentary breakfast and cocktail hour is served to all guests of the Embassy Suites (tel. toll free 800/EMBASSY). Guest Quarters Hotels (tel. toll free 800/424-2900) offer special weekend rates of $69 for up to four, fully-equipped kitchens, and some properties with breakfast and cocktails.

All in all, you may get more for your money at this kind of establishment: more space, facilities, and services, at the same cost as a hotel room.

Low-Cost Motel Chains

Something exciting has happened in the motel management field and that's the development of the low-cost motel chain. Based on the reasonable premise that travelers were getting tired of paying exorbitant prices for motel rooms, a few business people decided to build no-frills facilities that would not have to charge high rates to stay in business. This meant cutting out some of the extras such as restaurants on the property (they built across the street from the existing restaurants instead), wall-to-wall carpeting, etc. The first low-cost motel chain did so well that others have followed the lead, and now there are many all over the U.S. where you can spend the night comfortably and cheaply. We've included the following low-cost motel chains in our listings:

Allstar Inns, Best Inns of America, Budget Host Inns, Budgetel Inns, Comfort Inns, Days Inns of America, Drury Inns, E-Z 8 Motels, Econo Lodges of America, Exel Inns of America, Friendship Inns International, Hampton Inns, Imperial 400 Motor Inns, Knights Inns, Master Hosts Inns, Motel 6 Inns,

Quality Inns, Red Carpet Inns, Red Roof Inns, Regal 8 Inns, Scottish Inns, Select Inns of America, Super 8 Motels, Susse Chalet Inns, and TraveLodge Inns.

The rates of the various low-cost motels vary from chain to chain, and often even within the chain, but, in general, the more people you can fit into one room the more money you will save. It is always advisable to make reservations in advance at these motels, since they have become extremely popular with travelers. We've given approximate rates for each chain.

"The budget motels are very heavily booked especially during the summer and the chance of getting a room after 2 p.m. is slim indeed."

Remember that in order to stay at any of these motels, you will probably need to have a car (the bus and train books suggested in Chapter 1 will help with information on those places that are accessible by public transportation).

For free directories of all the facilities in any of the low-cost chains, you can write to the following addresses. If a chain has a toll-free telephone reservation number it's included below, along with facilities common to all or most of the member properties of each chain. In the body of this guide, an individual property listing will include only its name, address, and telephone number. Refer to this list for details on rates and facilities. Individual properties are listed by city within each state:

Allstar Inns
P.O. Box 3070
Santa Barbara, CA 93130-3070
Tel.: 805/687-3383
Handicapped facilities available.
Approximate Rates: $19.95 to $27.95 single; $23.95 to $30.95 double; $26.95 to $33.95 triple; $29.95 to $36.95 quad.

Best Inns, Inc.
P.O. Box 1719
Marion, IL 62959-7719
Tel.: 618/997-5454
Handicapped facilities available.
Discounts for senior citizens, and children under 18 years stay free.
Approximate Rates: $23.88 to $34.88 single; $27.88 to $38.88 double; $33.88 to $42.88 triple or quad.

Budget Host Inns
2601 Jacksboro Hwy., Caravan Suite 202, P.O. Box 10656
Fort Worth, TX 76114
Tel.: 817/626-7064
Reservations: toll free 800/835-7427
Handicapped facilities available in most inns.
Discounts for senior citizens, and bonus coupons available.

Approximate Rates: $16 to $36 single; $18.88 to $45 double; $24 to $54 triple; $35 to $65 suites.

Budgetel Inns
212 W. Wisconsin Ave.
Milwaukee, WI 53203
Tel.; 414/272-6020
Reservations: toll free 800/428-3438
Handicapped facilities available.
Discounts for senior citizens and children.
Approximate Rates: $23.95 to $37.95 single; $28.95 to $42.95 double; $31.95 to $48.95 triple; $36.95 to $53.95 quad.

Days Inns of America, Inc.
2751 Buford Hwy., NE
Atlanta, GA 30324
Tel.: 404/728-4451
Reservations: toll free 800/325-2525
Discounts vary from inn to inn. Applicable to senior citizens, military personnel, teachers, and students.
Approximate Rates: $20 to $40 single; $28 to $45 double.

Drury Inns, Inc.
10801 Pear Tree Lane
St. Ann, MO 63074
Tel.: 314/429-2255
Reservations: toll free 800/325-8300
Discounts for senior citizens, and children under 18 years stay free.
Approximate Rates: $24 to $40 single; $29 to $50 double; $4 to $6 each additional person.

E-Z 8 Motels, Inc.
2484 Hotel Circle Place
San Diego, CA 92108
Tel.: 619/291-4824
Approximate Rates: $16.88 to $32.88 single; $18.88 to $34.88 for two in one bed; $23.88 to $39.88 for three to four in two beds.

Econo Lodges of America, Inc.
6135 Park Rd., Suite 200
Charlotte, NC 28210-9981
Tel.: 704/554-0088
Reservations: toll free 800/446-6900
Handicapped facilities available.
Discounts vary from lodge to lodge. Applicable to senior citizens, families, and military personnel.

Approximate Rates: $21 to $40 single; $24 to $45 for two in one bed; $25 to $50 for two in two beds; $3 to $7 for each additional person.

Exel Inns of America, Inc.
4706 E. Washington Ave.
Madison, WI 53704
Tel.: 608/241-5271
Reservations: toll free 800/356-8013 or 800/362-5478 in Wisconsin
Handicapped facilities available.
Discounts for senior citizens, and children under 18 years stay free.
Approximate Rates: $21.95 to $36.95 single; $24.95 to $38.95 double; $31.95 to $45.95 triple; $33.95 to $47.95 quad.

Friendship Inns International, Inc.
2627 Paterson Plank Rd.
North Bergen, NJ 07047-2294
Tel.: 201/863-3443
Reservations: toll free 800/453-4511
Approximate Rates: $17 to $35 single; $20 to $45 for two in one bed; $22 to $50 for two in two beds; $2 to $7 for each additional person.

Hampton Inns, Inc.
6799 Great Oaks Rd., Suite 100
Memphis, TN 38138
Tel.: 901/756-2811
Reservations: toll free 800/HAMPTON, or 901/363-7777 in Memphis
Discounts for senior citizens, and children under 18 years stay free.
Approximate Rates: $25 to $40 single; $31 to $50 double, triple, or quad.

Hospitality International, Inc.: Scottish Inns, Red Carpet Inns, and Master Hosts Inns
1152 Spring St., Suite A
Atlanta, GA 30309
Tel.: 404/873-5924
Reservations: toll free 800/251-1962
Discounts for senior citizens.
Approximate Rates: $16 to $35 single; $18 to $40 for two in one bed; $20 to $45 for two in two beds; $3 to $6 for each additional person.

Imperial 400 National, Inc.
1000 Wilson Blvd., Suite 820
Arlington, VA 22209
Tel.: 703/524-4880
Reservations: toll free 800/368-4400, or 800/572-2200 in Virginia
Handicapped facilities at most locations.
Discounts for senior citizens, and children under 16 stay free.

Approximate Rates: $20 to $35 single; $22 to $40 for two in one bed; $24 to $50 for two in two beds.

Knights Inn
6561 E. Livingston Ave.
Reynoldsburg, OH 43068
Tel.: 614/755-9981
Handicapped facilities available.
Discounts for senior citizens, and children under 18 stay free.
Approximate Rates: $28.50 to $40 single.

Motel 6
51 Hitchcock Way
Santa Barbara, CA 93105
Tel.: 805/682-6666
Reservations: 505/891-6161
Children under 18 stay free.
Approximate Rates: $14.95 to $25.95 single; $19.95 to $30.95 double; $4 for each additional person.

Quality International: Quality Inns and Comfort Inns
10750 Columbia Pike
Silver Spring, MD 20901
Tel.: 301/593-5600
Reservations: toll free 800/228-5151 for Quality Inns; 800/228-5150 for Comfort Inns
Handicapped facilities at many inns.
Discounts available for senior citizens, families, and military personnel.
Approximate Rates: $22 to $40 single; $28 to $50 double.

Red Roof Inns, Inc.
4355 Davidson Rd.
Hilliard, OH 43026
Tel.: 614/876-3200
Reservations: toll free 800/848-7878
Handicapped facilities available at most inns.
Children under 18 stay free.
Approximate Rates: $21.95 to $37.95 single; $26.95 to $42.95 for two in one bed; $28.95 to $44.95 for two in two beds.

Regal 8 Inn
P.O. Box 1268
Mt. Vernon, IL 62864
Tel.: 618/242-7240
Reservations: toll free 800/851-8888
Handicapped facilities in most inns.
Discounts for senior citizens in most inns.
Approximate Rates: $23.88 to $27.88 single; $28.88 to $34.88 double; $33.88 to $39.88 triple or quad.

Select Inns of America, Inc.
Box 2603
Fargo, ND 58108
Tel.: 701/281-0140
Reservations: toll free 800/641-1000
Handicapped facilities available.
Discounts for senior citizens, and children under 13 stay free.
Approximate Rates: $19.50 to $23.95 single; $22.99 to $31.90 double.

Super 8 Motels, Inc.
P.O. Box 4090
Aberdeen, SD 57402-4090
Tel.: 605/225-2272
Reservations: toll free 800/843-1991
Handicapped facilities available.
Discounts for senior citizens, and children under 12 stay free in many motels.
Approximate Rates: $18.88 and up single; $24.88 and up double; $28.88 and up triple; $30.88 and up quad.

Susse Chalet
Chalet Dr.
Wilton, NH 03086
Tel.: 603/654-2000
Reservations: toll free 800/258-1980, or 800/572-1880 in New Hampshire.
Handicapped facilities available in most inns.
Approximate Rates: $29.70 to $41.70 single; $33.70 to $45.70 double.

TraveLodge
1973 Friendship Dr.
El Cajon, CA 92071
Tel.: 619/448-1884
Reservations: toll free 800/255-3050
Handicapped facilities available at most inns.
Discounts available for senior citizens and families, and children under 17 stay free.
Approximate Rates: $22 to $40 single; $25 to $40 for two in one bed; $29 to $50 for two in two beds.

Pilot Books, 103 Cooper St., Babylon, NY 11702, publishes a *National Directory of Budget Motels.* The 1987–88 edition is available for $4.95 postpaid.

"Motels can be a great value. Particularly at touristy places out of season, it really pays to bargain. For example, when we were in Fort Lauderdale, Fla., the first two places told us it would be $26 for a double everywhere. Next door we got it down to $24 and next door to that, to $22. We checked next to this last place and then returned to say the bloke next door was charging $18. We ended up with a magnificent room for $15."

Bed-and-Breakfast Accommodations
A relatively new and very welcome phenomenon is the development of bed-and-breakfast facilities throughout the U.S. Taking the cue from other countries where bed-and-breakfast establishments have been an institution for a long

time, many people are opening their homes to travelers—providing a room and breakfast in pleasant surroundings for a rate often much lower than that offered in many commercial hotels and motels.

Reservation Services: Many of these people who want to host travelers in their homes have joined organizations that serve to publicize their facilities and help them simplify their reservations process. Bed-and-breakfast reservation services for a particular state or city are listed in that state's introduction or with the city listing.

Here are a few reservation services that cover more than one state: Anyone traveling in Washington, Oregon, Idaho, Hawaii, or California who wants to stay in a private home or bed-and-breakfast inn can contact Northwest Bed and Breakfast, 610 S.W. Broadway, Portland, OR 97205 (tel. 503/243-7616). The annual membership fee is $15 for one person, $20 for a family, $5 trial membership for one reservation. Overnight rates vary from $22 to $35 for a single, $24 to $45 for a double. A directory of approximately 350 homes in the Northwest network is available for $5; $5 will be credited to your membership fee.

Another western bed-and-breakfast service is Bed and Breakfast Rocky Mountain, P.O. Box 804, Colorado Springs, CO 80901 (tel. 303/630-3433), with 100 listings in Colorado, New Mexico, Montana, Wyoming, and Utah. Their directory with quarterly updates is $9.50 for one year. Single rates are $25 and up, double $35 and up, and triple, quad, apartment or suite $45 and up. Discounts of 10% are offered at some ski areas during the summer, 10% for senior citizens at some properties, and 15% on a second room for families.

Now in their tenth year of operation, Bed & Breakfast International, 151 Ardmore Rd., Kensington, CA 94707, is another organization that places people in private homes in San Francisco, Los Angeles, San Diego, and other locations in California, as well as in Hawaii, New York City, Washington, D.C., Seattle, and Las Vegas. It is the oldest organization of its kind. The cost is $38 to $85 for two people, $6 less for the single traveler. Special rates are available to students. For an application, write to the address above and enclose a stamped, self-addressed envelope or call 415/525-4569 during business hours.

Bed and Breakfast Registry Ltd., P.O. Box 8174, St. Paul, MN 55108, has listings in 42 states, with rates from $20 to $55 for a single and from $25 to $90 for a double. There's no registration fee; call 612/646-4238 for information and reservations. They have a detailed directory available for $9.25 plus $3 postage and handling.

Pineapple Hospitality, Inc., 47 North Second St., New Bedford, MA 02740 (tel. 617/990-1696), acts as a reservation service for Maine, Vermont, New Hampshire, Massachusetts, Connecticut, and Rhode Island in the cities and way out in the country as well. Their directory costs $4.95 plus $1 handling and applicable sales tax.

The American Country Collection handles reservations at bed-and-breakfasts in northeastern New York, Vermont, and western Massachusetts. They are at 984 Gloucester Place, Schenectady, NY 12309 (tel. 518/370-4948). Single rates range from $20 to $75, doubles from $30 to $100. Budget accommodations are available for $20 to $45 per double. Their directory is $2.

Publications: Books specific to one state are listed in that state's introduction. The following guides cover the entire U.S. or a region of the country. A book that lists guesthouses, tourist homes, and bed-and-breakfasts throughout the U.S.—and one that we've seen grow from brochure size to a full-fledged paperback in only a few years—is *Bed and Breakfast USA: A Guide to Guest*

Houses and Tourist Homes, by Betty Rundback and Nancy Kramer. The book, published by E.P. Dutton, is available in bookstores or from Tourist House Associates, Inc., RD 2, Box 355A, Greentown, PA 18426 ($9.95). Besides the listing of 800 facilities in all 50 states and Canada, the authors also include over 100 reservation services—the kind we mentioned above—which give readers access to 11,000 homes. The average rate for two is $40. According to the authors: "You are always made to feel more like a welcome guest than a paying customer."

Bed & Breakfast in New England ($11.95) and *Bed and Breakfast in the Mid-Atlantic States* ($10.95), both by Bernice Chesler are published by Globe Pequot Press, Old Chester Rd., Chester, CT 06412. A long list of Bed & Breakfast registration services can lead to accommodations all over the U.S. and eastern Canada.

America Bed and Breakfast Association, 16 Village Green, Suite 203A, Crofton, MD 21114 (tel. 301/261-0180). "A Treasury of Bed and Breakfast" ($14.95 plus $3 for shipping and handling) lists 3000 bed-and-breakfasts from Hawaii to Nova Scotia.

The National Bed and Breakfast Association publishes *Bed and Breakfast Guide for the U.S., Canada, Bermuda, Puerto Rico and the U.S. Virgin Islands,* by Phyllis Featherstone and Barbara Ostler, which lists over 120 bed-and-breakfast homes and small family-owned and operated inns. Through their new Reservation Service Section, you'll have access to 8000 to 9000 additional bed-and-breakfast accommodations. The explanation and the "How to Use the Guide" sections are written in English, French, and Spanish. The book is sold in many U.S. bookstores or can be ordered from the Association at 148 E. Rocks Rd., P.O. Box 332, Norwalk, CT 06852 ($11.95 plus $2 for postage and handling).

John Muir Publications, P.O. Box 613, Santa Fe, NM 87504, has *The Complete Guide to Bed and Breakfasts, Inns and Guest Houses,* by Pamela Lanier ($12.95), with 2800 inn listings and 10,000 private guesthomes, and an appendix of reservation services in the U.S.

Two more regional guidebooks, published by Chronicle Books, One Halladie Plaza, San Francisco, CA 94102, are *Bed and Breakfast Northwest,* by Myrna Oakley, covering Oregon, Washington, British Columbia, southeastern Alaska, and Montana ($7.95), and *Bed and Breakfast Colorado and the Rocky Mountain West,* by Buddy Mays, covering Colorado and other Rocky Mountain states ($7.95).

And finally, there's a countrywide network of bed-and-breakfast services which at last count had 20 members. For a brochure listing the various members, send a self-addressed, stamped envelope to the Bed and Breakfast National Network, P.O. Box 4616, Springfield, MA 01101 or P.O. Box 162, Oreland, PA 19075.

Camping

Camping in the U.S. can be a fabulous experience. The facilities are widespread and generally excellent, and it shouldn't be too difficult for you to avoid the trailer set and enjoy the great outdoors. Our favorites are the state and national parks, which are much more beautiful than most private campgrounds. Be warned, though, that state and national parks are extremely popular with campers, and it's possible that some will be filled to capacity when you decide to go.

In our state listings we have room to list only national parks, with a few exceptions. For complete information on state parks, just write or call the state tourist office listed for each state. Most publish lists and accompanying maps describing facilities, and will send them to you—all free of charge, of course.

Two companies offer organized camping trips: American Adventures, 650 Cambridge St., Cambridge, MA 02141 (tel. 617/499-2730), with sales offices all over Europe and in Australia, New Zealand, Hong Kong, Japan, Israel, etc., offers camping expeditions all over the U.S. for people ages 18 to 38 in groups of 12 to 13 persons. 1987 prices range from 21 days at $649 for "California Dreaming," "The East Coast," and "Cross Country South," to 64 days at $1879 for the "Great American Adventure." Prices include transportation, campsite fees, hikes, tent, and all equipment except sleeping bag.

TrekAmerica/Europa, P.O. Box 1338, Gardena, CA 90249 (tel. 213/321-0734, or toll free 800/221-0596), isn't really a trek, but is another "cooperative camping" tour operator with ten North American itineraries from two to seven weeks long and daily costs of about $30 to $40 plus about $5 for food. Again the age range is 18 to 35 and you're transported in a mini-van.

Anyone who intends to use the national park system extensively should purchase a "Golden Eagle Passport," which is sold at all parks. The passport costs $25 and provides free entry to all areas of the national park system that charge entrance fees. The free entry applies to the permit holder and everyone accompanying him or her in a private, non-commercial vehicle; it is valid for the calendar year. Normally the entrance fee to the parks ranges from $3 to $7.50 per passenger vehicle.

The "Golden Age Passport" is issued free to any U.S. citizen age 62 or older upon presentation of proof of age at any park, and a Golden Access Passport is issued free to blind and disabled people who are eligible for federal disability benefits. Both permit free admission to all areas of the national park system and a 50% discount on recreation fees. Applicants must apply in person.

Most campsites in the national park system are available on a first-come, first-served basis only. Reservations can be made directly at only a few of the campgrounds. For reservations, write to the addresses given in the listings for these campgrounds, to the attention of the superintendent. Reservations may be made through Ticketron for Acadia National Park (Maine), Cape Hatteras National Seashore (North Carolina), Great Smoky Mountains National Park (North Carolina and Tennessee), Shenandoah National Park (Virginia), Grand Canyon National Park (Arizona), Rocky Mountain National Park (Colorado), Sequoia-Kings Canyon National Park (California), Whiskeytown-Shasta-Trinity National Recreation Area (California), and Yosemite National Park (California). Reservation forms are available at Ticketron outlets and the Ticketron Reservations Office, Dept. R, 401 Hackensack Ave., Hackensack, NJ 07601.

Since campsites in the national parks are so much in demand, it has been necessary for the park service to limit the number of days a person may occupy a site at some of the parks during the peak season This time limit, and all other information about the park, is available from the address listed in each state section. Remember that the address we list here for the park is not necessarily the location of the campground—it is a mailing address only. In some cases, campgrounds may be many miles from the town listed as the mailing address.

For a list of the 104 areas maintained by the National Park Service, and information on their facilities, send $3.50 to the Superintendent of Documents, U.S. Government Printing Office, Washington, D.C. 20402, and ask for *Camping in the National Park System* (number 024-005-00987-6).

One other useful publication available from the same source is *Lesser-Known Areas of the National Park System* ($1.50).

For a comprehensive listing of all campgrounds in the U.S., both public and private, we recommend the *Rand McNally RV Park and Campground Directory* ($12.95); the 1987 edition is available in most bookstores. The Rand McNally guide is especially useful, since it contains maps of each state with every campground listed marked on them. This makes it easy to plan your travel route according to available campgrounds. Rand McNally also publishes its guide in East and West editions and in six regional editions: California and Western States; Mid-Atlantic States; Midwest States; New York and New England States; Southern States; and Texas, Great Plains, and Rockies States. All are updated annually, prices subject to change.

If the idea of camping on Indian lands interests you, write to the U.S. Department of the Interior, Bureau of Indian Affairs, Washington, D.C. 20242. There are reservations in many of the western states. For information on which ones offer campgrounds, contact the local state tourist offices.

Not everyone knows that many of the state and national parks have cabins and lodges that are available to the public. To find out what's where and how to arrange a cabin stay, see *Traveling and Camping in the National Park Areas: Eastern, Mid-America or Western*, Globe Pequot Press ($4.95 each).

Crashing

There's not much one can say about this kind of accommodation. You find it where you can, and whether you do or not depends on your own resourcefulness. More and more areas of the country have gotten used to the idea of crashing, and if you carry a sleeping bag along you'll find crashing a lot easier. College towns are the most likely places to find crashing space; stop at some of the on-campus addresses given in the state listings to ask about the chances for crashing in the neighborhood. Many of the hotlines listed in *Where to Stay USA* will also be able to tell you whether there's any crashing space around.

Home Hospitality

An interesting organization that we discovered and one that doesn't really fit under any other heading is one called Innter Lodging Co-op. The Co-op is a group of families who agree to make their homes available to travelers for at least three months a year. In return, when they travel they can stay at other members' homes for $4 or $5 per night (no meals included). To find out more about the Co-op, write to Innter Lodging Co-op, P.O. Box 7044, Tacoma, WA 98407 (tel. 206/756-0343).

Visiting Friends, Inc., is a guestroom exchange network in the U.S. with a few Canadian members. It's a "flexible and useful association of friendly folks—an excellent supplement to other ways of travel." It is used by hikers and bikers, by sightseers and Elderhostelers (no pets or children allowed). A small fee is charged. They're at P.O. Box 231, Lake Jackson, TX 77566 (tel. 409/297-7367).

One organization that sponsors a worldwide program of exchange hospitality for travelers in over 90 countries including the U.S. is SERVAS. Its goal: to help build peace, goodwill, and understanding through home visits and other contact between people. Here's how SERVAS works: you apply and are interviewed; if accepted, you receive a personal briefing, written instructions, a list of SERVAS hosts in the area you are going to visit, and an introductory letter. You arrange your visits in advance by writing or calling the hosts. The usual stay with a SERVAS host is two nights. For information on SERVAS, contact the SERVAS office in your home country, or write to the U.S. SERVAS Committee, Inc., 11 John St., Room 706, New York, NY 10038. SERVAS asks for a donation of $45 for its services.

Last Resorts
"I met two guys who had had their packs ripped off and had nothing to their names. I went with them to the Salvation Army where they were able to get $4 worth of groceries and $6 worth of clothes—they also told them about churches, etc., that gave out free food. I'd advise anyone in trouble to check out a Salvation Army."

People Who Can Help
The idea of community switchboards, hotlines, free clinics, and help lines has caught on all over the country, and no matter where you roam help is always just a telephone call away. If you have a problem, need a place to stay or some medical care, or just want to hear a friendly voice, you can call the help lines listed in each state section.

In researching *Where to Stay USA,* we asked friends all over the country about the help lines and crisis centers that were located in their areas so that we could include them in our book. Hotlines seem to come and go with great rapidity; the telephone numbers that we have here were in service when we went to press and hopefully still are.

In the "Help" section of each state listing, besides the telephone numbers of hotlines and crisis centers you'll often find the addresses and telephone numbers of Travelers Aid offices. Travelers Aid (its full name is Travelers Aid Association of America) is a social-work agency with branches in airports, bus stations, and railroad stations that has been set up to assist people on the move by providing emergency assistance, protective care, and professional counseling service. Feel free to call on them if you need help.

The National Runaway Switchboard is operated by Metro-Help, Inc., in Chicago. It takes calls from around the country on a toll-free line. "Kids can call us from anywhere in the continental U.S. and get information on over 3000 runaway centers, central community switchboards, and counseling agencies around the country. In addition, we can also use a conferencing device on the phone to allow kids to talk directly with any of these agencies or their parents. If a runaway wants to let his or her parents know that he or she is all right, we'll also deliver the message. . . ." The toll-free number is 800/621-4000 and is available 24 hours a day. All services are confidential.

Paying Your Way
As you travel, it may be possible to pick up jobs here and there to give you enough money to keep you going.

State employment offices can usually offer good advice on the current work situation in any particular area—feel free to call on them for advice.

If you run out of money and need a job immediately in order to keep you going, you can try calling the help-line numbers. Sometimes they can refer you to a temporary job that will give you enough money to move on.

There are some sweeping generalizations that can be made about job-finding in the U.S. One is, don't count on finding work in California or Michigan, where too many others are job-seeking. If you're going across country and think you're going to need some more money to see you through, big cities are good places to look for a job—especially in the service industries, as waiters, waitresses, sales help, etc.

N.B. Foreign visitors with B (visitors) visas may not seek paid employment during their stay in the U.S. To work without the proper visa is illegal.

Volunteering

The National Park Service recruits volunteers to perform a variety of tasks at the parks in the areas of interpretation (helping visitors understand the natural and human history of the area), arts and crafts, history, archaeology, natural science, environmental study, and resource management. You can get a brochure, "Volunteers in Parks," and an application from the National Park Service, U.S. Department of the Interior, Washington, D.C. 20240.

Volunteer! The Comprehensive Guide to Voluntary Service in the U.S. and Abroad, lists full-time opportunities for teens and adults. It's available from CIEE, Pubs. Dept., 205 E. 42nd St., New York, NY 10017.

Eating

It's going to be tempting, as you travel, to do most of your eating at the fast-food chain restaurants that are springing up all over America. That's why we decided to list a few of our friends' favorite eating places in the state listings and have resisted mentioning any of the chains; we hope to prove that you can still find good, filling, low-cost meals without having to resort to the chains.

If you're trying to economize, why not forget eating in restaurants altogether; buy your food in supermarkets and have yourself a picnic.

Many of the accommodations listed in *Where to Stay USA* have cooking facilities available; whenever this is true, you can save money by taking advantage of them. We have one friend who used to cook hamburgers in his hotel room on a travel iron that he carried around with him—there are all sorts of ways to save money if you put your mind to it.

We can recommend one more book for those who care about what they eat. It is *Goodfood,* by Jane and Michael Stern, published by Knopf ($8.95). According to the Sterns, "It is possible to escape the homogenized cuisine that lines the highways and makes eating in Arizona indistinguishable from eating in Maine." They point the way, listing what they consider America's best regional restaurants.

CHAPTER 3

Special-Interest Groups: The Disabled, Senior Citizens, and Families

For People with Disabilities

For far too long, disabled travelers were ignored; there was very little information for them, and facilities that could make their travel at least possible, and at most pleasurable, were minimal. That has changed and much has been done to develop special facilities. Many new publications broadcast the news, and services arrange tours and transportation. Wheelchair Wagon Service, P.O. Box 1270, Kissimmee, FL 32742 (tel. 305/846-7175), offers non-emergency transportation to and from the airport and tours for the elderly and disabled in the Orlando, Florida area. Their newest venture "Rent-A-Vans" will allow folks to go off and explore on their own in vehicles equipped with raised roofs and hydraulic lifts. Their "Wheelchair Vacation Escort" service will provide personal assistance for persons traveling alone.

Whole Person Tours runs 5- to 15-day tours including visits to the cities of the Middle Atlantic States, Disney World, New England, Hawaii and more. For a catalog send $2 to Whole Person Tours, Inc., P.O. Box 1084, Bayonne, NJ 07002-1084. They also publish a bi-monthly magazine *The Itinerary,* at $9 a year.

Moss Rehabilitation Hospital, 12th Street and Tabor Road, Philadelphia, PA 19141 (tel. 215/329-5715), offers a travel information service where, for $5, they will send you a travel accessibility information package on up to three destinations. There is no charge for brief telephone inquiries and their general information sheet. From them we've learned of the following additional services for the disabled: "Access Amtrak," Public Affairs Office, AMTRAK, 400 N. Capital St. NW, Washington, DC 20001 (tel. toll free 800/523-6590), and "Helping Hand Services for the Handicapped," Greyhound Lines, Section S, Greyhound Tower, Phoenix, AZ 85077 (tel. toll free 800/345-3109).

A travel guide for the disabled is the *Wheelchair Traveler,* by Douglas Annand. The book lists 6,000 hotels, motels, restaurants, and sightseeing attractions that are accessible to the disabled. For information about the book, write to Douglas Annand, Ball Hill Road, Milford, NH 03055. An excellent guide is *Access to the World,* Henry Holt and Co. ($12.95), first published ten years ago with information and tips of all kinds. "Access Travel: Airports" is available through Access America, Washington, DC 20202 or Consumer Information Center, Pueblo, CO 81009 (item number 632k).

An excellent source of information for the disabled is Mobility International USA, an organization dedicated to integrating people with disabilities into travel and educational programs in the U.S. and abroad. *A World of Options: A Guide to International Educational Exchange, Community Service and Travel for Persons with Disabilities* offers firsthand information on successful wheelchair travel and a resource section on books and agencies that will help the disabled traveler. Contact MIUSA at P.O. Box 3551, Eugene, OR 97403 (tel. 503/343-1284).

And something new for "people with travel limitations" is LTD Travel, a newsletter published in California. One of the founders, who has traveled in a wheelchair for 30 years, has designed the newsletter to serve travelers with limitations and especially families "with one limited member who hates being a burden but also hates being left home." Recent issues have included articles on wheelchair camping and touring the northern California wine country. Subscriptions are $15 for four issues per year. Write to LTD Travel, 931 Shoreline Drive, San Mateo, CA 94404 (tel. 415/573-7998).

For Senior Citizens

The American Association of Retired Persons (AARP), with national headquarters at 1909 K St. NW, Washington, DC 20049, offers members a Purchase Privilege Program which includes discounts for major hotels and motels, car rentals, the AARP Motoring Plan with emergency and other road services for an annual fee and AARP travel services with group travel programs all over the U.S. and the world. For information on membership and these programs, write to AARP at the above address.

Another organization that serves senior citizens and has become extremely popular in the past few years is Elderhostel, a Boston-based group that sponsors study vacations on college campuses worldwide. Friends of ours who have participated in Elderhostel said that it was the best vacation they'd had in over 40 years. For a catalog of Elderhostel programs, write to the organization at 80 Boylston St., Suite 400, Boston, MA 02116 (tel. 617/426-8056).

Mature Outlook is an organization serving people 50 and older. Membership is $7.50 per year per couple. Services include consumer discounts, publications, and discounts on hotels, motels, cruises, vacations, car rentals and more. Contact them at P.O. Box 1209, Glenview, IL 60025-9935 (tel. toll free 800/336-6330).

Also of interest to senior citizens is *The Discount Guide for Travelers Over 55,* by Caroline and Walter Weintz; published by E.P. Dutton ($7.95).

Another useful guide published by Pilot Books is *The Senior Citizen's Guide to Budget Travel in the U.S. and Canada* ($4.95 postage included)

Many budget motel chains offer special discounts to senior citizens—check with the head offices of the individual chains (addresses on pages 28–32) for information.

For Families

More and more families are traveling with their children, and finding that they need advice and details in order to make their trips a success. Travel with Your Children is a resource information center—the only one of its kind—for parents and travel agents, and publishes *Family Travel Times,* a monthly newsletter on everything from camping to all-suite hotels, museum and city visits, air travel and African treks, and all for families with children under 12. They also publish annual guides called "Skiing with Children" and "Cruising with Children." Destinations are worldwide. Subscribers to the newsletter may call the Travel Information Hotline for special requests. Subscriptions to *Family Travel Times* are $35 a year. They're at 80 Eighth Ave., New York, NY 10011 (tel. 212/206-0688). As for travel guides for families, there are many, but they can be difficult to find. Two companies handle mail orders: Send for the free catalog "Families on the Go's" from 1259 El Camino Real #147, Menlo Park, CA 94025 (tel. 415/322-4203, or toll free 800/367-2934 in the U.S.; 800/752-9955 in California); and Carousel Press' "Family Travel Guides" catalog for $1, applicable toward purchase. They're at P.O. Box 6061, Albany, CA 94706.

A new guide promising to be quite terrific is by Dorothy Jordon, publisher of *Family Travel Times* and Marjorie Cohen, author of this guide. It is *Great Vacations With Your Kids*, E.P. Dutton ($9.95).

CHAPTER 4

Especially for Foreign Visitors

The U.S., often viewed by its natives with relative disinterest, caused, it seems, by a lack of a familiarity with its fascinations, usually gets rave reviews from foreign visitors. If you're anything like the people from abroad who stopped by to see us after their trips around the U.S., you're going to have a wonderful time here. One of the reasons for this, and probably the most important, is that Americans really are friendly people, especially the ones who live beyond the large cities and seem to have more time for everything, including enjoying a visitor from another country. One young Frenchman put it neatly: "Everywhere we are welcome."

In this section you'll find more about what you should know before you start out on your trip in the U.S.: special discounts available to you because you are an international visitor (remember that all special discounts are, unfortunately, subject to change or cancellation without warning), and everyday bits of information designed to save you the common traumas of travel; for instance, your first phone call from a pay telephone or your first taxi ride.

Don't forget to read the other introductory chapters, too, since they contain information that everyone—American or foreign—needs when traveling in this country.

Transportation Discounts

To know what travel discounts exist at any given time, you have to be an expert in the field. For help in finding what bargains exist once you are in the U.S., consult a Council Travel Services office (addresses on page 2, Chapter 1).

BY AIR: Air travel is extremely popular in the U.S. There are planes flying in and out of more than 1000 airports across the country. Aside from airport delays and traffic jams getting to the airport, it's the fastest way to get from one place to another, but not necessarily the cheapest unless you find a special fare and can live with its restrictions.

You will probably find that travel in the U.S. is less expensive mile for mile than it is at home, and if you use the following special discounts, you can travel by air and still keep to a modest budget: As a foreign visitor, you can take advantage of deals that are unavailable to U.S. citizens. Currently, airpasses are offered by Delta and Northwest Airlines and must be purchased outside of the U.S. by holders of non-U.S. passports. Delta's 60-day pass costs between $500 and $623. Northwest offers a 30-day pass at $389 and 60 days at $479.

BY BUS: Bus travel is inexpensive and a favorite with young people both because of the cost and because you get to see a lot of the U.S. from a seat in a bus—everything that you'd miss if you went by plane. See "Going by Bus" in Chapter 1 for details. Currently, Greyhound offers a "Visit USA" pass through travel agents all over Europe. Write to Greyhound International, 625 Eighth Avenue, New York, NY 10018 for complete details.

BY TRAIN: People who live outside the U.S. are entitled to two kinds of USA Rail passes on Amtrak—a national one and four regional ones. The national pass is good for periods of 14, 21, or 30 days and costs $375, $450, and $525 respectively (half-price for children under 12). The regional pass covers 14 days of travel over one of four sections of the country—Western ($225), Far Western ($125), Eastern ($215), and Northeastern ($125).

The USA Rail Pass is good for coach travel on any part of the Amtrak system with unlimited stopovers except on Metroliner Service trains or the Auto Train. However, a USA Rail Pass holder may travel aboard the Metroliner Service trains—as well as in club or sleeping cars—by paying the appropriate additional charge, subject to the availability of such accommodations.

A valid passport is required to purchase the rail passes. Details on the program and passes should be available in your country from most major travel agents or from Council Travel Services offices in France or Japan (see page 2 for addresses). Remember that on the more popular long-distance runs in the U.S., it is necessary to have reservations, preferably made well in advance of your train trip. In the U.S., USA Rail Pass holders should be sure to make reservations by calling 800/USA-RAIL or by visiting an Amtrak ticket or sales office. There is no charge for reservations.

Also note that the Rail Pass must be presented at an Amtrak ticket office where tickets for the particular trips will be issued.

BY CAR: To drive in the U.S. all you'll need is a valid driver's license from your own country, as long as it's one of the 161 countries that have agreed to the Geneva Road Traffic Convention of 1949. (If you are not from one of these countries, you'll have to obtain a U.S. driver's license at your point of entry into the U.S.) It is advisable to carry an International Driving Permit, which is printed in the official languages of the United Nations. It is especially helpful to local police speaking only English, and may be essential in case of an emergency.

Most car-rental companies require that Americans be at least 21 years of age to rent a car (it's age 25 in New York), but foreign visitors only have to be 18. When you rent a car, you'll have to make a fairly large deposit—the exact amount depends on the place where you pick up the car. Americans *must* pay the deposit with a credit card but foreign visitors may pay in cash. Don't forget the possibility of finding a "driveaway" car (see Chapter 1) or of buying a used car and then selling it when your trip is over.

Other Possibilities

Although there is no set nationwide policy, there are many hotels, motels, and tourist attractions that will give foreign visitors special rates. Always ask whether such a special rate exists—you have nothing to lose by trying.

Meeting Americans in Their Homes

Since there's no better way to get to understand the U.S. and Americans than by spending some time with them at home, you'll probably want to explore some of the following possibilities for arranging a visit to an American home. Chances are that if you do not prearrange such a visit through one of these organizations you will still get to meet Americans in their homes, since Americans are free with their invitations. When an American invites you to be his guest, don't feel he is just being polite—he wouldn't ask you to come if he didn't really want you to.

If you are interested in joining a summer or long-term program in the U.S. involving a family homestay, a partial listing of exchange programs is available on request from the Institute of International Education. Write for the *International Home Hospitality Programs List* from Communications Division, IIE, 809 United Nations Plaza, New York, NY 10017.

Christmas International House: This organization, based in Atlanta, places international students currently enrolled in American colleges (undergraduate and graduate) in American homes from mid-December to after the New Year, to share the holidays with an American family. For details, write to the organization, 341 Ponce de Leon Ave. NE, Atlanta, GA 30365 (tel. 404/873-1531). For more of such organizations see "Home Hospitality" on page 36.

Community Organizations

There are also community-based organizations around the country that have been set up specifically to cater to the needs of foreign visitors. These organizations are located all over the U.S., and most of them belong to a central organization, the National Council for International Visitors (NCIV), located in Washington, D.C.

Some of these organizations will place foreign students or visitors with families in their area for two- or three-day stays, although this is not necessarily their major function. These organizations should not be confused with accommodation bureaus; they are simply groups of people who wish to further international understanding and feel that one way to do this is to offer hospitality and program assistance to visitors from abroad. They are usually staffed by volunteers who give their time because they believe in what they are doing, and their help and hospitality should never be abused. Some community organizations can arrange home hospitality only for people who are visiting the U.S. as part of a prearranged program. Many of the ones we list below are willing to offer their sponsored services to unsponsored visitors. Understandably, all these organizations require advance notice of one week to one month to allow time to contact the host family and make arrangements.

In order to arrange a home visit with one of these groups in a specific state, you should contact the organization directly and give them some basic information about your interests and your background. Even if you are not planning a home visit, you can feel free to consult these organizations for general information on the area. Most are anxious to help you and many have 24-hour answering services so they can provide assistance in emergencies.

You may want to write to NCIV and ask for a copy of the "NCIV Pocket Directory," a brochure which provides a complete listing of the telephone numbers and addresses of NCIV members across the country. NCIV's address is Meridian House, 1623 Belmont St. NW, Washington, DC 20009.

ALABAMA: Birmingham Council for International Visitors, Suite 300, Commerce Center, 2027 First Ave. North, Birmingham, AL 35203 (tel. 205/252-9825). Will provide homestay and home hospitality for sponsored visitors with ten-day advance notice. Open 8:30 a.m. to 5 p.m., Monday to Friday.

Huntsville-Madison County Council for International Visitors, Room 525, Madison County Courthouse, Huntsville, AL 35801-9990 (tel. 205/532-3560). Open 9:30 a.m. to 4:30 p.m. Monday to Friday. Provides information on the community and assistance in an emergency.

ARIZONA: World Affairs Council of Phoenix, Inc., 401 North 1st St., Ramada Inn Downtown, Room 233, Phoenix, AZ 85004 (tel. 602/254-3345). Does professional and social programming for international visitors; provides home visits and overnight stays for visitors and hosts with common interests. Open 9:30 a.m. to 12:30 p.m. Monday through Friday.

Tucson Council for International Visitors, Aztec Inn, 102 North Alvernon Way, Tucson, AZ 85711 (tel. 602/795-0330, ext. 104). Provides foreign visitor volunteer programming and hosting and a language bank; provides home visits and escorts for sightseeing. Open 9 a.m. to 12 noon, Monday to Friday.

CALIFORNIA: International Visitor's Center, 312 Sutter St., Room 402, San Francisco, CA 94108 (tel. 415/986-1388). Open 9 a.m. to 5 p.m., Monday to Friday. Provides home hospitality in the form of dinner invitations on four-day notice.

Sacramento Council of International Visitors, 7645 Eastgate St., Citrus Heights, CA 95610 (tel. 916/967-0742). Provides home hospitality in the form of dinner invitations on 10-day notice, and some professional programming on 30-day notice. Open 8:30 a.m. to 5 p.m. Monday to Friday.

COLORADO: International Hospitality Center UNA-UNESCO Colorado Division, 980 Grant St., Denver, CO 80203 (tel. 303/832-4234 and 832-4765). Open 10 a.m. to 4 p.m., Monday to Friday. Arranges home visits and homestays with one month's notice. Drop-in visitors can pick up tourist information.

Institute of International Education, 700 Broadway, Suite 112, Denver, CO 80203 (tel. 303/837-0788). Open 8:30 a.m. to 4:30 p.m., Monday to Friday. Brochures, maps, and general information about Denver for drop-ins. With one month's notice and an adequate description of the students, will arrange a two- or three-day homestay. Student must also give exact date and time of arrival and departure.

CONNECTICUT: World Affairs Center, Inc., 1380 Asylum Ave., Hartford, CT 06105 (tel. 203/236-5277). Office open or answering service Monday to Friday, 9:30 a.m. to 4:30 p.m. With adequate notice, home hospitality is available in addition to professional contacts and reservations for low-cost lodging.

International Center of New Haven, P.O. Box 94A, 442 Temple Street, New Haven, CT 06520 (tel. 203/787-3531). Has volunteers in the community who help host, transport, arrange visits, and orient visitors to the area. Open 10 a.m. to 4 p.m. Monday to Thursday.

International Hospitality Committee, 28 Darbrook Rd., Westport, CT 06880 (tel. 203/227-3345). Arranges and provides home hospitality for a day to area students at holiday times and arranges visits for sponsored visitors. Open 9 a.m. to 5 p.m. Monday to Friday.

DISTRICT OF COLUMBIA: Foreign Student Service Council, 2337 18th St. NW, Washington, DC 20009 (tel. 202/232-4979). Open 9 a.m. to 5 p.m., Monday to Friday. Homestays of up to three nights may be arranged for international university students with host families or individuals in the area. At least two weeks' advance notice must be given. Send name, age, school, studies, nationality, date, time, and means of arrival in Washington, and address where you can be reached prior to your visit there. A $3-per-person registration fee, payable by check or money order, is required for this service. International Student Identity Cards are available, as well as advice on low-cost accommodation and sightseeing tours. Similar homestays can be arranged for national graduate students pursuing specific and advanced research. Three weeks' advance notice is necessary.

International Visitors Information Service, 733 15th St. NW, Suite 300, Washington, DC 20005 (tel. 202/783-6540). Open 9 a.m. to 5 p.m., Monday to Friday. Provides bilingual tourist information and 24-hour telephone language assistance.

FLORIDA: Council for International Visitors of Greater Miami, Inc., 607 Olympia Building, 174 East Flagler St., Miami, FL 33131 (tel. 305/379-4610 or 379-4615). Open Monday to Friday, 9 a.m. to 5 p.m. No homestays for unsponsored visitors, but "we never deny a welcome to foreign visitors. We welcome their inquiries, will assist by giving local orientation and, in general, make these students comfortable in our community."

Mid-Florida Council for International Visitors, Orlando International Airport, Box 80, Orlando, FL 32812 (tel. 305/826-2403). Arranges person-to-person "at home" hospitality with community host families, meetings with students, cultural, and recreational activities and assistance on accommodations, transportation, and restaurants. Open 9 a.m. to 5 p.m., Monday to Friday, and 7 a.m. to 11 p.m. every day at the International Information Kiosk (tel. 305/826-2352).

INDIANA: Council for International Visitors, 8753 Washington Blvd. East Dr., Indianapolis, IN 46240 (tel. 317/846-6806). If enough advance notice is given, a three-day homestay is possible. Overnight stays, sightseeing, and information are easily available. Some documentation is required from the visitor.

IOWA: Council for International Visitors to Iowa City, 202 Jefferson Bldg., Iowa City, IA 52242 (tel. 319/335-0335). Information center open 9:15 a.m. to 12:15 p.m. Monday, Wednesday, and Friday.

LOUISIANA: Council for International Visitors of Greater New Orleans, P.O. Box 24825, New Orleans, LA 70184 (tel. 504/242-3563 or 865-9704). Provides hotel reservations, sightseeing, and a home meal with a minimum of one week's advance notice. No specific office hours.

MARYLAND: International Visitors Center Baltimore, World Trade Center,

Suite 1353, Baltimore, MD 21201 (tel. 301/837-7150). With ten days advance notice, provides sightseeing and hotel information, arranges professional appointments, home visits, and brief homestays for individuals and small groups of sponsored professional visitors. Open 9 a.m. to 5 p.m. Monday to Friday.

MICHIGAN: International Visitors Council, 100 Renaissance Center, Suite 1405, Detroit, MI 48243 (tel. 313/259-2680). Open 9 a.m. to 5 p.m. weekdays. Helps with sightseeing information, maps, etc. No home hospitality for unsponsored visitors.

World Affairs Council of Western Michigan, 143 Bostwick, Grand Rapids, MI 49506 (tel. 616/458-9535). Open Monday to Friday, 9 a.m. to 5 p.m. "Some of our members have expressed an interest in acting as host families for short-term visits by foreign guests. We could also arrange visits to local colleges and places of business."

NEBRASKA: Grand Island Area Council for International Visitors, P.O. Box 505, Grand Island, NE 68802-0578 (tel. 308/384-0800). Provides transportation and sets up home stays.

NEW MEXICO: Council on International Relations, La Fonda Hotel, Mezzanine, Suite 3, 100 East San Francisco, P.O. Box 1223, Santa Fe, NM 87504-1223 (tel. 505/982-4931). Open 9 a.m. to noon weekdays. Provides homestays from one to a few days. Asks for a donation of $9 per night per person.

NEW YORK: The International Center of Syracuse, 500 South Warren St., Hotel Syracuse, Syracuse, NY 13202 (tel. 315/471-0252). Open 8:30 a.m. to 5 p.m. Monday to Friday. They can provide very few home stays but will gladly give information.

Buffalo-Western New York Council for International Visitors Inc., 140 North St., Suite 114, Buffalo, NY 14201 (tel. 716/883-5804). Provides information on tourism and hotels, and arranges homestays for sponsored international visitors and students. Open 9:30 a.m. to 2 p.m. weekdays.

OHIO: International Visitors Center, 10101 Alliance Rd., Cincinnati, OH 45242 (tel. 513/241-7384). Open 9 a.m. to 5 p.m. weekdays. With prior notice, provides homestays, dinner, and transportation for sponsored foreign visitors, and provides tourist information.

International Visitor Council, Inc., Port Columbus International Airport, 4600 E. 17th Ave., Columbus, OH 43219 (tel. 614/231-9610). Provides tourist information and, with at least two weeks notice, a short homestay. Open 10 a.m. to 7 p.m. every day but Saturday.

Cleveland Council on World Affairs, 601 Rockwell Ave., Suite 511, Cleveland, OH 44114 (tel. 216/781-3730). Provides tourist information and maps and, with two weeks advance notice, homestays. Open 9 a.m. to 5 p.m. weekdays.

OKLAHOMA: International Visitors Council, Oklahoma Chamber of Commerce, 1 Santa Fe Plaza, Oklahoma City, OK 73102 (tel. 405/278-8900). Open 8 a.m. to 4:30 p.m. Will provide bed-and-breakfast and some sightseeing help, but needs advance notice.

OREGON: World Affairs Council of Oregon, 1912 S.W. Sixth Ave., Room 252, Portland, OR 97201 (tel. 503/229-3049). Will recommend places to stay. Open 9 a.m. to 5 p.m. weekdays.

PENNSYLVANIA: Pittsburgh Council for International Visitors, 139 University Place, 263 Thackery Hall, Pittsburgh, PA 15260 (tel. 412/624-7800). Open 9 a.m. to 5 p.m., Monday to Friday. They are able to provide information about the city and make reservations for visiting foreign students.

International Visitors Center of Philadelphia, Civic Center Museum, 34th Street and Civic Center Blvd., Philadelphia, PA 19104 (tel. 215/823-7261). Open weekdays from 9 a.m. to 5 p.m. Offers 24-hour language assistance in an emergency by calling 215/879-5248.

RHODE ISLAND: Council for International Visitors, 180 Rhode Island Ave., Newport, RI 02840 (tel. 401/846-0222). Provides general information, maps, and referrals for accommodations and homestays with sufficient advanced notice.

TENNESSEE: Center for International Education, University of Tennessee at Knoxville, 201 Alumni Hall, Knoxville, TN 37996 (tel. 615/974-3177). Basic information and general assistance.

Tennessee Valley Authority (TVA), 400 West Summit Hill Dr., EP-B27, Knoxville, TN 37902 (tel. 615/632-3974). Open 8 a.m. to 4:45 p.m. With advance notice, conducts a general orientation to TVA, arranges professional and technical discussions, and gives tours of TVA dams.

TEXAS: The Institute of International Education, 1520 Texas Ave., no. 1A, Houston, TX 77002 (tel. 713/223-5454). Provides brochures, maps and general information about Houston. Open 8:30 a.m. to 5 p.m. weekdays.

UTAH: International Visitors—Utah Council West in Hotel Utah, Salt Lake City, UT 84111 (tel. 801/532-4747). Open 8 a.m. to 4 p.m., Monday to Friday. Usually able to provide a meal in a member's home and someone to take a visitor sightseeing; always happy to provide information on the area and make suggestions about what to do and see.

Study in the U.S.

The Institute of International Education (IIE), 809 United Nations Plaza, New York, NY 10017, publishes a book that can help you plan your study in the U.S. *English Language and Orientation Programs in the United States* ($8.95) is a directory of intensive and nonintensive English-language and orientation programs offered to foreign students admitted to U.S. postsecondary institutions.

The College Board, 888 Seventh Ave., New York, NY 10106 publishes three useful booklets: *The College Handbook: Foreign Supplement,* ($10.95) *Financial Planning for Study in the United States* ($25 for package of 50 copies) and *Entering Higher Education in the U.S.* ($25 for package of 50 copies).

Basic Survival Tips

This is the section that is meant to prepare you for some of the basic facts of life in the U.S.

THE TELEPHONE: Telephone numbers all over the U.S. have ten digits, for example, 212/661-1414. The first three digits are called the "area code," and the last seven digits are the number of the home or office you are calling.

A *local* call is one placed to a number within the same town as the telephone from which you are calling. The cost ranges from 10¢ to 30¢ and will be printed at the top of the telephone. Generally, the procedure when dialing a local call is to insert the money and dial the last seven digits of the number. On some phones, you may be instructed to dial first and pay when someone answers.

When dialing a *long-distance* call, have plenty of change on hand. To call someone in another town within the same area code (usually relatively nearby), dial "1" and the seven-digit number. To call someone in another state or another area code, dial "1" first and the area code and then the seven-digit number. The operator or a recorded message will answer first and tell you how much money to insert before the connection is made. This amount will allow you to talk for three minutes and then the operator or a recording will interrupt you, asking for more money. If you are using a private telephone, keep in mind that long-distance calls are discounted 35% from 5 p.m. to 11 p.m. and 60% from 11 p.m. to 8 a.m. weekdays, all day on Saturday, and until 5 p.m. on Sunday.

You may place a *person-to-person* call if you are not sure whether the person you are calling will be there. You will be charged only if the person you ask for is there, but the rates for these calls are higher. If the person you are calling is willing to pay for the call, you can place a *collect* call. When placing a person-to-person or collect call, dial "0" and the area code and then the seven-digit number and tell the operator what kind of call you are making.

If you need assistance, you can dial the operator ("0") and, when the operator answers, you will get your money back.

There are two types of telephone directories: the general directory or white pages, which lists alphabetically the telephone numbers and addresses for individuals and businesses, and the Yellow Pages, which classifies businesses alphabetically by type, listing together all bookstores, all cleaners, etc. In smaller cities or towns, the white and Yellow Pages will be combined into one book, with the Yellow Pages at the back. The Blue Pages lists city, state, and federal government offices.

If you do not have access to telephone books, you can get a telephone number from the operator. For a number in the local area, dial 411. For a number within the same area code, dial 555-1212, and for one in another area code, dial "1" and the area code of the person you are trying to call and then 555-1212. The operator will first ask "what city" and then the person's name. Many large companies, hotel and motel chains, and state tourist boards have "800" numbers which are toll free. Just dial 1-800 and the seven-digit number. For information about an 800 number call 1-800-555-1212.

TELEGRAMS: Telegrams are usually sent via Western Union, a privately owned company. The number of Western Union offices has diminished tremendously in the past few years. Telegrams are generally sent by telephone—check the telephone book under "Western Union" for the number to call. The price of a telegram depends on the number of words and where it is going. On telegrams sent overseas you are charged for the number of words in the address and for your signature, but not on telegrams sent within the U.S. A *night letter*, which is transmitted at night when the telegraph lines are less busy, is usually cheaper than a regular telegram; ask the Western Union operator for details.

You can also telegraph money to a stranded friend if necessary. Bring cash or a money order, which you may purchase at a bank or post office (they won't take checks), and for a fee—depending on where it is going—the money will be transferred to your needy friend.

MAIL: You can mail packages or letters at any of the post offices located throughout the cities and towns of the U.S. or, if you prefer, you can drop your stamped letters into a mailbox (they're dark blue boxes located on many street corners and say "U.S. Mail" on them). Post offices are generally open from 8 a.m. to 5 p.m., Monday through Friday, and from 8 a.m. to noon on Saturday. In large cities they may be open much longer hours. Stamps may be purchased from a post office or a vending machine in stationery or drug stores. If possible, avoid using the machines since stamps cost more that way.

Aerograms are the cheapest and most efficient way to send letters abroad. You can buy them at any post office.

The following postage rates are in effect at press time:

U.S.A., Canada, Mexico

postcard (first class and airmail)	14¢
letter (first class and airmail)	22¢ per first ounce plus 17¢ per each additional ounce

Overseas

aerogram	36¢
airmail letter	44¢ per half ounce
airmail postcard	33¢
surface postcard	25¢

When mailing a heavy letter or package, you must have it weighed at the post office. It's wise, too, to insure anything of value that you mail.

If you don't have a friend who can hold mail for you while you are traveling in the U.S., you can have mail addressed to you in care of General Delivery in any city of the U.S. The mail will be held at the main post office of that city for 30 days, after which unclaimed mail will be returned to the sender. To pick up mail sent to General Delivery, you will need to show official identification—your passport will do.

MONEY AND BANKS: Ours is a decimal system based on the dollar, which contains 100 cents. There are six coins: a penny or 1¢, a nickel or 5¢, a dime or 10¢, a quarter or 25¢, a half dollar or 50¢, and a dollar coin. As for paper money, the dollar bill is the most common denomination. There also are $2 bills (rare), and $5, $10, $20, $50, $100, $500, and higher bills.

You can check the exchange rate between your own currency and U.S. currency in any commercial U.S. bank or American Express office.

To protect yourself against loss or theft of money, you would be wise to buy travelers checks, which can be used just like cash. They usually cost one percent of your total purchase.

Banks are usually open from 9 a.m. to 3 p.m., Monday through Friday.

Some have evening hours on certain weeknights, but these vary from bank to bank. Banks and certain other businesses and shops are closed on the following national holidays, many of which are celebrated on Monday as a result of legislation:

New Year's Day	January 1
Martin Luther King Jr. Day	January 19
Washington's Birthday	Monday closest to February 22
Memorial Day	Monday closest to May 30
Fourth of July	July 4 (How could it be any other date?)
Labor Day	First Monday in September
Columbus Day	Monday closest to October 12
Veterans' Day	November 11
Thanksgiving Day	Fourth Thursday in November
Christmas Day	December 25

TIPPING: You are generally expected to tip waiters and waitresses, taxi drivers, porters, hairdressers, and sometimes doormen. You do not have to tip the usher at the theater. Porters should get 50¢ per bag if they carry your bags to your room, waiters and waitresses 15% of the bill, hairdressers approximately 15% of the bill, unless it is the owner of the business who cuts your hair, and taxi drivers 15%.

A good way to save money is to avoid situations where you are expected to tip; carry your own bags, have a friend cut your hair, and eat in a self-service cafeteria.

DRINKING: More and more states are passing legislation requiring that you be 21 years old to be served in a bar or buy liquor from a liquor store; in others you may be 18 or 19. If you look as if you are under the drinking age, you should carry proof of your age (your driver's license or passport, for example) if you intend to drink. There are all kinds of bars in the larger U.S. cities—bars for single people, bars for literary people, bars for gay people, bars for businesspeople.

DRUGS: At some point in your travels you may be offered illegal substances or whatever happens to be in fashion and in supply at the time. In some places people will approach you right out on the street, and you will be surprised at how open drug dealing seems to be. Remember that possession of any narcotic —and marijuana is included—is against the law, and penalties can be severe. Besides the legal problems involved in narcotic usage, it is possible that drugs sold on the streets may be impure and may very well contain lethal ingredients.

MEDICAL ADVICE: Medical care in the U.S. is very expensive. You must be aware of the fact that a visit to a doctor for a physical examination can cost $100 and to have a tooth extracted can cost as much, too. Hospitals charge as much as $300 per day per room—and that doesn't even include the doctor's fee, the high cost of medication, etc. *All this makes medical insurance a must.* Be sure to arrange for this in advance of your trip.

In case of emergency, you can get medical help, an ambulance, or the police by dialing "0" for an operator or 911. In some communities there are free clinics that will attend to your needs as best they can, but they are usually limited by lack of funds and lack of staff so you can't count on them as a substitute for adequate insurance. To find out about free medical services, check the local underground papers or call the help lines listed in each state section.

AIDS: Acquired Immuno Deficiency Syndrome (AIDS) is a very serious medical problem in the U.S., as it is becoming in other parts of the world. Hotlines have been set up in cities around the country. Several are nationwide:
- Center for Disease Control, toll free 800/342-AIDS
- Public Health Service, toll free 800/447-AIDS
- National Gay Task Force and AIDS Crisis, toll free 800/221-7044

No one seems to be immune from this virus transmitted through the exchange of body fluids (notably blood, semen, and vaginal secretions) usually during sex and intravenous drug use. The virus can be transmitted from men to men; men to women; women to men; women to their children, before, during or after birth (through breast milk); and possibly from women to women. What it boils down to is that you are not safe just because you're not gay and you don't use drugs.

Here are some ways to protect yourself:
- Know your sexual partners. Ask about their health and sexual history.
- Use condoms and a water-based lubricant during sex.
- Don't share needles. Note also that any drug use, intravenous or otherwise, can weaken the immune system.

Two booklets, for gay or straight people, published by the American College Health Association, 15879 Crabbs Branch Way, Rockville, MD 20855 (tel. 301/963-1100), are "Safe Sex" and "Making Sex Safer."

CHAPTER 5

State by State

This section is divided alphabetically into states and further into cities within each state. Each state chapter begins with a map of the state indicating the locations of cities listed in the section. The state introductions give some general and relatively objective commentary on the state; and they list special guidebooks to that area, some special events that might be fun to see, bed-and-breakfast reservation services and guides if they exist, and the address and telephone number of the state tourist office.

After the introductory material, the state chapter is divided alphabetically into cities. We have further divided the city listings into all or some of the following subheadings, depending on the information we were able to uncover: Tourist Information, Help, On Campus, Accommodations, and Camping; with additional details on places to stay, places to eat, things to do and see, how to get around, where to shop, etc. Fifteen of the most popular cities are described in even greater detail.

Tourist Information: The tourist office of any state or large city can send you brochures on their own areas. Use these information offices freely; you'll find some helpful information including maps, discount coupons, listings of accommodations of all sorts from motels to ranches, bed-and-breakfasts and campgrounds, information on nature programs at state and national parks, and free activities. Be sure to make your information requests as specific as possible.

Help: Here we list the telephone numbers of hotlines and crisis centers that can assist you in an emergency. Some are phone services; others are drop-in centers. Travelers Aid offices are also listed. See Chapter 2 for a description of how they can help you.

On Campus: This section tells you where to go on a particular campus to meet students, get information, find a good cheap meal, or just enjoy yourself. We had the cooperation of a lot of people on a lot of campuses throughout the U.S. in getting information for the on-campus sections and are grateful for it all.

Accommodations: These are the places to stay in each city or town. A variety of accommodation facilities are included, many of which offer some kind of discount and many have access facilities for people with disabilities. These different types of accommodations are all described in Chapter 2.

Camping: These are the National Park Service campgrounds that are open to individual travelers. Every once in a while you'll see a listing called "camping and accommodations"—this refers to campgrounds that have cabins to rent as well as tent space. See also "Camping" in Chapter 2, and check with the state or local tourist board for more listings.

To send you off on your journey, let us leave you with these thoughts. Each state and each town has its own character. You'll find spectacular scenery, outdoor opportunities, historical sites, unique museums and above all—people who want to meet you, everywhere.

Look for what's typical and unique in the regions you visit—restaurants, accommodations, museum collections. Try not to listen to others' generalizations, as they often omit the fine details. Do less, but in more depth so you have the time to experience a place and its people. You'll have a wonderful time!

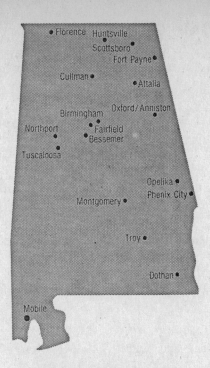

Alabama

Things are definitely looking up. In the first edition we complained that Alabama, with very few low-cost accommodations, made a discouraging beginning to a basically optimistic book. Since then, the Alabama listings have grown considerably. We're also delighted to pass on some good news about traveling in Alabama, and in the South in general. "Things have changed a great deal since the early '60s, and although we are stereotyped as intolerant and conservative . . . people are very tolerant and congenial to outsiders, and especially those who come to our area to visit and learn more about us."

One of the cities that you will want to visit is Birmingham, representing the growth of the New South while retaining the charms of the Old South, the latter displayed at the Arlington Antebellum Home and Gardens. In Montgomery, the first capital of the Confederacy, you can visit the Alabama Shakespeare Festival Theater Complex, the W.A. Gayle Space Transit Planetarium, the first White House of the Confederacy, and Jasmine Hill Gardens. For space and rocket buffs we recommend a visit to Huntsville, the home of the Alabama Space and Rocket Center, where you can take a simulated ride to the moon. South Alabama is the closest to the image of the Deep South as it has been portrayed in movies, books, and songs. Here the Spanish moss hangs heavy and azaleas bloom. In Bayou La Batre the city hall is a shrimp boat; Mobile has its own Mardi Gras, in fact, the original Mardi Gras; and near Mobile, in Theodore, is the quintessential reminder of the Deep South—Bellingrath

Gardens and Home. A good introduction to Alabama is the booklet, simply titled *Alabama,* available free from the Alabama Bureau of Tourism and Travel (address below).

Camping reservations at Alabama's 21 state parks may be made by calling 800/ALA-PARK.

Some Special Events: Mardi Gras in Mobile (February or March); Mobile Azalea Festival (March–May); Birmingham Festival of Arts (April); Eufaula Pilgrimage in Eufaula (April); Spirit of America Festival in Decatur (July); Alabama Shakespeare Festival in Montgomery (December–August); National Shrimp Festival in Gulf Shores, and National Peanut Festival in Dothan (October); Christmas on the River in Demopolis (December); and Christmas on the Coosa in Wetumpka (December).

Tourism Information: Alabama Bureau of Tourism and Travel, 532 South Perry St., Montgomery, AL 36104 (tel. in Montgomery 205/261-4169, toll free 800/252-2262 out of state, or 800/392-8096 in Alabama).

N.B. Two bed-and-breakfast reservation services are Bed & Breakfast Montgomery, P.O. Box 886, Millbrook, AL 36054 (tel. 205/285-5421); and Bed & Breakfast Mobile, P.O. Box 66261, Mobile, AL 36606 (tel. 205/473-2939).

Attalla

Accommodation: Red Carpet Inn, 507 Cherry St., 35954 (tel. 205/538-9925).

Bessemer

Accommodation: Motel 6, 1000 Shiloh Lane, 35020 (tel. 205/426-9646).

Birmingham

Tourist Information: Greater Birmingham Convention and Visitors Bureau, 2027 First Ave. North, Suite 300, 35203 (tel. 205/252-9825).

Help: Travelers Aid, 3600 Eighth Ave., Room 110-E, 35222 (tel. 205/322-5426).
- Crisis Center, 205/323-7777.

Accommodations: Ranch House Motel, 2127 Seventh Ave. South, 35233 (tel. 205/322-0691). $22 for one; $24 for two in one bed; $26 for two in two beds.
- Budgetel Inn, 513 Cahaba Park Circle, 35243 (tel. 205/995-9990).
- Super 8 Motel, 140 Vulcan Rd., Homewood, 35209 (tel. 205/945-9888).
- Days Inn, 1011 9th Ave. SW, 35020 (tel. 205/424-9690).
- Days Inn, I-65, Exit 260, 300 North 10th St., 35203 (tel. 205/328-8560).
- Hampton Inn, 1466 Montgomery Hwy., 35216 (tel. 205/822-2224).
- Econo Lodge, 103 Green Springs Hwy., 35209 (tel. 205/942-1263).
- Econo Lodge, 2224 Fifth Ave. North, 35203 (tel. 205/324-6688).
- Scottish Inn, 624 Decatur Hwy., 35068 (tel. 205/849-7431).
- Red Roof Inn, I-65 and Oxmore Road, 35209 (tel. 205/942-9414).

Cullman

Accommodation: Days Inn, I-65 and U.S. 278, 1841 4th St. SW, 35055 (tel. 205/739-3800).

Dothan

Accommodations: Days Inn, 2841 Ross Clark Circle SW, P.O. Drawer 1890, 36301 (tel. 205/793-2550).
- Econo Lodge, 2901 Ross Clark Circle SW, 36301 (tel. 205/793-5200).
- Quality Inn, 3591 Ross Clark Circle SW, 36303 (tel. 205/793-9090).

Fairfield

Accommodation: Knights Inn, I-20 at Valley Road, 5601 Flintridge Dr., 35064 (tel. 205/786-5577).

Florence

Accommodation: Master Hosts Inn, 1241 Florence Blvd., 35630 (tel. 205/764-5421).

Fort Payne

Camping: DeSoto State Park, Route 1, Box 210, 35967 (tel. 205/845-0051; reservations 205/845-5075). $5 per night for primitive campsites; $8 per night for sites with water and electricity; $9 per night for sites with water, electricity, and bath.

Huntsville

Accommodations: Budgetel Inn, 4890 University Dr. NW, 35805 (tel. 205/830-8999).
- Knights Inn, U.S. 72 at 3100 University Dr., 35816 (tel. 205/533-0610).
- Super 8 Motel, 3803 University Dr., 35805 (tel. 205/539-8881).
- Hampton Inn, 4815 University Dr., 35816 (tel. 205/830-9400).

Mobile

Tourist Information: Convention and Visitors Department, Mobile Area Chamber of Commerce, 451 Government St., P.O. Box 2187, 36652 (tel. 205/433-6951).
Help: Travelers Aid, 205/438-1625.
- Helpline, 205/432-1222.
Accommodations: Motel 6, 1520 Matzenger Dr., 36605 (tel. 205/473-1603).
- Motel 6, 5560 I-10 Service Rd., 36619 (tel. 205/660-1483).

- Drury Inn, I-65 and Airport Boulevard., 824 Beltline Hwy., 36609 (tel. 205/344-7700).
- Hampton Inn, 930 S. Beltline Hwy., 36609 (tel. 205/344-4942).
- Econo Lodge, 5550 I-10 Service Rd., 36619 (tel. 205/661-8181).
- Regal 8 Inn, 400 South Beltline Hwy., 36608 (tel. 205/343-8448).
- Red Carpet Inn, 1061 Government St., 36604 (tel. 205/438-4653).
- Red Roof Inn, I-65 and Dauphin Street, 33 S. Beltline Hwy., 36606 (tel. 205/476-2004).
- Red Roof Inn, I-10 and U.S. 90, Exit 15B, 5380 Coca-Cola Rd., 36619 (tel. 205/666-1044).

Montgomery

Help: Travelers Aid, Family Guidance Center, 925 Forest Ave., 36106 (tel. 205/265-0568 or 262-6669).

Accommodations: Motel 6, 1051 Eastern Bypass, 36117 (tel. 205/277-6748).

- Comfort Inn, 5175 Carmichael Rd., 36117 (tel. 205/277-4447).
- Hampton Inn, 1401 East Blvd., 36117 (tel. 205/277-2400).
- Budgetel Inn, 5225 Carmichael Rd., 36106 (tel. 205/277-6000).
- Scottish Inn, Rte. 1, Box 264, U.S. 231 South, 36064 (tel. 205/288-1501).
- Days Inn, I-65 and 1150 West South Blvd., 36105 (tel. 205/281-8000).
- Days Inn, Hope Hull Exit, I-65 and U.S. 31, 36043 (tel. 205/281-7151).
- Econo Lodge, 2625 Zelda Rd., 36107 (tel. 205/269-9611).
- TraveLodge, 1550 Federal Dr., 36109 (tel. 205/265-0586).

Northport

Accommodation: Budget Host—Travel Inn, 3020 Hwy. 82 West, 35476 (tel. 205/339-3900).

Opelika

Accommodations: Motel 6, 1015 Columbus Parkway, 36801 (tel. 205/745-0988).

- Red Carpet Inn, I-85, Exit 62, 1107 Columbus Parkway, 36801 (tel. 205/749-6154).

Oxford/Anniston

Accommodations: Days Inn, I-20 and Alabama 21, P.O. Drawer F, 36203 (tel. 205/831-5463).

- Hampton Inn, 1600 Highway 21, 36203 (tel. 205/835-1492).
- Quality Inn, I-20 at SR 21, Recreation Dr., 36203 (tel. 205/835-0300).

Phenix City

Accommodation: Econo Lodge, 1506 Phenix City Bypass, 36867 (tel. 205/298-5255).

Scottsboro

Accommodation: Econo Lodge, 1106 John T. Reid Pkwy., P.O. Box 518, 35768 (tel. 205/574-1212).

Troy

Help: Help-a-Crisis, Emergency Telephone Counseling, c/o East Central Mental Health/Mental Retardation, Inc. (tel. 205/566-3391).

Accommodation: Econo Lodge, 1013 U.S. Hwy. 231, P.O. Box 1086, 36081 (tel. 205/566-4960).

Tuscaloosa

Help: University Switchboard, 205/566-3000.

Accommodations: Days Inn, 3600 McFarland Blvd., 35405 (tel. 205/556-2010).

- Motel 6, 4700 McFarland Blvd., 35405 (tel. 205/759-4942).
- Super 8 Motel, 4125 McFarland Blvd. East, 35405 (tel. 205/758-8878).

On Campus: According to a friend at the University of Alabama, located near downtown Tuscaloosa, the school is "lovely and has a vibrant history." She told us that the Continuing Education Center on campus is open day and night and "offers housing for those on quasi-university business—that is, looking at the campus." If you're feeling lonely, go to the Side Track, Egan's, or Morgan's. Three good restaurants are Ruby Tuesday and The Landing, a steakhouse, both on McFarland Blvd., and Storyville, right off campus. You'll easily find someone to talk to at any of these.

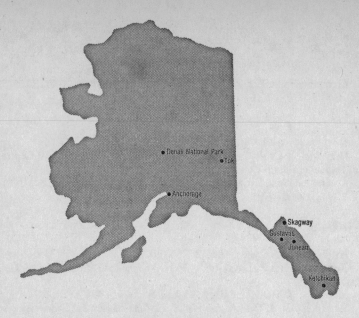

Alaska

Alaska is huge. Superimposed on a map of the U.S. it stretches from Seattle to Miami. And in all this space there are only 539,600 Alaskans.

Not many Americans get as far as Alaska, but one adventurous New York student told us about her two months in the town of Homer. "From Seattle I took a ferry that takes three days. I traveled fifth class and brought my own food. I got off at Haines and hitchhiked to Homer on the Alaskan Highway. There are quite a few kids in Homer and if you settle down for more than a week you're no longer considered a stranger. Alaska is a rather expensive place—food especially."

The Alaska Division of Tourism gave us some good news and some bad news about low-cost accommodations in their state. The good news: the U.S. Forest Service rents 135 cabins in the Tongass National Forest for $15 a night. The bad news: most of the cabins can be reached only after a plane ride in a single-engine De Havilland Beaver.

For all the tourist information you could want on Alaska, we recommend these publications:

One is *The Milepost,* published by Alaska Northwest Publishing Co., 130 Second Ave. South, Edmonds, WA 98020 ($14.95 plus $1 fourth-class or $3 first-class postage and handling). The book is a mile-by-mile log of the northern highways, including the Alaska Highway, with maps and specifics for everyone from fishermen to rock hounds. Also from Alaska Northwest Publishing Co. is *The Alaska Wilderness Milepost* ($14.95 plus $1 fourth-class or $3 first-class postage), a complete guide to Bush Alaska for business and recreational travelers.

Another guide is *Alaska Travel Guide,* published by Alaska Travel Guide, P.O. Box 15504, Salt Lake City, UT 84115 ($9.95 plus $2 postage). It contains information on hotels, motels, campgrounds, national parks, etc. It is released annually in April and includes a free copy of the Rand McNally map of Alaska and the Yukon. The fourth recommended guide is *The Inside Passage Traveler,* by Ellen Searby, Windham Bay Press, P.O. Box 34283, Juneau, AK 99803 ($8.95; add $2 for airmail postage). Written by a member of a ferry crew, this book tells you how to make the most of the ferry system and how to find your way from the dock around the town. It includes information on air, rail, and road connections, hotels, sights to see, etc.

Adventuring in Alaska, by Peggy Wayburn, is a Sierra Club book which explores wild and urban Alaska. Copies are $10.95 and available from Sierra Club Books, 730 Polk St., San Francisco, CA 94109.

Some Special Events: World championships including dog-sled races and snowmobile races (February); Fairbanks Winter Carnival (March); Break-Up Drama Festival in Dawson City, Yukon, Canada (May); Gold Rush Days in Valdez, an annual festival which celebrates the good old days of gold discovery in Alaska (August); Alaska Festival of Music in Anchorage (September); and Alaska Day in Sitka (October).

"Originally I was hitching from Houston to San Francisco to New York but then found a job with the U.S. Forest Service as a technician in Ketchikan and I'm still here."

Tourist Information: Alaska Division of Tourism, P.O. Box E, Juneau, AK 99811. Ask for *Alaska and Canada's Yukon Vacation Planner,* the official State of Alaska vacation booklet.

N.B. If you're going to Alaska, it might be wise to contact Stay With a Friend, Box 173-3605 Arctic Blvd., Anchorage 99503 (tel. 907/344-4006). A member of the American Bed and Breakfast Association, this service has homes for you to stay in Anchorage, Palmer, Hatcher Pass, Kenai, Homer, Seldovia, and None. According to the owner of the service, this is a chance to "get your information over a cup of coffee when you need it and enjoy privacy when you want it." Stay With a Friend also publishes a guide to Alaska called the *Cheechako Guide* ($3).

Anchorage

Help: CRISIS, Inc., 907/276-1600.

Accommodation: Anchorage International Hostel (AYH), 700 H St., number 3, 99501 (tel. 907/276-3635). $10 for AYH members; $5 for children under 18 traveling with parents; $1 for linen from May through September.

Denali National Park

Camping: Denali National Park and Preserve, P.O. Box 9, 99755 (tel. 907/683-2294). Walking distance from bus and train stations. Seven campgrounds with 225 sites. $10 per campsite per night at Riley Creek, Savage River,

Teklanika River, Wonder Lake, Igloo Creek, and Sanctuary River. There is no fee at Morino (walk-in camping).

Gustavus

Camping: Glacier Bay National Park, 99826 (tel. 907/697-2230). Wilderness camping from June 1 to mid-September. Access by plane or boat only from Juneau.

Accommodation: Salmon River Rentals, Box 13, 99826 (tel. 907/697-2245). Open May 15 to September 20. $40 per cabin (will accommodate four people); $200 per week; $4 for linen.

Juneau

Help: Juneau Information Center, c/o Davis Log Cabin, 907/586-2201.

Accommodation: Juneau International Hostel (AYH), 614 Harris St., 99801 (tel. 907/586-9559). Open year round. $7 for AYH members; $9 for non-members.

Ketchikan

Help: Women in Safe Homes, 907/225-9474.

Accommodations: Ketchikan Youth Hostel (AYH-SA), 400 Main St., P.O. Box 8515, 99901 (tel. 907/225-3319). Access to Ketchikan is by Alaska State Ferry or Alaska Airlines. Open Memorial Day to Labor Day. $4 for AYH members; $7 for non-members. Sleeping bags required.

• Rain Forest Inn, 2311 Hemlock St., 99901 (tel. 907/225-6302). $17 single dorm bed; $39 double; $6 each additional person; $45 furnished one-bedroom apartment, two nights minimum; $85 per week dorm; $196 per week room.

Skagway

Camping: Klondike Gold Rush National Historical Park, P.O. Box 517, 99840 (tel. 907/983-2921). Camping from May through September at primitive campsites.

Tok

Accommodation: Tok Youth Hostel (AYH), Box 532, 99780. One mile south on Pringle at mile 1322 ½ Alaska Highway (Alcan). Open May 15 to September 15. $5 for AYH members; $8 for nonmembers.

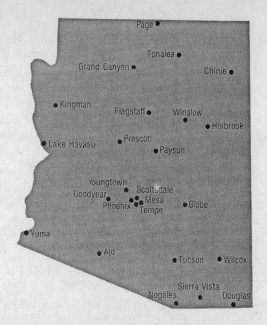

Arizona

Lots of the people who go to Arizona are there to see the Grand Canyon, a multicolored fissure 217 miles long, 3 to 17 miles wide, about a mile deep, and very probably one of the most spectacular natural sights you will ever see. Since the largest crowds come during the summer, visit if you can in the spring or fall when you can enjoy the relative solitude.

The state's southern half—with its largest cities, Tucson and Phoenix—has the kind of warm, dry air that makes people feel good, so many go to the area's resorts to do just that. Arizona may well be one of the most beautiful of our states. Besides the Grand Canyon, the attractions of the state include the Hoover Dam, Lake Mead, 21 national parks, several Indian villages and reservations, the Painted Desert, and the Petrified Forest.

Some Special Events: Cinco de Mayo Celebrations in Prescott, Phoenix, Tucson, Scottsdale, Winslow, Willcox, and Mesa (May); Fiesta de los Vaqueros in Tucson (February); Annual Old Timers' Picnic in Casa Grande (June); Navajo Pow Wow and Rodeo in Window Rock, and Homemakers' Ice Cream Social in Pine (July); Turkey Creek Rodeo in White River, and Navajo County Fair in Holbrook (August); Annual Gold Camp Days in Oatman, and Cochise County Fair in Douglas (September).

Tourist Information: Office of Tourism, 1480 East Bethany Home Rd., SR 180, Phoenix, AZ 85014 (tel. 602/255-3618). Their "Arizona by Auto" brochure provides an in-depth look at Arizona, especially useful for those going by ground transportation.

Ajo

Camping: Organ Pipe Cactus National Monument, Rt. 1, Box 100, 85321 (tel. 602/387-6849). Open year round. $6 per campsite per night, plus $3 park entrance fee per vehicle; 35' RV limit.

Chinle

Camping: Canyon de Chelly National Monument, P.O. Box 588, 86503. Camping at Cottonwood, one mile south of entrance, year-round.

Douglas

Accommodations: Motel 6, 111 16th St., 85607 (tel. 602/364-2457).
- TraveLodge, 1030 19th St., 85607 (tel. 602/364-8434).

Flagstaff

Accommodations: Weatherford Hotel (AYH), 23 North Leroux St., 86001 (tel. 602/774-2731). Open year-round. Near bus and train station. Restaurant on premises. Dormitory-style: $8.65 for AYH members; $3 charge for introductory pass for members. $15 to $18 for hotel rooms. Call and check on availability of rooms. Recommended by a reader who told us that "the Weatherford is named in Zane Grey's book *Call of the Canyon* and is very special."
- Motel 6, 2010 East Butler Ave., 86001 (tel. 602/774-1801).
- Regal 8 Inn, 2440 East Lucky Lane, 86001 (tel. 602/774-8756).
- Budget Host—Frontier Motel, 1700 East Santa Fe Ave., 86001 (tel. 602/774-8993).
- Super 8 Motel, 3725 Kasper Ave., 86004 (tel. 602/526-0818).
- Allstar Inn, 2500 Lucky Lane, 86001 (tel. 602/779-6184).
Camping: Sunset Crater National Monument, Rte. 3, Box 149, 86004 (tel. 602/527-7042). Camping at Bonito Campground (opposite the Visitor Center). Open May 15 to September 15. $7 per campsite per night.

Globe

Accommodations: Friendship Ember Motel, 1105 North Broad St., 85501 (tel. 602/425-5736).
- Budget Host—El Rey Motel, 1201 Ash St., 85501 (tel. 602/425-4427).

Goodyear

Accommodation: Super 8 Motel, 1710 N. Dysart Rd., 85338 (tel. 602/932-9622.

Grand Canyon

Accommodation: Grand Canyon International Hostel (AYH-SA), 76 Tonto St., P.O. Box 270, 86023 (tel. 602/638-9018). $8 per person. Written advance reservations of one month necessary. "Built in 1925, this was the first ranger dormitory in the park."

Holbrook

Accommodation: Motel 6, 2514 Navajo Blvd., 86025 (tel. 602/524-6106).

Kingman

Accommodations: Motel 6, 3270 East Andy Devine Ave., 86401 (tel. 602/757-7121).
● TraveLodge, 1001 Andy Devine Ave., 86401 (tel. 602/753-5541).
● Allstar Inn, 3351 West Andy Devine Ave., 86401 (tel. 602/757-7151).
● Econo Lodge, 3016 East Andy Devine Ave., 86401 (tel. 602/753-3339).

Lake Havasu

Accommodations: E-Z 8 Motel, 41 Acoma Blvd., 86403 (tel. 602/855-4023).
● Shakespeare Inn, 2190 McCulloch Blvd., 86403 (tel. 602/855-4157). $25 single; $28 double; $33 triple; $37 quad; $150 single per week.
● Super 8 Motel, 305 London Bridge Rd., 86403 (tel. 602/855-8844).

Mesa

Accommodations: Allstar Inn, 630 West Main St., 85201 (tel. 602/969-8111).
● Motel 6, 336 West Hampton Ave., 85202 (tel. 602/844-8899).
● Super 8 Motel, 6733 E. Main St., 85206 (tel. 602/981-6181).
● TraveLodge, 22 South Country Club Dr., 85202 (tel. 602/964-5694).

Nogales

Accommodation: Motel 6, 2210 Tucson Hwy., 85621 (tel. 602/281-2951).

Page

Camping: Glen Canyon National Recreation Area, P.O. Box 1507, 86040. Open year-round. $6 per campsite per night.

Payson

Accommodation: Super 8 Motel, 101 W. Phoenix St., 85541 (tel. 602/474-4526).

Phoenix

Wherever you go in Phoenix, you will be aware of the influence that Indian culture has had on its evolution. The city that is now the capital of Arizona began as a small settlement on the banks of the Salt River and has become quite a popular tourist stop. One of the biggest attractions is the weather—one Phoenician promises "absolutely sunny skies more than three hundred days of the year." There are several information booths in and around Phoenix. There are two at Sky Harbor International Airport—one in Terminal 2 and one in Terminal 3. They are open for business from 9 a.m. to 9 p.m. Monday through Friday, and from 9 a.m. to 5 p.m. Saturday and Sunday. The Phoenix and Valley of the Sun Convention and Visitors Bureau has two offices, one at 505 North 2nd Street, Suite 300 (tel. 602/254-6500), and one at the Hyatt Regency Hotel, located at 2nd Street and Adams Street on the first floor. The State Office of Tourism is a good source of information and is located at 1480 East Bethany Home Road (tel. 602/255-3618). The Visitors Bureaus and Chamber of Commerce are open from 8:30 a.m. to 4:30 p.m. Monday through Friday. None have accommodation reservation services.

One good area guidebook is *Arizona Handbook,* by Mel Weir, Moon Publications, 722 Wall St., Chico, CA 95928 ($10.95). Another is *Day Trips From Phoenix, Tucson and Flagstaff,* by Pam Hait, Globe Pequot ($8.95).

Radio station KTAR, AM 620, is *the* station in the Phoenix area to learn what's happening around the Valley—24-hour-a-day talk radio. Each Friday *The Arizona Republic* newspaper publishes an entire section entitled "Calendar," which lists attractions, festivals, films, lectures, benefits, cultural events, a nightlife guide, restaurant listings and much, much more. Each Tuesday a free, thick, chock-full-of-info newspaper/magazine called the *New Times* hits the racks all over the city. Some of its extensive listings include music of all types, theater offerings, film, politics, sports events, dance lessons, a kids section, a learning and self-help section and lots more.

Tempe, the location of Arizona State University, is not far from Phoenix, and it has its own listing in this chapter. There are some restaurants located in Tempe, though, that are listed here.

Getting There: From the airport, a taxi will cost about $6 to the downtown area; $5 for the Supershuttle. Airport limousine service costs $2.50 to downtown or $3 to Tempe, as long as there are other passengers; if not, it will cost $6. There's no airport bus service. The Continental Trailways terminal is at 433 East Washington (tel. 602/257-0257), and Greyhound's is nearby at 525 East Washington (tel. 602/248-4040). Amtrak is at 401 West Harrison (tel. 602/253-0121).

Getting Around: Once you're in the city, you can take a taxi for $2.05 for the first mile, $1.20 for each additional mile. Call Yellow Cab Company (tel. 602/252-5071), and a taxi will come and get you. Since local bus service is very poor (no service after 7 p.m. or on Sunday), you may want to rent a car. To do this, check Budget Rent-a-Car, 219 South 24th St. (tel. 602/249-6124). A Ford

Escort or similar car costs $17.95 per day, with 100 miles included, 17¢ per mile after that, and $134 for the week with 1,000 free miles. At Ajax Rental (tel. 602/244-9889), a Ford Escort costs $26.90 per day with unlimited mileage and $139 per week with 1,050 free miles. Bell Rent-a-Car, 1202 S. 24th St. at the airport (tel. 602/244-2406) has $22.95 daily and $134 weekly rates. If you want to use the bus, you can get a printed schedule and route map from the Phoenix Transit Corporation's information booth, First Street and Adams Street, and from most libraries, banks, and hospitals. The fare is 75¢. Flag the driver from a bus stop when you wish to board.

Help: Valley of the Sun Convention Bureau, 602/952-8687.

● Doctors' Referral Service, 602/252-6094.

● St. Luke's Medical Center, 1800 East Van Buren, 602/251-8100.

● Poison Control, 602/253-3334.

● Visitor Hot Line—what's happening in Phoenix, 602/840-4636.

Accommodations: Valley of the Sun International Hostel (AYH), 1026 North 9th St., 85006 (tel. 602/262-9439). $8 for AYH members in the winter, $7 in the summer; $10 for nonmembers.

● YMCA, 350 North First Ave., 85003 (tel. 602/253-6181). Near the Civic Plaza. Men and women. This hotel is well kept and centrally located. $15 single; $18 double. Weekly rate: $55 single. $5 refundable key deposit. Children 12 and over.

● Motel 6, 2323 East Van Buren St., 85006 (tel. 602/267-7511).

● Motel 6, 5315 East Van Buren St., 85008 (tel. 602/267-8555).

● Motel 6, 2330 West Bell Rd., 85023 (tel. 602/993-2353).

● Allstar Inn, 214 South 24th St., 85034 (tel. 602/244-1155).

● Allstar Inn, 4130 North Black Canyon Hwy., 85017 (tel. 602/277-5501).

● Budget Host—Del Ward's Motor Hotel, 3037 East Van Buren St., 85008 (tel. 602/273-1601).

● Days Inn, I-17 and 2735 West Sweetwater, 85029 (tel. 602/993-7200).

● Hampton Inn, 8101 N. Black Canyon Hwy., 85021 (tel. 602/864-6233).

● Regal 8 Inn, 2548 West Indian School Rd., 85017 (tel. 602/248-8881).

● Regal 8 Inn, 8152 North Black Canyon Hwy., 85051 (tel. 602/995-7592).

● TraveLodge, 2900 East Van Buren St., 85008 (tel. 602/275-7651).

● TraveLodge, 965 East Van Buren St., 85006 (tel. 602/252-6823).

● Valley O' The Sun Bed and Breakfast, Papago St. (tel. 602/941-1281). Near airport and Phoenix Zoo—call for exact directions from airport. $25 single; $35 double.

● Phoenix 6 Motel, 3644 East Van Buren St., 85008 (tel. 602/275-7661). Four miles east of downtown center. $35 single; $40 double; $45 triple; $48 quad; $45 to $55 for 3-bed suites.

Where to Eat: Earthen Joy, 36 East 5th St., Tempe (tel. 602/968-4710). Open 11:30 a.m. to 10 p.m. From fresh carrot juice to delicious cheesecake, sandwiches on 14-grain bread, and salads. Every evening there's a special entree. The setting is informal, and eating is done surrounded by bright-colored pillows, an aquarium, and lots of plants.

● Monti's Casa Vieja, 3 West 1st St., Tempe (tel. 602/967-7594). Open 11:30 a.m. to midnight. "One of the best Western steakhouses. The atmosphere is rustic; prices are reasonable."

● La Casita Cafe, 1021 South Central Ave. (tel. 602/262-9322). Open from 11 a.m. daily except Tuesday. This Mexican cafe serves all the dishes you'd expect and has been a landmark for decades.

● Willy and Guillermo's, 1120 East Apache Blvd., Tempe, and 5600 North Central Ave (tel. 602/266-1900). Mexican food in a comfortable setting.

● China Doll, 3336 North 7th Ave. (tel. 602/264-0538). Good and reasonably priced Chinese food with dim sum on weekends.

● Cafe Casino, 4824 North 24th St. (tel. 602/955-3430). Near the Arizona Biltmore Hotel, a marvelous example of Frank Lloyd Wright's architecture. This French-style cafeteria-boulangerie is modestly priced.

● Thai Lahna, 3738 East Indian School Rd. (tel. 602/955-4658). A small, comfortable place for good Thai food.

● Lucille's Soul Food, 1202 East Washington (tel. 602/262-9835). Not far from Heritage Square, downtown. Reasonably priced chicken, ribs, and other Southern goodies.

● Pinnacle Peak Patio, 10426 East Pinnacle Peak Rd., Scottsdale (tel. 602/563-5134). This is about 12 miles north of Phoenix and is a popular tourist attraction. Steak and beans in a Western atmosphere; entertainment includes a melodrama where it's perfectly acceptable—in fact encouraged—to hiss and boo the players.

● Mr. Lucky's, 3660 North Grand (tel. 602/246-0686). Located at the State Fair Grounds, this large nightclub offers buffet-style ribs, ham, and pot roast—$2.99 for all you can eat!

● Melany's Pizza, 1135 East Glendale (tel. 602/277-5322). This family-run restaurant serves spaghetti, gyros, dolmades, and pizza. No atmosphere but the food is fine.

● Ham's, 3302 North 24th St. (tel. 602/956-9911). Homestyle cooking—dishes like pork chops and meat loaf at low, low prices in this neighborhood tavern. Two people can eat for about $10 and that includes a couple of beers.

● Po' Folks, 3301 West Indian School Rd (tel. 602/263-0910). Country cooking—things like chicken and dumplings or red beans and rice for less than $5. Popular, so expect a crowd.

● Pa Clark's, 3317 West Van Buren (tel. 602/272-0851). "The best Philly-style steak sandwiches in Phoenix. Nothing to look at, but a real bargain."

● Garcia's del Metro, 3301 West Peoria Ave. (tel. 602/866-1850). Open 11 a.m. to 10 p.m. daily, Garcia's serves all the usual Mexican dishes, plus many tasty, original recipe dishes from the Garcia family. Many meals priced lower than $5.

● Ed Debevic's, 2102 East Highland, in the Town and Country Shopping Center (tel. 602/956-2760). Open 11 a.m. to 10 p.m. Sunday through Thursday; 11 a.m. to midnight Friday and Saturday. Fresh, home cooked, liberal portions of food straight from the 50's era. They bake all their own bread, rolls, etc. A large meal for $7.

● South China Buffet, 1636–38 North Scottsdale Rd.—half block south of McKellips Road (tel. 602/994-8875). Open 11 a.m. to 3 p.m. and 4:30 p.m. to 9:30 p.m. daily. Tasty Chinese dishes—an all-you-can-eat place. Lunch is $2.95, dinner is $3.95.

● The Eggery, 5109 North 44th St.—corner of Camelback Road and 44th Street (tel. 602/840-5734). Open 6:30 a.m. to 2:30 p.m. daily. Superb, inexpensive egg-oriented meals.

● Mrs. White's Golden Rule Cafe, 808 East Jefferson (tel. 602/262-9256). Open 7:30 a.m. to 6:30 p.m. Monday through Friday. Inexpensive soul food—home cooking. No check—just tell the cashier what you ate. Average meal—$4.50.

What to See: Phoenix is a cornucopia of music, theater, film, sports, dance, cultural events, and fine dining. There are also enough major attractions to keep one busy from morning till night. A small sampling would include the following:

● Heard Museum of Anthropology and Primitive Art, 22 East Monte Vista Rd. (tel. 602/252-8848). Open Monday to Saturday from 10 a.m. to 5 p.m.; Sunday from 1 to 5 p.m. One of the West's finest collections of Indian arts and crafts, prehistoric and modern, from all over the world. Every year, during the first week in March, the museum sponsors an Indian arts-and-crafts fair with dancing, food, and craft demonstrations. It's a very popular fair, indeed.

● Wildlife World Zoo, 165th Ave. and Northern (tel. 602/935-9453). Open 9 a.m. to 5 p.m. daily. Display of more than 180 species of animals and birds, including zebras, kangaroos, deer, giraffes, and tigers in natural settings.

● Rawhide, 23023 N. Scottsdale Rd. (tel. 602/563-5600). Open 5 to 10 p.m. weekdays, and noon to 10 p.m. weekends. If the Old West intrigues you, step back in time to Rawhide, an authentic re-creation of an 1880's town—complete with stagecoach rides, old-time piano music, gunfights in the streets, the Golden Bell Restaurant, and much more.

● Hall of Flame Firefighting Museum, 6101 E. Van Buren (tel. 602/275-3473). Open 9 a.m. to 5 p.m. Monday through Saturday. Features over 30,000 square feet of exhibits; everything from 100 fully restored fire engines and vehicles, helmets, badges, and firemarks to lithographs, photographs, and drawings. Popular with all ages.

● Pueblo Grande Museum and Ruins, 4619 East Washington (tel. 602/275-3452). Open 9 a.m. to 5 p.m. weekdays, 1 to 5 p.m. Sunday; closed Saturday. Where the Hohokam Indians, the earliest inhabitants of Phoenix, lived. There's a museum with artifacts to visit, too.

● Japanese Flower Gardens. Along Baseline Road there's a two-mile stretch of flower farms. The peak of their beauty is from February to April. Citrus fruits and dates are sold at roadside stands along the way.

● South Mountain Park. The entrance to this municipal park is at the end of South Central Avenue. Within the park's boundaries are petroglyphs, picnic areas, and superb views of the city.

● Desert Botanical Gardens, 5800 East Van Buren St. 3,000 acres of Papago Park devoted to desert plants from all over the world.

● Phoenix Zoo, 5800 East Van Buren St. (tel. 602/273-7771).

● Taliesin West, East Shea Blvd. (tel. 602/948-6670). Located in an area of virgin desert, it was once the winter home and school of Frank Lloyd Wright. Now open to visitors October to May, 10 a.m. to 4 p.m. daily; noon to 4 p.m. Sunday.

● Paolo Soleri Cosanti Foundation, 6433 Doubletree Rd. (tel. 602/948-6145). Workshop for innovative architectural designers where you can see models of future city projects.

● Gila River Indian Arts and Crafts Center. Approximately 20 miles southeast of Phoenix, just off the Phoenix-Tucson Freeway. A museum and a crafts shop that features pottery, baskets, and jewelry made by various Arizona tribes. Open 9 a.m. to 5:30 p.m.

● For the sports-minded, check on the sporting events while you're in town. The possibilities include the Phoenix Suns (basketball), PGA golf tournaments, horse and dog racing, Indy and stock-car races, major-league baseball spring training, and the Phoenix Giants (AAA minor-league baseball).

At Night: For jazz: Boojum Tree Restaurant, Second Avenue and Osborn (tel. 602/248-0222). Open until 1 a.m. A place to go to hear well-known jazz recording stars.

● Timothy's, 6335 North 16th St (tel. 602/277-7634). Jazz gets started at 8 or 9 p.m. "The best local jazz in the valley."

● Mr. Lucky's, 3660 Grand Ave. (tel. 602/246-0686). Upstairs you can dance to country and western, downstairs to rock bands. Open 7 p.m. to 12:45 a.m. $2 cover charge.

● Rick's Café Americana, 8320 North Hayden Rd. (tel. 602/991-2233). Open 7 p.m. until 1 a.m., Monday through Saturday. This chic jazz club is straight out of the movie *Casablanca*, complete with ceiling fans, lots and lots of plants everywhere, fanback chairs, rattan and cane furniture.

● For dancing: El Bandido, 1617 East Thomas Rd. Open until 1 a.m. Good dancing and very good Mexican food.

● Champs, 4343 North Seventh Ave. Open 8 p.m. to 1 a.m. Wednesday through Saturday. A disc jockey spins oldies and current tunes continously; large dance floor and the ubiquitous strobe and colored lights overhead. A popular place.

● Barn Steak House, 6508 West Bell Rd. (tel. 602/252-5821). Open 6:30 p.m. until 12:30 a.m. Wednesday through Sunday. This popular haunt of Phoenicians is actually in the shape of a gigantic barn. Great food and dance music by Silverado (house band)—mostly country and western tunes.

● For theater: Phoenix Little Theater, 25 East Coronado (tel. 602/254-2151). Curtain rises at 8 p.m. at this, the oldest continuously operated community theater in the U.S.

● Max's Dinner Theater, 6727 North 47th Ave. (tel. 602/937-1671). Dining begins at 6 p.m., showtime is 8 p.m.

● For movies: Valley Art Theater, 509 Mill Ave., Tempe (tel. 602/967-6664). If you're in the mood for a film, you'll find either a classic, a foreign film, an underground movie, or a current new feature at this theater near the university.

● Glenfair Cinema, 59th Avenue and Bethany Home Road in Glenfair Plaza. $.99 for all ages, all movies, except $.49 each Tuesday and Wednesday.

● Valley West Cinemas, 59th Avenue and Northern, inside Valley West Mall. $1.50 for all ages, except Tuesdays when admission is $.50.

● For classical music: Phoenix Symphony, Symphony Hall, 225 East Adams (tel. 602/264-4754). The season runs from October through May at Symphony Hall in the new Civic Plaza.

● Scottsdale Center for the Arts, 7383 Scottsdale Mall—crossroads are 2nd St. and Civic Center Plaza (tel. 602/994-2787). Performances usually begin at 8 p.m.

● For dance/ballet performances: Kerr Cultural Center, 6110 North Scottsdale Rd. Known for presenting both modern and ballet performances by dance companies of high caliber. Performances at 8 p.m.

● Arizona Ballet Theater, Symphony Hall, and Scottsdale Center for the Arts (tel. 602/258-2354). This resident professional dance company performs classical and modern ballet world premieres and classical revivals.

● For folk and country music: Funny Fellows Restaurant, 1814 West Bethany Home Rd. Open 8 p.m. to 1 a.m. A favorite haunt for those who like not only folk music, but country and western fare as well as soft rock.

Shopping: For books: Changing Hands, 9 East 5th St., Tempe (tel. 602/966-0203). The emphasis here is on "humanistic self-growth books"—everything from solar energy to vegetarian cooking.

- Al's Family Bookstore, 1454 East Van Buren St. (tel. 602/258-6922). For a wide range of books, new and secondhand.
- Dushoff Books, Ltd., 3106 East Camelback Rd. (tel. 602/957-1176). A good general bookstore.
- Guidon Books, 7117 East Main, Scottsdale (tel. 602/945-8811). Specializing in Arizona lore and western Americana.
- For records: Circles, 800 North Central Ave. (tel. 602/254-4765). An impressive variety of records.
- Odyssey Records and Tapes, 1127 East Camelback Rd. Jazz, rock, and classical music for sale.
- Prickly Pear Records and Tapes, 3444 West Dunlap Ave. (tel. 602/956-2030). Today's and yesterday's top hits; thousands of out-of-print records.
- For camping equipment: Holubar, 232 W. Southern, Tempe (tel. 602/955-3391), and 3925 East Indian School Rd. Good for camping equipment and outdoor gear.
- Arizona Hiking Shack, 11645 North Cave Creek Rd. (tel. 602/943-2722). Another source of camping equipment.
- Popular Outdoor Outfitters, 4315 Glendale Ave., Glendale (tel. 602/937-3751). A basic surplus store.
- For gifts: Gilbert Ortega's, 7215 East Main St., Scottsdale (tel. 602/947-2805; locations all over the valley). Arts and crafts store.

Prescott

Accommodations: Motel 6, 1111 East Sheldon St., 86301 (tel. 602/776-0161).
- Super 8 Motel, Bus. 89 at Gurley Street, 86301 (tel. 602/776-1282).

Scottsdale

Accommodations: Motel 6, 6848 East Camelback Rd., 85251 (tel. 602/946-2280).
- Allstar Inn, 1612 North Scottsdale Rd., 85281 (tel. 602/945-9506).
- Scottsdale's Fifth Avenue Inn, 6935 Fifth Ave., 85251 (tel. 602/994-9461: reservations 800/528-7396). Rates vary: from May 1 to January 14, $32 to $42 single; $40 to $50 double; $48 to $58 triple; $56 to $66 quad. From January 15 to April 30, $69 single; $80 double; $88 triple; $96 quad. Two-week advance reservations necessary.

Sierra Vista

Accommodations: Motel 6, 1551 East Fry Blvd., 85635 (tel. 602/459-5035).
- Super 8 Motel, 100 Fab Ave., 85635 (tel. 602/459-5380).

Tempe

Note: See Phoenix listing for restaurants, etc., in Tempe, which is a suburb of that city.

Accommodations: Allstar Inn, 513 West Broadway, 85282 (tel. 602/967-8696).
- Regal 8 Inn, 1720 South Priest Dr., 85281 (tel. 602/968-4401).

Tonalea

Camping: Navajo National Monument, 86044 (tel. 602/672-2366). Open May 15 to October 15. Reservations must be made with the superintendent for trips to Keet Steel Ruin. No charge.

Tucson

Help: Information and Referral, 602/881-1794.
- El Pueblo Clinic, 101 W. Irvington, 85714 (tel. 602/573-0096).
Accommodations: YMCA, 516 North Fifth Ave., 85705 (tel. 602/624-7471). Men only. $16 per night plus $5 refundable key and towel deposit. Weekly rate: $75. Monthly rate: $195.
- Hotel Congress, Ⓢ √, 311 E. Congress St., 85701 (tel. 602/622-8848). $20 single; $23 double; $27 triple; $30 quad; $7 for AYH members; $3 charge for linen. "Best deal in downtown!"
- Days Inn, I-10 at Palo Verde and Irvington, Exit 264, 3700 East Irvington, 85714 (tel. 602/571-1400).
- Regal 8 Inn, 1222 South Freeway, 85713 (tel. 602/624-2516).
- Motel 6, 960 South Freeway, 85745 (tel. 602/628-1339).
- Motel 6, 1031 East Benson Hwy., 85714 (tel. 602/628-1264).
- Super 8 Motel, 4950 S. Outlet Center Dr., 85714 (tel. 602/746-0030).
- Lamp Post Motel, Ⓢ√, 1990 S. Craycroft, 85711 (tel. 602/790-6021). $26 single; $29 double; $32 triple; $35 quad. Kitchens are $5 per day extra. Swimming pool.
- E-Z 8 Motel, 720 West 29th St., 85713 (tel. 602/624-8291).
- E-Z 8 Motel, 1007 South Freeway, 85745 (tel. 602/624-9843).
- Allstar Inn, 1388 West Grant Rd., 85745 (tel. 602/622-4784).
- Allstar Inn, 755 East Benson Hwy., 85713 (tel. 602/622-4614).
- TraveLodge, 1136 North Stone Ave., 85705 (tel. 602/622-6714).
- TraveLodge, 222 South Freeway, 85705 (tel. 602/791-7511).
- TraveLodge, 2803 East Valencia Rd., 85706 (tel. 602/294-2500).
- Budget Host—Sandman Inn, 3020 S. 6th Ave., 85713 (tel. 602/623-5881).

Wilcox

Accommodation: Motel 6, 921 North Bisbee, 85643 (tel. 602/384-2201).

Winslow

Accommodations: TraveLodge, 1216 East 3rd St., 86047 (tel. 602/289-2491).
- Motel 6, 725 West 3rd St., 86047 (tel. 602/289-3903).
- Budget Host—Mayfair Motel, 1925 West Hwy. 66, 86047 (tel. 602/289-5445).

● Super 8 Motel, 1916 West Third St., P.O. Box 986, 86047 (tel. 602/289-4606).

Youngtown

Accommodation: Motel 6, 11133 Grand Ave., 85363 (tel. 602/977-1318).

Yuma

Accommodations: Motel 6, 2730 Fourth Ave., 85364 (tel. 602/344-3890).
● Motel 6, 1640 Arizona Ave., 85364 (tel. 602/782-6561).
● TraveLodge, 2050 Fourth Ave., Box 4608, 85364 (tel. 602/782-3831).
● Friendship Pikes Motel, 200 South Fourth Ave., 85364 (tel. 602/783-3391).

Arkansas

Here's one of the strangest stories ever told—how Arkansas got its name. It started with the name of a tribe called Quanaw, which the Algonquins pronounced Oo-ka-na-sa. Marquette wrote it as Arkansoa, La Salle as Arkensa, De Tonti as Arkancas, and La Harpe as Arkansas. In 1881 the legislature had to appoint a committee to decide on the right pronunciation of the last syllable. May we suggest a similar committee, preferably of Algonquins, to decide how Quanaw could possibly have been pronounced Oo-ka-na-sa?

Probably the biggest tourist attraction in Arkansas is the world-famous Hot Springs National Park, with 47 thermal springs that are collected and distributed to bathhouses throughout the park and the city of Hot Springs. Fifty-four miles from Hot Springs is Little Rock, the capital of Arkansas, where you can visit the Arkansas Art Center; Arkansas Territorial Restoration; and the first state capitol, the Old State House. The downtown area of the Victorian resort of Eureka Springs in the Ozark Mountains is on the National Register of Historic Places. From May to October the Ozark Folk Center preserves, interprets, and displays the arts, crafts, music, and lore of the mountain people. Nearby is the impressive Blanchard Springs Cavern. Lakeside beaches, farmland, wild and placid rivers, and historical sites complete the picture. Get off the beaten track!

As in many states, in Arkansas there are a number of state parks that offer housekeeping cottages for rent within the boundaries of each park. The overnight rental for two people is well within this book's budget, and the settings are quite beautiful. For information, write to the Arkansas Department of Parks and Tourism at the address below.

Some Special Events: Annual Jonquil Festival in Old Washington State Park, and the Annual Pioneer Craft Festival in Rison (March); Annual Arkansas Folk Festival in Mountain View (April); Arkansas Heritage Week held statewide, Annual Historic Helena Tour in Helena, and Riverfest in Little Rock (May); Annual Hope Watermelon Festival in Hope (August); Annual Prairie

Grove Battlefield Clothesline Arts and Crafts Fair in Prairie Grove (Labor Day weekend); Ozarks Art and Craft Festival on War Eagle Mills Farm, Arkansas Oktoberfest in Hot Springs, and the Annual Family Harvest Festival at Ozark Folk Center (October); and the Annual Ozark Christmas at Ozark Folk Center (December).

Tourist Information: Arkansas Department of Parks and Tourism, One Capitol Mall, Little Rock, AR 72201 (tel. 800/643-8383 out of state, 800/482-8999 in state).

N.B. A bed-and-breakfast reservation service for Arkansas is B & B of the Arkansas Ozarks, Rt. 1, Box 38, Calico Rock, AR 72519 (tel. 501/297-8764).

Bald Knob

Accommodation: Scottish Inn, 703 Hwy. Blvd, 72010 (tel. 501/724-3204).

Benton

Accommodations: Budget Host—Troutt Motel, I-30 West, Exit 116, 1901 W. South St., 72015 (tel. 501/778-3633).
- Super 8 Motel, 1221 Hot Springs Hwy., 72015 (tel. 501/776-1515).

Blythville

Accommodation: Days Inn, I-55 and Ark. 18E, P.O. Box 1342, 72315 (tel. 501/763-1241).

Camden

Accommodation: Econo Lodge, Rte. 3, Box 869, 71701 (tel. 501/574-0400).

Clarksville

Accommodation: Econo Lodge, I-40, Exit 58, P.O. Box 755, 72830 (tel. 501/754-2990).

Conway

Accommodation: Motel 6, Hwy. 65B and I-40, P.O. Box 567, 72032 (tel. 501/327-6623).

Dardanelle

Accommodation and Camping: Mt. Nebo State Park, Rte. 3, P.O. Box 374,

72834 (tel. 501/229-3655). Besides camping in the park ($3 to $6 per campsite), there are 14 natural stone cabins "with breathtaking views of the valley 1,800 feet below," with all-electric kitchens, full baths, a bedroom, living room, and fireplace. Cabins rent for $40 to $55 per night for two persons; $3 extra for each additional person up to six. You must be 18 or over to rent a cabin. Reservations are recommended two to three months in advance for cabins.

Eureka Springs

Tourist Information: Eureka Springs Chamber of Commerce, P.O. Box 551, 72632 (tel. 501/253-8737).

Eureka Springs has been described as a "unique and beautiful small town in the country and the center of an Ozark back-to-the-land movement." There are lots of young people passing through the Ozarks and many staying and homesteading. While you're in the area, "see the mountains, trees, lakes, rivers, Victorian architecture, and native crafts. Listen to the bluegrass, canoe, bicycle, or hike."

Accommodation: Budget Host—Country Holiday Motel, 102 Kingshighway, 72632 (tel. 501/253-8863). Open March to December 12.

Fayetteville

Help: Information Desk, Arkansas Union, University of Arkansas (tel. 501/575-2304).

Accommodation: Town House and Sands Motel, 215–229 North College, Bus. 62 and 71, 72701 (tel. 501/442-2315). Six blocks from the University of Arkansas. Swimming pool. $18 single; $20 for two in one bed; $22 for two in two beds; $24 to $27 triple; $26 quad. Higher rates apply during the three big football weekends in the fall. Children under 12 stay free.

Fort Smith

Accommodations: Regal 8 Inn, 1021 Garrison Ave., 72901 (tel. 501/785-2611).
- Motel 6, 6001 Rogers Ave., 72903 (tel. 501/484-0576).
- Budgetel Inn, 2123 Burnham Rd., 72903 (tel. 501/484-5770).

Harrison

Camping: Buffalo National River, P.O. Box 1173, 72601 (tel. 501/741-5443). Buffalo Point is open year-round. Canoe rentals. $8 per campsite per night for drive-ins; $5 for walk-ins.

Accommodation: Super 8 Motel, 1330 Hwy. 62/65 North, 72601 (tel. 501/741-1741).

Hope

Accommodation: Red Carpet Inn, I-30 and Hwy. 4, 71801 (tel. 501/777-9222).

Hot Springs

Tourist Information: Hot Springs Convention & Visitors Bureau, P.O. Box K, 71901 (tel. 800/543-BATH).

Camping: Hot Springs National Park, P.O. Box 1860, 71902 (tel. 800/543-BATH). Campsites at Gulpha Gorge, two miles east of Hot Springs. Open year-round. $6 per campsite per night.

● Lake Catherine State Park, Rte. 19, Box 360, 71913 (tel. 501/844-4176). 70 campsites and 17 fully equipped cabins on Lake Catherine. $7.50 per day campsites; $40 to $45 per day cabins (two persons per cabin).

Jonesboro

Accommodations: Motel 6, 2300 South Caraway Rd., 72401 (tel. 501/932-1050).

● Super 8 Motel, 2314 S. Caraway Rd., 72403 (tel. 800/843-1991).

Little Rock

Tourist Information: Little Rock Convention and Visitors Bureau, Markham and Broadway, P.O. Box 3232, 72203 (tel. 501/376-4781).

Accommodations: Motel 6, 9525 I-30, Southside Frontage Rd., 72209 (tel. 501/565-1388).

● Budgetel Inn, 1010 Breckenridge, 72205 (tel. 501/225-7007).
● Super 8 Motel, 7501 I-30, 72209 (tel. 501/568-8888).
● Regal 8 Inn, 9709 I-30, 72209 (tel. 501/568-1200).
● Red Roof Inn, I-30 at Scott Hamilton Drive, Exit 134 (tel. 501/562-2694).
● Hampton Inn, 6100 Mitchell Dr., 72209 (tel. 501/562-6667).
● Days Inn, 2600 W. 65th St., 72209 (tel. 501/562-1122).
● Imperial 400 Motor Inn, 322 East Capital Ave., 72202 (tel. 501/376-3661).

Marion

Accommodation: Scottish Inn, I-55, Exit 10, P.O. Box 398-B, 72364 (tel. 501/732-1640 or 734-3186).

North Little Rock

Accommodations: Days Inn, I-40 and Protho Jct., Exit 157, 2508 Jacksonville Hwy., 72117 (tel. 501/945-4167).

● Days Inn, I-40 and SR 107, 3100 North Main, 72116 (tel. 501/758-8110).
● Hampton Inn, 500 W. 29th St., 72114 (tel. 501/771-2090).

Pine Bluff

Accommodations: Comfort Inn, 210 North Blake St., 71601 (tel. 501/534-7222).

● Super 8 Motel, 4101 W. Barraque St., 71602 (tel. 501/534-7400).

Russellville

Accommodations: Merrick Motel, ⑤ √ ★, 10%, Hwy. 64 E., 1320 East Main St., 72801 (tel. 501/968-6332). $25 for one or two in one bed; $27 for two in two beds.

- Motel 6, I-40 and County Road, Rte. 6, Box 306, 72801 (tel. 501/968-3666).

Springdale

Accommodation: Scottish Inn, Hwy. 471 South, 72764 (tel. 501/751-4874).

Texarkana

Accommodations: Motel 6, 900 Realtor Ave., 75502 (tel. 501/772-0678).
- Super 8 Motel, 325 E. 51st St., 75501 (tel. 501/774-8888).

West Memphis

Accommodations: Scottish Inn, 2315 Hwy. I-55 and I-40, P.O. Box 1208, 72301 (tel. 501/732-2830).
- Motel 6, 2501 S. Service Rd., 72301 (tel. 501/735-0100).
- Days Inn, 1100 Ingram Blvd., 72301 (tel. 501/735-8600).

SAN FRANCISCO AREA

- Vallejo
- Pittsburg
- Berkeley
- Walnut Creek
- San Francisco
- Oakland
- Livermore
- Hayward
- Pleasanton
- Montara
- Newark
- Stanford
- Milpitas
- Los Altos
- Mountain View
- Santa Clara
- Sunnyvale
- Pescadero
- Campbell
- San Jose

- Crescent City
- Yreka
- Tulelake
- Weed
- Mount Shasta
- Dunsmuir
- Arcata
- Eureka
- Redding
- Mineral
- Red Bluff
- Quincy
- Chico
- Willows
- Oroville
- Ukiah
- Williams
- Truckee
- Marysville
- Yuba City
- South Lake Tahoe
- Woodland
- Santa Rosa
- Davis
- Sacramento
- Rancho Cordova
- Petaluma
- Napa
- Vacaville
- Point Reyes
- Fairfield
- Berkeley
- San Francisco
- Oakland
- Stockton
- Modesto
- Yosemite
- Tracy
- Saratoga
- San Jose
- Turlock
- Midpines
- Mammoth Lakes
- Santa Cruz
- Merced
- Gilroy
- Los Banos
- Palcines
- Monterey
- Salinas
- Fresno
- King City
- Three Rivers
- Coalinga
- Tulare
- Death Valley
- Paso Robles
- Porterville
- Atascadero
- Lost Hills
- Morro Bay
- San Luis Obispo
- Buttonwillow
- Ridgecrest
- Pismo Beach
- Bakersfield
- Santa Maria
- Los Alamos
- Mojave
- Lompoc
- Buellton
- Santa Barbara
- Lancaster
- Barstow
- Carpenteria
- Palmdale
- Victorville
- Needles
- Ventura
- Thousand Oaks
- Camarillo
- Simi Valley
- San Bernardino
- Big Bear
- Van Nuys
- Pomona
- Los Angeles
- Redlands
- Twentynine Palms
- Anaheim
- Riverside
- Beaumont
- Costa Mesa
- Banning
- Palm Springs
- Indio
- Blythe
- Oceanside
- Carlsbad
- Escondido
- El Centro
- San Diego
- La Mesa
- Imperial Beach
- San Ysidro

LOS ANGELES AREA

- Glendale
- Pasadena
- Arcadia
- Claremont
- Fontana
- Rosemead
- El Monte
- Los Angeles
- Ontario
- Pico Rivera
- Whittier
- Hacienda Heights
- Santa Fe Springs
- La Habra
- Norwalk
- Fullerton
- Carson
- Buena Park
- Stanton
- Westminster
- Long Beach
- Santa Ana
- San Pedro
- Huntington Beach

California

Everyone wants to visit California. Ask any Easterner, or anyone from abroad, and they'll tell you their dreams about California. California is now as much myth as reality, but no one is making a mistake when they decide to go there. It's a complex, vibrant, and interesting piece of the U.S. and has a lot to offer any traveler. Because California is so beautifully situated between the Pacific Ocean and the mountains, visitors can sail, surf, swim, ski, or hike. Of course, there is Disneyland, Sea World, lots of zoos, and historical missions up and down the state, not to mention Hollywood and all that the glamour capital has to offer. California has television studios, some of the best shopping areas in the world, and a major university, the University of California, with nine campuses covering the entire state. California is the number one producer of agricultural products in the world and supplies most of the U.S. with its harvests. Of course, California is a leading wine-producing state, and some of the finest wines in the country—some might even say the world—come from the northern part of the state.

San Francisco is a jewel city, not to be missed. Los Angeles is another "must visit" place. The Huntington Library in San Marino, near Los Angeles, has a famous collection of paintings and illuminated manuscripts of great interest to anyone who's interested in art history.

Then there's the Getty Museum near Santa Monica and the Hearst Castle in San Simeon. The Carmel Valley, home of many fine artists and craftsmen, is a fascinating place to visit, and finally, Monterey, with its Cannery Row made famous by John Steinbeck, is a lovely city that should be on every visitor's itinerary.

While you're in California, stop at the offices of CIEE at 2511 Channing Way, Berkeley, 94704 (tel. 415/848-8604); 1093 Broxton Ave., Los Angeles 90024 (tel. 213/208-3551); 14515 Ventura Blvd., Suite 250, Sherman Oaks, 91403 (tel. 818/905-5777); 4429 Cass St., San Diego, 92109 (tel. 619/270-6401); UCSD Student Center B-023, La Jolla, 92093 (tel. 619/452-0630); and 312 Sutter St., San Francisco, 94108 (tel. 415/421-3473). In addition to helping you find your way around California, they are a good source of information on low-cost travel all over the U.S. and the world.

"In California, I slept under the stars lots of times, on beaches or in the woods. On the coast there are lots of state parks where you can stay for almost nothing."

Some Special Events: Tournament of Roses Parade and Football Game in Pasadena, and the Winter Carnival in South Lake Tahoe (January); Chinese New Year Celebration in San Francisco (February); Festival of the Whales in Dana Point (mid-February to mid-March); San Luis Obispo Mardi Gras (March); California State Old Time Fiddlers Contest in Merced (April); Dixieland Jazz Jubilee in Sacramento (May); Railroad Days in Dunsmuir and

San Francisco Carnival (June); World's Biggest Salmon Barbecue in Fort Bragg, and Solano County Fair in Vallejo (July); County Fairs in San Mateo, Santa Clara, Humboldt, Lassen and San Joaquin Counties (August); and Harvest Festival in Riverside (September).

Tourist Information: California Office of Tourism, P.O. Box 9278, Van Nuys, CA 91409 (tel. 800/TO-CALIF). Offers an excellent visitor's map and other travel information.

N.B. A group that places people in private homes in San Francisco, Los Angeles, San Diego, and other locations in California, is Bed and Breakfast International, 151 Ardmore Rd., Kensington, CA 94707 (near Berkeley). The cost of a double, with breakfast included, is $36 to $86 (students may request lower rates); the minimum stay is two nights. To obtain an application, write to the address above and enclose a stamped, self-addressed envelope, or call 415/525-4569.

Two bed-and-breakfast reservation services are California Bed & Breakfast, P.O. Box 1551, Sacramento, CA 95807, and Bed & Breakfast Hospitality, P.O. Box 2407, Oceanside, CA 92054 (tel. 619/722-6694).

Anaheim

Accommodation: Motel 6, 921 S. Beach Blvd., 92804 (tel. 714/220-2866).

Arcadia

Accommodation: Motel 6, 225 Colorado Pl., 91006 (tel. 818/446-2660).

Arcata

Help: Humboldt Open Door Clinic, 770 10th St., 95521 (tel. 707/822-2957).
Accommodations: Arcata Crew House Hostel, Ⓢ★, 1390 Eye St., 95521 (tel. 707/822-9995). Open May 26 to August 25. $5.50 for AYH members and ISIC holders; $7.75 for nonmembers. "The hostel is an old Victorian house with some excellent redwood burlwork. It is homey and quiet." Bring your own linen.
- Motel 6, 4755 Valley West Blvd., 95521 (tel. 707/822-7061).
- Super 8 Motel, 4887 Valley West Blvd., 95521 (tel. toll free 800/843-1991).

Atascadero

Accommodation: Motel 6, 9400 El Camino Real, 93422 (tel. 805/466-6701).

Bakersfield

Accommodations: Motel 6, 350 Oak St., 93304 (tel. 805/362-1222).
- Motel 6, 5241 Olive Tree Ct., 93308 (tel. 805/392-9700).
- Motel 6, 2727 White Lane, 93304 (tel. 805/834-2828).
- Allstar Inn, 1350 Easton Dr., 93309 (tel. 805/327-1686).
- E-Z 8 Motel, 2604 Pierce Rd., 93308 (tel. 805/322-1901).
- E-Z 8 Motel, 5200 Olive Tree Ct., 93308 (tel. 805/392-1511).

Banning

Accommodation: Super 8 Motel, 1690 W. Ramsey St., 92220 (tel. 714/849-6887).

Barstow

Accommodations: Motel 6, 31951 E. Main St., 92311 (tel. 619/256-0653).
- Imperial 400 Motor Inn, 1281 E. Main St., 92311 (tel. 619/256-6836).
- Allstar Inn, 150 Yucca Ave., 92311 (tel. 619/256-1752).

Beaumont

Accommodation: Budget Host—Golden West Motel, 625 5th St., 92223 (tel. 714/845-2185).

Berkeley

On Campus: A branch of the University of California is here in this lively, diverse college town. "Everything passes by without comment in Berkeley—everything 'goes.'" To meet students in the area, stop at Sufficient Grounds, Cafe Roma, Henry's, Manuela's, or The Hermosa.

Accommodation: International House, ♿ (limited), University of California, 94720. (tel. 415/642-9470). To stay you "must have affiliation with the University of California as registered students, guests of residents, scholars visiting the campus, etc." Open to temporary visitors in summer only. Minimum one week stay. $250 single; $175 per person double. Includes 19 meals per week.

Big Bear

Accommodation: Motel 6, 1200 Big Bear Blvd., P.O. Box M28-6, 92315 (tel. 714/585-6666).

Blythe

Accommodations: Motel 6, 500 W. Donlon St., 92225 (tel. 619/922-6666).
- E-Z 8 Motel, 900 W. Rice St., 92225 (tel. 619/922-9191).
- Friendship Desert Inn, 850 W. Hobson Way, 92225 (tel. 619/922-5145).
- Friendship Dunes Inn, 9820 E. Hobson Way, 92225 (tel. 619/922-4126).

Buellton

Accommodations: Motel 6, 333 McMurray Rd., P.O. Box 1670, 93427 (tel. 805/688-7797).
- Allstar Inn, Second Street and Zaca Creek, 93427 (tel. 805/688-0336).

Buena Park

Accommodation: Friendship Gaslite Motel, 7777 Beach Blvd., 90620 (tel. 714/522-8441).

Buttonwillow

Accommodations: Motel 6, 3810 Tracy Ave., 93206 (tel. 805/764-5207).
● Allstar Inn, 20638 Tracy Ave., 93206 (tel. 805/764-5153).

Camarillo

Accommodation: Motel 6, 1641 E. Daily Dr., 93010 (tel. 805/388-3467).

Campbell

Accommodation: Allstar Inn, 1240 Camden Ave., 95008 (tel. 408/371-8870).

Carlsbad

Accommodation: Allstar Inn, 6117 Paseo del Norte, 92008 (tel. 619/438-1242).

Carpenteria

Accommodations: Motel 6, U.S. Hwy. 101 and Santa Monica Rd., 4200 Via Real, 93013 (tel. 805/684-6921).
● Friendship Reef Motel, 4160 Via Real, 93013 (tel. 805/684-4176).

Carson

Accommodation: Allstar Inn, 21321 Avalon Blvd., 90745 (tel. 213/835-0333).

Chico

Accommodations: Motel 6, 665 Manzanita Ct., 95926 (tel. 916/345-5500).
● Imperial 400 Motor Inn, 630 Main St., 95926 (tel. 916/895-1323).

Claremont

On Campus: There are six colleges in Claremont, "a small town in the old-fashioned sense—everyone knows each other in this town of beautiful old houses and lots of trees." The five undergraduate colleges are Pomona, Scripps, Pitzer, Claremont-McKenna, and Harvey Mudd. The graduate college is the Claremont Graduate School. At Pomona, the hub of student activity is the Edmunds Union. To meet students, go to Edmunds or the Coop at Pomona, the Motley Coffeehouse at Scripps, Red Baron Pizza at Harvey Mudd, the McConnell Center at Pitzer College, or Emmett Student Center at Claremont-McKenna. The general information number for the five colleges is 714/621-8000; the paper for the five colleges is called *Collage*.

Coalinga

Accommodations: Motel 6, 25278 W. Dorris Ave., 93210 (tel. 209/935-2063).
- Allstar Inn, 25008 W. Dorris Ave., 93210 (tel. 209/935-1536).

Costa Mesa

Accommodation: Allstar Inn, 1441 Gisler Ave., 92626 (tel. 714/957-3063).

Crescent City

Accommodation: Rustic Inn, 220 M St., 95531 (tel. 707/464-9553). Winter: $18 for one; $20 for two in one bed; $26 for two in two beds. Summer: $28 for one; $30 for two in one bed; $36 for two in two beds.

Davis

On Campus: There is a branch of the University of California in Davis, and you can get campus information by calling 916/752-2222. You'll find a ride board in the Memorial Union and housing possibilities in the Housing Office. There are two spots on campus where students tend to meet: The Housing Office and the Pub. You can also find students off campus at the Brewster House in the evening.
Accommodation: Motel 6, 4835 Chiles Rd., 95616 (tel. 916/753-3777).

Death Valley

Camping: Death Valley National Monument, Furnace Creek, 92328 (tel. 619/786-2331). Nine campgrounds with a total of approximately 1600 campsites. Furnace Creek, Mesquite Springs, and Wildrose are open year round; Texas Spring Sunset and Stove Pipe Wells are open November through April; Emigrant is open May through October; Thorndike, Pinyon Mesa, and Mahogany Flat are open March through November. No entrance fee; $5 per vehicle.

Dunsmuir

Accommodation: Cedar Lodge Motel, ⑤√, 4201 Dunsmuir Ave., 96025 (tel. 916/235-4331). $25 single; $30 for two in one bed; $32 for two in two beds; $36 for three in two beds; $40 for four in two beds; $10 extra for kitchen facilities. Family suite (bedrooms, kitchen, living room): $46 for two persons; $4 for each additional person. Near Mt. Shasta ski resort.

El Centro

Accommodations: Motel 6, 330 N. Imperial Ave., 92243 (tel. 619/352-6636).
- Motel 6, 395 Smoketree Dr., 92243 (tel. 619/353-6766).
- E-Z 8 Motel, 455 Wake Ave., 92243 (tel. 619/352-6620).

El Monte

Accommodation: Motel 6, 3429 Peck Rd., 91731 (tel. 818/448-6660).

Escondido

Accommodation: Motel 6, 509 W. Washington Ave., 92025 (tel. 619/743-6669).

Eureka

Accommodations: Allstar Inn, 1934 Broadway, 95501 (tel. 707/445-9631).
- Budget Host—Town House Motel, K St. and 933 4th St., 95501 (tel. 707/443-4536).
- Imperial 400 Motor Inn, 1630 4th St., 95501 (tel. 707/443-8041).

Fairfield

Accommodation: Motel 6, 2353 Magellan Rd., 94533 (tel. 707/427-0800).

Fontana

Accommodation: Motel 6, 10195 Sierra Ave., 92335 (tel. 714/823-8686).

Fresno

Accommodations: Motel 6, 933 N. Parkway Dr. at Hwy. 99, 93728 (tel. 209/233-3913).

- Motel 6, 4245 N. Blackstone Ave., Hwy. 41 North, 93726 (tel. 209/221-0800).
- Allstar Inn, 4080 N. Blackstone Ave., 93726 (tel. 209/222-2431).
- Allstar Inn, 1240 N. Crystal Ave., 93728 (tel. 209/237-0855).

Fullerton

Accommodations: Allstar Inn, 1415 S. Euclid Ave., 92632 (tel. 714/992-0660).
- Fullerton Hacienda Hostel, 1700 North Harbor Blvd., 92635 (tel. 714/738-3721). Located on the site of an old dairy farm. $8.50 per bed, dormitory style; $1 linen charge. AYH-IYHF members given preference. Two-week written advance reservation suggested.

Gilroy

Accommodations: Motel 6, 6110 Monterey Hwy., Hwy. 101, 95020 (tel. 408/842-9306).
- Super 8 Motel, 8435 San Ysidro Ave., 95020 (tel. 408/848-4108).

Glendale

Accommodation: YMCA, 140 North Louise St., 91206 (tel. 818/240-4130). Men only. Dormitory style, single rooms. $16.05 per night; $3 key deposit. Fitness facility.

Hacienda Heights

Accommodation: Allstar Inn, 1154 S. Seventh Ave., 91745 (tel. 818/968-9462).

Hayward

Accommodation: Allstar Inn, 30155 Industrial Pkwy. SW, 94544 (tel. 415/489-8333).

Huntington Beach

Accommodation: Colonial Inn Hostel (AYH), Ⓢ ★, 421 8th St., 92648 (tel. 714/536-3315). $9 dormitory or semiprivate. "In the heart of Orange County recreation area."

Imperial Beach

Accommodation: Imperial Beach Hostel (AYH), 170 Palm Ave., 92032 (tel. 619/423-8039). Near bus station. $7 for AYH members; $10 for non-members. Advance reservations of one week necessary during summer months.

Indio

Accommodation: Motel 6, 82195 Indio Blvd., 92201 (tel. 619/342-6311).

King City

Accommodation: Motel 6, 6 Broadway Circle, 93930 (tel. 408/385-5000).

La Habra

Accommodation: Allstar Inn, 870 N. Beach Blvd., 90631 (tel. 213/694-2158).

La Mesa

Accommodation: Allstar Inn, 7621 Alvardo Rd., 92041 (tel. 619/464-7151).

Lancaster

Accommodations: Allstar Inn, 43540 17th St. West, 93534, (tel. 805/948-0435).
● E-Z 8 Motel, 43530 N. 17th St. West, 93534 (tel. 805/945-9477).

Livermore

Accommodation: Allstar Inn, 4673 Lassen Rd., 94550 (tel. 415/449-0900).

Lompoc

Accommodations: Motel 6, 1415 E. Ocean Ave., 93436 (tel. 805/736-6514).
● Allstar Inn, 1425 North H St., 93436 (tel. 805/735-7631).

Long Beach

Help: Travelers Aid, 947 E. 4th St., 90802 (tel. 213/432-4743).
Accommodation: Allstar Inn, 5665 E. 7th St., 90804 (tel. 213/597-1311).

Los Alamos

Accommodation: Budget Host—Skyview Motel, 9150 U.S. Hwy. 101, Box 126, 93440 (tel. 805/344-3770).

Los Altos

Accommodation: Hidden Villa Ranch Hostel (AYH), 26870 Moody Rd., 94022 (tel. 415/941-6407). Closed June 1 to September 1. Located on 1,650 acres of farm and ranch. $5.50 for AYH members; $7.50 for nonmembers. Advance reservations necessary for weekends.

Los Angeles

Los Angeles is a legend. Here's the movie kingdom, the home of the leisure suit, 20th-century America at its extreme. L.A. can be a confusing city for a visitor—its sprawl is mind-boggling, its freeways are restless, and its beaches are endless.

In order to avoid "culture shock" when you arrive, consult any of these books: Arthur Frommer's *Guide to Los Angeles* ($5.95), an excellent guide to the city's sights and restaurants; *L.A. Access,* by Richard S. Wurman, Access Press ($9.95), not a budget guide but still good, which subdivides Los Angeles into sections and lists lots of interesting places to see; *The Moneywise Guide to California,* by Vicki Leon, published by Presidio Press ($9.95) with a good chapter on Los Angeles; *The Hip Pocket Guide to Los Angeles,* by Vanessa Weeks Page, Colophon/Harper and Row ($8.95), is a compilation of what's what in L.A. according to some people who live there; *The City Observed: Los Angeles,* by Charles Moore, Peter Becker, and Regula Campbell, Vintage Books ($11.95), is a guide to the architecture and landscapes of the city; and *A Marmac Guide to Los Angeles,* by Marvy Chapman, Pelican Publishing ($7.95).

Contact the Greater Los Angeles Visitors and Convention Bureau, 515 S. Figueroa St., 90071 (tel. 213/624-7300), for maps and information. And once you're there, check the *Los Angeles Times* entertainment section; *Los Angeles* magazine; *Reader,* a free weekly that comes out every Thursday; and *L.A. Weekly,* another free guide that is out on Thursday and "from an Angelino's perspective, the best guide to what's happening." And you can always check in with the people at Council Travel Services, 1093 Broxton Ave. (tel. 213/208-3551); Sherman Oaks, 14515 Ventura Blvd., Suite 250, Sherman Oaks, CA 91403 (tel. 818/905-5777); and 5500 Atherton St., Suite 212, Long Beach, CA 90815 (tel. 213/598-3338).

We've included one Angelino's unabashedly subjective guide to the "neighborhoods" of Los Angeles—just because we liked it and because it will give you a feel for what's out there:

Chinatown: *Not the same as San Francisco's Chinatown, but L.A.'s China-town still holds a certain charm and lots of good restaurants and shopping. Lo-*

cated downtown, its center is at the Mandarin Plaza Mall at #970 North Broadway.

Little Tokyo: *Another small ethnic center that's fun for shopping or just running around. It's in downtown L.A., located between Alameda and Los Angeles Street and 1st and 3rd Streets.*

Venice Beach: *Venice was once the center for hippie culture, then for artists, then for nudists. Now it has lots of stalls set up with food, handmade jewelry, posters, etc. . . . Sometimes there are street musicians too. "Last time I was there I saw a man with a boa constrictor, and another who likes just to stand in place and freeze." Watch the men and women at muscle beach (part of Venice), as they try to make their biceps as large as Arnold Schwarzenegger's—they love an audience!*

Beverly Hills: *Come see how the Los Angeles rich live. If you're interested in seeing stars, this is the place you'd most likely see them. For the most exclusive shops, walk down Rodeo Drive—you may even find a sale!*

Melrose Avenue: *Between LaBrea and Santa Monica Boulevard, Melrose Avenue is a very West Hollywood place to be. Very artsy area with lots of antique shops, little bars, restaurants, playhouses, etc. The clothing stores feature some of the vintage things—the first Hawaiian shirts, big jackets from the '40s, etc.*

Hollywood: *Once the Avenue of the Stars, now a twisted, perverse, and exciting place to be. So much history here! Walk on the huge stars planted in the sidewalk, each with a different star's name, as you browse through 100 huge shops. Today's Hollywood is still interesting but slightly sleazy; on any day you can usually see a couple of religious fanatics, a few punks, a drunk, and a few hookers.*

Santa Monica Boulevard: *Between Sunset Boulevard and Melrose Avenue, stretching from Hollywood to the ocean, this is the heart of L.A.'s gay community. The area is well kept and has some interesting shops, restaurants, and buildings, for example, the art deco bank on San Vicente.*

Westwood Village: *Located close to UCLA, Westwood still gives the appearance of a college town. Though a business area, with lots of interesting (if sometimes expensive) shops and restaurants, it is a very young area. Lots of movie houses are located here, and at night it becomes a massive "cruise" area.*

Hancock Park: *Located in the mid-Wilshire area, this park is lovely for a walk or a bike ride past houses of the rich on wide-laned, tree-lined streets.*

The Valley: *Otherwise known as the San Fernando Valley, made infamous by the song "Valley Girls." Not much to see or do here, hardly a cultural extravaganza. There are some nice clubs, though, and the Sherman Oaks Galleria is an excellent place to shop.*

Sunset Boulevard: *Another must, especially at night. Wall-to-wall cars cruising the flashy, well-lit street. Sunset is an odd mixture of the rich and sophisticated and the poor. The hills above Sunset are very lovely, with luxurious houses overlooking the lights of the city.*

Koreatown: *Centered on Olympic Boulevard between Crenshaw and Vermont, this ethnic community has sprung up quickly in the past couple of years. It has lots of interesting restaurants and markets.*

Fairfax Boulevard: *This traditionally Jewish part of Los Angeles is a great place for delicatessen food—lots of great bakeries too.*

Malibu: *Located off the Pacific Coast Highway just north of L.A., this area was made famous by the '50s and '60s beach movies. It's still a lovely beach, and it's especially nice to drive down Sunset Blvd. all the way to Malibu, a lovely drive to a lovely place.*

Olveras Street: *In the heart of downtown, across from the train station. This is where Los Angeles began. Now it's a touristy Mexican area with lots of shops and restaurants. It's fun to spend the afternoon.*

Some free events include: Pasadena Rose Parade—get there on New Year's Eve to see all the nightlife on the street and the rose floats being moved into position for the big parade (January 1); Concerts on the Green, Barnsdall Park, 4800 Hollywood—Sunday afternoons at 4—concerts with a range of music and performances of theater and dance at the Galley Theater in the Park (summer); Concerts in the Sky (summer); Bona Ventura Hotel, 404 S. Figueroa St. (tel. 213/972-7211); Watts Towers Jazz (summer—Sunday afternoons), 1765 E. 107th St. (tel. 213/569-8181); Music and Dance Series at John Auson Ford Theater (fall), (tel. 213/461-7140).

Getting There: From the Airport: Los Angeles International Airport is 17 miles southwest of downtown L.A. The least expensive way to get from there to downtown is via public bus, but it's inconvenient; try instead the Airport Bus Service (tel. 213/723-4636); the fare is $6.50 adults, $3.50 children to downtown, Beverly Hills, Hollywood, Wilshire District, and Fairfax near the Farmers Market.

● From the Bus and Train Stations: The bus station is located at 208 East 6th St., and the train station, Union Station, is right off the Hollywood Freeway at 800 North Alameda. To call Continental Trailways, dial 213/742-1200; Greyhound, 213/620-1200; and Amtrak, 213/624-0171. RTD (Rapid Transit District) bus transportation is available from the bus and train stations to other parts of the city.

Getting Around: If you travel by taxi (Santa Monica Checker Cab can be summoned by dialing 213/394-1144), you'll pay $1.90 for the first one-eighth mile and $1.40 for each additional mile (that's why we recommend taxis only for emergencies). L.A. Rapid Transit operates buses every 10 to 15 minutes that cost 85¢ locally and 10¢ for a transfer, but very few people depend on buses in L.A. Most people get around the city by car (or on skates). If you don't have a car but want to rent, two of the least expensive places to try are Rent-a-Wreck, 12333 West Pico Blvd., West L.A. (tel. 213/478-0676), $21.95 per day, first 100 miles free, 10¢ per mile after, $119 per week, 500 miles free; and Bob Leech's Autorental, 4810 West Imperial Hwy., Inglewood (tel. 213/673-2727), $15.95 per day with first 100 miles free and then 10¢ per mile for a subcompact car.

Keep in mind when planning your trip to L.A., that the car is king there; if you do not have access to a car, stay near Westwood where the public transportation is better than in other parts of the city.

Help: Los Angeles Free Clinic, 213/653-1990.

● Travelers Aid, 453 S. Spring St., Suite 901, 90013 (tel. 213/625-2501).
● Visitor Information Center, 505 S. Flower St. (tel. 213/689-8822).
● Community Access Line (for the handicapped), toll free 800/372-6641.
● Feminist Women's Health Center, 213/469-4844.
● Gay Community Hotline, 213/464-7400.

Accommodations: YMCA, 1006 E. 28th St., 90011 (tel. 213/232-7193). About 20 minutes by local bus from central bus station. Men only. $26.75.

● Mary Andrews Clark Home, YWCA, 306 Loma Dr., 90017 (tel. 213/483-5780). Women only. $30 single, including two meals, for members; $35 for non-members. The building was built in 1912, patterned after a French chateau.

● Bill Baker International Youth Hostel (AYH-SA), 8015 South Sepulveda Blvd., 90045 (tel. 213/670-4316 or 776-0922). Open June 1 to September 15. Must be 18 or older. $6 for AYH members; $7 for nonmembers.

● Hollywood Inn, 2011 North Highland Ave., 90068 (tel. 213/851-1800). $38 single or double.

● Mira Hershey Hall, UCLA, &, (limited), 801 Hilgard Ave., 90024 (tel. 213/825-3691). Open mid-June to mid-September. $32 single; $16 per person double. $3 per day for parking.

● Friendship Motel de Ville, 1123 W. 7th St., 90017 (tel. 213/624-8474).

● Carmel Hotel, Ⓢ★, 201 Broadway, Santa Monica, 90401 (tel. 213/451-2469). Discounted rates for above symbols: $31 single; $45 double. Regular rates: $45 to $50. The Airport Bus Service will take you right there. "The rooms are clean and it's a good place to start out your L.A. trip—a bit less mind-boggling than downtown L.A."

● The Crescent Hotel, 403 N. Crescent Dr., Beverly Hills, 90210 (tel. 213/274-7595). In the heart of Beverly Hills. Although singles are $30 to $40 and doubles are $35 to $45 (weekly rates $130 and up), this is really a low price considering the location.

● Los Angeles International Hostel (AYH), &, 3601 South Gaffey St., Bldg. 613, San Pedro, 90731 (tel. 213/831-8109). $7.25 for AYH members; $9 for nonmembers. Advance reservations of one week with first night's payment suggested.

● Hollywood YMCA Youth Hostel (AYH-SA), 1553 North Hudson Ave., 90028 (tel. 213/467-4161). $7 for AYH members; $9 for nonmembers. $25 single; $35 double. Must bring sleeping bag. Cafe on premises.

● Lincoln Hostel, &, 2221 Lincoln Blvd., Venice (tel. 213/305-0250). $10 per person.

Where to Eat: Farmers Market, West 3rd Street at Fairfax (tel. 213/933-9211). This popular tourist attraction is an open market with souvenirs for sale, restaurants, fresh produce stands, bakeries, candy stands, etc. You can have a Chinese platter at one of the stands—a main dish, tea, and a cookie for under $5. If Chinese food doesn't interest you, you can choose from Mexican, Italian, and American. Hours: Monday to Saturday, 9 a.m. to 6:30 p.m.; Sunday, 10 a.m. to 6 p.m.

● Side Walk Cafe, 1401 Ocean Front Walk, Venice (tel. 213/399-5547). American food and innovative omelets and sandwiches. Early in the day, enjoy brunch while you watch the skaters, or later on admire the Pacific sunset as you sip a sangria. A meal will cost about $5.

● Duke Tropicana Coffee Shop, 8585 Santa Monica Blvd (tel. 213/652-3100). A popular place with truck drivers, students, and artists in the heart of Hollywood's artist colony. There is a wait of at least a half an hour on a Saturday.

● King's Head, 116 Santa Monica Blvd., Santa Monica (tel. 213/394-9458). Fresh fish and chips, good beers, and delectable desserts in a British pub atmosphere complete with darts. Half an order of fish and chips at $2.50 should fill you up.

- Atomic Cafe, 422 East 1st St. (tel. 213/628-6433). In Little Tokyo near Chinatown. American and Japanese food; new wave and Japanese music from 4 p.m. to 4 a.m. every day.
- Lares Mexican Cafe, 2909 Pico Blvd., Santa Monica (tel. 213/829-4559). Open 7:30 p.m. to 12:30 a.m. Mexican food for under $7. "The greatest margaritas and sunrises and a chance to practice your Spanish."
- Barney's Beanery, 8447 Santa Monica Blvd., Hollywood (tel. 213/654-2287). Open 10 a.m. to 2 a.m. every day. Sandwiches and a vast selection of imported beers. Good service too.
- El Coyotes Restaurant, 7312 Beverly Blvd. (tel. 213/939-7766). In West Hollywood, Mexican food—a margarita, burrito, and chips—will fill you up for $3.50. The decor is tacky—very West Hollywood—but it's an interesting place with good food served in large portions.
- The Pantry, 877 South Figueroa (tel. 213/972-9279). A typical American steakhouse that makes up in value for what it lacks in decor. Said to be the oldest restaurant in L.A., it has some employees who have worked there for over 40 years. Prime ribs with French bread, vegetables, and a potato is only $6.75.
- The Hard Rock Cafe, 8600 Beverly Blvd. (tel. 213/276-7605). In the Beverly Center. The burgers are good, if a bit pricey, but the atmosphere is what you're paying for. This is a copy of the famous London spot and is the "place to be." The decor is, to say the least, unique, for example, a Cadillac protruding from the ceiling. "Great place to sit back and watch L.A. people at their best and their worst."
- Chan Daras, 1511 North Cahuenga, Hollywood (tel. 213/464-8585). Very reasonable Thai food in the heart of Hollywood.
- Canter's Delicatessen, 1119 North Fairfax Ave. (tel. 213/651-2030). A Jewish deli open 24 hours a day, whenever a craving for corned beef or pastrami strikes.
- Cafe Figaro, 9010 Melrose Ave. (tel. 213/274-7664). Dinners from $6 to $8 in a friendly Hollywood atmosphere. A great place for coffee and dessert, open weekends till 3 a.m.
- Falafel King, 10940 Weyburn Ave., Westwood (tel. 213/208-5782). Take-out or eat-in Lebanese food. Complete meals from $2 to $5.
- La Barbaras, 11813 Wilshire Blvd. Pizza, pasta and more. Very reasonable prices; open till 1:30 a.m.
- Casa Vallarta, 3360 Ocean Park Blvd., Santa Monica (tel. 213/450-8665). All-you-can eat Sunday brunch buffet for $5.50.
- Gorky's Russian Cafe, 536 East 8th St. (tel. 213/627-4060). A haven in the less-populated parts of downtown L.A.; an artist's hangout. Inexpensive Russian and American foods served buffet style. Meals from $4 to $7. Open 24 hours.
- Thai Dishes, 111 Santa Monica Blvd. (tel. 213/394-6189). Inexpensive Thai food—around $4.50 a meal.
- Gilberts, 2526 Pico Blvd., Santa Monica (tel. 213/450-8057). Cheap Mexican food with great margaritas.
- Islands, 10948 W. Pico Blvd., West L.A. (tel. 213/474-1144). In the Westwood Pavilion Shopping Center. Moderately priced burgers and salads. A big student hangout with a busy bar.

What to See and Do: NBC Studios, 3000 West Alameda, Burbank (tel. 818/840-4444). Take a look at the inside of a television studio, controls, wardrobes, departments, and sound stages. Tours run from 9 a.m. to 4 p.m., Monday through Sunday; $4.50 for adults; $3.25 for children.

● Universal Studios, 100 Universal City Plaza (tel. 818/508-9600). A two-hour guided tour aboard a tram winds through sound stages, the back lot, a star's dressing room. There are animal shows and special-effects demonstrations, including *Jaws.* Tours are available daily, 8 a.m. to 5 p.m. $15.95 for adults; $11.95 for children (under 3, free); seniors $11.50.

● Burbank Studios, 4000 Warner Blvd. (tel. 818/954-6000). Many popular shows are filmed here, and the tour that you'll get is highly technical and educational. Advance reservations are required and the tour costs a hefty $18. No children under 12 allowed.

● Disneyland, junction of Santa Ana Freeway and Harbor Boulevard in Anaheim, 27 miles from downtown Los Angeles. The world according to Disney—a fantasyland of theme parks, adventures, and rides. Call 714/999-4565 for hours and rates. "The happiest place on earth."

● Huntington Library, Art Gallery, and Botanical Gardens, 1151 Oxford Rd., San Marino (tel. 818/405-2275). The art gallery has 22 galleries of paintings, furniture, and tapestries; and the gardens cover over 200 acres. No admission fee; closed Monday.

● Farmer's Market. We mentioned it above under "Where to Eat," but it's a genuine tourist attraction too.

● J.P. Getty Museum, 17985 Pacific Coast Hwy., Malibu (tel. 213/459-2306). You may enter only by car and must make parking reservations in advance by calling 213/454-6541. Called "Pompeii by the Pacific," it has a beautiful colonnaded garden with Greek and Roman sculpture to admire.

● Mann's Chinese Theatre, 6925 Hollywood Blvd. (tel. 213/464-8111). Used to be Grauman's Chinese Theatre, where the footprints of the stars were immortalized in concrete. The name is changed but the footprints are still there to see.

● Griffith Observatory and Park, at the northern extremity of Vermont Boulevard above Hollywood. An excellent planetarium and laserium with shows every night. Call 213/664-1191 for the schedule. The park itself is a perfect spot for an outing or picnic, and there are horses to rent.

● Mulholland Drive. For a spectacular view of the city at night, drive up Mulholland Drive and park at one of the viewing spots.

● The *Queen Mary* and *Spruce Goose,* Long Beach Pier 7 (tel. 213/435-3511). See the old cruise ship in all her glory and Howard Hughes's plane that was too large to fly. Admission is $14.50 for adults; $8.50 to $10.50 for children; under 5 free. Open 9 a.m. to 9 p.m.

● George C. Page Laboratory Discovery Museum and the LaBrea Tar Pits, 5801 Wilshire Blvd. (tel. 213/936-2230). Closed Monday; open 10 a.m. to 5 p.m. every other day. Many prehistoric animals were caught in the small tar pits located here. The museum offers many reconstructed animals and other things of interest found in the pits. Surrounded by a little park, it's a nice getaway in the middle of the city. Admission is $3 for adults; $1.50 for seniors and students; and $.75 for children. Free second Tuesday of each month.

● Waddles Park is a small park at the top of Curson Boulevard north of Hollywood. It's a good place for a picnic or short hike with some good views of L.A.

● Los Angeles Zoo, in Griffith Park (tel. 213/666-4090). Admission is $4.50 for ages 16 and over; $2.50 for ages 2 to 12; under 2 free. Open 10 a.m. to 6 p.m.

- The Beverly Center. Located on the corner of LaCienega and Beverly, the Beverly Center is a huge new shopping complex where they'll sell you anything from clothes and jewels to dinner and a movie. Interesting for its architecture and its outside stairway.
- Watts Towers, 1765 E. 107th St. A work of folk art and architecture built by Simon Rocha of broken bottles, tile, and junk.
- Museum of Contemporary Art (MOCA), 250 S. Grand (tel. 213/621-2766). A permanent collection of modern art from the 1940s to the present.
- Bornstall Park, 4800 Hollywood Blvd. First California residence built by Frank Lloyd Wright converted to a park with an art gallery and theater.

At Night: In summer there are concerts—classical, rock, and jazz—and the Hollywood Bowl, 2301 North Highland Ave., probably the world's most famous amphitheater. Admission price varies with performance—from free to $15. Call 213/87-MUSIC for information.

- The Music Center for the Performing Arts, 1st Street and Grand Avenue, includes the Dorothy Chandler Pavilion, home of the Los Angeles Philharmonic Orchestra, the Ahmanson Theater, and the Mark Taper Forum. To find out what's on while you're in town, call 213/626-7210.
- From June to September there are outdoor performances by big-name stars in the Greek Theater in a natural canyon in Griffith Park, 2700 North Vermont Ave. Call 213/660-8400 for up-to-the-minute information.
- For country and western music, go to the Palomino Club, 6907 Lankershim, North Hollywood (tel. 213/765-9256). "The best country and western music in L.A." Casual atmosphere, drinks, and dinner. Well-known stars like Linda Ronstadt appear. On Thursday nights there's a talent showcase. $2.50 and up cover. Also McCabes Guitar Shop, 1301 Pico Blvd., Santa Monica 90404 (tel. 213/828-4497). Musical instruments for sale, lessons, and folk concerts, $7 to $10.
- For jazz, go to the Come Back Inn, 1633 West Washington Blvd. in Venice (tel. 213/396-7255). A different group every night; Wednesday and Saturday are the liveliest. $3 to $6 cover. The atmosphere is relaxed and the music is good. Also go to Baked Potato, 3787 Cahuenga (tel. 818/980-1615). Live jazz, big names, and potatoes any way you like!
- To dance, try The Palace, 1735 North Vine, Hollywood (tel. 213/462-8135). Cover can be $8 to $12, but on ladies' night there's no cover. This once-famous theater that dates from the '30s has retained some of its past glories—a huge dance floor, high ceilings, and three floors. Or for top 40 live rock, Sash, 11345 Ventura Blvd. (tel. 818/769-5555).
- For movies: For that rarity—the $2 movie—try the Gordon Theater at 614 North LaBrea on weekends (tel. 213/934-2944). Aero Theater, 1328 Montana Ave., Santa Monica (tel. 213/395-4990). First-rate double feature movies for $3.
- For comedy: The Comedy Store, 8433 Sunset Blvd., Hollywood (tel. 213/656-6225), is a place where lots of comedians got their start—some still stop by. Admission is $5. "A great place for a good time and lots of laughs."

Shopping: For books: B. Dalton Pickwick Books, 6743 Hollywood Blvd. (tel. 213/469-8191). One of the largest bookstores in southern California.

- A Change of Hobbit, 1853 Lincoln Blvd., Santa Monica (tel. 213/473-2873). Science fiction and fantasy books.
- Sisterhood, 1351 Westwood Blvd. (tel. 213/477-7300). Feminist bookstore.
- Crown Books, 10912 Lindbrook Dr., Westwood Village (tel. 213/208-1252). All books discounted 10%.

● For records: Tower Records, 8801 West Sunset Blvd. (tel. 213/657-7300). Large selection, low prices.

● Warehouse Records, 1093 Broxton Ave., Westwood Village. Good sales, a Westwood hangout.

● Aaron's Record Store, 7725 Melrose Ave. (tel. 213/653-8170). New, used, promos, and international records and tapes. "The cheapest I've found yet."

● Rino Records, 1720 Westwood Blvd. (tel. 213/474-8685). Wide range of used records.

● For clothes and gifts: Pier One, 5711 Hollywood Blvd. (tel. 213/483-8854). Handcrafts of wicker, glass, pottery. A good place to find a gift to take back home with you.

● Millers Outpost, 1100 Westwood Blvd. (tel. 213/208-7921). Good buys on the very popular jeans and shirts.

● Army and Navy Surplus Store, 5649 Santa Monica Blvd. (tel. 213/469-0488). Camping equipment—useful and cheap.

● Aahs, 1087 Broxton Ave., Westwood (tel. 213/824-1688). Everything and anything—our favorite is a toothbrush that plays "Strangers in the Night."

Los Banos

Accommodations: Motel 6, 12733 South Hwy. 33, Gustine, 95322 (tel. 209/826-6644).

● Allstar Inn, 13090 South Hwy. 33, Santa Nella, 95322 (tel. 209/826-0880).

Lost Hills

Accommodation: Motel 6, 14685 Warren St., 93249 (tel. 805/797-2346).

Mammoth Lakes

Camping: Devil's Postpile National Monument, P.O. Box 501, 93546 (tel. 619/934-2289). Open approximately mid-June through September. $5 per campsite per night.

Accommodation: Motel 6, 423372 Main St., P.O. Box 1260, 93546 (tel. 619/934-6660).

Marysville

Accommodations: Imperial 400 Motor Inn, 721 10th St., 95901 (tel. 916/742-8586).

● Holiday Lodge Motel, √ ($1), 530 10th St., 95901 (tel. 916/742-7147). $26.50 for one; $28.50 for two in one bed; $31.50 for two in two beds; $36.50 for three in two beds; $38.50 for four in two beds.

● Capri Motel, 803 E St., Hwy. 70, 95901 (tel. 916/743-5465). $24 single; $26 for two in one bed; $34 for two in two beds.

Merced

Accommodations: Allstar Inn, 1215 R St., 95340 (tel. 209/722-2737).

- Motel 6, 1983 East Childs Ave. & Hwy. 99 South, 95340 (tel. 209/384-3702).

Midpines

Accommodation: Budget Host—Muir Lodge, Hwy. 140, Rte. 140, Box 85, 95345 (tel. 209/966-2468).

Milpitas

Accommodation: Budget Host Inn, 485 S. Main St., 95035 (tel. 408/946-1615).

Mineral

Camping: Lassen Volcanic National Park, 96063 (tel. 916/595-4444). Six campgrounds open May or June to September or October. $3 to $6 per campsite per night.

Modesto

Accommodations: Allstar Inn, 1920 West Orangeburg Ave., 95350 (tel. 209/522-7271).
- Motel 6, 722 Kansas Ave., 95351 (tel. 209/524-3000).

Mojave

Accommodations: Motel 6, Calif. 58 and 14, 93501 (tel. 805/824-4571).
- Friendship Inn Mojave, 15620 Sierra Hwy., 93501 (tel. 805/824-4523).
- Imperial 400 Motor Inn, 2145 Hwy. 58, 93501 (tel. 805/824-2463).

Montara

Accommodation: Montara Lighthouse Hostel (AYH), P.O. Box 737, 16th Street at Cabrillo Hwy., 94037 (tel. 405/728-7177). Near bus stop and private beach; hostel is on a cliff overlooking the Pacific Ocean. Men, women, and children. $6 for AYH members; $9 for nonmembers; half price for children under 17. Advance reservations necessary during summer.

Monterey

Help: Mental Health Crisis Team, Community Hospital, 408/624-5311, extension 1623.

Accommodation: Motel 6, 2124 Fremont St. (Old Hwy. 1), 93940 (tel. 408/646-8585).

Morro Bay

Accommodation: Motel 6, 298 Atascadero Rd., 93442 (tel. 805/772-5641).

Mount Shasta

Accommodation: Swiss Holiday Lodge, √, P.O. Box 335, 96067, near jct. 15 & Calif. 89 (tel. 916/926-3446). $27.95 to $34.95 single; $31.95 to $38.95 double; $41.95 to $48.95 triple; $45.95 to $51.95 quad; $60 to $80 for apartments. Community kitchen.

Mountain View

Accommodation: Cozy 8 Motel, 1984 El Camino Real, 94040 (tel. 415/947-1284, or toll free 800/882-1984). $29.88 to $39.88 single; $32.88 to $43.88 double; $36.88 to $47.88 triple; $40.88 to $51.88 quad; $175 to $243 weekly rate.

Napa

Accommodation: Motel 6, 3380 Solano Ave., 94558 (tel. 707/257-6111).

Needles

Accommodations: Motel 6, 1420 J St., 92363 (tel. 619/326-3399).
- Imperial 400 Motor Inn, 644 Broadway, 92363 (tel. 619/326-2145).
- Allstar Inn, 1215 Hospitality Lane, 92363 (tel. 619/326-5131).

Newark

Accommodations: Motel 6, 5600 Cedar Ct., 94560 (tel. 415/791-5900).
- E-Z 8 Motel, 5555 Cedar Ct., 94560 (tel. 415/794-7775).

Norwalk

Accommodation: Allstar Inn, 10646 East Rosencrans, 90650 (tel. 213/864-2567).

Oakland

Help: Travelers Aid, 415/444-6834.

Accommodations: The Hotel Hamilton, ⑤ √, 2101 Telegraph Ave., 94612 (tel. 415/465-7600). $15 to $16 single; $19.75 double, shared baths; $77 to $83 single weekly rate; $98.75 double, shared baths, weekly rate. In the downtown area.
- Motel 6, 4919 Coliseum Way, 94601 (tel. 415/534-8185).
- Budget Host-Civic Center Lodge, 50 6th St., 94607 (tel. 415/444-4139).
- Hotel Touraine, ⑤★, 559 16th St., 94612 (tel. 415/832-2100). Short walk from bus stations, short cab ride from train station. Near Berkeley campus. $10 per night for AYH members; $17 single for nonmembers; $30 triple.

Oceanside

Accommodation: Motel 6, 1403 Mission Ave., 92054 (tel. 619/721-6662).

Ontario

Accommodation: Motel 6, 1515 North Mountain Ave., 91762 (tel. 714/986-6632).

Oroville

Accommodation: Motel 6, 505 Montgomery St., 95965 (tel. 916/532-9400).

Paicines

Camping: Pinnacles National Monument, East District, 95043 (tel. 408/389-4578 or 389-4579). Campgrounds are on the west side of the monument. Open year round at $5 per campsite per night. $3 entrance fee (good for 7 days).

Palm Springs

Accommodations: Motel 6, 595 East Palm Canyon Dr., 92262 (tel. 619/325-6129).
- Allstar Inn, 69-570 Hwy. 111, 92270 (tel. 619/324-8475).

Palmdale

Accommodations: Motel 6, 407 Palmdale Blvd., 93550 (tel. 805/272-0660).
- Super 8 Motel, 200 W. Palmdale Blvd., 93551 (tel. 805/273-8000).

Pasadena

Accommodation: Imperial 400 Motor Inn, 1203 E. Colorado, 91106 (tel. 818/449-3170).

Paso Robles

Accommodation: Allstar Inn, 1134 Black Oak Dr., 93446 (tel. 805/239-2114).

Pescadero

Accommodations: Pigeon Point Lighthouse Hostel (AYH), ♿, Pigeon Point Road (off Hwy. 1), 94060 (tel. 415/879-0633). $6 for AYH members; $9 for nonmembers ($16 members, double; $22 nonmembers, double). Advance reservations necessary for weekends; always call ahead. "Four modern bungalows, once U.S. Coast Guard family quarters, nestled beside a 115-foot tall lighthouse . . . beautiful coastline view."

Petaluma

Accommodations: Motel 6, 5135 Old Redwood Hwy., 94952 (tel. 707/664-9090).
- Allstar Inn, 1368 North McDowell Blvd., 94952 (tel. 707/792-1642).

Pico Rivera

Accommodation: Budget Host—Rivera Motel, 9118 Slauson Ave., 90660 (tel. 213/948-4044).

Pismo Beach

Accommodations: Motel 6, 860 4th St., 93449 (tel. 805/773-2665).
- E-Z 8 Motel, 555 Camino Mercado, Arroyo Grande, 93420 (tel. 805/481-4774).

Pittsburg

Accommodation: Motel 6, 2101 Loveridge Rd., 94565 (tel. 415/427-1600).

Pleasanton

Accommodation: Allstar Inn, 5102 Hopyard Rd., 94566 (tel. 415/463-2626).

Point Reyes

Help: Mental Health Emergencies, 415/663-8231.

Accommodation: Point Reyes Hostel (AYH), P.O. Box 247, Pt. Reyes Station, 94956 (tel. 415/663-8811). $6.50 for AYH members and nonmembers. Beach two miles from hostel. Advance reservations suggested for weekends.

Camping: Point Reyes National Seashore, 94956 (tel. 415/663-1092). Four hike-in campgrounds with approximately 12 sites each; open year round. No fees. Advance reservations of two months suggested in summer.

Pomona

Accommodation: Allstar Inn, 2470 South Garey, 91766 (tel. 714/591-1871).

Porterville

Accommodation: Motel 6, 935 West Morton Ave., 93257 (tel. 209/781-7600).

Quincy

Accommodation: Budget Host—Lariat Lodge, 2370 E. Main St., 95971 (tel. 916/283-1000).

Rancho Cordova

Accommodation: Allstar Inn, 10694 Olson Dr., 95670 (tel. 916/635-8784).

Red Bluff

Accommodations: Motel 6, 20 Williams Ave., 96080 (tel. 916/527-9200).
● Super 8 Motel, 203 Antelope Blvd., 96080 (tel. 916/527-8882).
● Friendship Kings Lodge, 38 Antelope Blvd., 96080 (tel. 916/527-6020).

Redding

Accommodations: Budget Host—Shasta Lodge, 1245 Pine St., 96001 (tel. 916/243-6133).
● Motel 6, 1640 Hilltop Dr., 96001 (tel. 916/221-1800).
● Imperial 400 Motor Inn, 2010 Pine St., 96001 (tel. 916/243-3336).
● Allstar Inn, 2385 Bechelli Lane, 96001 (tel. 916/221-0562).

Redlands

Accommodation: Motel 6, 1160 Arizona St., 92373 (tel. 714/792-3175).

Ridgecrest

Accommodation: Motel 6, 535 South China Lake Blvd., 93555 (tel. 619/375-6866).

Riverside

"A desert community, well-populated, one hour from L.A. with a campus of the University of California."

Help: Helpline, 714/686-HELP (24 hours).
Accommodations: Motel 6, 4045 University Ave., 92501 (tel. 714/686-6666).
● Motel 6, 23581 Alessandro Blvd., Moreno Valley, 92388 (tel. 714/656-4451).
● Motel 6, 6830 Valley Way, Rubidoux, 92509 (tel. 714/681-6666).
● Allstar Inn, 1260 University Ave., 92507 (tel. 714/784-2131).

Rosemead

Accommodations: Motel 6, 1001 San Gabriel Blvd., 91770 (tel. 818/572-6076).
● Friendship Flamingo Inn, 8621 East Garvey Ave., 91770 (tel. 818/571-0171).

Sacramento

N.B. A good guide book for Sacramento and vicinity is Sacramento and the Gold Country, by Karen Bachelis, Pelican Publishing ($9.95).
Help: Travelers Aid, 717 K St., Suite 501, 95814 (tel. 916/443-1719).
On Campus: You'll be able to find helpful information on the bulletin board at the Off-Campus Housing Office, 6000 J Street, Sacramento, 95819 at this branch of California State University. A friend there recommends the Graduate Restaurant and the Coffee House on campus.
Accommodations: Motel 6, 1415 30th St., 95816 (tel. 916/457-0777).
● Motel 6, 10271 Folsom Blvd., Rancho Cordova, 95670 (tel. 916/362-5800).
● Budget Host—Desert Sand Motel, 623 16th St., 95814 (tel. 916/444-7530).
● Allstar Inn, 227 Jibboom St., 95814 (tel. 916/441-0733).
● Allstar Inn, 5110 Interstate, 95842 (tel. 916/331-8100).
● Allstar Inn, 1254 Halyard Dr., West Sacramento, 95691 (tel. 916/372-3624).
● Imperial 400 Motor Inn, 1319 30th St., 95816 (tel. 916/454-4400).

Salinas

Accommodations: Motel 6, 1010 Fairview Ave., 93901 (tel. 408/758-2122).
● Allstar Inn, 140 Kern St., 93901 (tel. 408/424-0123).

San Bernardino

Accommodations: Motel 6, 111 Redlands Blvd., 92408 (tel. 714/825-6666).
- Motel 6, I-215 and State College Pkwy., 1960 Ostrem's Way, 92407 (tel. 714/887-8191).
- E-Z 8 Motel, 1750 South Waterman Ave., 92408 (tel. 714/888-4827).

San Diego

"We have the finest year-round climate in the world, but if you miss shoveling snow you'll find some just one hour away."

San Diego is the first and oldest city in California. For a glimpse of its beginnings, you can visit Old Town, a state park that re-creates the setting of life in California during its Mexican and early American periods. Two buildings here that have been restored are the Casa de Estudio and the Machado/Stewart Adobe. For a view of the more modern San Diego, you can take a cruise in San Diego Harbor and see the impressive skyline of the city, which has grown to be the second largest in the West. To read up on San Diego, we suggest *San Diego Welcomes You,* San Diego Chamber of Commerce, 110 West C St., San Diego, 92101 ($5), designed for residents and prospective residents but includes tourist-type information as well. Other useful guides are *Discover San Diego,* by Leander and Rosalie Peik, Peik's Enterprises ($2.50); *San Diego City & County,* by Carol Mendel ($4.95); and *Greater San Diego Metroguide,* by the San Diego Convention & Visitors Bureau, listed below.

Getting There: From the airport: The airport is only three miles northwest of the city. To get from there to downtown, you simply board a no. 2 bus—the fare is $.80.
- From the train and bus stations: Amtrak is located at 1050 Kettner Blvd.; the Greyhound bus station is at First Avenue and Broadway, and, Trailways is at 310 West C St (619/239-9171). All three stations are in the heart of downtown.

Getting Around: You can get a free copy of "Getting Around San Diego Without a Car" from UCSD Parking and Transit Systems, Q-040, La Jolla, 92093 (tel. 619/534-4235). You can also request a map and transportation brochure. For a free map of San Diego, contact the San Diego Convention and Visitors Bureau, 1200 Third Ave., Suite 824, 92101 (tel. 619/232-3101).
- City buses cost 80¢ and run every 15 to 20 minutes. For information, call San Diego Transit at 619/233-3004, or North County Transit at 619/222-6283. To get information on the San Diego Trolley, which goes downtown to the U.S.-Mexico border, call 619/231-8549. The trolley is the cheapest way to get to the border; it costs $1.50.
- The Molley Trolley, 739 5th Ave., Suite 20 (tel. 619/233-9177), operates 9 a.m. to 7 p.m. Tuesday through Sunday, $4 for a day pass, and connects Gaslamp, Horton Plaza, Hotel Circle, Sea World, Seaport Village, the Embarcadero, Shelter Island, Harbor Island, and the Zoo. A taxi costs $2.20 for the first mile and $1.20 for each additional mile. To rent a car, call San Diego Rent-A-Wreck, 619/224-8235, for a $17.95 daily deal.

Tourist Information: San Diego Convention and Visitors Bureau, 1200

Third Ave., Suite 824 92101 (tel. 619/232-3101, or toll free 800/522-1516). Open daily 8:30 a.m. to 5:30 p.m.

● International Visitors Center, 11 Horton Plaza, 92101 (tel. 619/236-1212). Multilingual attendants. Open daily 9 a.m. to 5 p.m.

● Mission Bay Visitors Information Center, 2688 E. Mission Bay Dr., 92101 (tel. 619/276-8200). Open Monday through Saturday, 9 a.m. to 6 p.m.; Sunday, 9 a.m. to 4:30 p.m.

● Chula Vista Visitors Center, 99 Bonita Rd., 92070 (I-805 and E St.) (tel. 619/425-2390).

● Escondido Visitors Information Bureau, 720 N. Broadway, 92025 (tel. 619/745-4741).

● State Parks Information for San Diego County, Old Town Visitors Center, 2645 San Diego Ave., 92110 (tel. 619/237-6770).

Help: Crisis Center/Hotline, 619/232-2753.

● Travelers Aid, 1122 Fourth Ave., 92101 (tel. 619/232-7991). At the airport: 619/231-7361.

● Health Clinic, 619/488-0644.

Accommodations: Tenochia Hall, San Diego State University, ♿, 92182 (tel. 619/265-5742). Open June 1 through August 13. $25 per night per room. A "reservations request" card should be requested from the Housing Office and returned two weeks prior to the first night of lodging.

● Motel 6, 2424 Hotel Circle North, 92108 (tel. 619/296-1616).

● Campus Hitching Post Motel, ♿, 6235 El Cajon Blvd., 92115 (tel. 619/583-1456). Near the college districts and public transportation. $32 to $40 single; $35 to $45 double; $40 to $50 triple; $45 to $55 quad. Higher rates apply in summer. Weekly rates available.

● San Diego's Elliott International Hostel (AYH) (right off bus 35, near Mission Bay Park and Sea World), 3790 Udall St., 92107 (tel. 619/223-4778). $8 for AYH members; $11 for nonmembers. "Large two-story stucco structure with room for 75 people." Advance reservations recommended during summer months.

● Clarke's Lodge, Ⓢ√ ♿ (all 10%), 1765 Union St., 92101 (tel. 619/234-6787). Near downtown. $33 for one or two in one bed; $43 for up to four in two beds. Pool and color television. Free airport, train, and bus pickup and return.

● Old Town Budget Inn, 4444 Pacific Hwy., 92110 (tel. 619/260-8024, or toll free 800/824-3051 in-state; 800/225-9610 out-of-state). $26.86 single; $28.86 double; $34 triple; $36 quad; $50 suite with kitchen.

● Friendship Town House, Ⓢ ★ 10%, 810 Ash St., 92101 (tel. 619/233-8826, or toll free 800/982-2020 in California). $30 to $40 single; $37 to $51 double; $45 to $56 triple; $49 to $61 quad.

● Budget Motel/Encinitas, 133 Encinitas Blvd (tel. 619/944-0260). $38 single or double; $48 triple; $50 quad.

● E-Z 8 Motel, 2484 Hotel Circle Place N., 92108 (tel. 619/291-8252).

● E-Z 8 Motel, 7851 Fletcher Pkwy., 92041 (tel. 619/698-9444).

● E-Z 8 Motel, 3333 Channel Way, 92110 (tel. 619/223-9500).

● E-Z 8 Motel, 4747 Pacific Hwy., 92110 (tel. 619/294-2512).

● E-Z 8 Motel, 7458 Broadway, 92045 (tel. 619/462-7022).

● E-Z 8 Motel, 1700 Plaza Blvd., 92050 (tel. 619/474-6491).

● E-Z 8 Motel, 1010 Outer Rd., 92154 (tel. 619/575-8808).

Where to Eat: Being so close to the Mexican border, it's not surprising that some of the popular kinds of restaurants in San Diego feature cooking from south of the border. Here are some possibilities:

- Las Olas, 2655 Hwy. 101, Cardiff-by-the-Sea, 92007 (tel. 619/942-1860). In the North County Beach Area. Low-priced Mexican food.
- El Indio Torita Shop, 3695 India St. (tel. 619/299-0333). One of the most popular fast-food Mexican restaurants in San Diego. The food is so good here that it's always busy but worth the wait. Nice outdoor patio, too.
- Casa de Pico, 2754 Calhoun Rd. (tel. 619/296-3267). Traditional Mexican food with mariachi music every day from 1 p.m. Tables outside on patio.
- Old Town Mexican Cafe, 2489 San Diego Ave. (tel. 619/297-4330). The best *carnitas* in town. From the sidewalk, you can watch Mexican women making the *tortillas* you are about to eat.
- Salazar's Taco Shop, 4101 Genesee Ave. (tel. 619/571-9352). Other locations throughout the city. You can get two rolled tacos, a bean tostada, or a beef taco for just $1.69! "Excellent food, especially the machaca burritos."
- Alfonso's, 12151 Prospect Ave., La Jolla (tel. 619/454-2232). Mexican food in an appropriate setting. A la carte ranges from $2 to $4; complete dinners from $6 to $10. "Great nachos and margaritas." Popular with UC/San Diego students.

When you tire of Mexican fare, you can try one of the following:

- Anthony's Fish Grotto, 1316 N. Harbor Dr., at Ash (tel. 619/232-5103). Located downtown on the Bay. Open daily 11:30 a.m. to 8:30 p.m. Fresh seafood—lunch specials.
- Sheldon's Cafe, 4711 Mission Bay Dr. (tel. 619/273-3833). In the Pacific Beach area. Open 24 hours-a-day weekdays; 2 p.m. to 11 p.m. Saturday and Sunday. Low-priced cafe.
- Harry's Cafe, 7545 Girard Ave. (tel. 619/454-7381). In downtown La Jolla. Open Monday through Saturday, 6 a.m. to 7:30 p.m.; Sunday, 6 a.m. to 2 p.m. A local favorite—popular for breakfast. Low-priced homestyle meals.
- Mongolian Beef House, 1856 E. Valley Pkwy., Suite 302, Escondido (tel. 619/480-7474). Open noon to 3 p.m. and 3:30 p.m. to 9:30 p.m. daily. Japanese and Chinese food. All-you-can-eat buffet.
- Boll Weevil (9 locations, check telephone directory). A real hamburger for just $1.99.
- Doodle Burgers (various locations throughout San Diego). Hamburgers in all styles to fit all needs.
- Board and Brew, 1212 Camino del Mar, Del Mar (tel. 619/481-1021). A great place to grab deli sandwiches and then head over to the 15th Street Park on the ocean for a picnic. Prices for sandwiches range between $2.45 and $4.25. They also have wines, beers, desserts, and frozen yogurt.
- O'Hungrys, 2547 San Diego Ave., Old Town (tel. 619/298-0133). Soups, sandwiches, yards of beer, and music from 9 p.m. to 11 p.m.
- Chicken Pie Shop, 3801 5th Ave. (tel. 619/295-0156). Cafeteria-style. Open every day. Lots of food for not much money.
- Baltimore Bagel, 7523 Fay Ave., La Jolla (tel. 619/456-0716). Open from 8 a.m. to 6 p.m. from Monday through Saturday. If you're a bagel-lover, you must taste these. They come in all varieties and to decorate yours, try cream cheese, lox spread, walnut spread, or egg salad.
- Firehouse Deli, 722 Grand Ave., Pacific Beach (tel. 619/272-1999). A good

place for Sunday brunch. All omelettes come with a basket of freshly baked sweet rolls. Sit upstairs on a nice day and enjoy the ocean view.

● Clay's Texas Pit Bar-B-Q, 5752 La Jolla Blvd. (tel. 619/454-2388). Delicious ribs, barbequed beef, and apple pie at the end. Prices start at $2.75.

● V.G.'s, 106 Aberdene, Cardiff-by-the-Sea (tel. 619/753-2400). People come for miles around for their donuts.

● Vieux Carre, 828 5th Ave. (tel. 619/238-0863). A taste of New Orleans in downtown San Diego. Morning special is three baguettes and a cup of coffee for $.99. "Dinners are southern style and delicious."

● Szechuan Restaurant, 4577 Clairemont (tel. 619/270-0251). The tastiest ethnic Szechuan in town. It's so good that a couple of friends come all the way from Denver just to eat here. Prices range from $5 to $8 for dishes.

● Phuong Nam, 540 University Ave., Hillcrest (tel. 619/298-0810). A second location at 1303 Fifth Ave., downtown (tel. 619/233-6090). Authentic Vietnamese cuisine at prices from $3.50 to $5.

● The Hong Kong Restaurant, 3871 4th Ave. (tel. 619/291-9449). Good Chinese food in this "neighborhood place that stays open to 4 a.m."

● Ichiban, 1449 University Ave. (tel. 619/299-7203). A small place with good and inexpensive Japanese food.

● Pasta la Vista, 808 West Washington, Hillcrest, (tel. 619/296-8010). Wine bar and fresh pasta—delicious and reasonable, too.

● Carino's Italian Restaurant and Pizza, 7408 La Jolla Blvd. (tel. 619/459-1400). If you like your pizza with thin crust and rich cheese, this is the place.

N.B. From 4 p.m. to 7 p.m. is happy hour in most San Diego restaurant bars. Food is free and drinks are reduced at many places around town. Some suggestions: Fat City, Mony Mony's, Shooters, Humphrey's, and Café Vid.

What to See and Do in and Around San Diego: Consult either the free *San Diego Reader* or the *North County Entertainer.* Also check the *San Diego Union* or the *Tribune*'s entertainment section for a guide to what's going on.

● Balboa Park. 1,400 acres of park with the world-famous San Diego Zoo, from June to September the city's Theater Festival in the Old Globe, and live shows during summer evenings in the Starlight Theatre. The park includes the Aerospace Museum, which displays a replica of the *Spirit of St. Louis,* the Museum of Man, the Museum of Art, and the Natural History Museum. For information, call 619/239-0512.

● Old Town. This is where San Diego began. The first Spanish settlement on the California coast began here. An historical walking tour of the area leaves every day at 2 p.m. from Casa Machado y Silvas. Don't miss Presidio Park and Padre Junipero Serra Mission. For a free brochure on Old Town, write to: Old Town Brochure, 2783 San Diego Ave., San Diego, CA 92110, or call 619/298-9167.

● Harbor Excursion. You can choose from a one- or two-hour cruise that goes daily and year round from the Broadway Pier at Harbor Drive. Adults pay $10 for the two-hour cruise, $7 for the one-hour cruise. Dinner cruise—dinner, dancing, and an open bar is $35. For information, call 619/234-4111.

● Sea World (tel. 619/226-3901). Everything aquatic plus a dolphin quiz show and the fabulous killer whale show starring "Shamu." Don't miss the penguins at the end of the park. Leave a whole day for this one! $13.95 for adults, $10.95 for children ages 4 to 12 and senior citizens.

● Maritime Museum, 1306 North Harbor Dr. (tel. 619/234-9153). Three restored ships to visit.

- Mission Bay. Sailing, swimming, frisbee, jogging, picnicking, and lots of other things on all the time.
- Beaches (as rated by a native). Black's Beach for nude bathing; La Jolla Shores, Torrey Pines, and Del Mar, all recommended; Pacific Beach, Mission Beach, Ocean Beach for young crowds; and for great waves Mission Bay, Coronado Island, and Cardiff-by-the-Sea.
- Navy Ship Tours. San Diego has the largest naval base on the West Coast so you should probably take a look. On weekends the Navy puts one of its ships on exhibition—tours are free.
- Cabrillo National Monument located at the tip of Point Loma. The view from here is spectacular! On a clear day you can see Mexico, Hotel del Coranado, the Bridge, North Island Naval Base, downtown, and Ballast Point (where the first Spanish landing occurred and now the home of the San Diego submarine base). You may even see as far as the Cleveland National Forest. During the migration of the California gray whale (January to March) this is an excellent lookout point, especially in the morning. This land is owned and operated by the National Park System and hours are 9 a.m. to sunset, daily. For more information call 619/557-5450.
- Scripps Institute of Oceanography and Aquarium Museum. Known worldwide for its research; admission to the aquarium is free.
- La Jolla Cove. A good place to watch the waves roll in and crash against the cliffs and a perfect place to scuba dive.
- Glider Port. The bluffs off the coast of La Jolla make this one of the best places for hang gliders and sail planes. To participate, you must be licensed or taking lessons. On a clear day the sky is filled with them.
- Mount Soledad. For a magnificent view of La Jolla, San Diego city, and the Pacific as far south as Mexico.
- Torrey Pines State Park. The Torrey pine tree grows in the park and it's the only place in the world where it grows. Rangers lead hikes which start at 1 p.m. daily.
- Palomar Mountain and Observatory. A good place to go to escape from the city and have a picnic. You can take a look at the inside of an observatory and see how it works.
- Coronado. San Diego's "Crown City" is reliving the Victorian era. The world-famous landmark, the Hotel del Coronado, has hosted many famous people from all over the world. It's worth a walk through the hotel just to see all the old photographs displayed on the walls. Coronado is situated at the end of a long peninsula, known as the Silver Strand, which forms the western land edge of San Diego Harbor; it is directly west of downtown San Diego.
- Bike Rides. Every Sunday morning at 9:30 a.m., American Youth Hostels sponsors a free bike ride around the city. The ride lasts about three hours and all you need is a bike. There's a slow, medium, and fast group, so you won't get left behind. Riders meet at the County Administration Building, south parking lot, downtown on Pacific Coast Highway.
- Hamel's Action Sports Center, 704 Ventura Place, Mission Beach. Bicycles and roller skates for rent at $3 per day.
- Del Mar Fair/Del Mar Racetrack and Fairgrounds. The fair takes place during the last 2 weeks of June and the first week of July. After that, the racetrack opens and operates through the summer.
- Gaslamp Quarter and Downtown. The newest tourist attraction is this re-

cently renovated part of town. Horton Plaza, a brand new mall, features boutiques, restaurants, and department stores.

At Night: Call 619/534-4090 to find out what's happening on the campus of UC/San Diego.

● Concerts: Often there are concerts at Balboa Park. For more information on what's happening in San Diego call the International Visitors' Information Center, 619/236-1212.

● For classical music, dance, or ballet: Civic Theater, 3rd and B Streets. (tel. 619/234-5855 or 236-6510).

● For theater: San Diego Repertory Theater, 1620 Sixth Ave. (tel. 619/235-8025).

● For jazz: Humphrey's Restaurant, 2241 Shelter Island Dr., Shelter Island (tel. 619/224-3577). Jazz concerts and easy rock all summer long on the lawn. Tickets are $12 to $20 Humphrey's is on the bay and the piano bar is open nightly with no cover charge.

● To dance: Belly Up Tavern, 143 South Cedros, Solano Beach (tel. 619/481-9022). $4 to $10 cover charge from 9 p.m. to 1:30 a.m.; free swing concerts on Wednesday, Friday, and Saturday from 6 to 8 p.m. Music every night of the week—could be blues, rock, reggae, country, or swing on the night you're there. Dancing and good food too.

● Cafe Vid, 7353 El Cajon Blvd., La Mesa (tel. 619/460-7353). A restaurant with video night club featuring Cajun cooking.

● Confetti's, 5373 Mission Center Rd., Mission Bay (tel. 619/291-8635). Drinks and dancing and confetti too.

● For movies: La Paloma, 471 1st St., Encinitas (tel. 619/436-7469).

Shopping: For books: Map Centre, 2611 University Ave. (tel. 619/291-3830). Travel books and maps of all kinds.

● B. Dalton 4525 La Jolla Village Dr. (tel. 619/453-8755).

● For records: Assorted Vinyl, UCSD, La Jolla. Co-op record store. New and used records at 30% to 50% off. Closed during the summer.

● Tower Records, 3601 Sports Arena Blvd. (tel. 619/224-3333). Super discount prices; open until midnight.

● For sporting goods: Eagle Creek Pack Factory, Ⓢ 10%, 143 South Cedros, Solana Beach. Travel gear, equipment for outdoor sports.

● For general shopping: Marshall's, 3902 Clairmont Square Shopping Center (tel. 619/272-5130). Brand names at discount.

● Seaport Village, on San Diego Bay, 849 West Harbor Dr. (tel. 619/235-4013). Boutiques for tourists, restaurants, and a carousel.

● Weekend Swap Meets. If you like the sport of bargain hunting, you might want to try one of the swap meets held on Saturday and Sunday—three are the Orange County Swap Meet, 88 Fair Drive, at the fairgrounds in Costa Mesa; the Spring Valley Swap Meet, 6377 Quarry Rd.; and the Sports Arena Swap Meet at the San Diego Sports Arena.

San Francisco

San Francisco: The Golden Gate Bridge, Chinatown, Fisherman's Wharf, Alcatraz, trolley cars—all well-known features of one of America's most charming cities, San Francisco. The Convention and Visitors Bureau boasts that

San Francisco has two big advantages over other cities—it's both scenic, with its rolling hills overlooking San Francisco Bay, and compact, making it easy for a visitor to get around.

To read up on what Somerset Maugham called "the most civilized city in America," try:

The Native's Guidebook: San Francisco Free and Easy, edited by William Ristow, Bay Guardian Books, Downwind Publications, San Francisco ($5.95). The ultimate guide to the city's entertainment, restaurants, bars, and other interesting places.

Arthur Frommer's Guide to San Francisco, Prentice Hall Press ($5.95). Another dependable guide to the city. Includes excursions to favorite spots in the Bay area.

San Francisco Access, Access Press ($9.95). A complete guide to San Francisco and the Bay Area in the Michelin mode.

San Francisco by Cable Car, by George Young, published by Wingbow Press ($7.95). Touring the city, using the cable cars which the author insists are like the city itself—"romantic, sweet, comic, exciting, and full of mystery and assorted unexpected sidetracks."

San Francisco on a Shoestring, by Louis Madison ($4.95). An excellent guide for travelers who are on a limited budget—includes restaurant listing.

San Francisco Insider's Guide, John K. Bailey, Non-Stop Books ($4.95). Another guide to low-cost attractions.

Weekend Adventures for City Weary People: Overnight Trips in Northern California, Carole Terwilliger Meyers, Carousel Press ($7.95).

And finally, a good restaurant guide, *Best Restaurants of San Francisco,* 101 Publications ($4.95).

The weekly *Bay Guardian* (every Wednesday) lists coming events. The pink section of the *Sunday Chronicle* is another all-inclusive list of the coming week's happenings. The San Francisco Convention and Visitors Bureau, at the Powell Street BART Station (Powell at Market), has a Dial-an-Event phone line, 415/391-2000, with tapes in French, Spanish, German, and Japanese. The staff there has helpful information and maps for drop-in visitors.

Getting There: From the Airport: The San Francisco International Airport is 15 miles south of the city. You can go by Airporter Express bus from the airport to a downtown terminal for $6; $11 round trip. These buses run every 15 minutes during the day, every half hour after 10 p.m., and take about 30 minutes for the trip. The Airporter terminal is at 301 Ellis St. (tel. 415/673-2433).

The privately run Super Shuttle picks up passengers anywhere in the city and brings them to the airport, or from the airport to the city. Call 415/558-8500. The service runs 24 hours a day and costs $7 per person one way.

From Oakland Airport, you can take the shuttle to Coliseum BART Station and then take the San Francisco/Daly City train to the city. The fare will be about $1.50 depending on your San Francisco destination.

The Greyhound Bus Station is at 50 Seventh St. From there local Muni buses connect to other points for 75¢. Call 415/433-1500 for information.

The Trailways station is located at the Transbay Terminal (tel. 415/982-6400), 1st and Mission in downtown San Francisco. The train station for Cal Train to the South Bay is located at 4th and Townsend; more Muni buses there. The Amtrak station is at 4th and Townsend (tel. 415/982-8512 or 872-7245).

Getting Around: Muni is the name of the city transit system that covers almost every corner of town. The fare is 75¢ with one transfer within 2 hours to another bus. Call 415/673-MUNI for information. A monthly Muni pass is $23. Muni Metro is the underground train that leads from downtown San Francisco to the outer boundaries of the city. L Taravel goes to the zoo, N Judah to the University of California Medical Center and the Sunset District, the K Line to San Francisco State. The cable cars are back in operation, under the auspices of Muni, running from Powell Street in the downtown area to the Wharf. The fare is $1.50 and you can use the Muni Monthly Pass on the cable cars, as well. BART (Bay Area Rapid Transit) underground trains criss-cross the Bay to reach main points in the East Bay, Berkeley, etc. The fare is charged according to the distance traveled—80¢ is the minimum. Call 415/788-7278.

AC Transit buses leave from Transbay Terminal for almost any point in the East Bay; Golden Gate Transit buses take you to Marin County and points north. Call 415/332-6600. A ferry to Sausalito from the San Francisco Ferry Terminal takes 30 minutes and costs $2.75 one-way on weekdays, $3 on weekends.

Taxis are difficult to flag down, unless you're in midtown.

To rent a car, try Reliable Rent-A-Car, 349 Mason (tel. 619/928-4414), one block from Union Square. The cost is $19 per day. Most car-rental places will offer you a special weekend deal. Another is Rent-a-Wreck, 555 Ellis Street (tel. 415/776-8700), located near the Airporter terminal in downtown San Francisco. Rates are $19.95 per day, and $99 for the week.

Help: Haight-Ashbury Switchboard, 415/621-6211. Stop in at their office at 1539 Haight St. and ask for a copy of the excellent, free *San Francisco Survival Manual*. Also pick up a copy of the one-page information sheet on *Job Resources in San Francisco*.

- Woman's Switchboard, 3543 18th St. (tel. 415/882-9191).
- Travelers Aid, 38 Mason St., 94102 (tel. 415/781-6738).
- Gay Switchboard and Counseling Service, 415/841-6224.
- San Francisco Women Against Rape, 415/647-7273.
- Options for Women Over Forty, 415/431-6944. This and the above organization are located in the Women's Building, 3543 18th St., 94110.
- Job resources: the San Francisco City College District Office, 33 Gough St. (tel. 415/239-3082); Jewish Vocational Services, 870 Market St., Suite 872, (tel. 415/391-3595)—$1 donation for job listings.

Accommodations: Mary Ward Hall, San Francisco State University, ♿, Housing Office, 800 Font Blvd., off I-280, 94132 (tel. 415/469-1067). Students, faculty, and educationally related visitors only. $32 single; $50 double. Guest meals available in nearby University Dining Center. Open June through August.

- The University of California at San Francisco Residence Halls, ♿, 500 Parnassus Ave., 94143 (tel. 415/476-2231). Open July 1 to September 8. $46 double; two rooms share one bath. Five minutes from Golden Gate Park and on main bus routes downtown. Swimming pool and cafeteria in building. Advance reservations suggested.
- Pensione San Francisco, 1668 Market St., 94102 (tel. 415/864-1271). $32 to $35 single; $38 double; $41 double (two in two beds). Hotel is convenient to BART, Muni Metro, and several bus lines. "Each room is individually decorated by a designer who is one of the owners. Room themes focus on the American West, with photos, antiques, etc. that owners gathered while contemplating opening the hotel. Great breakfast at the cafe."

- Hotel Sequoia, Ⓢ★ 🅑, 520 Jones St., 94102 (tel. 415/673-0234, or toll free 800/445-2631). $29 single; $34 double. Centrally located hotel (near Union Station); ". . . built in the 1920s with an art deco lobby and architecture . . . catering to the young student and international traveler . . . we try to keep an up-to-date, young, rock 'n roll image."

- San Francisco International Hostel (AYH), 🅑, Bldg. 240, Fort Mason, 94123 (tel. 415/771-7277). Two blocks inside Franklin & Bay Sts. Park entrance, behind park headquarters building. $9 for all guests. Must show photo ID. Advance reservations of at least two weeks recommended. "A spacious, historical Civil War building with an inspiring view of the Golden Gate Bridge."

- Golden Gate Hostel (AYH), 941 Fort Barry, Sausalito, 94965 (tel. 415/331-2777). Located within the Golden Gate National Recreation Area, follow the signs from Alexander Ave. The hostel was previously Officers' Headquarters and is listed in the National Register of Historic Places. $9. Photo ID required to register. Advance reservations recommended. "Scenic country setting only eight miles from San Francisco."

- Obrero Hotel and Basque Restaurant, 1208 Stockton St., 94133 (tel. 415/989-3960). $35 single; $42 double; $52 triple; $62 quad. If you bring a sleeping bag you can sleep for $7.50 a night or get a futon from the management and sleep for $10.50 a night. The bath is shared down the hall. Price includes breakfast. Inexpensive meals available daily. "European-style pension located in Chinatown."

- Golden Gate Hotel, Ⓢ★ (with passport), 775 Bush St., 94108 (tel. 415/392-3702). Walking distance from bus and train; one half block from cable car. Centrally located. Singles with shared bath $37, private bath $39; $40 to $42 double, depending on private baths; two people/two beds $57 to $59 depending on the bathrooms. There is a continental breakfast and afternoon tea served at the hotel as well. Advance reservations recommended during summer and holiday periods.

- Essex Hotel, Ⓢ✓★, 684 Ellis St., 94109 (tel. 415/474-4664, or toll free 800/44-ESSEX in state, 800/45-ESSEX out of state. Near bus and train stations. $32 to $40 single; $36 to $50 double; $68 quad; $78 suite; $8 for each additional person. Advance reservations of one day necessary. "A very elegant corner hotel in the heart of San Francisco with a charming European atmosphere and friendly, multilingual staff."

- European Guest House, 761 Minna St., 94103 (tel. 415/861-6634). $8 per night in dorm-style accommodations. No small children. "The place is run by hip Americans and caters primarily to foreign, young people. I've stayed there many times and it's the only place I stay in San Francisco. The atmosphere is friendly, laid-back, and free-wheeling."

- The Amsterdam Hotel, 749 Taylor St., 94108 (tel. 415/441-9014). Close to the Airporter Downtown Terminal. $45 single with private bath; $48 double; $36 single sharing bath with one other room; $41 double; $31 for single with a sink and shared bath; $36 double. "A little bit of Europe in one of America's most European cities."

- The Olympic Hotel, ✓ ($2), 140 Mason St., 94102 (tel. 415/982-5010). $20.25 single; $35 double with private bath; parking is available.

- The Windsor Hotel, ★, 238 Eddy St., 94102 (tel. 415/885-0101). $25 to $35 doubles only. Family suites at $50.

- Union Square Plaza, 432 Geary St., 94102. Near Union Square (tel. 415/776-7585). $35 single; $40 double.
- The Beresford Hotel, 635 Sutter St. (tel. 415/673-9900). Close to Union Square and the center of the city. $55 per room; $60 triple; $65 quad. Cribs and cots are available for an extra fee. An old, established hotel with a lot of charm.
- Laurel Motor Inn, Presidio Avenue and California (tel. 415/567-8467). $59 to $64 depending on city view; $7 for each additional person. There are kitchens available for an extra $5. Cribs available. Continental breakfast is served in the motel's coffee shop. The real plus here is the garage parking in a city where parking is at a premium. This motel is located not far from the city center in a quiet neighborhood and is serviced by many public transit lines.

Where to Eat: Salmagundi's. There are several locations but probably the most convenient is the one at Civic Center, near Symphony Hall and the San Francisco Museum of Modern Art. Cafeteria-style dining in a hi-tech interior, where you can sip a cup of coffee for hours without being bothered. Different soups every day; soup, salad, and roll with a drink costs about $5 to $7.

- United States Restaurant, 431 Columbus in North Beach (tel. 415/362-6251). Full Italian dinners for $5 to $7 in what looks like a greasy spoon but isn't. "Old-fashioned Italian; soggy vegetables but excellent calamari."
- La Mediterranee, 2210 Fillmore, with a new one on Market St. (tel. 415/921-2956). Middle Eastern atmosphere, the food is good in this small place. A dinner costs from $6 to $8.
- Tomasso's Famous Pizzeria, 1042 Kearny St. (tel. 415/398-9696). A great, late-night hangout in North Beach. Often crowded but worth the wait. Large pizzas are $7 to $14.
- Pasand Madras, 1857 Union St. (tel. 415/522-4498). Southern Indian food like masala dosas (large lentil pancakes filled with vegetarian curry) and biryianas (filling rice and curry dishes)—about $8.50 for a full meal including an appetizer. (There's another Pasand in Berkeley on Shattuck.) One friend eats here twice a week and considers it to be one of the best buys in town—especially good value compared to other high-priced restaurants on Union Street.
- La Taqueria, 2889 Mission St. (tel. 415/285-7117). One block from the 24th St. BART station and open every day from 10 a.m. to 10 p.m. Their burritos are supposed to be the best in the city. Mexican frescoes on the wall; there are two tables outside if the weather cooperates. $3 will buy you a large burrito and a fresh fruit drink. After dinner, walk one block to La Boheme Coffee House for a cappuccino.
- Hang Ah Tearoom, One Hang Ah St. (an alley off Sacramento St. below Stockton) (tel. 415/982-5686). A quiet dim sum place especially recommended for Sunday brunch. "My favorite is pork bow, a steamed doughy bun filled with barbequed pork." The interior is pleasant and two can eat here for $10."
- Pasta II, 381 South Van Ness (tel. 415/864-4116). A menu of nothing but pasta that's filling and usually good. The interior is black and white and funky with mismatched tables and chairs. Pasta II is not far from the Symphony and Ballet at Civic Center.
- Castro Gardens, 558 Castro (tel. 415/621-2566). Castro eggs with or without cheese, something like a souffle, or a "Denver" omelet—almost $12 for two.
- Mai's Vietnamese Restaurants on Union, Clement, and Irving Streets. (tel. 415/221-3046). A dependable selection of good Vietnamese food. Entrees average $5.

• Hong Kong Cafe, 651 Clement St. (tel. 415/387-2120). A small, Chinese bakery with dim sum to eat in or take out. Consider carrying some over to Mountain Lake Park for a picnic.

• Milano Pizza, 1330 Ninth St., between Irving and Judah (tel. 415/665-3773). A good pizza place in what real estate people call "an up-and-coming neighborhood."

• The Kublai Khan's Mongolian Barbecue, 1160 Polk at Fillmore (tel. 415/885-1378). All-you-can-eat Chinese buffet for $4.95 at lunchtime; $5.95 at dinner.

• The Mandalay, 4348 California (tel. 415/386-3895), within five blocks of Golden Gate Park. Recently named the best Asian restaurant in the city. This is the most delicious Burmese food you may ever have and there is something for everyone on the menu. The prices are in the medium range. Booster seats are available.

• The Red Crane, 1115 Clement St. (tel. 415/751-7226). Delicious vegetarian meals with no MSG. Weekday lunch specials, $2.95.

• 19th Avenue Diner, 19th Avenue and Lincoln (tel. 415/759-1517). The menu runs the gamut of fashionable diner fare; Sunday brunch and portable feasts to take to Golden Gate Park, directly across from the restaurant. Open Sunday through Thursday until 2 a.m.

• Il Pollaio, 55 Columbus Ave. (tel. 415/362-7727). Good and cheap Italian food—located in the heart of North Beach.

What to Do and See: Fisherman's Wharf. This is the home of the fishing fleet with seafood restaurants, shops, boat tours, and sailing ships. In October, the fishing fleet is blessed and the Procession of Maria del Lume follows.

• Golden Gate Park, 415/558-3706. There's lots going on here in the world's largest artificial park. You'll find the De Young Museum, the Asian Art Museum with its Avery Brundage Collection, the Academy of Sciences Museum with the aquarium, a planetarium, and a laserium. Other attractions of the park include the Japanese Tea Garden, a meadow full of roaming buffalo, a series of man-made lakes, and the Chinese Pavilion at Stow Lake, a gift from the People's Republic of China to the people of San Francisco.

• Chinatown. The largest and oldest Chinese colony outside China. Grant Avenue is the heart of the area. Enjoy a dim sum lunch in a basement restaurant and shop for small gifts.

• The Cannery. Leavenworth and Beach Sts. Once a Del Monte fruitpacking plant, now restored with art galleries, restaurants, shops, etc.

• Ghirardelli Square, Northpoint and Larkin Streets. Once a chocolate and spice factory but now redone as a miscellany of shops, restaurants, and inviting plazas.

• North Beach. The city's Italian section, which started out as the fishing center. Chinatown is beginning to spill over into this part of town. Many artists live around Columbus Avenue. Take a walk from Coit Tower. You'll get views of Alcatraz and find the quiet gardens of Telegraph Hill. St. Mary's Square is the center of the area; the large church dominates the plaza, just like a small European village.

• Haight-Ashbury. Not what it was in the '60s—in fact, it's become a chic area of shops for the affluent young. Full of old Victorian homes that are being lovingly restored. Worth the visit.

• Fort Mason Center, Bay and Laguna. Three old piers that have been renovated into theaters, galleries, and small museums, including the Mexican Museum, and the Italian-American Museum. The Liberty Ship, a fighting ship from World War II is docked at the end of the pier and is open to the public. From here, there are excellent views of the Golden Gate Bridge, and close to the marina is a nice spot for a picnic.

● Stern Grove Concert Series, 415/558-3706. Held every summer in a lovely park surrounded by eucalyptus trees. Free.

● Ferry Boat Ride, 415/332-6600. You can take a ferry from the San Francisco pier on the Embarcadero to Sausalito, across the bay in Marin County, Angel Island, and Alcatraz.

● San Francisco Art Institute, 600 Chestnut St. Close to North Beach (tel. 415/771-7020). Besides the art, the views from the cafeteria are remarkable. A lively place.

● The Mission District, 24th and Mission Streets, is the center of the Spanish-speaking part of the city. The food here is cheap and often Mexican. Visit the Cafe La Boheme at the crossing of 24th St. and Mission, and join the writers and artists of the city for an espresso. See also the Basilica and Museum of Mission Dolores, 18th and Dolores, the 19th-century church and one of the series of missions along the California coast.

● The Golden Gate National Recreation Area is a national park within the city's borders, extending from Fort Mason to Land's End, and it includes one of San Francisco's better beaches, Baker's Beach.

● The Zoo, Sloat Boulevard in the southern part of the city. The new primate center and a 19th-century carousel are two highlights.

● Palace of Fine Arts, Exploratorium Museum, Bay and Lyons Streets. The first hands-on science museum in the country, housed in a building dating from the 1915 World's Fair. Lots of fun!

● Legion of Honor Museum, on a bluff overlooking the ocean in Lincoln Park. Devoted to French art; the view on a clear day rivals the art.

● Civic Center, Pope Street between Grove and McAllister Sts. (tel. 415/558-3981). Here you'll find the Museum of Modern Art, Davie's Symphony Hall, City Hall complete with a Beaux-Arts rotunda and a public library that offers free walking tours of the city.

At Night: For jazz: Keystone Corner, 750 Vallejo St. (tel. 415/781-0697). "One of the country's best jazz clubs." Cover charge varies with the performer —can be quite expensive if it's someone famous. Call the KJAZ line, 415/769-4818, for an update on concerts and jam sessions in the Bay Area.

● To dance: I-Beam, 1245 Haight (tel. 415/668-6006). $5 cover every night.

● Trocadero Transfer, 520 4th St. (tel. 415/495-0185). Cover charge varies; starts at $5.

● Rockin' Robin's, 1840 Haight St. at Stanyan St. (tel. 415/221-1960). Dancing to '50s and '60s music; $3 cover on weekends, $1 other evenings.

● Club DV8, 55 Natoma (tel. 415/777-1419). Located in the new trendy neighborhood of SOMA, South of Market. With an $8 cover this is an expensive evening but is the place to be seen in San Francisco.

● For theater: For half-price theater tickets on the day of performance, try STUBS ticket outlet at Union Square facing Stockton St. (tel. 415/433-7827).

● Besides the well-established ACT Theater, there are lots of alternative, experimental plays being performed at places like the Magic Theater (tel. 415/421-8822); the One Act Theatre Company, near Union Square (tel. 415/421-6162); and the Theatre Artaud (tel. 415/621-7797). All of the above will give special prices to students.

- Castro Theater, 420 Castro (tel. 415/621-6120). It's worth a trip just to see the architecture or hear the organist.
- For movies: York Theater, 24th Street at Potrero Avenue (tel. 415/282-0316). A neighborhood movie theater with a '30s decor. $3.50 for a movie.
- For folk music: Ploughshares Coffeehouse, at Fort Mason (tel. 415/441-8910). About $3.50 cover. Good place for anyone serious about folk music.
- The Plough and The Star, 116 Clement St. (tel. 415/751-1122). An authentic Irish pub with dancing and an open microphone.
- For classical music: Davies Symphony Hall, Civic Center, Grove and Van Ness (tel. 415/431-5400). Where the San Francisco Symphony is located. Tours of the hall every day.
- For dance/ballet: Dance is an integral part of the life of the Bay Area. The San Francisco Ballet performs at the Opera House on Van Ness Avenue Grove Street across from Davies Hall. Tickets: $4 and up. There are lots of small dance companies in the area too, including the Margaret Jenkins Dance Studio, which performs at the Performance Gallery, 3153 17th St. (tel. 415/863-9834).

Shopping: For books: City Lights, 261 Columbus Ave. (tel. 415/362-8193). Lawrence Ferlinghetti's gift to San Francisco. One of the first paperback bookstores in the world and a literary meeting place.

- Green Apple Books, 506 Clement St. (tel. 415/387-2272). Friendly staff sells used books. You can browse for hours.
- A Clean and Well-lighted Bookstore, in the Opera Plaza on Van Ness. A friendly, new place that's well stocked.
- For records: Revolver Records, 520 Clement St. (tel. 415/386-6128). Used records, all types of music. Many records as low as $2.
- Tower Records, Columbus Ave. and Bay St (tel. 415/885-0500). Sells a large selection of records until midnight.
- Discount Records, 656 Market St. (tel. 415/398-4574). The name says it all.
- For sporting goods: California Surplus Sales, 966 Mission St. and also on Market Street For a large selection of camping equipment at reasonable prices.
- For general shopping: Union St. all the way from Steiner to Gough St. has all types of stores—selling antiques, gifts, art, clothing, and flowers. Try the Fillmore District between Fillmore and Bush, and California Street for a string of small boutiques with interesting art objects on display and some great used clothing places like Repeat Performance and Seconds to Go.
- Cost Plus, 2552 Taylor St. at Fisherman's Wharf (tel. 415/928-6200). A huge warehouse full of imports from all over the world. Two blocks for browsing.
- Clement Street Best part of town for bargain shopping. Many used clothing stores, factory outlets, small boutiques, coffeeshops, and cafes away from the regular tourist haunts.
- Noe Valley. Lots of "new wave" boutiques on the direct Metro line downtown on the J Church.

San Jose

Accommodations: Motel 6, 2560 Fontaine Rd., 95121 (tel. 408/270-3131).
- E-Z 8 Motel, 1550 North 1st St., 95112 (tel. 408/292-1830).
- E-Z 8 Motel, 2050 North 1st St., 95131 (tel. 408/436-0636).
- Friendship Inn, 1378 Oakland Rd., 95112 (tel. 408/437-0900).

San Luis Obispo

Accommodations: Motel 6, 1433 Calle Joaquin, 93401 (tel. 805/549-9595).
- Allstar Inn, 1625 Calle Joaquin, 93401 (tel. 805/541-6992).

San Pedro

Accommodation: Imperial 400 Motor Inn, 411 South Pacific Ave., 90731 (tel. 213/831-0195).

San Ysidro

Accommodation: Motel 6, 160 East Calle Primero, 92073 (tel. 619/690-6663).

Santa Ana

Accommodation: YMCA, 205 West Civic Center Dr., 92701 (tel. 714/542-3511). Three blocks from bus, half a mile from train. Men only. $18 single; $20 double. Weekly rate: $95 single; $140 double.

Santa Barbara

On Campus: The University of California has a branch in this city—"one of the most beautiful cities on the West Coast, right on the ocean." For organic food, try the Playa Azul, 902 South Santa Barbara.
Accommodations: Motel 6, 443 Corona Del Mar, 93103 (tel. 805/564-1392).
- Motel 6, 5897 Calle Real, Goleta, 93117 (tel. 805/964-3596).
- Motel 6, 3505 State St., 93105 (tel. 805/687-5400).
- Allstar Inn, 5550 Carpinteria Ave., 93013 (tel. 805/684-8602).

Santa Clara

Accommodations: Motel 6, 3208 El Camino Real, 95051 (tel. 408/241-0200).
- Madison Street Inn, 1390 Madison St., 95050 (tel. 408/249-5541). A comfortable Victorian inn with pretty gardens and old-fashioned hospitality. $55 single or double; $200 per week; $800 per month. $40 single with *Where to Stay*.

Santa Cruz

Accommodation: Santa Cruz Hostel Project (AYH-SA), P.O. Box 1241,

95061 (tel. 408/423-8304). Open mid-June to end of August. Reservations necessary.

Santa Fe Springs

Accommodation: Allstar Inn, 13412 Excelsior, 90670 (tel. 213/921-0596).

Santa Maria

Accommodation: Motel 6, 839 East Main St., 93454 (tel. 805/925-2551).

Santa Rosa

Help: Helpline, 707/544-HELP.
Accommodations: Motel 6, 2760 Cleveland Ave., 95401 (tel. 707/546-1500).
- Allstar Inn, 3145 Cleveland Ave., 95401 (tel. 707/525-9010).
- Super 8 Motel, 2632 N. Cleveland Ave., 95401 (tel. 707/542-5544).

Saratoga

Accommodation: Sanborn Park Hostel (AYH), 🚫, 15808 Sanborn Rd., 95070 (tel. 408/741-9555). $5 for AYH/IYHF members; $8 for nonmembers. "Beautiful old building listed in National Register of Historic Places and set in a forest of redwood, oak, and madrone trees." Kitchen available.

Simi Valley

Accommodation: Motel 6, 2566 North Erringer Rd., 93065 (tel. 805/526-3533).

South Lake Tahoe

Accommodations: Motel 6, 2375 Lake Tahoe Rd., P.O. Box 7756, 95731 (tel. 916/542-1400).
- South Lake Tahoe Hostel (AYH), 1043 Martin St., Box 7054, 95731 (tel. 916/544-3834). Closed April 1 to May 15 and October 1 to December 25. $8 for AYH members; $10 for nonmembers. Advance reservations suggested. Sleeping bag accepted.

Stanford

Accommodation: Stanford University Residence Halls, 🚫, Stanford Conference Office, 123 Encina Commons, 94305-6020 (tel. 415/723-3126). Men, women, and children. Open mid-June to mid-September. $24 single; $18 per person in shared room.

Stanton

Accommodation: Motel 6, 7450 Katella Ave., 90680 (tel. 714/891-0717).

Stockton

Accommodations: Motel 6, 4100 Waterloo Rd., 95205 (tel. 209/931-9511).
● Motel 6, 1625 French Camp Turnpike Rd., 95206 (tel. 209/467-3600).
● Allstar Inn, 817 Navy Dr., 95206 (tel. 209/946-0923).
● Allstar Inn, 6717 Plymouth Rd., 95207 (tel. 209/951-8120).

Sunnyvale

Accommodation: Motel 6, 806 Ahwanee Ave., 94086 (tel. 408/720-1222).

Sylmar

Accommodation: Motel 6, 12775 Encinitas Ave., 91342 (tel. 818/362-9491).

Thousand Oaks

"A beautiful city midway between Santa Barbara and Los Angeles, 30 minutes from Malibu."

Accommodations: Motel 6, 2850 Camino Dos Rios, Newbury Park, 91320 (tel. 805/499-0585).
● Allstar Inn, 1510 Newbury Rd., 91360 (tel. 805/499-5888).

Three Rivers

Camping: Kings Canyon National Park, 93633 (tel. 209/565-3341). Campgrounds at Azalea Canyon View, Crystal Springs, Sunset, and Cedar Grove. Azalea is open all year; the others are open from May to October. $6 per campsite per night.
● Sequoia National Park, 93271 (tel. 805/565-3381). Six campgrounds at Atwell Mill, Buckeye Flat, and Dorst, which are open during the summer sea-

son; and Lodgepole, South Fork, and Potwisha, which are open year round. $6 fee except for Atwell and South Fork, which have a $4 fee.

Tracy

Accommodation: Motel 6, 3810 Tracy Blvd., 95376 (tel. 209/836-4900).

Truckee

Accommodation: Star Hotel (AYH), P.O. Box 1227, 10015 W. River St., 95734 (tel. 916/587-3007). $10 for AYH members; $13 for nonmembers. Private hotel rooms, $40 single/double occupancy, $10 per person after that.

Tulare

Accommodations: Motel 6, 1111 North Blackstone, 93274 (tel. 209/686-1611).
● Tulare Inn, √, Hwy. 99 at East Paige Ave., 93274 (tel. 209/686-8571). $28 for one; $30 to $34 for two in one bed; $35 for two in two beds; $40 for three in two beds; $45 for four in two beds.

Tulelake

Camping: Lava Beds National Monument, 🔠, P.O. Box 867, 96134 (tel. 916/667-2282). Forty campsites open year round; water is shut off in winter. $5 per campsite per night in summer. Monument entrance fee $3.

Turlock

Accommodation: Motel 6, 250 South Walnut Rd., 95380 (tel. 209/667-4100).

Twentynine Palms

Camping: Joshua Tree National Monument, 74485 National Monument Dr., 92277 (tel. 619/367-7511). Eight campgrounds at Belle, Black Rock Canyon, Cottonwood Spring, Hidden Valley, Indian Cove, Jumbo Rocks, Ryan and White Tank are open from October 1 to June 1. Only Hidden Valley and A Loop at Cottonwood Spring are open during the summer. Entrance fee $5 per vehicle (good for 7 days); $5 per campsite at Black Rock Canyon and Cottonwood Spring. Group campsites can be reserved through the Ticketron Reservation System, these sites include Cottonwood, Indian Cove, and Sheep Pass.

Ukiah

Accommodation: Motel 6, 1208 South State St., 95482 (tel. 707/468-5404).

Vacaville

Accommodation: Motel 6, 107 Lawrence Dr., 95688 (tel. 707/447-5550).

Vallejo

Accommodations: Motel 6, 101 Maritime Academy Dr., 94590 (tel. 707/557-0777).
- Allstar Inn, 1455 Sears Point Rd., 94590 (tel. 707/643-7611).
- Allstar Inn, 597 Sandy Beach Rd., 94590 (tel. 707/552-2912).
- E-Z 8 Motel, 4 Mariposa St., 94590 (tel. 707/554-1840).

Van Nuys

Accommodation: Allstar Inn, 15711 Roscoe Blvd., 91343 (tel. 818/894-9341).

Ventura

Accommodation: Motel 6, 2145 East Harbor Blvd., 93003 (tel. 805/643-5100).

Victorville

Accommodations: Motel 6, 16901 Stoddard Wells Rd., 92392 (tel. 619/243-0666).
- E-Z 8 Motel, 15401 Park Ave., East, 92392 (tel. 619/243-1227).
- E-Z 8 Motel, 15366 La Paz Ave., 92392 (tel. 619/243-2220).

Walnut Creek

Accommodation: Motel 6, 2389 North Main St., 94596 (tel. 415/935-4010).

Weed

Accommodation: Motel 6, 466 North Weed Blvd., 96094 (tel. 916/938-4101).

Westminster

Accommodation: Motel 6, 6266 Westminster Ave., 92683 (tel. 714/891-5366).

Whiskeytown

Camping: Whiskeytown National Recreation Area, √ ⧉, P.O. Box 188, 96095 (tel. 916/241-6584). R.V.'s only at Brandy Creek with no fee, Oak Bottom—$5 per night for R.V.'s, $7 per night for tents. 37 R.V. sites at Brandy Creek, 105 tent sites and 50 R.V. sites at Oak Bottom. Handicapped access to fishing and marina access. Some campsites also set up for handicapped use.

Whittier

Accommodation: Motel 6, 8221 South Pioneer Blvd., 90606 (tel. 213/692-9101).

Williams

Accommodation: Motel 6, 455 4th St., 95987 (tel. 916/473-5337).

Willows

Accommodation: Super 8 Motel, 457 Humboldt Ave., 95988 (tel. 916/934-2871).

Woodland

Accommodation: Motel 6, 1564 East Main St., 95695 (tel. 916/666-6777).

Yosemite

Accommodations: The Yosemite Park and Curry Company, √, Yosemite National Park, 95389 (tel. 209/252-4848), operates several accommodations within Yosemite National Park. Reservations are requested as far in advance as possible and may be made by phone. Some of these accommodations are out of the price range of this book, but the following aren't:
- Yosemite Lodge Cabins. Without bath or water. $33 for one or two people; $5 for each additional person; $2.50 for each child under 12. Use central bathhouse. Linen supplied.
- Curry Village Tent Cabins. $22.65 for one or two people; $4 for each additional person; $2 for each child under 12. Use central bathhouse. Linen supplied.
- Housekeeping Camp. Units for one to four persons. $26.25 per day. Summer only. You supply your own linen and use central bathhouse.

● White Wolf Lodge Tents. $25.75 for one or two people; $5 for each additional person. Use central bathhouse. Linen supplied.

N.B. In summer, Yosemite Valley is filled to capacity. It is suggested that you try outlying and remote areas of the park if you want to experience wilderness.

Yreka

Accommodation: Motel 6, 1785 South Main St., 96097 (tel. 916/842-4111).

Yuba City

Accommodation: Motel 6, 700 North Polara, 95991 (tel. 916/674-1710).

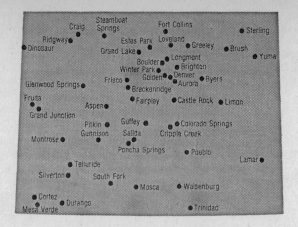

Colorado

Most of Colorado is located in the Rocky Mountains, and its natural beauty is extraordinary. Boulder is the student center of the state, and Vail and Aspen are where everyone from the East Coast wants to go skiing.

The Colorado Tourism Board promises 300 days of sunshine and crisp, clean air in what they call their 104,000-square-mile outdoor amphitheater. About one-third of Colorado is protected under government jurisdiction: 11 national forests, three national recreation areas, two national parks, six national monuments, and one national historic site. Whatever your outdoor fun is, you can probably do it in Colorado. Before the snow falls, backpacking is a favorite Colorado activity, and you can hike to your heart's content in the wilderness areas of Rocky Mountain National Park; south of Pikes Peak, near Colorado Springs; west of Denver in the Mount Evans area; in the San Juan mountain range in the southwest; north of Glenwood Springs, in the Flattops and Rabbit Ears Pass Area near Steamboat Springs; and in the Ten Mile Range south of Vail.

When winter comes, everyone in Colorado talks "ski." The Rocky Mountains have a powder snow that dreams are made of! For a free guide to Colorado's 28 ski resorts, write to Colorado Ski Country USA, One Civic Center Plaza, 1560 Broadway, Suite 1440, Denver, CO 80202, or telephone 303/837-0793.

Another favorite Colorado activity is river tripping. The state tourist office (see address below) will supply you with a list of 14 companies that operate river trips—trips that last from one hour to a week or more and can be booked with a guide who does all the paddling, or without, for a do-it-yourself experience!

A useful guide book for Colorado is *Colorado Off the Beaten Path,* by Curtis Casewit, Globe Pequot ($7.95).

N.B. Colorado has an active and ever-growing number of youth hostels. At some you must be an AYH card holder; at others you may buy introductory passes. Call individual hostels for details.

Some Special Events: Ullrfest Winter Carnival in Breckenridge and National Western Stock Show in Denver (January); American Ski Classic in Vail (March); Subaru Freestyle Nationals in Winter Park (April); Annual Kinetic Sculpture Challenge in Boulder (May); Annual Bluegrass and Country Music Festival in Telluride, and Aspen Music Festival (June); Colorado Indian Market in Denver (July); Jazz Festival in Central City (August); Scottish Highland Festival in Estes Park and Fall Rendezvous of Mountain Men in La Junta (September); Parade of Lights in Denver (December).

Tourist Information: Colorado Tourism Board, 1625 Broadway, Suite 1700, Denver, CO 80202 (tel. 303/592-5410; for their *Adventure Guide* only toll free 800/433-2656).

Two bed-and-breakfast reservation services are Bed & Breakfast Colorado, Box 6061, Boulder, CO 80306 (tel. 303/442-6664), and B & B Rocky Mountains, P.O. Box 804, Colorado Springs, CO 80901 (tel. 303/630-3433).

Aspen

Accommodation: The St. Moritz, √ ★, 334 W. Hyman Ave., 81611 (tel. 303/925-3220). $36 to $46 single; $40 to $56 double; $50 to $66 triple; $60 to $76 quad; higher rates during winter; children under 12 stay free.

Aurora

Help: COMITIS Crisis Center, 9840 East 17th Ave., 80010 (tel. 303/343-9890). 24-hour switchboard for information, referrals, help lines, emergency housing, counseling, food, and showers.

Boulder

Help: Women's Line, 303/492-8910.

On Campus: A friend from the University of Colorado calls this " 'Mork and Mindy' land, or East Coast/West Coast slick with a little hint of Western laidback for flavor." He goes on to explain that a few years ago Boulder was summer headquarters for the street people and the locals didn't like it at all. Some of the feelings persist, but in general young travelers are welcome—"if you're reasonably clean, sober at noon, and don't try to sleep in Central Park you won't be hassled."

When you're hungry in Boulder and want vegetarian food, try Hanna's New Age Foods (tel. 303/443-0755, open at lunchtime only), located above the New Age Food Store at 10th and Pearl. For not-so-organic eating, try Don's Cheese and Sausage Mart (tel. 303/444-0464), 28th and Baseline. Other possibilities: The Harvest, at 18th and Pearl, for healthful food; Marie's on North Broadway, for reasonable prices and an occasional Czech specialty; and the New York Deli (tel. 303/449-5161), on the Pearl St. Mall. Tulagi (tel. 303/442-1369) is a restaurant and nightclub located at 1129 13th, on "The Hill," near campus. They serve lunch and dinner from the same menu offering "stuffer" sandwiches for about $2.50. All drinks are $1.50. The best deal in town is probably the food service in the University Memorial Center on campus at either the Tabor Inn or the Alfred E. Packer Memorial Grill, named after the U.S.'s only convicted cannibal.

If you're in Boulder during the warm weather you'll surely walk along the Mall with a Haagen-Dazs ice cream cone and enjoy the jugglers, magicians, tightrope walkers, belly dancers, musicians, and all the other people. And if you're around in the beginning of April, you'll get to enjoy the annual campus Trivia Bowl.

To know what's going on, check the *Colorado Daily,* the campus paper, or the *Grapevine.* For disco, the place to be seen is Anthony's Gardens in the Harvest House Hotel, and if your desires run to an English/Irish pub-type place, try the James, just off the Mall. When it's time to leave Boulder, you can check the rider board next to Mr. Tomato's in the University Memorial Center—it's divided into geographical areas and gets lots of use.

"If you're clean, tan, and play Frisbee, there's a place for you."

Accommodation: Boulder International Hostel (AAIH), √ ★, 1107 12th St., 80302 (tel. 303/442-0522). Near bus station. $9 per person per night in the dorm. Private rooms are often available: $20 single; $25 double. Bring your own sleeping bag, sheet, sleeping sack, or linen—or rent linen package for $2. Kitchen and laundry facilities are provided.

Breckenridge

Tourist Information: Breckenridge Resort Chamber of Commerce, 303/453-2918.

Accommodation: Fireside Inn (AYH-SA), 200 Wellington St., 80424 (tel. 303/453-6456). Summer: $24 single; $29 double; $11 in dorm. Winter: $45 single or double; $16 in dorm. Continental breakfast included in summer prices. "A cozy, friendly place in an interesting refurbished western mining town." Excellent summer and winter recreational facilities.

Brighton

Accommodation: Super 8 Motel, 1020 Old Brighton Rd., 80601 (tel. 303/659-6063).

Brush

Accommodation: Budget Host—Empire Motel, 1408 Edison, 80723 (tel. 303/842-2876).

Burlington

Accommodations: Sloan's Motel, 1901 Rose Ave., 80807 (tel. 303/346-5333). $24 for one; $28 for two in one bed; $32 for two in two beds.
- Super 8 Motel, 2100 Fay, Box 485, 80807 (tel. 303/346-5627).
- Econo Lodge, 450 South Lincoln, P.O. Box 188, 80807 (tel. 303/346-5555).

Byers

Accommodation: Longhorn Motel, √ (10%), junction of I-70 and Hwy. 36 at Exit 316, P.O. Box 196, 80103 (tel. 303/822-5205). $28 to $34 for one; $32 to $37 for two in one bed; $34 to $42 for two in two beds. Heated swimming pool.

Castle Rock

Accommodation: Super 8 Motel, 1020 Park St., Exit 182, 80104 (tel. 303/688-0880).

Colorado Springs

Help: Terros, 303/471-4127. "We would be sympathetic to and interested in helping any travelers who should contact us." Terros can help you to find low-cost housing in this fast-growing town. They also mentioned that "the hitchhiker isn't really hassled but he isn't welcomed either."

Accommodations: Motel 6, 3228 North Chestnut St., 80907 (tel. 303/520-5400).

● Budget Host—Frontier Motel, 4300 North Nevada Ave., 80907 (tel. 303/598-1563).

● Econo Lodge, I-25 and Garden of the Gods Road, 4604 Rusina Rd., 80907 (tel. 303/594-0964).

● Econo Lodge, 6875 East Hwy. 94, 80915 (tel. 303/594-0964).

● Hampton Inn, 7245 Commerce Ctr. Dr., 80919 (tel. 303/593-9700).

● Imperial 400 Motor Inn, 714 North Nevada Ave., 80903 (tel. 303/636-3385).

● Imperial 400 Motor Inn, 1231 South Nevada Ave., 80903 (tel. 303/634-1545).

Cortez

Accommodation: Super 8 Motel, 505 E. Main St., 81321 (tel. 303/565-8888).

Craig

Accommodation: Super 8 Motel, 200 Hwy. 789, 81625 (tel. 303/824-3471).

Cripple Creek

Accommodation: Westward Ho Motel, 236 West Bennett, 80813 (tel. 303/689-2374). Open May 10 to October 5. $25 single; $31 double; $35 triple; $38 quad; $28 to $46 for cottages. "A small motel with 'Old West' exterior and modern interior; located in an old goldmining district."

Denver

Denver is the mile-high capital of Colorado, exactly 5,280 feet above sea level. One native says that anyone visiting the city should first "see Red Rocks Park—an incredibly beautiful natural amphitheater right outside Denver—and then move on to the mountains." Before heading for the mountains, though, there are some things that one should see in the city: Larimer Square, between 13th and 15th Streets, is a rebuilt section of downtown reminiscent of the 1890s; the Denver Art Museum, adjacent to the City Center and housed in an ultramodern building, is worth a visit; and the Denver Museum of Natural History is well known for its collections, including scenes of native birds and animals, meteorites, and Indian artifacts. For what's happening where, check the *Denver Post*'s weekend section that comes out on Friday and *Rocky Mountain News*.

Two recommended guidebooks to the city are *Denver Guidebook,* by Tami Abell, Johnson Publishing Co., 1880 South 57th Court, Boulder, CO 80301 ($3.95), a basic book on eating, drinking, dancing, etc. in Denver, and *Off the Mall,* published by the Denver Partnership, Inc., 511 16th St., Denver, CO 80202 ($10.95).

Getting There: Stapleton International Airport is seven miles from downtown and bus 32 connects the two at a cost of 70¢ from 6 to 9 a.m. and from 4 to 6 p.m.; 35¢ at other times. You can catch bus 32 on the lower level, between doors 1 and 5. A taxi ride on the same route will cost more than $8. The bus terminals are located at Broadway and Colfax and 16th and Market; the train station is at 17th and Wynkoop. For Amtrak information, call 800/421-8320; for Rio Grande Railroad, call 303/629-5533.

Getting Around: By Bus: The city buses run frequently—seven days a week from 5 a.m. until midnight. At rush hour, from 6 to 9 a.m. and from 3 to 6 p.m., the fare is 70¢; 35¢ any other time. Call 303/778-6000 for information. A free shuttle bus goes along the 16th Street Mall from Broadway to Market Street.

By Taxi: Yellow Cab (tel. 303/777-7777) charges $2.05 for the first mile and $1 for each mile after that. Each additional passenger is 40¢. Zone Cab (tel. 303/861-2323) charges $1.25 when you get in; $1 for each additional mile. Metro Cab (tel. 303/333-3333) charges $1.25 for the first one-fifth mile; $1 per mile afterwards; 40¢ for each extra person.

By Car: To rent a car, try one of these: Budget Rent-a-Car, 2150 Broadway (tel. 303/861-4125) charges $20 to $50 per day with unlimited mileage for an economy car; American International Rent-a-Car, 4000 Quebec (tel. 303/399-5020) charges $29.95 per day with unlimited mileage; and at Rex on Wheels, 4690 Pecos (tel. 303/477-1635) five- to ten-year-old cars rent for $11.95 per day, with the first 20 miles free and $.10 per mile after that.

Help: Denver and Colorado Convention and Visitors Bureau (one block west of Civic Center Park), 225 West Colfax Ave., 80202 (tel. 303/892-1112). Information booth at airport, too.

● Travelers Aid, 1245 East Colfax Ave., no. 408, 80218 (tel. 303/832-8194).

● COMITIS, 9840 East 17th Ave., Aurora (tel. 303/343-9890). 24-hour switchboard for information, referrals, and help.

● Emergency contact: Denver General Hospital, 777 Bannock (tel. 303/893-6000).

Accommodations: YMCA, 25 East 16th Ave., 80202 (tel. 303/861-8300). Men and women. $16.30 to $21.25 single; $19 to $31.25 double; $34 to $38 family suite (3 to 4 persons). Convenient to downtown. Small cafeteria.

● Ranch Manor Motor Inn, 1490 South Sante Fe, 80223 (tel. 303/733-5581). $22.20 for one; $27 for two; $31 for three. Two heated pools (summer only).

● Regal 8 Inn, 12033 East 38th Ave. at Peoria St., 80239 (tel. 303/371-0740).

● Regal 8 Inn, 3050 West 49th Ave. at Federal, 80221 (tel. 303/455-8888).

● Motel 6, 12020 East 39th Ave., 80239 (tel. 303/371-1980).

● Motel 6, 6 West 83rd Place, Thornton, 80221 (tel. 303/429-1550).

● Motel 6, 480 Wadsworth Blvd., 80226 (tel. 303/232-4924).

● Econo Lodge, 930 Valley Hwy., 80204 (tel. 303/592-1555).

● Denver Budget Inn, Ⓢ √ ★ (10%), 1490 S. Santa Fe, 80223. Tel.: (303)733-5581. $19.88 single; $24.88 double; $29.88 triple and quad.

Where to Eat: Beau Jo's, 2700 S. Colorado Blvd (tel. 303/758-1519). Open 11:30 a.m. to 9:30 p.m., until 10:00 p.m. on weekends. A pizza big enough for three costs $5.95.

● Red Moon Pizzeria, 329 East Colfax (tel. 303/861-9930). Open 11 a.m. to 9 p.m., closed on Sunday.

● Good Friends, 3100 E. Colfax (tel. 303/399-1751). Children's menu $2.25. Varied menu—vegetarian, Mexican, American entrees. Reasonable.

● Fuji En, 930 Lincoln (tel. 303/837-1178). Japanese. Accommodates children. Dinner: $9 to $11.

● Paris on the Platte, 1553 Platte Street (tel. 303/455-2451). Bookstore and café for light meals.

● Saucy Noodle, 727 South University (tel. 303/733-6977). Very Italian, just like being in Rome.

● La Bola, 900 Jersey (tel. 303/333-3888). Mexican food dished out in generous portions. Busy neighborhood-type place. Margaritas are a specialty.

● Ohle's, 1520 East Colfax (tel. 303/832-5086). A German deli that shares space with a small food market. Open until 6 p.m., on Saturday to 4 p.m.

● Rick's Cafe, 80 South Madison (tel. 303/399-4488). Popular watering hole for lunch and after work. Lots of young professional types.

● Le Central, 8th and Lincoln (tel. 303/863-8094). For French cuisine that's not too expensive.

● Buckhorn Exchange, 1000 Osage at 10th Avenue (tel. 303/534-9505). This is the oldest eatery and bar in Colorado. The building dates from 1886. The ambiance is strictly Old West—big game trophies, a gun collection, and a carved wooden bar. Buffalo, elk, and quail are on the menu; lunches from $4.95 to $7.95, dinners from $11.95 to $20.95.

● Le Peep, 915 17th St. (one block from 16th Street Mall at Curtis St.) (tel. 303/298-7337). Open 6:30 a.m. to 2 p.m. for breakfast and brunch of eggs, pancakes, and sandwiches.

● Chili Pepper, 2150 Bryant (tel. 303/433-8406). Mexican food for less than $6 a meal. An outdoor patio and a lovely nighttime view. 10 a.m. to 11 p.m. weekdays.

● Goldie's Delicatessen, 511 16th St. (tel. 303/623-6007). Right in the 16th Street Mall between Glenarm and Welton. A popular deli with an outdoor patio.

What to See and Do: Skiing: November through June is ski season in Colorado, and Denver is headquarters for skiers on their way to any one of the state's slopes. Colorado Ski Country, 1410 Grant St. (tel. 303/831-7669) has ski information and the latest snow reports.

● Cowboys: Every year Denver hosts a ten-day celebration of its cowboy heritage with a rodeo and show and sale of the finest blue-blooded cattle in the world. Stockmen come from all over the country to look and to buy; the world champion bull is exhibited right in the plush lobby of the Brown Palace Hotel. For ten days, *everybody*'s a cowboy.

● Larimer Square, between 13th and 15th Streets on Larimer Street. A recreation of the area as it appeared in the 1890s with antiques, restaurants, galleries, movies, etc. Often there are street fairs and other celebrations in the square.

● Denver Art Museum, in the Civic Center, 100 W. 14th St. (tel. 303/575-2793). Interesting collection in a controversial building designed by Gio Ponti. Admission is $4; $1.50 for students and seniors. Closed Monday. Wednesday night jazz, $3.

● Denver Botanic Gardens, 1005 York St. (tel. 303/575-2547). Outdoor gardens and a unique conservatory with lush native and exotic plants. Adults, $3; ages 7–15, $1; under 7, free. Open 9 a.m. to 4:45 p.m. every day. Summer concerts outdoors.

● Colorado Heritage Center, 1300 Broadway (tel. 303/866-3682). Dioramas, exhibits, and multimedia shows depicting the colorful history of the city and the state. $2.50 for adults; 50¢ for children and seniors.

● U.S. Mint, Colfax Avenue and Cherokee Street (tel. 303/844-3582). The largest depository of gold bullion outside Fort Knox, the mint makes over 1,000,000 coins per year. Free 20-minute tours every 30 minutes. There's a numismatic shop adjacent to the mint.

● Denver Museum of Natural History, in City Park on Colorado Blvd. (tel. 303/370-6363). Everything you'd expect in a natural history museum, plus daily shows in the Gates Planetarium and the IMAX Theater that are spectacular. "Definitely worth a visit."

● Denver Zoo, 23rd Avenue and Steele (tel. 303/575-2754). Open 10–5. Admission $4; children and senior citizens $2.

● Interesting neighborhoods: Old South Gaylord Street and South Pearl Street/Washington Park.

At Night: For folk music: Swallow Hill Music Association (tel. 303/393-6202) presents programs of folk and acoustic music in different locations around the city.

● For jazz: Two possibilities are The Bay Wolf, 231 Milwaukee (tel. 303/388-9221) in Cherry Creek Shopping Center and The Mall Exchange, corner of 16th and Lawrence (tel. 303/573-1400).

● City Spirit, 1434 Blake (tel. 303/575-0022). Jazz, books, art.

● For classical music: The Denver Symphony Orchestra performs September to April at Boettcher Concert Hall, 14th and Curtis. Call 303/592-7777 for ticket information.

● To dance: Rock Island, 1614 15th St. (tel. 303/572-7625). Rock/avant garde. $4 Friday and Saturday. $2 weeknights. No charge Sunday.

● Bangles, 4501 East Virginia Ave. (tel. 303/377-2701). Open 1 p.m. to 2 a.m., Monday through Saturday; 7 p.m. to midnight Sunday. Live rock and roll. The cover charge is $3 on Friday and Saturday. This is the place to dance—it looks like a ski lodge and has a restaurant on the second floor. There's a free buffet if you get there by 7:30 p.m.

● For theater: Denver Center Theater, at the Denver Center for Performing

Arts, 14th and Curtis, is headquarters for a repertory company. Twenty original productions a year, many by local playwrights, are given at Changing Scene, 1527 ½ Champa (tel. 303/893-5775) on Thursdays, Fridays, Saturdays, and Sundays.

● For ballet: Denver has its own professional resident ballet company performing at the Center for Performing Arts, 14th and Curtis. Tel.: (303)298-0677.

Shopping: 16th Street Mall, 16th Street from Broadway to Market Street A street devoted to shopping—no traffic, and there are free buses running from one end to the other.

● Wax Trax, 638 E. 13th Ave. (tel. 303/831-7246). Records, new and used.

● Together Books, 200 East 13th Ave. at 13th and Sherman (tel. 303/388-5171). Books on philosophy, survival, women, yoga, the occult, etc.

● Pickwick Discount Books, University Hills Shopping Center, 2553 South Colorado Blvd. (tel. 303/753-6495). Over 10,000 current titles discounted.

● Eastern Mountain Sports, 1428 East 15th St. (tel. 303/571-1160). Backpacking, camping, climbing, ski touring supplies, and jogging gear. Open until 8 p.m. on Monday, Thursday, and Friday.

● Gart Brothers, 1000 Broadway (tel. 303/861-1122). A large retail store specializing in sports and photographic equipment. (By now you've caught on to the fact that Denverites are very outdoorsy types.)

● Cherry Creek Shopping Center. This is a large complex in the middle of a residential area bounded by University Avenue, Third Avenue, Steele Street, and North Cherry Creek Drive. It includes a wide variety of stores, large and small—from Sears to exclusive specialty shops, restaurants, and cinemas. Some shops in the center are open on Sunday.

● The Tattered Cover, 2955 E. 1st Ave. (tel. toll free 800/833-9327). A wonderful place to browse for books, maps, posters, and cards.

● Budget Tapes and Records, 250 Detroit Ave. (tel. 303/329-9041).

Dinosaur

Camping: Dinosaur National Monument, P.O. Box 210, 81610 (tel. 303/374-2216). Split Mountain and Green River Campgrounds, developed, $5 fee. Lodore Campground, the primitive Deerlodge Park, Echo Park, and Rainbow Park Campgrounds are free. Backcountry river sites: primitive, most accessible only by boat. $5 entrance fee.

Durango

Accommodations: Durango Hostel, P.O. Box 1445, 543 East 2nd Ave., 81301 (tel. 303/247-9905 or 247-5477). $8 members; $9 nonmembers. $1 higher after October 15. Advance reservations advised. Hostel is located in a turn-of-the-century lodging house in the historic district of Durango.

● Super 8 Motel, 20 Stewart Dr., 81301 (tel. 303/259-0590).

Estes Park

Accommodation: H-Bar-Ranch Hostel (AYH), 3500 H-Bar-G Rd., 80517.

Six miles northeast of Estes Park, near Rocky Mountain National Park (tel. 303/ 586-3688). Open May 25 to September 12. Six miles from bus station. Hostel owner will pick you up at the Chamber of Commerce Tourist Information Center at 5 p.m. $5.50 for AYH and IYHF members; membership available at hostel. Advance reservations recommended July 10 to August 25. Bring food to cook because the nearest grocery store is six miles away. "Formerly a dude ranch, the hostel has a main building and several cabins with a superb view of the Rocky Mountains."

Camping: Rocky Mountain National Park, U.S. 36, two and one half miles west of Estes Park, 80517 (tel. 303/586-2371). Five campgrounds at Aspenglen, Glacier Basin, Longs Peak, Moraine Park, and Timber Creek. $6 per campsite per night; reservation period from June 25 to August 15 in Moraine Park and Glacier Basin; additional reservation fee required; trail camps with no fee, permit required, however. During peak season, you may have to wait a few days for permit issuance.

"For family-style cooking, go to Mountain Man Restaurant, Estes Kountry Kitchen, the Mountaineer, or Crowley's Hi Country Restaurant."

Fairplay

Accommodation: The Historic Fairplay Hotel, ⓢ (20%), 500 Main St., 80440, (tel. 303/836-2565). $23.95 to $30.95 single, $24.95 to $33.95 double without bath; $28.95 to $35.95 single, $29.95 to $38.95 double with bath. "A Victorian resort hotel in the Rocky Mountains with a restaurant and bar."

Fort Collins

Help: Community Crisis Center, 303/493-3888.

On Campus: Fort Collins is the home of Colorado State University, and the town has a good attitude toward young people. A student there told us that hitchhiking is common but that it is sometimes difficult to catch rides.

The United Campus Ministry at 629 South Howes might be able to help you find an inexpensive or free place to stay. You can call them at 303/482-8487. For outdoor recreational information, call the CSM Experimental Learning Program at 303/491-7226.

There are inexpensive movies at the Student Center throughout the weekends and a number of concerts and theater performances on and off campus throughout the year. Call 303/491-5402 for details.

The least expensive place to eat is Freebie's on College Avenue, near the University. *The Collegian,* the student newspaper, can provide all kinds of useful information on entertainment, rides, accommodations, and the like.

Accommodations: Motel 6, 3900 East Mulberry, 80521 (tel. 303/482-6466).
• Days Inn, 3625 East Mulberry, 80524 (tel. 303/221-5490).

Frisco

Accommodation: Woods Inn (AYH-SA), 205 South 2nd Ave., 80443 (tel.

303/668-3389). Daily, weekly, and monthly rates available (in winter, rates are higher and no weekly rates are offered). $15 to as high as $29 single (depending on type of room); $18 to $32 double; $27 to $39 triple; $32 to $44 quad. Breakfast and linens included in price. Advance reservations of two weeks necessary in winter.

Fruita

Camping: Colorado National Monument, 81521 (tel. 303/858-3617). Camping at Saddle Horn, four miles south of the West Entrance. Open year round. $6 per campsite per night.

Glenwood Springs

Accommodation: Pinon Pines Apartments, 3210 County Rd., 81601 (tel. 303/945-8102). One- or two-bedroom furnished apartments. Heated swimming pool and sauna on premises, surrounded by 300 acres of open mountain area. Forty minutes from Aspen. $35 for room with twin beds; $45 for room with four beds. Advance reservations of two to seven days necessary.

Golden

Accommodation: Budget Host—Mountain View Motel, 14825 West Colfax Ave., 80401 (tel. 303/279-2526).

Grand Junction

Accommodations: Motel 6, 776 Horizon Dr., 81501 (tel. 303/243-2628).
● Super 8 Motel, 728 Horizon Dr., 81506 (tel. 303/248-8080).

Grand Lake

Accommodation: Shadowcliff Lodge (AYH), 405 Summerland Park Rd., 80447 (tel. 303/627-9966). Situated at the southwest entrance to the Rocky Mountain National Park. Sixteen miles from bus and train stations in Granby. You can hitch a ride to Grand Lake with local residents. Open June 1 to October 1. $5 for AYH members.

Greeley

On Campus: For general information about this college town, home of the University of Northern Colorado, stop at the Office of International Student Services, 1925 10th Ave. The University Center is the central spot on the UNC campus; it's there that you'll find a bulletin board with rides and a cafeteria that's a popular meeting place on campus. During the summer, contact the director of housing at the university—there may be a place for you to stay on campus. For collectors of curious facts: Greeley is the home of the number one cattle feed manufacturer in the world—Monfort of Colorado. You can visit one of their feed lots if you'd like.

Accommodation: Motel 6, 3015 8th Ave., Evans, 80620 (tel. 303/351-6481).

Guffey

Accommodation: Currant Creek Hostel (AYH-SA), 6121 Rte. 9, 80820. No phone. $2.50 for AYH members; $2.75 for nonmembers. Primarily tent camping. There are three 8' × 10' wall tents and an 18' teepee or use your own tent. On the trans-America bicycle route. Open year round unless winter is too severe. Advisable to contact ahead of time for winter weather conditions.

Gunnison

Camping: Curecanti National Recreation Area, 102 Elk Creek, 81230 (tel. 303/641-2337). Camping at Elk Creek (open year round), Lake Fork, Old Stevens Creek, and Cimarron (open April through November), all on Blue Mesa Lake or Hwy. 50. $5 to $6 per campsite per night. Facility is operated by the National Park Service.

Accommodation: Friendship Colorado West Motel, 400 East Tomichi, 81230 (tel. 303/641-1288).

• Budget Host—Western Motel, 403 East Tomichi Ave., 81230 (tel. 303/641-1722).

Lamar

Accommodation: Plaza Motel/Restaurant and Lounge, 905 East Olive, 81052 (tel. 303/336-4315). $18 to $22 for one; $22 to $27 for two in one bed; $24 to $30 for two in two beds.

• Budget Host—Stagecoach Motor Inn, 1201 North Main St., 81052 (tel. 303/336-7471).

Limon

Accommodations: Budget Host—Silver Spur Motel, 514 Main St., 80828 (tel. 303/775-9561).

• Super 8 Motel, I-70 and Hwy. 24, P.O. Box 1038, 80828 (tel. 303/775-2889).

Longmont

Accommodation: Super 8 Motel, 10805 Turner Blvd., 80501 (tel. 303/772-0888).

Loveland

Accommodation: Super 8 Motel, 1655 E. Eisenhower Blvd., 80525 (tel. 303/663-7000).

Mesa Verde

Camping: Mesa Verde National Park, 81330 (tel. 303/529-4461). Campground at Morefield Canyon. Open May 1 to October 15. $6 per campsite per night; $11 per full hook-up site per night.

Montrose

Accommodations: Friendship Black Canyon, one mile east on U.S. 50, 1605 E. Main St., 81402 (tel. 303/249-3495).
- Super 8 Motel, 1705 E. Main, 81401 (tel. 303/249-9294).

Mosca

Camping: Great Sand Dunes National Monument, 81146 (tel. 303/378-2312). Campgrounds at Dunes open April 1 to October 31. $5 per campsite per night during summer season. Park is open year round. "Biggest sandbox in the state!"

Pitkin

Accommodation: Pitkin Hotel & Hostel (AYH-SA), Ⓢ √ ★, 400 Main St., mailing address, P.O. Box 53, Ohio City, CO 81237 (tel. 303/641-2757). Call ahead to arrange ride from Gunnison bus station. Dorm: $5 summer, $7 winter for AYH members. Private rooms: $7 per person. Advance reservations of one week suggested; call first in winter.

Poncha Springs

Accommodation: Rocky Mountain Lodge, √, 446 East Hwy. 50, Box 172, 81242 (tel. 303/539-6008). $24 for one; $26 for two in one bed; $30 for two in two beds.

Pueblo

Accommodations: Regal 8 Inn, 960 Hwy. 50 West 81008 (tel. 303/543-8900).
- Super 8 Motel, 1100 Hwy. 50 West, 81008 (tel. 303/545-4104).
- Hampton Inn, 4703 North Freeway, 81008 (tel. 303/544-4700).
- Motel 6, 4103 North Elizabeth, 81008 (tel. 303/543-6221).

Ridgway

Accommodation: The Pueblo Hostel & Cantina (AYH-SA), 251 Liddell

Dr., 81432 (tel. 303/626-5939). $12 per person in dorms. $20 single, $25 double in private rooms. Breakfast included. Advance reservations of two weeks suggested for July 4th and Labor Day.

Salida

Accommodation: Friendship Ranch House Motor Lodge, 7545 West U.S. Hwy. 50, 81201 (tel. 303/539-6655).

Silverton

Accommodation: Teller House Hotel and Hostel (AYH-SA), P.O. Box 467, 1250 Greene St., 81433 (tel. 303/387-5423). $8.50 for AYH members; $11 for nonmembers; $22 single hotel room; $28 double hotel room. "European-style hotel with breakfast included in price of room. In a small goldmining town (population 800) in the San Juan Mountains."

South Fork

Accommodation: Spruce Lodge (AYH-SA), ⑤√, 29432 S.W. Hwy. 160, 81154 (tel. 303/873-5605). $9 for AYH members. Families welcome. "Christian homelike atmosphere."

Steamboat Springs

Accommodation: Super 8 Motel, U.S. Hwy. 40 East, 80477 (tel. 303/879-5230).

Sterling

Accommodation: Budget Host—Blue Bird Motel, Hwy. 6 at Iris Drive, 80751 (tel. 303/522-5300).

Telluride

Accommodation: Oak Street Inn (AYH-SA), ⑤√ ★ 🔖, 134 North Oak St., 81435 (tel. 303/728-3383). $12.50 summer, $14 winter for AYH members; $16 single; $27 double; $40 triple; $50 quad for nonmembers. Open year round. Transportation arrangements from bus ($15 one way) or train ($30 one way) station must be made 24 hours in advance with Telluride Transit (tel. 303/728-4105). "Inn built in 1893 as a church and is in National Historic Register."

Trinidad

Accommodation: Budget Host—Derrick Motel, RR 1, Box 427B, 81082 (tel. 303/846-3307).

Walsenburg

Accommodation: Budget Host—Country Host Motel, 553 U.S. 85, 87, P.O. Box 190, 81089 (tel. 303/738-3800).

Winter Park

Accommodation: Winter Park Hostel (AYH-SA), behind Conoco gas station, P.O. Box 3323, 80482 (tel. 303/726-5356. $5 summer, $9 winter for AYH members; $6 summer, $11 winter for nonmembers. Equipped kitchen. Continental Trailways stops 100 yards from hostel door. Advance reservations suggested December 15 to April 15.

Yuma

Accommodation: Super 8 Motel, 421 W. 8th Ave., 80759 (tel. 303/848-5853).

Connecticut

Connecticut is diverse: the southwestern part of the state is dotted with New York's bedroom communities—everything from farmland and seaside to villages and large cities throughout the rest of the state. No point in the state is more than two hours from any other, so even if your time is limited, you can see quite a bit of Connecticut.

The capital city, Hartford, is enjoying a renaissance of its downtown area, but it is as proud of its past as it is of its present. Within the city are several interesting historical sites to visit: the Mark Twain House and, right next to it, the Harriet Beecher Stowe House are faithfully restored reminders of a gracious, literary 19th century; the Old State House on Main St., the oldest in the nation, has become a tourist attraction with its restored Senate and House chambers; and the Wadsworth Athenaeum, Hartford's art museum, has an appealing collection of paintings, sculpture, silver, textiles, etc.

New Haven is another Connecticut town worth a visit. The home of Yale University, it has two art museums of international repute—the Yale Center for British Art and the Yale University Art Gallery—and all of the cultural events you'd expect from a university town. The Long Wharf Theater, also in New Haven, in a former food-terminal warehouse, can usually be counted on for top-rate performances of new and revived plays.

In summer, the place to go is the Connecticut shore—to Westbrook, Saybrook, Lyme, and to Mystic with its Seaport, which is the state's number one tourist attraction, a living museum that re-creates a 19th-century maritime village with ships, shops, homes, and the last of the wooden whalers, the *Charles W. Morgan.* Throughout the state there are wooded hillsides, lakes, streams, colonial villages, and historic homes.

For general information on Connecticut and its attractions, send for the *Connecticut Vacation Guide* from the address given under tourist information below. For more specific books on Connecticut, consider the following:

Fifty Hikes in Connecticut, by Gerry and Sue Hardy, Backcountry Publications, P.O. Box 175, Woodstock, VT 05091 ($8.95; add $2 postage and handling).

Globe Pequot Press, P.O. Box Q, Chester, CT 06412, publishes *Where to Eat in Connecticut, The Best and the Very Best Deals,* by Jane and Michael Stern ($8.95), and *Short Bike Rides in Connecticut,* by Edwin Mullen and Jane Griffith ($5.95).

Some Special Events: A Battle for Madison in Madison, and Dogwood Festival in Fairfield (May); Rose and Arts Festival in Norwich, and Barnum Festival (P.T. Barnum, founder of the Greatest Show on Earth, was also the mayor of Bridgeport for a while) in Bridgeport (early June); Bluegrass Music Festival in Preston (early June); Audubon Festival in Sharon, and Railroad Days (July); the Oyster Festival in Milford, and Outdoor Arts Festival in Mystic (August); Chrysanthemum Festival in Bristol (late September to mid-October); and the Apple Harvest Festival in Southington (early October).

Tourist Information: Connecticut Department of Economic Development, Vacation-Travel Promotion, 210 Washington St., Hartford, CT 06106 (tel. toll free 800/842-7492 in-state, and 800/243-1645 out-of-state. They have lots of good material.

N.B. An excellent reservation service for bed-and-breakfast facilities throughout Connecticut is Nutmeg Bed and Breakfast, 222 Girard Ave., West Hartford, CT 06105 (tel. 203/236-6698). Accommodations range from modest homes to restored brownstones, historic farmhouses, and beachfront estates. The Nutmeg directory is available for $2.89.

Bolton

Accommodation: Bolton Home Hostel (AYH), Ⓢ★, 42 Clark Rd., 06043 (tel. 203/649-3905). $8 for AYH members. Open April 15 to October 15. Must arrive on foot or by bicycle; no cars or motorcycles allowed. Hostel is four miles from bus station. Call hostel from station on arrival. Advance reservations suggested by calling after 5 p.m. Introductory AYH passes available for $5. Complete kitchen facilities, hot shower, swimming pool.

Branford

Accommodation: Econo Lodge, 309 East Main St., 06405 (tel. 203/488-4035).

East Hartford

Accommodation: Imperial 400 Motor Inn, 927 Main St., 06108 (tel. 203/289-7781).

Enfield

Accommodation: Red Roof Inn, 5 Hazard Ave., 06082 (tel. 203/741-2571).

Hartford

Help: University of Hartford General Info, 203/243-4204.

● Info Line, 999 Asylum Ave., 06105 (tel. 203/522-4636). "Information, referral, advocacy."

● Travelers Aid, 30 High St., Suite 4, 06103 (tel. 203/522-2247).

Accommodations: YMCA, 160 Jewell St., 06103 (tel. 203/522-4183). Men and women. $18.70 with private bath; $14.90 with shared bath. "One of the newest YMCA's in America. All rooms are carpeted and air-conditioned. Full-service YMCA with all facilities—health and fitness centers, pool and two gyms."

● YWCA, ⑤, 135 Broad St., 06105 (tel. 203/525-1163). Women only. $15.05 single with shared bath; $21.50 single with private bath; $9.68 dorm room (4 beds). This is a new building with a kitchen and a laundry on each of the seven floors. Reservations preferred one or two weeks in advance. Two blocks from bus and train stations.

● Susse Chalet Inn, I-91, Exit 27, on Brainard Road, 06114 (tel. 203/525-9306).

● Super 8 Motel, 57 W. Service Rd., I-91, Exit 33, 06120 (tel. 203/246-8888).

Morris

Accommodation: Bantam Lake Youth Hostel (AYH), East Shore Road, Lakeside, 06758 (mailing address), (tel. 203/567-9258). $7 for AYH members and guests. Advance reservations necessary for groups; individuals may call in reservations. "Historic area of great national beauty offering a variety of outdoor activities in all seasons."

New Britain

Accommodation: YMCA, 50 High St., 06051. Two miles from Exit 35 off Hwy. 84, via Rte. 72 to Columbus Avenue exit (tel. 203/229-3787). Men only. Single: $69 per week. Two blocks from bus station.

New Haven

Help: Travelers Aid, One State St., 06511 (tel. 203/787-3959).

● Info Line: 203/624-4143.

● New Haven Convention and Visitors Bureau, 900 Chapel St., Suite 1225, 06510 (tel. 203/787-8822); with a branch office right off I-95 at Long Wharf.

On Campus: Yale University is here and students are everywhere. "This is a beautiful historic campus—surrounded by a depressed neighborhood, surrounded by scenic New England." Two favorite student restaurants are Clark's Dairy, 68 Whitney Ave., for sandwiches, salads, omelets, etc., and the Educated Burger, 51 Broadway. Tours of Yale are available, and if you want to get out of the urban setting, you can go to Sleeping Giant State Park in nearby Hamden for hiking and picnicking. To meet someone in a comfortable atmosphere, try any pizza or ice cream place around campus or Lourdes Cafeteria at the Commons. For rock, go to Toad's Place on York Street.

Accommodations: Hotel Duncan, Ⓢ √ ★, 1151 Chapel St., 06511 (tel. 203/787-1273). Walking distance from bus and train. $28 without bath, $35 with bath single; $48 double; $58 triple; $65 quad. Advance reservations of one week suggested.

● International Center Residence, 442 Temple St., P.O. Box 94A, 06520. (tel. 203/787-3531). Men and women. Summer only. $20 (There may be room for one person to stay for a night or two during the academic year—call ahead to check.) "This was once a private home and is situated in an attractive residential area."

● YMCA, 52 Howe St., 06511 (tel. 203/865-3161). Men and women. $17.20 single. Weekly rate: $80. Coffeeshop in building.

New London

Accommodations: Susse Chalet Motor Lodge, I-95 (Exit 74), 06357 (tel. 203/739-6991).

● Red Roof Inn, I-95 and 707 Colman St., 06320 (tel. 203/444-0001).

Norwich

Accommodation: YMCA, 337 Main St., 06360 (tel. 203/889-7349). Men only. $60 per week.

Southington

Accommodation: Susse Chalet Motor Lodge, I-84 off of exit 32 (tel. 203/621-0181).

Stamford

Help: Info-Line, 203/324-1010.

Accommodation: YMCA, 909 Washington Blvd., 06901 (tel. 203/357-7000). Men and women 18 and over. Although the single rate is $32 in this high-rise facility with private baths, color TV, phone, and maid service, a double is $44, and the weekly rate is within our budget at $137. Advance reservations necessary.

"Forget any story you may have heard before about other Y's—some facilities are suffering 'old age' symptoms but not here."

Torrington

Accommodation: Super 8 Motel, 492 E. Main St., 06790 (tel. 203/496-0811).

Windsor

Accommodation: Windsor Home Hostel (AYH), c/o Lois Macomber, 126

Giddings Ave., 06095 (tel. 203/683-2847 or 726-8950). $7 for AYH members. Advance reservations necessary.

Woodstock

Accommodation: Woodstock Home Hostel, c/o Henri Caldwell, Rte. 171, Box 278, South Woodstock, 06267 (tel. 203/974-0490). Open April 16 to October 14. $6.25 for AYH members. Advance reservations necessary; call between 5 and 8 p.m.

Delaware

It's a ministate, and most of it either belongs or belonged to the Du Ponts, one of the world's richest families. In 1802, Eleuthere Du Pont built a powder mill on Brandywine Creek, and in the 150 years since, Delaware has, with the help of the Du Ponts, become the chemical capital of the world. Other corporations have been lured by the state's attractive incorporation and tax laws.

One of the nicest things the Du Ponts did for Delaware was to give it the Henry Francis Du Pont 198-room pied-a-terre in Winterthur. Now the Winterthur Museum contains a collection of American decorative arts from 1640 to 1840 and is definitely worth seeing. Some day-long tours are available by reservation only; they vary in price with the season. Another tourist attraction in Delaware is also Du Pont-related. It's the Hagley Museum, a 185-acre complex where visitors are told the story of American industry from the Du Pont point of view. It should come, then, as no great surprise that the name of Delaware's governor is Pierre S: Du Pont.

Look for the *Go . . . Don't Go Guide to Delaware and Nearby Pennsylvania*, a comprehensive guide to Delaware (Helen A. and Elliot R. Detchon, $4.95).

Some Special Events: Day in Old New Castle in Old New Castle, and Old Dover Days in Dover (May); Crafts Fair in Delaware Arts Museum in Wilmington (June); An Old-Fashioned Fourth with fireworks on the boardwalk in Lewes (July); Arts Festival in Bethany (August); and Nanticoke Tribe Pow Wow, six miles east of Millsboro (September).

Tourist Information: Delaware Tourism Office, 99 Kings Hwy., P.O. Box 1401, Dover, DE 19903 (tel. 302/736-4271 or 800/441-8846).

N.B. A good bed-and-breakfast service is Bed and Breakfast of Delaware, Box 177, 3650 Silverside Rd., Wilmington, 19810 (tel. 302/479-9500). Open Monday to Thursday, 9 a.m. to 9 p.m. Rates: $30 to $45 single; $40 to $60 double.

Dover

Accommodations: Econo Lodge, 561 North DuPont Hwy., 19901 (tel. 302/678-8900).
- Comfort Inn, 222 S. DuPont Hwy., 19901 (tel. 302/674-3300).

Fenwick Island

Accommodation: Seaside Motel, Rte. 1, Ocean Hwy. (tel. 302/539-7684). $30 and up single; $37 and up double.

Greenwood

Accommodation: Holiday Motel, Rte. 13, P.O. Box 170, 19950 (tel. 302/349-4270). $25 to $35 double; $4 for a roll-away.

New Castle

Accommodations: Motel 6, 1200 West Ave., State Hwy. 9, 19720 (tel. 302/571-1200).
- Quality Inn Dutch Village, 111 S. DuPont Hwy. (tel. 302/328-6246). $35 and up single; $39 and up double.
- Deville Motel, 160 S. DuPont Hwy., 19720 (tel. 302/328-1600). $27.56 single; $31.80 double; $3.18 for each additional person. Children under 12 free.

Newark

On Campus: This is where you'll find the University of Delaware. To meet the students, go to the Student Center Scrounge or to the International Center at 52 West Delaware Ave. To get something inexpensive to eat, someone at the university suggests Jimmy's Diner or the Post House Restaurant, both on East Main St. A popular Sunday brunch spot is Klondike Kate's, also on East Main Street. To meet students, try the Deer Park or the Stone Balloon—both on (you guessed it) Main Street. The Down Under is a new favorite of students. According to someone on the staff at the U of D, the school is "a commuter institution, and consequently loses most of its students over the weekends when they go home."

Odessa

Accommodation: Pleasant Hill Motel, Rte. 13, 19730 (tel. 302/378-2468). $27 to $29 single; $31 to $37 double.

Rehoboth Beach/Dewey Beach

Accommodations: Admiral Motel, 2 Baltimore Ave. (tel. 302/227-2103). $29 and up single; $33 and up double.

● Bay Resort, West Bellevue Street on the Bay, P.O. Box 461 (tel. 302/227-6400). $30 and up double. Children under 12 free.

● The Commodore Motel, 50 Rehoboth Ave. (tel. 302/227-9446, or toll free 800/245-2112). $29 and up single; $32 and up double; $10 additional weekend surcharge.

● Oceanus Motel, 6 Second St., P.O. Box 324, (tel. 302/227-9436). $28 and up single; $29 and up double. Children under 12 free.

Seaford

Accommodation: Sunrise Motel, U.S. Hwy. 13, RFD 4, P.O. Box 95, 19973 (tel. 302/629-5511). $28 to $38 single; $38 to $48 double; $8 for roll-aways and cribs.

Wilmington

Help: Travelers Aid, 809 Washington St., 19801 (tel. 302/658-9885).

Accommodation: YWCA, 908 King St., 19801 (tel. 302/658-7161). Women only. $13 to $15 single. Weekly rate: $40 to $45. Advance reservations of two weeks necessary.

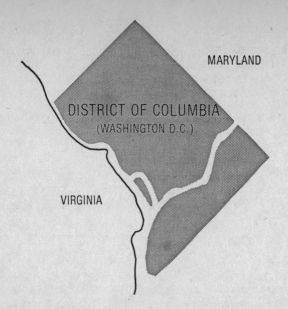

MARYLAND

DISTRICT OF COLUMBIA
(WASHINGTON D.C.)

VIRGINIA

District of Columbia (Washington, D.C.)

Washington, D.C., is ready if you are. When you get there, you'll want to stop at one of the information centers that are available to assist visitors to the capital district. They include the International Visitor Information Service, with an office at 733 15th St. NW (tel. 202/783-6540), which provides 24-hour language assistance in over 50 languages; Visitors Association, Suite 250, 1575 I St. NW (tel. 202/789-7000); and the Information Center for Handicapped Individuals, 605 G St. NW (tel. 202/347-4986; teletype 202/347-8320). For a recording of current events in the district, call 202/737-8866. Information booths are scattered throughout the Mall area and on all monument grounds—help is never far away.

Two guidebooks to the city are *Washington, D.C., in Your Pocket,* published by Baron's, 250 Wireless Blvd., Hauppauge, NY 11788 ($3.95), a directory of stores, museums, landmarks, etc., and *Washington, D.C., and Historic Virginia on $40 a Day,* by Rena Bulkin, published by Prentice Hall Press ($10.95). For maps of everything, get *Instant Guide to Washington,* by Tony Lasher, Flashmaps Publishing ($4.95). For more information consult the *City Paper,* distributed free at newsstands weekly; "The Weekender," a very extensive listing of activities available with the Friday evening edition of the *Washington Post;* and *The Smithsonian Magazine,* which lists Smithsonian activities and displays in the back of each monthly issue. Also listen to WGMS 103.5 FM or 570 AM.

Some events include the Washington Flower and Garden Show in the Convention Center (March); the National Cherry Blossom Festival, a week of festivities at or near the tidal basin (Jefferson Memorial area) capped by a parade and highlighted by the blooming of the cherry trees (early April); Fourth of July Parade on Constitution Avenue.

Getting There: Washington's National Airport is about five miles south of town. The best way to get from there to downtown is to take the Metro, an elevated train. The fare is 80¢ during non-rush hours, and during rush hour it depends on the distance traveled. Taxi fare from the airport is about $11. The Greyhound station is at 1110 New York Ave. NW (tel. 202/565-2662), and Trailways is at 1101 First St. NE (1st and L Sts.), one block from Union Station. The train station, Union Station, is at 50 Massachusetts Ave. NE (tel. 202/484-7540).

Getting Around: The best way to get from place to place is the quiet and fast subway system or Metro. Be aware, though: Metro runs only from 6 a.m. to midnight on weekdays, 8 a.m. to midnight on Saturday, and 10 a.m. to midnight on Sunday. Trains run every five minutes during rush hour (6 to 9:30 a.m. and 3 to 6:30 p.m.); every ten minutes during nonrush hours. Fare is 80¢ during nonrush hours; during rush hours the fare depends on distance traveled. Many of the buses connect with the Metro and are free, with a transfer within DC. The fare on the regular bus is 75¢ to 80¢ for nonrush; prices vary for rush hours. A Flash Pass allows unlimited bus use and $4 worth of subway use, and costs $15 per 2-week period. Metro stops are marked by a large sign that says "M." For bus and Metro information call 202/637-7000.

● Taxis charge by the zone. One zone is $2.10 and each additional zone is about 75¢. One Washingtonian advises: "When taking a cab, always establish the fare before you get in—otherwise it may double or triple by the time you get to where you're going—especially at night." You can call Diamond Taxi (tel. 202/387-6200), or Yellow Taxi (tel. 202/544-1212). Red Top (tel. 202/522-3333) charges $1.20 per mile. Don't be surprised if your taxi driver stops to pick up additional passengers en route to your destination. That's what they do in DC!

● If you're going to tour within the city, avoid using a car. If you do bring your car, you'll just end up buying it back from the parking lot at the end of the day. The most popular sites are close together and the subway, bus, and tourmobiles are inexpensive and uncomplicated. The tourmobiles stop at 17 sites, and tourists are able to get on and off wherever they want, as often as they want. Fares are $7 for adults and $3.50 for children for a full-day ticket, 9 a.m. to 6:30 p.m. in summer; 9:30 a.m. to 4:30 p.m. in winter. For touring outside the center city area, you might consider renting a car from Hertz (tel. 202/659-8702), Budget Rent-a-Car (tel. 202/628-2750), or Avis (tel. 800/467-6588).

Help: Travelers Aid, 1015 12th St. NW, 20005 (tel. 202/347-0101); Washington National Airport (tel. 202/684-3472); Union Station (tel. 202/347-0101); and Foreign Student Service Council, Adams Morgan at 2337 18th St. NW (tel. 202/232-4979).

● International Visitors Information Services, 801 19th St. NW (tel. 202/872-8747). Language assistance in over 50 languages is available 24 hours a day.

● Foreign Service Lounge, State Department (tel. 202/632-3432). Foreign students can get information on how to reach any embassy.

On Campus: The American University is here. For information on rides, apartments, etc, check the bulletin board in the Mary Graydon Student Center or look at a copy of the campus newspaper, *The Eagle*. When you're hungry or thirsty, try the Pub or the Cafeteria on the AU campus, or Quigley's, a favorite student hangout nearby. Other local colleges and universities include George Washington and Georgetown.

Accommodations: The Women's Information Center, 3918 West St. NW, 20007 (tel. 202/338-8163), finds housing for women and foreign visitors. Their bed-and-breakfast network specializes in finding inexpensive, comfortable, and friendly accommodations. They also have information on long-term housing (group housing, apartments, etc.), jobs, rides, and local organizations.

● Washington International Hostel (AYH-SA), 1009 11th St. NW, 20001 (tel. 202/737-2333. Three blocks north of Metro Center. Dormitory rooms $10. There's a dining room and cooking facilities too. Reservations recommended April to September.

● International Student House, 1825 R St. NW, 20009 (tel. 202/232-4007). Students only. Very few vacancies, but worth a try. $510 to $575 single per month; $475 to $535 (per person) double per month; $470 (per person) triple per month. All rates include breakfast and dinner seven days a week. Advance reservations required. This is a grand mansion built in 1912 with a dormitory wing built in 1969. It is primarily for long-term graduate students; during Christmas vacation, travelers planning to stay at least a week are welcome. Weekly rates are $160 to $180 single; $150 to $170 per person double; $150 per person triple.

● Bed & Breakfast Ltd. of Washington, D.C., P.O. Box 12011, 20005 (tel. 202/328-3510). A network of 80 homes, almost all located in the city's historic downtown areas, providing bed-and-breakfast. Advance reservations recommended. $30 to $65 single; $40 to $75 double.

● Allen Lee Hotel, 2224 F St. NW (tel. 202/331-1224). $30 to $40 single ($25 to $30 without bath); $37 to $45 double ($30 to $40 without bath).

● University Inn, 2134 G St. NW, 20037 (tel. 202/342-8020). In the heart of George Washington University campus. $39 single; $45 double.

● The Connecticut-Woodley Guest House, 2647 Woodley Rd. NW, 20008 (tel. 202/667-0218). Half block from Woodley Park Zoo metro. $28 to $41 single; $34 to $47 double; $38 to $49 triple for families, $40 to $52 for groups; $39 to $50 quad for families, $46 to $58 for groups. "Large, old house converted into a guesthouse."

● The "2005" Guest House, ⑤∨★(10%), 2005 Columbia Rd. NW, 20009 (tel. 202/265-4006). $19 to $25 single; $25 to $35 double; $30 to $45 triple; $40 to $60 quad.

● Meg's International Guest House, ⑤∨★, 1315 Euclid St. NW, 20009 (tel. 202/232-5837, 387-9623, or toll free 800/824-7008). $25 single; $49 to $55 double; $10 per extra person. Complimentary breakfast included. Reserve space prior to arrival. The house is located in a diverse cosmopolitan area which is close to all the national monuments and the Capitol.

● Columbia House, 800 E. St. NE, 20002 (tel. 202/543-8800). Within walking distance of the congressional offices, monuments, and galleries. $114 to $140 per week. No private bath.

● International Guest House, 1441 Kennedy St. NW, 20011 (tel. 202/726-5808). $15 per person. Foreigners are preferred, but anyone, including children, can be accommodated. "A home away from home for traveling internationals." Advance reservations of one month preferred.

● Davis House, 1822 R St. NW, 20009 (tel. 202/232-3196). Near Metro and bus lines. $18 per person. Advance reservations of one month necessary. "Small, nonprofit guesthouse with priority given to international visitors."

● The Kalorama Guest House at Kalorama Park, √ ★, 1854 Mintwood Pl. NW, 20009 (tel. 202/667-6369). Near Metro and bus. $25 to $65 single; $35 to $75 double; $80 to $95 triple; $10 per extra person, $25 July and August weekend rate. Prices include continental breakfast. "Large Victorian townhouse furnished with antiques."

● The Kalorama Guest House at Woodley Park, Ⓢ√, 2700 Cathedral Ave. NW 20008 (tel. 202/328-0860). $25 to $65 single; $35 to $75 double; $75 to $80 triple; $10 per extra person, $25 July and August weekend rate. Seventh night free if you stay the week. Complimentary continental breakfast included. Advance reservations necessary March to October. Rates slightly higher March 1 to October 31. "Turn-of-the-century townhouse near Metro and bus stop."

● Econo Lodge, 1600 New York Ave. NE, 20002 (tel. 202/832-3200).

● Adams Inn Bed and Breakfast, 1744 Lanier Place NW, 20009 (tel. 202/745-3600). Adams Morgan neighborhood. $30 to $45 single; $35 to $70 double; $5 per extra person. "The rooms are small but nice and clean. It's a friendly place in a good location." Some rooms have kitchenettes.

Where to Eat: Timberlakes, 1726 Connecticut Ave. NW (tel. 202/483-2266). Open 11:30 a.m. to 2 a.m. weekdays, 9:30 a.m. to 3 p.m. weekends. A very typical bar and grill with good service and inexpensive food.

● Sholl's Colonial Cafeteria, 1990 K St. NW (tel. 202/296-3065). Open 7 a.m. to 8 p.m. Monday to Saturday. Nothing fancy, but good size helpings of "home-cooked" food. Dinner $5; lunch $3.50; breakfast $2.

● Viet Huong Cafe-Restaurant, 2928 M St. NW (tel. 202/337-5588) in Georgetown. Open 5 p.m. to 10:30 p.m. Good assortment of Vietnamese cuisine. Excellent food, generous helpings, moderate prices.

● Red Sea, 2463 18th St. NW (tel. 202/483-5000) in the Adams Morgan neighborhood. Open noon to 2 a.m. every day. Very popular Ethiopian place. Moderate prices.

● Montego Bay, 2437 18th St. NW (tel. 202/387-7222) in Adams Morgan. Open 10 a.m. to 8:30 p.m. Monday to Friday; 10 a.m. to 8 p.m. on Saturday. Jamaican food. Average meal $5.

● Patent Pending, in courtyard between National Collection of Fine Arts (8th and G Sts. NW) and the National Portrait Gallery (7th and F Sts. NW). Perfectly located if you're sightseeing around the mall. This cafeteria offers an interesting menu including courtyard salad, nitrite-free hot dogs made interesting, and big bowls of soup. You can eat outdoors or indoors. Open every day for lunch.

● Kramerbooks and Afterwords, 1517 Connecticut Ave. NW (tel. 202/387-1400). Just north of Dupont Circle. Popular indoor/outdoor cafe with an adjoining bookstore. Croissants for breakfast, quiches and salads for dinner.

● Tucson Cantina, 2605 Connecticut Ave. NW (tel. 202/462-6410). Near the National Zoo. The food is Mexican via the Southwest—tacos, burritos, enchiladas. Service is fast and entrees are $3.50 or under.

● The Dubliner, 4 F St. NW, directly across from Union Station (tel. 202/737-3773). Irish-American food; conveniently located near Capitol Hill, traditional Irish music performed live every night with no cover charge.

● The Booeymonger, 5250 Wisconsin Ave. NW (tel. 202/686-5805). Indoor and outdoor seating attracts a young crowd who like the salads and sandwiches like "The Exorcist," a roast beef "possessed" by bleu cheese with sprouts on French bread, $3.25. Open 24 hours.

● The Tune Inn, 331 ½ Pennsylvania Ave. SE (tel. 202/543-2725). On a popular strip; filled with people who work on Capitol Hill. Burgers and fries. A pitcher of beer is $3.25.

● The Omega, 1856-58 Columbia Rd. NW (tel. 202/462-1732). Spanish food very close to Dupont Circle. "Lots of food for your money."

● Millie and Al's, 2440 18th St. NW (tel. 202/387-8131). A favorite for cheap pizza and beer by the pitcher. Open every day.

● Geppetto, 2917 M St. NW (tel. 202/333-4315). In Georgetown and winners of *The Washingtonian* magazine's best-tasting pizza competition.

● Trio's, 1537 17th St. NW (tel. 202/232-5611). This diner is popular because of its cheap, good food, and in spite of its nasty waitresses.

● New Orleans Cafe, 1790 Columbia Rd. (just north of Dupont Circle) (tel. 202/234-5111). As you'd expect, New Orleans cooking—dishes like oyster loaf, ham and sausage gumbo, crayfish bisque. Long lines on weekends for brunch but worth the wait.

● Mi Riconcito, 1703 Connecticut Ave. NW (tel. 202/387-4515). A quaint Mexican restaurant with an outdoor cafe, bar, and international coffees.

● Florida Avenue Grill, 11th and Florida NW (tel. 202/265-1586). Soul food —ham hocks, peanut pie, short ribs and breakfasts of eggs, grits, bacon, and toast in a crowded and noisy spot.

● Au Pied du Cochon, 1335 Wisconsin Ave. NW, Georgetown (tel. 202/333-5440). An old D.C. favorite for food and people-watching. Menu prices from $4.25 to $8.

What to See: Although Washington, D.C., is a relatively small metropolitan area, it outdoes itself in the variety and number of activities it offers. Most museums and typical tourist activities are free (except for transportation) and, as an established tourist spot, Washington handles her crowds easily with few long waits.

● The Mall and its Museums: From the Capitol to the Washington Monument lies the National Mall, laid out in 1791. All along the Mall are buildings that you'll want to visit. Seven of these are Smithsonian Institution Museums, including the Freer Gallery of Art, Arts and Industries Building, the Hirshhorn Museum and Sculpture Garden (20th-century art indoors and sculpture outdoors), the National Museum of History and Technology, the National Museum of Natural History, the Smithsonian Institution Building (where the Visitors Information Center is located), the National Gallery of Art, and the extraordinarily popular National Air and Space Museum. At the National Air and Space Museum you can trace the history of flight as you look at the Wright Flyer, Lindbergh's *Spirit of St. Louis,* John Glenn's Mercury Capsule, *Gemini 4,* the Apollo 11 command module *Columbia,* and finally, a moon rock. The Albert Einstein Spacearium on the second floor presents sky and space spectaculars. For information on the Smithsonian Institution buildings, hours, exhibits, etc., call 202/381-6270. The Smithsonian has constructed a new wing, called the Quadrangle Building, next to the Castle on the mall. It holds the National Museum of African Art and the Arthur M. Sackler Gallery of Near Eastern and Asian Art (tel. 202/357-1300).

● National Portrait Gallery, 7th and F Sts. NW (tel. 202/357-1300). Life portraits of "men and women who have made significant contributions to the history, development, and culture of the people in the United States." Is yours there? This is a part of the Smithsonian Institution, and although it's not in the Mall, it's not far away at all.

● National Collection of Fine Arts, 8th and G Sts. NW (tel. 202/636-7040). Another Smithsonian Institution, right across from the Portrait Gallery, which contains a panorama of American painting, graphic art, and sculpture from the 18th century to the present.

● The U.S. Capitol, Capitol Hill (tel. 202/224-3121). Of all the buildings in Washington, this most symbolizes the federal government. You can visit the House and Senate galleries with passes that can be obtained from your representative or senator. Foreigners can go to the third floor of the Capitol, Senate or House side depending on which you want to see, for a morning pass. There are tours every day starting from the Rotunda from 9 a.m. to 3:45 p.m. daily.

● U.S. Supreme Court, 1st and Maryland Avenue NE (tel. 202/252-3211). Tours of the highest court in the land are conducted from 9:30 a.m. to 4 p.m.

● Washington Monument, Constitution Avenue at 15th Street NW (tel. 202/426-6841). You can take an elevator up and enjoy the view from 8 a.m. to midnight in summer.

● The White House, 1600 Pennsylvania Ave. NW (tel. 202/456-1414). Tours are conducted from 10 a.m. to noon, Tuesday to Saturday. If there's an official function on the day you want to go, you won't be able to take the tour.

● Lincoln Memorial, foot of 23rd Street NW (202/426-6985). A very moving tribute to Lincoln and worth a quiet visit.

● Federal buildings: Just about every government agency offers a tour of its premises. Some possibilities are: Bureau of Engraving and Printing (tel. 202/566-2000), Federal Bureau of Investigation (tel. 202/324-3447), and the Department of State (tel. 202/632-3241).

● Dumbarton Oaks and Gardens, 1703 32nd St. NW (tel. 202/342-3200). The house is headquarters for the Colonial Dames of America. Adjacent to it you can enjoy 16 acres of beautiful gardens with terraces and reflecting pools.

● Washington National Zoo, 3000 Connecticut Ave. NW (tel. 202/673-4800). Easily reached by buses L-2 and L-4, and the Metro (Woodley Park Zoo stop). The stars of the zoo are two giant pandas: 11 a.m. and 3 p.m. feeding times are the best times to see them. The zoo is divided into six trails that are well marked and easy to follow. The grounds are open from 8 a.m. to 8 p.m., the animal houses from 10 a.m. to 6 p.m. (hours vary seasonally). Admission is free. Parking $3 a day. Picnicking permitted.

● Library of Congress, 10 First St. SE (tel. 202/287-6400). Over 80 million items in 470 languages. Free tours.

● Old Post Office Pavillion, 1100 Pennsylvania Ave. (tel. 202/289-4224). No longer a post office but rather a courtyard surrounded by boutiques and restaurants where people-watching is the sport of choice.

● Vietnam Veterans Memorial, Constitution Avenue between Henry Bacon Drive and 21st Street NW (tel. 202/426-6700). A very moving memorial inscribed with the names of the nearly 58,000 Americans who died in Vietnam.

● Arlington National Cemetery, Arlington, VA 22111 (tel. 703/692-0931). The burial place for many of America's heroes. Every hour there's a changing of the guard at the Tomb of the Unknown Soldier.

● Adams Morgan is the most culturally diverse area of the city. It is located in northwest D.C., centered around 18th Street and Columbia Road. There's a wide range of restaurants and bars (reasonably priced) as well as many artistic shops. Great bargains await your discovery!

- Georgetown is a popular hangout for students. There are hundreds of bars, discos, restaurants, and shops. Georgetown is attractive and fun, but very expensive.

- Old Town Alexandria is across the river from the District of Columbia, but easily accessible by taxi or metro. A historic area with interesting shops and restaurants. Prices are more reasonable here—a good place for strolling and buying souvenirs.

- Beyond Washington: Two recommended day trips are to Annapolis, Maryland (40 minutes away), a charming small town that's the home of the U.S. Naval Academy, and to Harpers Ferry in West Virginia (about 1 ½ hours away), a national historic park with a visitors' center that explains the history of the community and John Brown's raid and capture here in 1859. Visitors can explore the park grounds and even do a bit of mountain climbing. Baltimore is only 40 miles from D.C.

At Night: For arts performances: Kennedy Center, New Hampshire Avenue at F Street NW. This is where you can see a play, enjoy a concert, listen to opera, see a dance performance, or watch a film. For information on what is going on at the Eisenhower Theater, the Opera House, the Concert Hall, the American Film Institute, or the Terrace Theater, call 202/872-0466. Student discounts are available at times. Free concerts take place at the Washington and Jefferson Memorials and at the Capitol steps on summer evenings. For 50% discounts on tickets (on the day of performance) go to Ticketplace, Metro Center Station, F Street Plaza (between 12th and 13th Sts. NW).

- For jazz: Blues Alley, 1073 Wisconsin Ave. NW (tel. 202/337-4141). This restaurant/nightclub presents big-name and local jazz performers and serves New Orleans-style food. The cover is between $10 and $15.

- One Step Down, 2517 Pennsylvania Ave. NW (tel. 202/331-8863). Big-name jazz bands in a small, smoky, and crowded atmosphere. Cover charge on weekends can go as high as $7; during the week it may be only $1.50 on some nights.

- Applause Restaurant, 1101 King St., Alexandria. Jazz in a modern atmosphere.

- Park Place Cafe, 2651 Connecticut Ave. NW. $5 to $7.50 cover. Fun, "uptown" jazz place.

- To dance: Pier 9, 1824 Half St. SW. (tel. 202/488-1205). There's room for 700 people to dance to a disco beat. Minimum every night; closed Monday and Tuesday nights.

- Deja Vu, 2119 M St. NW (tel. 202/452-1966). No cover or minimum. Enormous stained-glass windows, palm trees, and working fireplaces set the scene of this very colorful dance hall/bar that's always busy. Every night there's bopping (remember that?) to the tunes of the '50s and '60s. You can let loose on the dance floor or go to one of the quieter adjoining rooms. No food is served, and drinks are reasonable.

- Pier Street Annex, 1210 19th St. NW (tel. 202/466-4040). Enormous dance hall with disco and rock. Drinks served outdoors. "Attracts all kinds."

- The Kilimanjaro, 1724 California Ave., NW (tel. 202/328-3838). Dancing to live music until 3:30 a.m. A favorite of many Africans.

- Tracks, 80 M St. SE (tel. 202/488-3320). $10 cover. New wave music, large dance floor inside, volleyball court and dancing outside.

- Cagney's, One Dupont Circle (tel. 202/659-8820). Classy, new-wave music. $3 cover before 10 p.m., $5 after 10 p.m.

● For movies: Biograph Theater, 2819 M St. NW (tel. 202/333-2696). $3.50 will buy you a double feature of either a golden oldie or a more recent classic; film festivals, celebrity actors, directors, countries, etc., are featured periodically.

● Bethesda Cinema and Draft House, 7719 Wisconsin Ave. (tel. 301/656-3337). Food and drinks served during $3 movies.

● P&G New Carrollton, Annapolis Road, New Carrollton Metro Stop (tel. 301/588-1667). 99¢ movies.

● For country and folk music: Gallagher's Pub, 3319 Connecticut Ave. NW (tel. 202/686-9189). A large pub that serves great hamburgers and often features folk and country music.

● Folklore Society of Greater Washington, 7750 16th St. NW (tel. 202/281-2228. Folk performances.

● Washington Harbour, 3050 K St. NW in Georgetown (tel. 202/944-4140). Many free folk performances.

● The Birchmere, 3901 Mt. Vernon (tel. 703/549-5919). Bluegrass and acoustic music. Very big and *very* popular right now.

● For punk music: The 930 Club, 930 F St. NW (tel. 202/993-0930). The premier punk club of D.C. Cover ranges from $6 to $12.

● For theater: Arena Stage, 6th and Maine Avenue SW (tel. 202/488-3300); Marvin Center Theatre, George Washington University Campus, 800 21st St. NW (tel. 202/994-6178). Many free performances.

● Be sure to see a play at Ford's Theater, 511 10th St., NW (tel. 202/638-2941), the place where President Lincoln was assassinated. The theater has been restored beautifully and has a wonderful offering of plays every season.

● For classical music: International Conservatory of Music, 4835 MacArthur Blvd. NW (tel. 202/835-9669)—most performances are free; Levine School of Music, 1690 36th St. NW—most performances are free.

● For modern dance/ballet: Dance Place, 3225 8th St. NE (tel. 202/269-1600, near Catholic University); The Kennedy Center and university theaters are the best places to turn to for dance performances but they do not perform on a regular basis.

Shopping: For books: Globe Book Shop, 1700 Pennsylvania Ave. NW (tel. 202/393-1490, near White House). Large selection and variety of books.

● Yes! Bookshop, 1035 31st St. NW (Georgetown, tel. 202/338-7874). Inner development, travel needs, new-age music, Asian studies.

● Crown Books, 1710 G St. NW, and 2020 K St. NW and other locations. General selection of books at a hefty discount.

● Sidney Kramer Books, 1722 H St. NW (tel. 202/298-8010). Possibly the best selection of economics, area studies, and social sciences books in any East Coast store.

● Second Story Books, 2000 P St. NW (tel. 202/659-8884). Rare, used, and out-of-print books.

● International Learning Center, 1715 Connecticut Ave. NW (tel. 202/232-4111). The stock includes international cookbooks, travel guides to the U.S., and dictionaries in 100 languages.

● Common Concerns, 1347 Connecticut Ave. NW (tel. 202/463-6500). Books on political and international topics.

● The Newsroom Cafe, 1753 Connecticut Ave. NW (tel. 202/332-1489). This spot, at a lively intersection near Dupont Circle, has newspapers and magazines from all over the U.S. and the world.

- For records: Tower Records, 2000 Pennsylvania Ave. NW (tel. 202/331-2400). Biggest record store in the city.
- Sam "K" Midtown Records and Tapes, 1839 7 St. NW (tel. 202/234-6540). "What the DJ's play you'll find at Sam "K'"—priced at a discount.
- Melody Record Shop Inc., 1523 Connecticut Ave. NW (Dupont Circle, tel. 202/232-4002). All types of music at "maximum" discounts.
- Olsson's Books and Records, 19th and L Sts. NW (tel. 202/785-5037) or 1239 Wisconsin Ave. NW (tel. 202/338-9544 or 338-6712). Everything at a discount.
- Serenade Record Shop, 1710 Pennsylvania Ave. NW (tel. 202/638-5580) and 1800 M St. NW (tel. 202/452-0075). Jazz, popular, classical, rock, and soul at a discount.
- For sporting goods: Hudson Trail Outfitters, 4437 Wisconsin Ave. NW (tel. 202/363-9810). Sleeping bags, clothing, and other outdoor gear.
- For general shopping: The Shops, 1331 Pennsylvania Ave. NW (tel. 202/783-9090). This is a shopping mall and food emporium with lots of little boutiques—right in the heart of downtown D.C.
- Garfinkel's, 1401 F St. NW (tel. 202/628-7730). Washington's best-known department store—with a nice selection of gifts if you don't have to worry too much about prices.
- Georgetown. The whole area—an eight-square-block area with hub at Wisconsin Avenue and M Street NW—teems with galleries, specialty shops, boutiques, and eateries. Georgetown Park on M Street is a big neighborhood attraction.
- For secondhand clothing: Secondhand Rose, 1516 Wisconsin Ave. NW (tel. 202/337-3378). In Georgetown, a popular source of resale clothes and accessories for women.

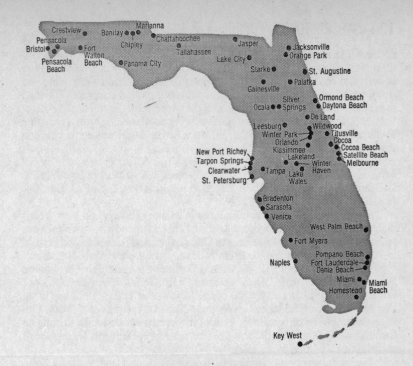

Florida

Florida means vacation for most people. When the winter winds blow up north, down they all come. The biggest tourist attraction in all of Florida is Disney World, about 20 miles south of Orlando. Everyone seems to agree that the place is a lot of fun. One friend's favorite Florida sight is the Stephen Foster Memorial on the Suwannee River (near White Springs), which is a sight in itself with its oak-lined banks and Spanish moss.

There are lots of sea attractions in Florida, like Sea World in central Florida, Marineland in St. Augustine, and the Seaquarium in Miami. A real must-see, if you can stand the traffic, is Miami Beach with its famous hotel row where each hotel vies with the next for splendor.

The farthest point south in the U.S. is Key West, with the Atlantic on one side and the Gulf of Mexico on the other. Here you can still see men practicing the old art of shelling conch.

If you're attracted by state capitals, then you'll want to visit Tallahassee. But one city that you should really try to include in your plans is St. Augustine, just 50 miles south of the Georgia-Florida line. This was the first place in the U.S. settled by the Spaniards in the 1500s, and its original fort still stands. Tampa, on the west coast, still has an Hispanic flavor, too.

The southern portion of Florida, from the Keys to the Broward County area, has become home for many who have left Castro's Cuba. One section of Miami is called Little Havana, more than 20 years after the first exodus. Southern Florida is still home to many natives, but in the last 30 years many northerners have relocated to take advantage of the climate. Central and northern Florida are still mostly "home-grown" people, but they too are being "colonized" by people who can't stand the northern winters. Camping abounds, in state and private campgrounds, and many areas retain their natural character. The state publishes a camping directory and state park brochure. "Free Florida Attractions" will lead you to such possibilities as self-guided walking tours, free cattle auctions, and factory tours à la Donald Duck Citrus World, museums, concerts and more.

Two useful guidebooks to the state are *Florida Off the Beaten Path*, by Bill and Diana Gleasner, Globe Pequot ($7.95), and *Guide to the Small and Historic Lodgings of Florida*, by Herbert Hiller, Pineapple Press, Inc., P.O. Box 314, Englewood, FL 33533 ($14.20).

Some Special Events: Orange Bowl in Miami (January, on New Year's night); Seafood Festival in Grant (February); Old Island Days in Key West (February to March); Frontier Days in Orange City, and Ponce de Leon Festival in Port Charlotte (March); Rodeo in Palatka, and Catfish Festival in Crescent City (April); Billy Bowlegs Festival (Billy Bowlegs was a pirate) in Fort Walton Beach (May); Sea Turtle Watch in Jensen Beach (June); Everglades Outdoor Music Festival (the annual festival of the Miccosukee Tribe) in Miami (July); Fun Day and Possum Festival in Wausau (August); International Worm Fiddling Contest (who can create the best vibration on a wooden stake to bring up the most worms) in Caryville and Seafood Festival in Pensacola (September); and Hispanic Heritage Week in Dade County (October).

Tourist Information: Division of Tourism, Florida Department of Commerce, Collins Bldg., Tallahassee, FL 32301 (tel. 904/488-8230).

Bonifay

Accommodation: Econo Lodge, I-10 & S.R. 79, Rte. 1, Box 202J, 32425. (tel. 904/547-9345).

Bradenton

Accommodation: Knights Inn, I-75 & S.R. 64, 668 67th St. Circle East, 33508 (tel. 813/748-1876).

Bristol

Camping: Torreya State Park, Rt. no. 2, Box 70, 32321 (tel. 904/643-2674). Campground along the Apalachicola River with 35 sites open year round. $6 per campsite per night; $8 for electric site.

Chattahoochee

Accommodation: Morgan Motel, U.S. 90 East, 32324 (tel. 904/663-4336). $24 for one; $26 for two in one bed; $29 for two in two beds.

Chipley

Camping: Falling Waters State Recreation Area, Rte. 5, Box 660, 32428 (tel. 904/638-4030). Campground with 24 sites open year round. $6 per campsite per night for inland areas; $8 for coastal areas; $10 for Florida Key areas.

Clearwater

Accommodations: Red Carpet Inn, 2940 Gulf-to-Bay Blvd., 33519 (tel. 813/799-0100).
● TraveLodge, 711 Cleveland St., 33515 (tel. 813/446-9183).

Cocoa

Accommodation: Scottish Inn, 4150 West King St., 32922 (tel. 305/632-5721).

Cocoa Beach

Accommodation: Motel 6, 3701 North Atlantic Ave., 32931 (tel. 305/783-3103).

Crestview

Accommodations: Scottish Inn, 564 U.S. 90 W., 32536 (tel. 904/682-3832).
● Econo Lodge, I-10 and Fla. 85, Exit 12, P.O. Box 1466, 82536 (tel. 904/682-6255).

Dania Beach

Accommodation: Motel 6, 825 East Dania Beach Blvd., 33004 (tel. 305/921-5505).

Daytona Beach

Tourist Information: Convention and Tourism Department, Destination Daytona!, P.O. Box 2775, 32015 (tel. 904/255-0981).
Help: Travelers Aid, 771-B Briarwood Dr., 32014 (tel. 904/252-4752).
Accommodations: Days Inn, I-95 and U.S. 92, 2800 Volusia Ave., 32015 (tel. 904/255-0541).
● Days Inn, 1909 South Atlantic Ave., 32018 (tel. 904/255-4492).
● Days Inn, 3209 South Atlantic Ave., 32018 (tel. 904/761-2050).

- Rip Van Winkle Motel, 1025 North Atlantic Ave., 32018 (tel. 904/252-6213). $18 for one; $22 for two in one bed; $24 for two in two beds.
- Scottish Inn, 133 South Ocean Ave., 32018 (tel. 904/253-0666).
- YWCA, 344 South Beach St., 32014 (tel. 904/252-3253). Women only. $15 single; $12.50 per person double; $11 per person in dorm-style accommodations. Weekly rates: $70 single; $65 per person double; $55 per person in dorm. Advance reservations of three weeks necessary. "A comfortable, clean establishment with its own outdoor pool."
- Daytona Beach Youth Hostel (AYH-SA), 140 South Atlantic Ave., 32018 (tel. 904/258-6937). $9.98 for AYH members; $12.99 for nonmembers.
- Econo Lodge, 2250 Volusia Ave., 32014 (tel. 904/255-3661).

DeLand

On Campus: At Stetson University, your first stop, if you want help finding your way around, is the Carlton Union (center of campus). Stetson students should be easy to meet at the Commons (in the Carlton Union building).

Fort Lauderdale

Accommodations: Motel 6, 1801 S.R. 84, 33315 (tel. 305/760-7999).
- Days Inn, I-95 & Fla. 84, Exit 27, 2640 S.R. 84, 33312 (tel. 305/792-4700).

Fort Myers

Accommodations: Days Inn, 1099 Cleveland Ave., U.S. 41 North, 33903 (tel. 813/995-0535).
- Days Inn, 11435 Cleveland Ave., 33907 (tel. 813/936-1311).
- Red Carpet Inn, 4811 Cleveland Ave., 33907 (tel. 813/936-3229).
- Econo Lodge, 1089 U.S. Hwy. 41 North, 33903 (tel. 813/995-0571).
- Knights Inn, U.S. 41 at Marinatown Boulevard., 13251 N. Cleveland, 33903 (tel. 813/656-5544).
- TraveLodge, 2038 West First St., 33901 (tel. 813/334-2284).

Fort Walton Beach

Accommodation: Econo Lodge, 100 Miracle Strip Pkwy., 32548 (tel. 904/244-0121).

Gainesville

On Campus: The University of Florida is in Gainesville, and according to one student, "there are so many students in Gainesville that strangers will blend right in." For food, go to the Copper Monkey, Purple Porpoise II, or Knife and Fork. At night, try Richenbacher's for jazz and Spectrum Disco for dancing.

The J. Wayne Reitz Union on the Univ. of Florida campus has a ride board on the ground floor and cheap movies are shown on the second floor. Buses in town are a bargain at $.50. The student newspaper, *Independent Florida Alligator,* is distributed all over town free, and the Corner Drug Store has leads on places to stay.

Accommodations: Econo Lodge, 2649 S.W. 13th St., 32608 (tel. 904/373-7816).

● Econo Lodge, 700 N.W. 75th St., 32601 (tel. 904/322-2346).

● Days Inn, I-75 and Fla. 26, 6901 N.W. Eighth Ave., 32601 (tel. 904/376-1601).

● Knights Inn, I-75 and S.R. 24, 4021 S.W. 40th Blvd., 32608 (tel. 904/373-0392).

● Motel 6, 4000 S.W. 40th Blvd., 32608 (tel. 904/373-1604).

● TraveLodge, 413 West University Ave., 32601 (tel. 904/376-1224).

Homestead

Camping: Everglades National Park, P.O. Box 279, 33030. (tel. 305/247-6211). If you plan to visit the park, it is strongly recommended that you have a private vehicle to get there and around. There are 29 backcountry campsites and two regular campgrounds (Long Pine Key and Flamingo) with a total of over 300 sites. Backcountry campsites are accessible by boat only, and a permit is required for their use. $4 to $7 per campsite per night in regular campgrounds. $5 entrance fee for occupants with cars or motorcycles; $2 for all others.

● Biscayne National Park Campground, P.O. Box 1369, 33090 (tel. 305/247-7275). Camping year round at Elliot Key. Access by boat only. No fee. "One of the largest marine preserves administered by the National Park Service. There is a self-guiding nature trail from Biscayne Bay to the Atlantic. Campers must bring their own tents."

Jacksonville

Tourist Information: Convention and Visitors Bureau of Jacksonville and Its Beaches, 33 S. Hogan St., no. 250, 32202 (tel. 904/353-9736).

Help: Travelers Aid, 217 W. Church St., 32202 (tel. 904/356-0249).

● First Call for Help, 904/632-0600.

Accommodations: YWCA, 325 East Duval St., 32202 (tel. 904/354-6681). Women and up to two children (boys up to age 8). $27.75 to $37 single; $36.75 to $47 double. $8 key deposit.

● Best Inns of America, I-95 at Baymeadows Road Exit, 8222 Dix Ellis Trail (tel. 904/739-3323).

● Econo Lodge, 5018 University Blvd. West, 32216 (tel. 904/731-0800).

● Econo Lodge, 6560 Ramona Blvd., 32205 (tel. 904/786-2794).

● Econo Lodge, 2300 Phillips Hwy., 32207 (tel. 904/396-2301).

● Econo Lodge, 1055 Golfair Blvd., 32209 (tel. 904/764-2551).

● Days Inn, I-95 and Jax International Airport Exit, P.O. Box 18217, 32229 (tel. 904/757-5000).

● Knights Inn, I-95 at Baymeadows Road, 8285 Dix Ellis Trail, 32216 (tel. 904/731-8400).

● Red Carpet Inn, 5331 University Blvd. West, 32216 (tel. 904/733-8110).

- Red Roof Inn, I-95 and Airport Road, 14701 Duval Rd., 32218 (tel. 904/751-4110).
- Red Roof Inn, I-295 and Blanding Boulevard., 6099 Youngerman Circle, 32244 (tel. 904/777-1000).
- Motel 6, 10885 Harts Rd., 32218 (tel. 904/757-8600).
- Motel 6, 6107 Youngerman Circle, 32244 (tel. 904/777-6100).
- Scottish Inn, I-295 and Hwy. 17, 337 Park Ave., 32073 (tel. 904/264-0511).
- Budget Host—Friendly Inn, 731 1st St., North, 32250 (tel. 904/249-5006).
- Super 8 Inn, 10901 Harts Rd., 32218 (tel. 904/751-3888).
- TraveLodge, 881 Golfair Blvd., 32209 (tel. 904/764-7511).

Jasper

Accommodation: Scottish Inn, I-75 and S.R. 6, Rte. 3, Box 136, 32052 (tel. 904/792-1234).

Key West

Accommodations: Key West Hostel and Sea Shell Motel, Ⓢ★, 718 South St., 33041 (tel. 305/296-5719). Within walking distance of bus station. $32 to $39 single; $16 to $19.50 per person double; $11 to $14.50 per person triple; $9 to $12 per person quad. Rates vary according to season; highest in winter. Advance reservations are necessary.

Kissimmee

Accommodations: Days Inn, 5840 Spacecoast Pkwy., 32741 (tel. 305/396-7969).
- Days Inn, 5820 Spacecoast Pkwy. 32741 (tel. 305/396-7900).
- Knights Inn, 7475 W. Space Coast Pkwy., 32741 (tel. 305/396-4200).
- Knights Inn, 2800 Poinciana Blvd., 32741 (tel. 305/396-8186).
- Motel 6, 7455 West Space Coast Pkwy., 32741 (tel. 305/396-6422).

Lake City

Accommodations: Days Inn, I-75 and U.S. 90, Rte. 13, P.O. Box 1140, 32055 (tel. 904/752-9350).
- Econo Lodge, I-75 at U.S. 90, P.O. Box 430, 32055 (tel. 904/752-7891).
- Motel 6, U.S. 90 & Ross Allen Road, 32055 (tel. 904/755-4664).

Lake Wales

Accommodation: Econo Lodge, 501 South Hwy. 27, P.O. Box 1637, 33853 (tel. 813/676-7963).

Lakeland

Accommodations: Scottish Inn, 244 North Florida Ave., 33801 (tel. 813/687-2530).
- Red Carpet Inn, 3410 U.S. 98 North, 33805 (tel. 813/858-3851).

Leesburg

Accommodation: Econo Lodge, 1115 West North Blvd., U.S. N. Hwy. 441, 32748 (tel. 904/787-3131).

Marianna

Camping: Florida Caverns State Park, √, 2701 Caverns Rd., 32446 (tel. 904/482-3632). Area surrounding Florida's only publicly accessible limestone caverns. Campground with 32 sites open year round. $6.30 per campsite per night for nonelectric sites; $8.40 for electric.
Accommodation: Econo Lodge, 1119 West Lafayette St., 32446 (tel. 904/526-3710).

Melbourne

Accommodations: Econo Lodge, 4505 West New Haven Ave., 32904 (tel. 305/724-5450).
- Red Carpet Inn, 1423 South Harbor City Blvd., 32901 (tel. 305/727-2950).
- TraveLodge, I-95 and U.S. 192, 32901 (tel. toll free 800/255-3050).

Miami Beach/Miami

Sixty years ago this was swampland but now it's high-rise hotel land. People flock to Miami every winter for the sun and the ocean, and many have decided to stay, so the Miami area is full of transplants (mostly retirees) from other, more northerly spots. Because Miami is such a popular resort area, prices can be high. One friend writes: "In September the hotels are not as busy and the rates are still low; later on it's too crowded and earlier it's too hot." Events include the Miami Grand Prix and the Coconut Grove Arts Festival in February, Dade County Youth Fair, an outstanding family outing in March, and Goombay Festival in June.

One neighborhood you'll want to visit is Little Havana, in southwest Miami, which was established back in 1959 by Cubans and has been growing ever since. There you'll find restaurants, shops, discos, and hotels all in the Cuban tradition—a lively place to visit and practice your Spanish. Other neighborhoods include the Art Deco District, which you can tour on Saturdays at 10:30 a.m. (call the Miami Design Preservation League at 305/672-1836), and Cauley Square, 22400 Old Dixie Highway (tel. 305/258-3543), which offers a collection of charming shops, plus the Tearoom—a wonderful place to browse for antiques and collector's items. To know what's going on in Miami, check with *Miami/South Florida Magazine* or contact the Greater Miami Convention and Visitors Bureau, 4770 Biscayne Boulevard, Penthouse A, Miami, 33139 (tel. 305/573-4300). The airport also has an information booth/area.

For more information on Miami read Fodor's *Greater Miami and the Gold Coast* (current price $5.95). On Fridays *The Miami Herald* publishes a "Weekend" section guide to all current movies, events, theater, concerts, restaurants, etc. The magazine *Miami/South Florida* is published monthly with a calendar of all current events. The same magazine publishes a good basic guide to the area called "South Florida Made Easy" ($1).

Getting There: Miami International Airport is five miles northwest of the city. A taxi ride from the airport will cost about $10 to $12, but you can take a bus—no. 5, 7, 37, 42, or J—and it will cost only 75¢. The bus station is at 300 N.W. 32nd Ave. in Miami (tel. 305/638-6700), with another terminal in downtown Coral Gables.

Getting Around: Taxi fares start at $1 plus $1.20 for each additional mile. The bus fare is 75¢, 35¢ for children, with a discount for senior citizens between 9 a.m. and 4 p.m. and after 6 p.m. Be sure to check your schedule, too, of the new rapid Metrorail System which services limited areas of the city and costs $1. Information is available by calling 305/638-6700. To rent a car, you might try Way-Lo Rent-a-Car, at locations in Miami Beach, downtown Miami, and near the airport. Rates are $109 per week for Ford Escorts and Toyotas. You might also try Value-Rent-a-Car.

Or take a self-guided bike tour through Coral Gables and around the University of Miami. You can rent a bike for approximately $10 per day at the Dade Cycle Shop, 3216 Grand Ave. (tel. 305/443-6075).

Help: United Way Information Referral, 600 Brickell Ave., third floor, 33131 (tel. 305/579-2200). Will help travelers in need contact family or helpful organizations.

Accommodations: Haddon Hall Hotel (AYH-SA), ⓢ, 1500 Collins Ave., 33139 (tel. 305/531-1251). In Miami's art deco area, one block from Greyhound station. Men, women, and children. April 15 to December 1, $18 to $25 single or double. Higher rates apply in winter. Rooms have refrigerators, sinks, and cooking facilities. "We have our own Olympic-size pool and are a block from the ocean. We're in the heart of Miami Beach." These are special rates for *Where to Stay* readers.

● Hotel Netherland, ★, 1330 Ocean Dr., Miami Beach, 33139 (tel. 305/534-4791). Summer: $23 single; $25 double; $28 triple; $32 quad. Higher rates from December 1 to May 1—call for information.

● Winterhaven Hotel, ⓢ★, 1400 Ocean Dr., 33139 (tel. 305/531-5571). $18 to $26 single. Rooms face the ocean and have kitchenettes. Recommended by a reader who said the management was "very friendly." Advance reservations suggested during winter.

● Clay Hotel/Miami Beach Youth Hostel (AYH), ⓢ★, 1438 Washington Ave., 33139 (tel. 305/534-2988). $16.50 single; $22 double; $33 triple; $8 per person member, $10 per person nonmember quad. Rates slightly higher December to March. Advance reservations suggested December to April.

● Sagamore Hotel, 1671 Collins Ave., Miami Beach (tel. 305/538-7211). $28 single or double; $32 triple; $44 quad.

● Marseilles Hotel, 1741 Collins Ave., Miami Beach (tel. 305/538-5711). $33 single; $35 double; $40 triple; $45 quad.

● The Ritz Plaza Hotel, Ⓢ ★ (10%), 1701 Collins Ave., Miami Beach, 33139 (tel. 305/531-6881). $22 single; $26 to $32 double; $4 each additional person. Weekly rate: $175. A 1930s hotel, recently renovated. Located on the beachfront, it also includes a 90-foot swimming pool. Reservations necessary.

Where to Eat: El Viajante, 1676 Collins Ave., Miami Beach (tel. 305/534-2101). Recommended for good, moderately priced American and Spanish food. Typical dinner—$7.99.

● Bobby Rubino's for Ribs, 8600 Mills Drive, Town and Country Mall (tel. 305/596-3939). Wonderful ribs in a pleasant atmosphere. Typical meal—$8.95.

● New Chinatown, 5958 South Dixie Hwy. (tel. 305/662-5649). All types of Chinese food. Average price—$8.

● Bagel Emporium, 1238 South Dixie Hwy., Coral Gables, across from University of Miami (tel. 305/666-9519). Nine varieties of bagels.

● Uncle Tom's Cabin Barbecue, S.W. 8th Street and 40th Avenue (tel. 305/446-9528). Relaxing, old-style western setting. $4 to $6 for a meal consisting of barbecued chicken, ribs, or pork with cole slaw and bread.

● La Carreta, four locations with the original at 3632 S.W. 8th St. (tel. 305/444-7501). A good place to try typical Cuban food.

● Monty Trainers, 2560 Bayshore Dr. (tel. 305/858-1431). Dine outdoors by the water in a casual atmosphere.

● Sakura Japanese Restaurant, 440 South Dixie Hwy. (tel. 305/665-7020). Authentic and good Japanese food.

What to See: You'll probably want to stay and bask on the beach for most of your stay, but if the weather is bad or you get tired of sun and sand, there are lots of tourist attractions in the area. These include the Miami Seaquarium, a 60-acre aquatic park on Rickenbacker Causeway in Biscayne Bay complete with performing whales. Call 305/361-5703 for information.

● Monkey Jungle, 14805 S.W. 216th St. (tel. 305/235-1611). Gorillas, orangutans, and chimpanzees doing what they do in the open while the visitors watch from enclosed walkways.

● Villa Vizcaya, 3251 South Miami Ave. (tel. 305/579-2708). This 70-room Italian-style extravaganza was once the home of the industrialist James Deering and is now the property of the Dade County Art Museum. Inside the villa you'll see rugs, tapestries, and sculpture, and outside you can walk through formal gardens.

● Art Deco District. All-day tours begin each Saturday at 10:30 a.m. Tour guides are designers, architects, writers, and historians. Call 305/672-1836.

● Six Flag Atlantis—The Water Kingdom, 2700 Stirling Rd., Hollywood (tel. 305/926-1000). About a 15-minute ride from Miami Beach. A water theme park, with a song-and-dance revue and a water-ski show.

● Museum of Science Planetarium, 3280 South Miami Ave. (tel. 305/854-2222).

● Fairchild Tropical Gardens, 10901 Old Cutler Rd. (tel. 305/667-1651). A paradise of tropical plants from around the world. Train rides or a self-guided walking tour.

● Jai-alai, 3500 N.W. 37th Ave. (tel. 305/633-6400). From December to September. One of Miami's most exciting spectator sports.

At Night: The big hotels have shows at night—big-name stars and some not-so-big-name stars. Check *Miami/South Florida Magazine* to see who's where while you're in town. For discount tickets call Bass Ticket Agency at 305/653-0450 and Select-a-Seat at 305/625-5100. Some other possibilities:

● For arts events: Dade County Auditorium, 2901 West Flagler St. (tel. 305/547-5414). This is the heart of Miami's cultural life—call to see whether there's a concert, a play, or a dance company booked into this popular theater and whether there are any tickets.

● For jazz: Greenstreets-Holiday Inn, 2051 Le Jeune Rd. (tel. 305/445-2131). Open 7-12 p.m. except Sunday. Also call the Jazz Hotline at 305/382-3938.

● For folk music: Call the "Folk Hot-Line" at 305/531-3855.

● For classical music: Gusman Cultural Center, 174 East Flagler St. (tel. 305/372-0925).

● To dance: Copacabana Supper Club, 3600 S.W. 8th St. (tel. 305/443-3801). A Latin dance club; Ronnie's, 2373 Le Jeune Rd., across from the airport. Open from 9:30 p.m. to 5 a.m. for dancing to big-band sounds, disco, and other kinds of music, too.

● For theater: Coconut Grove Playhouse, 3500 Main Hwy. (tel. 305/442-4000); Theatre of the Performing Arts, 1700 Washington Ave., Miami Beach (tel. 305/673-7300 or 673-8300.

● For movies: Dadeland (tel. 305/279-9990), across from the Dadeland Mall; Riviera, 1560 South Dixie Hwy. (tel. 305/559-8920). All movies are currently $4.50 to $4.75, although most theaters have matinee prices of $2.50 to $3.

● For modern dance/ballet: Colony Theater, 1040 Lincoln Mall, Miami Beach (tel. 305/538-0900).

● Coconut Grove is a fun place to hang out—lots of open-air cafés, discos, and people-watching!

Shopping: For books: The Grove Book Worm, 3025 Fuller St. (tel. 305/443-6411). All hard- and soft-cover books.

● Books and Books, Inc., 296 Aragon Ave., Coral Gables (tel. 305/442-4408). A thoughtful selection of books; frequent guest appearances by well-known authors.

● For records: Spec's Music Shop, Dadeland Mall, 7535 North Kendall Dr. and other locations (tel. 305/666-5941). Records galore.

● Q Records, 11600 North Kendall Drive (tel. 305/271-4487). Discount prices.

● For clothing & gifts: Shoe Villa, 17220 Collins Ave., Sunny Isles (tel. 305/949-9276). All kinds of shoes with a 25% discount to ISIC holders.

● Malls include Dadeland at 7535 N. Kendall Drive, Town and Country at N. Kendall Drive and 117th, and The Falls at 8778 S.W. 136th St. Here you'll find most everything.

● And more: Southwest 8th St. ("Calle Ocho" to most) is for shopping with a Latin flavor—you can bargain with shopkeepers here. A must if you want to get a feel of what today's Miami is all about.

Naples

Accommodation: Days Inn, U.S. 41 and Fla. 84, Alligator Alley, 1925 Davis Blvd., 33942 (tel. 813/774-3117).

New Port Richey

Accommodation: Knights Inn, 7631 U.S. Hwy. 19, 33552 (tel. 813/845-4990).

Ocala

Accommodations: Days Inn, I-75 and Fla. 40, 4040 W. Silver Springs Blvd., 32675 (tel. 904/629-8850).
● Budget Host—Western Motel, 4013 N.W. Blichton Rd., 32675 (tel. 904/732-6940).
● Econo Lodge, 3951 N.W. Blichton Rd., 32675 (tel. 904/629-7021).
● Red Carpet Inn, 3960 N.W. Blichton Rd., Exit 70 on I-75, 32675 (tel. 904/629-8681).
● Quality Inn, 3767 N.W. Blichton Rd., 32675 (tel. 904/732-2300).
● TraveLodge, 1626 S.W. Pine Ave., 32670 (tel. 904/622-4121).

Orange Park

Accommodation: Knights Inn, I-295 at U.S. 17, 141 Park Ave., 32073 (tel. 904/264-5107).

Orlando

All of the budget motels in the Orlando area are here to accommodate all of the people who come to Disney World and to Sea World.
Help: We Care, Inc., 112 Pasadena Place, 32803 (tel. 305/628-1227). 24-hour crisis/suicide prevention. Someone from We Care, Inc., told us that if you're really in a bind, a place called Daily Bread will serve you a free meal at noon.
Accommodations: Young Women's Community Club (AYH-SA), ♿, 107 East Hillcrest St., 32801 (tel. 305/425-2502). Women ages 16 to 37 only. $9 in dorm-style room. Breakfast and dinner served on the premises daily.
● Budget Host—Loch Haven Motor Inn, 1820 North Mills Ave., 32803 (tel. 305/896-3611).
● Orlando International Youth Hostel (AYH), 420 Highland Ave., 32801 (tel. 305/841-8867). $10 per person per night—welcomes members and non-members of AYH. Five blocks from bus station, near downtown.
● Days Inn, I-4 and Fla. 46, Sanford, 32771 (tel. 305/323-6500).
● Days Inn, I-4 and 33rd St., 2500 West 33rd St., 32809 (tel. 305/841-3731).
● Days Airport Inn, 2323 McCoy Rd., 32809 (tel. 305/859-6100).
● Days Inn—Landstreet Inn and Lodge, 1221 West Landstreet Rd., 32824 (tel. 305/859-7700).
● Econo Lodge, 5870 Orange Blossom Trail South, 32809 (tel. 305/859-5410).

Ormond Beach

Accommodation: Econo Lodge, 1634 North U.S. 1 at I-95, 32074 (tel. 904/672-6222).

Palatka

Accommodation: Budget Host—Town House Motel, 100 Moseley Ave., 32077 (tel. 904/328-1533).

Panama City

Accommodations: Scottish Inn, 4907 West Hwy. 98, 32401 (tel. 904/769-2432).
● Scottish Inn, 11000 West Alternate Hwy. 98, 32407 (tel. 904/234-3351).
● Super 8 Inn, 207 U.S. Hwy. 231, 32405 (tel. 904/784-1988).

Pensacola Beach

Camping: Gulf Islands National Seashore, 1400 Fort Pickens Rd., 32561 (tel. 904/932-5018). Campground with 200 sites open year round. $8 to $10 per campsite per night. $3 entrance fee per carload, good for 7 days.

Pensacola

Help: Help Line, 904/438-1617.
● Information & Referral, 904/436-9011.
Accommodations: Econo Lodge, I-10 & Hwy. 291, Plantation Road, 32504 (tel. 904/474-1060).
● Knights Inn, I-10 at S.R. 291, 1353 Northcross Lane, 32514 (tel. 904/477-2554).
● Regal 8 Inn, 7827 North Davis Hwy., 32514 (tel. 904/476-5386).
● Motel 6, 5829 Pensacola Blvd., 32505 (tel. 904/477-7522).
● Red Roof Inn, I-10 and S.R. 291, Exit 5, 7340 Plantation Rd., 32504 (tel. 904/476-7960).
● Red Carpet Inn, 4448 Mobile Hwy., 32506 (tel. 904/456-7411).
● Super 8 Inn, 7220 Plantation Rd., 32504 (tel. 904/476-8038).

Pompano Beach

Accommodations: Days Inn, 1411 N.W. 31st Ave., 33069 (tel. 305/972-3700).
● Motel 6, 1201 N.W. 31st Ave., 33069 (tel. 305/977-8011).

St. Augustine

Accommodations: Econo Lodge, 3101 Ponce de Leon Blvd., 32084 (tel. 904/829-3461).
- Scottish Inn, Rte. 2, Box 277X, 32084 (tel. 904/829-5643).
- Scottish Inn, 427 Anastasia Blvd., 32084 (tel. 904/824-5055).
- Days Inn, I-95 and Fla. 16, Rte. 2, Box 277Y, 32084 (tel. 904/824-4341).
- Days Inn, 2800 Ponce de Leon Blvd., 32084 (tel. 904/829-6581).
- Red Carpet Inn, I-95 and S.R. 16, P.O. Box D-1, 32084 (tel. 904/824-4306).
- Scottish Inn, 110 San Marco Ave., 32084 (tel. 904/824-2871).

St. Petersburg

Tourist Information: Convention and Visitors Bureau, St. Petersburg Area Chamber of Commerce, P.O. Box 1371, 33731 (tel. 813/821-4069).
Accommodation: Days Inn, 9359 U.S. 19 North, 33565 (tel. 813/577-3838).

Sarasota

Accommodations: Econo Lodge, 5340 North Tamiami Trail, 33580 (tel. 813/355-8867).
- Cadillac Motel, 4021 North Tamiami Trail, 33580 (tel. 813/355-7108). $24 for one or two in one bed; $26 for two in two beds.
- TraveLodge, 270 North Tamiami Trail, 33577 (tel. 813/366-0414).

Satellite Beach

Accommodation: Econo Lodge, 180 Hwy. A1A, 32937 (tel. 305/777-3552).

Silver Springs

Accommodation: Scottish Inn, 5331 N.E. Silver Springs Blvd., 32688 (tel. 904/236-2383).

Starke

Accommodation: Dixie Motel, 744 North Temple Ave., 32091 (tel. 904/964-5590). $22 to $26 for one; $24 to $28 for two in one bed; $28 to $32 for two in two beds.
- Econo Lodge, 1101 N. Temple, P.O. Box 1090, 32091 (tel. 904/964-7600).

Tallahassee

On Campus: If you're in Tallahassee and want to meet some of Florida

State University's students, stop at Poor Paul's Poorhouse, The Alley, The Phyrst, Radcliff's, or Bullwinkle's, all friendly local pubs with music.

Accommodations: Best Inns of America, I-10 at S.R. 27, 2738 Graves Rd., (tel. 904/562-2378).

- Econo Lodge, 2681 North Monroe St., 32303 (tel. 904/385-6155).
- Knights Inn, I-10 at U.S. 27, 2728 Graves Rd., 32303 (tel. 904/562-4700).
- Motel 6, 1481 Timberlane Dr., 32308 (tel. 904/668-2600).
- Master Hosts Inn, 1630 North Monroe St., 32303 (tel. 904/224-6183).
- Red Roof Inn, 2930 Hospitality Rd., 32303 (tel. 904/385-7884).

Tampa

On Campus: You can contact the Overseas Information Center, SOC 107, Room 301, at the University of South Florida (tel. 813/974-3104), for help in finding temporary accommodations with someone from the University Community. You might also find apartment listings in the *Oracle,* the University of South Florida's newspaper.

A good place to meet people is the Empty Keg, the student bar at the University Center. There are also several pubs along Fletcher Ave. where students burn the midnight oil. For good pizza, ask directions to the popular C.D.B. Pizza.

Tourist Information: Tampa/Hillsborough Convention and Visitors Association, 100 S. Ashley Dr., Suite 850, 33601 (tel. 813/223-1111, or toll free 800/826-8358 outside Florida.

Accommodations: Econo Lodge, 11414 Central Ave., 33612 (tel. 813/933-7831).

- Econo Lodge, 321 East Fletcher Ave., 33612 (tel. 813/933-4545).
- Budgetel Inn, 4811 U.S. Hwy. 301 North, 33610 (tel. 813/626-0885).
- Budgetel Inn, 602 S. Faulkenburg Rd., 33619 (tel. 813/684-4007).
- Motel 6, 333 East Fowler Ave., 33612 (tel. 813/932-4948).
- Days Inn, I-75 & Fla. 54 W., Zephyrhills, 34249 (tel. 813/973-0155).
- Days Inn, 701 East Fletcher Ave., 33612 (tel. 813/977-1550).
- Days Inn, 2901 East Busch Blvd., 33612 (tel. 813/933-6471).
- Days Inn, 6010 Fla. 579, North Seffner, 33584 (tel. 813/621-4681).
- Red Carpet Inn, 4528 East Columbus Dr., 33605 (tel. 813/621-4651).
- Red Roof Inn, 5001 North U.S. 301, 33610 (tel. 813/623-5245).

Tarpon Springs

Accommodation: Days Inn, 816 U.S. 19 S., P.O. Box 786, 33589 (tel. 813/934-0859).

Titusville

Accommodations: Rodeway Inn, √ (10%), 3655 Chaney Hwy., 32780 (tel. 305/269-7110). $30 to $35 single; $35 to $42 double. Higher rates apply during shuttle launches.

- Days Inn, 3480 Garden St., 32796 (tel. 305/269-9310).

Venice

Accommodation: Motel 6, 281 Venice Bypass North, 33595 (tel. 813/485-8255).

West Palm Beach

Help: The Center for Family Services (Travelers Aid), 2218 S. Dixie Hwy., 33401 (tel. 305/655-4483).
- Crisis Line, 305/686-4000.
  Accommodation: Days Inn, 2300 West 45th St., 33407 (tel. 305/689-0450).

Wildwood

Accommodations: Days Inn, I-75 and Fla. 44, Rte. 2, Box 65E, 32785 (tel. 904/748-2000).
- Econo Lodge, Rte. 2, Box 62, 32785 (tel. 904/748-2005).
- Red Carpet Inn, I-75, Exit 65, P.O. Box 159, 32785 (tel. 904/748-4488).
- Red Carpet Inn, I-75 and S.R. 44, Exit 66, P.O. Box 939, 32785 (tel. 904/748-1133).

Winter Haven

Accommodations: Budget Host—Banyan Beach Motel, 1630 6th St. NW, 33880. (tel. 813/293-3658).
- Red Carpet Inn, 2000 Cypress Gardens Blvd., S.R. 540, 33880 (tel. 813/324-6334).
- Scottish Inn, 3525 U.S. Hwy. 17 North, 33880 (tel. 813/294-2804).

Winter Park

On Campus: In this "charming, small town next to Orlando in Central Florida," you'll find Rollins College, the oldest private institution of higher learning in Florida. The center of life on campus is in the Student Center and right outside the Center and the Rose Skillman Dining Hall, there's a bulletin board where rides, apartments, and other available commodities are listed. To meet students, try Decades, Two Flights Up, East India Ice Cream Parlor, and The Olive Garden, all on Park Avenue. Right on campus you can visit the Cornell Art Gallery and the Beall-Maltbie Shell Museum.

Accommodation: Days Inn, I-4 & Lee Road, 650 Lee Rd., 32810 (tel. 305/628-2727).

Georgia

The image of the Deep South just doesn't jibe with what goes on in its most popular city, Atlanta, however much of the countryside retains a traditional Southern personality.

The tourist office people have recently mounted a campaign to entice visitors their way, and they've divided Georgia into eight travel regions, each with its own brochure, listing sights, information resources, and more. Georgia's mountains include Chickamauga Battlefield, scene of one of the Civil War's bloodiest battles, and many outdoor attractions. The Classic South includes hundreds of antebellum mansions, the Cotton Exchange Building and the Old Slave Market Column in Augusta, and the preserved home of Alexander H. Stephens, vice-president of the Confederacy, in Crawfordsville. The Colonial Coast is where you'll find the city of Savannah and the vast and intriguing Okefenokee Swamp. Historic Heartland is the center of the state which includes the city of Macon and its restored Grand Opera House and 24-room Renaissance Hay House and Ocmulgee National Monument, the largest archeological restoration of ancient Indian civilization in the East. The Presidential Pathways area is home of two U.S. Presidents, Jimmy Carter and Franklin D. Roosevelt. Plantation Trace designates the southwest corner with its large quail and hunting preserves and native roses and pine. Magnolia Midlands, in southeast Georgia, echoes with memories of the Civil War, sprinkled with three state parks and rivers and lakes for outdoor pleasures. And finally, what the tourist people call the Big "A," with Atlanta at its hub.

Some recommended guidebooks include Rand McNally's *Atlanta Getaway*

Guide (what to do within a 200 mile radius of Atlanta), edited by Mike Michaelson ($7.95); *A Guide to the Georgia Coast,* by the Georgia Conservancy (1984, $10); and *Sojourn in Savannah,* by Betty Ravers and Franklin Traub, Sojourn in Savannah, 134 E. 45th St., Savannah, GA 31405 ($3.75).

Some Special Events: St. Patrick's Day (March 17) in Savannah, Oktoberfest in Helen, Arts Festival of Atlanta, Cherry Blossom Festival (March) in Macon, Rose Festival (April 18–23) in Thomasville, Praters Mill County Fair (twice a year in May and September) in Dalton, National Pecan Festival (third weekend in October) in Albany, and Dogwood Festival (April 9–17) in Atlanta.

Tourist Information: Tourist Division, Georgia Department of Industry and Trade, P.O. Box 1776, Atlanta, GA 30301 (tel. 404/656-3590). Ask for their information book, "Georgia on My Mind".

Adel

Accommodations: Econo Lodge, I-75, Exit 10, and West 4th St., 31620 (tel. 912/896-4574).

● Comfort Inn, I-75, Exit 10, and S.R. 37, 31620 (tel. 912/896-4523, or toll free 800/228-5150).

● Quality Inn, I-75, Exit 10, and 1103 West 4th St., 31620 (tel. 912/896-2244, or toll free 800/228-5151).

Albany

Accommodations: Motel 6, 301 South Thornton Dr., 31705 (tel. 912/439-0078).

● Super 8 Motel, 2444 N. Slappey Blvd., 31707 (tel. 912/888-8388).

Arabi

Accommodation: Red Carpet Inn, I-75 and Arabi Rd., Exit 30, 31712 (tel. 912/273-8586).

Ashburn

Accommodation: Quality Inn, I-75 and Ashburn-Amboy Exit 29, P.O. Box 806, 31714 (tel. 912/567-3334).

Athens

On Campus: A friend at the University of Georgia describes Athens as a "serene and ruggedly beautiful southern town with very hospitable people." Athens and the surrounding areas are rich in Civil War history, particularly

Madison, "the town Sherman would not burn," and the many pre-Civil War plantations that still stand.

Accommodations: Days Inn, 2741 Atlanta Hwy., 30606 (tel. 404/546-9750).
- Scottish Inn, 410 Macon Hwy., 30606 (tel. 404/546-8161).
- Red Carpet Inn, 2715 Atlanta Hwy., 30606 (tel. 404/549-1530).

Atlanta

"This city is cosmopolitan, alive, friendly, slower-paced than many other big cities, and less conservative than other areas of the South."

Atlanta started out as a railroad worker's camp right near today's Omni International Complex. The camp was called "The Terminus," and one civil engineer at the time noted that the place had little future. Atlanta is now home to 2.2 million people, a veritable boomtown American-style. The phoenix is the symbol of Atlanta, commemorating the city's amazing resurrection after General Sherman put it to the torch. That was in 1864, when eight out of every nine homes were burned. Who can ever forget the scene of a burning Atlanta in Margaret Mitchell's *Gone with the Wind*?

Much of the old Atlanta is disappearing and being replaced with new highrise offices and hotels. You can still find evidence of the "Old South" atmosphere, however, in Atlanta's many older neighborhoods, such as Inman Park and Midtown. Of particular interest to visitors are tours offered by the Atlanta Preservation Center, 404/522-4345, and by the Georgia Department of Natural Resources, 404/656-3530, or trips to one of the parks of Atlanta (Stone Mountain Park with its famous Easter Sunrise Service, 404/498-5600; Chattahoochee Recreation Center, 404/952-4419). On the more cosmopolitan side, Atlanta has great shopping centers (Lenox Square is probably the best), the High Museum, and many theaters for plays or movies.

In the '80s Atlanta is thriving. The city celebrates itself several times a year. In the summer, Atlanta has a "Concerts in the Park" series at Piedmont Park, during which the Atlanta Symphony Orchestra gives free outdoor concerts (ASO Box Office Information, 404/892-2414). In the fall they have the Piedmont Arts Festival, during which the park is full of local arts and crafts persons selling their wares, as well as a varied schedule of musicians. In the spring there is the dogwood festival in late March-early April, which is a tour of the city under blooming dogwood trees. There is also the Renaissance Festival (404/964-8575—admission $8 for adults and $4 for children 5–12 years old) during the month of May, and the Inman Park Festival of Homes in late April.

To find out what's happening and when, check the "Weekender" supplement to the Saturday *Atlanta Constitution and Journal,* and on Sunday, its Arts and Entertainment section; *Creative Loafing,* an alternative newspaper; *Southline,* a weekly on arts and political events; and the monthly *Atlanta Magazine.* For a useful guidebook to the city see *A Marmac Guide to Atlanta,* by William Schemmel and Marge McDonald, Pelican Publishing Co. ($7.95).

Getting There: From the Airport: Hartsfield International Airport, with the largest passenger terminal complex in the world, is about eight miles from the city. You can get from the airport to town on MARTA (Metropolitan Atlanta Rapid Transit Authority) Bus 300 "Airport Express" to Lakewood subway station where you take the train to Five Points station (downtown) or North Avenue station on the North/South line or Inman Park station on the East/West line. A taxi from the airport will cost $14 to $25. The Atlanta Airport Shuttle has regular service to the downtown and metropolitan area from 6 a.m. to 1 a.m.; the ride costs $7 one way and $12 round trip to downtown, $10 one way and $15 round trip to midtown. For shuttle information, call 404/524-2400. For the Northside Shuttle call 404/952-1601. The fare is $10 one way, $17.75 round trip to the northern part of town. They have guided tours, too!

● From the Bus Stations: The Greyhound Terminal is at 81 International Blvd., right behind the Peachtree Center area (tel. 404/522-6300); Trailways is at 200 Spring St. (tel. 404/524-2441).

Getting Around: Atlanta streets follow old rail rights-of-way and cow paths; no symmetrical grid-like pattern here. The city is divided into quadrants, which come together at the junction of Peachtree Street, Edgewood Avenue, and Marietta-Decatur Streets.

● MARTA is constructing a rapid rail system (see those "MARTA at Work" signs). MARTA bus and train fares are 75¢. Call 404/522-4711 for MARTA information. The train station is on Peachtree near I-75/I-85 (tel. toll free 800/872-7245). Taxis cost $1 plus $1 per mile, with 50¢ extra for each additional passenger. Call Checker Cab at 404/525-5466. For car rentals, Budget Car Rental offers the best deal, 404/530-3000.

Tourist Information: Atlanta Convention and Visitors Bureau, 233 Peachtree St. NW, Suite 200, 30343 (tel. 404/521-6600).

Help: Travelers Aid, 40 Pryor St., 30303 (tel. 404/527-7400).

● Emergency Mental Health Services, 404/522-9222.

● Centers for Disease Control, 404/329-2888.

Accommodations: Bed & Breakfast Atlanta, 1801 Piedmont Ave., Suite 208, 30324 (tel. 404/875-0525, 9 a.m. to noon and 2 p.m. to 5 p.m. Monday through Friday). $24 to $36 single; $28 to $40 double. Price includes continental breakfast. Advance reservations necessary.

● Alamo Plaza Motel, 2370 Stewart Ave. SW, 30315 (tel.404/767-1521). On MARTA routes nos. 19 & 41. $32.75 single or double.

● Georgian Motel, √, 4300 Buford Hwy., 30329 (tel. 404/636-4344). Accessible from downtown on MARTA bus 44, 65, or 130. $25 single or double.

● Best Way Inn, √ (10%), 144 14th St. NW, 30318 (tel. 404/873-4171). Six blocks from Georgia Tech to the southwest and Piedmont Park to the east. $34 single; $36 double.

● YMCA, 22 Butler St. NE, 30303 (tel. 404/659-8085). Men only. $13.54 single without bath.

● Motel 6, 4427 Commerce Dr., 30344 (tel. 404/762-5201).

● Motel 6, 4100 Wendell Dr. SW, 30336 (tel. 404/696-0757).

● Scottish Inn, 1848 Howell Mill Rd., 30318 (tel. 404/351-1220).

● Red Carpet Inn, 4552 Old Dixie Hwy., Forest Park, 30050 (tel. 404/363-4250).

● Atlanta Motel, 277 Moreland Ave., 30316 (tel. 404/659-2455). $30 single or double.

● Scottish Inn/Six Flags, 4430 Frederick Dr. SW, 30336 (tel. 404/691-6310).

● Flag View Motel, √ ★, Hwy. 6 & I-20, Exit 12, Austell, 30001 (tel. 404/941-6600). Weekdays: $24 single; $28 double. Weekends: $30 single; $40 double.

- Scottish Inn, 3118 Sylvan Ave. at I-85 and Sylvan Road, 30354 (tel. 404/762-8801).
- Red Carpet Inn, 1360 Virginia Ave., 30344 (tel. 404/761-5201).
- Days Inn, I-75 Frontage Rd. and Farmer's Market, Forest Park, 30050 (tel. 404/363-0800).
- Days Inn, 2788 Forest Hills Dr., 30315 (tel. 404/768-7750).
- Dogwood Motel, 5140 Buford Hwy., Doraville, 30340 (tel. 404/457-7246). $28.96 for single or double.
- Red Roof Inn, I-75 and Windy Hill Exit 110, 2200 Corporate Plaza, Smyrna, 30080 (tel. 404/952-6966).
- Red Roof Inn, I-285, I-85 and Old National Hwy., Exit 16, College Park, 30349 (tel. 404/761-9701).
- Red Roof Inn, I-85 and Druid Hills, 1960 North Druid Hills Rd., 30329 (tel. 404/321-1653).
- Red Roof Inn, I-20 and Fulton Industrial Blvd., Exit 14, 4265 Shirley Dr. SW, 30336 (tel. 404/696-4391).
- Red Roof Inn, I-75 and S.R. 54, Exit 76, 1348 South Lake Plaza Dr., Morrow, 30260 (tel. 404/968-1483).
- Pinetree Motel, 2533 McClave Dr. and Buford Hwy., Doraville-Atlanta, 30345 (tel. 404/451-4700). $27 single; $30 double.

Where to Eat: Mary Mac's, 224 Ponce de Leon Ave. NE (tel. 404/876-6604). About ten minutes by car from Peachtree Plaza. Family-style downhome cooking in just the right atmosphere. Country-fried steak, two vegetables, and dessert costs $5 to $6 at dinnertime.

- Eat Your Vegetables Cafe, 438 Moreland Ave. (tel. 404/523-2671). Good vegetarian food as well as chicken and fish dinners. Salads are great! Try the house tofu dressing. Lunch: $3 to $5. Dinner: $6 to $10. Open Monday through Saturday, 11 a.m. to 10 p.m., later on weekends.
- The Mansion, 179 Ponce de Leon Ave. NE, (tel. 404/876-0727). An unusual and charming restaurant in an old Victorian house surrounded by trees. Lunch is about $6 to $10; dinner from $10 to $20.
- Capo's Cafe, 992 Virginia Ave. NE (tel. 404/876-5655). Large menu includes chicken salad nora (chunks of chicken, apples, walnuts, and raisins with a curry cream dressing, $6.25; scallops Parisienne, $8.95; fettuccine Alfredo, $5.95; and the house specialty, chicken diable, $9.75. "One of the least expensive good restaurants around."
- Cha Gio Vietnamese Restaurant, 998 Peachtree St. NE (tel. 404/876-1817). This unimposing downtown restaurant has a friendly atmosphere, good Oriental food, and lots of followers. A substantial dinner for two of spring rolls, soup, pork fried rice, garlic beef, and broccoli and chicken, flan, and tea is only $12. Lunch: $3 to $6. Dinner: $5 to $12.
- Tortillas, 752 Ponce de Leon (tel. 404/892-3493). Open 11:30 a.m. to 9:30 p.m. Monday to Thursday, until 10 p.m. Friday and Saturday, and closed Sunday. Very good vegetarian and Mexican food and nice artsy-type people who own the place. Average meal—$3.50.
- The Majestic, 1031 Ponce de Leon (tel. 404/875-0276). A landmark in Atlanta, the Majestic is an old diner which serves very cheap food 24 hours a day—situated in the bohemian side of town.
- Max's Stage Door, 654 Peachtree (tel. 404/881-0223). Open 11:30 a.m. to 11 p.m. Monday to Saturday, noon to 4 p.m. on Sunday. In the same building as

the Fox Theater, Max's offers a good dinner before or after a show—they also have a very good and inexpensive brunch on Saturday and Sunday. An interesting Art Deco atmosphere.

- Atkins Park, 794 N. Highland Ave. (tel. 404/876-7249). Open 11 a.m. to 11 p.m., until 4 a.m. on the weekends. Meals in the $5 to $7 range. Famous for its great location and for its delicious brunches. This is also a neighborhood restaurant frequented by the locals.

What to See and Do: For tickets: Seats, 404/577-2626, at many locations including any Turtles Record Store; and Tic-x-press, 404/252-9191, at many locations.

- Stone Mountain Park. About 16 miles east of Atlanta. A 3200-acre park complete with museums, skylift, riverboat, scenic railroad, campground, and more. MARTA bus marked "120 Stone Mountain" from the Avondale rail station will get you there.
- Six Flags Over Georgia, 7561 Six Flags Rd., Mableton, 30059, 15 minutes from downtown Atlanta (tel. 404/948-9290). A family entertainment park with 100 rides, shows, and attractions. Open weekends during the fall and spring, daily from May 20 to September 1. Accessible from downtown by MARTA rail and bus: take rail line to Hightower Station and from there take bus marked "201 Six Flags." The trip costs $1.25 plus 60¢ rail fare each way; a one-price ticket to Six Flags costs $16 and entitles you to all rides and most shows.
- Toy Museum of Atlanta, 2800 Peachtree St. (tel. 404/266-8697). Antique toys and dolls dating from the 1850s. $2 adults; $1.50 children 6 to 12.
- Martin Luther King Historic District. This two-block area includes King's birthplace, the Ebenezer Baptist Church where he preached, and Dr. King's gravesite. Information center for the area is on the tour site; further information available by calling 404/524-1956.
- Grant Park and Atlanta Zoo, Boulevard Avenue, SE (tel. 404/658-6374 or 658-7059). The largest reptile collection in the country. $2.50 adults; $1.25 for children 4 to 11.
- Fernbank Science Center, 156 Heaton Park Dr., Decatur (tel. 404/378-4311). Science exhibits, botanical gardens, 65-acre forest with two miles of walking trails, and the third-largest planetarium in the U.S. Museum admission is free; planetarium is $2 for adults, $1 for students.
- Wren's Nest, 1050 Gordon St. (tel. 404/753-8535). Once the home of Joel Chandler Harris, creator of the Uncle Remus stories, with some of the original furniture on display. $2.50 adults; $1.25 teens; 75¢ children; $2 seniors.
- Woodruff Arts Center, 1280 Peachtree St. NE (tel. 404/892-3600). Home of the High Museum of Art, the Atlanta Symphony Orchestra, and the Alliance Theater.
- For sports: The Omni is a large stadium with sports events of all kinds, 100 Techwood Dr. Ticket information, 404/577-2626. The Atlanta Braves play baseball at the Atlanta-Fulton County Stadium. Call SEATS for tickets.

At Night: For jazz: Walter Mitty's, 816 N. Highland Ave. (tel. 404/876-7127). Open weeknights until 2 a.m., Friday until 4 a.m., and until 3 a.m. on Saturday. A very nice jazz bar and restaurant; The Point, 420 Moreland Ave. A neighborhood bar in Little Five Points, a diverse and exciting neighborhood; Dantes Down the Hatch, 3380 Peachtree Rd. (tel. 404/266-1600).

- To dance: Limelight, 3330 Piedmont Rd. (tel. 404/231-3520). An entertainment complex which includes disco and a screening room; Club Rio, 195 Luckie

St. (tel. 404/525-7467). Open until 3 a.m. A varied club of 3 levels—discotheque on the lower level, an outside bar, and an upstairs Latin dance floor.

● For folk music: Country Cork Pub, 56 E. Andrews Dr. (tel. 404/262-2227). Open 9 p.m. to 2 a.m. Specializes in Irish and Scottish music.

● For classical music: Atlanta Symphony Orchestra—Woodruff Arts Center, 1280 Peachtree St. (tel. 404/892-2412).

● For modern dance/ballet: Dancers Collective Theater, 1105 Euclid Ave. (tel. 404/659-3267).

● For dinner or drinks and a film: Buckhead Cinema 'n' Drafthouse, 3110 Roswell Rd. NE (tel. 404/231-5811).

● For films: Toco Hills, 2983 North Druid Hills Rd. (tel. 404/636-1858). 99¢ at all times.

● For theater: Academy Theater, corner of 11th St. and Juniper in Midtown (tel. 404/892-0880); Alliance Theater, 1280 Peachtree St., in the Woodruff Arts Center, next to High Museum (tel. 404/892-2414).

Shopping: Atlantans love shopping! Check out Lenox Square at 3393 Peachtree Rd. NE, and the Virginia Highlands Area.

● For books: Oxford Books, 2345 Peachtree St., in Peachtree Battle Shopping Center (tel. 404/262-3332). A huge bookstore with a coffeeshop upstairs.

● Oxford, Too, 2395 Peachtree St. (tel. 404/262-3411). Great selection of used and discounted books.

● McGuires Books, 1055 Ponce de Leon (tel. 404/875-7323). New books, good poetry, art and fiction section.

● For records: Wax and Facts, 432 Moreland Ave. (tel. 404/525-2275). Used records, "new music," new records and tapes.

● Metronome Records, Monroe Drive (tel. 404/888-9800). Great selection of classical music, as well as all other types.

● Turtle's Records and Tapes, 3337 Buford Hwy. NE and other locations (tel. 404/663-2539). More records and tapes at discount.

● For sporting goods: Blue Ridge Mountain Sports, Ltd., Lenox Square Shopping Center. (tel. 404/266-8372). Sells all kinds of outdoor equipment and rents backpacking and canoeing equipment.

● Britches Great Outdoors, in Lenox Square (tel. 404/262-1621). Camping equipment.

● Old Sarge Army-Navy Surplus Store, 5316 Buford Hwy., Doraville (tel. 404/451-6031) and three other locations. All kinds of surplus outdoor gear.

● For clothing: Marshall's, in the mall at Buford Highway and Clairmont Road. (tel. 404/329-0200). All kinds of name-brand clothing at substantial discounts.

Augusta

Accommodations: Econo Lodge, 906 Molly Pond Rd., 30901 (tel. 404/722-6841).

● Econo Lodge, 3034 Washington Rd., 30907 (tel. 404/860-8485).

● Hampton Inn, 3030 Washington Rd., 30907 (tel. 404/737-1122).

● Knights Inn, I-20 at Washington Road, 210 Boyscout Rd., 30909 (tel. 404/737-3166).

● Uptowner Inn, 801 Reynolds St., 30902 (tel. 404/722-5361). $35 single or double. Higher rates apply in April.

Austell

Accommodation: Knights Inn, I-20 at Thornton Road, 1595 Blair Bridge Rd., 30001 (tel. 404/944-0824).

Brunswick

Help: Crisis Line, 912/264-7311.
Accommodations: Hostel in the Forest (AYH), U.S. Hwy. 84, P.O. Box 1496, 31521 (tel. 912/264-9738). Call for ride to hostel between 8 a.m. and 8 p.m. for $2. $5 for AYH members; $6 for nonmembers. "Housing in two geodesic domes and two tree houses situated on 90 acres of Georgia forest."
● Budgetel Inn, 105 Tourist Dr., 31520 (tel. 912/265-7725).
● Days Inn, 409 New Jesup Hwy., 31520 (tel. 912/264-4330).
● Knights Inn, I-95, Exit 7-A at U.S. Hwy. 341, 31520 (tel. 912/267-6500).
● Super 8 Motel, 472 Jesup Hwy., 31520 (tel. 912/264-8800).

Byron

Accommodations: Scottish Inn, I-75 and S.R. 49, 31008 (tel. 912/956-5100).
● Red Carpet Inn, I-75, Exit 45, Rte. 3, Box 114-X, 31008 (tel. 912/956-3800).

Calhoun

Accommodations: Budget Host—Shepherd Motel, Jct. I-75 and S.R. 53, 30701 (tel. 404/629-8644).
● Scottish Inn, I-75, Exit 130, 30701 (tel. 404/629-8261).
● Red Carpet Inn, I-75, Exit 129, Rte. 5, Box 167, 30701 (tel. 404/629-9501).
● Days Inn, I-75 and Ga. 53, Rte. 6, 30701 (tel. 404/629-8271).

Cartersville

Accommodations: Days Inn, I-75 and Cassville-White Road, P.O. Box 1088, 30120 (tel. 404/386-0350).
● Super 8 Motel, Rte. 294 and Rte. 20, 30120 (tel. 404/382-8881).
● Quality Inn, U.S. 41 and Dixie Avenue, P.O. Box 158, 30120 (tel. 404/386-0510).

Chula

Accommodation: Red Carpet Inn, I-75 at Brookfield Road, Exit 23, 31733 (tel. 912/382-2686).

Clarksville

Accommodation: LaPrade's Cabins, Restaurant and Marina, Rte. 1, Hwy. 197, 30523 (tel. 404/947-3312). Open April 1 to December 1. $26 per person (includes three meals). Rustic mountain fisherman cabins accommodate one to ten people. Advance reservations of two weeks necessary. Closed on Wednesdays.

Columbus

Accommodations: Motel 6, 3050 Victory Dr., 31903 (tel. 404/687-7214).
- Budgetel Inn, 2919 Warm Springs Rd., 31097 (tel. 404/323-4344).
- Hampton Inn, 5585 Whitesville Rd., 31904 (tel. 404/576-5303).
- Super 8 Motel, 2935 Warm Springs Rd., 31907 (tel. 404/322-6580).

Commerce

Accommodation: Quality Inn, I-85 and U.S. 441, 30529 (tel. 404/335-5581).

Conyers

Accommodation: Knights Inn, I-20 at West Avenue, 1297 Dogwood Ave., 30207 (tel. 404/483-1332).

Cordele

Accommodation: Days Inn, I-75 and Tremont Road, P.O. Box 736, 31015 (tel. 912/273-6161).

Dalton

Accommodations: Quinton Inn, 1407 Chattanooga Rd., 30720 (tel. 404/278-3693). $20.55 single; $22.83 for two in one bed; $24.91 for two in two beds. Children under 12 stay free.
- Best Inns of America, 1529 W. Walnut Ave., I-75, Exit 136 (tel. 404/226-1100).

Douglas

Accommodation: Super 8 Motel, Hwy. 221 South, 31533 (tel. 912/384-0886).

Eulonia/Townsend/North Brunswick

Accommodation: Days Inn, I-95 and Ga. 99, P.O. Box 156, 31331 (tel. 912/832-4411).

Folkston

Accommodation: Red Carpet Inn, 1201 South Second St., 31537 (tel. 912/496-2514).

Forsyth

Accommodations: Days Inn, I-75 and Ga. 42, Box 714, 31029 (tel. 912/994-5168).
- Hampton Inn, I-75 at Tift College Drive, 31029 (tel. 912/994-9697).
- Quality Inn, I-75 and S.R. 83, Exit 62, 55 North Dr., 31029 (tel. 912/994-5161).

Gainesville

Accommodation: Days Inn, U.S. 129 and Ga. 985, P.O. Drawer CC, 30503 (tel. 404/532-7531).

Hahira

Accommodation: Days Inn, I-75 and Ga. 122, Rt. 2, Box 14, 31632 (tel. 912/794-3000).

Jekyll Island

Accommodation: Days Inn, 60 South Beachview Dr., 31520 (tel. 912/635-3319).

Kingsland

Accommodation: Super 8 Motel, 60 South off Boone Avenue, P.O. Box 2247, 31548 (tel. 912/729-6888).

Locust Grove

Accommodations: Scottish Inn, I-75, Exit 68, 4679 Hampton-Locust Grove Rd., 30248 (tel. 404/957-9001).
- Red Carpet Inn, I-75, Exit 68, P.O. Box 613, 30248 (tel. 404/957-2936).

Macon

Accommodations: Red Carpet Inn, I-475 at U.S. 80, 4606 Chambers Rd., 31206 (tel. 912/781-2810).
- Hampton Inn, 3680 Riverside Dr., 31204 (tel. 912/471-0660).
- Scottish Inn, I-475 at U.S. 80, 4952 Romeiser, 31206 (tel. 912/474-1661).
- Days Inn, 4295 Pio Nono Ave., 31206 (tel. 912/788-8910).
- Motel 6, 4991 Harrison Rd., 31206 (tel. 912/474-2870).

Madison

Accommodation: Quality Inn, I-20 and U.S. 441, 30650 (tel. 404/342-1839).

McDonough

Accommodations: Red Carpet Inn, I-75 and S.R. 81, Exit 70, P.O. Box 477, 30253 (tel. 404/957-5821).
- Days Inn, 1311 McDonough Rd., Box 761, 30253 (tel. 404/957-5818).

Milledgeville

Accommodation: Days Inn, 3001 Heritage Rd. NW, 31061 (tel. 912/453-3551).

Moultrie

Accommodation: Red Carpet Inn, 600 South Main St., 31768 (tel. 912/985-3980).

Perry

Accommodation: Scottish Inn, I-75 and U.S. 341, Exit 3, 704 Mason Terrace, 31069 (tel. 912/987-1515).

Rome

Accommodation: Super 8 Motel, 1590 Dodd Blvd., SE, 30161 (tel. 404/234-8182).

Sautee

Accommodation: The Stovall House, ⑤★ &, Hwy. 255, Rte. 1, Box 152, 30571. (tel. 404/878-3355). Transport from bus station available with prior notice only. $36.50 single; $65 double; $67.50 triple; $80 quad. Includes continental breakfast. Advance reservations of two months in fall and one month any other time necessary. Sunday through Thursday nights: 10% discount for ISIC holders. "Provide guests with a relaxing 'country experience' in the cozy surroundings of an historical house."

Savannah

Tourist Information: Savannah Visitors Convention Bureau, 222 W. Oglethorpe Ave., 31499 (tel. 912/944-0456). Free 12-minute slide show, literature, and tour information to give you an idea of what to see. Open every day.

Help: Travelers Aid, 912/236-4241.

Accommodations: Bed & Breakfast Inn, c/o Robert McAlister, Ⓢ(10%), 117 Gordon St. West at Chatham Square, 31401 (tel. 912/238-0518). Walking distance to bus station and waterfront. "1853 town house in the historic district." $30 single; $38 double. Price includes a full breakfast.

● Budget Inn, Ⓢ(10%), 3702 Ogeechee Rd., 31405 (tel. 912/233-3633). All rooms $26.95 one or two people; suites $34.95 one or two people. Cherokee Restaurant and Waffle House are right next door).

● Budgetel Inn, 8484 Abercorn St., 31406 (tel. 912/927-7660).

● Econo Lodge, 7500 Abercorn St., 31406 (tel. 912/352-1657).

● Econo Lodge, I-95 and U.S. 17, P.O. Box 47, Richmond Hill, 31324 (tel. 912/756-3312).

● Knights Inn, 5711 Abercorn St., 31402 (tel. 912/354-0434).

● TraveLodge, 512 West Oglethorpe Ave., 31401 (tel. 912/233-9251).

● Motel 6, I-95 and U.S. Hwy. 17, Exit 14, Richmond Hill, 31324 (tel. 912/756-3543).

Statesboro

Accommodation: Master Hosts Inn, 461 South Main St., 30458 (tel. 912/764-5666).

Thomasville

Accommodation: Days Inn, U.S. 19 Bypass & U.S. 319, 31792 (tel. 912/226-6025).

Tifton

Accommodations: Days Inn, I-75 and U.S. 82, Exit 18, P.O. Box 1310, Virginia Avenue, 31793 (tel. 912/382-8100).

● Scottish Inn, P.O. Box 1087, I-75 and U.S. 82 West, 31794 (tel. 912/386-2350).

● Quality Inn, I-75, Exit 19 and Second Street, 31794 (tel. 912/386-2100).

● Carson Motel, √, 309 West 7th St., 31794 (tel. 912/382-3111). $16 to $17 single; $18 to $20 for two in one bed; $21 to $22 for two in two beds.

● Red Carpet Inn, 1025 West 2nd St., 31794 (tel. 912/382-0280).

Unadilla

Accommodation: Days Inn, I-75 and U.S. 41, Exit 39, P.O. Box 405, 31091 (tel. 912/627-3211).

Valdosta/Lake Park

Accommodations: Days Inn, I-75 and U.S. 84 W., P.O. Box 911, 31603 (tel. 912/247-2440).

- Budget Host—Azalea City Motel, 2015 West Hill Ave., Box 644, 31601 (tel. 912/244-4350 or 244-4647).
- Motel 6, 2003 West Hill Ave., 31601 (tel. 912/333-0047).
- Scottish Inn, 2525 North Ashley St., Hwy. 41 North, 31602 (tel. 912/242-7676).
- Quality Inn, I-75 and S.R. 94, Exit 5, 31601 (tel. 912/244-8510).
- Quality Inn, 1902 West Hill Ave., 31601 (tel. 912/244-4520).
- Comfort Inn, I-75, Exit 6 and North Valdosta Road, 31602 (tel. 912/244-4460, or toll free 800/228-5150).

Warner Robins

Accommodation: Super 8 Motel, 105 Woodcrest Blvd., 31093 (tel. 912/923-8600).

Waycross

Accommodations: Days Inn, 2016 Memorial Dr., U.S. 1 South, 31501 (tel. 912/285-4700).
- Super 8 Motel, 132 Havanna Ave., 31501 (tel. toll free 800/843-1991).

Hawaii

James Michener calls the islands of Hawaii "unbelievably beautiful. They rise from the sea like a strand of pearls, each one with its own peculiar beauty, yet all suffused with the same grace and charm." Mark Twain called them "the loveliest fleet of islands that lies anchored in any sea." The state of Hawaii, 2,000 miles west of California, is actually a cluster of islands and Hawaii is only one of these islands. The other largest ones are Kauai, Oahu (where Honolulu is), Molokai, Lanai, and Maui. Downtown Honolulu is a busy city with typical urban problems, but beyond it the island is not heavily populated and is characterized by mountains, volcanoes, tropical foliage, sandy beaches, and rocky coast.

Because Hawaii is so far away from the mainland, air fares to and from it may be high depending on the ever-changing airline picture: check for inexpensive hotel-air packages before you go.

One friend suggests that you do what she did for six months: "Get a camping permit at Oahu's Department of Parks and Recreation, 650 South King St., rent camping equipment if you don't have your own (the Visitors Bureau will supply names and addresses), and camp around the island. The weather is always good, between 69 and 90 degrees . . . and as long as you renew your permit every two weeks you can go on like this forever."

There are more than 50 parks, most of which are public, located at the water's edge, high on the slopes and some are even inside a crater! Camping is very popular so make your reservations early.

"Hawaii's a great place, but don't be fooled into expecting a paradise or utopia."

A good guide to the islands is *Hawaii on $50 a Day*, by Faye Hammel and Sylvan Levey, Prentice Hall Press ($11.95). Another is *Hidden Hawaii: The Adventurer's Guide*, by Ray Riegert, published by Ulysses Press, Box 4000-H, Berkeley, CA 94704 ($12.95). The book, which includes history as well as travel information, is special because it takes the reader behind the flashy facade of

Hawaii and back to the parks, trails, campsites, beaches, and volcanoes. *The Maverick Guide to Hawaii* is written by a local author, Bob Bone, Pelican Publishing ($11.95).

Some Special Events: Buffalo's Annual Big Board Surfing Classic in Makaha Beach, Oahu (late February, early March); Prince Kuhio Festival in Lihue, Kauai, and Prince Kohio Day in Honolulu, Oahu (March); May Day/Lei Day Celebration in Wailea, Maui (April); Lei Day in Honolulu, Oahu, and Western Week in Honokaa, Hawaii (May); Annual Festival of the Pacific in Honolulu, Oahu, and King Kamehameha Celebration on all islands (June); Annual Hilo Orchid Society Show, and International Festival of the Pacific, both in Hilo, Hawaii (July); Hula Festival in Honolulu, Oahu, and Macademia Nut Harvest Festival in Honokaa, Hawaii (August); Aloha Week Festivals on all islands (September); Annual Waimea Falls Makahiki Festival (October).

Tourist Information: Hawaii Visitors Bureau, Waikiki Business Plaza, 2270 Kalakaua Ave., Honolulu, HI 96815 (tel. 808/923-1811). On the mainland, there are branch offices in Chicago, Los Angeles, New York, and San Francisco. The Visitors Bureau has prepared driving itineraries of each island describing sights and including distances and driving times. Their *Accommodation Guide* includes everything from resorts and condominiums to motels, cabins and B&B's. Camping, by tent or cabin, is detailed in a special "Fact Sheet."

N.B. For a bed-and-breakfast reservation service, try Bed & Breakfast International. A double, breakfast included, is $40 to $60; the minimum stay is three nights. For an application, write to the organization at 151 Ardmore Rd., Kensington, CA 94707, and enclose a stamped, self-addressed envelope, or telephone 415/525-4569. Another service is Bed and Breakfast Hawaii, Box 449, Kapaa, HI 96746 (tel. 808/822-7771).

Honolulu, Oahu

Ray Riegert, the author of *Hidden Hawaii* (see first page of this section) has written a book on Honolulu called, not surprisingly, *Hidden Honolulu*. A pocket-size guide, the book covers everything from the good life to the great outdoors—both of which exist in abundance in Honolulu, according to the author.

Tourist Information: Hawaii Visitors Bureau, 2270 Kalakaua Ave., 96815 (tel. 808/923-1811).

Help: Information and Referral, 808/521-4566.
● Suicide and Crisis Center, 808/521-4555.

"Try to get out of the city and into the rural areas—great scenery!"

Accommodations: Fernhurst YWCA, 1566 Wilder Ave., 96822 (tel. 808/941-2231). Women only, over 18. $18 plus linen charge and key deposit of $5 for room shared with one other person and bath shared with two others (dorm style). Lesser rate for YWCA members. Includes breakfast and dinner Monday through Saturday. City bus stops nearby and goes to Waikiki and the U. of Hawaii.
● YMCA, 401 Atkinson Dr., 96814 (tel. 808/941-3344). Men only. $17 single without bath; $20 with bath. Call from airport to see if there is a room.

Coffeeshop in building; restaurants in Ala Moana Shopping Center across the street.

- Honolulu International Youth Hostel (AYH), 2323A Seaview Ave., 96822 (tel. 808/946-0591). Open year round. Open 7 a.m. to 9 a.m. and from 4:30 p.m. to 9 p.m. $7 per night for AYH members; $10 for nonmembers. Advance reservations necessary; send stamped, self-addressed envelope and one night's deposit (money order or bank draft) for reservation. Near bus stop. "City bus system an excellent way to sightsee."
- Hale Aloha Hostel, 2417 Prince Edward St., 96815 (tel. 808/946-0591). Open 8 a.m. to 10 a.m. and from 5 p.m. to 8 p.m. $9 per night for AYH/IYHF members only. A few studios available for $21 per night. Advance reservations necessary. Send a self-addressed stamped envelope and one night's deposit (money or bank draft). In the heart of Waikiki—near the beach and busline.

"Don't expect to live on the beach or in any free housing. Jobs are difficult to find. Living expenses are very high. Don't carry expensive jewelry or large amounts of cash."

Keanae, Maui

Accommodation: Camp Keanae Maui YMCA (AYH), Box 820, Wailuku 96793 (tel. 808/244-3253). $5 for AYH members. Advance reservations of at least two weeks suggested. "We're thirty-two miles from the airport so we suggest you rent a car. Also buy food before arriving."

Kihei, Maui

Accommodation: Lihi-Kai Cottages and Apartments, 2121 Iliili Rd., 96753 (tel. 808/879-2335). $40 per studio per night; $43 per apartment and cottage per night for one or two persons; $8 per each extra person. Reservations necessary. Near beach and tennis courts.

Makawao, Maui

Camping: Haleakala National Park, P.O. Box 369, 96768 (tel. 808/572-9306). $3 entrance fee per vehicle; $1 for others on foot, bike, commercial vehicle, etc. Limit of three-night stay. Four undeveloped campgrounds and three primitive cabins. $5 per person per night, plus $2.50 per person per night firewood fee. Advance reservations of three months necessary for cabins. Accessible by horseback or on foot only; located in Haleakala Crater. "Haleakala weather can change rapidly, sometimes going through the entire temperature range within one day. January to late May or early June is generally considered the wet season; July to October the dry. Be prepared at any time of year for rain and cold wind."

Waimea, Kauai

Accommodation: Kokee Lodge, P.O. Box 819, 96796 (tel. 808/335-6061).

Cabins that sleep three to seven and come equipped with linens and kitchen supplies, hot showers, and fireplaces. $25 per cabin per night. Breakfast and lunch available in restaurant on premises. Advance reservations necessary with $25 deposit (refundable if cancellation is made at least two weeks prior to reservation date); send a stamped, self-addressed envelope for confirmation. "Located high in Hawaii's 4,345-acre Kokee State Park."

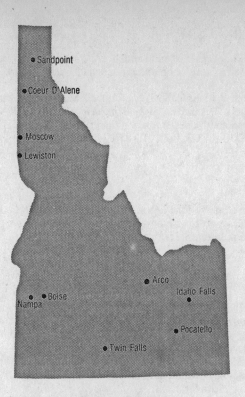

Idaho

We're convinced, having read through so many tourist office brochures, that there's one public relations man or woman who puts out the materials for all 50 states and just changes the name of the state to suit the latest client. Each claims that its state has it all, with "something for everyone," "a year-round playground," and "site of the Lewis and Clark expedition." In the case of Idaho it all happens to be true. There may not be many people in Idaho, but there certainly is a variety of landscape, sports opportunities from trailrides and rafting to skiing and backpacking, a chance to visit pioneer and Indian sites, and much more. The brochures don't fib. In central Idaho there's the Primitive Area where there are no roads, the Salmon River, and the Craters of the Moon National Monument (this is a weird and wild landscape where the astronauts trained for their moon walk). Northern Idaho has beautiful rivers, lakes, and mountains. In southeastern Idaho there are more mountains and rivers, plus an incredible combination of dry desert plains and rich farmland. The latest guidebook on the area is *Idaho for the Curious* by Cort Conley (Backeddy Books, Cambridge, ID).

Some Special Events: Salmon River Rodeo in Riggins (May); Old Timer's Celebration in Harrison, featuring a theater revue, dance, and parade, and Idaho State Square and Round Dance Festival (July); a Roundup in Lewiston, including a cowboy breakfast and a rodeo, and Labor Day Festival in Bellevue, which includes a parade, a shootout, oldtime fiddlers, and a barbecue (September).

Tourist Information: Idaho Travel Council, State Capitol Building, Room 108, Boise, ID 83720 (tel. 208/334-2470 or toll free 800/635-7820).

N.B. A bed-and-breakfast reservation service for the state is Bed & Breakfast Idaho, P.O. Box 7323, Boise, ID 83707 (tel. 208/336-5174).

Arco

Camping: Craters of the Moon National Monument, P.O. Box 29, 83213 (tel. 208/527-3257). At Lava Flow Campground you can camp from April 15 to October 15. $5 per campsite per night.

Boise

Help: Hotline, 208/345-7888 (7 to 11 p.m., Sunday to Thursday; 7 p.m. to 3 a.m. Friday and Saturday).
- Information and Referral, 208/378-0111 (during business hours).
- Emergency, 208/334-5474.
  Accommodations: Motel 6, 2323 Airport Way, 83705 (tel. 208/344-3506).
- Super 8 Motel, 2773 Elder St., 83705 (tel, 208/344-8871).
- TraveLodge, 1314 Grove St., 83702 (tel. 208/342-9351).
- Allstar Inn, 2275 Airport Way, 83705 (tel. 208/336-7788).

Coeur D'Alene

Accommodations: Motel 6, 416 Appleway, 83814 (tel. 208/664-6600).
- Comfort Inn, 280 W. Appleway, 83814 (tel. 208/765-5500).
- Days Inn, 2200 North West Blvd., 83814 (tel. 208/667-8668).
- Super 8 Motel, 505 W. Appleway, 83814 (tel. 208/765-8880).

Idaho Falls

Help: Information Referral Agency, 208/524-2433.
  Accommodations: Motel 6, 1448 West Broadway, 83401 (tel. 208/522-0112).
- Quality Inn Westbank, 475 River Pkwy., 83401 (tel. 208/523-8000).
- Super 8 Motel, 705 Lindsay Blvd., 83401 (tel. 208/522-8880).

Lewiston

Accommodation: Super 8 Motel, 3120 North South Hwy., 83501 (tel. 208/743-8808).

Moscow

Accommodations: Motel 6, 101 Baker St., 83843 (tel. 208/882-5511).
● Super 8 Motel, 175 Peterson Dr., 83843 (tel. 208/883-1503).

Nampa

Accommodation: Pepper Mill Inn, 908 3rd St. South 83651 (tel. 208/466-3594, toll free 800/433-2639 or 800/432-2639 in Washington). $26 for one; $28 for two in one bed; $32 for two in two beds.

Pocatello

Accommodations: Motel 6, 291 West Burnside Ave., 83201 (tel. 208/237-7880).
● Imperial 400 Motor Inn, 1055 South Fifth Ave., 83201 (tel. 208/233-5120).
● Super 8 Motel, 1330 Bench Rd., 83204 (tel. 208/234-0888).

Sandpoint

Accommodation: Super 8 Motel, 3245 Hwy. 95 North, 83864 (tel. 208/263-2210).

Twin Falls

Accommodations: Motel 6, 1472 Blue Lakes Blvd. North, 83301 (tel. 208/734-3993).
● Imperial 400 Motor Inn, 320 Main Ave. South, 83301 (tel. 208/733-8770).
● Super 8 Motel, 1260 Blue Lakes Blvd. North, 83301 (tel. 208/734-5801).
● TraveLodge, 248 Second Ave. West, 83301 (tel. 208/733-5630).

Illinois

Chicago is the pulse of Illinois, and, in many ways, of the Midwest. It's where many of the young people from midwestern states head when they leave school and it's most definitely worth a visit. See the special section on Chicago to help plan your days there.

If you have more time to explore the state, go beyond Chicago to the area around Springfield where Abraham Lincoln spent many years of his life. Lincoln's New Salem State Historic Site is a restoration of the village where Lincoln lived from 1831 to 1837. At New Salem, visit the building where he pored over his law books, the store where he clerked, and the post office he tended. Lincoln memorabilia are exhibited in an indoor museum within this village and tourists can visit 23 buildings that are meant to conjure up Lincoln's past. During the summer months, the Talisman Riverboat runs daily and the Great American People Show, a Lincoln presentation, is presented in an open-air theater.

Although it is the state of Utah that is most often thought of when Brigham Young is mentioned, it was in Illinois, on the banks of the Mississippi, where Joseph Smith founded the headquarters of the Church of Latter-Day Saints. The group was persecuted there and after Smith was murdered, Brigham Young led the exodus to Utah. Left behind in the town of Nauvoo are Smith's first log homestead, the restored Joseph Smith Mansion House, the Brigham Young Home, the Jonathan Browning Home, and the Temple Lot.

Anyone planning to visit Illinois should send for a free copy of the *Illinois* book, which is an overview of Illinois including information on attractions/ historic sites; festivals and annual events; camping, biking, skiing, etc. Copies are available from the Illinois Department of Commerce and Community Affairs, address listed below.

A useful guidebook for Illinois is *Illinois Off the Beaten Path* by Rod Fensom and Julie Foreman, Globe Pequot ($7.95).

Some Special Events: Rock Cut Winter Festival in Loves Park and Central Illinois Jazz Festival in Decatur (January); Maple Syrup Time in Springfield (February); Annual Orchid Display in Naperville (March); Old Settlers Day in Sumner (April); Dogwood Festival in Quincy, Lilac Festival in Lombard, and Old Capitol Art Fair in Springfield (May); Fort de Chartres Rendezvous at Prairie du Rocher, Vermilion County Civil War Days in Danville, Grand Levee in Vandalia, and Old English Faire in Brimfield (June); Ravinia Festival in Highland Park (all summer); Taste of Chicago in Chicago, Petunia Festival in Dixon, Lincolnfest in Springfield, and Catfish Days in Wilmington (July); Illinois State Fair in Springfield, Indian Pow Wow in Arcola, and National Sweetcorn Festival in Mendota (August); Grape Festival in Nauvoo, Henry County Hog Festival in Kewanee, Apple Festival in Murphysboro, and Jordbruksdagarna in Bishop Hill (September); Spoon River Scenic Tour in Fulton County, Knox County Scenic Drive in Knox County, Fall Crafts Festival in Clayville, Fort Massac Encampment at Metropolis, and Burgoo Festival at Utica (October); Pope County Deer Festival in Golconda, Way of Lights in Belleville; Julmarknad at Bishop Hill and Country Christmas in Galena (November); Way of Lights in Belleville, Christmas at New Salem State Historic Site, Old Fashioned Christmas Walk at Galena and Lucia Pageant and Festival in Chicago (December).

Tourist Information: Illinois Department of Commerce and Community Affairs, Office of Tourism, 620 E. Adams, Springfield, IL 62701 (tel. 217/782-7139).

Alton

Accommodation: TraveLodge, 717 East Broadway, 62002 (tel. 618/462-1011).

Aurora

Accommodation: Regal 8 Inn, 2380 North Farnsworth Ave. and East West Tollway 5, 60507 (tel. 312/851-3600).

Belleville

Accommodation: Imperial 400 Motor Inn, 600 East Main St., 62220 (tel. 618/234-9670).

Bloomington

Accommodations: Best Inns of America, I-74, I-55, and Market Street, 61701 (tel. 309/827-5333).
● Super 8 Motel, 818 IAA Dr., 61701 (tel. 309/663-2388).

Carbondale

Accommodation: Best Inns of America, 1345 E. Main St. (tel. 618/529-4801).

Champaign-Urbana

On Campus: The University of Illinois is in this fair-size town on the Illinois prairie. You may be able to stay at the Student Union for $30 single; $36 double, per night—contact the Guest Room Reservations at 217/333-1241. For a true "taste" of Champaign-Urbana, you have to visit Murphy's Pub for a steak sandwich or the Deluxe Lunch for a fish sandwich on Friday or Saturday. To meet students, you can also go to Cochrane's, R&R Sports Grill, or Garcia's Pizza. The Deluxe Lunch & Billiards, Inc. has a delicious fish sandwich and is open Friday and Saturday.

The *Daili Illini* newspaper can help you find out about rides and accommodations.

"Champaign-Urbana is an oasis of culture, fun, and entertainment on an otherwise barren prairie. It's a good stopover for anyone going cross country since it's at the intersection of Interstates 74 and 57."

Accommodations: Best Inns of America, 914 West Bloomington Rd., 61820 (tel. 217/356-6000).
● Super 8 Motel, 202 Marketview Dr., 61820 (tel. 217/359-2388).

Chicago

Chicago's most striking feature is its lakefront. Because of Lake Michigan, Chicago has beaches, parks, and marinas that give lots of pleasure to Chicagoans and visitors as well. While you're in Chicago, be sure to walk, bicycle, or jog along the lakefront, admiring the skyline on one side and the lake on the other. For example, you can walk through Grant Park's Rose Garden, watch the boats on the lake, Buckingham Fountain in the center, the skyline of the city beyond, and end up at the Field Museum, the Shedd Aquarium, and the Adler Planetarium. Another way to enjoy the lakeshore is to take a picnic to the Grant Park bandshell (Columbus Drive at Jackson, across from the back door of the Art Institute), listen to a concert, then watch the evening color display at Buckingham Fountain. If you walk up Michigan Avenue to the Chicago River, you'll find the spot where the first Fort Dearborn has been outlined on the street, pick up a snack, and picnic along either side of the river. Or try this: rent a bike from the Village Cycle, 1337 N. Wells, or a moped from Scooters, 874 N. Wabash and

Delaware; take a horse-drawn carriage ride to see the sights; or order a picnic basket from Kenesseys, 403 W. Belmont Ave.

For anyone with an interest in architecture, Chicago is a dream—you'll find the works of Louis Sullivan, Frank Lloyd Wright, and Mies van der Rohe, and two outstanding examples of the architecture of the '70s—the Sears Tower (the world's tallest) and the John Hancock Building. You can go to the Chicago Architecture Foundation's ArchiCenter, 330 South Dearborn, for information on Chicago's treasures. The Center also conducts walking tours that cost $4—the most popular is the Loop tour which visits several downtown buildings. To see some outstanding outdoor sculpture, walk from the ArchiCenter north on Dearborn to see Calder's *Flamingo* on the Federal Center Plaza; Chagall's *Four Seasons* on the First National Bank Plaza (in summer, be there at lunch time so that you can catch the free entertainment); Miro's *Chicago* and Picasso's *Lady* facing each other on Daley Plaza across from City Hall; and, Dubuffet's *Monument with Standing Beast* in front of the brand-new State of Illinois building designed by Helmut Jahn. There are no formal tours of the new building, but visitors can wander in, explore the atrium, and ride the glass elevators.

Chicago starts to celebrate every year as soon as the weather gets nice. From June to August, there are concerts by the Chicago Symphony Orchestra at the Ravinia Festival in Highland Park (can be reached by special train on the Chicago and Northwestern lines during concert season). Tickets for indoor seating are available, but most people prefer to picnic on the lawns just beyond the concert shell, frequently bringing their own crystal, linen, and cuisine. During the summer, there are also free concerts in Grant Park. Just bring a picnic supper along and make yourself comfortable on the lawn.

For exploring Chicago, *Chicago in Your Pocket* is especially helpful; for an excellent pocket-size guide to the city, buy a copy of Marilyn Appleberg's *I Love Chicago Guide* ($7.45). Other helpful guides include *Fodor's Chicago* ($6.95) and *Zagat Chicago Restaurant Survey* ($8.95).

To know what's going on in Chicago while you're visiting, check the *Sun Times,* the *Tribune,* or the alternative paper *The Reader,* which can be picked up free in many stores especially on the North Side. *Chicago Magazine* ($1.95) is another good source of information—it comes out monthly and includes articles, restaurant listings, etc. *Chicago Scene* ($1.50) tells what's happening too.

In May, you can enjoy the Chicago International Art Expo on Navy Pier. This is an impressive assemblage of art from all over the world. The Chicago Jazz Festival in late August is another very special event in Chicago. Foreign college students visiting Chicago may want to contact the International Visitors Center, 520 North Michigan Ave., 60611 (tel. 312/645-1836). Ask about some of the special programs they organize.

Getting There: From the Airport: O'Hare is about 17 miles from the city and Midway is about ten miles away. Continental Air Transport services both airports and the fare is $6.75 from O'Hare and $6 from Midway to the Loop. Taxis cost between $8 and $15 to town. The subway is the quickest way and costs $1 from O'Hare.

Or you can go by public transport from O'Hare to the Loop in about a half hour. The "El" goes all the way to O'Hare and operates 24 hours a day ($1 plus

10¢ for transfer). From Midway take Dearborn and Washington Douglas B train to Cicero (90¢) or ride bus 54B to the Douglas El (90¢ plus 15¢ transfer).

From the Train and Bus Stations: The Greyhound station is at Clark and Randolph and the Trailways station is at Randolph and State, in the heart of downtown. From these terminals you can catch a bus or the El. The Union Station train terminal is located at Canal and Adams; the Northwestern Station is at Canal and Madison; and the Illinois Central Station is at Randolph and Michigan. There are many bus routes that go to and from the train stations.

Getting Around: Taxis are expensive; it will cost you $1 to get in, then 10¢ per one-tenth mile.

● The Chicago Transit Authority operates trains and buses that arrive from north, south, and west of the city and circle the central business and shopping district. The train fare is $1 plus 25¢ for a transfer. Exact change is necessary on buses.

● The bus fare is 90¢ plus 15¢ for a transfer and buses run every 5 to 15 minutes, usually. Look for rectangular signs that say CTA (Chicago Transit Authority), with the number and route of the bus, at each bus stop. Exact change is required.

● The CTA distributes a Downtown Transit Map, which explains its routes in both English and Spanish. Their travel information number is 312/836-7000.

● CTA "Culture Buses" run June to September on north, south, and west routes starting at the Art Institute. The fare of $2 entitles riders to unlimited travel along the route from 10:35 a.m. to 4:45 p.m.

Tourist Information: Chicago Tourism Council, Historic Water Tower in-the-Park, 806 N. Michigan Ave. at Pearson Street, 60611 (tel. 312/280-5740). All you need to know in this new center for tourists. Open seven days a week.

Help: Travelers Aid, O'Hare Airport, Concourse G between Air Canada and U.S. Air (tel. 312/686-7562); Greyhound Station, 74 West Randolph (tel. 312/435-4537); Union Station, 210 South Canal (tel. 312/435-4543).

Accommodations: For a brochure describing *Chicago Holidays* (two-in-a-room weekend specials), write to the Chicago Convention and Tourism Bureau, McCormick Place and the Lake, 60616.

"Some of the most elegant Chicago hotels offer special weekend rates that are not very widely publicized. A few phone calls might get you an elegant double for about $35 per person for two nights."

● Parkway Eleanor Club, 1550 North Dearborn Pkwy., 60610 (tel. 312/664-8245). Women only. $21 single or double with breakfast and shared bath. Membership fee of $2.50 required. Advance reservations necessary.

● International House at the University of Chicago, 1414 East 59th St., 60637 (tel. 312/753-2270 or 753-2280). Open June 1 to September 7. $21 per person per night single rooms. Advance reservations of three to seven days necessary. A neo-Gothic limestone building with 507 single rooms and a full-service cafeteria. During the academic year, it is a residential and program center for foreign and American graduate students, although a few vacant rooms are usually available for transient guests.

● Lincoln Belmont YMCA, 3333 North Marshfield Ave., 60657 (tel. 312/248-3333). Men over 18 only, $11.50 per night in private room with shared washroom and shower. Weekly rate: $45 to $52. Advance reservations of one month necessary.

- Lawson YMCA, ⑤√ ★ 🅰, 30 West Chicago Ave., 60610 (tel. 312/944-6211). Men and women. $22 to $35 per day; $65.50 to $105 per week.
- Regal 8 Inn, 2448 North Mannheim, Franklin Park, 60131 (tel. 312/455-6500).
- Admiral Oasis Motel, 9353 Waukegan Rd., Morton Grove, 60053 (tel. 312/965-4000). $19.71 to $23.71 single; $21.71 to $25.71 double.
- Red Roof Inn, 17301 South Halsted Rd., South Holland, 60473 (tel. 312/331-1621).
- Red Roof Inn, Ill. 5 and Highland Avenue, 1113 Butterfield Rd., Downers Grove, 60515 (tel. 312/963-4205).
- Red Roof Inn, I-90 and Arlington Hts. Road, 22 West Algonquin Rd., Arlington Hts., 60005 (tel. 312/228-6650).
- Red Roof Inn, 2450 E. 173rd St., Lansing, 60438 (tel. 312/895-9570).
- Days Inn, I-80 and 294, 17220 Halsted St., Hazelcrest, 60429 (tel. 312/957-5900).
- Econo Lodge, 510 East End Ave., 60409 (tel. 312/862-2500).
- Delaware Towers, 25 E. Delaware, 60601 (tel. 312/944-4245). Discount rates for *Where to Stay* readers, and special family rates. $68 double.
- Cass Hotel, ⑤, 640 N. Wabash, 60601 (tel. 312/787-4030). "Best find in Chicago." $20 to $30 single; $25 to $35 double.
- Cedar Motel, 1118 N. State St., 60601 (tel. 312/787-5560). Located downtown in the center of the nightlife district. $25 single or double; $2 key deposit.

Where to Eat: One chain that can be recommended is the Original Pancake House (at 2020 North Lincoln Park West and 30 other Chicago locations). It serves an apple pancake that's more like a soufflé with apple slices and a cinnamon glaze on top. There's usually a long wait on weekends. The Pancake House is a popular restaurant for people with children.

- The Sears, IBM, and Standard Oil Building cafeterias are open Monday through Friday for breakfast and lunch. Most museums have cafeterias that are open daily for lunch and for dinner (on the nights the museums stay open late). Marshall Field's, the huge department store on State Street, has nine restaurants—the least expensive are the Bowl and Basket and the Buffet on the seventh floor, the Dinette in the basement, and the Punch Bowl on the third floor. Use the *I Love Chicago Guide* or the *Chicago Magazine Guide* for restaurant suggestions. Here are a few of ours:
- The Berghoff, 17 West Adams (tel. 312/427-3170). Open Monday to Saturday, 11 a.m. to 9:30 p.m. In this German restaurant right in the heart of the Loop, you'll find one of the best food bargains in the city. Portions are generous and the price is reasonable. The restaurant is huge, one of the oldest in the city, and extremely busy at lunchtime. Try the Berghoff's own beer—which they've brewed since before Prohibition.

"For stuffed pizza, which is a layered deep-dish pie, go to one of the branches of Giordano's (North Rush St., North Clark, West Irving Park, and South Blackstone), which Chicago Magazine *voted the best in the city."*

- French Baker, 26 West Madison (tel. 312/346-3532). Good, light food right in the center of town.
- Greek Islands, 766 West Madison (tel. 312/782-9855). One of several good restaurants in the Halsted Street Greek area.

- Acorn on Oak, 116 East Oak (tel. 312/944-6835). For burgers and late-night piano.
- Belden Corned Beef Center, 2315 North Clark (tel. 312/935-2752). Never closes.
- Carson's, 612 North Wells (tel. 312/280-9200). The place in town for ribs (and Chicago loves ribs).
- Pizzeria Uno, 29 East Ohio (tel. 312/321-1000); and Due, 619 North Wabash (tel. 312/943-2400). Famous Chicago-style deep-dish pizza.
- Tenkatsu, 3365 North Clark (tel. 312/549-8697). Good tempura and teriyaki in a no-frills atmosphere.
- Water Tower Place, 845 North Michigan (tel. 312/440-3165). Twelve eating places all together—try Vie de France, a bakery on the mezzanine; Theatre Cafe, a coffeeshop and chocolatier on two; or D.B. Kaplan's, a delicatessen, on seven.
- Morry's Deli, 5500 South Cornell Ave. (tel. 312/363-3800). Good sandwiches; a branch in the University of Chicago bookstore.
- Chances R, 5225 South Harper (tel. 312/363-1550). A mellow combination of burgers and Saturday-night jazz.
- Gino's Pizzeria, 932 Rush St. (tel. 312/337-7326). Graffitti ridden—but all part of the decor. "Best place in town for pizza." Open for lunch and dinner.
- Twin Anchors, 1655 N. Sedgewick (tel. 312/266-1616). Near Lincoln Park, north of the city. Famous for their zesty ribs. A slab of ribs goes for $12.

What to See: A CTA elevated train ride to the end of the line and back gives visitors a unique view of the city skyline. The American, tel. 312/427-3100; Gray Line, tel. 312/346-9506; and Keeshin, tel. 312/427-9400, companies offer bus tours. To see the city by boat from the Chicago River and Lake Michigan from May to September, call Mercury, tel. 312/332-1353; Wendella, tel. 312/337-1446; or Shoreline Marine, tel. 312/427-2900. Many places will give guided tours with advance reservations, for example, the Merchandise Mart, the Police Department, the *Chicago Sun-Times*, and the Quaker Oats Test Kitchens. For a good introduction to Chicago, see the dual-theater shows at the Water Tower Pumping Station, Michigan at Pearson Street. *Heartbeat Chicago* is a 63-projector, quadraphonic sound show, and *City of Dreams* is a 70-mm film with aerial and special effects. Open every day from 10 a.m. to 10:30 p.m.; $3.75 admission.

- A site of historical interest is the Old Water Tower and Pumping Station, across from Water Tower Place, 835 North Michigan Ave. This limestone structure is the sole building to have survived the Great Chicago Fire, over a century ago. Inside is a museum, featuring the history of Chicago.
- Art Institute of Chicago, Michigan Avenue at Adams (tel. 312/443-3500). The well-known institute houses one of the best collections of French impressionist paintings in the world and the renowned Thorne miniature replicas of rooms from the 16th to mid-20th centuries. Admission is $4.50 for adults; $2.25 for students, children, and senior citizens; and Tuesday it's free for all.
- Field Museum of Natural History (tel. 312/922-9410). In Grant Park, Roosevelt Road at Lake Shore Drive, this museum features animal dioramas, Indian art and archaeology collections, and exhibits tracing human history. On Thursday, admission is free; otherwise it's $2 for adults; $1 for students with ID. Right near the Field Museum are the Adler Planetarium, tel. 312/322-0300, and the John G. Shedd Aquarium, tel. 312/939-2426. Both are worth a side trip.
- Sears Tower. You'll find this 110-story building at the intersection of

Wacker Drive and Adams (tel. 312/875-9696). For $1.50 you can enjoy a view from the top, seeing not only Chicago but also the suburbs, and parts of Indiana, Michigan, and Wisconsin. Open from 9 a.m. to midnight.

- John Hancock Center, 875 North Michigan (tel. 312/751-3681). The world's fourth-tallest building. Get a drink plus a view from the windows of Images, the bar on the 96th floor.

- Museum of Science and Industry, East 57th Street and South Shore Drive (tel. 312/MU4-1414). The admission is free and the exhibits include an enormous model of the human heart and the Apollo 8 lunar module. Fun for anyone who likes to know how things work.

- Chicago Public Library Cultural Center, Washington at Michigan (tel. 312/269-2837). Stunning Tiffany mosaics and windows in halls and central room of 1897 landmark. Art and photo exhibits, concerts, and films. Free.

- Chicago Historical Society, Clark at North Avenue (tel. 312/642-4600). The history of Chicago and Illinois on exhibit. $1 on Tuesday to Sunday; Monday is free.

- Expressway Children's Museum, 75 East Washington St. (tel. 312/269-3222). Hands-on exhibits designed for children 3 to 12.

- Peace Museum, 430 West Erie St. (tel. 312/440-1860). Dedicated to peace education through the arts, it is the first and only such institution in the U.S. It's open Tuesday through Sunday, noon to 5 p.m., Thursday until 8:00 p.m. An interesting gift shop has posters, books, and crafts from various countries.

- Lincoln Park Conservatory and Zoo, 2200 N. Cannon Dr., 60614 (tel. 312/294-4660). Three acres of gardens under glass and 35 acres of natural habitat for 2000 animals. Free seven days a week.

- Neighborhoods: Greektown is located around the 200 South block of Halsted; Chinatown around the 2300 South block of Wentworth. There are two art gallery districts; Superior/Huron and Michigan Avenue.

At Night: Try sampling the scene at the intersection of Rush and State Street going north on State to Division; the bars, shops, and restaurants along Halsted from Armitage to Webster, west on Webster to Racine, south on Racine, and east on Armitage; or on the stretch along Lincoln Avenue from Armitage to Webster. Some telephone numbers that will come in handy as you plan your nights in Chicago are:

- Jazz Hotline, 312/666-1881.
- Jam's Rock Concert Hotline, 312/666-6667.
- Eventline, 312/225-2323.
- Fine Art Line, 312/346-3278.
- Sportsline, 312/976-1313.
- Hot Tix at 24 S. State St. sells half-price day-of-performance tickets for theater, dance, and music events. Open noon to 6 p.m. Monday, 10 a.m. to 6 p.m. Tuesday to Friday, and 10 a.m. to 5 p.m. Saturday. Call 312/977-1755 for information.

- Rick's Cafe American, in the Holiday Inn, 644 North Lake Shore Dr. (tel. 312/943-9200). In this re-creation of Rick's from the film *Casablanca*, the jazz is good, whether there are big names featured or local talent.

- Andy's, 11 East Hubbard St. (tel. 312/642-6805). *The* place for jazz these days.

- Orphan's, 2462 North Lincoln (tel. 312/929-2677). More jazz.

- The Bulls Jazz Club, 1916 North Lincoln Park West (tel. 312/337-3000). Outstanding contemporary jazz groups, good food, and pleasant service give this spot, long popular with the Chicago jazz lovers, an increasingly widespread reputation in the rest of the country and even abroad. On weekends, you'd better make reservations.

● B.L.U.E.S., 2519 North Halsted St. (tel. 312/327-3331). It's near to Lincoln Park's nightlife area and features blues seven nights a week.

● To dance: The Smart Bar, 3730 N. Clark (tel. 312/549-4140). Avant garde club located beneath the metro—$6 cover; Clubland, 3145 N. Sheffield (tel. 312/248-7277). New music, great dance floor, 50 TVs playing videos. $5 cover.

● To see modern dance/ballet: The Dance Center of Columbia College, 4730 N. Sheridan Rd. (tel. 312/271-7928); The Auditorium, 70 E. Congress Parkway (tel. 312/922-2110).

● To see a play: Apollo Theater, 2540 N. Lincoln (tel. 312/935-6100); Blackstone Theater, 60 E. Balbo (tel. 312/236-4300).

"Chicago theaters should not be underrated even if they still operate from storefront locations. Steppenwolf, Wisdom Bridge, Victory Gardens, The Remains Theater, The Court Theater, and Body Politic—all deserve a try."

● To hear classical music: Orchestra Hall, 220 South Michigan (tel. 312/435-8111). This is the home of the Chicago Symphony Orchestra, whose principal conductor is Georg Solti. Guest artists perform during the symphony's season which runs from fall through spring.

● Civic Opera House, 20 North Wacker (tel. 312/346-0270). The Lyric Opera, a first-rate company, attracts top operatic talent during its fall season. Chicago is also visited each year by many famous dance companies, for example, the Joffrey, Alvin Ailey, American Ballet Theater, etc.

● For comedy: Second City, 1616 North Wells St. (tel. 312/337-3992). This improvisational comedy theater was the starting place for most of "Saturday Night Live's" original cast as well as Alan Alda. Call for details.

● For movies: Music Box Theater, 3733 North Southport (tel. 312/871-6604). Popular film revival house. Two inexpensive movie houses are Village Theater, 1548 N. Clark (tel. 312/642-2403), and 3 Penny, 2424 N. Lincoln Ave. (tel. 312/281-7200).

Shopping: Barbara's Book Store, 1434 North Wells, 2907 North Broadway, and 121 North Marion, Oak Park (tel. 312/642-5044). A fine selection of hard- and softcover books, specializing in small press literature and poetry, mysteries, fiction, and children's books.

● Joseph O'Gara, 1311 East 57th St. (tel. 312/363-0993) and a warehouse on Wabash. For used paperbacks and hardcovers.

● Rizzoli's, Water Tower Place, 835 North Michigan Ave. (tel. 312/642-3500). Books, records, foreign and domestic newspapers and magazines.

● Rose Records, 214 South Wabash (tel. 312/987-9044). Huge selection of records and tapes, especially well stocked in the classics, opera, and jazz departments. The second floor has budget and out-of-print records. If they don't have the record you want in stock, they'll order it for you. Other branches are at 1122 North State Parkway, 3155 North Broadway, 3259 North Ashland, and 4821 West Irving Park.

● Wax Trax, 2449 N. Lincoln Ave. (tel. 312/929-0221). Best selection of imports, oldies, unconventional, and hard-to-find records around.

● Marshall Field, 111 North State (tel. 312/781-1000). One reader insists that all visitors take a look at this, the city's most famous department store—a full city block with luxuries and bargains in a building with Tiffany mosaic domes.

● Eddie Bauer, Inc. 123 North Wabash Ave. (tel. 312/263-6005) across from Marshall Field. Specializes in high-quality down gear, ski wear, and backpacking equipment.

● Morrie Mages Sports, 620 N. Lasalle St. (tel. 312/337-6151). All types of sporting goods.

● Crate and Barrel, 850 North Michigan Ave., and also at 101 North Wabash. Here you'll find anything and everything you need to equip a kitchen—glassware, dishes, good gift possibilities. Most things are reasonably priced and the basements at the Michigan Ave. store and the Outlet Store at 1510 North Wells carry basics, closeouts, and discontinued merchandise—all worth checking out.

● Water Tower Place, north of Old Water Tower and Pumping Station. A shopping mall, a great place to meet friends and spend a day shopping, eating, and seeing a film.

● Woodfield Mall, in suburban Schaumburg, was touted as the "world's largest indoor shopping mall" upon its completion in the '70s. You'll find just about anything amongst its hundreds of stores. The mall is serviced by CTA and RTA buses.

Collinsville

Accommodations: Super 8 Motel, 2 Gateway Dr., I-55/70, Exit 11, 62234 (tel. 618/345-8808).

● Drury Inn, I-55/70 and IL 157, 602 N. Bluff, 62234 (tel. 618/345-7700).

Crystal Lake

Accommodation: Super 8 Motel, 577 Crystal Point Dr., 60014 (tel. 815/455-2388).

Danville

Accommodation: YWCA, 201 North Hazel St., 61832 (tel. 217/446-1217). Women only. $12 single with shared bath. Weekly rate: $40.

Decatur

Accommodations: Econo Lodge, 333 Wyckles Rd., 62522 (tel. 217/422-5900).

● Budgetel Inn, 5100 Hickory Point Frontage Rd., 62526 (tel. 217/875-5800).

● Super 8 Motel, 3141 N. Water St., 62526 (tel. 217/877-8888).

De Kalb

Help: Crisis Line, 815/758-6655.

On Campus: Northern Illinois University is in De Kalb, and for $31.08 for a single or $36.63 for a double, you can stay in one of the hotel-like rooms in the Holmes Student Center there. Call 815/753-1444 for information. Also in the Holmes Center is the Pow Wow Room where a full meal—meat, potatoes, vegetables, roll, and beverage—will be inexpensive. There are three other restaurants in the Student Center to choose from. Off campus, try Rosita's at 642 East Lincoln Hwy., where Mexican food is featured, or Hop's Cantonese at 1822 Sycamore Rd. Also, there are many fast-food restaurants near campus.

Accommodation: Motel 6, 1116 West Lincoln Hwy., 60115 (tel. 815/756-3398).

Effingham

Accommodations: Days Inn, West Fayette Road and I-57 and 70, Box 1168, 62401 (tel. 217/342-9271).
● Best Inns of America, 1209 N. Keller Dr. (tel. 217/347-5141).
● Budget Host—Lincoln Lodge, Exit 162 on I-70 and I-57, 62401 (tel. 217/342-4133).
● Super 8 Motel, 1400 Thelma Keller Ave., 62401 (tel. toll free 800/843-1991).

Evanston

Help: Crisis Intervention Referral Services, 312/492-6500.
On Campus: In Evanston, the suburban area adjacent to Chicago, you'll find the campus of Northwestern University. Northwestern students gather at The Spot, Fritz's, Jay's, Yesterday's, and The Main. There's a bulletin board you might want to check at Norris Center; pick up a copy of the *Daily Northwestern* to see what's going on when you arrive.

Accommodations: YMCA, 1000 Grove St., 60201 (tel. 312/475-7400). In downtown Evanston, one block south of Davis Street Men only, age 18 and over. $24 single.
● Margarita Inn, 1566 Oak Ave., 60201 (tel. 312/869-2273). $30 to $40 single; $35 to $45 double; $40 to $45 triple. "Gracious residential hotel with a European ambience." Located near downtown Evanston and Northwestern University.

Galesburg

Accommodation: Regal 8 Inn, 1487 North Henderson, 61401 (tel. 309/344-2401).

Greenville

Accommodation: Budget Host—Bel Air Motel, Rte. 4, Box 183, 62246 (tel. 618/664-1950).

Jacksonville

Accommodation: Motel 6, 1716 West Morton Dr., 62650 (tel. 217/243-7157).

Joliet

Accommodations: Kings Inn, Ⓢ√ ★, 2219 ½ West Jefferson, 60435 (tel. 815/744-1220). $19.88 single; $24.88 for two in one bed; $27.88 for two in two beds.
● Red Roof Inn, 1750 McDonough, 60436 (tel. 815/741-2304).

Kankakee

Accommodations: Regal 8 Inn, Ill. 50 and Armour Road, Bourbonnais, 60914 (tel. 815/933-2300).
● Scottish Inn, RR 7, Box 336, 60901 (tel. 815/939-4551).

LaSalle

Accommodation: Motel 6, 1900 May St., Peru, 61354 (tel. 815/224-2785).

Libertyville

Accommodation: Doe's Motel, Rtes. 45 and Ill. 137, 60048 (tel. 312/362-0800). $32.75 for one; $35.75 for two in one bed; $37.95 for two in two beds.

Lombard

Accommodation: Highland Manor Motel, 19 West 545 Roosevelt Rd., 60418 (tel. 312/627-5700). $26.50 for one or two in one bed; $30.70 for two in two beds.

Macomb

Accommodation: Olson Conference Center, Western Illinois University, West Adams St., 61455 (tel. 309/298-2461). $16.40 single; $19 double. Rooms have two single beds, which are used as couches during the day. Each floor of the guest area has a lounge and a community bathroom. Meals in adjacent building. On Western Illinois University campus, one-half mile from train station.

Marion

Accommodations: Regal 8 Inn, I-57 and Rte. 13, 62959 (tel. 618/993-2631).
● Best Inns of America, I-57 and New Rte. 13 (tel. 618/997-9421).
● Super 8 Motel, Hwy. 57 and Rte. 13, Exit 54B, 62959 (tel. 618/993-5577).

Moline

Accommodations: Regal 8 Inn, Quad City Airport Road, 61265 (tel. 309/764-8711).
- Exel Inn, 2501 52nd Ave., 61265 (tel. 309/797-5580).
- Hampton Inn, 6920 27th St., 61265 (tel. 309/762-1711).

Monmouth

Accommodation: Fulton Hall, 300 block of North 7th Street, 61462 (tel. 309/457-2345). $8 per person dormitory style. Advance reservations necessary.

Mount Vernon

Accommodations: Regal 8 Inn, I-57 and Ill. 15, 62864 (tel. 618/244-2383).
- Best Inns of America, Rte. 15 and I-57, 62864 (tel. 618/244-4343).
- Drury Inn, I-57/64 and IL 15, P.O. Box 805, 62864 (tel. 618/244-4550).
- Super 8 Motel, 401 S. 44th St., 62864 (tel. 618/242-8800).

Normal

On Campus: Illinois State University is in this town. Activities there center around the Bone Student center and sometimes move to one of the local bars— the Cellar, Garcia's, The Gallery, Benningan's, or Rocky's II. For information on campus events check *Vidette,* the student newspaper.
Accommodation: Motel 6, 1600 North Main St., 61761 (tel. 309/452-0422).

Okawville

Accommodation: Super 8 Motel, I-64 and Rte. 177, P.O. Drawer 515, 62271 (tel. 618/243-6525).

Palos Park

Accommodation: Community Center Foundation, 12700 Southwest Hwy., 60464. (tel. 312/361-3650). $16.50 single; $33 for two twin beds. Advance reservations suggested.

Peoria

Accommodations: YWCA, 301 N.E. Jefferson St., 61602 (tel. 309/674-1167). Women only. $13 single. Weekly rate of $60 includes linens. Centrally located. "1928 building with front parlors, tearoom, swimming pool, and a sauna."
- Motel 6, 104 West Camp St., 61611 (tel. 309/699-7281).
- Imperial 400 Motor Inn, 202 N.E. Washington, 61602 (tel. 309/676-8961).
- Red Roof Inn, 4031 North War Memorial Dr., 61614 (tel. 309/685-3911).
- Days Inn, 2726 West Lake Ave., 61615 (tel. 309/688-7000).

Rock Falls

Accommodation: Super 8 Motel, 2100 1st Ave., 61071 (tel. 815/626-8800).

Rockford

Help: Contact Rockford, information and referral line, as well as crisis line, 815/964-4044.

Accommodations: Motel 6, 4205 11th St., 61109 (tel. 815/398-0066).
- Regal 8 Inn, 3851 11th St., 61109 (tel. 815/398-6080).
- Exel Inn, 220 South Lyford Rd., 61108 (tel. 815/332-4915).
- Red Roof Inn, I-90 at East State St. Bus. Rte. 20, 7434 East State St., 61108 (tel. 815/398-9750).

Rolling Meadows

Accommodation: Best Inns of America, 2801 Algonquin Rd., S.R. 62 (tel. 312/259-5900).

Salem

Accommodation: Super 8 Motel, I-57 and U.S. 50, Exit 116, 62881 (tel. 618/548-5882).

Springfield

"The state capital of Illinois is not, as many people think, Chicago—but Springfield 200 miles to the south in the heart of the state."

Accommodations: Red Roof Inn, I-55 at South Grand Ave., Exit 96B (tel. 217/753-4302).
- Regal 8 Inn, I-55 and Toronto Road, 62703 (tel. 217/529-1633).
- Motel 6, 3125 Wide Track Dr., 62703 (tel. 217/789-1063).
- Days Inn, 3000 Stevenson Dr., 62703 (tel. 217/529-0171).
- Super 8 Motel, 1330 S. Dirksen Pkwy., 62703 (tel. 217/528-8889).

Tuscola

Accommodation: Super 8 Motel, Rte. 36, I-57 at Hwy. 36, 61953 (tel. 217/253-5488).

Urbana (see also Champaign-Urbana)

Accommodations: Motel 6, 1906 North Cunningham Ave., 61801 (tel. 217/344-1082).
- Hendrick House, 904 West Green St., 61801 (tel. 217/328-8000). Open May 1 to August 15. $12.50 single; $10 per person double. Advance reservations of two months necessary.

Vandalia

Accommodation: TraveLodge, 1500 North 6th St., 62471 (tel. 618/283-2363).

Waukegan

Accommodations: Best Inns of America, 31 N. Greenbay Rd., I-94, Exit 120 (tel. 312/336-9000).
* Super 8 Motel, 630 Greenbay Rd., 60085 (tel. 312/249-2388).

Indiana

Most people think of the Indianapolis 500 when they think of Indiana; the race is probably Indiana's biggest claim to fame. It's held on Memorial Day and has attracted huge crowds since 1911 (with time off for the two World Wars). Other things to see in Indiana are Indiana Dunes National Lakeshore; Wayandotte Cave, a five-level cavern; the Indianapolis Motor Speedway, once a testing ground for vehicle performance and now the scene of the 500 and a museum of the racing art; Lincoln Boyhood National Memorial, the cabin and the grave of Lincoln's mother with a visitor center that features a film on the family's four years in Indiana; and New Harmony, the remains of what was once a utopian village.

Indiana Off the Beaten Path, by Bill and Phyllis Thomas ($6.95, published by Globe Pequot Press, P.O. Box Q, Chester, CT 06412) is recommended if you're going to explore this state. "When the mood strikes, you can visit the world's largest underground mountain, a singular circus town, a one-of-a-kind jail, a walking sand dune, a small town with the most concentrated collection of contemporary architecture in the country, America's biggest navigable lost river, an extraordinary children's museum, the graves of James Dean and John Dillinger, the birthplace of Michael Jackson, and many other whacky, wonderful attractions."

Some Special Events: Parke County Maple Syrup Fair in Rockville (February); Indianapolis 500 Festival (May); Civil War Days in Rockville, and Hey Days in New Harmony (June); Circus City Festival in Peru (once winter headquarters for many great circuses), and Three Rivers Festival in Fort Wayne (July); Popcorn Festival in Van Buren, and State Fair in Indianapolis (August);

Auburn-Cord-Duesenberg in Auburn (September); and the Parke County Covered Bridge Festival in Rockville (October). Hoosier hospitality will be especially evident during the Hoosier Celebration '88 with special events planned statewide.

Tourist Information: Tourism Development Division, Indiana Department of Commerce, One North Capitol, Suite 700, Indianapolis, IN 46204 (tel. 317/232-8860, or toll free 800/2-WANDER. Ask for their *Wander Book* booklet, which lists the state's major historical, recreational, and scenic attractions.

N.B. A reservation service for Indiana is InnServ, P.O. Box 301G, Eaton, IN 47338 (tel. 317/396-3209).

Anderson

Accommodation: Motel 6, 5810 Scatterfield Rd., 46013 (tel. 317/642-9023).

Angola

Accommodation: Red Carpet Inn, Rte. 7, Box 392, 46703 (tel. 219/665-9561).

Bloomington

On Campus: Have you seen the film *Breaking Away?* That's Bloomington, scene of the Little 500 bicycle race and home of the University of Indiana, one of the "Big Ten."

Two places on campus where you may be able to spend a night are the Indiana Memorial Union and the Poplar's Research and Conference Center. If you're hungry, try The Commons, the IMO Cafeteria, or the Garden Patch—all in the Memorial Union on 7th and Park. Off-campus, try Runcible Spoon, 6th and Grant (great coffee, teas, and brunches); and Daily Grind, Dunn and 5th (good for lunch). Local taverns such as The Bluebird, Jake's, and The Second Story have live music every weekend. For great pasta, shop at Mamma Girisanti's, 850 Auto Mall Rd. For things to do, the IU Music School presents operas and concerts that are of very high quality, and student tickets are usually discounted. IU has its own art museum, which, along with the Nather's Museum of History, Anthropology, and Folklore, has year-round exhibits and are open to the public. For an outdoor experience, you can go to nearby Lake Monroe, Hoosier National Forest, Brown Co., and McCormick's Creek State Park.

Accommodations: Motel 6, 126 South Franklin Rd., 47401 (tel. 812/332-0337.

● Down Town Motel, 509 North College Ave., 47401 (tel. 812/336-6881). $19.95 single; $24.95 double; $28.95 triple; $30.95 quad. Advance reservations of three days necessary; a check or credit card number must be given with reservations.

● Hampton Inn, 2100 N. Walnut St., 47401 (tel. 812/334-2100).

● Knights Inn, 1800 N. Walnut St., 47402 (tel. 812/332-0820).

Columbus

Accommodations: Imperial 400 Motor Inn, 101 3rd St., 47201 (tel. 812/372-2835).
● Knights Inn, I-65 at S.R. 46, 101 Carrie Lane, 47201 (tel. 812/378-3100).
● Super 8 Motel, 110 Brex Park Dr., 47201 (tel. 812/372-8828).

Dale

Accommodation: Budget Host—Stones Motel, 410 South Washington St., 47523 (tel. 812/937-4448).

Elkhart

Help: Switchboard Concern, 219/293-8671.
Accommodations: Red Roof Inn, 2909 Cassopolis St., 46514 (tel. 219/262-3691).
● Days Inn, 2820 Cassopolis St., 46514 (tel. 219/262-3541).
● Knights Inn, I-80/90 at 52188 S.R. 19, 46514 (tel. 219/264-4262).
● Super 8 Motel, 345 Windsor, 46514 (tel. 219/264-4457).

Evansville

Accommodations: Regal 8 Inn, 4201 Hwy. 41 N. & Yokel Road, 47711 (tel. 812/424-6431).
● Drury Inn, 3901 Hwy. 41 N., at Lynch Road, 47711 (tel. 812/423-5618).

Fort Wayne

Tourist Information: Greater Fort Wayne Chamber of Commerce, 826 Ewing, 46802 (tel. 219/424-1435).
Help: Switchboard, Inc., 316 West Creighton Ave. (tel. 219/456-4561). 24-hour crisis and information line.
Accommodations: Hallmark Inn, U.S. 24 & City Rte. 30 at junction of U.S. 30, 46803 (tel. 219/424-1980). $21.70 to $25.70 for one; $28.70 to $32.70 for two; $3 for each additional person.
● Best Inns of America, 3011 W. Coliseum Blvd., 46808 (tel. 219/483-0091).
● Budgetel Inn, 1005 W. Washington Center Rd., 46825 (tel. 219/489-2220).
● Motel 6, 1020 Coliseum Blvd. North, 46805 (tel. 219/422-8551).
● Motel 6, 3003 Coliseum Blvd. West, 46808 (tel. 219/482-3972).
● Knights Inn, I-69 at U.S. 30/33, 2901 Goshen Rd., 46808 (tel. 219/484-2669).
● Red Roof Inn, 2920 Goshen Rd., 46808 (tel. 219/484-8641).
● Days Inn, 3527 Coliseum Blvd., 46808 (tel. 219/482-4511).
● Red Carpet Inn, 4606 Lincoln Hwy. East, 46803 (tel. 219/422-9511).

Goshen

On Campus: If you find yourself in need of conversation, the Leaf Raker is a popular place for food and fellowship. The Student Union of Goshen College has a bulletin board that might provide helpful information about rides, accommodations, and so forth. Goshen is a typical midwest town of 20,000 and is in the heart of a large Mennonite-Amish community dotted with neatly kept farms and horse-and-buggy travel.

Hammond

Accommodation: Super 8 Motel, 3844 179th St., 46324 (tel. 219/844-8888).

Indianapolis

Tourist Information: Indianapolis Convention and Visitors Association, Suite 100, 200 S. Capitol Ave., 46225 (tel. 317/639-4282).

Accommodations: YMCA, 860 West 10th St., 46202 (tel. 317/634-2478). Men and women. $14 single; weekly rate, $49 single. "The people there were very friendly. Don't walk from the bus station—you have to go through a pretty raunchy neighborhood." Higher rates during race week.

- Motel 6, 2851 Shadeland, 46219 (tel. 317/546-5864).
- USA Inn, Ⓢ √ ★, 6990 Pendleton Pike, 46226 (tel. 317/546-4971). $20.70 single; $25.70 double; $28.95 triple; $31.95 quad.
- Regal 8 Inn, 5241 West Broadway at Lynhurst, 46241 (tel. 317/248-1231).
- Budgetel Inn, 2650 Executive Dr., 46241 (tel. 317/244-8100).
- Red Roof Inn, 6415 Debonair Lane, 46224 (tel. 317/293-6881).
- Red Roof Inn, 9520 Valparaiso Ct., 46268 (tel. 317/872-3030).
- Red Roof Inn, 5221 Victory Dr., 46203 (tel. 317/788-9551).
- Days Inn, 7314 East 21st St., 46219 (tel. 317/359-5500).
- Days Inn, 5151 Elmwood Dr., 46203 (tel. 317/785-5471).
- Days Inn, 450 Bixler Rd., 46227 (tel. 317/788-0811).
- Econo Lodge, 1501 East 38th St., 46205 (tel. 317/926-4401).
- Knights Inn, I-70 at 7101 E. 21st St., 46219 (tel. 317/353-8484).
- Knights Inn, I-465 at S.R. 431, 9402 Haver Way, 46240 (tel. 317/848-2423).

Kokomo

Accommodation: Econo Lodge, 2040 South Reed Rd., 46902 (tel. 317/457-7561).

Lafayette

Accommodation: Red Roof Inn, 4201 S.R. 26 East, 47905 (tel. 317/448-4671).

LaPorte

Accommodation: Super 8 Motel, 438 Pine Lake Ave., 46350 (tel. 219/325-3808).

Merrillville

Accommodations: Red Roof Inn, 8290 Georgia St., 46410 (tel. 219/738-2430).
- Knights Inn, I-65 at U.S. 30, 8250 Louisiana St., 46410 (tel. 219/736-5100).
- Super 8 Motel, 8300 Louisiana St., 46410 (tel. 219/736-8383).

Michigan City

Accommodations: Red Roof Inn, 110 West Kieffer Rd., 46360 (tel. 219/874-5251).
- Knights Inn, I-94 at U.S. 21, 201 W. Kieffer Rd., 46360 (tel. 219/874-9500).
- Super 8 Motel, 5724 S. Franklin, 46360 (tel. 219/879-0411).

Muncie

Accommodation: Super 8 Motel, 3601 W. Fox Ridge Lane, 47304 (tel. 317/286-4333).

New Albany

On Campus: Indiana University Southeast is located in New Albany. According to one friend there, the place to eat is Lancaster's, one-half mile from campus on Grant Line Road. Also recommended is the Cellar at 13th and Floodwall.

Plymouth

Accommodation: Motel 6, 2535 North Michigan, 46563 (tel. 219/935-5911).

Portage

Accommodation: Motel 6, 6101 Melton Rd., Rte. 20, 46368 (tel. 219/763-3121).

Remington

Accommodation: Days Inn, I-65 and U.S. 24, Rte. 2, Box 2408, 47977. (tel. 219/261-2178).

Richmond

Accommodation: Knights Inn, I-70 at U.S. 40, 419 Commerce Dr., 47374 (tel. 317/966-6682).

Seymour

Accommodation: Days Inn, 302 Frontage Rd. SE, 47274 (tel. 812/522-3678).

South Bend

"We have beautiful parks, two Frank Lloyd Wright houses, the Notre Dame and Indiana State University campuses, and an auto museum."

Help: Hotline-Crisis Intervention, 219/232-3344.
● Community Resource Center, information and referral, 219/232-2522.
Accommodations: YWCA, 🦽, 802 North Lafayette Blvd., 46601 (tel. 219/233-9491). Women only. $15 plus $2.50 key deposit single. Weekly rate: $34 to $55 plus a deposit of one week's rent. Advance reservations of one week necessary. Cooking facilities available.
● Motel 6, 52624 U.S. Hwy. 31 North, 46637 (tel. 219/272-7072).
● Knights Inn, I-80/90 at U.S. 33, 236 Dixie Hwy., 46637 (tel. 219/277-2960).

Spencer

Accommodation: McCormick's Creek State Park, 🦽, RR1, P.O. Box 72, 47460 (tel. 812/829-2235). Eighteen miles from Bloomington. Accommodations at the Canyon Inn (tel. 812/829-4881) for $31 to $33 and at cabins in the park for a full week only for $90 per week, April to October. These cabins accommodate six people and have two sleeping rooms, a kitchen, a lavatory, and showers. Advance reservations suggested.

Terre Haute

Accommodations: Regal 8 Inn, I-70 and U.S. 41, 47802 (tel. 812/238-1586).
● Super 8 Motel, 3089 S. 1st St., 47802 (tel. 812/232-4890).

Wabash

Accommodation: Scottish Inn, Jct. U.S. 24 and S.R. 13, Rte. 2, Box 35, 46992 (tel. 219/563-2195).

Iowa

You probably never thought about it before, but wherever you are in the U.S. you're no more than 2 ½ driving days from Iowa. Lots of people pass through Iowa on their way across country on Interstate 80 and some, who like farmland and open spaces, decide to stay.

It was, in fact, Iowa's rich prairie soil that attracted people from all over Europe since the mid-1800s. The farmer is king in Iowa—the state is patterned with farms that grow corn and soybeans and raise hogs and cattle. The major attractions in Iowa are the Amana Colonies, not far from Cedar Rapids, which represent an experiment in communal utopianism; the Herbert Hoover National Historic Site in West Branch, which includes the two-room cottage where the one-time president was born, a replica of his father's blacksmith shop, the Quaker meeting house where the family worshipped, and the Hoover Presidential Library Museum; Fort Dodge Historical Museum, Fort, and Stockade, reproduction of a fort where pioneers withstood hostile Indians; and Vesterheim in Decorah, a folk museum honoring the Norwegian pioneers of the area.

The Iowa Department of Economic Development has eight information centers located on Interstate highways throughout the state which are open from mid-May to mid-September; check with them for maps and travel advice.

Some Special Events: Tulip Time in Pella (May); Grant Wood Festival in Stone City, All Iowa Fair in Cedar Rapids, and Steamboat Days American Music Festival in Burlington (June); RAGBRAI Bike Race (different starting point each year), Riverboat Days in Clinton, and Bix Beiderbecke Memorial Jazz Festival in Davenport (July); Sidney Championship Rodeo in Sidney, Threshers and Collectors Show in Albert City, Iowa State Fair in Des Moines (August); Tri-State Rodeo in Fort Madison (September); and Covered Bridge Festival in Winterset (October).

Tourist Information: Iowa Department of Economic Development, 200 East Grand, Des Moines, IA 50309 (tel. toll free 800/345-IOWA).

N.B. A bed-and-breakfast reservation service for Iowa is Bed & Breakfast in Iowa, P.O. Box 430, Preston, IA 52069 (tel. 319/689-4222).

Albia

Accommodation: Holiday Motel, Hwy. 34 East, 52531 (tel. 515/932-7181). $26 for one; $30 for two in one bed; $32 for two in two beds.

Algona

Accommodation: Super 8 Motel, 201 E. Norwood Dr., Box 164, 50511 (tel. 515/295-7225).

Ames

Help: Open Line, 515/292-7000. "We are a free, confidential listing and info-referral service."
- University Switchboard, 515/294-4111.
- Campus Information, 515/294-4357.

On Campus: The campus of Iowa State University is in Ames. A place for the night on campus may be found at the Memorial Union ($28 for a single, $34 for a double); or by contacting the Office of International Educational Services, whose personnel will assist you in finding accommodations (tel. 515/294-1120). For rides, etc., check the bulletin board in the Memorial Union. To meet students, go to That Place, 205 Main St. or the Memorial Union's Commons. For good food, all in the university area and all in a $2 to $5 price range, try Grubstake Barbecue, 2512 Lincoln Way for ribs, sandwiches, and beer; Thumbs Up, 113 Welch Ave. for pizza, salad bar, and beer; or Dugan's Deli, 2900 West St. for deli sandwiches and salads.

Accommodations: Comfort Inn, I-35 and Hwy. 30, 50010 (tel. 515/233-6060).
- Super 8 Motel, 1418 Dayton Rd., 50010 (tel. 515/232-6510).

Burlington

Accommodation: Super 8 Motel, 3001 Kirkwood, 52601 (tel. 319/752-9806.

Carroll

Accommodation: Super 8 Motel, Hwy. 71 North, 51401 (tel. 712/792-4753).

Cedar Falls

Accommodations: Motel 6, 4117 University Ave., 50613 (tel. 319/277-6931).
- Exel Inn, 616 33rd Ave. SW, 52404 (tel. 319/366-2475).

Cedar Rapids

Accommodations: Red Roof Inn, 3325 Southgate Ct. SW, 52404 (tel. 319/366-7523).
● Heartland Inn, 3315 Southgate St., 52404 (tel. 319/362-9012 or toll free 800/334-3277). $29 single; $34 double; $39 triple; $44 quad.
● Super 8 Motel, 400 33rd Ave. SW, 52404 (tel. 319/363-1755).

Clear Lake

Accommodation: Super 8 Motel, I-35 at Exit 193, P.O. Box 340, 50428 (tel. 515/357-7521).

Clinton

Accommodations: Imperial 400 Motor Inn, 1111 Camanche Ave., 52732 (tel. 319/243-4621).
● TraveLodge, 302 6th Ave. South, 52732 (tel. 319/243-4730).

Council Bluffs

Accommodations: Motel 6, 1846 North 16th St., 51501 (tel. 712/328-8300).
● Heartland Inn, 1000 Woodbury Ave., 51501 (tel. 712/322-8400 or toll free 800/334-3277. $29 single; $34 double; $39 triple; $44 quad.
● Super 8 Motel, 2712 S. 24th St., 51501 (tel. 712/322-2888).

Creston

Accommodation: Super 8 Motel, 804 W. Taylor, 50801 (tel. 515/782-6541).

Davenport

Accommodations: Motel 6, 6111 North Brady St., 52806 (tel. 319/391-8997).
● Exel Inn, 6310 North Brady St., 52804 (tel. 319/386-6350).
● Hampton Inn, 3330 E. Kimberly Rd., 52807 (tel. 319/359-3921).
● Budget Host—Town House, 7222 Northwest Blvd., 52806 (tel. 319/391-8222).
● Super 8 Motel, 410 E. 65th St., 52807 (tel. 319/388-9810).

Des Moines

Tourist Information: Greater Des Moines Convention and Visitors Bureau, 309 Court Ave., Suite 300, 50309 (tel. 515/286-4960).
Help: First Call for Help (Travelers Aid), 700 Sixth Ave., 50309 (tel. 515/244-8646).

Accommodations: YMCA, 🚻, 101 Locust St., 50309 (tel. 515/288-0131). Men only. $19.50 single; $51.11 per week (available after a three-day stay at the regular rate). Advance reservations suggested.

● YWCA Residence, 717 Grand Ave., 50309 (tel. 515/244-8961). Women only. Eight blocks from bus station. $10 single. Weekly rate: $59 in single room. Pool and gym.

● Kirkwood Civic Center Hotel, Ⓢ√★, 400 Walnut St., 50309 (tel. 515/244-9191 or 800/345-8629. $30 single; $36 double; $48 triple or quad.

● Motel 6, 4817 Fleur Dr., 50321 (tel. 515/287-6364).

● Econo Lodge, 5626 Douglas Ave., 50310 (tel. 515/278-1601).

● Super 8 Motel, 4755 Merle Hay Rd., 50323 (tel. 515/278-8858).

Dubuque

Accommodations: Regal 8 Inn, 2670 Dodge St., 52001 (tel. 319/556-0880).

● Heartland Inn, 4025 Dodge St., 52001 (tel. 319/582-3752 or toll free 800/334-3277). $29 single; $34 double; $39 triple; $44 quad.

● Super 8 Motel, 2730 Dodge St., 52001 (tel. 319/582-8898).

Fort Dodge

Accommodations: YWCA, 826 First Ave. North, 50501 (tel. 515/573-2911). Women only. $9 single. Weekly rate: $23.

● Super 8 Motel, 3040 E. 5th Ave., 50501 (tel. 515/576-8000).

Iowa City

Help: Crisis Center, 321 E. First St., 52240 (tel. 319/351-0140).

On Campus: The University of Iowa has a ride board in the Iowa Memorial Union. One eating place recommended by an Iowa City native is Bushnell's Turtle, on the mall on East College (for large subs, homemade soup, and hot apple cider). The Bijou, the movie theater at the Iowa Memorial Union, shows old and new films for only $2.

Accommodations: Wesley House Youth Hostel (AYH), 120 North Dubuque St., 52240 (tel. 319/338-1179). Two miles south of I-80. Closed November 23 to 26 and December 21 to January 3. Students only. $7 for AYH members.

● Motel 6, 810 First Ave., Coralville, 52241 (tel. 319/354-0030).

● Super 8 Motel, 611 1st Ave., Coralville, 52241 (tel. 319/337-8388).

Keokuk

Accommodations: A&B Globe Motel, Main Street Road on Hwy. 218 North, 52632 (tel. 319/524-4312) $15.95 for one; $18.95 to $23 double; $27 triple; $31 quad.

● Super 8 Motel, 3511 Main St., 52632 (tel. 319/524-3888).

Lamoni

On Campus: According to a friend from Graceland College, people are generally friendly toward strangers. When it's time to eat, all of the restaurants are "good and inexpensive compared with big-city prices." If you're in Lamoni on a Thursday, visit the cattle auction at the Sale Barn. The cafe attached to the barn serves "a very country, very wholesome, filling meal for about $3.50." To meet students, stop in at the K Bar C, T/D Corral, the Pizza Shack, the Out Post, the Swarm Inn, or Pizza Hut. There is also a dance club in the basement of the Coliseum movie theater—open Thursday, Friday, and Saturday evenings when school is in session. Contact the director of housing for temporary on-campus housing. Varsity Drug (downtown) also offers a wide variety of travel services.

Le Mars

On Campus: Westmar College is here and you can spend a night or two at the College Residence Hall—contact the dean of students for information. "We're just corn fields—Sioux City is 25 miles south." Three good eating spots are the Pantry Cafe, Central Avenue and 1st Street NE; the Club Cafe, 20 Plymouth St. SW; and Munro's, south on Highway 75. For a bit of culture, ask someone about the "excellent collection of exotic musical instruments" in the city. There's a museum on 4th Street SW and Second Avenue.

Marshalltown

Accommodation: Super 8 Motel, Hwy. 14 South, P.O. Box 156, 50158 (tel. 515/753-8181).

Mason City

Accommodations: Days Inn, 2301 4th St. SW, 50401 (tel. 515/424-0210).
● TraveLodge, 24 5th St., 50401 (tel. 515/424-2910).

Muscatine

Accommodation: Super 8 Motel, U.S. Highway 61 and Highway 38, 52761 (tel. toll free 800/843-1991).

Newton

Accommodation: Days Inn, 1605 West 19th St. South, 50208 (tel. 515/792-2330).

Oskaloosa

Accommodations: Friendship Mahaska Motel, 1315 A Ave. East, 52577. (tel. 515/673-8351).
● Super 8 Motel, 306 S. 17th St., 52577 (tel. 515/673-8481).

Ottumwa

Accommodation: Heartland Inn, Highway 63 North, 52501 (tel. 515/682-8526, or toll free 800/334-3277). $29 single; $34 double; $39 triple; $44 quad.

Sioux City

Help: A.I.D. Center, 206 6th St., 51101 (tel. 712/252-1861).

Accommodations: Motel 6, 6166 Harbor Dr., c/o General Delivery, Sergeant Bluff, 51054 (tel. 712/277-3131).

● Super 8 Motel, 4305 Stone Ave., 51106 (tel. 712/274-1520).

Spencer

Accommodation: Super 8 Motel, 209 11th St. SW, 51301 (tel. 712/262-8500).

Walcott

Accommodation: Super 8 Motel, Walcott I-80 Industrial Park, 52773 (tel. 319/284-5083).

Waterloo

Accommodations: YWCA, 425 Lafayette, 50703 (tel. 319/234-7589). Call in advance. Women only. $10 per night per single; $25 to $30 per week per single. Kitchen privileges included.

● Exel Inn, 3350 University Ave., 50701 (tel. 319/235-2165).

● Heartland Inn, 1809 La Porte Rd., 50702 (tel. 319/235-4461 or toll free 800/334-3277). $29 single; $34 double; $39 triple; $44 quad.

Kansas

Kansas is the geographic center of the U.S. and the breadbasket of the world. When Dwight Eisenhower told a European audience "I come from the heart of America," he was referring to Abilene, Kansas, the town where he grew up. The Eisenhower family home is preserved and the Eisenhower library and museum were opened in 1962.

Many historic trails crossed through early Kansas—you can almost hear the wagonmaster's cry of "Wagons Ho!" in parts of the Chisholm Trail, along which Indian trader Jesse Chisholm drove his cattle on the way from Texas to Abilene; Lewis and Clark's route, which follows the Missouri River along the northeastern boundary of the state; the Oregon Trail, which was so heavily traveled in the years after 1848 by people heading for California gold; the Santa Fe Trail, which was used as a trade route with Mexico; and the Smoky Hill Trail, which was the quickest way to the Denver goldfields discovered in 1859. There's an organization that operates one-day covered-wagon trips through the Scenic Flint Hills. Write to Flint Hills Overland Wagon Train Trips, P.O. Box 1076, El Dorado, KS 67042 (tel. 316/321-6300).

Some Special Events: Messiah Festival in Lindsborg (during Easter Week); After Harvest Czech Festival in Wilson, and Mexican Fiesta in Topeka (July); Walnut Valley Bluegrass Festival, Flat-Picking Championship Contest in Winfield, and Renaissance Festival in Bonner Springs (September); Neewollah Celebration in Independence, and Maple Leaf Festival in Baldwin City (October). Write to the Department of Commerce for a *Calendar of Events*.

Tourist Information: Travel and Tourism Division, Kansas Department of Commerce, 400 W. 8th St., 5th Floor, Topeka, KS 66603 (tel. 913/296-2009). The Department operates information centers in Topeka, I-70 in Kansas City, I-70 in Goodland, and I-35 at South Haven.

N.B. Kansas City Bed and Breakfast is a reservations service, with accommodations in Kansas City, Leawood, Lenexa, Overland Park, Parkville, Independence, and St. Joseph. For details, write to P.O. Box 14781, Lenexa, KS 66215 or call 913/888-3636.

Clay Center

Accommodation: Budget Host—Cedar Court Motel, 9th & Hwy. 24, Box 186, 67432 (tel. 913/632-2148).

Coffeyville

Accommodation: Budget Host—Townsman Motel, 600 Northeast St., 67337 (tel. 316/251-2010).

Colby

Accommodations: Budget Host—Country Club Motel, 460 Country Club Dr., 67701 (tel. 913/462-7568).
● Super 8 Motel, 1040 Zelfer Ave., Box 628, 67701 (tel. 913/462-8248).

Dodge City

Accommodations: Budget Host—Thunderbird Motel, 2300 West Wyatt Earp Blvd., 62801 (tel. 316/225-4143).
● Super 8 Motel, 1708 W. Wyatt Earp Blvd., 67801 (tel. 316/225-3924).

Ellsworth

Accommodation: Budget Host—Garden Motel, Jct. Hwys. 156 and 140, Box 44, 67439 (tel. 913/472-3116).

Emporia

Accommodations: TraveLodge, 3021 West Hwy. 50, 66801 (tel. 316/342-3770).
● Econo Lodge, 2630 West 18th Ave., 66801 (tel. 316/343-1240).
● Super 8 Motel, 2913 W. Hwy. 50, 66801 (tel. 316/341-7567).

Goodland

Accommodation: Motel 6, I-70 and Hwy. 27, Rte. 1, Box 96E, 67735 (tel. 913/899-5672).

Great Bend

Accommodations: Econo Lodge, 4701 10th St., P.O. Box K, 67530 (tel. 316/792-8235).
● Super 8 Motel, 3500 10th St., 67530 (tel. 316/793-8486).

Greensburg

Accommodation: Kansan Inn, √, 800 East Kansas Ave., 67054 (tel. 316/

723-2141). $19.75 to $23.75 for one; $27.75 to $30.75 for two in one bed; $29.75 to $32.75 for two in two beds.

Hays

Accommodations: Motel 6, 3404 Vine St., 67601 (tel. 913/625-4282).
● Budget Host—Villa Budget Inn, 810 East 8th at Vine Street, 67601 (tel. 913/625-2563).
● Econo Lodge, I-70 & 3503 Vine St., 67601 (tel. 913/625-4839).
● Hampton Inn, 3801 N. Vine St., 67601 (tel. 913/625-8103).
● Super 8 Motel, 3730 Vine St., 67601 (tel. toll free 800/843-1991).

Hesston

Accommodation: Budget Host—Heritage Inn, 606 East Lincoln, 67062 (tel. 316/327-4231).

Hill City

Accommodation: Budget Host—Western Hills Motel, 800 West Hwy. 24 (Box 389), 67642 (tel. 913/674-2141).

Hutchinson

Accommodation: Super 8 Motel, 1315 East 11th Ave., 67501 (tel. 316/662-6394).

Junction City

Accommodations: Budget Host—Golden Wheat Budget Inn, 820 S. Washington, 66441 (tel. 913/238-5106).
● Super 8 Motel, 211 W. Flinthills Blvd., 66441 (tel. 913/238-8181).

Kansas City

Accommodations: YMCA, 900 North 8th St., 66101 (tel. 913/371-4400). Men only. $9.50 per night plus $3 key deposit.
● Days Inn, 9630 Rosehill Rd., Lenexa, 66215 (tel. 913/492-7200).
● Red Roof Inn, 6800 West 108th St., Shawnee Mission, 66211 (tel. 913/341-0100).
● Motel 6, 9725 Lenexa Dr., Lenexa, 66215 (tel. 913/541-1266).

Lawrence

On Campus: The University of Kansas is in Lawrence and the Union is a good place to meet KU students. At night the scene switches to the minibars and restaurants on Massachusetts, the town's main street. You'll find Dos Hombres, Liberty Hall, Paradise Cafe, and The Wheel among others. When hunger strikes, there's the Tin Pan Alley, where you can get sandwiches and salads, or La Tropicana, serving Mexican food. There is also the Haskell Indian Junior College in South Lawrence.

Help: KU Information Center, 105 Burge Union, 66045 (tel. 913/864-3506). Open 24 hours. "We'll help with questions about directions, where to eat, what to do . . . The country around Lawrence is beautiful with a number of small and large lakes for swimming and fishing. The Information Center is here to tell you what is happening."

Help and Emergency Accommodation: Headquarters, Inc., 1419 Massachusetts, 66044 (tel. 913/841-2345). Headquarters is a crisis-intervention center with volunteers who can help if you're going through a bad time and will tell you who else can help. Open 24 hours daily. For emergencies there's a bedroom available. There is usually a one-night limit and one hour's worth of housework is required as payment.

Accommodations: Econo Lodge, 2907 West 6th St., 66044 (tel. 913/843-6611).
- Super 8 Motel, 515 McDonald Dr., 66044 (tel. 913/842-5721).

Leavenworth

Accommodation: Super 8 Motel, 303 Montana Crt., 66048 (tel. 913/682-0744).

Liberal

Accommodations: TraveLodge, 564 East Pancake Blvd., 67901 (tel. 316/624-6203).
- Super 8 Motel, 747 E. Pancake Blvd., Box 297, 67901 (tel. 316/624-8880).

Manhattan

Tourist Information: Chamber of Commerce, 505 Poyntz, 66502 (tel. 913/776-8829).

On Campus: When you visit Kansas State University in Manhattan, the first thing you realize is that it doesn't look like what you thought it would look like. There are hills and trees and lakes and its fun! Since it's the home of the Kansas State University Wildcats, the students have one of the biggest and best student unions around, the K-State Union. KSU also has an International Student Center to accommodate foreign visitors. The off-campus hangout is Aggieville, a section right off campus. It's been said that if you put a roof over Aggieville, you'd have the biggest bar in the country. Since Kansas State is a state institution there are restrictions on alcoholic beverages allowed on campus, so you'll find the action either in Aggieville or at Tuttle Creek Reservoir when the weather's nice (there's camping there, too). The University Master Calendar, located in the Reservations Office, second floor of the K-State Union, is the place to find out what's going on—call 913/532-6591.

, Manhattan has all the typical hamburger, taco, and fried-chicken places you'd expect, but for good down-home cooking try the Chef at 111 South 4th or Last Chance Restaurant and Saloon at 1215 Moro in Aggieville.

For rides out of town, there's a ride board on the second-floor concourse in the K-State Union that really works.

Accommodation: Motel 6, 510 Tuttle Creek Blvd., 66502 (tel. 913/537-1022).

McPherson

Accommodations: Budget Host—Wheat State Motel, 111 Roosevelt (Box 374), 67460 (tel. 316/241-4230).

● Super 8 Motel, 2110 E. Kansas, 67460 (tel. 316/241-8881).

Medicine Lodge

Accommodation: Budget Host—Rancho Motel, 500 Black Gold, 67104 (tel. 313/886-3453).

Newton

Accommodation: Super 8 Motel, 1620 E. 2nd St., 67114 (tel. 316/283-7611).

Norton

Accommodation: Budget Host—Hillcrest Motel, West Hwy. 36 and 383, Box 249, 67654 (tel. 913/877-3343).

Oakley

Accommodations: Budget Inn-Country Club Motel, 709 Center, 67748 (tel. 913/672-3161).

● TraveLodge, 708 North Center Ave., 67748 (tel. 913/672-3226).

Olathe

Accommodation: Econo Lodge, 209 East Flaming Rd., 66061 (tel. 913/829-1312).

Ottawa

Accommodation: Econo Lodge, 2331 S. Cedar, 66067 (tel. 913/242-3400).

Quinter

Accommodation: Budget Host—Q Motel, I-70 and 212 Hwy., Box 398, 67752 (tel. 913/754-3337).

Sabetha

Accommodation: Budget Host—Koch Motel, U.S. Hwy. 75 South, Box 235, 66534 (tel. 913/284-2145).

Salina

Accommodations: Budget Host—Vagabond Inn, 217 South Broadway, 67401 (tel. 913/825-7265).
● Super 8 Motel, 1640 W. Crawford, 67401 (tel. 913/823-9215).
● TraveLodge, 245 South Broadway, 67401 (tel. 913/827-9351).

Smith Center

Accommodation: Budget Host—Modern Aire Motel, 117 West Hwy. 36, Box 34B, 66967 (tel. 913/282-6644).

Topeka

Accommodations: Motel 6, 3846 South Topeka Ave., 66609 (tel. 913/267-1222).
● Motel 6, 709 Fairlawn Rd., 66606 (tel. 913/272-8283).
● Super 8 Motel, 5968 S.W. 10th St., 66604 (tel. 913/273-5100).

WaKeeney

Accommodation: TraveLodge, I-70 and Hwy. 283, 67672 (tel. 913/743-2121).

Wichita

Tourist Information: Wichita Convention and Visitors Bureau, 100 S. Main St., Suite 100, 67202 (tel. 316/265-2800).
Accommodations: Motel 6, 5736 West Kellogg, 67209 (tel. 316/945-8440).
● Budget Host—English Village Motor Lodge, 6727 East Kellogg, 67207 (tel. 316/683-5613).

Kentucky

The theme is horses. They take them very seriously in Kentucky—from the breeding to the racing. If you're planning to go to the Kentucky Derby in May this year, be sure to check to see if there's room at the Derby Hostel at the University of Louisville.

Some of the major attractions in Kentucky are: in the north-central part of the state, the Abraham Lincoln Birthplace in Hodgenville, the "Stephen Foster Story" outdoor drama at My Old Kentucky Home in Bardstown, Shaker Village at Pleasant Hill, and the unique Kentucky Horse Park near Lexington; in eastern Kentucky, Cumberland Gap in Middlesboro, the 672,000 acre Daniel Boone National Forest, Cumberland Falls near Corbin, and world-renowned handcrafts; in western Kentucky, the National Boy Scout Museum in Murray, Kentucky and Barkley lakes, and 170,000-acre Land Between the Lakes; and in the south-central part of the state, Mammoth Cave National Park, Lake Cumberland, and the Big South Fork National River and Recreation Area.

The 42 Kentucky state parks include luxury resorts, recreational parks, and historic sites. Most parks offer camping, swimming, beaches or pools, boating, fishing, golf, tennis, and hiking. The 15 resort parks also offer lodges, cottages, and fine dining. Reservations can be made by calling toll free 800/255-PARK.

A free booklet, *Kentucky Trails,* which lists trails and areas for backpacking, day hiking, bikeways, equestrian trails, canoe routes, ORV trails, and state park maps, is available from the State Naturalist, Kentucky Department of Parks, Capital Plaza Tower, Frankfort, KY 40601.

Other free literature, available from the Kentucky Department of Travel Development (address below), includes *The Traveller's Guide to Kentucky, Kentucky State Parks, Outdoor Recreation Guide, Calendar of Events,* and the "Official Highway Map."

According to the Kentucky Department of Travel Development, "Natural Bridge State Resort Park and the Red River Gorge are a fantastic draw among young people. They flock there for the beauty and solitude, camping and canoeing."

Some Special Events: Kentucky Derby Festival in Louisville (late April to early May); Harlan Homecoming and Poke Sallet Festival in Harlan (late June); Berea Craft Festival in Berea and Bluegrass Festival in Renfro Valley (mid-July); Wheel Horse Draft Horse Show at the Kentucky Horse Park (early September); Cave City Good Ole Days, and Black Patch Tobacco Festival in Princeton (mid-September); and Carter County Sorghum Festival in Grayson (early October).

Tourist Information: Travel, Department of Travel Development, Capital Plaza Tower, Frankfort, KY 40601. Call toll free 800/225-TRIP.

N.B. A bed-and-breakfast reservation service for Kentucky is Bluegrass Bed & Breakfast, Rte. 1, Box 263, 40383 (tel. 606/873-3208).

Ashland

Accommodation: Knights Inn, U.S. 60 West, 7216 S.R. 60, 41101 (tel. 606/928-9501).

Berea

Accommodation: Econo Lodge, I-75 and Ky. 21, P.O. Box 183, 40403 (tel. 606/986-9323).

Bowling Green

On Campus: A friend at Western Kentucky University told us that his campus is not really used to transients, but that if you want to help them get more used to them you should probably head for the Downing Center on campus. He says there are good camping areas—it costs only $7.50 to get a campsite at Beech Bend Park. For good eating he recommends a popular truck stop on the Bypass called Mary's Restaurant.

Accommodations: Motel 6, 3139 Scottsville Rd., 42101 (tel. 502/843-0140).
- Days Inn, 181 Cumberland Trail, 42101 (tel. 502/781-6330).
- Econo Lodge, I-65 and Hwy. 31 West, Rte. 14, Box 61, 42101 (tel. 502/781-6181).
- Scottish Inn, 3140 Scottsville Rd., 42101 (tel. 502/781-6550).
- Super 8 Motel, 250 Cumberland Trace Rd., 42101 (tel. 502/781-9594).

Cave City

Accommodation: Quality Inn, I-65 at Exit 53, 42127 (tel. 502/773-2181).

Central City

Accommodation: Economy Inn, Hwys. 62 and 431 and West Kentucky Parkway 42330 (tel. 502/754-2441). $20.90 for one; $24.95 for two in one bed; $28.50 for two in two beds.

Corbin

Accommodations: Days Inn, I-75 and U.S. 25 West, P.O. Box 10, 40701 (tel. 606/528-8150).
- Knights Inn, I-75 at U.S. 25, RR 11, Box 256, 40701 (tel. 606/523-1500).
- Scottish Inn/Town House, 804 South Main St., 40701 (tel. 606/528-3434).

Elizabethtown

Accommodations: Days Inn, I-65 and U.S. 62, Exit 94, P.O. Box 903, 42701 (tel. 502/769-5522).
- Friendship Cloverleaf Inn, 711 E. Dixie Ave., 42701 (tel. 502/765-2194).
- Motel 6, U.S. Hwy. 62 and I-65, 42701 (tel. 502/769-3102).
- Super 8 Motel, 2028 N. Mulberry St., 42701 (tel. 502/737-1088).

Florence

Accommodation: Super 8 Motel, 7928 Dream St., 41042 (tel. 606/283-1221).

Frankfort

Accommodations: Days Inn, I-64 and U.S. 127 South, 40601 (tel. 502/875-2200).
- Scottish Inn, 711 East Main St., 40601 (tel. 502/223-2041).
- Super 8 Motel, 1225 U.S. Hwy. 127 South, 40602 (tel. 502/875-3220).

Fulton

Accommodation: Quality Inn, U.S. 51 and Purchase Parkway, Rte. 1, Box 366, 42041 (tel. 502/472-2342).

Georgetown

Accommodation: Days Inn, I-75 and Delaplain Road, Exit 129, 40324. (tel. 502/863-5000).

Horse Cave

Accommodation: Budget Host Inn, I-65 Exit 58, S.R. 218, Box 332, 42749 (tel. 502/786-2165).

Lexington

"The place to visit if you are interested in horses or bluegrass."

On Campus: Visiting students can call Student Housing (tel. 606/257-3721) to rent a room for $20 a night. Favorite eating places near campus are High on Rose, a crowded bar with beer and Mexican food; Alfalfa, a mostly vegetarian restaurant; Joe Bologna, for pizza and Italian food; Jefferson Davis Inn, corner of Limestone and High Street; Two Keys Tavern, Limestone Street; and Charlie Brown's on Euclid Avenue.

Accommodations: YMCA, 239 East High St., 40507 (tel. 606/254-9622). Men only. $20 per night. Weekly rate: $85.

● Red Roof Inn, 483 Haggard Lane, 40505 (tel. 606/293-2626).

● Days Inn, 1675 North Broadway, 40505 (tel. 606/293-1421).

● Knights Inn, I-75 at Winchester Pike, 2250 Elkhorn Rd., 40505 (tel. 606/299-8481).

● Super 8 Motel, 2351 Buena Vista Rd., 40505 (tel. 606/299-6241).

Louisville

Tourist Information: Louisville Visitors Bureau, Founders Square, 40202 (tel. 502/582-3732).

Help: Family and Children's Agency, Travelers Aid Service, 1115 Garvin Place, 40203 (tel. 502/584-8186).

● Crisis and Information Center, 502/589-4313.

On Campus: The University of Louisville's International Center can help foreign visitors find their way around. Call 502/588-6602 to find out how to get there. To meet students, stop at the Butchertown Pub, 1335 Story Ave.; Bristol Bar and Grill, 1321 Bardstown Rd.; City Lights, 117 West Main; or Cardinal's Nest and Red Barn restaurants in the student center. The people at the university's Red Barn run a hostel during Derby weekend. For information, call 502/588-6691. For discounts in the area, contact the Student Government Association at 502/588-6695.

Accommodations: Kentucky Derby Student Hostel, 2011 South Brook St., 40292 (tel. 502/588-6691). "A tent city located in a secure area of campus offering indoor showers, continental breakfasts, and parking areas." Open Thursday through Sunday afternoon of Derby weekend. Advance reservations suggested. $5 per night.

● Days Inn, I-71 and Ky. 53, LaGrange, 40031 (tel. 502/222-7192).

● Days Inn, I-65 and Ky. 44, 40165 (tel. 502/543-3011).

● Hampton Inn, 1902 Embassy Square Blvd., 40299 (tel. 502/491-2577).

● Motel 6, 3304 Bardstown Rd., 40218 (tel. 502/456-2861).

● Knights Inn, I-64 at Hurtsbourne Lane, 1850 Embassy Square Blvd., 40299 (tel. 502/491-1040).

● Red Roof Inn, 9330 Blairwood Rd., 40222 (tel. 502/426-7621).

● Red Carpet Inn, 9512 Hurstbourne Lane, 40220 (tel. 502/491-7320).

Madisonville

Accommodations: Econo Lodge, 1117 East Center St., P.O. Box 187, 42431 (tel. 502/821-0364).

● Red Carpet Inn, U.S. Hwy. 41 North, P.O. Box 470, 42431 (tel. 502/821-7677).

Mammoth Cave

Camping and Accommodation: Mammoth Cave National Park, 42259. There's camping at headquarters ($6 per campsite per night) and at Houchin's Ferry (no fee) all year.
- Mammoth Cave Hotel, 🖾, Mammoth Cave National Park, 42259 (tel. 502/758-2225). $20 to $40 single; $25 to $47 double; $29 to $52 triple; $34 to $57 quad. Hotel and cottages available. Advance reservations of two weeks necessary.

Middlesboro

Camping: Cumberland Gap National Historical Park, √, P.O. Box 1848, 40965 (tel. 606/248-2817). 160 developed campsites; four backcountry campsites accessible by hiking. $7 per campsite per night. Showers available.

Mount Sterling

Accommodation: Days Inn, I-64 and U.S. 460, Ragland Avenue, 40353 (tel. 606/498-4680).

Owensboro

Accommodations: Motel 6, 4585 Frederica St., 42301 (tel. 502/686-8606).
- Days Inn, U.S. 231 and 60 Bypass, 42301 (tel. 502/684-9621).

Paducah

Accommodations: Days Inn, I-24 and U.S. 60 West, 42001 (tel. 502/442-7501).
- Drury Inn, I-24 and U.S. 60, Hinkleville Road, P.O. Box 9246, 42001 (tel. 502/443-3313).
- Best Inns of America, 5001 Hinkleville Rd., I-24 & U.S. 60 (tel. 502/442-3334).

Pippa Passes

Accommodation: Pippa Passes Home Hostel (AYH), c/o Ed and Charlotte Madden, P.O. Box 15, 41844 (tel. 606/368-2753). $5.25 for AYH members.

Richmond

Accommodations: Super 8 Motel, 107 N. Keenland, 40475 (tel. 606/624-1550).
- Knights Inn, I-75 at Exit 90-A, U.S. 421, 40475 (tel. 606/624-2612).

Russell

Accommodation: YMCA, Mulberry Street, 41169 (tel. 606/836-6344). Men only. $13.50. Weekly rate: $45.

Somerset

Accommodation: Super 8 Motel, 302 S. Hwy. 27, 42501 (tel. 606/679-9279).

Williamstown

Accommodation: Econo Lodge, 2110 Ky. 36 West, 41097 (tel. 606/824-5025).

Winchester

Accommodation: Scottish Inn, 1510 W. Lexington Ave., 40391 (tel. 606/744-9220).

Louisiana

The big attraction is New Orleans with its Vieux Carré, Preservation Hall Jazz, and two weeks of Mardi Gras celebration that falls 47 days before Easter. It's a shame that most travelers making the typical cross-country trips never make it as far south as Louisiana—a detour is worth considering.

Although New Orleans is probably the reason you'll be coming to Louisiana, there is more to see if you have the time. (See the New Orleans section, page 230.) To get a feeling for the state's past there are two historical sites, each about three hours from New Orleans, that deserve a visit. The first, the Acadian House Museum in St. Martinville, in the very heart of Cajun country, displays artifacts of the early French period of the area. Some say that this home may have once belonged to Louis Arcenaux, the model for Longfellow's Gabriel in his poem "Evangeline." The Acadians, or Cajuns, still keep their distinct subculture alive and well in the 20th century. The second is the Rosedown Plantation and Gardens, a restoration of an 1835 mansion that is lavishly furnished and surrounded by fabulous formal gardens designed in the 17th-century French manner; a tour of the house is available.

On the River Roads, on both sides of the Mississippi River between New Orleans and Baton Rouge, are several other plantations that also capture the flavor of Louisiana's past. They are San Francisco, Destrehan, and Houmas House on the east bank, and Oak Alley and Nottoway on the west. All are open to the public for a fee of from $3 to $4 and some have restaurant facilities.

One book recommended by the Office of Tourism for those interested in Louisiana is *The Pelican Guide to Plantation Homes of Louisiana,* by Nancy Harris Calhoun and James Calhoun, Pelican Publishing Company ($4.95). The

Louisiana Office of Tourism (address below) offers a guidebook and highway map free of charge to travelers.

Some Special Events: New Orleans Jazz and Heritage Festival, and Christmas and Tomato Festival in Chalmette (May); Jumbalga Festival in Gonzales, and Louisiana Peach Festival in Ruston (June); New Orleans Food Festival, and Cajun Festival in Montegut (July); Seafood Festival in Lafitte (August); and the North Louisiana Cotton Festival and Fair in Bastrop (September).

Tourist Information: Department of Culture, Recreation, and Tourism, located at 666 N. Foster Dr., Baton Rouge, 70806, or write P.O. Box 94291, Baton Rouge, LA 70804-9291 (tel. 504/925-3850, or toll free 800/227-4386).

N.B. New Orleans Bed & Breakfast is a reservations service listing homes in all areas of New Orleans and throughout Louisiana and Mississippi, and can accommodate "one or a bunch." Rates run from $15 to $40 per person. For information, write to them at P.O. Box 8128, New Orleans, LA 70182, or call 504/822-5038 or 822-5046. Another service for Louisiana and other areas of the South is Southern Comfort B & B Reservation Service, 2856 Hundred Oaks, Baton Rouge, LA 70808 (tel. 504/346-1928 or 928-9815).

Alexandria

Tourist Information: Rapides Parish Convention and Visitors Bureau, P.O. Box 8110, 71306 (tel. 318/443-7049).

Baton Rouge

Tourist Information: Baton Rouge Area Convention and Visitors Bureau, 838 North Blvd., 70802 (tel. 504/383-1825).

On Campus: You may be able to spend a night or two on campus in Pleasant Hall, but first you must obtain special permission from the International Student Office, Raphael Semmes Road, 70803–1201 (tel. 504/388-3191) at Louisiana State University.

If you go to Murphy's or the Bengal, 2286 Harlem Rd. (tel. 504/387-5571), you'll be able to meet LSU students. They suggest Round-the-Corner, 3347 Highland, for inexpensive food.

There is a bulletin board located in the Union near "Tiger Lair" cafeteria, and you might be able to find helpful information in the Student Government Office, 327 Union.

Accommodations: Motel 6, 2800 I-10 Frontage Rd., Port Allen, 70767 (tel. 504/343-5945).

- Budgetel Inn, 10555 Rieger Rd., 70809 (tel. 504/291-6600).
- Regal 8 Inn, 9901 Gwen Adele, 70816 (tel. 504/924-2130).
- Days Inn, 215 Lobdell Hwy., Port Allen, 70767 (tel. 504/387-0671).
- Days Inn, 10245 Airline Hwy., 70815 (tel. 504/293-9680).
- Hampton Inn, 10045 Gwen Adele Dr., 70816 (tel. 504/924-4433).
- Hampton Inn, 4646 Constitution Ave., 70808 (tel. 504/926-9990).
- Red Carpet Inn, 2445 South Acadian Thruway, 70808 (tel. 504/925-8141).
- Scottish Inn, 2142 West Hwy. 30, 70737 (tel. 504/647-8787).

Bossier City

Accommodation: Motel 6, 210 John Wesley Blvd., 71112 (tel. 318/742-3472).

Lafayette

Tourist Information: Lafayette Convention and Visitors Commission, P.O. Box 52066, 70505 (tel. 318/232-3737).

On Campus: Lafayette is the capital of Acadiana and the home of the University of Southwestern Louisiana. The multiple festivals in Acadiana—Music Festival, Crawfish Festival, Boudin Festival, La Grande Boucherie, Mardi Gras, Bayou Food Festival—depict the "joie de vivre" of the French-speaking Cajun people expressed in music and food. The joy and gentleness of the people are captivating.

For inexpensive seafood, there's Pat's in Henderson or Don's in Lafayette. To be with the young people of the area, you can go to Grant St. Dance Hall, 52nd Street, America's Favorite Bar, Antler's, the Keg, or Mulate's.

Accommodations: Imperial 400 Motor Inn, 410 West Vermilion, 70501 (tel. 318/235-9051).

- Motel 6, 2724 N.E. Evangeline Thruway, 70501 (tel. 318/233-2055).
- Superior Motor Inn, 711 Frontage Rd., 70501 (tel. 318/232-0070, or toll free 800/445-1773). $19.95 for one or two persons; $24.95 for two or three persons (in two beds); $28.95 for four persons (in two beds).
- Econo Lodge, 1605 North University, P.O. Box 3783, 70501 (tel. 318/232-6131).
- Super 8 Motel, 2224 N.E. Evangeline Thwy., 70501 (tel. 318/232-8826).

Lake Charles

Tourist Information: Southwest Louisiana Convention and Visitors Bureau, P.O. Box 1912, 70602 (tel. 318/436-9588).

Accommodations: Motel 6, 335 Hwy. 171, 70601 (tel. 318/433-1773).

- Imperial 400 Motor Inn, 825 Broad St., 70601 (tel. 318/436-4311).
- Econo Lodge, 1101 West Prien Lake Rd., 70601 (tel. 318/474-5151).

Monroe

Accommodations: TraveLodge, 401 Grammont St., 71201 (tel. 318/322-5430).

- Motel 6, 1501 U.S. I-65 Bypass, 71202 (tel. 318/322-5430).

Natchitoches

Accommodation: Super 8 Motel, 801 Hwy. 3110 Bypass, 71457 (tel. 318/352-1700).

New Orleans

Two hundred fifty years of French, Spanish, Italian, West Indian, and finally American influence have made New Orleans the appealing place it is today, probably the most European city in all of North America. Narrow streets, antebellum mansions, old-time jazz, Creole culture, and the busy Mississippi River are all reminiscent of another time, one recalled so well in the books of Mark Twain, William Faulkner, and Tennessee Williams. In spite of the ultra-contemporary hotels and the space-age Superdome, much of New Orleans is not new at all. Many old ways are alive and well in this city. Mardi Gras is, of course, New Orleans's big event. It always falls on the Tuesday 47 days before Easter. New Orlean's Carnival Parades begin many days before the actual Mardi Gras, on Fat Tuesday.

"During Mardi Gras, the French Quarter is just one long party."

Two guidebooks published by Pelican (1101 Monroe St., Gretna, LA 70053, tel. toll free 800/843-4558 in Louisiana, 800/843-1724 out of state) are *A Marmac Guide to New Orleans* and *The Pelican Guide to New Orleans*. Both include suggested itineraries in and around the city as well as restaurants, accommodations, events, etc. The first one even has discount coupons in the back and special chapters called "The International Visitor" and "Special People" (for senior citizens, disabled, children, and students).

Jazz Fest is always held during the last weekend in April and the first weekend in May. The festival is held on the infield of the Fair Grounds Race Track. Approximately 10 stages are set up with continuous music of blues, cajun, reggae, gospel, jazz, etc. There are local entertainers and a few "name" entertainers. The added attraction is the huge selection of local food such as red beans and rice, gumbos, alligator, pasta dishes, desserts, boiled and fried seafood, "po-boys," and much more.

Getting There: New Orleans (Moisant) International Airport is 5 miles west of the central business district and the French Quarter. Cab fares vary: the fare for one person to downtown is $18. Cheaper still is the Rhodes Airport Transport Service's limousine service between the airport and the downtown hotels, which costs $7 per person. Call 504/469-4555 for limo reservations at least one day in advance for the trip from the hotel to the airport. And least expensive of all is the Louisiana Transit Company's express bus service, which will get you from the airport to a terminal on Tulane Avenue (near the Civic Center, downtown) for only 90¢. Call 504/737-9611 for information. The Trailways bus terminal is at 1314 Tulane Ave., near downtown (tel. 504/525-4201), and Greyhound's terminal is at 1001 Loyola Ave., downtown (tel. 504/525-9371).

Getting Around: If you need a map of the city, get a free one at the Tourist Commission, 529 St. Ann, in the French Quarter. The city bus system (called RTA) also has an information desk in the French Quarter, at 317 Baronne (tel. 504/529-4545), where you can pick up a map of bus routes. Bus service is inexpensive (60¢ for regular service) and generally efficient. The trolley line that links the French Quarter with the uptown district of the city is more than just a relic—it's a popular source of public transportation, day and night; at 60¢ there is no better self-guided tour of the city. Several bus companies provide transportation to the outlying parishes. St. Bernard Bus Lines, Inc. (tel. 504/279-5556), goes to Arabi, Chalmette, and places nearby. Gretna, Harvey, and various suburbs across the river are served by Westside Transit Lines, Inc. (tel. 504/366-3258). The airport and the surrounding East Jefferson Parish are served by the Louisiana Transit Company (tel. 504/737-9611). Algiers and communities on the West Bank are connected by a free ferry which leaves from the Canal and Jackson Street docks; the trip takes ten minutes and is especially beautiful at night.

Tourist Information: Greater New Orleans Tourist and Convention Commission, Inc., 1520 Sugar Bowl Drive, 70112 (tel. 504/566-5011). Maps, hotel information, and a calendar of events are all here and are free.

Help: Volunteer and Information Agency, 504/524-HELP. "During Mardi Gras, a Mardi Gras coalition is formed to help visitors."

Accommodations in the French Quarter: St. Peter Guest House, Ⓢ ★ (25%) 1005 St. Peter, 70116 (tel. 504/524-9232, or toll free 800/535-7815). $40 to $65 for one or two people. "An historic building in the center of the French Quarter with antique and period-furnished rooms, balcony, and courtyard."

● Old World Inn, 1330 Prytania St., 70130 (tel. 504/566-1330). $27.50 to $39 single; $35 to $45 double. Price includes breakfast. "Atmosphere combines European warmth with Southern hospitality." Highly recommended.

● St. Charles Guest House, Ⓢ∨ ★ (10%), 1748 Prytania St., 70130 (tel. 504/523-6556). $20 to $42 single; $25 to $48 double; $40 to $55 triple; $45 to $70 quad. Advance reservations suggested. "A simple, cozy, affordable bed-and-breakfast near French Quarter with patio and pool." Another hotel that gets high marks from a native of the city.

● A Creole House, 1013 St. Ann, 70116 (tel. 504/524-8076). Rates start at $39.50 single; $49.50 double.

● Andrew Jackson Hotel, 919 Royal, 70116 (tel. 504/561-5881). Low season rates start at $40 single and $45 double. Peak season rates (Mardi Gras, Jazz Fest, and during the summer) start at $50 single and $55 double.

● Burgundy Inn, 911 Burgundy, 70116 (tel. 504/524-4401). Rooms starting at $38 and up. Convenient parking, located in quieter section of French Quarter.

● Nine-O-Five Royal Hotel, 905 Royal, 70116 (tel. 504/523-0219). Single $35; double $45. Courtyard, kitchenettes, quaint European-style hotel.

● Bed and Breakfast Inc., 1360 Moss St., Box 52257, 70152, (tel. 504/525-4640, or toll free 800/228-9711). Have various B&B homes throughout New Orleans. Rates start at $25 single and $35 double. Cribs are available in some homes.

Accommodations near the French Quarter within easy access via trolley: Columns Hotel, 3811 St. Charles, 70115 (tel. 504/899-9308). Rates begin at $35 for a double room. Rooms with balconies in a nice neighborhood. Continental breakfast included.

● YMCA, ♿, 936 St. Charles, 70130 (tel. 504/568-9622). Men, women, and children. $15.40 single; $22 double. "More than a room, with safety, comfort, convenience, cleanliness."

● India Hotel, 124 South Lopez, 70119 (tel. 504/822-7833). $12 single; $14 double; $5 for dormitory room. Primarily for international students who are backpacking. Complimentary breakfast. "A bit like a European hostel."

● La Salle Hotel, Ⓢ∨ ★, 1113 Canal St., 70112 (tel. 504/523-5831, toll free in Louisiana 800/643-4955; out of state 800/521-9450). $25 to $36 single; $30 to $42 double; $33 to $45 triple; $36 to $48 quad. Discounts do not apply during Mardi Gras when rates are slightly higher. Advance reservations suggested.

● Hummingbird Hotel and Grill, ⑤ √ ★ (10%), 804 St. Charles, 70130. (tel. 504/561-9229). $16 for one or two people; $20 to $22 for three or four. Breakfast, lunch, and dinner served in the grill, which is open 24 hours every day of the year. "Family-run historical landmark hotel . . . in a convenient location."

● Parkview Guest House, ⑤ √ ★ (10%), 7004 St. Charles, 70118 (tel. 504/861-7564). $40 to $55 single; $50 to $65 double; $62 to $75 triple; $70 to $85 quad. Advance reservations preferred. "A Victorian guesthouse listed in the National Register of Historic Landmarks."

● St. Charles Inn, 3636 St. Charles Ave., 70118 (tel. 504/899-8888). Convenient location on St. Charles Ave., streetcar runs in front of hotel. $42 single; $52 double. Que Sera, a sidewalk restaurant, is downstairs. Nice for having an afternoon drink.

● Marquette House (AYH), ⑤ ★ (10%), 2253 Carondelet St., 70130 (tel. 504/523-3014). $9 per night for AYH members, slightly higher for nonmembers. $17 single and $23 double for members in private room; $19 single and $25 double for nonmembers; add $6 for each additional person. Advance reservations of one month necessary during Mardi Gras, and suggested during summer. "Housed in a 100-year-old home reminiscent of antebellum New Orleans."

Accommodations outside of Downtown: A car is required to reach downtown or the Garden District from these hotels—approximately 15 to 20 minute drive.

● Superior Motor Inn, 4861 Chef Menteur Hwy., 70126 (tel. 504/283-1531). $29 single; $32 double. No cribs available.

● Days Inn, 1300 Veterans Blvd., Metairie, 70002 (tel. 504/469-2531).

● Days Inn, 5801 Read Blvd., 70127 (tel. 504/241-2500).

Where to Eat: New Orleans is known for its food and its restaurants. Here's a list of some of the more popular, but not too expensive, restaurants. Keep in mind the fact that many of the city's restaurants are closed on Monday.

In the French Quarter and Downtown: Buster Holmes, 721 Burgundy St., (tel. 504/561-9375). Average meal $1.50 to $4.

● Cafe du Monde Coffee Stand, in the French Market, by the river. Try the beignets. "Great restaurant!"

● Central Grocery, 923 Decatur St. (tel. 504/523-1620). Sandwiches are $3.50; try the muffulettas.

● Chez Helene, 1540 North Robertson St. (tel. 504/947-9155). A good soul-food restaurant where a meal costs anywhere from $8 to $14.

● Felix, 739 Iberville St. (tel. 504/522-4440). Have oysters on the half shell, at the bar, and be prepared to splurge.

● Gumbo Shop, 630 St. Peter St. (tel. 504/525-1486). The gumbo is among the best in town; a meal costs from $8 to $10; a sandwich is about $4.

● Mother's, 401 Poydras St. (tel. 504/523-9656). Taste the roast beef "poor boy," dressed. $2.75 to $3.50 *"Probably the most famous and best 'poor boys' in town."*

● The Coffee Pot, 714 St. Peter St. (tel. 504/523-8215). For a breakfast served in a courtyard. A meal is about $5. Open all night. "The food is delicious."

● Cafe Maspero's, 601 Decatur St. (tel. 504/523-8414). Nice setting with lots of dark varnished wood. A small menu but huge sandwiches that are excellent.

● Houlihan's, 315 Bourbon St. (tel. 504/523-7412). A Creole bistro featuring French onion soup, spinach salad, and quiche Lorraine.

● Vera Cruz, 1141 Decatur, also uptown at 7537 Maple St., (tel. 504/523-9377). The food is Mexican, the portions are huge, and the quality is somewhere between good and excellent.

● Mama Rosa's Slice of Italy, 616 N. Rampart (tel. 504/523-5546). Wonderful pizza and homebaked bread. A small pizza, which is really large enough for 3 or 4 people, costs $8.

Uptown: Camellia Grill, 626 South Carrollton Ave. (tel. 504/861-9311). Located on the trolley line. The cheeseburger is always a winner, but if you're feeling more adventurous try a "Cannibal Special." The freezes and the pecan pie are excellent. Omelettes, for $4, are great.

● Casamento's, 4330 Magazine St. (tel. 504/895-9761). Many people think that their oyster loaf is the best in town. Closed in summer.

● Parasol's, 2533 Constance (tel. 504/899-2054). "Po' boy" sandwiches. Neighborhood bar and restaurant in the Irish part of town.

● Cafe Savanna, 8324 Oak St. (tel. 504/866-3223). A nice place with an open patio, ceiling fans, and other accessories. Meals are $7 to $10; sandwiches and omelets about $4.

● Mais Oui, 5908 Magazine St. (tel. 504/897-1540). Cajun/Creole-soul food meals for $7 to $12.

What to Do: "The best things to do in New Orleans are walk and eat and drink. Other activities include antique shopping on Magazine Street and plantation tours outside the city."

For listings of what's going on in New Orleans, check the *Times Picayune* (especially Friday edition's "Lagniappe"), *Gambit,* the uptown weekly, and *New Orleans Magazine,* a monthly publication. *Wavelength* is another monthly with good information on the where's and when's of local bands. It's free in record stores and bars.

● In the French Quarter, begin by walking; stroll around Jackson Square, see the Cabildo and the Presbytere. Ride the New Orleans Steamboats for a fascinating journey on the Mississippi or into bayou country. Boats dock at Toulouse Street and Canal Street wharves. Call the tourist office for information at 504/568-5661. Be sure, too, to walk along the Moonwalk in the evening. It's along the river, just opposite Jackson Square. Some places that we recommend visiting are:

● New Orleans Museum of Art, Lelong Avenue, City Park, 70179 (tel. 504/488-2631). Open Tuesday through Sunday from 10 a.m. to 5 p.m. Free admission to ISIC-holders.

● Casa Hove, 723 Toulouse St., one of the oldest buildings in the Mississippi Valley, furnished in period pieces and open Monday to Saturday, 10 a.m. to 4:30 p.m. A tour costs $1.50.

● Gallier House, 1118–1132 Royal St. (tel. 504/523-6722). To tour this fine example of 19th-century architecture and furnishings costs $2.50. The house is open Monday to Saturday, 10 a.m. to 4:30 p.m.; Sunday, 1 to 4:30 p.m.

● Musee Conti Wax Museum, 917 Conti St. (tel. 504/525-2605). Here you'll see the history of New Orleans from 1682 to the 20th century unfold. Open Monday to Friday, 9:30 a.m. to 5:30 p.m.; Saturday and Sunday, 10 a.m. to 9 p.m. Admission is $3.

● At the corner of Canal and Carondelet Streets you can step onto the St. Charles streetcar for a journey along broad St. Charles Avenue into uptown New Orleans and its magnificent Garden District. Between 1st and 7th Streets, from St. Charles to Magazine, the area has some of the finest antebellum architecture in the South. See the Old Cemetery in the Garden District, bounded by 6th, Coliseum, Prytania, and Washington Streets; Audubon Park and Zoo, farther uptown than the Garden District, near the trolley line; and Audubon Place, across from the park, a palm-tree-lined boulevard which is literally out of another century.

● Jazz and Heritage Festival, P.O. Box 2530, New Orleans, 70176 (tel. 504/522-4786). At the end of April, beginning of May, two weekends are crammed full of music—jazz, blues, gospel, and rock. There's food, crafts, and unbeatable people-watching possibilities.

● The Audubon Zoo, 6400 Magazine St. (tel. 504/861-2537). Open 10 a.m. to 6 p.m. You can take a "zoo cruise"—a riverboat from downtown to the zoo where the animals lie in a "natural" setting. A nice afternoon activity.

● The controversial Superdome, at 1500 Poydras St. (tel. 504/587-3645), seats over 95,000 spectators for sports events, concerts, conventions, and even an indoor Mardi Gras Parade! It's located on nine acres.

At Night: For jazz: As with our restaurant suggestions, the following listing is only meant as an appetizer. After all, jazz was born in New Orleans and it can be heard all over the French Quarter. Some favorites: Preservation Hall, 726 St. Peter (tel. 504/522-2238), "the classic place" to hear oldtime jazz; Storyville New Jazz Hall, 1104 Decatur (tel. 504/525-8199), for traditional and progressive jazz; Muddy Waters, 8301 Oak, behind the French Quarter; Snug Harbor, 626 Frenchmen (tel. 504/944-0696), behind the French Quarter; Pete Fountain's Place, Hilton Hotel, Poydras Street (tel. 504/523-4374) and the river; or Crazy Shirley's, 640 Bourbon St.

● You'll find jazz outside the Quarter too, as well as blues, rock, Cajun, reggae, and just about any other type of music you can name. Some popular music spots beyond the Quarter are the Dream Palace, 534 Frenchmen (tel. 504/943-6860), a popular nightclub near the French Quarter; the Maple Leaf Bar, 8316 Oak (tel. 504/866-9359), featuring a relaxed atmosphere and music anywhere from reggae to blues; Jimmy's, 8200 Willow (tel. 504/861-8200), where you'll hear mostly rock, country, and new wave, and across the street from Jimmy's, Carrollton Station (tel. 504/865-9190) for jazz, blues, or rock—in a neighborhood bar.

● To dance: La Boucherie, 339 Chartres. Lives up to its name—a loud, disco-type place—or Maple Leaf Bar, 8301 Oak (tel. 504/866-9359) a down-to-earth dance spot.

● For films: The Prytania, 5339 Prytania (tel. 504/895-4513), has $5 double features—a favorite for foreign films.

● For classical music: The New Orleans Symphony's season runs from fall to spring; tickets run from $5 to $15. The symphony's home is the beautifully restored Orpheum Theater, 129 University Pl (tel. 504/525-0340).

● For theater: Try one of these: Le Petit Theatre du Vieux Carre, 616 St. Peter (tel. 504/522-2081); Contemporary Arts Center, 900 Camp St. (tel. 504/523-1216); Theatre Marigny, 616 Frenchmen (tel. 504/944-2653); Saenger Performing Arts Center (tel. 504/587-3200).

● For neighborhood bars: Two we like are the Mayfair, 1505 Amelia, corner of Prytania (tel. 504/895-9163), and Charity's, 1005 Lowerline (uptown off Broadway).

● Cooter Brown's, 5095 Carrollton (tel. 504/865-9166). A good bar with darts, videos, a large selection of imported beers, and pool tables, too. Oysters on the half shell, 15¢ a piece.

● Napoleon House, 500 Chartres (tel. 504/524-9752). A very old bar in the French Quarter with lots of character—French doors open onto patio and street. Nice place for a drink.

Shopping: For books: Maple Street Bookshop, 7523 Maple (tel. 504/866-4916). All kinds of books.

● For records: Leisure Landing Records, 5500 Magazine. Best in the city for whatever kind of music you like.

● South Warehouse, 5500 Magazine. Complete selection of music.

● Record Ron's, 1129 Decatur (tel. 504/524-9444). Current and rare records —will buy and trade.

● For sporting goods: Canoe and Trail Shop, 624 Moss (tel. 504/488-8528). For all types of camping equipment.

● For general shopping: Uptown Square Shopping Center, 200 Broadway (tel. 504/866-4513). Lots of boutiques with tempting things inside.

● Jax Brewery, at Jackson Square and the Mississippi River (tel. 504/529-1211). Shops, cafes, and restaurants.

● The Riverwalk, at the foot of Canal Street. A shopping area along the river —cafes and restaurants. Located on the former site of the Louisiana World's Fair.

Shreveport

Tourist Information: Shreveport-Bossier Convention and Tourist Bureau, P.O. Box 1761, 629 Spring St., 71166 (tel. 318/222-9391, or toll free 800/551-8682 outside of Louisiana).

Accommodations: Motel 6, 4915 Monkhouse Dr., 71109 (tel. 318/631-9691).

● Econo Lodge, 4911 Monkhouse Dr., 71109 (tel. 318/636-0771).

● Super 8 Motel, 5204 Monkhouse Dr., 71109 (tel. 318/635-8888).

Slidell

Tourist Information: St. Tammany Parish Tourist and Convention Commission. P.O. Box 432, 2020 First St., 70459 (tel. 504/649-0730).

Accommodations: Econo Lodge, I-70 and Gause Boulevard., P.O. Box 1358, 70459 (tel. 504/641-2153).

● Days Inn, 1645 Gause Blvd., 70458 (tel. 504/641-3450).

● Motel 6, 136 Taos St., 70458 (tel. 504/649-7925).

Maine

Maine is a beautiful state—its coastline attracts lots of visitors in the summer months, and Acadia National Park on Mount Desert Island is a mecca for campers, hikers, fishers, and nature lovers. In this park you'll find mountains, lakes, seashore, and more than 75 carriage trails that are a hiker's dream. If you can get to Acadia in the spring or early fall you'll be able to appreciate it all the more. If the summer crowds get to you, head north of Bar Harbor to the miles of unspoiled wilderness and wooded area that stretch to the Canadian border.

Many tourists favor the southern coast of Maine from York to Bath, which includes Ogunquit, home of a well-known summer playhouse. And those who have even the mildest interest in camping and things out-of-doors really should treat themselves to a visit to the headquarters of L.L. Bean, a store that campers and sportsmen dream about. Located in Freeport, L.L. Bean is open every single day of the year, 24 hours a day.

"We stopped at L. L. Bean at midnight on a summer Tuesday night and you might have thought, by the size of the crowd, that it was the day before Christmas!"

More attractions in Maine are Mt. Katahdin, the state's highest peak and the beginning of the Appalachian Trail, and Lily Bay State Park on Moosehead Lake, the largest natural lake within one state in the U.S.

When you get hungry in Maine, take advantage of the bean suppers, barbecues, and seafood festivals that are held in small towns all over the state, especially during the summer. The food is inexpensive, plentiful, and, best of all, homemade with love. Check for posters outside supermarkets and along the road.

The Appalachian Mountain Club publishes two very good outdoor guides to Maine, which are available from AMC, 5 Joy St., Boston, MA 02108. They are *AMC Maine Mountain Guide* ($10.95), and *AMC Guide to Mount Desert and Acadia National Park* ($3.50); include $1.50 per book for shipping and handling. Another recommended guidebook is *Maine—An Explorer's Guide,* by Christina Tree and Mimi Steadman, The Countrymen Press, Woodstock, VT 05091 ($13.95).

Some Special Events: Annual Chicken Barbecue and Fiddlers Contest in Bowdoinham, Clam Festival in Yarmouth, and Seacoast Festival in Kennebunkport (July); Blueberry Festival in Union, and Downeast Jazz Festival in Camden (August); Common Ground Country Fair in Windsor (September); and Fair in Fryeburg (October).

Tourist Information: Maine Publicity Bureau, 97 Winthrop St., Hollowel, ME 04347 (tel. 207/289-2423).

N.B. A bed-and-breakfast reservation service for Maine is Bed & Breakfast of Maine, 32 Colonial Village, Falmouth, ME 04105 (tel. 207/781-4528).

Alfred

Accommodation: The Olde Berry Inn, c/o Kathe and Lloyd Gallegos, Kennebunk Road, P.O. Box 286, 04002 (tel. 207/324-0603). $30 to $35 double. Three rooms with shared baths in 1804 Colonial in village near Bunganut Lake. Includes full breakfast. Call for reservations.

Augusta

Help: Crisis Counseling, 207/623-4511.

Accommodations: Susse Chalet Motor Lodge, Maine Turnpike, I-95, Winthrop Exit, on Whitten Road, 04330 (tel. 207/622-3776).

● Crosby's B&B, c/o David and Joyce Crosby, 51 Green St., 04330 (tel. 207/622-1861). $34 to $36 double. Includes full breakfast. 1870s home near Capitol complex.

Bangor

Accommodation: Susse Chalet Lodge, I-95 Exit 45B, Rte. 2, West 1100 Hammond St., 04401 (tel. 207/947-6921).

Bar Harbor

Camping: Acadia National Park, Rte. 1, P.O. Box 177, 04609. Blackwoods and Seawall are the two campgrounds with over 500 sites altogether. Blackwoods, five miles south of Bar Harbor, is open year round. Seawall is open May to late September. $8 per campsite per night without reservations; $10 with reservations.

Bass Harbor

Accommodation: Pointy Head Inn, c/o Doris and Warren Townsend, Rte. 102A, 04653 (tel. 207/244-7261). $35 to $45 double. Sea captain's seashore home with trails. Full breakfast included. Open April to October. Call for reservations.

Belfast

Accommodation: Hiram Alden Inn, c/o James and Jacquelyn Lovejoy, 19 Church St., 04915 (tel. 207/338-2151). $35 to $40 double. Sea captain's 1840 home. Full breakfast included. Call for reservations.

Blanchard

Accommodation: Crossroads Inn, RFD 1, Box 54, Abbot Village, 04406. (tel. 207/997-3920). Open May 15 to October 15 and February 1 to 28. $5 summer, $7 winter. Sleeping bags required. Reservations strongly advised.

"Appalachian Trail passes the door; canoeing the Piscataquis River even closer."

Camden

Accommodation: Blue Harbor House B&B, c/o Thomas and Lorraine Tedeschi, 67 Elm St., 04843 (tel. 207/236-3196). $18 to $70 double. Full breakfast included. Call ahead for reservations.

Carmel

Accommodation: Ring Hill Hostel (AYH), Rte. 2, Box 235, 04419 (tel. 207/ 848-2262). Open June 1 to September 30 and February 1 to 28. Transportation from Bangor International Airport available. $6 for AYH members. Advance reservations necessary.

Eastport

Accommodation: Weston House, c/o Jett and John Peterson, 26 Boynton St., 04631 (tel. 207/853-2907). $30 to $45 double. Five rooms in landmark 1810 Federal home. Full breakfast included. Call for reservations.

Fort Kent

Accommodation: Residence Hall, ♿, Pleasant Street, University of

Maine at Fort Kent, 04743 (tel. 207/834-3162). Open May 1 to September 1. Shuttle service from bus station (43 miles away) available at certain times of the year. Near Allagash Waterways. $10 per person; $2 deduction if guest provides own linen or sleeping bag. Advance reservations of one week necessary. Cafeteria on premises.

Harrington

Accommodation: S.E.A.D.S., Inc. Hostel (AYH), Georgetown Road, P.O. Box 262A, 04643 (tel. 207/483-9763). $5 for AYH members.

Kennebunk

Accommodation: Friendship Inn, ME Turnpike (I-95), Exit 3, P.O. Box 575, 04094 (tel. 207/985-3541).

Monson

Accommodation: The Old Church, Ⓢ★, 04464 (tel. 207/997-3691). Open June 15 to October 15. $8 for AYH members; $11 for nonmembers.

Ogunquit

Accommodation: Yardarm Village Inn, c/o Phyllis and Lawrence Drury. 130 Shore Rd., P.O. Box 773, 03907 (tel. 207/646-7006). $34 double. Open May 15 to October 15. Includes continental breakfast. Call for reservations.

Orono

On Campus: The University of Maine is in Orono, and the Memorial Union Building is the hub of life there. For good food and entertainment, go to Margarita's on Mill Street; to meet students, just stop at the Bear's Den in the Union. You might be able to pay a reasonable price for a dorm room in the summer—just check with the Student Affairs Office on the Main Floor of Memorial Union.

"I'm from Tennessee and I think this place is great—the people are friendly and there's lots and lots of snow for winter fun."

Peaks Island

Accommodation: Moonshell Inn, c/o Elinor Clark, Island Ave., 04108. (tel. 207/766-2331). $29 to $53 double. Old house with stairs to beach. Continental breakfast included. Call for reservations.

Portland

Help: Hotline, 207/774-4357.

Accommodations: YWCA, 87 Spring St., 04101 (tel. 207/874-1130). Women only, at least 18 years of age. $18 single; $15 per person double. Advance reservations of one week suggested.

● Susse Chalet Motor Lodge, Maine Turnpike I-95, Exit 8, on Brighton Ave., 04102 (tel. 207/774-6101).

● Super 8 Motel, 208 Larrabee Rd., Westbrook, 04092 (tel. 207/854-1881).

Surry Village

Accommodation: Time and Tide Bed and Breakfast, RFD 1, Box 275-B (on Rte. 172), 04684 (tel. 207/667-3382 or 667-4696). Open mid-June to Labor Day, and the last week in September to the last week in October. $19.50 single; $27 double; $39 triple; $51 quad; rates 10% higher in August. Breakfast included.

West Bethel

Accommodation: Kings Inn, c/o Mac and Bunny MacMunn, Box 92, 04286. (tel. 207/836-3375). $40 double. Wilderness inn three miles inside National Forest. Full breakfast included. Call for reservations.

West Gouldsboro

Accommodation: The Sunset House, c/o Dan and Ruth Harper, Rte. 186, HCR 60, Box 62, Gouldsboro, 04607 (tel. 207/963-7156). $35 to $45 double. Full breakfast with afternoon tea included. Three-story 1898 Victorian house on 2 ½ acres. Call for reservations.

Maryland

Although many people limit their travel in Maryland to the suburban belt around Washington, D.C., there's lots of breathtaking farmland, oceanside, and wildlife beyond. One of the most interesting features about Maryland is the Eastern Shore, named after the three states of Delaware, Maryland, and Virginia—the Delmarva Peninsula. On "The Shore" is a mixture of farmland, fishing villages, colonial towns, large estates, and a seaside resort. To set the mood for a visit, read James Michener's *Chesapeake.*

Annapolis, Maryland's historic capital, was the country's first peacetime capital and since 1845 it has been the home of the U.S. Naval Academy. The U.S. Department of the Interior has designated one square mile of downtown Annapolis as a historic district—and many landmarks still stand. A walking tour of Annapolis should include a look at the City Dock area with its restored City Market, shops, and seafood restaurants.

Baltimore is a city with a maritime atmosphere and a reputation for excellent seafood. Also well known for its association with the national anthem (Francis Scott Key wrote "The Star-Spangled Banner" there), it has many landmarks worth visiting: Fort McHenry, U.S.S. *Constellation,* B & O Railroad Museum, Harborplace, National Aquarium, and the Maryland Science Museum with its IMAX Theater.

Two books that concentrate on travel from Baltimore are *Day Trips from Greater Baltimore,* by Gwyn Willis, Globe Pequot Press ($7.95), and *The Baltimore One-Day Trip Book,* by Elois Paananen, EMP Publications ($8.95). A book that covers all of Maryland is *The Pelican Guide to Maryland* by Victor and Tom Block, Pelican Publishing ($9.95).

For help in finding your way around Maryland, write to the Office of Tourist Development (address below) and ask for *Maryland Travel Guide,* a Calendar of Events, an Outdoor Guide for camping and recreational information, and a Bicycle Map.

Some Special Events: NASA Goddard Flight Center Model Rocket Launching in Greenbelt (first and third Sunday of every month); Winterfest in McHenry and Maryland Day Celebration in St. Mays City (March); Children's Festival in Annapolis and Main Street Festival in Laurel (May); Barbara Fritchie Motorcycle Race in Frederick (July); Jonathan Hager Frontier Crafts Day in Hagerstown and Crab Feast in Gaithersburg (August); Prince George's

County Fair in Upper Marlboro (September); and Harvest Weekend in Ellicott City (October).

Tourist Information: Office of Tourist Development, 45 Calvert St., Annapolis, MD 21401 (tel. 301/974-2686).

Aberdeen

Accommodation: Super 8 Motel, Rte. 22 and Beards Hill Road, 21001 (tel. 301/272-5420).

Baltimore

This is famous for its Harborplace, which includes plenty of food markets, boutiques, and an aquarium. The Marble Bar is a rock-and-roll club within walking distance of the Harbor, and it gets its name from the genuine-marble bar that Gene Kelly danced on once upon a time. Fells Point is another popular spot with its neighborhood bars and Bertha's Mussels, a popular spot specializing in mussels and other seafood treats as well. Another recommended Baltimore sight is the city's Museum of Art, at 10 Museum Dr. off North Charles Street, where the collection of impressionist paintings is certainly worth a visit.

If you are going to spend a while in Baltimore, you may want a copy of *Day Trips from Greater Baltimore,* by Gwyn Willis ($7.95), published by Globe Pequot Press.

Tourist Information: Baltimore Office of Promotion and Tourism, 34 Market Place, Suite 310, 21204 (tel. 301/752-8632).

Help: Travelers Aid, 204 N. Liberty, Suite 200, 21201 (tel. 301/685-3569).

Accommodations: The Shirley Guest House, ⑤∨ ★ (10%), 205 W. Madison St., 21201 (tel. 301/728-6550). Beautifully restored Victorian house, furnished entirely with antiques. $27.50 to $42.50 single or double; $26.66 to $30 triple. Includes continental breakfast and sherry aperitif in the evening. Reservations necessary.

● Baltimore International Hostel (AYH), 17 W. Mulberry St., 21201 (tel. 301/576-8880). $9 for AYH-IYHF members only. Closed December 24 to January 2.

● Friendship Inn, 306 W. Franklin St., 21201 (tel. 301/539-0227).

"Make sure you stop at the Lexington Market on Lexington and Eutaw Streets for the freshest seafood around. Another place I really enjoyed was the Peabody Book Store on Charles Street. It was an old, comfortable, dusty bar which looks like a library and has a wonderful fireplace."

Berlin

Camping: Assateague Island National Seashore, Rte. 2, Box 294, 21811 (tel. 301/641-1441). Three campgrounds on the island about ten miles south of Ocean City. Two primitive facilities open year round ($5 per campsite), one modern facility open April through October ($15 per campsite).

Betterton

Accommodation: Ye Lantern Inn (AYH), P.O. Box 29, Ericsson Ave., 21610 (tel. 301/348-5809). $7 summer, $8 winter for AYH members. Advance reservations necessary.

Capitol Heights

Accommodation: Motel 6, I-95 and Central Aveune West, 75 Hampton Park Blvd., 20743 (tel. 301/499-0800).

Edgewood

Accommodation: Econo Lodge, I-95, Exit 9, 21040 (tel. 301/679-3133).

Frederick

Accommodation: Super 8 Motel, 5579 Spectrum Dr., 21701 (tel. 301/695-2881).

Gaithersburg

Accommodation: Red Roof Inn, 497 Quince Orchard Rd., 20878 (tel. 301/977-3311).

Greenbelt

Camping: Greenbelt Park, 6565 Greenbelt Rd., 20770 (tel. 301/344-3944). Twelve miles from Washington, D.C. 174 sites open all year. $4 per campsite per night.

Hagerstown

Accommodations: YMCA, 149 North Potomac St., 21740 (tel. 301/739-3990). Four blocks from the bus station. Men only. $10 single. Weekly rate: $40.
- Budget Host Inn, 1716 Dual Hwy., 21740 (tel. 301/739-6100).
- Econo Lodge, Rte. 6, Box 195C, 21740 (tel. 301/791-3560).

244 WHERE TO STAY USA

Hancock

Accommodation: Budget Host—Timber Ridge Inn, Rte. 2, Box 308, I-70 (Exit 5) (tel. 301/678-6276).

Hanover

Accommodation: Red Roof Inn, 7306 Parkway Dr., 21076 (tel. 301/796-7700).

Jessup

Accommodation: Parkway Inn, Rte. 175 and Baltimore-Washington Pkwy., P.O. Box 367, 20794 (tel. 301/799-0300 or 776-5510). $26.95 for one; $29.95 for two in one bed; $33.95 for two in two beds.

Knoxville

Accommodation: Harpers Ferry Hostel (AYH), RR. 2, P.O. Box 248E, 21758 (tel. 301/834-7652). $7 per night in bunk rooms for AYH members, summer; $8 winter; $3 per night camping for members; additional $5 a night for nonmembers, good toward AYH membership.

Laurel

Accommodation: Budget Host—Valencia Motel, 10131 Washington Blvd., 20707 (tel. 301/725-4200).

Salisbury

Accommodation: Lord Salisbury Motel, ✓ ★, Rte. 13 N., 21801 (tel. 301/742-3251). $28 to $35 for one; $42 double.

Sharpsburg

Camping: Chesapeake and Ohio Canal National Historical Park, P.O. Box 4, 21782 (tel. 301/739-4200). Free camping along the canal year round at hiker-biker units located approximately every six miles along the towpath. Campsites are accessible by trail, boat, bike, and horseback. Water is available from mid-April to mid-November. The Antietam Creek Walk-In campground is open from Memorial Day to Labor Day. Primitive facilities. No fee.

Thurmont

Camping: Catoctin Mountain Park, 21788 (tel. 301/663-9330). Owens Creek campground open from mid-April to November 20. $4 per campsite per night.

Waldorf

Accommodations: Waldorf Motel, U.S. Rte. 301, Box 55, 20601 (tel. 301/645-5555). $32.55 for one; $35.70 for two in one bed; $38.85 for two in two beds.; $3.15 for each additional person.
- Super 8 Motel, 5050 Hwy. 301 South, 20601 (tel. 301/932-8957).

Williamsport

Accommodation: Days Inn, I-81 and U.S. 11, 310 East Potomac, 21795 (tel. 301/582-3500).

Massachusetts

At first look the Commonwealth of Massachusetts seems typically New England, but it has lots about it that's unique. Massachusett's beauty, although somewhat showy in the fall, is more hidden and unexpected in the other seasons. Winter is a difficult time to travel in this state since the weather, at best, is unpredictable. Summer and fall, although unbearably hot or disappointingly short, are the most sensible times to travel and sightsee.

If you travel through Massachusetts, try to include the Berkshires and the musical events at Tanglewood, the Amherst region with its rich cultural life that is rooted in the area's many colleges and universities, lovely but sometimes overcrowded Cape Cod, and of course the cities of Boston and Cambridge. Massachusetts can show you rocky shores, sandy beaches, salt marshes, cranberry bogs, gentle hills, valleys, woods, meadows, and fields. Nearly every town has a river, a lake, or a pond to be proud of.

Because so much of the important early history of the U.S. took place in Massachusetts, there are many historic sights to visit—Lexington and Concord, Boston Harbor, Salem. But there's more than the reminders of the past to see. There are lots of offbeat, lesser-known sights that will amuse; a medieval castle in Gloucester, a church built like an upturned ship in Hingham, the "Littlest House," also in Hingham, and on and on. According to one native, every town has its oddity—just ask.

You'll have no trouble at all gathering information about Massachusetts. Not only is there information from a vast number of public sources, but most of the people you'll meet will be happy to pass information on, to tell the legends and scandals of their town, and of course, to throw in a few complaints about their government.

Three books about Massachusetts that are recommended for the city-weary are the *AMC Massachusetts and Rhode Island Trail Guide* ($12.95), the *More Country Walks Near Boston,* by William Scheller ($7.95), both available from the Appalachian Mountain Club, 5 Joy St., Boston, MA 12108, and *Short*

Walks on Cape Cod and the Vineyard, by Hugh and Heather Sadlier, Globe Pequot Press ($5.95).

Some Special Events: The 26-Mile Patriot's Day Marathon Race in Boston (April); Flea Market in Brimfield (May); Blessing of the Fleet in Gloucester and Provincetown (June); Tanglewood Music Festival in Lenox (June through August); Heritage Days in Salem, Boston's Harbor Festival (July); New England Renaissance Festival in South Carver, Colonial Fair and Fife Drum Master in Sudbury, and Cranberry Festival in South Carver (September); Haunted Happenings in Salem (Halloween weekend); and First Night in Boston (December).

Tourist Information: Division of Tourism, Massachusetts Department of Commerce and Development, 100 Cambridge St., Boston, MA 02202 (tel. 617/727-3201). Call for a free "Spirit of Massachusetts Vacation Planner."

Amesbury

Accommodation: Susse Chalet Motor Lodge, I-95 at Rte. 110, 10913 (tel. 617/388-3400).

Amherst

Help: First Call for Help, 413/256-0121.
• Council Travel Services, 79 South Pleasant St., 2nd Floor, 01002 (tel. 413/256-1261).

Bass River

Accommodations: The Anchorage, 122 S. Shore Dr., 02664 (tel. 617/398-8265). $18 to $38 per room. Call for reservations.
• Captain Isaiah's House, 33 Pleasant St., 02664 (tel. 617/394-1739). $25 to $40 per room with shared bath. Includes continental breakfast. Restored old sea captain's house. Call for reservations.

Boston/Cambridge

The Boston/Cambridge area is a haven for students. Harvard, Radcliffe, MIT, Boston University, Northeastern, and Boston College are the largest schools in town and there are lots of smaller ones. You'll see students everywhere, but probably nowhere in greater concentration than in Harvard Square in Cambridge.

Boston is a well-loved city that's easy to walk around and easy to get to know in a fairly short time. A city of neighborhoods: there's Beacon Hill; Back Bay, with the Boston Common and the Public Gardens; and the North and South Ends. Adjacent to the North End are Haymarket Square, the Faneuil Hall Marketplace, which attracts tourists by the droves, Waterfront Park and

Boston's historic wharves. Boston's Chinatown is the third largest in the U.S. and a nice place for wandering.

To find out what's going on in the area, check the "Calendar" section of the *Boston Globe* on Thursdays, *Boston Magazine,* and *The Phoenix,* an alternative paper that comes out on Fridays.

Boston is famous for outdoor concerts where you can relax and picnic under the stars, accompanied by anyone from Madonna to the Boston Symphony. Look for series like "Concerts on the Common" and on the Esplanade. The North End hosts colorful and friendly Italian street fairs in the summer and fall. The Waterfront Festival takes place in the summer, and the famous Boston Marathon in the spring. "First Night" is Boston's New Year's Eve arts celebration.

Good guides are:

Flashmaps' Instant Guide to Boston, Flashmaps Publication Inc., 1985. A handy tourist information booklet with excellent area and localized maps.

Stepping Out, a year-round guide to 215 arts and entertainment attractions in Massachusetts. Available through the Massachusetts Cultural Alliance, 53 Harrison Ave., Boston, MA 02111.

The Complete Guide to Boston's Freedom Trail, Newtowne Publishing, P.O. Box 1882, Cambridge, MA 02238 ($3.95).

Car-Free in Boston: The Guide to Public Transit in Greater Boston and New England, Association for Public Transportation, Inc., P.O. Box 192, Cambridge, MA 02238. ($3.95 plus $1 shipping and handling). Explains how to use the transit system with routes and schedules.

Arthur Frommer's Guide to Boston, by Faye Hammel, Prentice Hall Press, $5.95. The familiar guidebook to points of interest, hotels, shopping, and nightlife.

Foreign visitors who plan to spend more than just a few days in Boston may want a copy of *Hello Boston,* a publication of the World Affairs Council of Boston, 22 Batterymarch St., 02109 (tel. 617/482-1740).

The Globe Pequot Press publishes *Guide to Recommended Thrift Shops of New England,* by L.A. Collins, Julie Hatfield, and Ruth Weinstein, 1982. An excellent guide for budget-minded clothes shoppers; *AIA Guide to Boston,* by Susan and Michael Southworthy ($14.95); *Historic Walks in Old Boston* and *Historic Walks in Cambridge,* by John Harris ($9.95), *Greater Boston Park and Recreation Guide,* by Mark Primack ($9.95); *In and Out of Boston With or Without Children,* by Bernice Chesler ($10.95), and *Boston's Freedom Trail,* by Robert Booth ($6.95 book; $9.95 cassette). See also the many New England area guides listed in our "Some Books to Read" section of Chapter 1.

Getting There: From the Airport: Logan Airport is only about two miles from the city. To get to town from Logan, simply take the free shuttle bus that stops at each major airline terminal and takes passengers to the Airport station on the Blue Line of the MBTA (subway). Take the Blue Line to Government Center (the fourth stop), change to the Green Line, and go one stop to the Park St. station, the heart of the city, or ask for directions on getting where you want to go. The MBTA fare is 60¢. A taxi will be about $10 to downtown, and as much as $20 to Cambridge.

● From the Bus Station: The Greyhound station is at 10 St. James Ave. near the Green Line's Arlington St. subway station (tel. 617/542-4304). The

Trailways station is at 555 Atlantic Ave., across from South Station on the Red Line (tel. 617/482-6620). Both are close to the center of town.

● From the Train Stations: Trains may stop at North Station or South Station. Both North and South Stations are also stops on the subway system.

Getting Around: Taxi: There are taxi stands at major intersections. You can either hail a cab or call one. The fare is 90¢ for the first one-sixth of a mile and 20¢ for each additional one-sixth.

● Subway: The fare is 60¢ for rides underground; 20¢ or more if you go above ground. All MBTA stations are color coded according to line (orange, red, blue, and green) and are marked with a large "T."

● Bus: The bus fare is 50¢. A special double-decker bus runs along the major shopping streets. MBTA transit information: 617/722-5657 or 722-5700.

● Car Rentals: Just check the Yellow Pages for the rates. Expect to be quoted about $30 per day for a compact car.

Tourist Information: There are information booths on Tremont Street next to the Park Street subway station or in the National Park Building at 15 State St. next to the Old State House.

● Greater Boston Convention and Visitors Bureau, Prudential Plaza, P.O. Box 490, 02199 (tel. 617/536-4100). Call 617/267-6446 for events of the day.

● Council Travel Services, 729 Boylston St., Suite 201, Boston, MA 02110 (tel. 617/266-1926).

Help: Travelers Aid, 711 Atlantic Ave. at East Street (tel. 617/542-7286).

● Project Place, 32 Rutland Pl. (tel. 617/267-9150). Drop in from 9 a.m. to 10 p.m. or call 24 hours a day, seven days a week. "From stubbed toes to suicide calls."

● Bridge Over Troubled Waters, Inc., 147 Tremont at West Street (tel. 617/ 423-9575). Counseling and free medical service.

● For information about Cambridge (and just about anywhere else you're going) contact Harvard Student Agencies, Thayer Hall-B, Cambridge, 02139 (tel. 617/495-5230).

On Campus: At Northeastern University, check the bulletin board at the Student Lounge in the ELL Center for apartments and rides. Some of the recommended places to eat nearby are the Mandalay Restaurant, 329 Huntington Ave., for Burmese food; Thai Cuisine on Westland Avenue for Thai food, and Kyoto Restaurant on Huntington Avenue for Japanese food. NU students can usually be found at Our House East at 55 Gainesborough St. or at the very inexpensive Husky Rest, 280 Huntington Ave.

Accommodations in Boston: Bed and Breakfast of Cambridge and Boston, P.O. Box 665, Cambridge, 02140 (tel. 617/576-1492). Place guests in private homes throughout the area. $40 to $70 single; $50 to $80 double; $15 extra per person.

● Berkeley Residence Club, 40 Berkeley St., between Copley Square and Arlington Street MBTA stations, 02116 (tel. 617/482-8850). Women only. $23 single; $28 double; $2 extra for first night if guest is not a YMCA member. Advance reservations of one week necessary. There's a cafeteria in the building, "a lovely walled garden," and access to a swimming pool.

● Boston YMCA, 316 Huntington Avenue, 02115 (tel. 617/536-7800). Men and women. Near Northeastern University and the Museum of Fine Arts. On MBTA's Arborway/Huntington Avenue line. $27 single; $38 double; $5 key deposit. 10 day maximum stay. Must be at least 18 years old.

● Garden Hall Dormitories, 164 Marlborough St., 02116 (tel. 617/267-0079 or 266-5232). Men, women, and children. Open 9 a.m. to 1 p.m. weekdays. June 1 to August 20; $18 per night with a three-night minimum. Weekly rate: $72. Monthly rate: $325 single, $375 double per person (private bathroom and kitchen). Reservations and advance payment required. Bring a sleeping bag—there's no linen.

● Anthony's Town House, 1085 Beacon St., Brookline, 02146 (tel. 617/566-3972). Near Boston University, 15 minutes by subway to downtown Boston. $30 to $35 single; $40 double; $50 triple; $60 quad. This brownstone has 14 rooms; "it's a very nice, friendly place."

● Susse Chalet Motor Lodge, off the Southeast Expressway., 800 Morrissey Blvd., 02122 (tel. 617/287-9100).

● The Longwood Avenue Guest House, ★, 83 Longwood Ave., Brookline, 02146 (tel. 617/277-1620). Only 1½ blocks from MBTA at Beacon Street, which will transport you to the Boston area in ten minutes. $20 to $30 single; $30 to $40 double; $50 triple. Advance reservations necessary. "An old Victorian home converted to a ten-room guesthouse."

● Boston International Hostel (AYH), &, 12 Hemenway and Haviland Streets, 02115. One block from the subway, Green Line (tel. 617/536-9455). $9 for members only—can join at hostel—$20 if U.S. citizen, $18 if visitor. Advance reservations suggested June 15 to September 30. Open 7 a.m. to 10 a.m. and 5 p.m. to 12 p.m. Saturdays in summer until 2:30 a.m.

● Beacon Inn, 1087 and 1750 Beacon St., 02146 (tel. 617/566-0088). $28 single; $36 (shared bath) to $39 (private bath) double; $35 single (private bath). Nonrefundable deposit of one night's rate to hold all rooms. Advance reservations of one week necessary in summer. "Four-floor traditional brownstone with ornate fireplaces and modern facilities."

Cambridge: Cambridge Bed & Breakfast, P.O. Box 211, Cambridge, 02140 (tel. 617/491-6300). $40 to $80 single; $55 to $90 double; $15 each additional person. Main house and carriage house built in 1892. Minutes from public transportation in Porter Square, north Cambridge. Call for reservations.

● Cambridge Family YMCA, 820 Massachusetts Ave., Cambridge, 02139 (tel. 617/876-3860). Men only. $24 single. Near Harvard and MIT.

● YWCA-Tanner House, 7 Temple St., Cambridge, 02139 (tel. 617/491-6050). Near Central Square. Women only. $25 single for members; $28 for non-members; $10 key deposit. Advance reservations suggested. Inexpensive restaurants nearby; swimming pool.

Where to Eat: Note—we've included both Cambridge and Boston possibilities here (Boston, unless otherwise noted).

● Legal Seafoods, in the Park Plaza Hotel, Arlington Street and Columbus Avenue, and in Cambridge: 5 Cambridge St. and Chestnut Hill Mall (tel. 617/426-4444). Fish is featured, but the meat and chicken are just as good. This is a very popular place so expect up to an hour's wait at dinnertime.

● Jacob Wirth, 31 Stuart St. (tel. 617/338-8586). Open every day. The food is German and American, and you can choose from a generous-size sandwich to a full dinner. This is an old, popular eating place with a saloon atmosphere that's best known for its specially brewed dark beer.

● Wursthaus, 4 Boylston St., Cambridge (tel. 617/491-7110). Another German/American place with good hot pastrami, a wide choice of beers, and a friendly Bavarian atmosphere.

● Joe Tecce's Restaurant, 55 North Washington St. (tel. 617/742-6210). In the

Italian North end, off Haymarket Square and right by Government Center. A meal of pasta, meat, and vegetables can cost $10, and according to one fan, "is worth every penny."

● Rubin's Kosher Deli, 500 Harvard St., Brookline (tel. 617/566-8761). A short MBTA ride out of the city but worth it when you crave real kosher deli. A full meal will cost almost $6, but a good and filling sandwich is under $3.

● No-Name Restaurant, 15 ½ Fish Pier, just past Anthony's Pier Four on the Wharf (tel. 617/338-7539). Fresh seafood at reasonable prices; well known for the chowder. Bring your own wine or beer and expect to wait in line.

● Durgin Park, 340 Faneuil Hall Marketplace, North Market Building. (tel. 617/227-2038). "Established before you were born." In the same spot since the late 1800s, this place is a definite part of the Boston tradition and a favorite with tourists.

● Brandy Pete's, 82 Broad St. (tel. 617/482-4165). A little of everything—steak, spaghetti, seafood, sandwiches. A short walk from Quincy Market. Closed on weekends.

● Quadalaharry's, 20 Clinton St. (tel. 617/720-1190). Next to Quincy Market. Great Mexican food and margaritas—an average meal is $7 at night.

● Pizzeria Uno, 731 Boylston St. (tel. 617/267-8554) in Boston and 22 JFK St. (tel. 617/497-1530) in Cambridge. A pizza for one and a salad or soup is $3.25 at lunch time.

● Union Oyster House, 41 Union St., near Quincy Market, (tel. 617/227-2750). New England seafood favorites in Boston's oldest restaurant. The average cost of an entree at dinner time is $8.95.

● Nick's Beef and Grille, 1688 Massachusetts Ave., Cambridge. Burgers, sandwiches, salads, etc. $5 to $7 for two people; $3 pitchers of beer.

● The European Restaurant, 218 Hanover St. (tel. 617/523-5694). A renowned family restaurant near the North End and The Children's Museum—Italian food and friendly atmosphere.

What to See and Do: Boston Common and Public Garden: The Common is the oldest park in the U.S. and provides a nice piece of green in the heart of downtown. The Public Garden, right across Charles Street from the Common, is where you'll find the swan boats in summer.

● Freedom Trail: The Freedom Trail is 2½ miles long with 16 historic sites, all connected by a red line on the sidewalk.

● Hancock Tower Observatory: Go to the top of this Copley Square building for a view of the city. Open 9 a.m. to 10:15 p.m. $2.75 for adults; $2 for children ages 5 to 12; $2.25 for students.

● Prudential Center: For a different view of the city, go up to the Skywalk on the 50th floor of the "Pru." Open 9 a.m. to 11 p.m., until midnight on weekends. $2 for adults; $1 for children; $1 for college students.

● Museum of Fine Arts, 465 Huntington Ave. (tel. 617/267-9377). Egyptian, Classical, and Asiatic art; impressionist painting; and early-American furniture. The Huntington Avenue streetcar stops right in front of the museum and there's a restaurant inside and a place for you to eat if you bring your own lunch. $5 for adults; children under 6 free. Free on Saturdays, 10 a.m. to noon.

● Museum of Science, Science Park (tel. 617/723-2500). Take the Green Line from Park Street to Science Park station. Exhibits about man's natural world and the things he has invented. See the new Mugar Omnimax Theater. Wonderful for all ages. Open every day. $6.50 for adults; $4 for children.

● Isabella Stewart Gardner Museum, 280 The Fenway (tel. 617/734-1359). Isabella Gardner was a fascinating, eccentric Bostonian whose fabulous art collection is housed in this reconstruction of a Florentine palace. Included is a Titian, some Vermeers, and paintings by Botticelli, Corot, etc.—all arranged by Mrs. Gardner with the stipulation that they must never be moved. There are free chamber music concerts at the museum; call for the schedule which varies with the season.

● Faneuil Hall Marketplace: One of the major tourist attractions in the country, Faneuil Hall/Quincy Market is a conglomeration of small shops and restaurants. Be prepared to elbow through crowds wherever you go, but do go. Especially popular Irish bars are The Purple Shamrock and The Black Rose.

● Beacon Hill: Originally, the hill was twice as high and it had a beacon on top of it so that sailors could find the city. The New Statehouse (the old one stands on Washington Street) was designed by Charles Bulfinch and built in 1797 and is the prototype for many other capitols, including the one in Washington. Louisburg Square with its lovely town houses and Charles Street are the epitome of Boston charm. Get off at Charles Street station on the T Red Line, walk down Charles Street halfway and turn left on any side street.

● Haymarket: In the North End near Faneuil Hall, this open-air market attracts crowds, especially on Friday and Saturday.

● New England Aquarium, Central Wharf, near Faneuil Hall Marketplace (tel. 617/742-8870). The world's largest fish tank and dolphin, whale, and scuba-diving shows. $5 for adults; $3 for children.

● John F. Kennedy Library, Columbia Point on Dorchester Bay (tel. 617/929-4567). $1.50 for adults; children under 16, free. The life and times of John F. Kennedy as shown through photos, memorabilia, and a 30-minute film.

● Harbor cruises go on the hour and whale-watching boats leave the wharf near Faneuil Hall every weekend during the summer. Call Boston Harbor Cruises, 617/227-4320; Bay State-Spray and Provincetown Steamship Company 617/723-7800; or AC Cruise Line, 617/426-8419.

● For a sightseeing tour of Boston by bus, contact The Gray Line, 617/481-3840, which offers a 50% discount to ISIC holders on any tour on a space-available basis.

● Charles River Esplanade. At the bottom of Beacon Hill, this is a wonderful park along the Charles River, for running, hiking, or strolling.

● For a free walking tour of the Harvard campus, go to the Admissions Office in Byerly Hall, 8 Garden St., Cambridge (tel. 617/495-5000). Tours on weekdays and Saturdays. For a look at MIT's campus, go to the school's information office inside the main entrance at 77 Massachusetts Ave.

● All in the Harvard area of Cambridge are the Fogg Art Museum, 32 Quincy St. (tel. 617/495-4544), with medieval, Oriental, and impressionistic works; the Busch-Reisinger Museum (tel. 617/495-2338), a collection of the art of central and northern Europe; and the Peabody Museum, 11 Divinity Ave., a collection of archeological, botanical, and geological exhibits and home of the famous glass models of nearly every flower on earth.

At Night: For music and dancing: Jack's, 952 Massachusetts Ave., Cambridge. The cover here is $1 to $3, and the style is casual. The music is blues, southern rock, rock and roll, and new wave. There's a small dance floor.

● For jazz: Ryle's, 212 Hampshire St., Inmar Square, Cambridge (tel. 617/876-9330). A good place to hear jazz. The music begins at 9:00. Take bus 69 to the Lechmere stop.

- The 1369 Club, 1369 Cambridge St., Cambridge (tel. 617/661-1369). Jazz nightly 9:30 to 1 a.m. Music all day on Sundays.
- Nightstage, 823 Main St., Central Square, Cambridge (tel. 617/497-8200). Local jazz/blues artists. Cover varies between $7 and $12. Shows start at 9 p.m.
- For dancing: Lynx Club, 120 Boylston St., Boston. Open dance floor with a disc jockey—contemporary/pop music. Open every night until 2 a.m. Cover charge usually $4.
- Metro and Spit, 15/13 Landsdowne St. (tel. 617/262-2424). Popular with college students and local young people. "Metro's a disco, Spit's a little more punk." Both clubs are gay on Sundays.
- For folk music: Passim's, 47 Palmer St., Harvard Square (tel. 617/492-7679). This daytime cafe turns into folk music headquarters at night. It's small and nice.
- Nameless Coffeehouse, First Parish Church, Main Sanctuary, 3 Church St., Cambridge (tel. 617/864-1630). Folk music. Performances start at 7:30 p.m.
- For classical music: Symphony Hall, 301 Massachusetts Ave. (tel. 617/266-1492). The home of the Boston Symphony. Call for performance schedule and prices—the season runs from September through April. "One of the most acoustically perfect concert halls in the world."
- New England Conservatory, 290 Huntington Ave., Boston (tel. 617/262-1120). Classical music, usually free. Usually begin at 8 p.m.
- For dance and ballet: Boston Ballet Company, the Metropolitan, 553 Tremont St. (tel. 617/542-3945). The season runs from November to March.
- For theater: Resident theater groups like Boston Shakespeare, the Lyric Stage, the Next Move Theater, and the American Rep offer good theater at prices that are reasonable.
- Shubert Theater, 265 Tremont St., Boston (tel. 617/426-4520). Ballet in this beautiful restored old theater.
- For movies: Somerville Theater, Davis Square, T stop Red Line. Cheap movies and music performances.
- The showings of movies each day at the Harvard Square Theater, 10 Church St., Cambridge (tel. 617/864-4580), are at reduced rates—their movies often start in the afternoons.
- For comedy: Catch a Rising Star, 1330 John F. Kennedy St., Cambridge. (tel. 617/661-9887).

Shopping: For books: Barnes and Noble, with several branches in the city, has popular books at discount prices.
- Reading International, corner of Brattle and Church Streets, Cambridge (tel. 617/864-0705 at Harvard Square). Mostly paperbacks; large selection of periodicals and some foreign-language magazines, journals, and papers.
- Wordsworth, 30 Brattle St., Cambridge (tel. 617/354-5201). Good selection, all books discounted—10% for paperbacks and 15% for hardcovers.
- Harvard Bookstore, Newbury Street (tel. 617/661-1515). Great collection of paperbacks, postcards, stationery, etc.
- Harvard Coop, 1400 Massachusetts Ave., Cambridge (tel. 617/492-1000). Books, records, clothing, and just about everything else.
- For records: Strawberries, 709 Boylston St., Boston (tel. 617/354-6232) and 30 Boylston St. in Harvard Square, Cambridge. Contemporary records and tapes.
- For camping equipment: Hilton Tent City, 272 Friend St. (tel. 617/227-9242). Discount store for camping and hiking gear.

● For clothing and gifts: Filene's, 426 Washington St. A specialty store with a well-known bargain basement that's the oldest in the U.S. All the merchandise is dated and every 15 days the price drops 30%.

● Faneuil Hall Market Place in Boston is consumer heaven, the place to be seen, and the place to snack!

● Copley Place Shopping Complex, at Copley Square. A shopping "heaven" —restaurants, shops, etc.

Bourne

Accommodation: Bay Breeze Guest House, Monument Avenue, 02553 (tel. 617/759-5069). $25 to $51 per room with shared bath. Kitchen facilities available. On the water at Monument Beach. Call for reservations.

Brewster

Accommodations: Captain Freeman Inn, 15 Breakwater Rd., 02631 (tel. 617/896-7481). $30 to $40 per room with shared bath; $38 to $62 per room private bath. Call for reservations.

● Old Sea Pines Inn, 2553 Main St., 02631 (tel. 617/896-6114) $29 to $32 per room with shared bath; $36 to $60 per room private bath. Call for reservations.

Cambridge

(See Boston/Cambridge listing.)

Dennisport

Accommodation: Innisfree of Dennisport, 32 Inman Rd., 02639 (tel. 617/394-5356). $25 to $45 per room shared bath; $30 to $55 private bath. Across from ocean. Call for reservations.

Eastham

Accommodation: Mid-Cape Hostel (AYH), RR1, Box 167, 02642 (tel. 617/255-2785). Open May 15 to October 15. $8 for AYH members.

Falmouth

Accommodation: Hastings By the Sea, 28 Worcester Ave., 02540 (tel. 617/548-1628). $15 to $25 per room shared bath. Ocean view from every room. Call for reservations.

Gloucester

Accommodations: Blue Shutters Inn, 1 Nautilus Rd., 01930 (tel. 617/281-2706). $30 to $45 per room shared bath; $46 to $70 per room private bath. All rooms overlook the beach and ocean.

● Williams Guest House, 136 Bass Ave., 01930 (tel. 617/283-4931). $30 to $38 per room shared bath; $40 to $50 per room private. Located at Cape Ann, Good Harbor Beach. Call for reservations.

Holyoke

Accommodation: Susse Chalet Inn, Rte. 5, I-91, Exit 17, 17A, Northampton Street, 01040 (tel. 413/536-1980).

Hyannis

Accommodations: AYH-Hostel/Cape Cod, 465 Falmouth Rd., 02601 (tel. 617/775-2970 after 5 p.m.). $8 to $14. Open year round. Reservations usually needed for July and August.
● Captain Bearse Lodge, 39 Pearl St., 02601 (tel. 617/771-2700). $30 to $45 per room shared bath. Call for reservations.

Lawrence

Accommodation: YMCA, 40 Lawrence St., 01841 (tel. 617/686-6191). Men over 18 only. $18 per night; $5 refundable key deposit required. Weekly rate: $50; $50 security deposit required.

Lenox

Accommodation: Susse Chalet Motor Lodge, Mass. Turnpike, Exit 2, on Rtes. 7 and 20, 01240 (tel. 413/637-3560).

Leominster

Accommodation: Susse Chalet Motor Lodge, Rte. 2 at Rte. 13 Exit near Searstown, 01453 (tel. 617/537-8161).

Littleton

Accommodation: Friendly Crossways Youth Hostel (AYH), 🛦, Whitcomb Ave., mailing address P.O. Box 2266, 01460 (tel. 617/456-3649 or 456-9386). $10 AYH members; $20 for nonmembers. Advance reservations necessary with a 50% deposit and a stamped, self-addressed envelope. "A privately owned country conference center that prides itself on being homey."

Martha's Vineyard

Accommodations: Titticut Follies Guest House, 43 Narragansett Ave., Box

103, Oak Bluffs, 02557 (tel. 617/693-4986). Two blocks from the ferry. Open June 1 to September. $45 for a double. Reservations recommended. "An old house restored to its original gingerbread style in the tradition of the Victorian seaside resort."

● Manter Memorial International Youth Hostel (AYH), 🚹, Edgartown Road, P.O. Box 158, West Tisbury, 02575 (tel. 617/693-2665). Open April 1 to November 30. $8 for AYH members; $13 for nonmembers. Advance reservations necessary; send a stamped, self-addressed envelope for confirmation. Buy food before arrival at hostel. "Bikers and hikers only; no motorists."

Newburyport

Help: Turning Point, 5 Middle St. (tel. 617/462-8251).

Accommodation: Newburyport Family YMCA (AYH-SA), 96 State St., 01950 (tel. 617/462-6711). Open July 1 to Labor Day. $6 for AYH members; $8 for nonmembers. Advance reservations necessary.

Northampton

On Campus: This vibrant town of 33,000 is the home of Smith College, America's largest liberal arts college for women. Smith features a renowned art museum, a wide range of public events during the academic year, and free carillon concerts during the summer. Northampton boasts intriguing architecture, stylish stores, dozens of restaurants, ethnic to elegant; well-stocked bookstores, and free buses connecting the five area colleges. There is live music nightly, foreign films, sidewalk cafes, even a sushi bar. Northampton thinks like a city yet retains a small-town flavor.

Northfield

Accommodation: Monroe and Isabel Smith Hostel (AYH), Highland & Pine Streets, Box 2602, 01360 (tel. 413/498-5311, ext. 502, summers only, or 498-5983 before June 12). Open June 12 to August 20. $6.50 for AYH members. "Victorian house in a quiet, beautiful residential area."

Oak Bluffs

Accommodations: Narragansett House, 62 Narragansett Ave., P.O. Box 1746, 02557 (tel. 617/693-3627). $25 to $40 per room shared bath; $30 to $50 per room private bath. Includes continental breakfast. Call for reservations.

● Nashua House, Kennebec and Park Avenues, Box 803, 02557 (tel. 617/693-0043). $29 to $55 per room shared bath. 1873 Victorian guesthouse near beach. Call for reservations.

Rockport

Accommodation: The Inn on Cove Hill, 37 Mt. Pleasant St., 01966 (tel. 617/546-2701). $30 to $32 per room shared bath; $41 to $67 per room private bath. 200-year-old Federal-style home within walking distance of town and shore. Call for reservations.

South Deerfield

Accommodation: Motel 6, Rte. 5-10, 01373 (tel. 413/665-7161).

Springfield

Accommodations: Metropolitan Springfield YMCA, 275 Chestnut St., 01104 (tel. 413/739-6951). Men and women. $21 to $35 single; $3 each additional person. Health facilities available to guests.
• Susse Chalet Motor Lodge, Massachusetts Turnpike, Exit 6 (tel. 413/592-5141).

Truro

Accommodation: Little America Youth Hostel (AYH), P.O. Box 402, 02666 (tel. 617/349-3889 or 349-3726). Open June 12 to September 4. Advance reservations necessary; contact AYH National Office, P.O. Box 37613, Washington, D.C. 20013. $8 for AYH members. "An old Coast Guard Station converted to dorm-like accommodations." Buy food before arrival at hostel.

Washington

Accommodation: Bucksteep Manor, Camp Karu, Washington Mountain Road, 01223 (tel. 413/623-5535). Ten miles east of Pittsfield, in the Berkshires. "We offer you a mellow blend of the rural life, mixed as you like it with sports, entertainment, and cultural attractions." Cabins $10 to $12.50 per person. They also have rooms in the Manor Inn which cost $54 to $60 double.

Williamstown

Accommodation: River Bend Farm, 643 Simonds Rd., 01267 (tel. 413/458-5504 or 458-3121). $30 to $40 per room shared bath. Call for reservations.

Worcester

Help: Crisis Center, 617/791-6562.
Accommodation: Budgetel Inn, 444 Southbridge St., 01501 (tel. 617/832-7000).

Wrentham

Accommodation: Stardust Motor Inn, 900 Washington St., 02093 (tel. 617/384-3176). $30 for one or two in one bed; $39 for two in two beds.

Michigan

Your first thoughts when you hear "Michigan" are probably Detroit and cars. Michigan is, after all, America's leading producer of automobiles and the headquarters of the United Auto Workers, the second-largest union in the country.

But there's much of Michigan beyond Detroit—much that's beautiful, rustic, and serene. The state motto, "If You Seek a Pleasant Peninsula, Look Around You," can quite accurately describe the Upper Peninsula of Michigan, where there are streams to fish, forests to camp and hike, mines to explore, and where in winter there's skiing, snowmobiling, tobogganing, and skating. You'll enjoy taking a ferry from Mackinaw City to Mackinac Island during the summer; there are no cars on the island, but hundreds of bicycles are available to rent for exploring this popular summer resort.

The Henry Ford Museum and Greenfield Village, not far from Detroit in Dearborn, are popular tourist attractions where Americana is king: Ford had famous homes, laboratories, stores, and other buildings gathered from all over the U.S. and deposited in his park.

Ann Arbor, the home of the University of Michigan, is a lively town, certainly worth a visit, especially if you're a student.

Some Special Events: Blossomtime Festival in Benton Harbor and Tulip Festival in Holland (May); Rose Festival in Jackson, and Seaway Festival in Muskegon (June); National Cherry Festival in Traverse City, and Bass Festival in Crystal Falls (July); Country Festival in Canton, and Indian Pow Wow in Cross Village (August); Peach Festival in Romeo, and Riverfest in Lansing (September).

Tourist Information: Travel Bureau, Michigan Department of Commerce., P.O. Box 30226, Lansing, MI 48909.

N.B. A bed-and-breakfast reservation service for Michigan is Betsy Ross Bed & Breakfast, P.O. Box 1731, Dearborn, MI 48121 (tel. 313/561-6041).

Alpena

Accommodation: Budget Host—Thunder Bay Motel, 2717 South U.S. 23, 49707 (tel. 517/354-8001 or 35-MOTEL, or for reservations call toll free (800/835-7427, ext. 443).

Ann Arbor

"A unique blend of cosmopolitan opportunities and small-town charm."

Help: Ann Arbor Conference and Visitor Hotline, 313/995-7281.
● Washtenaw Crisis Center, 313/996-4747 or 994-1616.
On Campus: The University of Michigan is in Ann Arbor, and according to one Ann Arborite "the university is the whole town." A good source of help there, especially for foreign visitors, is the University of Michigan International Center, 603 East Madison St., 48109 (tel. 313/764-9310).

Be forewarned: Finding low-cost accommodations in Ann Arbor is difficult, according to one person who's tried it and another who lives there, and on football weekends it's impossible. It may be possible for students to stay at the residence halls of the University of Michigan during the summer—call the International Center for information.

For an inexpensive meal, try Del Rio, 122 W. Washington St., for Mexican food and Seva, 314 E. Liberty, for vegetarian.

Accommodations: Red Roof Inn, 3621 Plymouth Rd., 48105. (tel. 313/996-5800).
● Knights Inn, I-94 at 3764 S. State St., 48104 (tel. 313/665-9900).

Battle Creek

Accommodations: Regal 8 Inn, 4775 Beckley Rd. (Capital Ave. at I-94), 49017 (tel. 616/979-1141).
● Econo Lodge, 90 North Division St., P.O. Box 1103, 49017 (tel.: 616/965-7761.
● Comfort Inn, 165 Capital Ave. SW, 49015 (tel. 616/965-3976).
● Knights Inn, I-94 at 2595 Capital Ave. SW, 49015 (tel. 616/964-2600).
● Super 8 Motel, 5395 Beckley Rd., 49017 (tel. 616/979-1828).

Benton Harbor

Accommodations: Red Roof Inn, 1630 Mall Dr., 49022 (tel. 616/927-2484).
● Super 8 Motel, 1950 E. Napier Ave., 49022 (tel. 616/926-1371).

Center Line

Accommodation: Gatewood Home Hostel (AYH), c/o Harold and Gloria

Gatewood, 8585 Harding Ave., 48015 (tel. 313/756-2676). Ten miles from Detroit. $5 for AYH members. "A unique home filled with odds and ends from all over the world and assorted pets."

Coldwater

Accommodation: Econo Lodge, 884 W. Chicago, U.S. 12, 49036 (tel. 517/278-4501).

Delton

Accommodation: Circle Pines Center (AYH-SA), 8650 Mullen Rd., 49046 (tel. 616/623-5555). $15 adults; $7.50 children ages 3 to 13; under age 3, free. $8.25 summer, $10.25 winter for AYH members. Rooms sleep four to six. Twenty-five miles from bus or train stations; guests may contact the center at least 48 hours in advance for a ride at a special fee. Chores required. Bring sleeping bags. Meals are served daily in the summer. When meals are not available, kitchen use is $2.50 per day. "We are an educational cooperative established in 1938. We own 284 acres of woods and meadows, with one-third mile of lakefront with a sandy beach. There are 40 buildings, a lodge, a farmhouse, and many cabins. Tenting is also available."

Detroit

Tourist Information: Visitors Information Center, 2 East Jefferson, 48226 (tel. 313/567-1170).
Help: Travelers Aid, 211 E. Congress, 48226 (tel. 313/962-6740).
● Travelers Aid, 130 East Congress (Greyhound Bus Station), 48226 (tel. 313/961-1532).
● Hotline: 313/298-6262. What's happening in Detroit.

"Detroiters do not wear mechanics' coveralls to the symphony!"

Except possibly when it plays under the stars at Meadowbrook at Oakland University on summer nights—call 313/370-2100 for information. Also look into the free jazz and blues concerts sponsored by the Jefferson-Chalmen Citizens' District Council in summer—call 313/822-0006. Check with the housing office of Oakland University in suburban Rochester, or the University of Detroit—they might have a room available for a night or two.
Accommodations: YMCA, 2020 Witherell, 48226 (tel. 313/962-6126). Men only; must be at least 18 years old. $18 per person in dormitory-style rooms. Fully equipped health facilities.
● Manning Hall, Mercy College, 8200 West Outer Dr., 48219 (tel. 313/592-6170). Ask for Director of Housing. Men, women, and children. Open May to August. $18.50 single; $13.50 per person double. Advance reservations of two weeks necessary.
● Budgetel Inn, 20675 13 Mile Rd., Roseville, 48066 (tel. 313/296-6910).
● Knights Inn, I-94 at Merriman Road, 8500 Wickham Rd., Romulus, 48174 (tel. 313/722-8500).

- Knights Inn, I-696 at 26091 Dequindre Rd., Madison Heights, 48071 (tel. 313/545-9930).
- Knights Inn, I-94 at 31811 Little Mack Rd., Roseville, 48066 (tel. 313/294-6140).
- Red Roof Inn, 24300 Sinacola Ct., Farmington Hills, 48018 (tel. 313/478-8640).
- Red Roof Inn, 32511 Concord, Madison Heights, 48071 (tel. 313/583-4700).
- Red Roof Inn, 39700 Ann Arbor Rd., Plymouth, 48170 (tel. 313/459-3300).
- Red Roof Inn, 31800 Little Mack Rd., Roseville, 48066 (tel. 313/296-0310).
- Red Roof Inn, 2350 Rochester Rd., Troy, 48083 (tel. 313/689-4391).
- Red Roof Inn, 26300 Dequindre Rd., Warren, 48091 (tel. 313/573-4300).
- American Fort Wayne Hotel (AYH-SA), ⑤V★, 408 Temple, 48201 (tel. 313/831-7150). Near bus and train. $10.75 single; $8.75 per person double; $7.75 per person triple; $6.75 per person quad.

East Lansing

Help: Listening Ear, 547 1/2 East Grand River Ave., 48823 (tel. 517/337-1717). Phone or drop in, seven days a week.

On Campus: Michigan State University is here, and, according to a member of the Union Activities Board, the attitude toward people on the road in the area is "liberal because of the college atmosphere." Nearly all of the local meeting places are just across the street from campus on Grand River Avenue. When hunger strikes, you can find an inexpensive meal at Beggar's Banquet, 218 Abbott; Al Azteco, 203 M.A.C.; or Olga's Kitchen, 131 East Grand River.

Empire

Camping: Sleeping Bear Dunes National Lakeshore, 49630 (tel. 616/326-5134). Camping all year at D.H. Day and Platte River for $6 per campsite per night. Wilderness camping available April to November at North and South Manitou Island; permit required.

Flint

Tourist Information: Flint Area Convention and Visitors Bureau, 400 North Saginaw St., Suite 101, 48502 (tel. 313/232-8900, or toll free within Michigan 800/482-6708).

Help: Voluntary Action Center, 202 East Boulevard Dr., Room 110, 48503 (tel. 313/767-0500). For information and referral.

Accommodation: Mott Lake Hostel (AYH), 6511 North Genesee Rd., 48506 (tel. 313/736-5760). Bring a sleeping bag or your own linens. Their backyard is a 4000-acre park that includes a 600-acre lake. Under age 18: $3.75 summer, $4.75 winter. Over age 18: $5.75 summer, $6.25 winter for AYH members.

Anyone who reserves with full payment receives $1 discount first night. Bike, canoe, sailboat, and sled rentals available. Kitchen facilities provided; bring your own food. Twelve miles from downtown Flint.
- Red Roof Inn, G-3219, Miller Road, 48507 (tel. 313/733-1660).
- Econo Lodge, 2002 South Dort Hwy., 48503 (tel. 313/235-6621).
- Knights Inn, I-75 at G-3277 Miller Rd., 48507 (tel. 313/733-5910).

Frankfort

Accommodation: Brookwood Home Hostel (AYH), c/o Marjorie Pearsall-Groenwald, 538 Thomas Rd., 49635 (tel. 616/352-4296 summer or 301/544-4514 winter.) Open June 15 to September 5. $4.75 for AYH members; $5.75 for non-members. Advance reservations necessary.

Gaylord

Accommodation: Budget Host—Royal Crest Motel, 803 South Ostego Ave., 49735 (tel. 517/732-6451).

Grand Marais

Accommodation: Budget Host—Welker's Lodge, end of Mich. 77 on Lake Superior Coast Guard Point, Canal St. (Box 277), 49839 (tel. 906/494-2361).

Grand Rapids

Help: Switchboard Crisis Center, 616/774-3535. Open 24 hours.
Accommodations: Red Roof Inn, 5131 East 28th St., 49508 (tel. 616/942-0800).
- Exel Inn, 4855 28th St. SE, 49508 (tel. 616/957-3000).
- Knights Inn, I-96 at 5175 E. 28th St., 49508 (tel. 616/956-6601).
- Motel 6, 3524 28th St. SE, 49508 (tel. 616/949-8112).
- Motel 6, 777 Three Mile Rd., Walker, 49504 (tel. 616/784-9375).
- Super 8 Motel, 44th Street and Aldrich Avenue, Wyoming, 49501 (tel. 616/530-8588).
- Cascade Inn, ⓺, 2865 Broadmoor SE, 49508 (tel. 616/949-0850). $23.95 to $25.95 for one; $26.95 to $29.95 for two; $5 for each additional person. Cash payment required for accommodations Thursday through Sunday.

Holland

Help: Crisis Intervention, 616/396-4357.
Accommodation: Budget Host—Wooden Shoe Motel, 465 U.S. 31 and 16th Street, 49423 (tel. 616/392-8521).

Houghton

Camping: Isle Royale National Park, 87 North Ripley St., 49931 (tel. 906/

482-0984). Thirty-six campgrounds, with 253 campsites, some accessible only by trail, some only by boat. Open mid-June to October. The park is a large island on Lake Superior and 50 miles from Houghton. There is ferry service from Houghton and Copper Harbor to Isle Royale.

Iron Mountain

Accommodation: Cooney's Mountaineer Motel, Jct. 141, 49801 (tel. 906/774-2918). $20 for one; $30 for two in one bed; $35 for two in two beds.

Jackson

Accommodations: Budgetel Inn, U.S. 127 North, 2035 Service Dr., 49201 (tel. 517/750-1550).
● Knights Inn, I-94 at U.S. 27, 830 Royal Dr., 49204 (tel. 517/789-7186).

Kalamazoo

Help: Helpline, 616/381-4357.
On Campus: Kalamazoo College and Western Michigan University are in Kalamazoo. A friend of ours who is a student there describes his town as having a "strong academic and cultural flavor" and a friendly attitude toward young people on the road. Knollwood Tavern is a popular student spot, and you can find a low-priced meal in the college dining rooms. One of the best spots for an inexpensive breakfast, lunch, or dinner is Theo's right in the center of town at 234 West Michigan.
Accommodations: Knights Inn, I-94 at Sprinkle Road, 3704 Van Rick Rd., 49002 (tel. 616/344-9255).
● Red Roof Inn, 3701 East Cork St., 49001 (tel. 616/382-6350).
● Red Roof Inn, 5425 West Michigan Ave., 49009 (tel. 616/375-7400).
● Super 8 Motel, 618 Maple Hill Dr., 49009 (tel. 616/345-0146).

Lansing

Help: Emotional Crisis, 517/372-8460.
Accommodation: Motel 6, 112 East Main St., 48933 (tel. 517/484-8722).
● Knights Inn, I-96 at Cedar Street, 1100 Ramada Dr., 48910 (tel. 517/394-9255).
● Knights Inn, I-96 at S.R. 43, 7326 W. Saginaw Hwy., 48917 (tel. 517/321-1444).
● Red Roof Inn, 3615 Dunckle, 48910 (tel. 517/332-2575).
● Red Roof Inn, 7412 West Saginaw Hwy., 48917 (tel. 517/321-7246).
● Regal 8 Inn, 6501 South Cedar St., 48910 (tel. 517/393-2030).

Mancelona

Accommodation: Northwoods Lodge at Schuss Mountain (AYH-SA), 2000 E. Village Dr., Box 728, 49659 (tel. 616/587-5223). $8 to $12 per person per night. Advance reservations necessary.

Marquette

Accommodation: Wahlstrom's Parkway Motel and Restaurant, 5057 U.S. 41 South, 49855 (tel. 906/249-1404). $25 for one; $28 for two in one bed; $31 for two in two beds.

Midland

Accommodation: Northwood Institute, NADA Center, 3225 Cook Rd., 48640 (tel. 517/835-7755). Open year round. $25 single; $30 double. College cafeteria available to guests.

Monroe

Accommodation: Knights Inn, I-75 at 1250 N. Dixie Hwy., 48161 (tel. 313/243-0597).

Munising

Camping: Pictured Rocks National Lakeshore, P.O. Box 40, 49862 (tel. 906/387-2607). Camping at three drive-in campgrounds: Little Beaver Lake, Twelvemile Beach, and Hurricane River. Fee is $4 per night; register upon arrival. Thirteen backcountry campsites available to backpackers and hikers. Permits required for backcountry camping (no fee). Open year round.

Accommodation: Terrace Motel, 420 Prospect St., 49862 (tel. 906/387-2735). $28 to $30 for one or two in one bed; $32 to $38 for two in two beds.

Muskegon

Accommodations: Days Inn, 150 Seaway Dr., 49444 (tel. 616/739-9429).
● Super 8 Motel, 3380 Hoyt St., 49444 (tel. 616/733-0088).

Newberry

Accommodation: The New Falls Hotel, Ⓢ √ ★, 301 South Newberry Ave., 49868 (tel. 906/293-5111). $22 to $26 for one; $30 to $36 for two in one bed; $32 to $40 for two in two beds. Price includes continental breakfast.

Port Huron

Accommodation: Knights Inn, I-94 at 2160 Water St., 48060 (tel. 313/982-1022).

Saginaw

Accommodations: University Center, Saginaw Valley (AYH-SA), Department of Residential Life, Saginaw State Valley College, 2250 Pierce Rd., 48710 (tel. 517/790-4255). Open May through August 15. $5 for AYH members. Advance reservations necessary.
- Comfort Inn, 3425 Holland Ave., 48601 (tel. 517/753-2461).
- Knights Inn, I-675 at 2225 Tittabawassee Rd., 48604 (tel. 517/791-1411).
- Red Roof Inn, 966 South Outer Dr., 48601 (tel. 517/754-8414).
- Super 8 Motel, 4848 Town Centre Rd., 48603 (tel. 517/791-3003).

St. Ignance

Accommodation: Budget Host—Chalet North Motel, 1140 North State St., 49781 (tel. 906/643-9141).

Sault Ste. Marie

Accommodation: Bavarian Motor Lodge, 2006 Ashmun St., 49783 (tel. 906/632-6864). Summer: $36 single. Winter: $26 single.

Sturgis

Accommodation: Green Briar Motor Inn, 71381 South Centerville Rd., 49091 (tel. 616/651-2361). $28 to $30 for one or two in one bed; $32 to $35 for two in two beds.

Tawas City

Accommodation: Tawas Motel, Ⓢ√ ★, P.O. Box 248, 1124 U.S. 23 S., 48764 (tel. 517/362-3822). $30 to $38 for one; $33.50 to $41.75 for two in one bed.

Traverse City

Accommodations: Hampton Inn, 1000 U.S. 31 North, 49684 (tel. 616/946-8900).
- Knights Inn, U.S. 31 at 618 E. Front St., 49684 (tel. 616/929-0410).

Twin Lake

Accommodation: Home Hostel (AYH), c/o Mary Payne, 3175 First St.,

49457 (tel. 616/828-6675). Canoeing on the lake in summer; cross-country skiing in winter. Advance reservations necessary.

Warren

Accommodations: Budgetel Inn, 30900 Van Dyke Rd. (tel. 313/574-0550).
● Knights Inn, S.R. 53 at Chicago Road, 7500 Miller Dr., 48092 (tel. 313/978-7500).

White Cloud

Accommodation: North Country Trail Association Schoolhouse Hostel (AYH), 3962 North Felch, 49349 (tel. 616/689-6876). $4 for AYH members. Bring sleeping bag.

Ypsilanti

On Campus: If you're at Eastern Michigan University, call for information on possible accommodations at Hoyt Conference Center (tel. 313/487-4109).

Minnesota

With 12,000 lakes and 3,000 miles of rivers, "the land of the sky-blue waters" is famous for water activities from wilderness canoeing in the Boundary Waters Canoe area to lakeside cabin camping, stepping across the headwaters of the Mississippi River at Itasca State Park, bass fishing, water-skiing, and just plain swimming.

One of the most beautiful canoe trips in the country is down the St. Croix River, which divides Minnesota and Wisconsin. You can rent canoes at several points along the river and travel from four hours to several days, camping along the shores as you go. At the end you can leave your canoe and get transportation back at a moderate price.

Nature programs, hikes, and canoe trips are run out of such sites as the Voyageur National Park with its new Visitor Center. At the Canadian border, Minnesota is nearly 40% water. One interesting camping site in this area is Rainy Lake. A number of islands in the lake have tidy campsites on them, owned and maintained for the general public by an area lumber company. The lake is rock-bottomed, very deep, and has many underwater rock mountains. The cold water is excellent for fishing, scuba diving, and snorkeling. Winters find hardy Minnesotans camping with snowshoes and cross-country skiing.

For those who like the bigger cities, Minneapolis and St. Paul have lots to offer. Cultural activities include the nationally renowned Guthrie Theater, Minneapolis Children's Theater, the Minneapolis Institute of Arts, St. Paul Chamber Orchestra concerts at the new Ordway Music Theatre, the Science Museum of St. Paul and its Omnitheater, and Walker Art Center. The University of Minnesota has a number of concert, dance, and opera series throughout the year. Minnesota Orchestra concerts, held year round, are exceptional and shouldn't be missed on any trip to the area. Professional sports include baseball, football, hockey, and soccer.

In Minnesota, the Scandinavian and German influence is quite noticeable. Other ethnic groups exist, but not in any great numbers, comparatively. In fact, it's been said that there are as many Lutheran churches in Minnesota as there are lakes.

A recommended guidebook on the state is *Minnesota Travel Companion*, by Richard Olsenius, Bluestem Productions, Box 334, Wayzata, MN 55391 ($12.95).

Some Special Events: Smelt Fry in Garrison (April); Festival of Nations in St. Paul, and Syttende Mai Fest in Spring Grove featuring Norwegian food, crafts, and dances (May); Minnesota Orchestra Somerfest, featuring marketplace and outdoor concerts (summer); Good Times Days in Boyd, Noble County Dairy Days in Ellsworth, Swedish Festival in Cambridge, and International Polka Festival and Tug of War in Pine City (all in June); Taste of Minnesota in St. Paul (July); Aquatennial in Minneapolis (July); St. Paul Winter Carnival (January); Minnesota Renaissance Festival in Shakopee (August, September); Whiz Bang Days in Robbinsdale, Lake of the Woods County Fair in Baudette, Lumberjack Days in Cloquet, and Song of Hiawatha Pageant in Pipestone (all in July); Strawhat and Sunbonnet Days in Verndale, Victorian Crafts Festival in St. Paul, and Sweet Corn Festival in Ortonville (August); Cherry Area Fair and Rodeo in Iron and Lac Qui Parle County Fair in Madison (September).

Tourist Information: Minnesota Office of Tourism, 375 Jackson St., 250 Skyway Level, St. Paul, MN 55101 (tel. 612/296-5029, or toll free 800/652-9747 within Minnesota, 800/328-1461 outside Minnesota). The center is open Monday through Friday from 8 a.m. to 5 p.m.

N.B. A recommended bed-and-breakfast registration service for Minnesota is the Bed & Breakfast Registry, P.O. Box 8174, St. Paul, MN 55108-0174 (tel. 612/646-4238).

Albert Lea

Accommodation: Super 8 Motel, 2019 W. Main St., 56007 (tel. 507/377-0591).

Alexandria

Accommodations: Days Inn, 4810 Hwy. 29 South, 56308 (tel. 612/762-1171).
● Super 8 Motel, 4620 Hwy. 29 South, 56308 (tel. 612/763-6552).

Austin

Accommodation: Super 8 Motel, 1401 14th St. NW, 55912 (tel. 507/433-1801).

Bemidji

Accommodations: Paul Bunyan Motel, 915 Paul Bunyan Dr. NE, 56601

(tel. 218/751-1314). $20 to $32 single; $24 to $40 double; $36 to $50 triple; $42 to $55 quad.
- Days Inn, 2420 Paul Bunyan Dr., 56601 (tel. 218/751-0390).
- Super 8 Motel, 1815 Paul Bunyan Dr. NW, 56601 (tel. 218/751-8481).

Blue Earth

Accommodation: Super 8 Motel, Jct. I-90 and U.S. Hwy. 169, Exit 119, P.O. Box 394, 56013 (tel. 507/526-7376).

Brainerd

Accommodations: Days Inn, Jct. 210 West and 371, P.O. Box 364, 56401 (tel. 218/820-0391).
- Econo Lodge, Hwy. 371 South and Andrew Street, 56401 (tel. 218/828-0027).
- Super 8 Motel, Hwy. 371 North, P.O. Box 2505, Baxter, 56425 (tel. 218/828-4288).

Burnsville

Accommodation: Red Roof Inn, I-35 at Burnsville Pkwy., 12920 Aldrich Ave., 55337 (tel. 612/890-1420).

Cloquet

Accommod: tion: Driftwood Motel, 1413 Hwy. 33 South, 55720 (tel. 218/879-4638). $25⁵fo two in one bed; $35 for two in two beds.

Detroit Lakes

Accommodat on: Super 8 Motel, 400 Morrow Ave., 56501 (tel. 218/847-1651).

Duluth

Help: Information and Referral, 218/727-8538.
Accommodations: College of St. Scholastica, 🚹, 1200 Kenwood Ave., 55811 (tel. 218/723-6000, ask for Director of Housing). Men, women, and children. Near local bus. Open June 7 to August 17. $15 single; $30 double. Weekly rate available. Advance reservations of one week necessary.
- Days Inn, 909 Cottonwood St., 55811 (tel. 218/727-3110).
- Super 8 Motel, 4100 W. Superior St., 55807 (tel. 218/628-2241).

Eveleth

Accommodation: Super 8 Motel, U.S. Hwy. 53, P.O. Box 745, 55734 (tel. 218/744-3603).

Faribault

Accommodation: Super 8 Motel, 2509 Lyndale Ave. North, 55021 (tel. 507/334-1634).

Fergus Falls

Accommodation: Super 8 Motel, 2454 College Way, 56537 (tel. 218/739-3261).

Glencoe

Accommodation: Super 8 Motel, 717 Morningside Dr., 55336 (tel. 612/864-6191).

Grand Marais

Accommodations: East Bay Hotel, Box 246, 55604 (tel. 218/387-2800). Near bus station. $13 single with shared bath, $23 with private bath; $18 double with shared bath, $23 to $39 with private bath; $20 triple with shared bath, $33 to $39 triple or quad with private bath. "An historic hotel located on Lake Superior—clean and comfortable with a fabulous view."
● Super 8 Motel, 1902 S. Pokegama Ave., Box 335, 55744 (tel. 218/327-1108).

Hendricks

Accommodation: Triple L Farm Bed and Breakfast, Rte. 1, Box 141, 56136 (tel. 507/275-3740). Bed-and-breakfast on a family farm. $20 single; $25 double; $30 triple or quad. Advance reservations of one week suggested.

Hibbing

Accommodation: Days Inn, 1520 Hwy. 37 East, 55746 (tel. 218/263-8306).

International Falls

Camping: Voyageurs National Park, P.O. Box 50. 56649 (tel. 218/283-9821). Campgrounds accessible only by boat. Open year round. No fee.

Accommodation: Days Inn, Hwy. 53, P.O. Box 182, 56679 (tel. 218/283-9441).

Lake City

Accommodation: Chateau Frontenac, RR2, Box 197, Old Frontenac, 55026 (tel. 612/345-3146). A restored 1865 resort. $20 single; $27.50 double; $34.50 triple; $40 quad. During midweek, September 15 to May 15, 25% discount.

Little Falls

Accommodation: Super 8 Motel, 300 12th St. NE, 56345 (tel. 612/632-2351).

Mankato

Accommodation: Super 8 Motel, Hwy. 169 North and Hwy. 14 Jct., 56001 (tel. 507/387-4041).

Marshall

Accommodation: Super 8 Motel, Hwys. 59 and 23, 56258 (tel. 507/537-1461).

Minneapolis

N.B. See St. Paul too, since Minneapolis and St. Paul are "twin cities" divided only by the Mississippi River.

Minneapolis is a well-kept secret according to a friend there. It has a rich cultural life, it is an easy place to get around (the transit service is generally reliable and easy to use) and hiking in the lakes area is a special pleasure.

Tourist Information: City of Minneapolis Information, 612/348-4313.
● Park and Recreation Information, 310 4th Ave. South. 612/348-2226.
● Luxton, Cultural Activities Information, 612/348-3541.

Help: First Call For Help (Travelers Aid), 404 South 8th St., 55404 (tel. 612/340-7431).
● Contact-Twin Cities, 612/341-2896.

On Campus: The University of Minnesota is in Minneapolis. A good place to go on campus for travel information (primarily international travel) is the International Study and Travel Center, 44 Coffman Memorial Union, 300 Washington Ave. SE (tel. 612/625-1150).

Accommodations: Days Inn, Hwy. 12 West, 6300 Wayzata Blvd., 55416 (tel. 612/546-6277).

- Budgetel Inn, 7815 Nicollet Ave. Street, Bloomington, 55420 (tel. 612/881-7311).
- Budgetel Inn, 6415 James Circle North, Brooklyn Center, 55430 (tel. 612/561-8400).
- Budget Host—Gopher Campus Motor Lodge, 925 S.E. 4th St., 55414 (tel. 612/331-3740).
- Exel Inn, 2701 East 78th St., Bloomington, 55420 (tel. 612/854-7200).
- Imperial 400 Motor Inn, 2500 University St. SE, 55414 (tel. 612/331-6000).
- Super 8 Motel, 7800 2nd Ave. South, Bloomington, 55420 (tel. 612/888-8800).
- Super 8 Motel, Burnsville Parkway and Aldrich Avenue, Burnsville, 55337 (tel. 612/894-3400).
- Super 8 Motel, 11500 W. 78th St., Eden Prairie, 55344 (tel. 612/829-0888).
- Super 8 Motel, 581 S. Marschall Rd., Shakopee, 55379 (tel. 612/445-4221).

Moorhead

On Campus: Moorhead State University is located here. For information while you're there, call Campus Information, 218/236-2011, or the Exchange in the Comstock Union, 218/236-2261. At night, try Mick's Office, Chumley's, the Trader and Trapper, or East Gate Lounge to meet people.

Accommodation: Super 8 Motel, 3621 S. 8th St., Box 516, 56560 (tel. 218/233-8880).

Northfield

On Campus: Visitors to Carleton College can get snacks and light meals at the snack bar in the student union, Sayles-Hill. Just a few blocks from campus on Division Street, the Archer House Hotel features two fine eating places: The Tavern, with cozy rathskeller atmosphere overlooking the river, and Treats, serving delicatessen specialties for indoor or outdoor seating or for take-out.

Accommodation: Red Carpet Inn, 1420 Riverview Dr., 55057 (tel. 507/663-0371).

Owatonna

Accommodation: Super 8 Motel, I-35 and Hwy. 14 West, P.O. Box 655, 55060 (tel. 507/451-0380).

Park Rapids

Accommodation: Super 8 Motel, Hwy. 34 East, Box 388, 56470 (tel. 218/732-9704).

Rochester

Accommodations: Colony Inn Motel, Hwy. 52 and 2nd St. SW, 55902 (tel. 507/282-2733). $22.99 for one person; $25.99 to $27.99 for two persons; $3 each extra person.

- Friendship Centre Towne Travel Inn, 116 S.W. 5th St., 55902 (tel. 507/289-1628).
- Motel 6, 2107 West Frontage Rd., 55901 (tel. 507/282-6625).
- Super 8 Motel, 1230 S. Broadway, 55901 (tel. 507/288-8288).
- Super 8 Motel, Hwy. 52 and 2nd St. SW, 55902 (tel. 507/281-5100).
- Econo Lodge, 519 Third Ave. SW, 55901 (tel. 507/288-1855).
- Comfort Inn, 111 S.E. 28th St., 55904 (tel. 507/286-1001).

Roseau

Accommodation: Guest House Motor Inn, 216 Main Ave. North, 56751. (tel. 218/463-2542). $23 to $27 for one; $4 for each additional person.

Roseville

Accommodations: Northwestern College, 🔥 (limited), 3003 North Snelling Ave., 55113 (tel. 612/631-5217). $25 single; $38 double; $45 triple. If you stay longer than one night the rates become lower. "Spectacular—new—similar to a fine hotel room."
- Comfort Inn, I-35 West and County Rd. C, 55113 (tel. 612/631-0284).

St. Cloud

Accommodations: Days Inn, 40 South 10th Ave., Waite Park, 56387 (tel. 612/253-7070).
- Super 8 Motel, 50 Park Ave. South, 56301 (tel. 612/253-5530).

St. Joseph

Accommodation: Super 8 Motel, Minnesota St. and 15th Ave. SE., County Rd. 75, 56374 (tel. 612/363-7711).

St. Paul

Tourist Information: St. Paul Convention Bureau, 445 Minnesota St., 600 NCL Tower, 55101 (tel. 612/297-6985 or toll free 800/328-8322, ext. 983).

On Campus: Students at the St. Paul campus of the University of Minnesota congregate at the student center, Valli Pizza, and Sammy D's. They also recommended contacting the Hennepin City and Ramsey City Historical Societies for information on the wonderful architecture in St. Paul, which includes art deco and late Victorian. The Ramsey number is 612/222-0701; Hennepin's is 612/870-1329.

Not far from the St. Paul campus of the University of Minnesota you'll find the Muffuletta, 2260 Como Ave. (tel. 612/644-9116), a friendly neighborhood restaurant. For a good meal in St. Paul, you can go to the Caravan Serai, an Afghani restaurant, at 2046 Pinehurst Ave. (tel. 612/690-1935).

The students at Hamline University in St. Paul head mainly to Bandanna Square—a wonderfully restored old railroad maintenance area next to the campus with restaurants, shops, cafes, etc.

Accommodations: Red Roof Inn, 1806 Woodlane Dr., Woodbury, 55125 (tel. 612/738-7160).

● Exel Inn, 1739 Old Hudson Rd., 55106 (tel. 612/771-5566).

● Hall Home Hostel (AYH), c/o Lyle Hall, 1360 Lafond, 55104 (tel. 612/647-0611 or 612/645-1539). $6.25 for AYH members; $7.25 for nonmembers. Advance reservations suggested.

Stillwater

Accommodation: Driscolls for Guests B&B (AYH), c/o Mina Driscoll, 1103 South 3rd St., 55082 (tel. 612/439-7486). $6.75 for AYH members; $49 double for bed-and-breakfast accommodations.

Willmar

Accommodation: Super 8 Motel, 2655 S. 1st St., P.O. Box 286, 56201 (tel. 612/235-7260).

Winona

Help: Winona Volunteer Services, 507/452-5591.

Accommodations: Sterling Motel, √, Jct. 14-61 and Gilmore Avenue, 55987 (tel. 507/454-1120). $22 for one; $28 for two in one bed; $32 to $36 for two in two beds.

● Carriage House Bed and Breakfast, 420 Main, 55987 (tel. 507/452-8256). An elegant 1870 carriage house in country decor. $40 for 1 person; $45 for 2 persons. Rooms are $5 less from November 1 through April 30. No children under 12 permitted.

● Budget Host-Westgate Motel, 1501 W. Service Dr., Hwy. 61 and Gilmore Ave., 55987 (tel. 507/454-2980).

● Days Inn, 420 Cottonwood Dr., 55987 (tel. 507/454-6930).

● Super 8 Motel, 1025 Sugar Loaf Rd., 55987 (tel. 507/454-6066).

Worthington

Accommodations: Sunset Motel, 207 Oxford St., 56187 (tel. 507/376-6155). $23 single; $26 double; $32 triple; $35 quad.

● Super 8 Motel, I-90 and 266, Exit 42, P.O. Box 356, 56187 (tel. 507/372-7755).

Mississippi

Mississippi has made rich contributions to the literature of the U.S. with such native authors as William Faulkner, Eudora Welty, and Richard Wright. Rural and quite poor by national standards, Mississippi has much natural beauty, especially in some of its state parks. For a free guide to these parks, write to the Department of Natural Resources, Bureau of Recreation and Parks, P.O. Box 10600, Jackson, MS 39209.

Must-see sights in Mississippi include the Natchez antebellum homes, the largest and—some say—most beautiful collection of preserved homes from the era before the Civil War. Cotton was king in Natchez, a Mississippi River port, and wealth was everywhere in the beginning of the 1800s. Natchez Trace Parkway is administered by the National Park Service, and on the portion between Tupelo and Natchez, drivers can stop at well-marked sites of historic or natural interest. Probably the most unsettling sight near the parkway is the view of the ruins of Windsor—40 columns are all that's left of a once-fabulous mansion.

And for those who are interested in the history of the Civil War, there's a national military park at Vicksburg, site of the 47-day Union siege after which the field was surrendered to General Grant. At the Visitors Center, the story of the battle is told through film and a variety of exhibits.

Some Special Events: Gum Tree Festival in Tupelo (May); Blessing of the Fleet in Biloxi (June); Deep-Sea Fishing Rodeo in Gulfport, and Choctaw Indian Fair in Philadelphia (July); Neshoba Country Fair in Philadelphia (August); and the Delta Blue Festival in Greenville (September).

Tourist Information: Division of Tourism, Mississippi Department of Economic Development, Box 22825, Room 1301, Walter Sillers Building, Jackson, MS 39205 (tel. toll free 800/647-2290).

Biloxi

Accommodation: Scottish Inn, 4660 West Beach Blvd., 39531 (tel. 601/388-2610).

Corinth

Accommodation: Econo Lodge, Hwy. 72 and 45, P.O. Box 510, 38834 (tel. 601/287-4421).

Durant

Camping: Holmes County State Park, Rte. 1, Box 153, 39063 (tel. 601/653-3351). Well-equipped rustic cabins in great condition, with a view of the lake, from $32 to $34 per night; modern duplex cabins from $42 to $44 per night. Room for four to six people in cabins. Advance reservations necessary.

Grenada

Accommodation: Econo Lodge, I-55 & Hwy. 8, Frontage Road, 38901 (tel. 601/226-6666).

Gulfport

Accommodation: Red Carpet Inn, 3314 West Beach Blvd., 39502 (tel. 601/864-1381).

Hattiesburg

Camping and Accommodation: Paul B. Johnson State Park, Rte. 3, Box 408, 39401 (tel. 601/582-7721). Besides camping at $5.50 per campsite, there are cabins that hold up to six people and rent for $42 per night. Bed linens and cooking utensils are furnished and four cabins have a fireplace.

Accommodations: Days Inn, 3320 Hwy. 49 North, 39401 (tel. 601/268-2251).
- Motel 6, 3109 Hwy. 49 North, 39401 (tel. 601/544-6096).
- Econo Lodge, 3501 Hwy. 49 North, 39401 (tel. 601/544-3475).

Holly Springs

Camping and Accommodation: Wall Doxey State Park, Hwy. 7 South, 38635 (tel. 601/252-4231). Modern vacation cabins with kitchen. $37.10 to

$44.52 per night per cabin. Four to seven people per cabin. Camping: $5.50 to $13.50 per night. Advance reservations suggested. "A family-oriented park."

Iuka

Camping and Accommodation: J.P. Coleman State Park, √, Rte. 5, Box 504, 38852 (tel. 601/423-6515). Vacation cabins with bedroom, bath, kitchen, and some with living rooms. $39 to $47 per night per cabin. Motel rooms at park for $55. Tent camping $5.50 per night; camping, electricity and water included, $10 per night.

Jackson

Accommodations: Motel 6, 970 I-20 West, North Frontage Rd., 39201 (tel. 601/969-3423).
- Days Inn, 616 Briarwood Dr., Box 12864, 39236 (tel. 601/957-1741).
- Days Inn, I-20, U.S. 49 and U.S. 80 East, P.O. Box 6034, 39208 (tel. 601/939-8200).
- Red Carpet Inn, 2275 Hwy. 80 West, 39204 (tel. 601/948-5561).
- Red Roof Inn, 700 Larson St., I-55 and High Street, 39202 (tel. 601/969-5006).
- Red Roof Inn, 828 Hwy. 51 North, 39157 (tel. 601/956-7707).
- Regal 8 Inn, 6145 I-55 North, 39213 (tel. 601/956-8848).
- Scottish Inn, 2263 U.S. 80 West, 39204 (tel. 601/969-1144).

McComb

Camping and Accommodation: Percy Quin State Park, ♿, Rte. 3, 39648 (tel. 601/684-3931). Men and women over 21. Besides rustic camping there are cabins furnished with linens and a kitchen. $38 per night. Some of the cabins can hold up to 12 people. Reservations necessary well in advance for cabins. Camping area is first-come, first-served for most sites.

Meridian

Accommodations: Motel 6, 2305 South Frontage Rd., 39300 (tel. 601/482-1182).
- Comfort Inn, 2901 St. Paul St., 39301 (tel. 601/485-2722).
- Hampton Inn, U.S. 80 at I-59, P.O. Box 5497, 39302 (tel. 601/483-3000).

Natchez

Accommodation: Scottish Inn, 40 Sargent Prentiss Dr., 39120 (tel. 601/442-9141).

Oakland

Camping and Accommodation: George Payne Cossar State Park, Rte. 1,

Box 64, 38648 (tel. 601/623-7356). $42 per cabin which accommodates four people. Advance reservations suggested. "Eight duplex cabins with central air conditioning and heat, kitchens, screened porch, and fireplace—very modern." Designed to accommodate four people but roll-away beds are available for $3 each. Limit of three-night stay during summer months.

Oxford

On Campus: A friend at the University of Mississippi told us you can go to the Grill at the Student Union and find someone there who will be glad to help you find a place to stay. According to this same friend, the people at the university are very helpful and friendly. Foreign student visitors who need help may call the foreign student advisor's office. Call 601/232-7404.

One friend's favorite bar is the Gin, in the old cotton gin, because it's "cheap, informal, and has good sandwiches and loud music," and Forrester's, where it's easy to meet students.

To find a ride to wherever you're going, check the Ole Miss Union Ride Board.

Oxford was the home of William Faulkner and one Oxfordian wants you to be sure to visit the Faulkner home there. At the end of July there's a week-long Faulkner festival in the town which attracts writers from all over the world.

There are rooms available at the Residence Halls. The charge is $5 per person in a double room; you must provide your own linens. For information, call the Miller Housing Office at 601/232-7328.

Accommodation: Ole Miss Motel, 1517 East University Ave., 38655 (tel. 601/234-2424). About four blocks from the campus of U. Miss. $21.60 single; $27 and up double.

Pescagoula

Accommodation: Hampton Inn, 6800 Hwy. 63 North at I-10, P.O. Box 660, Moss Point, 39563-0150 (tel. 601/475-2477).

Sardis

Camping and Accommodation: John W. Kyle State Park, Rte. 1, P.O. Box 115, 38666 (tel. 601/487-1345). Twenty cabins that rent for $36 to $42 per night. 200 campsites available (electricity, water, and bath houses). Advance reservations of two months suggested. Three-night minimum Memorial weekend through Labor Day weekend; two-night minimum at other times.

Accommodation: Scottish Inn, Rte. 1, Box 28, 38666 (tel. 601/487-2311).

Tupelo

Camping and Accommodation: Natchez Trace Parkway, RR1, NT-143, 38801. Campgrounds at Jeff Busby and Rocky Springs. Open year round. No fee.

● Tombigbee State Park, Rte. 2, Box 336E, 38801 (tel. 601/842-7669). Open year round. Cabins, large enough for four to six people, rent for $26 to $46 per night; campsites at $10 per night regular camping; $7 per night senior citizens or disabled; $5.50 per night tent camping.

Accommodation: Comfort Inn, 1190 N. Gloster St., 38801 (tel. 601/842-5100).

Yazoo City

Accommodation: Budget Host-Robie Knight Motor Inn, E. 15th St., Box 622, at 49 W. Hwy., 39194 (tel. 601/746-8780).

Missouri

Missouri is partly southern and partly western in philosophy and has produced such diverse personalities as Jesse James, Mark Twain, T.S. Eliot, and Harry S. Truman.

The northwestern part of the state is called the Pony Express Region, since it was from St. Joseph, in 1860, that the first Pony Express rider galloped on his way. Camping, picnicking, and water sports abound—and some people like to take a look at the home where the outlaw Jesse James was shot and killed. In the Mark Twain Region in the northeast, the town of Hannibal has preserved the author's boyhood home and has a Twain museum and the restored Becky Thatcher home.

In the center of the state, the huge Lake of the Ozarks attracts water lovers. And then there are the cities—Kansas City and St. Louis. Going south, the Ozark Playground Region has two of the area's best-known attractions: Silver Dollar City, a re-created 1880s town and entertainment park, and the outdoor pageant at Shepherd of the Hills Homestead, which depicts the story of Ozarks frontier life.

Some Special Events: Dogwood Festival in Camdenton (April); Valley of Flowers Festival in Florissant, and Family Bluegrass Music Weekend in Hermitage's Pomme de Terre State Park (May); International Festival in St. Louis, and Hillbilly Days in Bennett Spring State Park, Lebanon (June); National Tom Sawyer Fence Painting Contest in Hannibal (July 4); Bootheel Rodeo in Sikeston (August); Cotton Carnival in Sikeston (September); and Crafts Festival in Arrow Rock (October).

Tourist Information: Missouri Division of Tourism, P.O. Box 1055, Jefferson City, MO 65102 (tel. 314/751-4133).

N.B. Two bed and breakfast reservation services for Missouri are Ozark Mountain Country Bed & Breakfast Service, Box 295, Branson, MO 65616 (tel. 417/334-4720); and Midwest Host Bed & Breakfast, P.O. Box 27, Saginaw, MO 64846 (tel. 417/782-9112).

Branson

Accommodation: Econo Lodge, 1166 West Hwy. 76, 65616 (tel. 417/334-3946).

Cameron

Accommodation: Budget Host—Country Squire Inn, 509 Northland Dr., Box 375, 64429 (tel. 816/632-6623).

Cape Girardeau

Accommodation: Drury Inn, I-55 and Rte. K, William Street, P.O. Box 910, 63702 (tel. 314/335-1201).
● Drury Lodge, Rte. K at I-55, 63701 (tel. 314/334-7151).

Cassville

Accommodation: Holiday Motel, 85 South Main St., 65625 (tel. 417/847-3163). $22 for one; $26 for two in one bed; $28 for two in two beds.

Chillicothe

Accommodation: Budget Host—Capri Motel, Hwys. 36 and 65, 64601 (tel. 816/646-5660).

Columbia

Accommodations: Red Roof Inn, 201 East Texas Ave., 65202 (tel. 314/442-0145).
● Super 8 Motel, 3216 Clark Lane, 65202 (tel. 314/474-8488).
● Motel 6, 1718 North Providence Rd., 65203 (tel. 314/442-9390).
● Regal 8 Inn, 1800 I-70 Dr. SW, 65201 (tel. 314/445-8433).

Concordia

Accommodation: Econo Lodge, I-70 and Missouri 23 Hwy. 64020 (tel. 816/463-7987).

Fulton

Accommodation: Budget Host—Westwoods Motel, 422 Gaylord Dr., 65251 (tel. 314/642-5991).

Hannibal

Tourist Information: Visitors and Convention Bureau, 308 N. Main St., P.O. Box 624, 63401 (tel. 314/221-2477).
Accommodations: Budget Host—Hannibal House Inn, 3601-11 McMasters, at Jct. Hwys. 36 and 61, 63401 (tel. 314/221-7950).
● Super 8 Motel, 120 Huckleberry Heights Dr., P.O. Box 669, 63401 (tel. 314/221-5863).

Harrisonville

Accommodation: Budget Host—Cortez Motel, 1302 North Commercial, 64701 (tel. 816/884-3208).

Hayti

Accommodation: Drury Inn, I-55 and Rte. 84, P.O. Box 9, 63851 (tel. 314/359-2702).

Higginsville

Accommodation: Super 8 Motel, State Hwy. 13 at I-70, Exit 49, P.O. Box 306, 64037 (tel. 816/584-7781).

Jefferson City

Accommodations: Regal 8 Inn, 808 Stadium Dr., 65101 (tel. 314/634-2848).
● Super 8 Motel, 1624 Jefferson St., 65101 (tel. 314/634-4220).

Joplin

Accommodations: Motel 6, 3031 South Rangeline Rd., 64801 (tel. 417/781-6400).
● Best Inns of America, 3508 S. Rangeline Rd., Exit 8B on I-44 (tel. 417/781-6776).
● Budget Host—Tropicana Motel, 2417 Rangeline, 64801 (tel. 417/624-8200).

- Drury Inn, I-44 and U.S. 71, 3510 Rangeline Rd., 64804 (tel. 417/781-8000).
- Super 8 Motel, 2830 E. 36th St., 64801 (tel. 417/782-8765).

Kansas City

Tourist Information: Convention and Visitors Bureau of Greater Kansas City, Visitor Information Office, City Center Square, 1100 Main St., Suite 2550, 64105 (tel. 816/221-5242).

Accommodations: Red Roof Inn, 3636 N.E. Randolph Rd., 64161 (tel. 816/452-8585).

- Red Roof Inn, 13712 East 42nd Terrace, Independence, 64055 (tel. 816/373-2800).
- Motel 6, 901 West Jefferson St., Blue Springs, 64015 (tel. 816/228-9133).
- Motel 6, 8230 N.W. Prairie View Rd., 64152 (tel. 816/741-6400).
- Super 8 Motel, 4032 S. Lynn Court Dr., Independence, 64055 (tel. 816/833-1888).
- Super 8 Motel, 115 N. Stewart Rd., Liberty, 64068 (tel. 816/781-9400).
- TraveLodge, 921 Cherry St., 64106 (tel. 816/471-1266).
- Regal 8 Inn, 6400 East 87th St., 64138 (tel. 816/333-4468).
- Budget Host—Royale Inn, 600 Paseo, 64106 (tel. 816/471-5544).
- Schuyler Hotel (AYH-SA), 1017 Locust, 64106 (tel. 816/842-6550). $10 for AYH members.
- Days Inn, 2232 Taney St., 64116 (tel. 816/421-6000).
- Budgetel Inn, 2214 Taney St., 64116 (tel. 816/221-1200).

Kirksville

On Campus: Northeast Missouri State University is in this town, which is described by a friend there as "all-American." We're told that the general attitude toward young people "on the road" is good, but that hitchhiking is not recommended.

An inexpensive place to stay in town is the Village Inn Motel, at 1304 South Baltimore, 63501. For moderate-priced meals, try Manhattan Restaurant, 108 South Elson St.; Golden Corral, 1707 South Baltimore; Country Kitchen, 2700 South Baltimore; or any of the fast-food chains in the area. A favorite gathering place for young people is The Oz. For information on apartments, rides, etc., check the bulletin board in the Student Union Building or the campus newspaper, *The Index*.

Accommodation: Super 8 Motel, 1101 Country Club Dr., 63501 (tel. 816/665-8826).

Lebanon

Accommodation: Econo Lodge, I-44, Exit 127, P.O. Box 992, 65536 (tel. 417/588-3226).

Marston

Accommodation: Scottish Inn, P.O. Box K, 63866 (tel. 314/643-2201).

Moberly

Accommodation: Super 8 Motel, 300 Hwy. 24 East, 65270 (tel. 816/263-8862).

Mount Vernon

Accommodation: Budget Host—Ranch Motel, Jct. I-44 and Hwy. 39 (Box 6B), 65712 (tel. 417/466-2125).

Nevada

Accommodation: Super 8 Motel, 2301 E. Austin, 64772 (tel. 417/667-8880).

Oak Grove

Accommodation: Econo Lodge, 300 South Outer Belt Rd., P.O. Box 178, 64075 (tel. 816/625-3681).

Perryville

Accommodation: Park-Et Motel, Hwy. 61 South, 63775 (tel. 314/547-4516). $22 for one; $24 for two; $31 for three; $34 for four.
● Town House Motel, √ (10% with cash only), 1207 Kings Hwy., 65401 (tel. 314/341-3700). $21.95 single; $24.95 double; $29.95 triple; $32.95 quad.

Rolla

Accommodations: Econo Lodge, I-44 and 1417 Martin Spring Dr., 65401 (tel. 314/341-3130).
● Budget Host—Interstate Motel, 1631 Martin Spring Dr., 65401 (tel. 314/341-2158).

St. Charles

Accommodations: Budget Host—Budget Motel, 3717 I-70, 63301 (tel. 314/724-3717).
● Knights Inn, I-70 at Exit 225, 3800 Harry S. Truman Blvd., 63301 (tel. 314/925-2020).

St Louis

Lewis and Clark launched their two-year expedition from St. Louis, at the confluence of the Mississippi and Missouri Rivers. The Gateway Arch is the symbol of modern St. Louis, but not far from it are reminders of St. Louis's past: the Old Courthouse and the Basilica of St. Louis King of France, the oldest cathedral west of the Mississippi River, where Mass is celebrated daily. Not far away is Laclede's Landing, the last remaining historic area of the city's waterfront where buildings dating from 1830 have been restored and converted into restaurants, shops, and offices. A long time ago, in 1904, St. Louis hosted a World's Fair in a 1400-acre Forest Park, which has since become a well-loved tourist attraction with its Zoo, Planetarium, Municipal Opera, Art Museum, and Historical Society.

Good sources of information on what's happening in St. Louis are *St. Louis Magazine* and the magazine's annual, *Inside St. Louis* ($3.95), Thursday's edition of the *Post Dispatch,* radio station KMOX-AM, or Fun Phone (tel. 314/421-2100). You'll also want to have a copy of the Convention and Visitors Commission's *St. Louis Visitor's Guide;* it's free. *The Riverfront Times,* a free weekly publication available in restaurants, public buildings, college cafeterias, etc., and *The West End World,* another free publication, are particularly good for events in the Central West End. The Convention and Visitors Commission is at 10 South Broadway, 63102. In state call 314/421-1023 or 421-2100; out of state call toll free 800/325-7962 or 800/247-9791 for a special events recording. If you're driving into the city you may want to stop at the Missouri Tourism-St. Louis office on the I-270 at the Riverview exit in North St. Louis (tel. 314/869-7100). Another information bureau is the St. Louis Visitors Center. There are two locations; one is the promenade level of the Mansion House Center at the east end of Locust on 4th Street; the other is a wharf boat on the levee. The Visitors Center is at 330 Mansion House Center, Suite 211, St. Louis, MO 63102 (tel. 314/241-1764).

St. Louis loves holidays and likes to celebrate in grand style. The Veiled Prophet Fair, held over the 4th of July weekend, is the largest 4th of July celebration in the U.S. The National Ragtime and Jazz Festival is held in the early part of June. Strassenfest takes place in late July, and on St. Patrick's Day St. Louis has not one but *two* parades. Check the Calendar of events in the *Post Dispatch* for current information.

Getting There: The airport is about ten miles from town and a limousine connection costs $5.90 one way. The limousine will also take you to St. Louis and Washington Universities. A taxi costs about $18. The public bus from the airport to downtown—the Natural Bridge Bus—costs only 75¢, leaving the airport from exits 6 and 7 on the lower level between the hours of 6 a.m. and 7 p.m. The Bi-State public transportation information number is 314/231-2345. The Greyhound Terminal is at 801 North Broadway; Trailways is just a few steps away at no. 706. The train station is at 550 South 16th St. Transportation from both stations is available by bus or taxi.

Getting Around: The bus fare is 75¢; 85¢ if you want a transfer. Bus stop signs are posted on lampposts, at just about every corner. Taxis can be flagged or called ahead. They charge 90¢ a mile. Express buses are $1.

Accommodations: Bed & Breakfast St. Louis is a reservation service which lists accommodations in private homes in the St. Louis area for $30 to $50 for a single or double. For details, write to them at 4418 West Pine St., St. Louis, MO 63108 (tel. 314/533-9299).

● Other bed-and-breakfast services include Bed & Breakfast of St. Louis County, 11005 Manchester, St. Louis, 63122 (tel. 314/965-4328); and Bed & Breakfast Lafayette House, 1825 Lafayette, St. Louis, 63108 (tel. 314/772-4429).

● Washington University Guest Housing, 6515 Wydown Blvd., P.O. Box 1075, 63015 (tel. 314/889-5073). Men, women, and children. Open June 1 to August 15. $14 single; $12 per person double. Meals available during weekdays. Advance reservations preferred.

● Huckleberry Finn Youth Hostel (AYH), 1904-1906 South 12th St., 63104 (tel. 314/241-0076). $9 for AYH members; $2 extra for nonmembers. Advance reservations necessary June to August.

● Air-Way Motel, √ (10%), 4125 North Lindbergh Blvd., Bridgeton, 63044 (tel. 314/291-3414). $29 to $38 for one or two in one bed; $35 for two in two beds. Price includes continental breakfast.

● Regal 8 Inn, 3655 Pennridge, Bridgeton, 63044 (tel. 314/291-6100).

● Motel 6, 4576 Woodson Rd. (at airport), 63134 (tel. 314/427-1313).

● Motel 6, I-270 and Bellefontaine Rd., 1405 Dunn Rd., 63138 (tel. 314/869-9400).

● Red Roof Inn, 3470 Hollenberg, Bridgeton, 63044 (tel. 314/291-3350).

● Red Roof Inn, 307 Dunn Rd., Florissant, 63031 (tel. 314/831-7900).

● Red Roof Inn, 5823 Wilson Ave., 63110 (tel. 314/645-0101).

● Red Roof Inn, 11837 Lackland Rd., 63146 (tel. 314/991-4900).

● Knights Inn, I-270 at 12433 St. Charles Rock Rd., 63044 (tel. 314/291-8545).

● Econo Lodge, 4575 North Lindbergh Blvd., Bridgeton, 63044 (tel. 314/731-3000).

● Super 8 Motel, 6602 Lindbergh Blvd. South, 63123 (tel. 314/894-9449).

● Super 8 Motel, 12705 St. Charles Rock Rd., Bridgeton, 63044 (tel. 314/291-8845).

Where to Eat: One of the best areas of town to find good food at reasonable prices is the Loop in University City on the 6200 to 6500 blocks of Delmar Boulevard. This area has the highest concentration of ethnic restaurants in the city. Some possibilities:

● Zorba the Greek, 6346 Delmar Blvd. (tel. 314/721-5638). Serves appetizers —tzantziki ($1.25), spanakopita ($1.95), gyros ($2.75), and full dinners of mousaka, rice, salad, and pita for $4.95. Combine dinner at Zorba's with a film at the Tivoli next door.

● Cicero's, 6510 Delmar (tel. 314/862-0009). A typical Italian restaurant with an all-you-can eat special on weekdays.

● Koh-I-Noor, 6271 Delmar (tel. 314/721-3796). Simple and basic decor— delicious Pakistani food.

● Saleems, 6501 Delmar (tel. 314/721-7947). A beautiful atmosphere and excellent Lebanese food. There are dinners but the sandwiches like shish-taouk (marinated broiled chicken in pita bread with vegetables and tahini sauce for $4.95) are filling enough for a meal.

● La Patisserie, 6269 Delmar (tel. 314/725-4902). A perfect breakfast place for the pastry lover.

- Blueberry Hill, 6504 Delmar (tel. 314/727-0880). This rock'n'roll memorabilia haven has darts, pinball machines, poetry readings, and other unexpected treats along with food.
- The Red Sea, 6511 Delmar Blvd. (tel. 314/863-0099), offers Ethiopian Cuisine.
- Riddles Penultimate, 6307 Delmar (tel. 314/725-6985), has received great praise.

The Central West End is a wonderful area for the visitor to St. Louis to explore. Many of the restaurants in the area have tables outside in fair weather. It's fun to stroll along Euclid Street or to sit and watch the passing parade. Some possibilities:

- West End Cafe, 2 North Euclid (tel. 314/361-2020). For night hawks; open until 3 a.m. and offers a fairly extensive menu with most dishes under $5. Chicken wings are a St. Louis specialty.
- Magic Wok, Maryland Plaza (tel. 314/367-2626 or 367-2657). Good for a Chinese lunch.
- Dressels, 419 N. Euclid (tel. 314/361-1060), and Llewelyn's Pub, 4747 McPherson (tel. 314/361-3003), are two Welsh-style pubs. "I like Llewelyn's best—the homemade potato chips are great and the beer selection is extensive."
- Talayna's, 276 North Skinker (tel. 314/863-2120), offers excellent Italian food at reasonable prices.
- The Majestic, 4900 Laclede and Euclid (tel. 314/361-2011), offers good solid fare at very reasonable prices.
- The Silk Road, 510 N. Euclid (tel. 314/367-9370), has a great luncheon buffet for $4.50.
- Bar Italia, 4656 Maryland (tel. 314/361-7010), has particularly good ices.
- Zimfels, 238 N. Euclid (tel. 314/367-3155), is a favorite of the natives because of its good food and outdoor tables.
- Shalimar Garden, 4569 Laclede (tel. 314/361-6911), an Indian restaurant, has particularly good vegetarian food.

What to See and Do: Gateway Arch, 111 North 4th St. Designed by Eero Saarinen, the 630-foot arch is the nation's tallest memorial. Each leg of the arch has a passenger train to carry visitors to the top for a 30-mile-wide view. The ride costs $2.50 for adults, 50¢ for children.

- Museum of Westward Expansion, in the underground area beneath the arch, which tells the story of the pioneers and the people who made St. Louis.
- Huck Finn, Becky Thatcher, and Tom Sawyer Riverboat, foot of Washington Ave. (tel. 314/621-4040). Cruises from Memorial Day to Labor Day. $5. Dinner-dance cruises are $19.75 and include dinner and cocktails.
- Soulard Market, 7th and Lafayette. An interesting public market in South St. Louis.
- Laclede's Landing. Near the Gateway Arch and Mississippi River. The newly remodeled S.S. *Admiral* is now on the levee at the foot of Washington Street. The ship was formerly the world's largest excursion boat and now offers enough entertainment to satisfy just about anyone. The nine-block area of Laclede's Landing is continually being improved and diversified so that now there are places for casual lunches and for elegant dining, for dixieland, jazz, folk, country, and rock music. Laclede's Landing represents the only surviving portion of the historic St. Louis riverfront, so wear comfortable shoes as the streets are the original cobblestone.
- Grant's Farm, 10501 Gravois (tel. 314/843-1700). Land once farmed by

Ulysses S. Grant. A train without tracks takes you through a game preserve. The Clydesdale stallion barn is home of the Anheuser-Busch Clydesdales. Free, call for reservations.

● Jewel Box, Forest Park (tel. 314/535-4111). A floral conservatory that's open all year.

● Six Flags Over Mid-America, in Eureka (tel. toll free 800/241-0805). A 200-acre theme park with rides, games, shops, etc. Admission for the day, $14.95.

● St. Louis Art Museum, Forest Park (tel. 314/721-0067). Over 70 galleries displaying representative pieces of art of the last 3000 years. Free admission. Tours on Wednesday, Friday, Saturday, and Sunday.

● Municipal Opera, in Forest Park (tel. 314/361-1900). World's largest outdoor summer and musical theater—seats 12,000. In summer, features a ten-week repertory of light operas, musicals, and dance performances. Come early and you may get one of the 1500 free seats.

● Central West End, with Euclid Ave. at its heart, is only a few blocks away from Forest Park. Most of the fun here is walking around, looking at the stately mansions, the outdoor cafes, and the lively street life. Two blocks from Euclid, at the corner of Lindell and Newstead is the New St. Louis Cathedral, built in 1907, which combines Byzantine and Romanesque architecture and has an outstanding collection of mosaics.

● Laumeier Sculpture Park, Geyer and Rott Roads (tel. 314/821-1209). A 97.8-acre park with art, nature trails, picnic facilities, and an amphitheater for summer plays and concerts.

● Missouri Botanical Gardens, 4344 Shaw (tel. 314/577-5100). A national historic landmark; home of the Climation, the world's largest geodesic-dome greenhouse, a traditional Japanese Garden, and more. $1 admission.

● St. Louis Science Center, Forest Park, 5050 Oakland (tel. 314/289-4444), is the first phase of a major science center in St. Louis. The Center is composed of the former McDonnell Planetarium, the Medical Museum and the Museum of Science and Natural History, the New McDonnell Star Theatre, Discovery Room, and the Computer Connection.

● St. Louis Zoological Park, Forest Park (tel. 314/781-0900). In a garden-like setting of 83 acres, you can visit more than 2800 animals in naturalistic exhibits with a children's zoo and a zoo line railroad, too. Admission is free.

● Tour the Anheuser-Busch brewery, the largest one in the world, at 1227 Pestalozzi St. (tel. 314/577-2626). There are continuous, free guided tours daily from June to August, Monday to Friday from September through May.

● The National Museum of Transport at 3015 Barrett Station Rd. (16 miles southwest of downtown, near I-270 Big Bend & Dougherty Ferry exits) (tel. 314/965-7998). Newly expanded with an extensive collection of locomotives, railway cars, buses, trams, streetcars, and urban public transport conveyances.

Shopping: The 6200-6500 blocks of Delmar, are as good for shopping as they are for ethnic eating. Try Paul's Books (there really is a Paul), 6691 Delmar (tel. 314/721-4743); Streetside Records, 6314 Delmar for classical, rock, and soul; Vintage Vinyl, 6354 Delmar, for used records. With the St. Louis conservatory of music a few blocks away, this is a good place for sheet music and musical instruments, too.

Two new shopping centers in the downtown area have won instant acceptance from St. Louisans and visitors. The first of the major shopping centers is the 1894 train station, Union Station, which has been renovated into a hotel/shopping/restaurant complex. The second is the St. Louis Center, downtown's enclosed four-story mall, which offers a wide choice of eating and shopping spots.

Another shopping area to mention is Lower Cherokee Street, a favorite haunt for antique collectors, one of the places where "real finds" are still to be had.

Salem

Accommodation: Steelman Lodge, 🦽, in Montauk State Park, Rte. 5, RFD Box 278, 65560 (tel. 314/548-2434). Accommodations include a modern motel with a restaurant, 14 housekeeping cabins, and ten individual nonhousekeeping cabins. Facilities are open March 1 to October 31 and cost from $31 to $58. Specialties of the area are trout fishing and floating on Current River.

Sedalia

Accommodation: Super 8 Motel, 3402 W. Broadway, 65301 (tel. 816/827-5890).

Sikeston

Accommodations: Econo Lodge, I-55 and Exit 67, P.O. Box 701, 63801 (tel. 314/471-7400).
● Drury Inn, I-55 and U.S. 62, 2602 Rear East Malone, 63801 (tel. 314/471-8660).
● Super 8 Motel, 2609 E. Malone, 63801 (tel. 314/471-7944).

Springfield

Accommodations: Best Inns of America, 2355 N. Glenstone at I-44 (tel. 417/866-6776).
● Budget Host—Skyline Motel, 2120 N. Glenstone Ave., 65803 (tel. 417/866-4356).
● Motel 6, 2455 North Glenstone Ave., 65803 (tel. 417/869-4343).
● Regal 8 Inn, 3114 North Kentwood Ave., 65803 (tel. 417/833-0880).
● Super 8 Motel, 3022 N. Kentwood Ave., 65803 (tel. 417/833-9218).

Stockton

Accommodation: Lake Stockton Motel, 506 East Hwy. 32, Box 538, 65785 (tel. 417/276-5151). $20 single; $23 double.

Sweet Springs

Accommodation: Budget Host—Marmaduke Inn, Rte. 2, Box 2A, 65351 (tel. 816/335-6315).

Van Buren

Camping: Ozark National Scenic Riverway, P.O. Box 490, 63965. Eleven campgrounds open year round. Canoe rentals available at three of them. $5 per campsite per night.

Accommodation: Smalley's Budget Host Motel, √ ($1), Hwy. 60, Box 358, 63965 (tel. 314/323-4263 or toll free 800/835-7427, ext. 433). Besides the motel, there are two cabins available. $20 for one; $28 for two in one bed; $37 for two or more people in two beds; $55 for a cabin with three beds; $79.95 for a cabin with four beds and kitchen.

Warrenton

Accommodation: Budget Host—Coach Light Inn Motel, 220 Arlington Way, 63383 (tel. 314/456-4301).

Wentzville

Accommodations: Budget Host Inn, I-70 at Hwy. 61, Box 412, 63385 (tel. 314/327-5212).
● Comfort Inn, 1400 Continental Dr., 63385 (tel. 314/327-5515).

West Plains

Accommodation: Budget Host—Way Station Motel, N. Hwy. 63, Box 278, 65775 (tel. 417/256-4135).

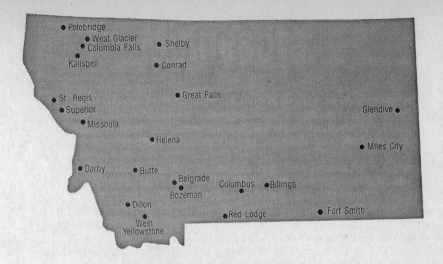

Montana

Montana, especially the western part with its mountains and mountain valleys, is camping, hiking, and horseback-riding country. The scenery is spectacular and there's enough space for everyone. Montana is home to the awesome Glacier National Park, miles of hiking trails, incredible wildlife, and seven Native American tribes. If you visit any of the reservations you'll discover some very small museums, filled with samples of some absolutely exquisite Indian crafts. Three of the entrances to Yellowstone National Park are in Montana, but since most of the park is in Wyoming, see the section on that state for the Yellowstone listing.

Falcon Press, P.O. Box 279 M, Billings, MT 59103, publishes five guides to the state—*The Angler's Guide to Montana,* by Mike Sample ($7.95); *The Hiker's Guide to Montana,* by Bill Schneider ($7.95); *The Nordic Skier's Guide to Montana,* by Elaine Sedlach ($6.95); *The Rockhound's Guide to Montana,* by Bob Feldman; and *The Traveller's Guide to Montana,* by Gary Turlach ($7.95).

Some Special Events: North American Ski Yachting Championships in Whitefish (April); Bucking Horse Sale in Miles City (May); College National Finals Rodeo in Bozeman (June); Montana Plainsmen Annual Grand Gathering in Fort Benton, North American Indian Days in Browning, Fiddlers Championships in Polson, and Sweet Pea Festival in Bozeman (all in July); Festival of Nations in Red Lodge, and Crow Fair in Crow Agency (August); Bison Roundup up in Moiese, and Bald Eagle Gathering in Glacier National Park (October).

Tourist Information: Travel Montana, Department of Commerce, 1424 9th Ave., Helen, MT 59620 (tel. 406/444-2654 or toll free 800/548-3390).

N.B. Two bed-and-breakfast reservation services are: Western Bed and Breakfast Hosts, P.O. Box 322, Kalispell, MT 59901 (tel. 406/257-4476); and Bed and Breakfast Rocky Mountain, P.O. Box 804, Colorado Springs, CO 80901 (tel. 303/630-3433).

Belgrade

Accommodation: Super 8 Motel, 6460 Jackrabbit Lane, 59714 (tel. 406/388-1493).

Billings

Accommodations: Motel 6, 5400 Midland Rd., RR9, 59102 (tel. 406/252-0093).
● Budget Host—Elliot Inn, 1345 Mullowney Lane, 59101 (tel. 406/252-2584).
● Regal 8 Inn, I-90 and Midland Road, 59102 (tel. 406/248-7551).
● Kings Rest Motel, 1206 East Main St., 59105 (tel. 406/252-8451). $24 for one; $26 for two in one bed; $28 for two in two beds.
● Lewis & Clark Inn, 1709 First Ave. North, 59101 (tel. 406/252-4691). $23 single; $29 double; $31 triple; $35 quad.
● Super 8 Motel, 5400 Southgate Dr., 59102 (tel. 406/248-8842).
● Juniper Motel, 1315 North 27th St., 59101 (tel. 406/245-4128). $26 to $28 for one; $30 to $32 for two in one bed; $32 to $34 for two in two beds.
● Imperial 400 Motor Inn, 2601 Fourth Ave. North, 59101 (tel. 406/245-6646).
● Picture Court Motel, ✓, 5146 Laurel Rd., 59101 (tel. 406/252-8478). $22 for one; $28 for two in one bed; $33 for two in two beds.

Bozeman

Accommodations: Rainbow Motel, 510 North Seventh Ave., 59715 (tel. 406/587-4201). $18 to $22 for one; $20 for two in one bed; $26 for two in two beds; $30 for three in three beds. Rates are $2 lower in winter months.
● Imperial 400 Motor Inn, 122 West Main St., 59715 (tel. 406/587-4481).
● Days Inn, 1321 North Seventh Ave., 59715 (tel. 406/587-5251).
● Super 8 Motel, 800 Wheat Dr., 59715 (tel. 406/586-1521).

Butte

Accommodations: Mile Hi Hotel, ✓ ★, 3499 Harrison Ave., 59701 (tel. 406/494-2250). $22 to $29 single bed, two persons; $28 to $35 two beds, three to four persons; $32 to $38 three beds, five to six persons. Advance reservations suggested. Heated pool.
● Super 8 Motel, 2929 Harrison Ave., 59701 (tel. 406/494-6000).

Columbia Falls

Accommodation: Mountain Shadows Motel, Box O, junction U.S. 2 and 206, 59912 (tel. 406/892-7686). $21 for one; $24 for two in one bed; $29 for two in two beds.

Columbus

Accommodation: Super 8 Motel, 602 8th Ave. North, 59019 (tel. 406/322-4101).

Conrad

Accommodation: Super 8 Motel, 215 N. Main St., 59425 (tel. 406/278-7676).

Darby

Accommodation: Tipi Hostel, c/o Jenny Sweet, Box 16, 59829 (tel. 406/821-3792). Open in late spring to late September. $2 per night per person. Set up own tent. $1 per person for shower. Cooking and facilities free. Bikers preferred.

Dillon

Accommodation: Super 8 Motel, 550 N. Montana St., 59725 (tel. 406/683-4288).

Fort Smith

Camping: Bighorn Canyon National Recreation Area, P.O. Box 458, 59035 (tel. 406/666-2233). Camping May 1 to November 1 at Black Canyon Boat Camp (access by boat only) and all year at Horseshoe Bend, Barry's Landing, and Black Canyon Boat Camp (access by boat only). $3 per campsite per night at Horseshoe Bend.

Glendive

Accommodations: Days Inn, 2000 North Merrill Ave., 59330 (tel. 406/365-6011).
● Super 8 Motel, 1904 N. Merrill Ave., P.O. Box 198, 59330 (tel. 406/365-5671).

Great Falls

Help: Crisis Center, 406/453-6511
Accommodations: Imperial 400 Motor Inn, 601 Second Ave. North, 59401 (tel. 406/452-9581).
● Super 8 Motel, 1214 13th St. South, 59405 (tel. 406/727-7600).

Helena

Accommodations: Motel 6, 800 North Oregon, 59601 (tel. 406/442-9990).

- Imperial 400 Motor Inn, 524 North Last Chance Gulch, 59601 (tel. 406/442-0600).
- Days Inn, 2001 Prospect Ave., 59601 (tel. 406/442-3280).
- Super 8 Motel, 2201 11th Ave., 59601 (tel. 406/443-2450).

Kalispell

Accommodations: Motel 6, 1540 Hwy. 93 South, 59901 (tel. 406/752-6355).
- Super 8 Motel, 1341 1st Ave. East, 59901 (tel. 406/755-1888).

Miles City

Accommodations: Motel 6, 1314 Haynes Ave., Rte 2, Box 3396, 59301 (tel. 406/232-7040).
- Budget Host—Custer's Inn, 1209 W. Haynes, Box 1235, 59301 (tel. 406/232-5170).
- Super 8 Motel, I-94 and Hwy. 59, P.O. Box 1625, 59301 (tel. 406/232-5261).

Missoula

Help: Crisis Center, 406/543-8277.
Accommodations: University of Montana Residence Halls, c/o Room 101 Turner Hall, 59812 (tel. 406/243-2611). Ask for Ron Brunell. For men and women who are affiliated with the university in some capacity, for example, visiting faculty, students, those attending workshops on campus, prospective students, etc. Open June 15 to August 10. $9.50 single; $7.50 per person double (rates subject to change). Advance reservations necessary.
- The Birchwood Hostel, 600 South Orange St., 59801 (tel. 406/728-9799). Closed December 15 to December 30. $4.50 to $5. Priority given to members of AYH/IYHF, bicycle tourists, backpackers, and foreign visitors; others welcome as space permits. Reservations recommended during the summer. Fully equipped kitchen, bicycle storage, and self-service laundry.
- Super 8 Motel, 3901 S. Brooks, 59801 (tel. 406/251-2255).
- TraveLodge, 420 W. Broadway, 59802 (tel. 406/728-4500).

Polebridge

Accommodation: North Fork Hostel (AYH), Ⓢ √ ★, end of Beaver Drive; mailing address: P.O. Box 1, 59928 (tel. 406/862-0184). Open year round. Large rustic log cabin adjacent to Glacier National Park. No electricity. $7 per night per person. Shower and complete kitchen. Bring sleeping bag. Advance reservations of two weeks suggested.

Red Lodge

Accommodations: Friendship Yodeler Motel, 601 South Broadway, Rte. 212, P.O. Box 1336 (tel. 406/446-1435).
- Super 8 Motel, 1223 S. Broadway, Rte. 2, 59068 (tel. 406/446-2288).

St. Regis

Accommodation: Super 8 Motel, Old Hwy. 10, P.O. Drawer L, 59866 (tel. 406/649-2422).

Shelby

Accommodation: O'Haire Manor Motel, 204 2nd St. South, 59474 (tel. 406/434-5555). $24 for one; $30 for two in one bed; $36 for two in two beds.

Superior

Accommodation: Budget Host—Big Sky Motel, 103 4th Ave. East, Box 458, 59872 (tel. 406/822-4831).

West Glacier

Camping: Glacier National Park, 59936 (tel. 406/888-5441). Fifteen campgrounds open June to September (except for Apgar, which is open May to October). Horseback riding nearby at Sprague Creek, Many Glacier Corral, Lake McDonald Corral, and Apgar Corral. $5 to $7 per campsite per night; Bowman Creek and River (North Fork) are free.

West Yellowstone

Accommodation: Alpine Motel, 120 Madison, 59758 (tel. 406/646-7544). Across from bus station. Open May 1 to November 1. $25 single; $33 double; $55 triple. Recommended by a reader from West Germany.

● Madison Hotel-Motel, 139 Yellowstone Ave., 59758 (tel. 406/646-7745). $20 to $22 single; $24 to $26 double; $26 to $28 triple; $26 to $30 quad.

● Super 8 Motel, 1547 Targhee Pass Hwy., 59758 (tel. 406/646-9584).

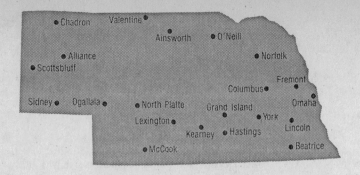

Nebraska

Not surprisingly, the people at the Division of Travel and Tourism in Nebraska want you to save time to "Discover the Difference" in Nebraska. You'll be surprised at what you uncover both indoors and out! Canoeists should write for *Canoeing Nebraska* and bikers should ask for *Backpacking: Trails to Nebraska's Great Outdoors*, both available free from the address below.

For those who prefer museums, Nebraska has many pioneer history sites that may interest you. Some of the other special places are: the Joslyn Art Museum in Omaha, which has a well-received collection of art from ancient to modern times and a group of paintings and artifacts from the Maximillian expedition to the upper Missouri in the mid-1800s; the Museum of the Fur Trade, near Chadron, which tells the story of that lively enterprise from the point of view of the traders, trappers, and Indians; and the University of Nebraska State Museum in Lincoln, a museum of natural history which features, among other things, "Ceres the Transparent Woman."

Since the sport of rodeo began in Nebraska in 1882, it would seem appropriate to attend at least one while you're in that state. North Platte, Burwell, and Omaha host three of the biggest rodeos.

Some Special Events: National Arbor Day Celebration in Nebraska City (April), NEBRASKA-land Days and the Buffalo Bill Rodeo in North Platte, and Homestead Days in Beatrice (June), Fur Trade Days in Chadron, and Annual Homecoming Celebration/Winnebago Pow Wow (July), Czech Festival in Wilber (August), Nebraska State Fair in Lincoln (September).

Tourist Information: For information on sights, lodging, camping, museums, events, fishing, state parks, backpacking, hiking, or canoeing, contact the Division of Travel and Tourism, Nebraska Department of Economic Development, P.O. Box 94666, 301 Centennial Mall South, Lincoln, NE 68509 (tel. 402/471-3796, or toll free 800/228-4307 out of state, 800/742-7595 in Nebraska).

Ainsworth

Accommodation: Super 8 Motel, 1025 E. 4th, 69210 (tel. 402/387-0700).

Alliance

Accommodations: Budget Host—McCarroll's Motel, 1028 East 3rd, Box 519, 69301 (tel. 308/762-3680).
● Super 8 Motel, W. Hwy. 385, 69301 (tel. 308/762-8300).

Beatrice

Accommodations: Budget Host—Holiday Villa, 1820 North 6th St., 68310 (tel. 402/223-4036).
● Super 8 Motel, 3210 N. 6th St., 68310 (tel. 402/223-3536).

Chadron

Accommodations: Budget Host—Grand Motel, 1050 West Hwy. 20 (three blocks east of 385 Jct.), 69337 (tel. 308/432-5595).
● Super 8 Motel, Hwy. 385 and Hwy. 20 West, 69337 (tel. 308/432-4471).

Columbus

Accommodations: Budget Host—Gembol's Motel, 3220 8th St., 68601 (tel. 402/564-2729).
● Super 8 Motel, 3324 20th St., 68601 (tel. 402/563-3456).

Fremont

Accommodation: Super 8 Motel, 1250 E. 23rd St., 68025 (tel. 402/727-4445).

Grand Island

Tourist Information: Visitor Information, Hall County Convention and Visitors Bureau, P.O. Box 1486, 309 West 2nd St., 68802 (tel. 308/382-9210 or toll free 800/247-6167, ext. 625).
Accommodations: TraveLodge, 507 West 2nd St., 68801 (tel. 308/384-1000).
● Super 8 Motel, 2603 S. Locust St., 68801 (tel. 308/384-4380).

Hastings

Accommodation: Budget Host—Rainbow Motel, 1000 West J St., 68901 (tel. 402/463-2989).

Kearney

Accommodations: Budget Host—Western Inn, 1401 2nd Ave., Box 1903, 68847 (tel. 308/234-3153).

- Budget Host—Hammer Budget Inn, West Hwy. 30, 68847 (tel. 308/237-2123).
- Super 8 Motel, 15 W. 8th St., 68847 (tel. 308/234-5513).

Lexington

Accommodation: Super 8 Motel, Rte. 2, Box 149, 68850 (tel. 308/324-7434).

Lincoln

On Campus: There are three universities in Lincoln. The University of Nebraska is the largest—25,000 students. There are also Nebraska Wesleyan University and Union College. For travel information and advice on accommodations, stop at the Overseas Opportunities Center, 1237 R St., and for counterculture-type information go to Dirt Cheap, 217 North 11th St.

The people from the University of Nebraska were anxious to recommend places to eat in the city-center area, where the food is good, and inexpensive, too. Here's their list: Duffy's Bar, 1412 O St. (tel. 402/474-3543), a college tradition, with beef stew; Kuhl's, 1038 O St. (tel. 402/476-1311), home-cooked chicken dinners; Arturo's Taco Hut, 249 North 11th (tel. 402/476-0761), the best Mexican food in eastern Nebraska; Valentino's, 232 North 13th (tel. 402/475-1501), pizza and salad; and for late-night eaters there's Stoney's Kitchen at 1640 Holdenige (tel. 402/476-3537) and the Zoo Bar at 136 North 14th (tel. 402/435-8754).

"Football Saturdays are a great time for strangers to see what football mania can do to a town."

Accommodations: Cornerstone Youth Hostel (AYH-SA) (on University of Nebraska Campus), 640 North 16th St., 68508 (tel. 402/476-0355). Open year round. $3.50 for AYH members.
- Days Inn, 2920 N.W. 12th St., 68521 (tel. 402/475-3616).
- Motel 6, 3001 N.W. 12th St., 68521 (tel. 402/475-3211).
- Budget Host—Great Plains Motel, 2732 O St., 68510 (tel. 402/476-3253).
- Scottish Inn, 2001 W. O St., 68528 (tel. 402/477-4488).
- Super 8 Motel, 2635 W. O St., 68528 (tel. 402/476-8887).
- Super 8 Motel, 2545 Cornhusker, 68521 (tel. 402/476-4488).

McCook

Accommodation: Super 8 Motel, 1103 E. B, 69001 (tel. 308/345-1141).

Norfolk

Accommodations: Econo Lodge, U.S. Hwy. 275 Bypass, 1909 Krenzien Dr., 68701 (tel. 402/371-7157).
- Super 8 Motel, 1223 Omaha Ave., 68701 (tel. 402/379-2220).

North Platte

Accommodations: Motel 6, 1520 South Jeffers St., 69101 (tel. 308/534-6200).
- Budget Inn—Park Motel, 1302 North Jeffers St., 69101 (tel. 308/532-6834).
- Super 8 Motel, 220 Eugene Ave., 69101 (tel. 308/532-4224).

Ogallala

Accommodations: Quality Inn, 201 Stagecoach Trail, 69153 (tel. 308/284-3656).
- Super 8 Motel, 500 East A St. South, 69153 (tel. 308/284-2076).

Omaha

Tourist Information: Omaha Convention and Visitors Bureau, Suite 1200 —Civic Center, 1819 Farnam St., 68183 (tel. 402/444-4660 or toll free 800/332-1819 outside Nebraska; 800/334-1819 in state).
Accommodations: Imperial 400 Motor Inn, 2211 Douglas St., 68102 (tel. 402/345-9565).
- Budget Host—Hiway House Motor Inn, I-80 and Hwy. 370, 68138 (tel. 402/332-3911).
- Budgetel Inn, 10760 M St., 68127 (tel. 402/592-5200).
- Hampton Inn, 10728 L St., 68137 (tel. 402/593-2380).
- TraveLodge, 3902 Dodge St., 68131 (tel. 402/558-4000).
- Motel 6, 10708 M St., 68127 (tel. 402/331-3161).
- Super 8 Motel, 7111 Spring St., 68106 (tel. 402/390-0700).
- Super 8 Motel, 10829 M St., 68137 (tel. 402/339-2250).

O'Neill

Accommodation: Super 8 Motel, E. Hwy. 20, 68763 (tel. 402/336-3100).

Scottsbluff

Accommodations: Budget Host—Capri Motel, 2424 Ave. I, 69361 (tel. 308/635-2057).
- Super 8 Motel, 2202 Delta Dr., 69361 (tel. 308/635-1600).

Sidney

Accommodation: Super 8 Motel, 2115 Illinois St., Box 314, 69162 (tel. 308/254-2081).

Valentine

Accommodations: Budget Host—Raine Motel, W. Hwy. 20, Box 626, 69201 (tel. 402/376-2030).

● Super 8 Motel, Jct. Hwy. 20 and 83, P.O. Box 653, 69201 (tel. 402/376-1250).

York

Accommodation: Super 8 Motel, I-80 and U.S. 81, P.O. Box 532, 68467 (tel. 402/362-3388).

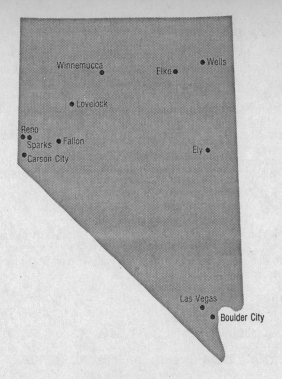

Nevada

Nevada has more neon lights than people. In fact, we'd give Las Vegas the neon city award hands down.

In case you hadn't heard, gambling is legal in Nevada, and practically all of the population depends on the industry for its livelihood. One good thing about Las Vegas and Reno is that any poor traveler over 21 years old can get a good, cheap meal in the casinos and hotels. The idea behind the "bargain" is that once you're there you'll gamble, so if you just eat and run you can save quite a bit.

"You hit the secret of Vegas on the nose—if you stay away from gambling, you can really get off cheap. Pick up some of the tourist newspapers available in every hotel lobby. They feature free coupons for nickels to play the slots, free meals at some casinos, and other give-aways like a three-minute phone call to anywhere in the U.S."

Try desert camping in Nevada; the stars are fantastic, the air is cold and clean, and the sand makes a good mattress.

For a guidebook to Nevada that's a combination of history and travel information, look for *The Complete Nevada Traveler,* by David W. Toll, available in bookstores for $7.95; or from the Gold Hill Publishing Co., P.O. Drawer F, Virginia City, NV 89440, for $9.45 ($9.95 for Nevada residents).

Some Special Events: Cowboy Poetry Gathering in Elko (January); Snowfest in North Lake Tahoe (late February to early March); America's Cup Land Sailing in Jean (April); Fallon's Wild Bunch Stampede, and Silver State Square Dance Festival in Reno-Sparks (May); National Basque Festival in Elko (June); Carson Valley Heritage Days in Minden/Gardnerville (July); Lincoln County Fair and Rodeo in Panaca (August); Numaga Days Celebration in Reno/Sparks (September); The Nevada Day Celebration and Parade in Carson City (October).

Tourist Information: Nevada Commission on Tourism, Capitol Complex, Carson City, NV 89710 (tel. 702/885-4322, or toll free 800/237-0774).

Boulder City

Camping: Lake Mead National Recreational Area, 601 Nevada Hwy., 89005 (tel. 702/293-8906). Ten campgrounds with 1148 sites open year round. Be prepared to share most of the campgrounds with trailers. $5 per campsite per night. No reservations.

Carson City

Accommodations: Motel 6, 2749 South Carson St., 89701 (tel. 702/885-7710).
● Super 8 Motel, 2829 S. Carson St., 89701 (tel. 702/883-7800).

Elko

Accommodations: Motel 6, 3021 Idaho St., 89801 (tel. 702/738-4337).
● Super 8 Motel, 1755 Idaho St., 89801 (tel. 702/738-8488).

Ely

Accommodation: Motel 6, 7th & Ave. O, 89301 (tel. 702/289-6671).

Fallon

Accommodation: TraveLodge, 70 East Williams Ave., 89406 (tel. 702/423-2194).

Las Vegas

"Eating out in Las Vegas is cheaper than cooking at home. Most of the casinos have smorgasbords with all of the extras for less than you can buy groceries. Every casino has what are called 'fun books,' and if you utilize them you can have a lot of fun for very little money. I have a free pancake, egg, and coffee breakfast every morning, and where it's not free, breakfast can be found in many hotels for $1.99. As a rule, prices are cheaper downtown than in the luxurious Strip hotels. If you are a gambler, you'll find the odds more in your favor downtown."

Accommodations: Motel 6, 195 East Tropicana Blvd., 89109 (tel. 702/798-0728).
- Allstar Inn, 4125 Boulder Hwy., 89121 (tel. 702/457-8051).
- Allstar Inn, 5085 South Industrial Rd., 89118 (tel. 702/739-6747).
- Budget Host—Koala Motel, 520 South Casino Centre Blvd., 89101 (tel. 702/384-8211).
- E-Z 8 Motel, 5201 South Industrial Rd., 89118 (tel. 702/739-9513).
- Imperial 400 Motor Inn, 3265 Las Vegas Blvd., 89109 (tel. 702/735-5102).
- Friendship King Albert, 185 Albert Ave., 89109 (tel. 702/735-1741).
- Budget Host—Tam O'Shanter Inn, 3317 Las Vegas Blvd., 89109 (tel. 702/735-7331).
- Super 8 Motel, 5288 Boulder Hwy., 89122 (tel. 702/435-8888).

Lovelock

Accommodation: Budget Host—Lovelock Inn, Hwy. 40 West & Cornell Avenue, 89419 (tel. 702/273-2937).

Reno

Help: Crisis Call Center, 702/323-6111. For 24-hour telephone crisis counseling, information, and referral.

Accommodations: Motel 6, 1901 South Virginia, 89502 (tel. 702/827-0255).
- Motel 6, 866 North Wells Ave., 89512 (tel. 702/786-9852).
- Motel 6, 1400 Stardust St., 89503 (tel. 702/747-7390).
- Allstar Inn, I-80 at 666 North Wells Ave., 89512 (tel. 702/329-8681).
- Chalet Motel, 515 N. Center, 89501 (tel. 702/322-0405 or toll free 800/367-7366). $20 to $38 single; $24 to $50 double; $35 to $52 triple; $37 to $54 quad. Higher rates given apply to weekends.
- Shamrock Inn, 505 N. Center St., 89501 (tel. 702/786-5182 or toll free 800/367-7366). $20 to $38 single; $24 to $50 double; $35 to $52 triple; $37 to $54 quad. Higher rates apply to weekends.

Sparks

Accommodation: Blue Fountain Inn, Ⓢ√ ★, 1590 B St., 89431 (tel. 702/359-0359 or toll free 800/367-7366). $24 to $35 single; $31 to $39 double; $35 to $45 twin; $37 and $50 quad. Higher rates apply on weekends.

Wells

Accommodation: Motel 6, I-80/U.S. 40 and U.S. 93, 89835 (tel. 702/752-2116).

Winnemucca

Accommodation: Motel 6, 1600 Winnemucca Blvd., 89445 (tel. 702/623-1180).

New Hampshire

New Hampshire is one place to go when you've had enough of cities. Its mountains, lakes, and wilderness are delicious to anyone who needs some space to move around. It's a small state, just 180 miles from north to south and no more than 100 miles wide at any point. Some of the choicest land is owned by the state, with more than 50 state parks to enjoy swimming, boating, camping , and picnicking. Enjoy the vivid leaves in the fall. Ski, sleighride, and skate come winter. New Hampshire has the highest mountains in the Northeast. Taste maple sugar and syrup in the spring. And swim at the beach or lakeside as the weather warms.

Some Special Events: Annual Sheep and Wool Festival in New Boston (May); Portsmouth Market Square Weekend in Portsmouth (June); Mt. Washington Valley Equine Classic, Attitash in Bartlett (July); Annual League of New Hampshire Craftsmen's Fair at Mt. Sunapee State Park in Newbury (August); New Hampshire Highland Games at Loon Mountain in Lincoln (September); Warner Fall Foliage Festival in Warner (October).

Tourist Information: New Hampshire Vacations, P.O. Box 856, Concord, NH 03301.

N.B. Two bed-and-breakfast reservation services for New Hampshire are New Hampshire Bed & Breakfast, RFD 3, Box 53, Laconia, NH 03246 (tel. 603/279-8348); and Valley Bed & Breakfast, Box 1190, North Conway, NH 03860 (tel. 207/935-3799).

Alton

Accommodation: Green Tops Youth Hostel (AYH), 400 yards from Lake Winnipesaukee, ♿, R.D. 1, from Rte. 28, Robert's Cove Road, 03809 (tel. 603/569-9878). Open May 20 to September 7. $6 for AYH members, $7 for nonmembers in dorm-style accommodations. Cabins: $25 for one or two people; $40 for three or more. Advance reservations necessary. Waterskiing, sailing available, lake and pool swimming nearby, "with an island yet!"

Boscawen

Accommodation: Daniel Webster Motor Lodge, Ⓢ√ ★, U.S. Rtes. 3 and 4, RFD 14, Box 246, 03303 (tel. 603/796-2136). $32 to $38 single; $36 to $44 for two. Lower rates apply in winter.

Franconia

Accommodation: Pinestead Farm Lodge, Easton Road, Rte. 116, 03580 (tel. 603/823-8121). Lodge will pick up guests from bus station, by prior arrangement only $15 per night. "An old farmhouse located in the White Mountains offering simple rooms for guests seeking country pleasure."

Gorham

Accommodation: Appalachian Mountain Club, Pinkham Notch Camp, Box 298, 03581 (tel. 603/466-2727). Men, women, and children. $24.50 for one adult including one meal, $12.50 for children; $32.50 including two meals, $16.50 for children (at least one meal must be purchased). $4 discount for AMC members. Advance reservations strongly advised for weekends and holiday periods. "Modern, rustic lodge with small bunk rooms with two, three, or four beds per room."

Hanover

On Campus: Here in this quaint New England town you'll find Dartmouth College. The heart of the college activities seems to be at the Hopkins Center (theater, music, film) and at Collis Center (student activities). The Hopkins Center bulletin boards, *The Dartmouth* (the daily newspaper), and the information desk in Collis should keep you informed of what's going on. While you're in the area consider going tubing on the White River (you need to have your own tube), canoeing or kayaking on the Connecticut River from Ledyard Canoe Club (rentals), cross-country skiing, golfing, windsurfing and sailing on Mascoma Lake, and swimming at the Ledges. For inexpensive meals try the Hopkins Center Cafeteria and Collis Cafe (vegetarian) in the Collis Center. In town, try Lou's Restaurant (famous for its freshly made crullers), EBA's—Everything But Anchovies, or Raphael's Cucina. For Mexican food go to Molly's Balloon.

Keene

Accommodation: Doyle House (AYH-SA), Keene State College, Main Street, 03431 (tel. 603/352-9602 between 4 and 8 p.m.; 603/352-1909, ext. 230, between 9 a.m. and 4:30 p.m.). Open June 1 to August 1. $7.25 for AYH members.

Lyme

Accommodation: Loch Lyme Lodge and Cottages, ⑤, Rte. 10, 03768 (tel. 603/795-2141). The Lodge will provide transportation from bus and train stations. Twenty-five cabins open from late May to September; the main lodge, a farmhouse built in 1784, is open year round. Advance reservations of up to one year are strongly suggested. $24 to $31 for one; lower rates for children. Price includes breakfast. Various meal plans are available in the dining room. All types of summer and winter recreational facilities are available, including swimming, skiing, and ice fishing.

Nashua

Accommodation: Susse Chalet Lodge, Everett Tpke., Rte. 3, Exits 5W (north) and 5E (south) (tel. 603/889-4151).

Randolph

Accommodation: Bowman Base Camp (AYH), U.S. Rte. 2, 03570 (tel. 603/466-5130). Open May 30 to October 12. $10 for AYH members. Advance reservations suggested. Hiking trails nearby.

Raymond

Accommodation: Walnut Hill Seminar House, Rte. 102, 03077 (tel. 603/895-2437). Open Memorial Day to Labor Day. Group reservations accepted year round. $7 summer, $8 winter for AYH members. Advance reservations of two weeks necessary during winter months.

West Ossipee

Accommodation: Chocorua Camping Village, P.O. Box 1180, 03890 (tel. 603/323-8536 summer; 603/659-2790 winter). Open May 30 to October 12. $10 to $28 single or double; $8 to $12 per person triple or quad. Advance reservations necessary July 1 to September.

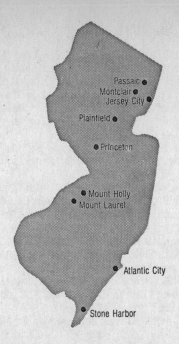

Passaic
Montclair
Jersey City
Plainfield
Princeton
Mount Holly
Mount Laurel
Atlantic City
Stone Harbor

New Jersey

New Jersey is a much-maligned member of the Middle Atlantic States. It's true that part of northeastern New Jersey represents the worst of what can happen when industrialization hits an area. But trust us: the state really does deserve to be called the Garden State. Once you're off the New Jersey Turnpike, you'll enter a New Jersey that's unknown to most of the rest of the country.

The New Jersey coast—Cape May, Long Beach Island, and Barnegat Light —is an area of exceptional beauty. The farther south you go, the more beautiful it seems to become. Its 127 miles of wide beaches are quiet on the mild days of fall and spring and busy with vacationers in summer.

On the western border of New Jersey is the Delaware River and in the far northwest, along the river, there are rolling hills, streams, and ponds. The Appalachian Trail passes through the area at the Delaware Water Gap, which has been made a national recreation area. Along this part of the river there are a number of places to rent canoes. If you do so, you'll experience rapids and calm stretches, passing high banks, cliffs, and rolling fields.

The Pine Barrens, in southeastern New Jersey, are more than 100 miles of scraggly pine and cedar trees that live in a series of swamps and on the banks of freshwater streams. This region is ideal for spring and fall camping and canoeing. The Bass River State Forest in New Gretna is the center of activity for the area.

New Jersey boasts more than 800 lakes and ponds, more than 100 rivers and creeks, more than 1400 miles of freshly stocked trout streams, 40 state parks, and 11 state forests.

There's no lack of historic sites to visit in New Jersey. Over 100 Revolutionary War battles were fought on New Jersey soil, including the important Battle of Trenton. Some of the names from New Jersey's proud past are Von Steuben, Livingston and Molly Pitcher, Edison, Whitman, and Wilson. For those who want to visit New Jersey's history preserved, we recommend the New Jersey Division of Travel and Tourism's booklet *A Guide to New Jersey's Unique Heritage* and their "Vacation Kit."

Another guide is *Discovering New Jersey* by Thomas Radco, Rutgers University Press, which describes countless sights and activities that "I didn't discover in eighteen years living in the state!"

Some Special Events: New Jersey Folk Festival at Douglass College in New Brunswick (April); Hollybush Festival of the Arts at Glassboro State College in Glassboro (May); Ethnic Festivals at the Garden State Arts Center in Holmdel and at Action Park in McAfee (weekends throughout the summer); New Jersey Festival of Ballooning at Solberg Airport in Readington (July); New Jersey State Fair at the Garden State Racetrack in Cherry Hill (July to August); Sussex County Farm and Horse Show at Sussex County Fairgrounds in Augusta (August); and Waterloo Folk Festival at Waterloo Village in Stanhope (September).

Tourist Information: Division of Travel and Tourism, One W. State St., CN-826, Trenton, NJ 08625 (tel. 609/292-2496).

N.B. A bed-and-breakfast reservation service for New Jersey is B&B of New Jersey, 103 Godwin Ave., Suite 132, Midland Park, NJ 07432 (tel. 201/444-7409).

Atlantic City

Accommodation: Econo Lodge, 328 White Horse Pike, Absecon, 08330 (tel. 609/652-3300).

Jersey City

Help: CONTACT Hudson County, 201/831-1870 (covers Bayonne, Jersey City, North Bergen, Weehawken, Guttenberg, West New York, and Union City).

Accommodation: YMCA, 654 Bergen Ave., 07304 (tel. 201/434-3211). Men and women. Weekly rate: $65 first week; $55 and up second week. Reservations necessary. Twenty minutes from New York City.

Montclair

Help: Help Line, 201/744-1954.

Accommodation: YMCA, 25 Park St., 07042 (tel. 201/744-3400). The bus from New York City stops at the Y. Men only. $14. Weekly rate: $41.

Mount Holly

Accommodation: Friendship Mount Holly Concord Inn, Rte. 38, 08060 (tel. 609/267-7900).

Mount Laurel

Accommodation: Red Roof Inn, 603 Fellowship Rd., I-295 at Hwy. 73, Exit 36A, 08054 (tel. 609/234-5589).

Passaic

Accommodation: YWCA, 114 Prospect St., 07055 (tel. 201/779-1770). Women only. $15 single. Weekly rate: $50 to $60. Reservations requested two weeks in advance.

Plainfield

Accommodation: YMCA, 518 Watchung Ave., 07060 (tel. 201/756-6060). Men only. $15 single; $10 key deposit required. Transient rooms are scarce. Advance reservations necessary.

Princeton

Help: Council for Community Services in Princeton, 609/924-5865.

On Campus: The well-known Princeton University is here as well as the Institute for Advanced Studies. It's a good place to see "well-preserved, lived-in American architecture of the 18th and 19th centuries." While you're there you can visit the university's excellent art museum or take the "Orange Key" tour of the campus.

A popular student hangout which also happens to have very good, inexpensive meals is the Annex, 128 ½ Nassau St. For Greek food and pizza, try the Athenian, 25 Witherspoon St. For excellent homemade ice cream in a variety of flavors, try Thomas Sweet, 179 Nassau St. And for fine dining, try Nassau Inn, Palmer Square.

Accommodations: Red Roof Inn, 3203 Brunswick Pike, I-295 and U.S. 1, Lawrenceville, 08648 (tel. 609/896-3388).

● McIntosh Inn, 🛇, 3270 Brunswick Pike at U.S. 1 and Quaker Bridge Mall, Lawrenceville, 08648 Tel: (609)896-3700. $31.95 single; $37.95 double; $40.95 triple; $43.95 quad.

Stone Harbor

Accommodation: Fairview Guest House, 8700 Pennsylvania Ave., 08247 (tel. 609/368-2065 in season, 609/848-4371 off-season). Open mid-May to late September. $26 to $48 double in-season; $18 to $31 double off-season.

New Mexico

Certain states attract dreamers, and New Mexico is one. In the late '60s and early '70s, young Americans considered New Mexico their Utopia. Communes formed, young people arrived, and all seemed well. By now lots of those communes have dissolved, and the people have moved on. But the reality of New Mexico is almost as beautiful as their dream, so do try to spend some time there.

What will you see while you're there? Carlsbad Caverns National Park, with more than 50 caves; White Sands National Monument; Taos Pueblo, 2½ miles north of Taos, where you can wander and watch some of the 1400 Indians who make their home in this terraced pueblo. New Mexico is a state to explore and a state where there is much to be learned about the Spanish and Indian cultures of the American Southwest.

Some Special Events: Spring Arts Celebration in Taos, and Four Corners Super Balloon Rally in Farmington Lake (May); Summer Festival in Ruidoso (June); Indian Pueblo Cultural Center Arts and Crafts Fair in Albuquerque, and Fiesta de Taos (July); Indian Market in Santa Fe, and Inter Tribal Indian Ceremonial in Gallup (August); State Fair in Albuquerque, Chili Festival in Hatch, and Santa Fe Fiesta (September); and Albuquerque International Balloon Fiesta (October).

Tourist Information: New Mexico Travel Division, Economic Development and Tourism Department, Joseph Montoya Building, 1100 St. Francis Dr., Santa Fe, NM 87503 (tel. 505/827-0291 or toll free 800/545-2040).

N.B. For information on bed-and-breakfast facilities in New Mexico write to New Mexico Bed and Breakfast, P.O. Box 2925, Santa Fe, NM 87504–2925.

Alamogordo

Accommodations: Motel 6, 251 Panorama Blvd., 88310 (tel. 505/434-5970).
- Econo Lodge, 907 S. White Sands Blvd., 88310 (tel. 505/437-5090).
- Super 8 Motel, 3204 N. White Sands, 88310 (tel. 505/434-4205).
- TraveLodge, 508 South White Sands Blvd., 88310 (tel. 505/437-1850).

Albuquerque

Tourist Information: Albuquerque Convention and Visitors Bureau, P.O. Box 26866, 87125 (tel. 505/243-3696).
Accommodations: Allstar Inn, 3400 Prospect Ave., NE, 87107 (tel. 505/883-8813).
- Allstar Inn, 1000 Stadium Blvd. SE, 87102 (tel. 505/243-8017).
- Comfort Inn, 13031 Central Ave. NE, 87123 (tel. 505/294-1800).
- Motel 6, 13141 Central Ave. NE, 87123 (tel. 505/294-4600).
- Motel 6, 1701 University Blvd. NE, 87102 (tel. 505/843-9228).
- Regal 8 Inn, 5701 Iliff NW at Coors, 87105 (tel. 505/831-8888).
- The Royal Hotel, Ⓢ √ ★ (10% to 15%), 4119 Central Ave. NE, 87108 (tel. 505/265-3585). $31.90 to $49.90 single; $36.90 to $39.90 double; $39.90 to $43.90 triple; $4 each additional person.
- Super 8 Motel, 2500 University Blvd. NE, 87107 (tel. 505/888-4884).
- Days Inn, 13317 Central Ave. NE, 87108 (tel. 505/294-3297).
- Red Carpet Inn, 12901 Central Ave. NE, 87123 (tel. 505/298-6861).

Bloomfield

Camping: Chaco Culture National Historical Park, Star Rte. 4, P.O. Box 6500, 87413 (tel. 505/786-5384). Campground with 46 sltes at Gallo Wash, one mile east of Visitors Center. Open year round. No fee for camping. Entrance fee: $1 per adult or $3 per car load, whichever is less.

Carlsbad

Accommodations: Motel 6, 3824 National Parks Hwy., 88220 (tel. 505/885-0011).
- Econo Lodge, 3820 National Parks Hwy., 88220 (tel. 505/887-0341).
- TraveLodge, 401 East Greene St., 88220 (tel. 505/885-3117).

Clovis

Accommodations: Motel 6, 2620 Mabry Dr., 88101 (tel. 505/762-2995).
- Super 8 Motel, 2920 E. Mabry Dr., 88101 (tel. 505/769-1953).

Deming

Accommodation: Motel 6, I-10 and Motel Drive, P.O. Box 970, 88031 (tel. 505/546-2623).

Farmington

Accommodations: Regal 8 Inn, 510 Scott Ave., 87401 (tel. 505/327-0242).
- Motel 6, 1600 Bloomfield Hwy., 87401 (tel. 505/326-4501).
- Super 8 Motel, 1601 Bloomfield Hwy., 87401 (tel. 505/325-1813).

Gallup

Accommodations: Motel 6, 3306 West Hwy. 66, SR 2, Box 18, 87301 (tel. 505/863-4492).
- Econo Lodge, 3101 West Hwy. 66, 87301 (tel. 505/722-6677).
- Allstar Inn, 3101 W. Hwy. 66, 87301 (tel. 505/722-6655).

Grants

Accommodations: Friendship Desert Sun Motel, Hwy. 66, 1121 East Santa Fe Ave., 87020 (tel. 505/287-7925).
- Motel 6, East Santa Fe Ave. (I-40 Interchange), P.O. Box 1478, 87020 (tel. 505/285-4607).
- TraveLodge, 1204 East Santa Fe Ave., 87020 (tel. 505/287-2991).
- Allstar Inn, Grants Spur Hwy., 87020 (tel. 505/287-2952).

Hobbs

Accommodations: Econo Lodge, 309 N. Marland Ave., 88240 (tel. 505/397-7171).
- Motel 6, 509 N. Marland Blvd., 88240 (tel. 505/393-0221).
- Super 8 Motel, 722 N. Marland Blvd., 88240 (tel. 505/397-7511).

Las Cruces

Accommodations: Motel 6, 235 La Posada Lane, 88001 (tel. 505/525-1010).
- Allstar Inn, 3091 South Main St., 88001 (tel. 505/525-0994).
- Hampton Inn, 755 Avenida de Mesilla, 88001 (tel. 505/526-8311).
- Super 8 Motel, 245 La Posada Lane, 88001 (tel. 505/523-8695).
- TraveLodge, 755 North Valley Dr., 88005 (tel. 505/524-7753).

Los Alamos

Camping: Bandelier National Monument, 87544 (tel. 505/672-3861). Campground at Juniper (one-tenth mile inside entrance). Open March 1 to November 30. $5 per campsite per night. Entrance fee per car, $5. Golden Eagle, Golden Age, and Golden Access passes honored.

Pilar

Accommodation: The Plum Tree Cafe and Hostel (AYH), ⑤★, Hwy. 68, Box 1-A, 87571 (tel. 505/758-4696 or toll free 800/552-0070, ext. 822).

Domes: $15 single, $17.50 breakfast included. Hostel: $7.50 for AYH members; $8.50 for nonmembers, $11 breakfast included. Honeymoon suite: $24.50 for two, $29.50 breakfast included. Bus stops in front of hostel. The Plum Tree offers fine art workshops, llama treks in the mountains, nature hikes, and raft trips. Discount applies to rooms only.

Ramah

Camping: El Morro National Monument Campground, 87321 (tel. 505/783-4226). Campground one-half mile from headquarters with nine free sites. Open year round. No fee.

Raton

Accommodations: Motel 6, 1600 Cedar St., 87740 (tel. 505/445-2777).
● Super 8 Motel, 1610 Cedar St., 87740 (tel. 505/445-2355).

Roswell

Accommodation: TraveLodge, 2200 West 2nd St., 88201 (tel. 505/623-3811).

Santa Fe

"The very old Indian and Spanish heritage and culture of the majority of people here is almost sacred."

Accommodations: Private homes of members of the Council on International Relations, P.O. Box 1223, 100 East San Francisco St. (La Fonda Hotel, Suite #3, Mezzanine), 87501 (tel. 505/982-4931, mornings only). Foreign visitors only. Donation of $9 per night requested for a stay of no more than three to four days, breakfast included. Advance reservations preferred. The Council office is closed weekends and holidays.

"The Council is really fantastic. The members are very friendly and helpful."

● Santa Fe International Hostel, 1412 Cerrillos Rd., 87501 (tel. 505/988-1153 or 505/983-9896). Limousine service from Lamay bus station. $8 for dorm; $20 single or double; $24 triple; $28 quad.
● Motel 6, 3007 Cerrillos Rd., 87501 (tel. 505/473-1380).
● Allstar Inn, 3383 Cerrillos Rd., 87501 (tel. 505/471-4140).
● Super 8 Motel, 3358 Cerrillos Rd., 87501 (tel. 505/471-8811).

"It is always worth checking at both the College of Santa Fe and St. John's College for dormitory space."

"Don't miss the Opera Under the Stars in the summer for $3. Standing room is usually available."

Santa Rosa

Accommodations: Motel 6, 3400 Will Rogers Dr., 88435 (tel. 505/472-3045).
- Super 8 Motel, 1201 Will Rogers Dr., 88435 (tel. 505/472-5388).

Socorro

Accommodation: Motel 6, 807 South U.S. 85, 87801 (tel. 505/835-4300).

Taos

Accommodations: The Abominable Snow-mansion and "Indian Country International Hostel" (AYH-SA), Ⓢ★, P.O. Box 3271, 87571 (tel. 505/776-8298). Shuttle bus to hostel. Summer: $10.50 ($7 for AYH members and *Where to Stay* readers). Winter: $15 for bed-and-breakfast. Meeting and study facilities available for groups of up to 75 people. Camping sites available. Family-style meals served at hostel.
- Sagebrush Inn, Ⓢ∨★, P.O. Box 557, 87571 (tel. 505/758-2254). $35 and up, single; $40 and up, double, triple, and quad; $75 and up for suites.

Tucumcari

Accommodations: Motel 6, 2900 East Tucumcari Blvd., Rte. 4, Box 196, 88401 (tel. 505/461-4791).
- TraveLodge, 1214 E. Tucumcari Blvd., 88401 (tel. 505/461-1401).
- Comfort Inn, 1023 E. Tucumcari Blvd., 88401 (tel. 505/461-0360).

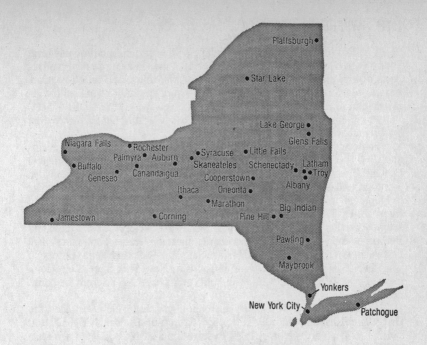

New York

What can you say about New York that hasn't already been said? Like California, New York is a place that people want to see. But most people think of New York as New York City. It's especially hard for New York City residents to remember that all those other people in the state are New Yorkers, too. If you visit New York, don't leave without immersing yourself in New York City for at least a few days, but leave yourself enough time to see some of the beautiful upstate and ocean areas of the state, too.

With a little exploring, you'll find that much of New York State is rural with miles of farmland, small towns, and abundant wildlife. Outdoor recreational opportunities are endless. The southwestern part of the state offers beautiful countryside, especially during early to mid-October, unbounded recreation in the Finger Lakes region, and some very special tourist possibilities like Genesee Gorge in Letchworth State Park; Watkins Glen for racing; and Timespell, a laser light and sound spectacular; Corning Glass Works and Museum; and the many wineries that dot the area from Watkins Glen to Hammondsport. For hikers or campers, what could be more inviting than the Adirondacks or the Catskills? And who hasn't heard of the grand Niagara Falls? Anyone with a car should try to do some exploring, too, along the Hudson where there are so many restored homes, museums, and pretty little towns just a few hours' ride from the New York City area. And don't forget the ocean beaches of Long Island, easily reached on the Long Island Railroad.

And without going too far from the city, you can also enjoy some lovely hikes and walks—just consult the *New York Walk Book,* Doubleday ($7.95).

The Rough Guide to New York will help you survive, and probably love, your stay in New York City and State. Loads of moneysaving details on all aspects of city life: food, accommodations, sights, tours, and an off-beat approach. Martin Dunford and Jack Holland, Routledge and Kegan Paul Inc., in association with Methuen Inc., 29 W. 35th St., New York, NY 10001.

Another useful guide to the city and state is *New York Off the Beaten Path* by William Scheller, Globe Pequot ($7.95).

Some Special Events: General Clinton Canoe Regatta on the Susquehanna and Civil War Encampment in Youngstown (May); Allentown Art Festival in Buffalo, Clearwater Hudson River Revival in Croton, Newport Jazz Festival in Saratoga, and Northeast Craft Fair in Rhinebeck (June); German Alps Festival in Hunter, Folk Fair in Panama, War of 1812 Pageant in Sackets Harbor, and International Theater Festival in Stony Brook, Long Island (July); Shaker Museum Festival in Old Chatham (August); Chowder Society Celebration in Old Bethpage, and New York State Fiddler's Contest in Osceola (September); Fall Festival in Lake Luzerne and Fall Foliage Sailplane Rides in Elmira (October).

Tourist Information: Division of Tourism, New York State, One Commerce Plaza, Albany, NY 12245 (tel. toll free 800/CALLNYS from the continental U.S.

N.B. Three bed and breakfast reservation services for New York State are Bed & Breakfast USA Ltd., P.O. Box 606, Croton-on-Hudson, NY 10520 (tel. 914/271-6228); North Country B&B Reservation Service, Box 286, Lake Placid, NY 12946 (tel. 518/523-3739); and Tobin's Bed & Breakfast Guide, Rd. 2, Box 64, Rhinebeck, NY 12572.

Albany

Tourist Information: Albany County Convention and Visitors Bureau, 52 South Pearl St., 12207 (tel. 518/434-1217).

Accommodations: Red Roof Inn, 188 Wolf Rd., I-87 at Albany Shaker Rd., Exit 4, 12205 (tel. 518/459-1971).

● Susse Chalet Inn, I-87, Northway Exit 2E, on Wolf Road (tel. 518/459-5670).

● Econo Lodge, 1632 Central Ave., 12205 (tel. 518/456-8811).

Auburn

Accommodation: Sleepy Hollow Motel, Rte. 20, 13021 (tel. 315/253-3281). $28 to $34 single; $32 to $36 double; $34 to $45 triple.

Big Indian

Accommodation: Cold Spring Lodge, ★ (10% midweek and spring), Box 37 Oliverea Rd., 12410 (tel. 914/254-5711). Modern efficiency cabins with fireplaces which accommodate up to eight people. $30 per person per night. Firewood supplied. They also have boarding-house-style rooms for $30 single; $40 double; $50 triple or quad. Restaurant on premises; cabins have kitchens. "We own forty acres of land situated in a beautiful valley in the Catskill Mountains."

Buffalo

Accommodations: YWCA Residence (AYH-SA), 245 North St., 14201 (tel. 716/884-4761). Women only. $7 for AYH members; mothers can bring small children age 6 and under. $10 single; $12 double. Advance reservations requested with advance deposit of $2. Cafeteria in building. Bring sleeping bag or bedsheets.

● Knights Inn, I-90 at S.R. 75, S-5245 Camp Rd., Hamburg, 14075 (tel. 716/648-2000).

● Red Roof Inn, 42 Flint Rd., I-290 and Millersport Hwy. North, Amherst, 14226 (tel. 716/689-7474).

● Red Roof Inn, 5370 Camp Rd., Hamburg, 14075 (tel. 716/648-7222).

● Hotel Lenox, Ⓢ√ ★ 🖢, 140 North St., 14201 (tel. 716/884-1700). $42 single; $50 double; $58 triple; $66 quad. Student rates: $32 single; $40 double.

● Super 8 Motel, Flint Road & Millersport Highway, Amherst, 14226 (tel. 716/688-0811).

Canandaigua

Accommodations: Econo Lodge, 170 Eastern Blvd., 14424 (tel. 716/394-9000).

● Budget Host—Heritage Motor Inn, Rte. 5 and 20 East, 14424 (tel. 716/394-2800).

Cooperstown

Accommodation: Cooperstown Hostel (AYH), Box 704, 13326 (tel. 607/293-7324). Open May 15 to October 15. $5 for AYH members. Advance reservations suggested. Rental tents, trailers, and cabins for nonmembers; $10 and up.

Corning

Accommodation: Super 8 Motel, 255 S. Hamilton, Painted Post, 14870 (tel. 607/937-5383).

Geneseo

On Campus: For travel information, contact the Travel Center at SUNY/College at Geneseo, located in Room 326 of the College Union (tel. 716/245-5864 or 245-5851).

On campus, the College Union Snackbar provides meals. In the area, students recommend the Davis Cafe, Bronze Bear, Club 41, and several fast-food spots, all on Main Street. Chinese cuisine is available at K-Gardens Restaurant on Park Street (adjacent to campus). Route 20A, just east of the village, is dotted with McDonalds, Burger Kings, and Pizza Huts. Nearby Conesus Lake features the Tee and Gee, Bojangles, and Cottonwood. For drinks and new friends, the Idle Hour on Center Street offers "happy hour" daily; the Vital Spot, Gentleman Jim's (GJ's), and the Inn Between are all within an area adjacent to the east side of campus.

Glens Falls

Accommodations: Susse Chalet Motor Lodge, I-87, Northway Exit 18, 12801 (tel. 518/793-8891).
● Friendship Landmark Motor Lodge, P.O. Box 376, 12801 (tel. 518/793-3441).

Ithaca

On Campus: There are thousands of students in Ithaca—at Cornell or Ithaca College—and either campus will welcome you. To find out what's happening on the two campuses, pick up copies of the *Ithaca Journal,* the *Cornell Daily Sun,* the *Grapevine,* or the *Ithaca New Times.* For a bulletin board with rides and apartments listed, go to Willard Straight Hall at Cornell and to the third floor of the Student Union building at Ithaca.

Our friend at Ithaca College tells us that "the city is on a lake, and during the warm months, there are boating trips and sailing facilities. There's also a wide selection of summer stock theaters in the area. . . ."

Accommodation: International Living Center, North Campus 8, Cornell University, 14853 (tel. 607/255-5299). Men and women (children with difficulty). Accommodation only for those with official business at Cornell. Preference is given to foreign students. June 1 to August 14. $9.50 single; $7.75 per person double. Linen is supplied. Advance reservations suggested. Cooking facilities available.

Jamestown

Accommodation: YWCA, 401 North Main St., 14701 (tel. 716/485-1137). Three blocks from bus station. Women only over age 18. $10 to $13.50 single. Weekly rate: $35 to $40.

Lake George

Accommodation: Lake George Youth Hostel (AYH), 🏛 (partial), Iroquois Street, P.O. Box 176, 12845 (tel. 518/668-2634, May 1 to September 15; 518/668-2001, rest of year, for information only). Open May 22 to September 15. $6 for AYH members. Advance reservations helpful July to August. No check-in after 8 p.m. without deposit.

Latham

Accommodation: Super 8 Motel, Troy-Schenectady Road, I-87, Exit 6 (tel. toll free 800/843-1991).

Little Falls

Accommodation: YMCA, 15 Jackson St., 13365. (tel. 315/823-1740). Ten miles from Adirondack Mountains in Mohawk Valley. Men only. $10. Weekly rate: $30.

Marathon

Accommodation: Friendship Three Bear Inn, Interstate 81, Exit 9, P.O. Box 507, 13803 (tel. 607/849-3258).

Maybrook

Accommodation: Super 8 Motel, Neelytown Road 1, P.O. Box 98, Montgomery, 12549 (tel. 914/457-3143).

New York City

"I agree with Comden and Green, 'a wonderful town.'"

It doesn't matter how you get to New York just as long as you make sure to get there. New York is an incredible city. There's no place quite like it anywhere, and everyone should see it for themselves at least once. In fact, most people aren't satisfied with just one visit—they keep coming back again and again. Since New York is so big and so fast-paced, you'll need a little help getting acquainted with this small and crowded island. Here are some books that will help:

Arthur Frommer's Guide to New York, by Faye Hammel, Prentice Hall Press ($5.95). A good, general guide to what there is to see and do. Particularly helpful to orient you to where you are and what you can do there.

New York City: The Best Things in NY are Free, by Marian Hamilton, Harvard Common Press, 535 Albany St., Boston, MA 02118 ($10.95).

The Carefree Getaway Guide for New Yorkers (Day and Weekend Trips without a Car), by Theodore Scull, Harvard Common Press ($8.95).

New York City—It's a Great College Town!, compiled by the Association of a Better New York, Globe Pequot ($9.95).

New York on $50 a Day, by Joan Hamburg and Norma Ketay. Prentice Hall Press ($10.95). Another Frommer Guide, this one with emphasis on the bargain spots.

The Hip Pocket Guide to New York City, compiled and edited by Tim Page. Harper/Colophon Books ($6.95). Thirty-one people give their opinions on restaurants, the performing arts, discos, clubs, record shops, and just about everything else that's New York. It is well-written and comprehensive—we recommend it.

Michelin Guide to New York City, Michelin ($9.95). New York done the classic Michelin way, that is, thoroughly researched and fascinating.

I Love New York Guide, by Marilyn J. Appleberg, Collier Macmillan ($5.95). Dedicated to helping you find it in New York—whatever "it" may be. This is a terrific pocket guide to everything and everywhere in New York.

Another easily carried guide to the city is *New York in Your Pocket,* Barron's ($3.95). Very brief—a bit like a mini-yellow pages for visitors.

The City Observed: A Guide to Architecture, by Paul Goldberger, Vintage Press ($8.95). A thorough and thoughtful guide to the buildings when you have enough time to do some exploring.

For anyone who needs to get away from it all for a day or so, we recommend *Natural New York,* by Phyllis and Bill Thomas, published by Holt, Rinehart and Winston ($10.95). The book leads you to the parks, wildlife sanctuaries, recreation areas, and other open spaces within 50 miles of New York City.

Also, to know what's going on when you're in town, refer to the *Village Voice, New York* magazine, the *New Yorker,* or the *New York Times* (especially the Sunday "Arts and Leisure" section and the Friday "Weekend" section).

"This is a city that's culturally diverse, intellectually alive, and vigorous."

A first stop in New York, especially for student visitors, should be CIEE's New York Student Center, which offers up-to-the-minute information on what's happening in the city, and discount tickets for a variety of activities in town. A Council Travel Services office there provides help in planning travel throughout the United States and the world. What's more, the Student Center is an ideal place to stay (see listing on page 322), as well as a great spot to meet other travelers. You can book a room by sending a cashier's check or money order made payable to CIEE. Send reservations to the Student Center, located in the William Sloane House, 356 W. 34th St., New York, NY 10001 (tel. 212/695-0291). Confirmation vouchers will be sent to you.

N.B. A little while ago, two major changes were made in telephone service in New York. Pay phone calls went from 10¢ to 25¢ and the people who live in Brooklyn, Queens, and Staten Island were given a new area code. Now it's necessary to dial 1-718 before any number in these three boroughs. This doesn't affect the cost of the call, though, it's still considered "local."

Getting There: From the Airports: You'll land in the borough of Queens at either JFK or La Guardia, or at Newark Airport in New Jersey. Banish thoughts of a taxi—the fare is $25 or more from JFK. Fortunately, there are several alternatives. Call 800/AIR-RIDE for most possible means of transportation to and from the airports. Call from a touchtone telephone and you'll be able to get all the information automatically by pressing the indicated numbers. A few years ago, a new subway route from JFK Airport through Manhattan called the JFK Express was inaugurated and is generally one of the less expensive and more efficient ways to get to and from JFK. The "Express," which is really a combination bus and train ride, takes about one hour and costs $6.50, leaving every 20 minutes from 6 a.m. to 1 a.m. From JFK, the bus takes passengers to the Howard Beach-JFK Airport station where they board the train for stops at Jay Street in Brooklyn, and seven stops in Manhattan: Broadway-Nassau, Chambers

Street (World Trade Center), West 4th Street (Washington Square), 34th Street (Sixth Avenue), 42nd Street (Sixth Avenue), 47th-50th Streets (Rockefeller Center), and 57th Street (Sixth Avenue).

A somewhat slower but less expensive ($2) bus and train combination has been around a lot longer than the JFK Express: From JFK take a Q10 bus to the Union Turnpike-Kew Gardens station, the Lefferts Boulevard-Liberty Avenue station of the IND subway, or the 121st Street and Jamaica Avenue station. From the first station you can take an E or F train; from the second, board an A train right into the heart of Manhattan; and from the third, you can catch a J train. Allow two hours for this method.

From LaGuardia, take the Q33 bus to 82nd Street and Jackson Heights and then switch to the 7 train which goes to Times Square ($1.50 total). From there you can get just about anywhere in the city.

If you have lots of luggage or are unwilling to spend your first hour in New York on the subway, take a Carey Transportation, Inc. bus from either JFK or La Guardia to Grand Central Station or Port Authority. From JFK the ride costs $8, and takes about one hour; from La Guardia it's $6, and takes one-half hour. Carey buses run approximately every 30 minutes from JFK between 5 a.m. and 1 a.m., and from La Guardia every 20 minutes between 6:45 a.m. and midnight. The Carey number is 718/632-0500.

Two bus lines run to and from Newark Airport and the Port Authority Bus Terminal on the West Side of Manhattan at Eighth Avenue and 40th Street. The 45-minute trip costs $4 on Olympia Trails, running 5 a.m. to 1 a.m. (tel. 212/964-6233 or 201/981-2015 at the airport); and $5 on New Jersey Transit Coaches, running 24 hours a day (tel. 201/762-5100).

● By Train: If you come by train, you'll arrive at either Grand Central Station on the East Side at 42nd Street and Vanderbilt Avenue or at Pennsylvania Station at 32nd Street and Seventh Avenue. Both stations have information booths where you can find out how to get where you're going by public transportation. There are subway stations in both terminals, and there are bus stops right outside.

● By Bus: Anyone coming by bus will arrive at the recently renovated Port Authority Bus Terminal, 40th Street and Eighth Avenue. There's a subway station entrance in the terminal and buses outside.

Getting Around: The best way to get around Manhattan is on foot. Just remember that most streets and avenues are laid out on a grid, that streets are numbered consecutively north of 4th Street, and that the avenues (with some exceptions) are numbered, lower to higher, from the East to the West Side. Fifth Avenue divides east and west; uptown is north of where you are, downtown is south, and crosstown is east or west toward either the East River or the Hudson River. The New York Convention and Visitors Bureau has a free map, but it's not very detailed, so we recommend either buying the paperback *New York in Flash Maps* or a Hagstrom map.

For bus and subway travel information between any two points in the five boroughs, call the Travel Information Bureau, 718/330-1234.

● By Bus: For visitors who don't want to walk, the bus is best. Buses go up and down the avenues and across the major streets, and on most routes they run frequently during the day and with limited service at night. The bus fare is $1 (exact change or a subway token), and free transfers are available: for example, when you go crosstown on a bus, you can get a free transfer to take you uptown or downtown on any of the avenues that have bus routes.

● Subway: Since 1904, New Yorkers have been riding on and complaining about the subway. It's noisy, it's dirty, and it's graffiti-scarred—but it's usually fast and costs only $1 to go anywhere on the system. You need to buy a token before you can enter the platform. Token booths usually have a supply of subway maps, and sometimes they have bus maps.

● Taxis: You'll be able to tell whether or not a taxi's free by the light on top—if it's lit up, it's vacant. A taxi ride costs $1.15 for the first one-seventh mile and 15¢ for each additional one-ninth mile. At night and on weekends you must pay a 50¢ surcharge. The tip should be 15% of the fare. Try to avoid taking a taxi because they're expensive and slow—especially when you're making a crosstown trip in rush hour. Most taxis are yellow—these are the ones licensed by the City of New York. Taxis by any other colors are called gypsy cabs and their drivers boast: "We're not yellow—we'll go anywhere."

Tourist Information: New York Convention and Visitors Bureau, 2 Columbus Circle, 10019 (tel. 212/397-8222). Everything here is free—from maps to calendars of events to tickets for television shows.

Help: Travelers Aid Society of New York, 158-160 W. 42 St. (tel. 212/944-0013). Open 9 a.m. to 5 p.m. Monday to Friday; 9:30 a.m. to 3 p.m. Saturday.

● Victim Service Agency, 2 Lafayette St., 10007 (tel. 212/577-7777). 24-hour hotline for crime victims, service referrals.

● Catholic Charities, 191 Joralemon St., Brooklyn (tel. 718/596-5500).

● Gay Men's Health Crisis, 258 W. 18th St. (tel. 212/807-6655).

● Gay & Lesbian Switchboard, 212/777-1800. Open daily noon to midnight.

Accommodations: Look for special bargains in weekend and holiday hotel rates and in New York City's "Tour Package Directory" available at the Convention and Visitors Bureau (see above, Tourist Information).

● Urban Ventures, Inc., P.O. Box 426, 10024 (tel. 212/594-5650). A bed-and-breakfast service run by Mary McAulay, with a total of 850 properties in New York and New Jersey. "We inspect every room; we list and interview every host." Here's one sample listing: "A twin-bedded room on East 80th Street and York Avenue in the home of a vivacious teacher. The bus to Bloomingdale's stops right in front of the door." $34 to $60 single; $45 to $80 double. Student discounts. Write for more details.

● New World Bed and Breakfast, 150 Fifth Ave., Suite 711, 10011 (tel. 212/675-5600 in New York state, toll free 800/443-3800 out of state). This reservation service offers hundreds of possibilities for your overnights in New York City, from "a loft in Soho . . . to . . . a midtown brownstone." $40 to $70 single; $50 to $85 double.

● New York City Youth Hostel, ⑤★, 255 W. 43rd St., 10036 (tel. 212/944-6390, or toll free 800/242-4343, must ask for Youth Hostel). This is the world's largest youth hostel with room for 1200 people per night! $30 to $55 single; $45 to $65 double; $55 to $75 triple; $65 to $85 quad; $10 per dorm room, two to six persons, $5 linen, or bring own.

● Hotel Chelsea, 222 West 23rd St., 10011 (tel. 212/243-3700). $35 single; $65 double with one bed; $75 with two beds; $85 for an efficiency; $85 and up for a quad. Advance reservations of one week necessary. "The Chelsea has been, and is still, an artistic and creative haven for many of New York's and the world's famous characters including Thomas Wolfe, Arthur Miller, Jane Fonda, Dylan Thomas, Sid Vicious, and Lenny Bruce."

● New York Student Center, ⑤, William Sloane House, 356 West 34th St., 10001 (tel. 212/695-0291). Six blocks from Port Authority Bus Station; two blocks from Penn Station. Huge 1485-room facility. Rates: $24 single; $17 per person for a twin-bedded room. Rates are for rooms without baths, although a few rooms with bath are available at a higher price. Weekly rates and meal plans are also available for resident students. Facilities available to guests include a newly renovated cafeteria, lounges, reading rooms, game room, television room, gymnasium, and laundry. CIEE and YMCA cooperate in offering the services at the Student Center. The Council Travel Services office at Sloane House issues airline and bus tickets, and arranges low-cost transportation and tours while helping students plan their travels in the U.S. and abroad. ISIC holders receive 10% discount on New York City bus and boat tours. The Hospitality Center offers information on activities in New York, including walking tours and discount tickets to plays and other events. The Student Center is also a good meeting place, especially in summer. Other plusses are the ride board and multilingual staff at the center.

● International Student Center, Ⓢ, 38 West 88th St., 10024 (tel. 212/787-7706). Open year round. $8. Foreign students under age 30 only.

● West Side YMCA, Ⓢ, 5 West 63rd St., 10023 (tel. 212/787-4400). Male and female students. $28 and up single; $40 and up double. Reservations preferred three weeks in advance with first night's deposit. Cafeteria in the building.

● Vanderbilt YMCA, Ⓢ, 224 East 47th St., 10017 (tel. 212/755-2410). Men and women. $27 to $36 single; $36 to $42 double; $51 triple; $64 quad; $99 per week for students. Excellent cafeteria.

● Greenpoint YMCA, 99 Meserole Ave., Brooklyn, 11222 (tel. 718/389-3700). Men only. $20 per person; $70 per week. One block from Nassau Avenue subway stop. Newly renovated. Health facilities available. One-half hour by subway from midtown Manhattan.

● Brooklyn YWCA, 30 Third Ave., Brooklyn, 11217. (tel. 718/875-1190). By subway, take the "A" train to Hoyt Schermerhorn. Single women only, ages 18 to 55, employed at least 1 year. $20 single. Weekly rate: $65 to $85. Advance reservations of one to two weeks necessary.

● Parkside Evangeline Residence, 18 Gramercy Park South, 10003 (tel. 212/677-6200). Women only. "This is a women's residence offering permanent residency (at least one month) for 300 women." During the summer, a transient can stay for $20 a night. Weekly rate: $123 including two meals a day. Advance reservations of one to two months necessary. Application and personal interview for those living nearby; others write, including a self-addressed stamped envelope.

● McBurney YMCA, 206 West 24th St., 10011 (tel. 212/741-9226). Men only. $23 to $31 single; $44 double.

● Consulate, 224 W. 49th St. (tel. 212/246-5252). $55 to $65 single; $75 to $85 double. 200 small rooms in the heart of the theater district.

● Excelsior, 45 W. 81st St. (tel. 212/362-9200). $55 to $65 single; $65 to $75 double. Across the street from the Museum of Natural History and Central Park, on the Upper West Side.

● Malibu Studios Hotel, Ⓢ★, 2688 Broadway, 10025 (tel. 212/663-0275 or 222-2954). $99 and up single per week; $140 and up double per week; $165 and up triple per week. Reservations recommended.

● Pickwick Arms, 231 East 51st St. (tel. 212/355-0300). $46 single; $60 to $70 double.

● Wales, 1295 Madison Ave. at 92nd St. (tel. 212/876-6000). $50 to $75 single;

$60 to $110 double. Good-sized rooms in a residential Upper East Side neighborhood.

● Westpark, 308 W. 58th St. (tel. 212/246-6440). $45 to $65 single; $65 to $85 double. A small hotel facing Columbus Circle. Some rooms have a view of Central Park.

Where to Eat: There are two kinds of eating to be done in New York. First is the grab-it-while-you-can-get-it type and second are the more peaceful and leisurely meals that are best when shared with someone else. For the first kind you can depend on some of the chains like Blimpies, Nathan's Famous, or Arby's. And don't forget the "street pizza" that's usually $1 a slice and often filling and delicious. Another good "picnic" possibility are the salad bars in so many of the produce markets around town. Usually for $2.60 or $2.80 a pound, you can enjoy a salad that you can create from 20 or 30 choices of ingredients. You'll never be far from one of these wherever you are in the city.

If you're interested in saving money at dinnertime, why not take advantage of the "happy hour" that many restaurants observe. Usually the happy hour lasts from 5 to 7 p.m., and during these two hours it's possible to have a drink and all the hors d'oeuvres you can eat for the cost of the drink alone. Some places serve quite substantial hors d'oeuvres—like fried chicken, pepper steak, meatballs, etc. Some places you might consider in midtown are the Old Stand, 914 Third Ave. (tel. 212/759-4836); Molly Mog's, 65 W. 55th St., (tel. 212/581-5436); and for happy hour Indian style, Tandoor, 40 E. 49th St. (tel. 212/752-3334).

For the second type of eating, here are some possibilities. We've chosen these because we feel that they offer, above all, good value. (Remember that to save money it's always best to have your big restaurant meal at lunchtime since the prices on the dinner menu are much higher.) The following suggestions are some of our favorites, places where you can feel comfortable and won't have to spend a fortune. Call ahead for hours and don't be too shy to ask about prices.

● Chumley's, 86 Bedford St. in the West Village (tel. 212/675-4449). This quintessential Village bar and restaurant was once a speakeasy. Hearty food, surprisingly low prices, and plenty of beer. For a remembrance of things past.

● Spring Street Restaurant, 162 Spring St. in Soho (tel. 212/219-0157). One of the first restaurant/bars in Soho and still one of the most popular. The management doesn't mind if you sit and talk awhile over your drink or your meal. Lunch $8; dinner $15; brunch $8.

● Hard Rock Cafe, 221 W. 57th St. (tel. 212/489-6565). Loud music, great burgers, long lines.

● Hamburger Harry's, 157 Chambers St. (tel. 212/267-4446), and 145 W. 45th between 6th Avenue and Broadway (tel. 212/840-0566).

● Two working breweries serving food and drinks are Manhattan Brewing Co., 40 Thompson St. at Broome (tel. 212/219-9250); and New Amsterdam Brewery, 235 11th Ave. at 26th Street (tel. 212/255-4100).

● Hudson Bay Inn, 1454 2nd Ave. (tel. 212/861-5683). Free spaghetti and salad Monday nights at 7:30 at the bar with purchase of a drink. Lunch $3 to $7; dinner $6 to $15; brunch $7 to $9.

● Mitchell's, 122 E. 27th St. (tel. 212/689-2058). Sunday brunch $7.95 to $12.95, all you can drink from noon to 4 p.m.

● West End Cafe, 2911 Broadway between 113th and 114th Streets, near Columbia (tel. 212/666-9160). You can eat here—good omelettes, sandwiches, hamburgers, etc.—but it's the music that we recommend. Starting at about 9 every night, in a side room that's all dark and smoky, you can hear terrific swing jazz played by the people who worked with Ellington and others as famous. Lunch $3.95 to $6.95; dinner $4.95 to $11.95. Cover $3 to $7 for music.

● Rathbones, 1702 Second Ave. at 88th St. (tel. 212/369-7361); and 340 E. 79th between 1st and 2nd Avenues (tel. 212/734-5788). Relaxed, comfortable setting but can get noisy at times. The bar is buzzing at night. Dinner $3.95 to $10.95.

● Chirping Chicken, 350 Amsterdam Ave. at 77th St. (tel. 212/787-6631); 1260 Lexington Ave. at 85th St. (tel. 212/517-9888); and 918 3rd Ave. (tel. 212/750-5011). One friend whom we consider an expert on such matters gives Chirping Chicken a four-star rating—the chicken is charcoal-broiled with a tasty marinade and sauce. It's inexpensive too—only $3.59 for a half chicken, $6.19 for a whole. Eat in or take out—how about a picnic starring a chirping chicken?

● Spring Street Natural Restaurant and Bar, 62 Spring St. in Soho (tel. 212/966-0290). The food is good—soups, vegetable tempura, etc.—and the staff, at least when we've been there, is eager to please. Lunch $5 to $8; dinner $6 to $11.

● Hisae's Place, 35 Cooper Square (tel. 212/228-6886). 4:30 to 6:30 dinner specials—$12.95 for two. Sushi half price on Mondays.

● Shojin, 23 Commerce St., off 7th Avenue (tel. 212/989-3530). All vegetarian cuisine. Non-dairy dishes. No alcohol and no smoking. Dinner $6 to $7.

● Leshko's, 111 Ave. A, near E. 7th Street (tel. 212/473-9208). An order of meat-filled pirogi (a pocket of dough with meat inside) is filling and inexpensive. Other Polish and Ukrainian specialties, too.

● Kiev, 117 Second Ave. at 7th Street (tel. 212/674-4040). A good bargain—fabulous *challah* French toast, homestyle soups, apple pancakes, and kasha. Colorful crowd, right by NYU's film school.

● Yaffa Cafe, 97 St. Marks Place (tel. 212/674-9302). Vegetarian food (like broccoli over brown rice with melted cheese) and "regular" dishes, too. You can bring your own wine or beer and enjoy it all on the back patio in nice weather. Three people can eat here for under $20.

● Mitali, 334 E. 6th St., between First and Second Avenues (tel. 212/533-2508). An Indian restaurant on a block that's lined with Indian restaurants. Explore the block; there are lots of good possibilities. Entrees here are $4 or $5. Bring your own wine.

● Romna, 322 E. 6th St. (tel. 212/475-9394 or 673-4718). Delicious curries. Bring your own wine or beer. Lunch $3.75 to $5.50; dinner $5.95 to $7.95.

● Bangkok Cuisine, 885 Eighth Ave. at 52nd Street (tel. 212/581-6370). For wonderful Thai food within an easy walk of the theater district. Most fun with a large group of people. Lunch specials $5.95; dinner $9 to $10.

● Nom Wah Tea Parlor, 13 Doyers St. (tel. 212/962-6047). Featured in this Chinatown restaurant is the dim sum lunch consisting of an assortment of dumpling-like creations that are stuffed with pork, seafood, bean curd, and vegetables. Lunch $1 to $2 per item; dinner $3 per item.

● Hee Seung Fung Restaurant and Teahouse, 46 Bowery (tel. 212/374-1319). Another very popular Chinatown restaurant. At lunchtime waiters carry around trays of dim sum specialties and you pick what looks good. At the end of the meal you pay according to the number of empty plates left on your table.

● Silver Palace Restaurant, 50 Bowery (tel. 212/964-1204). What fun this place is on a Sunday morning. Dim sum and lots of people enjoying it all in this enormous (particularly for Chinatown) space.

● Hunan Garden, 1 Mott St. (tel. 212/732-7270). A popular Chinatown restaurant with enclosed sidewalk cafe. Varied menu with Hunan specialties—hot and spicy dishes printed in red on the menu. Lunch $5 to $6; dinner $6 to $7.

● Luna's, 112 Mulberry St. (tel. 212/226-8657). In the very heart of Little Italy, Luna's serves southern Italian-style food. Usually crowded, always noisy, and rude help but still fun.

● Manganaro's Hero-Boy Restaurant, 492 Ninth Ave. (tel. 212/947-7325). In the middle of the Italian market section; serves all kinds of hero sandwiches.

● Symposium, 544 W. 113th St. (tel. 212/865-1011). Near Columbia University, this is a friendly, popular Greek restaurant with a pleasant year-round garden. Lunch $4.50 to $6.95; dinner $5.75 to $9.25.

● Delphi Restaurant, 109 West Broadway, corner of Reade Street, a short walk from the World Trade Center (tel. 212/267-5463). Greek food in a pleasant atmosphere. "Everything I tasted was so good, and I was amazed at the low prices."

● Second Avenue Deli, 156 Second Ave. at 10th Street (tel. 212/677-0606). Everything you've always wanted from a kosher deli—pastrami, borscht, chicken soup, chopped liver—in an atmosphere that's noisy, crowded, and fun.

● All up and down Columbus Ave.: The Upper West Side's a revitalized and very trendy strip—you'll find restaurants and cafes. For the price of a drink you can usually sit out at a sidewalk table and watch the passing parade. (One friend is sure it won't be long before the self-service laundries on Columbus will put tables and chairs out front, too.) And now, Amsterdam Avenue, one block west, is going the way of Columbus—new boutiques, restaurants, and bars open almost daily.

● And then there are the boroughs. Brooklyn: A short subway ride from Manhattan (the 2 or 3 train to Court Street or the 4 or 5 train to Borough Hall) are the glories of Atlantic Avenue and its variety of restaurants. Two we can recommend are the Moroccan Star, 205 Atlantic Ave. (tel. 718/596-1919); and Adnan's, 129 Atlantic Ave. (tel. 718/625-2115). After you've eaten there or at any other Atlantic Avenue spot, walk over to the Brooklyn Heights Promenade for a beautiful view of the lower Manhattan skyline. The Brighton Beach area is also known as "Little Odessa," and Eastern European treats abound.

In Queens, take the 7 train from Manhattan to Main Street, Flushing, with its Korean and Indian influences. You'll find Latin American restaurants on 82nd St. in Jackson Heights.

Arthur Avenue in the Bronx offers Italian cuisine. City Island is famous for seafood.

What to See and Do: We can only scratch the surface here; there's so much to do. Here are a few suggestions if your time is limited.

● Free in the Parks: The New York Philharmonic, the Metropolitan Opera, and the Shakespeare Festival Company all perform in the parks of New York every summer for free. Take a picnic along and enjoy some of the world's most creative people in a superb setting. Call 212/360-1333 for a recorded message about what's going on in the parks.

"I'd encourage visitors to check the papers for any street fairs that might be on during their stay; they strike me as New York at its very best."

● Museums: There are 150 museums in New York, each with something special to offer. With a limited time to spend in the city you will probably want to choose from some of the better known: the American Museum of Natural History, 79th Street and Central Park West (tel. 212/873-1300); the Metropolitan

Museum of Art, Fifth Avenue between 80th and 84th Streets (tel. 212/535-7710); the newly expanded and beautified Museum of Modern Art, 11 W. 53rd St. (tel. 212/708-9400); the Guggenheim Museum, 1071 Fifth Ave. at 89th Street (tel. 212/360-3500); the Cooper-Hewitt Museum (the Smithsonian Institution's National Museum of Design) at 2 E. 91st St. (tel. 212/860-6868); the Frick Collection, 1 E. 70th St. (tel. 212/288-0700); and the Museum of the City of New York, 5th Avenue and 103rd Street (tel. 212/534-1672).

To find out what exhibits are where, the hours of the museums, and admission policies (most have fees), check a copy of *New York* magazine, *The New Yorker,* or the free calendar of events distributed by the New York Convention and Visitors Bureau.

- One museum with a difference is the South Street Seaport Museum, 207 Front St., along the East River in Lower Manhattan (tel. 212/669-9400). "This is not a building or a ship; it is what remains of New York's great nineteenth-century port." Admission: $4 for adults; $2 children. Open 10 a.m. to 6 p.m. daily.
- The Seaport is a group of historic properties, restored or to be restored, to the area's 19th-century glory, as well as chic restaurants, boutiques, malls, public terraces, and sightseeing boat excursions. The area is rather over-commercialized and crowded with young people and tourists. The ships are lovely, however.
- The Museum of Holography, 11 Mercer St., near Canal (tel. 212/925-0526), features a form of 3-D photography which involves the use of lasers. This is the place for a unique, interesting, "wave of the future" experience in Soho. Open noon to 6 p.m., Tuesday to Sunday.
- Intrepid Sea, Air, and Space Museum. One of New York's newest sights, this museum on an aircraft carrier that was built in 1943 and decommissioned in 1974 is docked at Pier 86, 46th Street and 12th Avenue. It's open from 10 a.m. to 5 p.m. every day, except Monday and Tuesday. Admission is $4.75 for adults; $2.50 for children under 12. Call 212/245-2533 for information.
- The United Nations at 45th Street and First Avenue (tel. 212/963-7713). Hour-long tours of the U.N. are available every 15 minutes from 9:15 a.m. to 4:45 p.m., every day of the week. Tickets are $2.50 for students, $4.50 for others. A "walk-through" exhibit explains it all. Children under 5 are not allowed on the tour. Free tickets to open sessions of the General Assembly are also available on a first-come, first-served basis; ask at the information desk at the 45th Street entrance.
- Central Park: The park—840 miraculous acres of it—is one of New York's greatest attractions. It's bigger than Monaco, has almost 25,000 trees (who do you suppose counted them?), and lately has been having its various parts restored and renovated. In the recent past the Dairy, Belvedere Castle, the skating rink, and the Conservatory Garden at 105th Street and Fifth Avenue have been restored, and improvements are being made constantly to other sections. "Central Park is our jewel; try to enjoy some while you're here."
- The Prospect Park Environmental Center sponsors interesting walks, workshops, bus and boat trips, all focusing on Brooklyn. Call 718/788-8500.
- The buildings: For a view from the top that you won't forget, go to the 107th floor of the World Trade Center, Tower 2, in the Wall Street area (tel. 212/466-3501). It costs $2.95 for adults ($1.50 for children 6 to 12; children under 6 are free) to go to the observation deck and from there you can go to an open walkway on the roof. Hours are from 9:30 a.m. to 9:30 p.m. The Empire State Build-

ing, 34th Street and Fifth Avenue, has another view of Manhattan to offer from its 86th and 102nd floors. Cost $3.25 for adults; $1.75 for children under 12. Open 9:30 a.m. to midnight every day. Call 212/736-3100. To combine a beautiful view of New York on one side and New Jersey on the other with a drink, go to the Top of the Park Restaurant, 60th Street and Broadway, in the Gulf and Western building (no sneakers, please). Rockefeller Center is dazzling at Christmas with skaters, tree, and lights, and beautiful year-round with changing floral exhibits. Atria, located in various buildings throughout the city, have gained due recognition lately, providing spectacular indoor oases of lush vegetation and waterfalls set in highrising indoor spaces. The Convention and Visitors Bureau offers a self-guided walking tour brochure which starts at their Columbus Circle center and moves in and amongst—would you believe—20 atria!

● Brooklyn Bridge: the bridge remained stately and serene amid all the hoopla of its centennial celebration and now, even with the centennial over, it's an enormously popular tourist spot. Walking tours of the bridge are given once a season by the Prospect Park Environment Center, 718/788-8500.

● Staten Island Ferry. For 25¢ round trip you can take this poor man's cruise across New York harbor. You'll pass the Statue of Liberty en route but if you want to actually visit the statue, take the special ferry from South Ferry and Battery Park. The round trip costs $3.25 for adults ($1.50 for children). A museum telling the story of American immigration and the construction of the statue is in the statue's base. Call 212/269-5755 for ferry information: 212/363-3200 for statue information.

● Circle Line. One of the nicest ways to see the island of Manhattan is from a boat which cruises around all of it in three hours. The boat ride is a good way to begin a trip to New York, helping you to orient yourself to what's where on the island. The first boat leaves at 9:30 a.m., and there's a sailing every 45 minutes. The ride costs $7.50 for children under 12, $15 for adults, and it begins at Pier 83 on the Hudson River at the foot of W. 43rd Street. It runs from April through mid-November. Call 212/563-3200 for information. (ISIC holders are entitled to a 10% discount on Circle Line tickets purchased at the NY Student Center, 356 W. 34th St.)

● Tour of Harlem. Since most visitors are curious about Harlem, a tour company called Penny Sightseeing has tours of the area on Tuesdays, Thursdays, and Saturdays. On Sunday the tour is called Harlem Gospel Tour, and it includes a stop at a church to hear gospel music; the Saturday tour is called "Harlem As It Is". Sunday's tour costs $18, the other is $15; both last three hours. Call 212/410-0080; reservations are required. Other tour companies are Harlem Spirituals, Inc., 95–02 65th Rd., Rego Park, Queens (tel. 718/275-1408), and Harlem Your Way! Tours Unlimited, 129 W. 130th St. (tel. 212/690-1687 or 866-6997).

● Neighborhoods. A walk in and around the neighborhoods of New York is the most fun of all. You can choose from the Financial District, Chinatown, Little Italy, the Lower East Side, SoHo, Greenwich Village, TriBeCa, Chelsea, the Garment District, Midtown, the Upper East Side, and the Upper West Side. Leave yourself lots of time to stroll, go in and out of shops, and explore any place that attracts you. One of the guides listed on pages 319–20 will help you find your way, or pick up the Convention and Visitor's Bureau's special travel guides to each borough.

● Swimming. When New York gets steamy, take a break and head for the John Jay Park Pool at York Avenue and 77th Street (tel. 212/397-3159). It's a big, luxurious public pool. For information on other public pools call 718/699-4219.

● More wildlife: Don't miss the New York Aquarium at the corner of the Boardwalk and W. 8th Street in Brooklyn and its blast-from-the-past neighbors, the Coney Island beach and the amusement park.

At Night: For theater: See at least one play while you're in New York. For up-to-the-minute listings of what is playing either on Broadway, off-Broadway, or off-off-Broadway, check the *New York Times* (the Sunday "Arts and Leisure" section especially) or *New York* magazine. Take advantage, too, of the bargains offered at the TKTS booths at 47th Street and Broadway in Duffy Square, on the mezzanine of 2 World Trade Center in Lower Manhattan, and on Cadman Plaza at the foot of Montague Street in Brooklyn Heights. At 3 p.m. on the day of the performance, leftover tickets go on sale for half their original price at the 47th St. booth and tickets for matinees are available at 10 a.m.; the World Trade Center booth opens at 11 a.m. and closes at 5:30 p.m.—it has tickets for evening performances and limited matinee and Sunday tickets available one day prior to performance. The line can be long and you may not get your first choice, but after all, a bargain is a bargain.

● For performing arts: Lincoln Center at the intersection of Broadway and Columbus Avenue. Whether it's dance, opera, symphony, or theater that excites you, you'll find some or all of them going on at once in the Lincoln Center complex. The Metropolitan Opera (tel. 212/362-6000), Avery Fisher Hall (tel. 212/874-2424), the New York State Theater, (tel. 212/870-5570), the Vivian Beaumont Theater (tel. 212/362-7600), Alice Tully Hall (tel. 212/362-1911) are all there. At times, student rush tickets are available to performances in the Lincoln Center halls—call the individual box offices for details.

● Not long ago a Music and Dance Booth was opened in Bryant Park, just behind the 42nd Street library between Fifth and Sixth Avenues. Tickets to performing arts presentations in all five boroughs are available at half price on the day of performance. The booth is open seven days a week. Hotline for music and dance booth and WOR Artsline: 212/382-2323. A gem of a hall where so many of New York's performing artists appear is up on the Upper West Side. It's called Symphony Space and at just about any time you're in town, you'll find something interesting on the schedule. Call 212/864-5400 for information. Performing events from Ringling Brothers Barnum and Bailey's Circus to world-class boxing take place at Madison Square Garden (tel. 212/563-8300). Radio City Music Hall (tel. 212/757-3100) hosts films, performers and, of course, those high-stepping Rockettes.

● For film. If you want to see a commercial release, it's easy enough to find out what's playing where in the listings in the daily newspapers. But for those who are attracted to the lesser-known films—films by "undiscovered" directors, independent films, or early or overlooked films by known directors—there are several possibilities. The Museum of Modern Art (tel. 212/708-9490), the Whitney Museum (tel. 212/570-0537), and the Little Theater in Joseph Papp's Public Theater (tel. 212/598-7150) are the most obvious; a bit less well-known are Film Forum, 57 Watts St. (tel. 212/431-1590); Millenium, 66 E. 4th St. (tel. 212/673-0090); and Collective for Living Cinema, 52 White St. (tel. 212/925-2111).

● For clubs. New York has lots of them. You'll hear the newest music in the Village at the following—Kenny's Castaways, 157 Bleecker St. (tel. 212/473-9870); 5&10 No Exaggeration, 77 Greene St (tel 212/925-7414); R.T Firefly's,

75 Bleecker St. (tel. 212/254-3130); and The Bottom Line, 15 W. 4th St. (tel. 212/228-6300). Call for cover and minimum information—it changes from day to day. The Duplex at 55 Grove St. (tel. 212/255-5438) is a sing-along piano bar.

● For jazz: Blue Note, 131 W. 3rd St. (tel. 212/475-8592); West End Jazz Room, 2911 Broadway (tel. 212/666-8750); and Jazz-Line (tel. 718/465-7500), to find out what's going on jazz-wise all over town.

● For comedy: Stand Up NY, 236 W. 78th St. (tel. 212/595-0850); Improvisation, 358 W. 44th St. (tel. 212/765-8268); Comic Strip, 1568 2nd Ave. (tel. 212/861-9386).

● To dance: Limelight, 660 6th Ave. at 20th Street (tel. 212/807-7850); Palladium, 126 E. 14th St. (tel. 212/319-6770); Tunnel, 220 12th Ave. (tel. 212/714-9886); Saint, 233 E. 6th St. (tel. 212/477-0866); and S.O.B.'s (Sound of Brazil—Latin music), 204 Varick St. (tel. 212/924-5221), $15 cover.

Shopping: Does anyone pay full price for anything in New York? We sometimes wonder.

Some specific suggestions for the shoppers among us:

● For Books: Barnes and Noble Sale Annex, two main locations, at 600 Fifth Ave. (tel. 212/765-0590) and at 18th Street and Fifth Avenue (tel. 212/807-0099), and branches all over town. A bookstore offering such good reductions on all bestsellers and others that it's worth a trip from wherever you are.

● Gotham Book Mart, 41 W. 47th St. (tel. 212/719-4448).

● Strand, 828 Broadway at 12th Street (tel. 212/473-1452).

● The Complete Traveller, 199 Madison Ave. at 35th Street (tel. 212/679-4339). Books, guides, and maps—old and new. Has a large selection on New York City.

● The Traveller's Bookstore, 22 W. 52nd St. (tel. 212/664-0995).

● For records: Sam Goody's, 666 Third Ave. and 43rd Street (tel. 212/986-8480), and 1290 Ave. of the Americas (tel. 212/246-8730). Check Goody's ads in the Sunday *New York Times* for special bargains on all kinds of records and tapes.

● The Record Hunter, 507 Fifth Ave. (tel. 212/697-8970). One reader insists it's "better than Sam Goody's."

● Disc-O-Mat, branches all over Manhattan. Cheap records and tapes.

● Tower Records, 692 Broadway at E. 4th (tel. 212/505-1500), and uptown at 66th Street and Broadway (tel. 212/799-2500). The place to see and be seen and find just about any record you can imagine while you're at it. Open 9 a.m. to midnight everyday. There's a video department here, too, and an entire store devoted to video up at 1975 Broadway at 67th Street.

● For sporting goods: Hudson's, Third Avenue and 13th Street (tel. 212/473-0981). For camping equipment, jeans, outdoor clothing, etc., head downtown to one of New York's best-loved stores.

● For clothing and gifts: Bloomingdale's, 59th Street and Lexington Avenue (tel. 212/705-2000). Stop at Fiorucci's (tel. 212/751-5638)—just up the block at 125 E. 59th—it's a "must-see" store for the 80s. Macy's, 34th Street at 7th Avenue (tel. 212/695-4400).

● The Pottery Barn, 231 10th Ave. and 24th Street (tel. 212/206-8118). There are other branches of this chain in other parts of the city but this is the biggest. It's filled with cooking accessories, ceramic ware, and gift-type things to bring home with you.

● United Nations Gift Shop, at the United Nations, 46th Street and First Avenue. Usually forgotten by New Yorkers, this is an excellent place to buy gifts for everyone. Merchandise is selected from all over the world and whoever does the choosing has excellent taste. (In general the museum gift shops are wonderful, with a good selection for the budget-minded too.)

● For photographic supplies: 47th Street Photo, 67 W. 47th St. (tel. 212/398-1410). What a place! Hectic and wild no matter when you go, but what bargains on everything electronic—video equipment, watches, typewriters, computers, cameras, and on and on. Others at 115 W. 45th St. and 38 E. 19th. Closed Saturdays.

● For bargains: The Lower East Side. Bargains galore along Orchard Street especially—stylish clothing for men, women, and children. Durable underwear, pretty lingerie, fashionable shoes—all at least 20% below "uptown" prices. Remember that most of the stores here are closed Saturdays but open on Sundays.

● Canal Street and 14th Street are big bargain shopping areas—crowded, not especially organized, but great finds.

Niagara Falls

Accommodation: Niagara Falls International Youth Hostel (AYH), 1101 Ferry Ave., 14301 (tel. 716/282-3700 or 282-8429). Closed December 15 to February 1. $9 summer, $8 winter for AYH members. Sleeping bags allowed in winter only. Sheet-sack bags required by rental in summer for sanitation protection. Advance reservations advised from June to August. Complete kitchen available.

Oneonta

On Campus: A branch of the State University of New York is here, and a student mentioned that Market Street has several bars where students meet. The Country Baker, located on Main Street (tel. 607/432-1969), offers a fine lunch at reasonable cost. Another reasonable meal is found at Brook's House of Bar-B-Q's on Rte. 7, East End (tel. 607/432-1782). Oneonta is also the home of the National Soccer Hall of Fame. Only 22 miles away is Cooperstown, the home of the Baseball Hall of Fame.

You'll find the most informative bulletin boards in the basement of Schumacher Hall and in the Administration Building across from the Housing Office.

Palmyra

Accommodation: Canaltown Home Hostel (AYH), c/o Robert Liesten, 119 Canandaigua St., 14522 (tel. 315/597-5553). $7.25 for AYH members. $10.25 for nonmembers. Advance reservations necessary in July.

Patchogue

Camping: Fire Island National Seashore, 120 Laurel St., 11772. Tel.: 516/289-4810). Twenty-nine campsites at Watch Hill on Fire Island. Ferry terminal across the street from Long Island Railroad on West Avenue in Patchogue. Open year round, but ferry operates from May to October only, requiring a private boat otherwise. No fee for camping; ferry charge of $3.75 one way. Advance reservations required.

Pawling

Accommodation: Holiday Hills YMCA, Charles Colman Blvd., 12564 (tel. 914/855-1550). $40 single; $50 double. "New York YMCA's finest vacation and conference center." Advance reservations of one to four weeks necessary.

Pine Hill

Accommodation: Belleayre Youth Hostel (AYH), P.O. Box 665, Bonnieview Avenue, 12465 (tel. 914/254-4200). $6 summer, winter weekdays , and nonholidays; $9 winter weekends and holidays for AYH members. Ski hostel located near Belleayre Ski Mountain. Advance reservations advised during ski season weekends.

Plattsburgh

Accommodation: Econo Lodge, 610 Upper Cornelia St., 12901 (tel. 518/561-1500).

Rochester

Accommodations: Red Roof Inn, 4820 West Henrietta Rd., I-390, Exit 46, Henrietta, 14467 (tel. 716/359-1100).
● Super 8 Motel, 1000 Lehigh Station Rd., Henrietta, 14467 (tel. 716/359-1630).

Schenectady

Accommodations: YMCA, 13 State St., 12305 (tel. 518/374-9136). Bus station across the street. Men only. $16.50 to $18.50 single. Weekly rate: $51 to $55. Advance reservations of one month required.
● YWCA, 44 Washington Ave., 12305 (tel. 518/374-3394). Two blocks from bus station. Women only. $15 single for members: $20 for nonmembers.

Skaneateles

Accommodation: Budget Host—Bel-Aire Motel, 797 West Genesee St., Box 605, 13152 (tel. 315/685-6720).

Star Lake

Accommodation: Star Lake Campus (AYH-SA), Potsdam College of SUNY, 13690 (tel. 315/848-3486, ask for Administrative Assistant). Open year round. Men, women, and children. $9.50 for AYH members. Reasonable full-service rates also available, including boating and swimming.

Syracuse

Help: Volunteer Center, 315/474-7011.

On Campus: Some suggestions for anyone who gets hungry around the campus of Syracuse University: Faegan's Pub, 734 South Crouse Ave., a pub with a garden; Hungry Charley's, 727 South Crouse Ave., a good place for sangria, sandwiches, and meeting friends; Cosmos on Marshall Street, an authentic diner with everything from toasted honey buns to pizza; and King David's on Marshall Street for Middle Eastern cuisine. The new Schine Student Center is the information hub of Syracuse University. It houses a cafeteria, bulletin boards, auditorium, lounges, and recreation rooms. For film buffs, inexpensive films are shown at many campus theaters; most are open to the public.

Accommodations: Downing International Hostel, 459 Westcott St., 13210 (tel. 315/472-5788). Open year round. $6 for AYH or IYHF members only.

● Downtown Branch YMCA, 340 Montgomery St., 13202 (tel. 315/474-6851). Men only. $27 single, plus $3 key deposit. Weekly rates: $62 to $78. Advance reservations of two weeks necessary.

● Econo Lodge, 6590 Thompson Rd., 13206 (tel. 315/463-0202).

● Super 8 Motel, 421 7th North St., at Buckley Road, Liverpool, 13088 (tel. 315/451-8888).

Troy

Accommodations: YWCA, 🚹, 21 1st St., 12180 (tel. 518/274-7100). Women only. $18 for members of YWCA; $20 for nonmembers.

● Super 8 Motel, Fourth Street, 12180 (tel. toll free 800/843-1991).

Yonkers

Accommodation: YWCA, 🚹, 87 South Broadway, 10701 (tel. 914/963-0640). Women only. $30. Advance reservations of one week necessary.

North Carolina

North Carolina shares the Blue Ridge Parkway with Virginia and the Great Smoky Mountains National Park with Tennessee. Both are spectacular to see. For those who like the seashore best, North Carolina has some of that too: the well-known Outer Banks project a jagged coastline where currents can sometimes be treacherous, marine life is prolific, and there are some of the loveliest beaches on the entire Atlantic Coast. In this same area you'll find Kitty Hawk, the stretch of land where the Wright Brothers made their first flight in 1903. Campers love North Carolina, and hikers can enjoy any or all of the 68 miles of the Appalachian Trail that run through the state.

The cities of North Carolina include Asheville in the mountainous west, where you can tour the Vanderbilts' Biltmore House and Gardens; Winston-Salem, "cigaretteville," a combination of the Moravian-founded town of Salem and the contemporary industrial town of Winston-Salem; Raleigh, the old state capital; Chapel Hill, the home of the University of North Carolina (Thomas Wolfe's alma mater), the Ackland Memorial Art Center, the Coker Arboretum, and the Morehead Planetarium; and Durham, the home of Duke University and the place where the tobacco industry got started. For a guide to the historical landmarks of the state listed by county, see Marguerite Schumann's *Tar Heel Sights: Guide to North Carolina's Heritage,* published by Globe Pequot ($8.95).

Some Special Events: "Confederate Camp of Instruction—1864" in Kure Beach, and Dixie Deer Classic in Raleigh (March); Shad Festival in Grifton, and Azalea Festival in Wilmington (April); Battle of Alamance Anniversary Celebration in Burlington (May); Bluegrass and Old Time Fiddlers Convention in Mount Airy, and National Hollerin' Contest in Spivey's Corner (June); Southeast Old Threshers' Reunion in Denton, and Highland Games at Linville (July); Annual Mountain Dance and Folk Festival in Asheville, and the Strange Seafood Exhibition (tasting marinated octopus, fried squid, and charcoaled shark) in Beaufort (August); Fall Pioneer Living Day in Weaverville, and Masters of Hang Gliding Championship in Linville (September).

Tourist Information: North Carolina Travel and Tourism, Department of Commerce, 430 North Salisbury St., Raleigh, NC 27611 (tel. 919/733-4171 in Raleigh, or toll free 800/VISIT-NC.

Asheboro

Accommodation: Econo Lodge, Rural Rte. 9, Box 1, 27203 (tel. 919/625-1880).

Asheville

Accommodations: Econo Lodge, 190 Tunnel Rd., 28805 (tel. 704/254-9521).
● Days Inn, I-40 and 70 East, Exit 55, Box 9708, 28815 (tel. 704/298-5140).
● Days Inn, I-40 and E. Canton Exit 37, Rte. 5, P.O. Box 95, Candler, 28715 (tel. 704/667-9321).
● Days Inn, 183 Underwood Rd., Fletcher, 28732 (tel. 704/684-2281).
● Budget Host—Four Seasons Motor Inn, 820 Merrimon Ave., 28804 (tel. 704/254-5324).
● Red Carpet Inn, 120 Patton Ave., 28801 (tel. 704/254-9661).
● Super 8 Motel, U.S. 19 and 23 at I-40 West, P.O. Box 6164 (tel. 704/667-8706).

Bakersville

Accommodation: Trailridge Mountain Camp (AYH), Rte. 2, Hughes Gap Rd., 28705 (tel. 704/688-3879). Open June 5 to August 31. $5 for AYH members; $7 nonmembers. Advance reservations suggested.

Benson

Accommodation: Friendship Inn, I-95 and N.C. 50, Exit 79, 27504 (tel. 919/894-2144).

Blowing Rock

Accommodation: Blowing Rock Assembly Grounds (AYH-SA), 🔣, Goforth Road, 28605 (tel. 704/295-7813). $5 summer, $8 winter for AYH members. $16 to $26 single; $26 to $32 double; $24 to $33 triple; $28 to $36 quad. Higher rates apply in winter.

Boone

Accommodation: Scottish Inn, 905 East King St., 28607 (tel. 704/264-9002).

Chapel Hill

"Chapel Hill has had a reputation for being progressive, diverse, and activist since the '60s. It's a great town. I grew up here, left for college, and chose to move back. Please come!"

On Campus: Some 23,000 students inhabit Chapel Hill, many of them studying at the University of North Carolina. One of them recommends that you check with the Department of University Housing, Carr Building, UNC Campus 103A, about possible dorm space for a night or two. You might check the bulletin board or information desk in Frank Porter Graham Union, the *Village Advocate,* or the *Daily Tarheel* (campus newspaper) for details on special events, rides, etc. Students meet at Four Corners, East Franklin St., and He's Not Here, 112 ½ West Franklin. You can find an inexpensive home-style meal at the Carolina Coffee Shop on Franklin Street or Dip's Country Kitchen, 405 West Rosemary.

The Student Consumers Action Union (located in the Student Union) researchers and rates all restaurants in Chapel Hill and then publishes the results in the *Franklin Street Gourmet.* "It's the best source of up-to-date quality and prices."

Accommodation: Hampton Inn, 1740 U.S. 15 and 501 Hwy., 27514 (tel. 919/968-3000).

Charlotte

Accommodations: Motel 6, 3430 St. Vardell Lane, 28210 (tel. 704/527-0144).
- Motel 6, 3433 Mulberry Church Rd., 28208 (tel. 704/394-0899).
- Days Inn, 4419 Tuckaseegee Rd., 28208 (tel. 704/394-5181).
- Days Inn, I-85 and 1408 W. Sugar Creek Rd., 28213 (tel. 704/597-8110).
- Econo Lodge, 505 Clanton Rd., 28217 (tel. 704/523-1404).
- Econo Lodge, I-85 and Little Rock Rd., P.O. Box 668203, 28266 (tel. 704/394-0172).
- Knights Inn, I-85 at Mulberry Church, 3200 S. I-85 Service Rd., 28208 (tel. 704/398-3144).
- Knights Inn, I-77 at 7901 Nations Ford Rd., 28217 (tel. 704/522-0364).
- Red Roof Inn, 5116 I-85 N., I-85 and Sugar Creek Road, 28213 (tel. 704/596-8222).
- Red Roof Inn, 3300 I-85 S., I-85 at Billy Graham Parkway, 28208 (tel. 704/392-2316).
- Red Roof Inn, 131 Greenwood Dr., I-77 at Nations Ford Rd., 28201 (tel. 704/529-1020).
- Super 8 Motel, 5125 N. I-85, 28213 (tel. 704/598-8820).

Concord

Accommodation: Days Inn, I-85 and N.C. 73, P.O. Box 3322, 28025 (tel. 704/786-9121).

Creedmoor

Accommodation: Econo Lodge, I-85, Rte. 2, Box 179-B, 27522 (tel. 919/575-6451).

Dunn

Accommodation: Comfort Inn, I-95 and 1125 East Broad St., 28334 (tel. 919/892-1293).

Durham

Accommodations: Days Inn, I-85 and Redwood Road, 27704 (tel. 919/688-4338).
- Econo Lodge, 2337 Guess Rd., 27705 (tel. 919/286-7746).
- Motel 6, 2101 Holloway St., 27703 (tel. 919/682-5100).
- Imperial 400 Motor Inn, 605 West Chapel Hill St., 27701 (tel. 919/682-5411).

Fayetteville

Accommodations: Days Inn, I-95 and U.S. 13, Exit 58, Rte. 1, Box 216BB, Wade, 28395 (tel. 919/323-1255).
- Knights Inn, I-95 at S.R. 210/53, RR 9, 28301 (tel. 919/485-8122).
- Motel 6, 525 South Eastern Blvd., 28301 (tel. 919/323-3938).
- Quality Inn Americana, I-95 Bus. & U.S. 301 South, 28306 (tel. 919/485-5161).
- Hampton Inn, I-95 and 53/210, Rte. 9, Box 502, 28301 (tel. 919/323-0011).
- Econo Lodge, 442 Eastern Blvd., 28301 (tel. 919/483-0332).

Gastonia

Accommodation: Days Inn, I-85 and Edgewood Road, P.O. Box 338, Bessemer City, 28016 (tel. 704/867-0231).

Gold Rock

Accommodation: Imperial 400 Motor Inn, Rte. 1, Box 877, 27809 (tel. 919/977-3505).

Goldsboro

Accommodations: Days Inn, U.S. 70 Bypass & 2000 Wayne Memorial Dr., 27530 (tel. 919/734-9471).
- Motel 6, 701 Bypass 70 East, 27530 (tel. 919/734-4542).
- Econo Lodge, 704 Hwy. 70 Bypass East, 27530 (tel. 919/736-4510).

Graham

Accommodation: Econo Lodge, I-85 and Hwy. 54, P.O. Box 852, 27253 (tel. 919/228-0231).

Greensboro

Accommodations: Econo Lodge, I-85 at Lee Street Exit, 3112 Cedar Park Rd., P.O. Box 16163, 27416 (tel. 919/697-9140).
● Econo Lodge, 135 Summit Ave., 27401 (tel. 919/370-0135).
● Best Inns of America, 6452 Burnt Poplar Rd. (tel. 919/668-9400).
● Motel 6, 831 Greenhaven Dr., 27406 (tel. 919/854-0993).
● Days Inn, 501 Regional Rd. St., 27409 (tel. 919/668-0476).
● Hampton Inn, 2004 Veasley St., 27407 (tel. 919/854-8600).
● Red Carpet Inn, 204 Seneca Rd., 27406 (tel. 919/273-1983).
● Red Roof Inn, 2101 West Meadowview Rd., I-40 at High Point Road., 27403 (tel. 919/852-6560).
● Super 8 Motel, I-40 and High Pt. Road, on West Meadowview Road., 27403 (tel. toll free 800/843-1991).

Greenville

Accommodations: Econo Lodge, 810 Memorial Dr., 27834 (tel. 919/752-0214).
● Comfort Inn, 301 E. Greenville Blvd., 27858 (tel. 919/756-2792).
● Hampton Inn, 3439 S. Memorial Dr., 27834 (tel. 919/355-2521).

Henderson

Accommodations: Econo Lodge, I-85 and Ruin Creek Road, Box 808, 27536 (tel. 919/492-4041).
● Scottish Inn, U.S. Hwy. 1 and 158 at I-85, 27536 (tel. 919/438-6172).

Hickory

Accommodation: Red Roof Inn, 1184 Lenoir-Rhyne Blvd., 28602 (tel. 704/323-1500).

High Point

Accommodations: Motel 6, 200 Ardale Dr., 27260 (tel. 919/841-7717).
● Red Carpet Inn, 120 S.W. Cloverleaf, 27260 (tel. 919/885-4011).
● Scottish Inn, 2429 W. Green Dr., 27260 (tel. 919/883-6101).
● TraveLodge, 425 South Main St., 27260 (tel. 919/884-8838).

Jacksonville

Accommodations: Econo Lodge, 497 Western Blvd., 28540 (tel. 919/347-3311).

- Super 8 Motel, U.S. 17, Marine Boulevard near Western Boulevard (tel. toll free 800/843-1991).

Kinston

Accommodation: Econo Lodge, 212 East New Bern Rd., 28501 (tel. 919/523-8146).

Lumberton

Accommodations: Days Inn, I-95 and N.C. 211, Exit 20, P.O. Box 937, 28358 (tel. 919/738-6401).
- Motel 6, I-95 Service Rd., Rte. 3, 28358 (tel. 919/738-2410).
- TraveLodge, I-95, Exit 14, at jct. of U.S. 74, 28358 (tel. 919/738-1444).
- Econo Lodge, I-95 and Rte. 211, P.O. Box 693, 28358 (tel. 919/738-7121).

Maggie Valley

Accommodation: Scottish Inn, 35 Soco Rd., 28751 (tel. 704/926-1251).

Manteo—Cape Hatteras

Camping: Cape Hatteras National Seashore, Rte. 1, P.O. Box 675, 27954. Five campgrounds at Cape Point, Frisco, Ocracoke, Oregon Inlet, and Salvo. $8 to $10 per campsite per night.

Morganton

Accommodations: Days Inn, I-40 and Hwy. 18 South, 2402 S. Sterling St., 28655 (tel. 704/433-0011).
- Econo Lodge, 2217 South Sterling St., 28655 (tel. 704/437-6980).

New Bern

Accommodation: Quality Inn Palace, U.S. 17 and 70, 28560 (tel. 919/638-1151).

Pembroke

Accommodation: The House (AYH-SA), c/o Allen and Sharon Oxendine, P.O. Box 5025, Odum Street, 28372 (tel. 919/521-8777). $5 for AYH members. Advance reservations suggested.

Raleigh

Accommodations: Econo Lodge, 5110 Holly Ridge Dr., 27612 (tel. 919/782-3201).
● Econo Lodge, 3500 Wake Forest Rd., 27609 (tel. 919/872-9300).
● Econo Lodge, 309 Hillsborough St., 27603 (tel. 919/833-5771).
● Friendship East Raleigh Inn, 3120 New Bern Ave., 27602 (tel. 919/834-4700).

Roanoke Rapids

Accommodations: Quality Inn, I-95 at SR 46, Exit 176, P.O. Box 716, 27870 (tel. 919/537-1011).
● Comfort Inn, 1911 Weldon Rd. at I-95, 27870 (tel. 919/537-5252).

Rocky Mount

Accommodations: Days Inn, I-95 and N.C. 48, Goldrock Exit 145, Rte. 1, Box 155, Battleboro, 27809 (tel. 919/446-0621).
● Econo Lodge, I-95 and Exit 145, Box 519, Battleboro, 27809 (tel. 919/446-2411).

Rowland

Accommodation: Days Inn, I-95 and U.S. 301, South of the Border exit, Rte. 2, Box 187, 28383 (tel. 919/422-3366).

Salisbury

Accommodation: Econo Lodge, 1011 East Innes St., 28144 (tel. 704/633-8850).

Sanford

Accommodation: Econo Lodge, 404 Carthage St., 27330 (tel. 919/775-2328).

Selma

Accommodations: Econo Lodge, P.O. Box 786, 27576 (tel. 919/965-5756).
● Days Inn, I-95 and U.S. 70A, Exit 97, 27576 (tel. 919/965-3762).

Southern Pines

Accommodation: Econo Lodge, Hwy. 1 and 15–501, P.O. Box 150, 28387 (tel. 919/944-2324).

Statesville

Accommodations: Scottish Inn, P.O. Box 1748, 28677 (tel. 704/872-9891).
● Comfort Inn, I-77 at Monroe Street, 28677 (tel. 704/873-2044).
● Red Roof Inn, 1508 East Broad St., 28677 (tel. 704/878-2051).
● Days Inn, I-40 West and U.S. 21 North, 28677 (tel. 704/873-5252).
● Econo Lodge, 725 Sullivan Rd., 28677 (tel. 704/873-5236).
● Hampton Inn, 715 Sullivan Rd., 28677 (tel. 704/878-2721).

Washington

Accommodation: Econo Lodge, 1220 West 15th St., 27889 (tel. 919/946-7781).

Weldon

Accommodation: Econo Lodge, 1615 Roanoke Rapids Rd., 27890 (tel. 919/536-2131).

Wilmington

Accommodations: Days Inn, U.S. 17 and U.S. 74, 5040 Market St., 28405 (tel. 919/799-6300).
● Econo Lodge, 4118 North Market St., 28403 (tel. 919/762-4426).
● Motel 6, 2828 Market St., 28403 (tel. 919/762-0120).

Winston-Salem

Accommodation: Motel 6, 3810 Patterson Ave., 27105 (tel. 919/773-1588).

North Dakota

The sunsets, the thunderstorms, the cloud formations, and the northern lights of August are bound to dazzle anyone who has never before experienced "the plains" of North Dakota. The summers there are hot and dry, and the winters are cold and snowy. No matter what the time of year, the wide-open spaces are breathtaking.

North Dakota is primarily an agricultural state, with flatlands and wheat fields in the east and the rugged Badlands in the west. Most of the people who live there are of Scandinavian or German descent, or they represent several tribes of Native Americans including the Mandan and the Sioux.

Ten percent of the state's population lives in Fargo, the home of North Dakota State University. Not surprisingly, Fargo boasts a very active arts community—a symphony orchestra, opera company, community theater, and dance troupe. It's also the location of Bonanzaville, a restored western pioneer village, and Trollwood, a park devoted to the arts. During fair weather there are free outdoor concerts and arts-and-crafts exhibits, and during the winter there's cross-country skiing and ice skating. Fargo is near the border of Minnesota and its "sister city" of Moorhead, Minnesota. Moorhead State University and Concordia College, both liberal arts schools, are in Moorhead. The university has an excellent theater department with a good performing arts series and a summer theater workshop.

Other places to visit in North Dakota include the capital city of Bismarck, located on the Missouri River and the site of the reconstructed Slant Indian Village; Fort Totten Indian Reservation; the International Peace Gardens, on the border between the U.S. and Canada; and most certainly, the Badlands at and around Medora, where you'll find the Theodore Roosevelt National Park. The park, definitely worth a visit, features restorations, museums, and on summer nights, outdoor performances commemorating the history of the area through drama and music.

Some Special Events: Winterfest in Minot (February); Jaycee Rodeo Days in Mandan, and Riverboat Days in Grand Forks (July); Pioneer Days at Bonanzaville, West Fargo (August); United Tribes Powwow in Bismarck (September).

Tourist Information: North Dakota Tourism and Promotion Division, State Capitol Grounds, Bismarck, ND 58505 (tel. 701/224-2525). Their *Visitors*

Planning Guide includes coupons for discounts at participating restaurants, motels, and many other attractions.

N.B. Old West Bed and Breakfast, at Box 211, Regent, ND 58650 (tel. 701/563-4542), can help you out with their type of friendly accommodation.

Beulah

Accommodation: Super 8 Motel, 720 Hwy. 49 North, 58523 (tel. 701/873-2850).

Bismarck

Accommodations: Days Inn, 1300 Capitol Ave. East, 58501 (tel. 701/223-9151).
● Motel 6, 2433 State St., 58501 (tel. 701/255-6878).
● Select Inn, I-94 and U.S. 83, 58501 (tel. 701/223-8060).
● Comfort Inn, 1030 Interstate Ave., 58501 (tel. 701/223-1911).
● Super 8 Motel, 1124 Capitol Ave., 58501 (tel. 701/255-1314).

Bowman

Accommodation: Super 8 Motel, Hwys. 12 and 85, 58623 (tel. 701/523-5613).

Devils Lake

Accommodation: Super 8 Motel, Hwy. 2 East, 58301 (tel. 701/662-8656).

Dickinson

Accommodations: Select Inn, I-94 and N.D. 22, 642 12 St. West, 58601 (tel. 701/227-1891).
● Econo Lodge, 529 12th St. West, Exit 13, 58601 (tel. 701/225-9123).
● Super 8 Motel, 637 12th St. West, 58601 (tel. 701/227-1215).

Fargo

On Campus: The Student Affairs Office at North Dakota State University is the best place to go for help in getting your bearings. Across the street from campus, the Bison Turf offers inexpensive luncheon specials. At the Trader and Trapper in Moorhead and the Old Broadway in Fargo you'll run into lots of students.
Accommodations: Motel 6, 2202 South University Dr., 58103 (tel. 701/235-0570).
● Select Inn, I-29 and 13th Avenue South, 58103 (tel. 701/282-6300).
● Regal 8 Inn, 1202 36th St. South, 58103 (tel. 701/232-9251).
● Super 8 Motel, 3518 Interstate Blvd., 58103 (tel. 701/232-9202).
● Econo Lodge, 1401 35th St. South, 58103 (tel. 701/232-3412).

Grafton

Accommodation: Super 8 Motel, 948 W. 12th St., 58237 (tel. 701/352-0888).

Grand Forks

Accommodations: Regal 8 Inn, 1211 47th St. North, 58201 (tel. 701/775-0511).
- Select Inn, I-29 and U.S. 2, 58201 (tel. 701/775-0555).
- Super 8 Motel, 1122 N. 43rd St., 58201 (tel. 701/775-8138).

Jamestown

Accommodations: Budget Host—Economy Motor Hotel, 824 S.W. 20th St., 58401 (tel. 701/252-5222).
- Super 8 Motel, I-94 at Hwy. 281 S., Box 1242, 58402 (tel. 701/252-4715).

Minot

Accommodations: Select Inn, U.S. 83 at 22nd Avenue NW, Box 460, 58702 (tel. 701/852-3411).
- Super 8 Motel, 1315 N. Broadway, 58701 (tel. 701/852-1817).

Tioga

Accommodation: Super 8 Motel, 210 2nd St. East, 58852 (tel. 701/664-3395).

Valley City

Accommodation: Super 8 Motel, I-94 at Exit 69, Rte. 2, Box 150, 58072 (tel. 701/845-1140).

Watford City

Accommodation: Super 8 Motel, Hwy. 85 West, 58854 (tel. 701/842-3686)

Williston

Accommodations: Select Inn, U.S. 2 and Hwy. 85, 58801 (tel. 701/572-4242).
- Super 8 Motel, 2324 2nd Ave. West, P.O. Box 907, 58801 (tel 701/572-8371).

Ohio

Ohio, the Iroquois word for "beautiful river," became a state in 1803. Its history dates back to the early Mound Builders, whose large earthworks can still be seen at places like Great Serpent Mound near Hillsboro and Fort Ancient near Lebanon.

There is rich farmland in the northwestern part of the state, while the southeastern lands abound with recreational areas, including the caves of the Hocking Hills. There's a famous Pumpkin Festival each fall at Circleville, the gateway to the Hocking Hills.

Ohio played an important role in the story of the underground railroad. Many runaway slaves came up the Scioto and Olentangy Rivers after crossing the Ohio River through Columbus and Worthington. In the Worthington Historical Society's annual tours of old homes, you can see some of the slave hiding places.

The first organized settlement in the Northwest Territory was founded in 1788 at Marietta on the Ohio River. Marietta College, the Lafayette Hotel (named for its most famous guest), and an old riverboat and museum are among the attractions there.

In northern Ohio, Blossom Music Center, an outdoor amphitheater near Akron, is the summer home of the Cleveland Symphony.

Springfield, home of Wittenberg University, is located just off I-70 between Columbus and Dayton. The old National Road ended here at one time and the Pennsylvania House was the inn at the "end of the trail." A town of 80,000, Springfield has a symphony, a theater group, an art center, and a long-established photographic society. The Summer Arts Festival offers performing arts throughout July, free to the public, in Cliff and Synder Parks near the campus. Just nine miles south of Springfield is Yellow Springs, an interesting village of small shops and the home of Antioch University.

Ohio has 71 state parks, 59 with lakes. One of them, Hueston Woods, is located near Oxford, the home of Miami University and the place where Mc-Guffey wrote his *Eclectic Readers.*

Ohio has produced eight presidents of the United States and a variety of other famous people from Thomas Edison (whose birthplace can be visited in Milan) to the Wright Brothers. The famous Air Force Museum near Dayton depicts the history of aviation and the Neil Armstrong Museum at Wapakoneta is named for the first man to walk on the moon.

Some Ohioans think of themselves as easterners, some as midwesterners. You'll have to decide for yourself whose side you're on. Ohio has many, many college towns where you'll be welcome.

For a guide to some of the lesser-known sights in Ohio, see *Ohio Off the Beaten Path,* by George Zimmermann, published by Globe-Pequot Press ($6.95). It's all about the less-discovered pleasures of the state. Also see *Day Trips From Cincinnati,* by David Hunter, Globe Pequot ($6.95).

Some Special Events: Sugar Maple Festival in Bellbrook (April); A Taste of Cincinnati (May); Budweiser Cleveland Grand Prix in Cleveland (July); Ohio State Fair in Columbus (August); Air Show in Cleveland, and Oktoberfest in Cincinnati (September); Pumpkin Show in Circleville (October); and Winterfest in Kings Island, Cincinnati (December).

Tourist Information: Ohio Division of Travel and Tourism, P.O. Box 1001, Columbus, OH 43266–0101. In the continental United States call toll free 800/BUCKEYE. The office is an excellent source of information, and on request will provide free maps and brochures.

N.B. A bed-and-breakfast reservation service for Ohio is Buckeye Bed & Breakfast, P.O. Box 130, Powell, OH 43065 (tel. 614/548-4555).

Akron

Accommodations: Red Roof Inn, 99 Rothrock Rd., I-77 at Ohio 18, 44321 (tel. 216/666-0566).
- Super 8 Motel, 79 Rothrock Rd., Montrose, 44321 (tel. 216/666-8887).
- Knights Inn, I-77 at 3237 S. Arlington, 44312 (tel. 216/644-1204).

Ashland

Accommodation: Scottish Inn, 1120 U.S. Rte. 250, 44805 (tel 419/289-8911)

Athens

On Campus: The Ohio University is in this small, lively university town. Traveling young people will find the people receptive. For sources of information on rides, apartments, odd jobs, etc., check the *Athens News* or the *Ohio University Post.* For good, inexpensive meals, there's Suzi Greentree's, The Pub, Wendy's, CJ's, Casa Que Pasa, and Dexters—all in the center of town.

Bowling Green

On Campus: Bowling Green State University is located in the heart of a rural agricultural area. It is your "typical" college town with local bars where the students congregate. Campus Fact Line (tel. 419/372-2445) boasts of having the answer to any question and can give you all the information on campus events. The University Union hotel has reasonably priced rooms.

Accommodation: Wintergarden Youth Hostel (AYH), S. Wintergarden Road, mail: c/o 618 S. Wintergarden Rd., 43402 (tel. 419/352-5953 or 352-9806). $3.25 summer, $3.75 winter for AYH members. Advance reservations necessary.

Canton

Accommodations: Red Roof Inn, 5353 Inn Circle St. NW, I-77 at Everhard Road , Exit 109, 44720 (tel. 216/499-1970).
● Knights Inn, I-77 at Whipple Avenue, 3950 Convenience Circle NW, 44718 (tel. 216/492-5030).

Chillicothe

Accommodation: Home Hostel (AYH) (tel. 614/775-3632 or 773-3989). $3.50 for AYH members and nonmembers. Advance reservations necessary.

Cincinnati

"The downtown area of Cincinnati is thriving, unlike lots of other cities."

Accommodations: Koenig Home Hostel (AYH), c/o Phillip Koenig, 972 Ludlow Ave., 45220 (tel. 513/961-7541). $5 for AYH members. Advance reservations necessary.
● Knights Inn, I-275 at S.R. 125, 3960 Nine Mile Rd., 45230 (tel. 513/752-2262).
● Budgetel Inn, 12150 Springfield Pike, 45246 (tel. 513/671-2300).
● Red Roof Inn, 5300 Kennedy Rd., 45213 (tel. 513/531-6589).
● Red Roof Inn, 11345 Chester Rd., Sharonville, 45246 (tel. 513/771-5141).
● Red Roof Inn, 4035 Mt. Carmel-Tobascco Rd., Beechmont, 45230 (tel. 513/528-2741).
● Red Roof Inn, 5900 Pfeiffer Rd., 45242 (tel. 513/793-8811).
● Days Inn, 150 Garver Rd., Monroe, 45050 (tel. 513/539-9221).
● Days Inn, I-275 and U.S. 42, 45241 (tel. 513/554-1400).
● Econo Lodge, 8367 Cincinnati-Dayton Rd., West Chester, 45069 (tel. 513/777-5121).

Cleveland

Tourist Information: Cleveland Convention and Visitors Bureau, 1301 East 6th St., 44114 (tel. 216/621-4110 or toll free 800/321-1001 out-of-state, 800/362-5100 in-state).
Help: Center for Human Services, 1240 Huron Rd., 44115 (tel. 216/241-6400).
● Travelers Aid, 216/781-1800.

Accommodations: Hampton Inn, 29690 Detroit Rd., Westlake, 44145 (tel. 216/892-0333).

● Budgetel Inn, 6161 Quarry Lane, Independence, 44131 (tel. 216/447-1133).

● Red Roof Inn, 6020 Quarry Lane, Independence, 44131 (tel. 216/447-0030).

● Red Roof Inn, 17555 Bagley Rd., Middleburg Heights, 44130 (tel. 216/243-2441).

● Red Roof Inn, 15385 Royalton Rd., 44136 (tel. 216/238-0170).

● Red Roof Inn, 29595 Clemens Rd., 44145 (tel. 216/892-7920).

● Red Roof Inn, 4166 S.R. 306, Willoughby, 44094 (tel. 216/946-9872).

● Scottish Inn, 9029 Pearl Rd., Strongville, 44136 (tel. 216/234-3575).

● Red Carpet Inn, 4353 Northfield Rd., North Randall, 44128 (tel. 216/475-4070).

Columbus

"Native son James Thurber, writer, said, 'Columbus is a town in which almost anything is likely to happen and in which almost everything has happened.'"

Tourist Information: Columbus Convention Bureau, 50 W. Broad St., Suite 1300, 43215 (tel. 614/221-6623, or toll free 800/821-5785 in-state, 800/821-5784 out-of-state).

On Campus: Ohio State is in Columbus. The Union is at 1739 North High St. Off-Campus Student Center is at 1712 Neil Ave. To meet students, go to the Ohio Union, the Oval, or any restaurant along High Street Nangees Cafe, 21 E. 15th Ave.; Bernie's Bagels and Deli, 67 East Gay St. and 1896 North High St.; or the Blue Danube, 2439 North High St.

Accommodations: Central Branch, YMCA, 40 West Long St., 43125 (tel. 614/224-1131). Men only. $18 single. Weekly rate: $47.50.

● Imperial 400 Motor Inn, 655 West Broad St., 43215 (tel. 614/224-5151).

● Knights Inn, I-70 at Brice Road, 5950 Scarborough Blvd., 43232 (tel. 614/864-4670).

● Red Carpet Inn, 849 Stringtown Rd., Grove City, 43123 (tel. 614/871-0440).

● Red Roof Inn, 441 Ackerman Rd., 43202 (tel. 614/267-9941).

● Heart of Ohio Hostel (AYH), 95 East 12th Ave., 43201 (tel. 614/294-7157). $6 summer, $7 winter for AYH members. Closed Christmas Day. Advance reservations suggested. No use of personal sleeping bags.

● Days Inn, 5930 Scarborough Rd., 43232 (tel. 614/868-9290).

● Days Inn, 3131 Broadway, Grove City, 43213 (tel. 614/871-0065).

● Red Roof Inn, 2449 Brice Rd., Reynoldsburg, 43068 (tel. 614/864-3683).

● Red Roof Inn, 750 Morse Rd., 43229 (tel. 614/846-8520).

● Red Roof Inn, 1900 Stringtown Rd., 43123 (tel. 614/875-8543).

● Red Roof Inn, 5001 Renner Rd., 43228 (tel. 614/878-9245).

● Red Roof Inn, 5125 Post Rd., Dublin, 43017 (tel. 614/764-3993).

● Red Roof Inn, 7474 North High St., Worthington, 43085 (tel. 614/846-3001).

Dayton

Help: Travelers Aid, 184 Salem Ave., 45406 (tel. 513/222-9481).

On Campus: For advice and general help during office hours you can call International Students Office at the University of Dayton (tel. 513/229-2638). There's a bulletin board in the lower level of the Kennedy Union and you can meet University of Dayton students in the snackbar of the Union. Some of the nearby restaurants for good, inexpensive meals are Milano's, Frisches, The Shed, Skyline Chili, Submarine House, and Westward Ho Cafeteria—all on Brown Street.

Accommodations: Central YMCA, √, 117 West Monument Ave., 45402 (tel. 513/223-5201). Men only. $16. Weekly rate: $42. Cafeteria in building.

● Hampton Inn, 20 Rockridge Rd., 45322 (tel. 513/832-2222).

● Knights Inn, I-75 at Little York Rd., 3663 Maxton Rd., 45414 (tel. 513/898-1212).

● Red Roof Inn, 222 Byers Rd. Miamisburg, 45342 (tel. 513/866-0705).

● Red Roof Inn, 7370 Miller Lane, 45414 (tel. 513/898-1054).

● Days Inn, 7470 Miller Lane, 45414 (tel. 513/898-4946).

● Days Inn, 2450 Dryden Rd., Moraine, 45439 (tel. 513/298-0380).

Dover

Accommodation: Knights Inn, I-77 at S.R. 39 West, 889 Commercial Parkway, 44622 (tel. 216/364-7724).

Elyria

Accommodation: Knights Inn, I-80 at S.R. 57, 325 Griswold Rd., 44035 (tel. 216/324-3911).

Findlay

Accommodations: Econo Lodge, 316 Emma St., 45840 (tel. 419/422-0154).

● Knights Inn, I-75 at U.S. 224, 1901 Broad Ave., 45840 (tel. 419/424-1133).

● Super 8 Motel, 1600 Fox St., 45839 (tel. toll free 800/843-1991).

Franklin

Accommodations: Econo Lodge, 4385 East 2nd St., 45005 (tel. 513/746-3627).

● Knights Inn, I-75 at S.R. 73, 8500 Claude-Thomas Rd., 45005 (tel. 513/746-2841).

Gallipolis

Accommodation: Econo Lodge, 389 Jackson Pike, 45631 (tel. 614/446-7071).

Kent

Help: Town Hall II Help Line, 223 E. College Ave., 44240. (tel. 216/678-4357 or toll free 800/533-4357, 24 hours a day). The people here are willing to help: "We will do our best to help those who call or come to our door." They cannot, however, provide shelter.

On Campus: You can get from the Kent campus to other parts of the city cheaply on the KSU bus—it's available to nonstudents, too. A good place to meet other students is at one of the cafeterias on the Kent State campus, or one of about 15 bars in the area—Filthy McNasty's, J.B.'s, Ray's Place, Loft, Genesis, Robin Hood, or Townhouse. "This town is oriented toward young people." You may be able to stay at Korb Guest Hall on campus; call 216/672-7000 for information.

Lucas

Accommodation: Malabar Farm Youth Hostel (AYH), Rte. 1, Box 465A, Bromfield Road, 44843 (tel. 419/892-2055). $3.25 summer, $4.25 winter for AYH members. Advance reservations and deposit for one night's stay necessary September to May.

Marietta

Accommodations: Econo Lodge, 702 Pike St., 45750 (tel. 614/374-8481).
- Knights Inn, I-77 at S.R. 7, 506 Pike St., 45750 (tel. 614/373-7373).

Medina

Accommodations: Budget Host—Suburbanite Motel, 2909 Medina Rd., 44256 (tel. 216/725-4971).
- Scottish Inn, 841 Lafayette Rd., 44256 (tel. 216/725-9814).
- TraveLodge, 2860 Medina Rd., 44256 (tel. 216/725-0561).

Middletown

Accommodations: Regal 8 Inn, 2425 North Verity Pkwy., 45052 (tel. 513/423-9403).
- Super 8 Motel, I-75 at S.R. 122, P.O. Box 2197, 45042 (tel. 513/422-4888).

New Philadelphia

Accommodation: Motel 6, 181 Bluebell Dr. SW, 44663 (tel. 216/339-6446).

North Canton

Accommodation: Super 8 Motel, 3970 Convenience Circle NW, 44718 (tel. 216/493-8883).

Oxford

On Campus: Miami University is in Oxford, a small college town which is very receptive to young travelers. There are three inexpensive motels in the area, and a private inn on campus. Oxford is known for its Apple Butter Festival and there are many campus events throughout the year. You can meet students at Lottie Moon's, CJ's, Ozzies, Dipaolo's, and Attractions.

"Oxford is definitely off any main path for travelers but provides a friendly student atmosphere and plenty of places to meet people, both on campus and in town."

Portsmouth

Accommodation: Days Inn, 8402 Ohio River Rd., Wheelersburg, 45694 (tel. 614/574-8431).

St. Clairsville

Accommodations: Friendship Twin Pines Motel, one-quarter mile east of I-70, Exit 213 on Rte. 40, 46079 National Rd., 43950 (tel. 614/695-3720).
● Knights Inn, I-70 at Banfield Road, 51260 National Rd., 43950 (tel. 614/695-5038).
● Red Roof Inn, 68301 Red Roof Lane, 43950 (tel. 614/695-4057).
● Super 8 Motel, I-70, Exit 218, 68400 Matthews Dr., 43950 (tel. 614/695-1994).

Sidney

Accommodation: Days Inn, I-75 & Ohio 47, Exit 92, Folkreth Avenue, 45365 (tel. 513/492-1104).

Strongsville

Accommodation: Budget Host—La Siesta Motel, 8300 Pearl Rd., 44136 (tel. 216/234-4488).

Toledo

Accommodations: Days Inn, I-75 & Ohio 20 at Exit 193 on I-75, Ohio Turnpike Exit 5, 43551 (tel. 419/874-8771).
● Knights Inn, I-75 at 1120 Buck Rd., Rossford, 43460 (tel. 419/666-9911).
● Red Roof Inn, 1570 Reynolds Rd., Maumee, 43537 (tel. 419/893-0292).
● Red Roof Inn, 1215 Corporate Dr., Holland, 43528 (tel. 419/866-5512).

● Toledo Hostel (AYH), 4027 McGregor Lane, 43623 (tel. 419/474-1993). Open in summer. $4.25 for AYH members. Advance reservations suggested.

Twinsburg

Accommodation: Super 8 Motel, I-480 and S.R. 82, 44087 (tel. toll free 800/843-1991).

Warren

"This is the most overcast section of the country; we never see the sun. The fall is usually very short, winters are cold and damp . . ."

Accommodation: Scottish Inn, 4258 Youngstown Rd. SE, 44484 (tel. 216/369-4100).

Wooster

Accommodation: Econo Lodge, 2137 Lincolnway East, 44691 (tel. 216/264-8883).

Youngstown

Help: Hotline, 216/747-2696.
Accommodations: YWCA, Ⓢ√ ★ 🅖, 25 West Rayen Ave., 44503 (tel. 216/746-6361). Women only. $10 plus $7 key deposit. Weekly rate: $50. Advance reservations suggested.
● Days Inn, 1610 Motor Inn Dr., Girard, 44420 (tel. 216/759-3410).
● Motel 6, 1600 Motor Inn Dr., Girard, 44420 (tel. 216/759-7833).
● Econo Lodge, 1615 East Liberty St., Girard, 44420 (tel. 216/759-9820).
● Econo Lodge, 1300 Youngstown-Warren Rd., 44446 (tel. 216/544-1301).
● Knights Inn, I-80 at S.R. 46, 5431 Seventy-Six Dr., Austintown, 44515 (tel. 216/793-9305).
● Red Carpet Inn, 9694 Mahoning Ave., 44451 (tel. 216/538-2221).
● Comfort Inn, 10076 Market St., North Lima, 44452 (tel. 216/549-2187).

Zanesville

Help: Crisis Center Hotline: 614/454-9766.
Accommodation: YWCA, ★ 🅖, 49 North 6th St., 43701 (tel. 614/452-2717). Women only. $7.50 per person. Weekly rate: $22 to $32. Bring sleeping bag.

Oklahoma

Oklahoma has the second-largest Indian population in the United States and has lots of Indian attractions within its borders. Oklahomans, according to one we know, are generally open, friendly, and hospitable in the western style. Spring and fall are the best times to visit. During the hot summer, cool off in one of the state's 200 lakes, camping, sailing, fishing and more. Find out more about state park cabins from the Oklahoma Tourism and Recreation Department Literature Distribution Center, 215 N.E. 28th St., Oklahoma City, OK 73105 (tel. 405/521-2464; in state toll free 800/522-8565; in surrounding states 800/654-8240).

As you plan your stay in Oklahoma, consider visiting Anadarko, a town with several Indian museums and Indian City USA, an outdoor museum that depicts the life of the various tribes. Also try to include in your itinerary the Cowboy Hall of Fame and Western Heritage Center in Oklahoma City; the Stovall Museum of Science and History at the University of Oklahoma in Norman; the Woolaroc Museum in Bartlesville; the Thomas Gilcrease Institute of American History and Art in Tulsa, which has a fine collection of western paintings, Aztec manuscripts, and manuscripts of the early Spanish explorers; and the Cherokee Heritage Center in Tahlequah, which has both a museum and a pageant called the Trail of Tears that runs from early June through August.

There's tent camping in all 36 Oklahoma state parks and 24 recreation areas. The Tourism and Recreation Department tells you to "just pitch your tent by a beautiful lake, enjoy the Sooner State's clean air and pure water and have a ball." There are also five state resorts located near lakes that are reasonably priced. For more information call the State Parks office at 405/521-3411.

Some Special Events: International Finals Rodeo in Tulsa (January); Rattlesnake Hunt in Waurika (March); Azalea Festival in Muskogee (April); Strawberry Festival in Stilwell, and Rooster Day Celebration in Broken Arrow (May); Kiamichi Owa Chito Festival of the Forest (Choctaw for "Happy Hunting Party") in Broken Bow (June); Huckleberry Festival in Jay, and Pow Wow in Tulsa (July); All-Night Gospel Sing in Konowa, and Watermelon Festival in Rush Springs (August); State Fair of Oklahoma (September); and Will Rogers Birthday Celebration in Claremore (November).

Tourist Information: Oklahoma Tourism and Recreation Department, 500 Will Rogers Memorial Bldg., Oklahoma City, OK 73105 (tel. 405/521-2406; toll free 800/652-6552 in neighboring states. To order any brochures about the state, call 405/521-2409. The Oklahoma Vacation Guide is $2, complete and detailed.

N.B. Redbud Reservations arranges bed-and-breakfast stays, P.O. Box 23954, Oklahoma City, OK 73123 (tel. 405/720-0212).

Altus

Accommodation: Econo Lodge, 3202 North Main St., 73521 (tel. 405/477-2300).

Ardmore

Accommodation: Motel 6, 120 Holiday Dr., 73401 (tel. 405/226-7666).

Blackwell

Accommodation: Super 8 Motel, 1014 W. Doolin, 74631 (tel. 405/363-5945).

Clinton

Accommodation: Comfort Inn, 2247 Gary Freeway, 73601 (tel. 405/323-6840).

El Reno

Accommodation: Red Carpet Inn, 2820 S. 81 Hwy., 73036 (tel. 405/262-8240).

Elk City

Accommodation: Motel 6, 2500 East Hwy. 66, 73644 (tel. 405/225-6661).

Erick

Accommodation: Econo Lodge, Rte. 1, Box 97A, 73645 (tel. 405/526-3315).

Frederick

Accommodation: Scottish Inn, 1015 S. Main St., 73542 (tel. 405/335-2129).

Lawton

Accommodation: Quality Inn, 202 S.E. 2nd St., P.O. Box 3034, 73502 (tel. 405/355-9765).

Miami

Accommodations: Budget Host—Townsman, 900 Steve Owens Blvd., 74354 (tel. 918/542-6631).
● Super 8 Motel, 2120 E. Steve Owens Blvd., 74354 (tel. 918/542-3382).

Muskogee

Accommodations: Motel 6, 903 South 32nd St., 74401 (tel. 918/683-8369).
● Quality Inn, 2300 E. Shawnee Ave., U.S. 62, 74401 (tel. 918/683-6551).

Norman

Help: Number NYNE, Oklahoma University Crisis Hotline, 650 Parrington Oval, 73019 (tel. 405/325-6963).

On Campus: For inexpensive lodging on campus, call 405/325-1011 and you might be able to stay in Walker Tower for $18 a night. To meet OU students, head for Mr. Bill's, Town Tavern, Service Station, Interurban, or The Mont. For a meal, try Town Tavern, corner of Boyd and Asp, or Love Light on Jenkins Street. The Union at 900 Asp seems to be the center of the OU universe—go there to meet students and check the ride board, too.

Accommodation: Econo Lodge, 1430 24th Ave. SW, 73069 (tel. 405/329-6990).

Oklahoma City

Accommodations: Motel 6, 820 South Meridian Ave., 73108 (tel. 405/946-6662).
● Motel 6, I-40 and Hudiburg Dr., Tinker Diagonal, Midwest City, 73110 (tel. 405/737-6676).
● Motel 6, 1417 North Moore Ave., Moore, 73160 (tel. 405/799-6616).
● Motel 6, 11900 N.E. Expressway, 73131 (tel. 405/478-8666).
● Regal 8 Inn, 5801 Tinker Diagonal, Midwest City, 73110 (tel 405/737-8851).
● Regal 8 Inn, 12121 N.E. Expressway, 73131 (tel. 405/478-4030).
● Red Carpet Inn, 11901 N.E. Expressway, 73111 (tel. 405/478-0243).
● Days Inn, 2801 N.W. 39th St., 73112 (tel. 405/946-0741).
● Econo Lodge, 8200 West I-40, 73127 (tel. 405/787-7051)

Ponca City

Accommodation: Super 8 Motel, 1415 E. Bradley, 74604 (tel. 405/767-1406)

Stillwater

Accommodation: Motel 6, 5122 West 6th Ave., 74074 (tel. 405/624-0433).

Sulphur

Camping: Chickasaw National Recreation Area, P.O. Box 201, 73086 (tel. 405/622-3163). Camping all year at Buckhorn, The Point, and Rock Creek, and from April to October at Cold Springs and Guy Sandy. $5 per campsite per night; $10 for groups or $1 per person with a minimum charge of $10.

Accommodation: Super 8 Motel, 2110 W. Broadway, 73086 (tel. 405/622-6500).

Tulsa

Tourist Information: Convention and Visitors Division, Metropolitan Tulsa Chamber of Commerce, 616 S. Boston Ave., 74119 (tel. 918/585-1201).

Accommodations: YMCA, ∨ ★ 🛇, 515 S. Denver, 74103 (tel. 918/583-6201). $10.50 single; $45.84 weekly; $159.60 monthly. Men only.

● Best Inns of America, 4717 S. Yale, I-44, Yale Exit (tel. 918/622-6776).

● Drury Inn, I-44, Exit 41st and Sheridan, 6030 E. Skelly Dr., 74135 (tel. 918/665-2630).

● Econo Lodge, 1016 N. Garnett Rd., 74116 (tel. 918/438-5050).

● Motel 6, 5828 Skelly Dr., 74107 (tel. 918/445-0223).

● Motel 6, 1011 South Garnett Rd., 74128 (tel. 918/234-6200).

● TraveLodge, 2600 North Aspen, Broken Arrow, 74012 (tel. 918/258-7085).

Weatherford

Accommodations: Scottish Inn, 616 East Main St., 73096 (tel. 405/772-3349).

● Econo Lodge, Hwy. 54 and I-40, Exit 80, P.O. Box 705, 73096 (tel. 405/772-7711).

Oregon

The population of Oregon is a little over two million, so for those of you coming from a highly populated area, Oregon will give you a chance to breathe. Oregon has mountains, deserts, fields, and the ocean. From Eugene, for example, one can travel an hour west and be at the coast, or an hour east and be in the mountains.

Green is the color of Oregon. There's a lot of rain in winter (it's snow in the mountains); for color and scenery, late spring is the most beautiful season. In summer and fall, the weather is perfect for swimming in mountain lakes and hiking in the wilderness. Winter in Oregon is usually gray, but ski resorts like Mt. Bachelor near Bend, Mt. Hood (approximately 50 miles east of Portland), and Mt. Ashland near Ashland, are worth a winter visit.

Most of Oregon's history is centered on Indian history, early settlers, explorers, and trappers. One of the small towns that has been restored to look as it did in the early days is Applegate, in southern Oregon near Ashland.

The major sightseeing attractions include Cannon Beach, Newport, and Gold Beach along the coast. Eastern Oregon is very different geographically from the west. There is a lot of cattle-raising in eastern Oregon, and the terrain is extremely dry. The area around Pendleton, the Steens mountains, and the Alvord desert are particularly attractive sections of the state.

Portland is an interesting city to visit. It's built into the trees so that it never seems as large as it is. It may not be spectacular as far as cities go (it could not really be compared to Seattle, San Francisco, Chicago, or New York, for example), but it is clean, quiet, and appealing. Eugene is somewhat more lively for a city of its size. The home of the University of Oregon, it has lots of ethnic restaurants, an extensive bike-path system, a public market, a Saturday market, some nice parks, and the cultural productions and sports activities that are part of the university. The Shakespeare Festival in Ashland in the summertime is quite well known and worth a stop.

"I guess the best thing I could say about Oregon is that it has lots more to offer than

just large urban centers and that Oregon is there to explore. I think many people would find out a lot about Oregon if they were left on their own just to hike through the mountains or spend a day at the coast, drive through the back roads or swim in a mountain lake." (This quote is from a homesick Oregonian, in exile in Ohio.)

Some Special Events: Pear Blossom Festival in Medford (April); Pacific Northwest Championship All-Indian Rodeo in Tygh Valley (May); Rose Festival in Portland (June); World Championship Timber Carnival in Albany, and Crooked River Round-Up in Prineville (July); Threshing Bee and Draft Horse Show in Dufur (August); Alpenfest in Wallowa Lake (September); Kraut and Sausage Feed and Bazaar in Verboot (November).

Tourist Information: Oregon Tourism Division, 595 Cottage St. NE, Salem, 97310 (tel. toll free 800/547-7842 in state, or 800/233-3306 out of state).

N.B. A bed-and-breakfast reservation service for Oregon is Gallucci Hosts Hostels B&B, P.O. Box 1303, Lake Oswego, OR 97034 (tel. 503/636-6933).

Albany

Accommodation: Friendship Inn of Albany, 3125 Santiam Hwy., 97321 (tel. 503/926-1538).

Ashland

Accommodations: The Ashland Hostel (AYH), 150 North Main St., 97520 (tel. 503/482-9217). Two blocks from bus station. $6.50 for AYH members; $8.75 for nonmembers. Kitchen facilities on premises.

● Super 8 Motel, 2350 Ashland St., 97520 (tel. 503/482-8887).

Bandon

Accommodation: Sea Star Hotel (AYH), 375 2nd St., 97411 (tel. 503/347-9533). Near bus station, river, and beach. Open year round. $5.50 for AYH and IYHF members; $8.50 for nonmembers. Private rooms for families and couples. No curfew—open all day.

"The hostel building was a condemned structure which was brought back to life by completely renovating it with walls of natural cedar, big skylights, and many personal touches—one would never know the state it came from nor the work that went in. The town itself is a unique coastal town with a beautiful ocean beach. Many artists live in the town of two thousand five hundred, which has two artist cooperatives and many shops."

Burns

Accommodation: Motel 6, 997 Oregon Ave., 97720 (tel. 503/573-3013).

Cave Junction

Accommodation: Fordson Home Hostel (AYH), c/o Jack and Mary Ann Heald, 250 Robinson Rd., 97523 (tel. 503/592-3203). $6 for AYH members. Advance reservations necessary by phone or mail May to November.

Eugene

Help: Eugene Switchboard, 503/686-8453. They'll help you find a place to stay in Eugene—stop at their office at 323 E. 12th St. Check with them, too, for rides, odd jobs, and general information on the area.

On Campus: The University of Oregon in Eugene is a popular stop for young people on their way from California to Canada. Erb Memorial Student Union Bldg., in the center of the campus at 13th and University Streets, is a good first stop. Pick up a copy of the *Daily Emerald,* the university's daily paper, which lists rides, jobs, housing, etc. For food, try Old Taylor's, which has a large variety of burgers and imaginative sandwiches on health breads, and Rennies Landing, which has a similar menu. There are also popular nightspots, like DeFrisco's, Duffey's, and Max's.

We hear that the switchboard on KZEL 96 FM has a ride-assistance service. There are many excellent bicycle paths in Eugene, keep an eye out for plays on the mall during summer, and stop by at the wonderful public market at 5th Street on Saturday and Sunday.

Accommodations: Motel 6, 3690 Glenwood Dr., 97403 (tel. 503/687-2395).
- Motel 6, 3752 International Ct., Springfield, 97477 (tel. 503/741-1105).
- TraveLodge, 540 East Broadway, 97401 (tel. 503/342-1109).
- Continental Motel, ⑤∨ ★ 🔲, 390 East Broadway, 97401 (tel. 503/343-3376). $24 single; $26 to $30 double; $30 triple; $34 quad.

Fort Klamath

Accommodation: Fort Klamath Lodge, Hwy. 62, 97626 (tel. 503/381-2234). $19.95 single; $24 double. Advance reservations of two weeks suggested in summer.

Grants Pass

Accommodations: Motel 6, 1800 N.E. Seventh, 97526 (tel. 503/474-1331).
- TraveLodge, 748 S.E. 7th St., 97526 (tel. 503/476-7793).
- Allstar Inn, 1835 N.E. 7th St., 97526 (tel. 503/479-7173).

Klamath Falls

Accommodations: Motel 6, 5136 South 6th St., 97601 (tel. 503/884-2110).
- Super 8 Motel, 3805 Hwy. 97 North, 97601 (tel. 503/884-8880).
- TraveLodge, 124 North 2nd at Main, 97601 (tel. 503/882-7741).

Medford

Accommodation: Motel 6, 950 Alba Dr., 97504 (tel. 503/773-4290).

Newport

Accommodation: Newport Hostel, 212 N.W. Brook St., P.O. Box 1641, 97365 (tel. 503/265-9816). $6 for AYH members. Excellent ocean view—spring and fall whale watching!

Ontario

Accommodation: Motel 6, 275 Butler St., 97914 (tel. 503/889-6617).

Pendleton

Accommodations: Motel 6, 325 S.E. Nye Ave., 97801 (tel. 503/276-3160).
● Imperial 400 Motor Inn, 201 S.W. Court Ave., 97801 (tel. 503/276-5252).

Portland

Tourist Information: Greater Portland Convention and Visitors Association, 26 S.W. Salmon St., 97204 (tel. 503/222-2223).

Help: Portland Metro Hotline, 503/223-6161.

On Campus: The University of Portland, Portland State University, and Lewis and Clark College are here. The city attracts many young people, especially from the East, who like its recreational opportunities, its reputation for being politically independent, and its friendly, liberal people.

There's no lack of places to eat in Portland: Hamburger Mary's, 840 S.W. Park; Dave's Delicatessen, 1110 S.W. 3rd, a kosher deli; the Fishmonger, 5262 N. Lombard, for good seafood; and Rose's, 315 N.W. 23rd, for fabulous pastries. The meeting place on the University of Portland's campus is the Pilot House; off campus it's the Twilight Room, 5242 N. Lombard, which has earned a solid reputation for its hamburgers. The Metro is supposed to be a good place to meet people downtown. It's on Broadway, right across from the Hilton. Another is Pioneer Courthouse Square, a recent addition to the downtown scene. The Square showcases musical performances, and its Pavilion, a french bistro, is a great place to relax.

Portland has an art museum, an historical museum, and the Oregon Museum of Science and Industry. The Saturday Market (open on Sunday too) gives local artists and craftsmen a chance to show their wares under the Burnside Bridge.

Accommodations: YWCA, 🦽, 1111 S.W. 10th Ave., 97205 (tel. 503/223-6281). Women only. $17.44 single; $8.72 per each additional person; $61 weekly. Advance reservations of one to three days necessary. "Exceptional value, very clean, with a friendly staff. A great supermarket next door."

● Budget Host—Viking Motel, 6701 North Interstate Ave., 97217 (tel. 503/285-6687).

- Friendship Sands Motel, 3800 North Interstate Ave., 97227 (tel. 503/287-2601).
- Imperial 400 Motor Inn, 518 N.E. Holladay St., 97232 (tel. 503/234-4391).
- Motel 6, 3104–06 S.E. Powell Blvd., 97202 (tel. 503/238-0600).
- Motel 6, 17950 S.W. McEwan Rd., Tigard, 97224 (tel. 503/620-2066).
- Motel 6, 1610 N.W. Frontage Rd., 97060 (tel. 503/665-2254).
- Allstar Inn, 17959 S.W. McEwan, P.O. Box 953, 97062 (tel. 503/684-0760).

Roseburg

Accommodation: TraveLodge, 315 W. Harvard Blvd., 97470 (tel. 503/672-4836).

Salem

Accommodations: YWCA, 768 State St., 97301. Behind State Capitol Building, next door to Willamette University and near train and bus stations (tel. 503/581-9922). Women only. $10 members of YWCA; $12 nonmembers. $60 to $70 weekly. Advance reservations of one week suggested.
- Friendship City Center Motel, 510 Liberty St. SE, 97301 (tel. 503/364-0121).
- Motel 6, 2250 Mission St. SE, 97302 (tel. 503/588-7191).
- TraveLodge, 1555 State St., 97301 (tel. 503/581-2466).
- Allstar Inn, 1401 Hawthorne Ave. NE, 97301 (tel. 503/371-8024).

Springfield

Accommodation: Mill Street Hostel (AYH), 542 Mill St., 97477 (tel. 503/726-5012). $6 for AYH members; $9 for nonmembers.

The Dalles

Accommodation: Budget Host—The Inn at The Dalles, 3550 S.E. Frontage Rd., 97058 (tel. 503/296-1167).

Wilsonville

Accommodation: Super 8 Motel, 25438 S.W. Parkway Ave., 97070 (tel. 503/682-2088).

Pennsylvania

Pennsylvania is rich in history. Philadelphia was the patriots' capital through most of the Revolutionary War period. In this state one can visit the site of the country's greatest agonies as well as some of its greatest joys.

In Philadelphia you can visit Independence Hall, which still looks as it did 200 years ago when the Second Continental Congress gathered there to choose George Washington as the commander-in-chief of the Continental Army, where it heard the Declaration of Independence read, and where it convened throughout the war.

Valley Forge National Historical Park, not far from Philadelphia, where Washington led over 10,000 ragged and starving men into an agonizing winter encampment in December 1777, has been called the most famous military camp in the world. More places to visit on the trail of the Revolutionary War are Washington Crossing State Park, the Betsy Ross House, and the Liberty Bell. And for those who are interested in the Civil War, Pennsylvania is the site of the Gettysburg National Military Park, where 51,000 men fell in the bloodiest battle of the entire war.

Besides an abundance of historic sites, Pennsylvania has some very beautiful country, particularly in the Poconos and the often-visited Pennsylvania Dutch country. Urban types will gravitate toward Philadelphia and Pittsburgh; country types will want to explore Lancaster County and the Pocono Mountain area instead.

If the idea of a farm vacation strikes you, write to the Pennsylvania Department of Agriculture, Bureau of Markets, 2310 North Cameron St., Harrisburg, PA 17110, for their *Farm Vacation Directory,* which lists 30 Pennsylvania farms that offer accommodations and activities. Most are within our price range and are generally family oriented.

Some Special Events: Mummers Parade in Philadelphia (January); Cherry Blossom Festival in Wilkes-Barre (April); Northern Appalachian Festival in Bedford (May); Delco Scottish Games and Country Fair in Devon, and Annual Snake Hunt (prize for the longest snake, the snake with the most rattles) in Cross Fork (June); Woodsmen's Festival in Cherry Springs State Park (August); and Mountain Craft Days in Somerset (September).

Tourist Information: Pennsylvania Department of Commerce, Bureau of Travel Development, 416 Forum Bldg., Harrisburg, PA 17120 (tel. toll free 800/ VISIT-PA, ext. 275). Write to Department SXA for a free copy of the state's travel guide. The Bureau also publishes another useful booklet, *Bed & Breakfast Country Inns*.

N.B. Two bed-and-breakfast reservation services for Pennsylvania are Rest & Repast B&B Service, P.O. Box 126, Pine Grove Mills, PA 16868 (tel. 814/238-1484); and Guesthouses, RD 9, West Chester, PA 19380 (tel. 215/692-4575).

Another alternative is described in the booklet *Pennsylvania Farm Vacation Directory* (Pennsylvania Department of Agriculture, 2301 North Cameron St., Harrisburg, PA 17110-9408). Rates dip as low as $15 per day, and many include meals. What a charming stay you'll have!

Allentown

Accommodations: Days Inn, I-78 and 15th Street Exit, Rte. 22 and 15th Street, 18104 (tel. 215/435-7880).
● Red Roof Inn, 1846 Catasauqua Rd., U.S. 22 and Airport Road South, 18103 (tel. 215/264-5404).

Bedford

Accommodations: Econo Lodge, Bus. Rte. 220 North, at Pa. Turnpike Exit 11, 15522 (tel. 814/623-5108).
● Quality Inn, Box 171, 15522 (tel. 814/623-5188).

Belle Vernon

Accommodation: Scottish Inn, Rte. 51 and I-70, 15012 (tel. 412/929-4501).

Bowmansville

Accommodation: Bowmansville Youth Hostel (AYH), Rte. 625, P.O. Box 157, 17507 (tel. 215/445-4831). Closed December 20 to January 2. Send stamped, self-addressed envelope with reservation request. $6 for AYH members. There are several Mennonite or Amish farmers who are willing to serve hostelers a meal—contact hostel for more information. Reservations for meals should be made a few days in advance.

Breezewood

Accommodation: Econo Lodge, I-70/76 and U.S. 30, 15533 (tel. 814/735-4341).

Bristol/Levittown

Accommodation: Friendship Del-Val, Rte. 13 and Beaver Dam Road, 19007 (tel. 215/788-9272).

Brookville

Accommodation: Gold Eagle Inn, RD 3, Rtes. 322/28/36, 15825 (tel. 814/849-7344). $27 to $32 for one; $30 to $37 for two in one bed; $32 to $42 for two in two beds.

Carlisle

Accommodation: Budget Host—Coast-to-Coast Motel, 1252 Harrisburg Pike, 17013 (tel. 717/243-8585).

Chambersburg

Accommodation: Econo Lodge, 1110 Sheller Dr., 17201 (tel. 717/264-8005).

Clarion

Accommodation: Knights Inn, I-80 at S.R. 68, Rte. 3, 16214 (tel. 814/226-4550).

Danville

Accommodation: Red Roof Inn, RD 2, I-80 at Pa. 54, Exit 33, Box 88, 17821 (tel. 717/275-7600).

Downington

Accommodation: Marsh Creek State Park Hostel (AYH), East Reeds Rd., P.O. Box 376, Lyndell, 19354 (tel. 215/458-5881). $6 for AYH members; $11 for nonmembers. Advance reservations suggested. "A beautiful old house, on the lake, surrounded by woods, fields, and farms in the Brandywine Valley."

Erie

Accommodations: Red Roof Inn, 7865 Perry Hwy., I-90 at Pa. 97, Exit 7, 16509 (tel. 814/868-5246).
• Knights Inn, I-90 at S.R. 97, 7455 Schultz Rd., 16509 (tel. 814/868-0879).

Gardners

Accommodation: Ironmaster's Mansion Youth Hostel (AYH), &, RD 2,

Box 3978, Pine Grove Furnace State Park, 17324 (tel. 717/486-7575). $6 for AYH members.

Geigertown

Accommodation: Shirey's Hostel (AYH), P.O. Box 49, 19523 (tel. 215/286-9537). Open March 1 to December 1. $6.25 summer, $7.25 winter for AYH members. Advance reservations necessary.

Gettysburg

Accommodation: Friendship Penn Eagle Motel, 1031 York Rd., 17325 (tel. 717/334-1804).

Greensburg

Accommodation: Knights Inn, U.S. 30 Bypass at U.S. 119, 1215 S. Main St., 15601 (tel. 412/836-7100).

Harrisburg

Accommodations: Days Inn, I-83 Exit 18 & I-76, Exit 18, 353 Lewisberry Rd., New Cumberland, 17070 (tel. 717/774-4156).
● Red Roof Inn, 400 Corporate Circle, I-81 at North Progress Ave, Exit 24, 17110 (tel. 717/657-1445).
● Red Roof Inn, 950 Eisenhower Blvd., I-283 at Pa. 441, Exit 1, 17111 (tel. 717/939-1331).

Indiana

Accommodation: Budget Host—College Motel, Rear 886 Wayne Ave., 15701 (tel. 412/463-8726).

Johnstown

Accommodation: Super 8 Motel, 1450 Scalp Ave., 15904 (tel. 814/266-8789).

Kittaning

Accommodation: Friendship Plaza Inn, RD 6, 422 East, P.O. Box 2796, 16201 (tel. 412/543-1100).

LaAnna

Accommodations: Pocono Youth Hostel (AYH), R.D. 2, P.O. Box 1026,

Rte. 191, Cresco, 18326 (tel. 717/676-9076). $6 per person per night AYH members. Advance reservations necessary.

• LaAnna Guest House, Rte. 191, 18326 (tel. 717/676-4225). $20 single; $30 double; $35 triple; $40 quad. "Victorian-style home, spacious rooms, furnished with Victorian and Empire antiques, situated on 25 acres in a quiet mountain village."

Lancaster

Tourist Information: Pennsylvania Dutch Visitors Bureau, 501 Greenfield Rd, 17601 (tel. 717/299-8901).

Help: Crisis Intervention, 717/394-2631.

Accommodations: YWCA, Ⓢ∨ ★ 🏷 (10% for all), 110 North Lime St., 17602. (tel. 717/393-1735). Women only. $14.84 single. Weekly rate: $74.80. Advance reservations suggested.

Media

Accommodation: McIntosh Inn, Rte. 1 and 352, 19063 (tel. 215/565-5800). $29.95 for one; $35.95 for two; $3 for each additional person. Five persons per room maximum.

Milesburg

Accommodation: Econo Lodge, I-80 and U.S. 150 N., P.O. Box 538, 16853-0538 (tel. 814/355-7521).

New Hope

Accommodation: Wedgwood Bed and Breakfast Inn, 111 West Bridge St., 18938 (tel. 215/862-2570). $45 single; $60 double; $64 triple; $80 quad. Price includes breakfast. Advance reservations necessary on weekends. "Hardwood floors, lofty windows, and antique furnishings re-create a warm, comfortable 18th-century feeling. Filled with Wedgwood pottery, original art, handmade quilts, and fresh flowers."

Newtown

Accommodation: Tyler State Park Hostel (AYH), P.O. Box 94, 18940 (tel. 215/968-0927). $6 for AYH members. Guest memberships available. Check-in time 6 p.m. to 8 p.m. daily.

Palmyra

Accommodation: Camp Seltzer Youth Hostel (AYH-SA), 697 South

Franklin St., 17078 (tel. 717/838-4957). Bunkhouse accommodations in a rustic retreat lodge. $6.50 for AYH members; groups of 10 or more only. Advance reservations necessary with deposit and stamped, self-addressed envelope.

Philadelphia

"Backpacking and hitchhiking types should try to get to the South Street area between 3rd and 6th—for all information and goings-on."

Tourist Information: Philadelphia Convention and Visitors Center, 1525 John F. Kennedy Blvd. 19102 (tel. 215/636-1666). Open 9 a.m. to 5 p.m. every day except Christmas. The bureau offers personalized itineraries, information for the handicapped including braille maps and free guidebooks for wheelchair users, and tickets to various events including the New Year's Day Mummers Parade and the Mann Music Center.

Help: Traveler's Aid, 311 South Juniper St., 19107, (tel. 215/546-0571).

"I would definitely recommend Philadelphia as a town to visit. I have been to many towns and have found Philadelphia to be the most exciting yet."

On Campus: Temple University and the University of Pennsylvania are in Philadelphia. At Temple there's a bulletin board at the Student Assistance Center, Student Activities Center, 13th and Montgomery, where apartments, rides, etc., are listed. For similar information, you can also listen to WRTI, the Temple radio station, or WXPN, the Penn Station; or you can get a copy of the city papers *Welcomat* or *City Paper*. For good, inexpensive meals near the Temple campus, there are many lunch trucks offering a variety of American and international foods. There is a Salad Alley Restaurant on campus featuring salads, soups, and sandwiches. To meet students on the Penn campus, go to one of the many college bars, such as La Terrasse, the White Dog Cafe, or Smokey Joe's, where there is a mixed crowd for dancing.

Accommodations: To locate a bed-and-breakfast accommodation in the Philadelphia area, contact Bed and Breakfast of Philadelphia, P.O. Box 630, Chester Springs, PA 19425 (tel. 215/827-9650). Rates in 1987 ranged from $25 to $60 for a single; $35 to $70 for a double.

● International House of Philadelphia, 🏠, 3701 Chestnut St., 19104 (tel. 215/387-5125). "For academically oriented Americans and foreign visitors." $38 single; $46 double (limited number); $52 apartments (limited number). Reservations requested; room is sometimes scarce. "Beautiful, modern, award-winning building." Residence facilities at the University of Pennsylvania are available to their residents who stay a month or more.

● Crozer Residence YWCA, 2027 Chestnut St., 19103 (tel. 215/564-3430). Women only. $23 single; $34.50 double for Y members. Advance reservations of one to two weeks necessary.

● Chamounix Mansion International Youth Hostel (AYH), West Fairmount Park, 19131 (tel. 215/878-3676, Monday through Thursday, 4:30 to 8 p.m.).

Three-quarters of a mile from bus 38 stop. In a house built in 1802. Open year round except December 15 to January 15. $7 for AYH-IYHF members; $10 for nonmembers. "A gracious summerhouse mansion located in a quiet area of Fairmount Park."

● Red Roof Inn, 49 Industrial Hwy., I-95 and U.S. 420, Essington, 19029 (tel. 215/521-5090).

Pittsburgh

Tourist Information: Greater Pittsburgh Convention and Visitors Bureau, Inc., 4 Gateway Center, 15222 (tel. 412/281-9222, or toll free 800/255-0855 in state, 800/821-1888 out of state).

Help: Travelers Aid, Greyhound Bus Station, 11th Street and Liberty Avenue, 15222 (tel. 412/281-5474).

On Campus: Duquesne University, Carnegie-Mellon University, the University of Pittsburgh, and Point Park College are in this city. To meet students from Duquesne, go to Frank and Wally's on Forbes Avenue or Van Braams Cafe on Van Braam off Forbes. Since the University of Pittsburgh is a commuter campus, it's harder to find students in any one place. The Student Union might be a good place, though—it's worth a try. In the Point College Park area, try Tramps on the Boulevard of the Allies.

Other places to meet people in a comfortable atmosphere are CJ Barneys and Peter's Pub, a bar in Oakland on the Pitt campus; Squirrel Hill Cafe, for cheap beer, or at the downtown YMCA's Tuesday night folk dancing.

For information on rides, apartments, odd jobs, etc., try the University of Pittsburgh Student Union's bulletin boards.

"Ethnic food abounds. Try Middle Eastern food restaurants in the Oakland area and for Italian food go to the Bloomfield section."

Accommodations: YMCA, 600 West North Ave., 15212 (tel. 412/321-8594). Men only. $21.12 single (includes $3 key deposit). Weekly rate: $48.87. "We are directly across the street from a park which is six blocks long and has everything you would want to do."

● Knights Inn, I-79 at S.R. 60, 4800 Steubenville Pike, 15205 (tel. 412/922-6900).

● Knights Inn, I-79 at S.R. 50, 111 Hickory Grade Rd., Bridgeville, 15017 (tel. 412/221-8110).

● Red Roof Inn, 20009 Rte. 19, U.S. 19 and I-76 (Pennsylvania Turnpike), Warrendale, 16046 (tel. 412/776-5670).

● Red Roof Inn, 6404 Steubenville Park, Old U.S. 22/30 at Pa. 60, 15205 (tel. 412/787-7870).

● Motel 6, Rte. 19, RD #7, Box 1316, 16046 (tel. 412/776-4333).

Quakertown

Accommodation: Weisel Youth Hostel (AYH), RD 3, 18951 (tel. 215/536-8749). $5 for AYH members; introductory passes available for nonmembers Advance reservations for weekends are strongly recommended. "Lovely rustic manor house in a state park."

Reading

Accommodation: Econo Lodge, 2310 Fraver Dr., 19605 (tel. 215/378-1145).

Schellsburg

Accommodation: Living Waters Hostel (AYH), RD 1, One Mile West, 15559 (tel. 814/733-4607). $8 for AYH members.

Shippensburg

Accommodation: Budget Host—Shippensburg Inn, I-81, Exit 10, Box 349, 17257 (tel. 717/530-1234).

State College

Accommodation: Imperial 400 Motor Inn, 118-120 South Atherton St., 16801 (tel. 814/237-7686).

Washington

Accommodations: Red Roof Inn, 1399 West Chestnut St., 15301 (tel. 412/228-5750).
• Knights Inn, I-70 at U.S. 19, 125 Knights Inn Dr., 15301.

West Reading

Accommodation: Budget Host—Penn-View Inn, 250 Penn Ave., 19602 (tel. 215/376-8011).

Wilkes-Barre

Accommodation: Red Roof Inn, 1700 East End Blvd., 18702 (tel. 717/829-6422).

Williamsport

Accommodation: Econo Lodge, 2401 East Third St., 17701 (tel. 717/326-1501)

Rhode Island

With 400 miles of winding coastline, beautiful white sandy beaches, quaint seaside resorts, and 2,300 acres of magnificent parks on six islands, Rhode Island offers distinctive vacation regions from historic Blackstone Valley and Greater Providence to the coastal resorts of South County. And they are all within an hour's drive!

You can go to Newport on the coast and absorb the splendor of the Newport mansions. Once upon a time, before there was an income tax, the richest of the rich anchored their yachts at Newport and built themselves summer cottages along the shore. No one wants to rough it, after all, even in a resort home, so they included Tiffany windows, French ballrooms, Italian dining rooms, and animal topiary gardens in their plans. Extraordinary to see.

The Appalachian Mountain Club publishes the *AMC Massachusetts and Rhode Island Trail Guide,* which is available from the publisher at 5 Joy St., Boston, MA 02108 ($12.95 plus $1.50 shipping and handling).

Some Special Events: Festival of Historic Houses in Providence (June); International Tennis Hall of Fame Championships, South County Hot Air Balloon Festival, Black Ships Festival in Newport, and Jazz and Folk Festivals in Newport (July); International Jumping Derby in Portsmouth (August); Providence Waterfront Festival (September); Ocean State Marathon in Newport (November); Christmas in Newport (December); and First Night Providence (New Year's Eve).

Tourist Information: Rhode Island Department of Economic Development, Tourism Division, 7 Jackson Walkway, Providence, RI 02903 (tel. 401/277-2601).

N.B. A bed-and-breakfast reservation service for Rhode Island is Guest House Association of Newport, P.O. Box 981, Newport, RI 02840 (tel. 401/846-5444).

Block Island

"This gorgeous island, just off the coast of Rhode Island, is a vacationer's dream. Beautiful beaches, good biking, eating, and relaxing. It's easy to reach any ferry from several points in Rhode Island including Galilee, Newport, and Providence. From Galilee the round-trip ferry fare is $8."

Block Island has more guesthouses than hotels. One good one is The Driftwind, High Street (tel. 401/466-5548). $30 single; $40 double.

Galilee

"Another picturesque harbor community with hundreds of working vessels to watch. It's probably best to stay at a guest house in Narragansett if you're going to visit Galilee. (See Narragansett listing further on.) While in Galilee, eat at George's—wear your bathing suit, everyone else does."

Kingston

Accommodation: University of Rhode Island Youth Hostel (AYH), Ⓢ★, Rte. 138, Memorial Union, 02881 (tel. 401/789-3929). Closed December 20. Men, women, and sometimes children. $4.25 for AYH members; $5.25 for nonmembers. Two-story farmhouse built around 1860; one mile west of the University of Rhode Island entrance.

Narragansett

"This is a beautiful seaside community with superb beaches, surfing, guesthouses, and restaurants."
Accommodation: Seagull Guest House, 50 Narragansett Ave., 02882 (tel. 401/783-4636). $34 single, $39 double weekdays; $39 single, $44 double weekends. Shared baths. A 50% nonrefundable deposit must accompany a reservation. One block from beach.

Newport

Tourist Information: Newport Chamber of Commerce, P.O. Box 237, 02840 (tel. 401/847-1600), or Newport Harbor Center, P.O. Box 782, 02840 (tel. 401/849-8048).
● Newport Council for International Visitors, 180 Rhode Island Ave., 02840 (tel. 401/846-0222). A member of the council has provided us with some good tips about the area; Salve Regina College is here and you might be able to find ride and apartment information on their bulletin board. Also check the bulletin board at O'Hare Academic Center and Miley Hall. You can meet students at Maximillian's and "many, many waterfront bars and grills." Basically, "Newport is wall-to-wall people in the summer, accommodations are hard to find and everything is expensive."

Providence

"Providence is a great little city—restaurants are wonderful. One of America's leading repertory companies (Trinity Repertory, tel.: 401/351-4242) is here. Art galleries are easy to find. There are lots of films, antique shops, boutiques, and two superb shopping galleries. It's an easy city to get around; the public transportation system is efficient and the train station is right downtown. For information on what's happening, pick up a copy of The New Paper."

Tourist Information: Greater Providence Convention and Visitors Bureau, 30 Exchange Terrace, 02903 (tel. 401/274-1636).

Help: Travelers Aid, 1 Sabin St., 02903 (tel. 401/521-2255). Has listings of shelter accommodations and hotel information. Information on local transportation.

On Campus: Brown University and the Rhode Island School of Design are in Providence, a town one citizen calls "the East Coast's best-kept secret." For food in Providence, try Rue de l'Espoir, 99 Hope St.; Taj Mahal, 230 Wickenden St.; and LaSerre on Angell Street.

Accommodations: International House of Rhode Island, 8 Stimson Ave., 02906 (tel. 401/421-7181). $40 one person; $45 two persons. Student prices: $20 for one; $25 for two.

● Susse Chalet Inn, U.S. 6 and 114A off I-95, Seekonk, MA 02771 (tel. 617/336-7900).

Where to Eat: Meeting Street Cafe, 220 Meeting St. (tel. 401/273-1066). A great lunch spot—enormous sandwiches.

● Montana, 272 Thayer St. (tel. 401/272-7573). Tex-Mex food and great ribs too.

● Little Chop Sticks, 488 Smith St., behind the State House (tel. 401/351-4290). Excellent Chinese cooking; low prices.

● Andreas, 268 Thayer St. (tel. 401/331-7879). Reasonably priced Greek food right on College Hill.

Wickford

"This is a lovely little harbor town that offers an annual art festival on the weekend after July 4th."

South Carolina

Most of South Carolina has been left in its original and natural state—and that's good. You'll find beaches, subtropical islands, mountains, streams, and lakes. The city of Charleston is as aristocratic, historic, and beautiful a city as the U.S. can claim. If your time in South Carolina is limited, you'll probably want to spend most of it in Charleston and the area around it.

Historic Charleston, founded in 1670, is a lovely place to explore on foot. Start your stroll along the Battery and then walk slowly by the beautiful 18th-century homes. Save time for a visit to the Heyward-Washington House; the second-oldest synagogue in the U.S.; the Charleston Museum; the Dock Street Theater (dating from 1736); and Cabbage Row, the inspiration for *Porgy and Bess*. And only ten miles from this wonderful city, you'll enjoy 500 acres of informal gardens at Magnolia Gardens, where the camellias, oaks, and cypresses draped with moss and wisteria are breathtaking. You may walk the trails, ride a bicycle, or rent a canoe.

Two areas that are enormously popular with young people, because of the beaches and the nightlife, are the Grand Strand and one of the beaches on it, Myrtle Beach. The Grand Strand is 55 miles of uninterrupted beach that stretches from Little River at the state line south to Georgetown.

Some Special Events: Springfest in Hilton Head Island (March); Governor's Frog Jump and Egg Striking Contest in Springfield (April); Mayfest in Columbia (May); Spoleto Festival USA—one of the world's most comprehensive arts festivals, in Charleston (May and June); Hampton County Watermelon Festival in Hampton, and Sun Fun Festival in Myrtle Beach (June); Water Festival in Beaufort, and Tobacco Festival in Lake City (July); South Carolina State Fair in Columbia (October); and Chitlin' Strut (a day of country music, dancing, a Pig Calling Contest, parade, and chicken barbeque) in Salley (November).

Tourist Information: Division of Tourism, South Carolina Department of Parks, Recreation and Tourism, P.O. Box 71, Edgar A. Brown Bldg., Columbia, SC 29202. Although it is possible to rent cabins in South Carolina's state parks, reservation requests must be received by November 1 of the year before. All requests, whether by mail or telephone, should be made to the specific park. Write to the tourist office (address above) for information and the brochures *South Carolina* and *South Carolina State Parks: Facilities, Activities and Fees.*

Aiken

Accommodations: Comfort Inn, I-20, Exit 22, U.S. 1 North, 2660 Columbia Hwy., 29801 (tel. 803/642-5692).
● Econo Lodge, 1850 Richland Ave., Hwy. 1 and 78, 29801 (tel. 803/648-6821).

Anderson

Accommodation: Super 8 Motel, 3302 Cinema Ave., 29621 (tel. 803/225-8384).

Charleston

Tourist Information: Charleston Trident Convention and Visitors Bureau, P.O. Box 975, 17 Lockwood Dr., 29402 (tel. 803/723-7641 in state, toll free 800/845-7108 out of state).
● Visitor Information Center, 85 Calhoun St., 29402 (tel. toll free 803/722-8330).
Accommodations: Econo Lodge, 4725 Arco Lane, 29405 (tel. 803/747-3672).
● Econo Lodge, 2237 Savannah Hwy., 29407 (tel. 803/571-1880).
● Days Inn, I-26 and West Montague Avenue, 2998 West Montague Ave., 29405 (tel. 803/747-4101).
● Hampton Inn, 4701 Arco Lane, North Charleston, 29406 (tel. 803/554-7154).
● Master Hosts Inn, 1468 Savannah Hwy., 29407 (tel. 803/571-6660).
● Motel 6, 2058 Savannah Hwy. (intersection of Hwy. 17 and Rte. 7), 29407 (tel. 803/556-5144).
● Red Roof Inn, 7480 Northwoods Blvd., 29418 (tel. 803/572-9100).

Clemson

On Campus: Clemson University is famous for its milk shakes and blue cheese, available at the Agricultural Sales Center beside the P & AS Building. Numerous historic sites include the Hanover House and Calhoun Mansion. Come see the Death Valley Stadium, where the Tigers roar, in front of crowds as large as 88,000. Littlejohn Coliseum features numerous big-name concerts and attractions each year. There is one place you are sure to meet people in Clemson—Edgar's Night Club in the University Union complex. There are also lots of nightclubs and restaurants downtown, within walking distance of the campus.
Accommodations: Days Inn, I-85 and SC 187, Exit 14, Anderson, 29621 (tel. 803/287-3550).
● Clemson Motel, SC 93 and 123, P.O. Box 249, 29631 (tel. 803/654-2744). $22 single; $25 double; $5 for each additional person.

Columbia

On Campus: Here in the largest city in the state, you'll find the state university. To eat well in Columbia, try one of the locations of Lizard's Thicket (southern cooking), The Parthenon, 734 Harden St. (tel. 803/799-7754; Greek food for a student's budget), Applegate's Landing 2600 Decker Blvd. (tel. 803/788-8501; a nice restaurant for those special evenings), or the Basil Pot, 2721 Rosewood Dr. (tel. 803/256-2721) for those interested in natural foods.

For campus news, listen to WUSC 90.5 FM, the campus-owned and operated radio station. All USC sports broadcasts are carried through WVOC AM 56. Be sure to check the *Gamecock,* the campus newspaper, to keep up with campus happenings.

To meet other college-age students, the five points area (at the corner of Harden and Blossom) has become very popular for USC students. For rides, apartments for rent, or items for sale, check the bulletin board at the Russell House Student Union.

Accommodations: Days Inn, 7128 Parklane Rd., 29223 (tel. 803/736-0000).
- Budgetel Inn, 911 Bush River Rd., 29210 (tel. 803/798-3222).
- Hampton Inn, 1094 Chris Dr., West Columbia, 29169 (tel. 803/791-8940).
- Knights Inn, I-26 at S.R. 302, 1987 Airport Blvd., Cayce, 29033 (tel. 803/794-0222).
- Red Roof Inn, 7580 Two-Notch Rd., 29204 (tel. 803/736-0850).
- Red Roof Inn, 10 Berryhill Rd., 29210 (tel. 803/798-9220).
- Red Carpet Inn, 505 Knox Abbott Dr., Cayce, 29033 (tel. 803/796-6550).
- Econo Lodge, 127 Morninghill Dr., 29210 (tel. 803/772-5833).
- Econo Lodge, 1617 Charleston Hwy., 29169 (tel. 803/796-3714).
- Comfort Inn, 827 Bush River Rd., 29210 (tel. 803/772-9672).

Dillon

Accommodations: Days Inn, I-95 and SC 9, Exit 193, Rte. 1, 29536 (tel. 803/774-6041).
- Econo Lodge, I-95 and SC 9, Exit 193, P.O. Box 76, 29536 (tel. 803/774-4181).
- Comfort Inn, I-95 at Exit 193, 29536 (tel. 803/774-4137).

Fair Play

Accommodation: Econo Lodge, I-85 and SC 59, P.O. Box 186, 29643 (tel. 803/972-9001).

Florence

Accommodations: Econo Lodge, I-95 and U.S. 52, P.O. Box 5688, 29501 (tel. 803/665-8558).
- Days Inn, I-95 and U.S. 76, Exit 157, P.O. Box 3806, 29502 (tel. 803/665-8550).
- Quality Inn, P.O. Box 1512, 29503 (tel. 803/669-1715).

Goose Creek

Accommodations: Econo Lodge, 401 Goose Creek Blvd. N., 29445 (tel. 803/797-8200).

Greenville

Accommodations: Econo Lodge, 536 Wade Hampton Blvd, 29609 (tel. 803/232-6416).
- Econo Lodge, U.S. 276, P.O. Box 643, Mauldin, 29662 (tel. 803/288-1770).
- Days Inn, I-85 at Bus. 25 and 291, Exit 45 B, 29605 (tel. 803/277-4010).
- Hampton Inn, 246 Congaree Rd., 29607 (tel. 803/288-1200).
- Red Roof Inn, 2801 Laurens Rd., I-85 & U.S. 276, 29607 (tel. 803/297-4458).
- TraveLodge, 10 Mills Ave., 29605 (tel. 803/233-3951).
- Quality Inn, 755 Wade Hampton Blvd., 29602 (tel. 803/233-5393).
- Comfort Inn, I-85 at U.S. Hwy. 25 (Bus.), Exit 45A at Frontage Road, 29605 (tel. 803/277-8630).

Greenwood

Accommodation: Super 8 Motel, 230 Birchtree Dr., 29646 (tel. 803/223-1818).

Hardeeville

Accommodation: Days Inn, I-95 and U.S. 17 29927 (tel. 803/784-2221).

Manning

Accommodations: Days Inn, I-95 and U.S. 301, Exit 115, Rte. 5, 29102 (tel. 803/473-2596).
- Econo Lodge, I-95 and U.S. 301, P.O. Box 268, 29102 (tel. 803/473-2525).

Myrtle Beach

Accommodation: Hampton Inn, 48th Avenue North and Hwy. 17, 28577 (tel. 803/449-5231).

Rock Hill

Accommodations: Econo Lodge, 962 River View Rd., 29730 (tel. 803/329-3232).
- Comfort Inn, 875 Riverview Rd., 29730 (tel. 803/329-2171).

Saint George

Accommodation: Econo Lodge, I-95 and U.S. 78, P.O. Box 247, 29471 (tel. 803/563-4027).

Santee

Accommodations: Days Inn, I-95 and SC 6, Exit 98, P.O. Box 9, 29142 (tel. 803/854-2175).
- Quality Inn Clark's, I-95 at 301/15, Exit 98, 29142 (tel. 803/854-2141).

Spartanburg

Accommodations: Days Inn, I-85 and SC 9, Exit 75, 1355 Boiling Springs Rd., 29303 (tel. 803/585-2413).
- Red Carpet Inn, Rte. 9, Box 553, I-85 & Sigsbee Road, 29301 (tel. 803/576-7270).
- Econo Lodge, I-85 and Boiling Springs Road, 29303 (tel. 803/578-9450).
- Hampton Inn, 6023 Alexander Rd., 29301 (tel. 803/576-6080).
- Quality Inn, 578 North Church St., P.O. Box 4335, 29305 (tel. 803/585-4311).
- TraveLodge, 416 East Main St., 29302 (tel. 803/585-6451).

Summerville

Accommodation: Econo Lodge, 110 Holiday Inn Dr., 29483 (tel. 803/875-3022).

Sumter

Accommodation: Econo Lodge, Hwy. 521 and 76, 378 Broad St., P.O. Box 2731, 29150 (tel. 803/469-9210).

Walterboro

Accommodation: Econo Lodge, 1057 Sniders Hwy., 29488 (tel. 803/538-3830).

South Dakota

As you plan your days in South Dakota, you'll concentrate on the natural wonders of the state because they are quite spectacular. The most interesting geological formations are the Black Hills and the Badlands. The Black Hills are the highest mountains east of the Rockies. The Badlands, caused by centuries of erosion, are beautifully colored cliffs, rides, and spires.

Once a prehistoric swamp, the Badlands National Monument is one of the richest fossil beds in the world. Along the Fossil Walk you can examine pieces of the past, like a dog-size camel, a three-toed horse, and a sabre-toothed cat. For children, there's a special "Feelie Room" at the Park Visitor Center.

And no one would want to leave the state before getting a look at sculptor Gutzon Borglum's Mount Rushmore National Memorial. This granite monument to Washington, Jefferson, Lincoln, and Theodore Roosevelt is bound to astound you. Every night during the summer there's a lighting ceremony at the monument.

For those who like the romance of the Old West, visit Deadwood, a town that once had wide-open gambling and bawdy houses and the Number 10 Saloon, where Wild Bill Hickok never did hear Jack McCall's six-gun go off.

Some Special Events: Old Time South Dakota Fiddlers Jamboree in Lake Norden (April); Jackrabbit Stampede (includes a rodeo) in Brookings (May); Czech Days in Tabor, Ft. Sisseton Historical Festival in Ft. Sisseton State Park, and Nordland Festival in Sioux Falls (June); Sitting Bull Stampede Rodeo in Mobridge, Black Hills Roundup in Belle Fourche, Mt. Rushmore Celebration at the Mt. Rushmore Monument, Expeditionary Volksmarch in Custer, and Gold Discovery Days in Custer (July); Days of '76 in Deadwood, Black Hills Motorcycle Rally in Stugis, Oahe Days in Pierre, and Sioux Empire Fair in Sioux Falls (August); State Fair in Huron, and Corn Palace Festival in Mitchell (September).

Tourist Information: South Dakota Department of Tourism, Capitol Lake Plaza, Pierre, SD 57501 (tel. 605/773-3301; statewide, toll free information and referral service 800/843-1930). Open 8 a.m. to 5 p.m. Monday through Friday. For a complete listing of facilities and things to see across the state, request the *South Dakota Vacation Guide*.

N.B. Two bed-and-breakfast reservation services for South Dakota are

Old West & Badlands B&B Association, P.O. Box 728, Philip, SD 57567-0728 (tel. 605/859-2040); and South Dakota Bed & Breakfast, P.O. Box 80137, Sioux Falls, SD 57116 (tel. 605/339-0759 or 528-6571).

Aberdeen

Accommodations: Budget Host—Sands Motel, 1111 Sixth Ave. SE, 57401 (tel. 605/225-6000).
* Super 8 Motel, 2405 6th Ave. SE, Box 1593, 57401 (tel. 605/229-5005).

Belle Fourche

Accommodation: Super 8 Motel, 501 National St., 57717 (tel. 605/892-3361).

Brookings

Accommodation: Super 8 Motel, 108 6th St., 57006 (tel. 605/692-6345).

Canova

Accommodation: Skoglund Farm Bed & Breakfast, Rte. 1, Box 45, 57321 (tel. 605/247-3445). $25 for adults, $20 for teenagers, $15 for children, free for children under age 5. Includes dinner and breakfast.

Chamberlain

Accommodation: Super 8 Motel, I-90 at Exit 263, Lakeview Heights, 57325 (tel. 605/734-6548).

Custer

Accommodation: Friendship Custer Motel, 109 Mt. Rushmore Rd., 57730 (tel. 605/673-2876).

Deadwood

Accommodation: Super 8 Motel, Hwy. 385 South, 57732 (tel. 605/578-2535).

Gary

Accommodation: Pleasant Valley Lodge (AYH), Rte. 1, Box 256, 57237 (tel. 605/272-5614). Open April to November. $8 for AYH members; $10 nonmembers. Hotel rooms: $14 single; $28 double; $32 triple or quad.

Hill City

Accommodation: Super 8 Motel, 201 Main St., P.O. Box 555, 57745 (tel. 605/574-4141).

Hot Springs

Camping: Wind Cave National Park, 57747 (tel. 605/745-4600). Camping at Elk Mountain (one-half mile north of headquarters) year round. $7 per campsite per night.

Accommodation: Super 8 Motel, 800 Mammoth St., 57747 (tel. 605/745-3888).

Huron

Accommodation: Super 8 Motel, Hwy. 37 South, 57350 (tel. 605/352-0740).

Lemmon

Accommodation: Super 8 Motel, U.S. Hwy. 12, 57638 (tel. 605/374-3711).

Milbank

Accommodation: Super 8 Motel, East Hwy. 12, 57252 (tel. 605/432-9288).

Mitchell

Accommodation: Motel 6, 1309 South Ohlman St., 57301 (tel. 605/996-0530).

• Super 8 Motel, P.O. Box 867, I-90 at U.S. Hwy. 37, 57301 (tel. 605/996-9678).

Murdo

Accommodation: TraveLodge, 302 W. 5th St., 57559 (tel. 605/669-2425).

Pierre

Accommodation: Super 8 Motel, 320 W. Sioux, 57501 (tel. 605/224-1617).

Rapid City

Accommodations: YMCA, 815 Kansas City St., 57701 (tel. 605/342-8538). Men and women. Open June 1 to August 24. $3.50 for readers of *Where to Stay*.

Must bring own bedding. Complimentary health facilities, including swimming pool.
- Motel 6, 620 East Latrobe St., 57701 (tel. 605/343-3687).
- Super 8 Motel, 2520 Mt. Rushmore Rd., 57701 (tel. 605/342-4911).

Sioux Falls

Accommodations: YWCA, 300 West 11th St., 57102 (tel. 605/336-3660). Women only. $9 single. Weekly rate: $47.70. $5 key deposit required.
- Motel 6, 3009 West Russell St., 57104 (tel. 605/336-7800).
- Budget Host—Plaza Inn, 2620 East 10th St., 57103 (tel. 605/336-1550).
- Super 8 Motel, 4808 N. Cliff Ave., 57104 (tel. 605/339-9212).
- TraveLodge, 809 West Ave. North, 57104 (tel. 605/336-0230).
- Exel Inn, 1300 West Russell St., 57104 (tel. 605/331-5800).
- Select Inn, 3500 Gateway Blvd., I-29 & 41st Street West, 57106 (tel. 605/361-1864).

Spearfish

Accommodations: Budget Host—Sherwood Lodge, 231 W. Jackson Blvd., 57783 (tel. 605/642-4688).
- Super 8 Motel, I-90 at Exit 14, P.O. Box 316, 57783 (tel. 605/642-4721).

Sturgis

Accommodation: Super 8 Motel, I-90, Exit 30, P.O. Box 703, 57785 (tel. 605/347-4447).

Vermillion

Accommodation: Super 8 Motel, 1208 E. Cherry St., 57069 (tel. 605/624-8005).

Watertown

Accommodation: Super 8 Motel, 13th Ave. South and Hwy. 81, P.O. Box 876, 57201 (tel. 605/882-1900).

Webster

Accommodation: Super 8 Motel, W. Hwy. 12, Box 592, 57274 (tel. 605/345-4701).

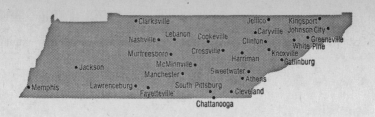

Chattanooga

Tennessee

Tennessee is rich in natural and man-made attractions. One of the best known is music. Is there anyone who hasn't heard of the Grand Ole Opry, or Elvis Presley's home Graceland, Beale Street Blues, or the folk ballads of the Appalachians? There's more than music, though, in Tennessee. The state boasts the Mud Island Mississippi River Museum in Memphis, which explains the history of the river and its importance in the life of the state; the Hermitage, Andrew Jackson's mansion in Nashville; in Greeneville, the home and shop owned by Andrew Johnson, the 17th president of the U.S.; the Casey Jones railroad museum in Jackson; the resort city of Gatlinburg, at the northern edge of the Smokies; Rock City Gardens, on the bluffs overlooking Chattanooga Valley; and the Jack Daniel Distillery in Lynchburg, now a National Historic Site.

Someone who lives in Tennessee put it this way: "The main things I like around here are the mountains and tiny towns where people live set apart from a lot of the world—like the tiny area about 90 miles from Knoxville where the Melungeons live. Stories vary about who the Melungeons are—some say they're descendants of Spaniards and some, escaped slaves. Whatever the truth is, they remain aloof and apart and have kept alive some old crafts like making buckets of wood with no nails. There are dulcimer makers here too, and I suppose I should mention Gatlinburg—the tourist center of Tennessee. Lots of people like it, but it's too touristy for me—too many Ye Olde Shoppes, etc. But on the way to Gatlinburg there's a grist mill dating back to 1850 where corn and wheat are still ground by water power. It's a pretty place."

Some Special Events: Dogwood Arts Festival in Knoxville (17-day salute to spring and the beauty of the dogwood trees), Mule Day in Columbia, and the World's Largest Fish Fry in Paris (all in April); Tennessee Crafts Fair in Nashville, and Spring Music and Crafts Festival in Rugby (May); Dulcimer and Harp Convention in Cosby, Country Music Days in Elizabethton, and Rhododendron Festival in Roan Mountain (all in June); Fiddler's Jamboree and Crafts Festival in Smithville, and Gatlinburg's Summer Craftsmen's Fair in Gatlinburg (July); Elvis International Tribute Week in Memphis (August); the Tennessee State Fair in Nashville (September); Tennessee Fall Homecoming in Norris (October); and Christmas at Twitty City in Hendersonville (late November to early January).

Tourist Information: Department of Tourist Development, P.O. Box 23170, Nashville, TN 37202 (tel. 615/741-2158).

N.B. Two bed-and-breakfast reservation services for Tennessee are Bed & Breakfast in Memphis, P.O. Box 41621, Memphis, TN 38174 (tel. 901/726-5920); and B&B Host Homes of Tennessee, P.O. Box 110227, Nashville, TN 37222-0227 (tel. 615/331-5244).

Athens

Accommodation: Scottish Inn, I-75 and Hwy. 30, 2541 Decatur Pike, 37303 (tel. 615/745-5800).

Caryville

Accommodation: Budget Host—Tennessee Motel, 101 Tennessee Dr., Box 16, 37714 (tel. 615/562-9595).

Chattanooga

Tourist Information: Chattanooga Area Convention and Visitors Bureau, 1001 Market St., 37402 (tel. 615/756-2121).
Accommodations: Days Inn, I-75, Exit 1, 1401 Mack Smith Rd., 37412 (tel. 615/894-7480).
- Days Inn, 101 East 20th, 37408 (tel. 615/267-9761).
- Scottish Inn, 6510 Ringgold Rd., East Ridge, 37412 (tel. 615/894-0911).
- Scottish Inn, 7707 Lee Hwy., 37421 (tel. 615/892-7707).
- Scottish Inn, 3210 South Broad St., 37408 (tel. 615/267-0414).
- Super 8 Motel, 20 Birmingham Rd., 37419 (tel. 615/821-8880).

Clarksville

Accommodations: Motel 6, 881 Kraft St., 37040 (tel. 615/552-0045).
- Comfort Inn, 1112 SR 76 and I-24, Exit 11, 37043 (tel. 615/358-2020).

Cleveland

Accommodations: Cleveland Motel, √ ★, 1510 South Lee Hwy., 37311 (tel. 615/472-9525). $20 to $26 single; $28 to $35 double; $35 to $42 triple; $42 to $50 quad. Higher rates during Labor Day week.
- Scottish Inn, 2650 Westside Dr. NW, 37311 (tel. 615/472-3281).

Clinton

Accommodation: Budget Host—Riverview Motel, 247 South Main St. and Hwy. 25 West, 37716 (tel. 615/457-3333).

Cookeville

Accommodation: Days Inn, I-40 and Tenn. 111, Exit 288, Rte. 8, 38501 (tel. 615/528-5411)

Crossville

Accommodation: Heritage Inn, Ⓢ√ ★ ⓖ, P.O. Box 581, 38555 (tel. 615/

484-9505). $25 single; $27.50 to $35 double; $30 to $40 triple; $30 to $45 quad. Advance reservations suggested.

Fayetteville

Accommodation: Budget Host—Bonanza Motel, 1651 Huntzville Hwy., 37334 (tel. 615/433-6121).

Gatlinburg

Camping: Great Smoky Mountains National Park, 37738. There are nine campgrounds in this immensely popular park, with three—Elkmont, Smokemont, and Cades Cove—open year round. There are also trail shelters along the Appalachian Trail—one day's journey apart. Permits required for backcountry use. Reservations can be made through Ticketron, May through October.

Accommodation: Bales Motel, √ ★, 10%, 118 Bishop Lane, 37738 (tel. 615/436-4773). $22 to $44 single or double; $25 to $47 triple; $28 to $50 quad. Open April 1 through October 31.

Greeneville

Accommodation: Star Motel, Ⓢ★, 1633 Tusculum Blvd., 37743 (tel. 615/638-8124). $21 single; $24 double; $26 triple; $28 quad.

Harriman

Accommodation: Scottish Inn, Rte. 8, Box 55, 37748 (tel. 615/882-6600).

Jackson

Accommodations: Budgetel Inn, 2370 N. Highland Ave., 38305 (tel. 901/664-1800).
- Days Inn, 1919 Hwy. 45 Bypass, 38305 (tel. 901/668-3444).
- Hampton Inn, 1890 Hwy. 45 Bypass & I-40, 38305 (tel. 901/664-4312).
- Quality Inn, 2262 N. Highland Ave., 38305 (tel. 901/668-1066).

Jellico

Accommodation: Days Inn, I-75 and U.S. 25 W., Exit 160, P.O. Box 299, 37762 (tel. 615/784-7281).

Johnson City

Accommodation: Super 8 Motel, 108 Wesley St., 37601 (tel. 615/282-8818)

Kingsport

Accommodation: Econo Lodge, 1704 East Stone Dr., 37660 (tel. 615/245-0286).

Knoxville

Tourist Information: Knoxville Area Council for Conventions and Visitors —Knoxville Convention and Visitors Bureau, P.O. Box 15012, 37901 (tel. 615/523-2316).

On Campus: According to someone at the University of Tennessee, Knoxville is "a great place to live, a fair place to visit, and a great place to travel through." If you are passing through, you can count on meeting students in the Student Center or at any of the bars and restaurants that appear and disappear on Cumberland Ave. between the 1500- and 2000-numbered blocks.

To find out what's going on on campus, get a copy of the *Daily Beacon,* the university paper. Everyone reads it, so if you want to put a notice somewhere about a ride, apartment, etc., put it in the *Beacon.* The various bulletin boards in the Student Center are also a good source of information.

Just off Cumberland Avenue, there's an area known as "The Strip." Fastfood spots, eating and drinking places, and small restaurants galore. Some possibilities: Old College Inn, sandwich platters for $3.95 to $4.95; Arnolds's deli-style sandwiches for $2.85 to $4.75; Varsity Inn, breakfast any time; Mom & Pop's Restaurant; and Ruby's, Cumberland & 21st Streets, a place that's popular with the drinking crowd at night. At the UT Student Center, try Smokey's Cafeteria, where plate lunches are under $3. Anyone can eat here— "institutional food but surprisingly good—build-your-own sandwiches, a salad bar, and a wide variety of desserts."

Accommodations: Days Inn, 200 Lovell Rd. NW, 37922 (tel. 615/966-5801).

- Red Roof Inn, 5640 Merchants Center Blvd., 37912 (tel. 615/689-7100).
- Scottish Inn, 104 Bridgewater Rd., 37923 (tel. 615/693-5331).
- Red Carpet Inn, 503 Merchants Rd., 37912 (tel. 615/689-7666).
- Motel 6, 10115 Watkins Blvd., 37922 (tel. 615/675-5700).
- Econo Lodge, 6712 Central Ave. Pike, 37912 (tel. 615/689-6600).
- Comfort Inn, 5334 Central Ave. Pike, 37912 (tel. 615/688-1010).

Lawrenceburg

Accommodation: Budget Host—David Crockett Motel, 503 East Gaines St., 38464 (tel. 615/762-7191).

Lebanon

Accommodations: Days Inn, I-40 and U.S. 231 South, Exit 238, 37087 (tel 615/449-2900).

- Quality Inn, I-40 and U.S. 231 South, 37087 (tel. 615/444-7400).

Manchester

Accommodations: Days Inn, I-24 and U.S. 41, Exit 114, Box 8131, 37355 (tel. 615/728-9530).
- Comfort Inn, I-24 and U.S. 41, Exit 114, Rte. 8, Box 8140, 37355 (tel. 615/728-0800).
- Scottish Inn, Rte. 8, Box 8580, 37355 (tel. 615/728-0506).

McMinnville

Accommodation: Scottish Inn, 1105 Sparta Rd., 37110 (tel. 615/473-2181).

Memphis

Tourist Information: Memphis Convention and Visitors Bureau, 203 Beale St., Suite 305, 38103 (tel. 901/526-4880).
Accommodations: Budgetel Inn, 6020 Shelby Oaks Dr., 38134 (tel. 901/377-2233).
- Days Inn, 5301 Summer Ave., 38122 (tel. 901/761-1600).
- Days Inn, I-55 and 1533 E. Brooks Rd., 38116 (tel. 901/345-2470).
- Hampton Inn, 1585 Sycamore View Rd., 38134 (tel. 901/388-4881).
- Red Roof Inn, 6055 Shelby Oaks Dr., 38134 (tel. 901/388-6111).
- Red Roof Inn, 3875 American Way, I-240 & Getwell Road at American Way, 38118 (tel. 901/363-2335).
- Regal 8 Inn, 1360 Springbrook Rd., 38116 (tel. 901/396-3620).
- Motel 6, 1321 Sycamore View Rd., 38134 (tel. 901/382-8572).

Murfreesboro

Accommodations: Motel 6, 114 Chaffin Pl., 37130 (tel. 615/890-8524).
- Hampton Inn, 2230 Old Fort Parkway, 37130 (tel. 615/896-1172).
- Quality Inn, I-24 and U.S. 231 South, 37130 (tel. 615/896-5450).

Nashville

Help: Travelers Aid, 535 5th Ave. South, 37203 (tel. 615/256-3168 or 256-3169).
Accommodations: Budgetel Inn, 531 Donelson Pike, 37214 (tel. 615/885-3100).
- Days Inn, 710 James Robertson Pkwy., 37219 (tel. 615/256-4800).
- Drury Inn, I-65 and Trinity Lane West, 2306 Brick Church Pike, 37207 (tel. 615/226-9560).
- Hampton Inn, 2407 Brick Church Pike, 37207 (tel. 615/226-3300).
- Knights Inn, I-24 at 323 Harding Place, 37211 (tel. 615/834-0570).
- Motel 6, 95 Wallace Rd., 37211 (tel. 615/333-9933).
- Motel 6, 311 West Trinity Lane, 37207 (tel. 615/227-9696).
- Red Roof Inn, 110 Northgate Dr., I-65 at Long Hollow Pike, Exit 97, 37072 (tel. 615/859-2537).
- Scottish Inn, 1501 Dickinson Rd., 37207 (tel. 615/226-6940).

● Econo Lodge, I-24 East and Old Hickory Blvd., Exit 62, 37211 (tel. 615/793-7721).
● Econo Lodge, 2460 Music Valley Dr., 37214 (tel. 615/889-0090).

South Pittsburg

Accommodation: Scottish Inn, I-24 jct. at Kimball, P.O. Box 1044, Jasper, 37347 (tel. 615/837-7933).

Sweetwater

Accommodations: Red Carpet Inn, South Main Street, 37874 (tel. 615/337-3585).
● Econo Lodge, I-75 and Hwy. 68, Exit 60, 37874 (tel. 615/337-9357).
● Comfort Inn, U.S. 11 and SR 68, South Main St., 37874 (tel. 615/337-6646).

White Pine

Accommodation: Red Carpet Inn, Rte. 1, Box 151, 37890 (tel. 615/674-2592).

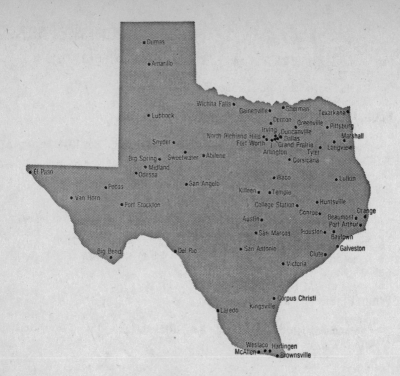

Texas

Texas is big—maybe not as big as Alaska but still very big (266,807 square miles —as large as all of New England, New York, Pennsylvania, Ohio, and Illinois combined!). Texans love the bigness and don't seem to mind being teased about it. Texas cities are some of the fastest growing and most prosperous urban areas in the U.S. at a time when most cities are on the decline. Northern, central, and eastern Texas are the most developed areas; western Texas is still a land of vast deserts, mountains, and prairies, with all the huge ranches that you've seen in John Wayne movies. There are tropical areas, too, in the south, along the Mexican border and Gulf of Mexico.

Because of the general prosperity in much of Texas, there are part-time unskilled jobs to be had in most of the cities—Houston and Dallas especially.

Some Special Events: Cotton Bowl Parade and Football Game in Dallas on New Year's Day; Livestock Shows and Rodeo in El Paso, San Antonio, and Houston, and Charro Days in Brownsville (February); Dogwood Trails Festival in Palestine (March); Neches River Festival in Beaumont, Buccaneer Days in Corpus Christi (April); Magnolia Homes Tour in Columbus (May); Watermelon Thump in Luling (June); Black-eyed Pea Jamboree in Athens (July); Texas Folklife Festival in San Antonio (August); National Championship Powwow in Grand Prairie (September); Czhilispiel in Flatonia (October); and Chili Cook-off in Terlingua (November).

Tourist Information: Texas, Dept. DHT, P.O. Box 5064, Austin, TX 78763. Ask for a copy of their 224-page booklet *Texas! Travel Handbook.*

N.B. Bed and Breakfast Texas Style, 4224 West Red Bird Lane, Dallas, 75237 (tel. 214/298-5433 or 298-8586). Arranges lodgings in private homes, historical mansions, ranches, lakesides, and new condos. Rates from $25 to $35 (budget), $36 to $50 (comfort for singles/doubles). Dallas, Austin, Houston, San Antonio, Waco, Galveston, Fort Worth, Amarillo. Directory $3.

The Sand Dollar Hospitality/Bed and Breakfast has a listing of residential homes, several of which are near the water, for $27 to $48 single; $30 to $51 double. For details, contact them at 3605 Mendenhall, Austin, 78415 (tel. 512/853-1222).

Abilene

Accommodations: Best Inns of America, 1702 E. Interstate 20, Exit Hwy. 351 (tel. 915/672-6433).
● Motel 6, 4951 West Stamford St., 79603 (tel. 915/672-8462).
● Econo Lodge, Rte. 1, Box 47, 79601 (tel. 915/673-5251).

Amarillo

Accommodations: Friendship Inn Broncho Lodge, 6005 Amarillo Blvd. W., 79106 (tel. 806/355-3321).
● Hampton Inn, 1700 I-40 East, 79103 (tel. 806/372-1425).
● Motel 6, 2032 Paramount Blvd., 79109 (tel. 806/355-6554).
● Motel 6, 3930 I-40 East, 79103 (tel. 806/374-6444).
● Regal 8 Inn, 6030 I-40 West, 79106 (tel. 806/359-7651).
● Allstar Inn, 4301 I-40 East, 79104 (tel. 806/373-3045).
● Super 8 Motel, Rte. 2, Box 1045, 79101 (tel. 806/335-2836).

Arlington

Accommodation: Motel 6, 2626 Randol Mill Rd. East, 76011 (tel. 817/649-0147).

Austin

Tourist Information: Tourist and Convention Information, Austin Convention and Visitors Bureau, P.O. Box 2990, 78767 (tel. 512/478-0098).
On Campus: The largest campus of the University of Texas is in Austin. Students can be found all over Austin with an especially high concentration in the Student Union. International students traveling in the area may contact the International Office at 512/471-1211 for general help and advice.
Accommodations: Motel 6, 2707 Interregional Hwy. South, 78741 (tel. 512/444-5882).
● Allstar Inn, 8010 North I-35, 78753 (tel. 512/837-9890).
● Drury Inn, I-35 and 290, 919 E. Koenig Lane, 78751 (tel. 512/454-1144).
● Drury Inn, I-35 and U.S. 290, 6511 Interregional Hwy. 35 North, 78752 (tel. 512/467-9500).
● Exel Inn, 820 E. Anderson Lane, 78752 (tel. 512/836-1436).
● Super 8 Motel, 2525 I Hwy. 35 South, 78741 (tel. 512/441-0143).

Baytown

Accommodation: Scottish Inn, 9032 U.S. Hwy. 146 North, 77580 (tel. 713/576-6521).

Beaumont

Accommodations: Motel 6, 2640 I-10 East, 77703 (tel. 409/898-7190).
- Allstar Inn, 2052 I-10 South, 77701 (tel. 409/842-0041).
- Super 8 Motel, 2850 Interstate 10 East, 77703 (tel. 409/899-3040).

Big Bend

Camping: Big Bend National Park, 79834. There's camping year round at Cottonwood, Chisos Basin, and Rio Grande Village. $3 to $5 per campsite per night.

Big Spring

Accommodation: Motel 6, 600 West I-20, Box 2384, 79720 (tel. 915/267-1695).

Brownsville

Accommodation: Motel 6, 2255 North Expressway, 78521 (tel. 512/546-4699).

Clute

Accommodation: Motel 6, 1000 Hwy. 332, 77531 (tel. 409/265-6766).

College Station

Accommodation: Motel 6, 2327 Texas Ave., 77840 (tel. 409/696-3379).

Conroe

Accommodation: Motel 6, 820 I-45 South, 77304 (tel. 409/760-4003).

Corpus Christi

Camping: Padre Island National Seashore, 9405 South Padre Island Dr., 78418-5597 (tel. 512/949-8173). Located 35 miles from downtown Corpus Christi. There are campgrounds at Malaquite Beach for $4 and primitive camping on other beaches.

Accommodations: Motel 6, 845 Lantana St., 78408 (tel. 512/289-9397).
- Motel 6, 8302 South Padre Island Dr., 78412 (tel. 512/991-8858).
- Drury Inn, I-37 and TX 358 Exit Leopard, 2021 N. Padre Island Dr., 78408 (tel. 512/289-8200).
- Econo Lodge, 6033 Leopard St., 78409 (tel. 512/289-1116).
- Gulf Beach II, Ⓢ∨ ★, 3500 Surfside, 78402 (tel. 512/882-3500 or toll free 800/882-3502). $22.77 to $39.95 single; $27.77 to $54.95 double.

Corsicana

Accommodation: Econo Lodge, 2021 Regal Dr., 75110 (tel. 214/874-4751).

Dallas

Tourist Information: Dallas Convention and Visitors Bureau, Dallas Chamber of Commerce, 400 South Houston (in person) or 1507 Pacific (mailing address), 75201 (tel. 214/954-1482).

Accommodations: Exel Inn, 1181 N. Watson Rd., 76006 (tel. 817/649-0993).
- Motel 6, 3629 Hwy. 80, 75150 (tel. 214/613-1662).
- Motel 6, 4610 South R.L. Thornton Freeway, 75224 (tel. 214/372-5924).
- Motel 6, 9626 C.F. Hawn Freeway, 75217 (tel. 214/286-7952).
- Red Roof Inn, 8150 Esters Blvd., Hwy. 114 & Esters Rd., Irving, 75063 (tel. 214/929-0020).
- Red Roof Inn, 1550 Empire Central Dr., 75247 (tel. 214/638-5151).
- Days Inn, U.S. 80 at Town East Boulevard, 3817 Hwy. 80 East, 75150 (tel. 214/270-7551).

Del Rio

Accommodation: Motel 6, 2115 Ave. F, 78840 (tel. 512/774-2115).

Camping: Amistad National Recreation Area, P.O. Box 420367, 78842 (tel. 512/775-7491). Camping all year at primitive campsites. No charge.
- American Campground/Cabins, Ⓢ ∨ ★, (10%), Hwy. 90W, Box 44, 78840 (tel. 512/775-6484). Cabins: $10 single; $15 double; $20 triple; $24 quad; $1 linen charge. Rustic recreation resort with horse stables and watersport center. Reservations suggested.

Denton

Accommodations: Motel 6, 4125 I-35 North, 76201 (tel. 817/566-4798).
- Exel Inn, 4211 I-35E North, 76201 (tel. 817/383-1471).

Dumas

Accommodation: Budget Host—Moore Rest Inn, 119 W. 17th, Box 1474, 79029 (tel. 806/935-6222).

Duncanville

Accommodations: Allstar Inn, 4220 Independence Dr., 75237 (tel. 214/296-3331).
- Hampton Inn, 4154 Preferred Place, 75237 (tel. 214/298-4040).

El Paso

Help: El Paso Crisis Services, 915/779-1800.
Accommodations: Gardner Hotel/El Paso International Youth Hostel (AYH-SA), 311 East Franklin Ave., 79901 (tel. 915/532-3661). Five blocks from bus; six blocks from train. $14.50 to $20 single; $19 to $23 double; $26 triple. $8.50 for AYH members, $10.50 for nonmembers in dorm beds. Listed on El Paso Historic Register and recently renovated. "It's a safe, clean, and friendly place to stay."
- Motel 6, 11049 Gateway Blvd. West, 79935 (tel. 915/594-8533).
- Motel 6, 7840 North Mesa St., 79932 (tel. 915/584-2129).
- Imperial 400 Motor Inn, 6363 Montana Ave., 79925 (tel. 915/778-3311).
- Allstar Inn, 1324 Lomaland Dr., 79935 (tel. 915/592-6386).

Fort Stockton

Accommodation: Motel 6, 3001 West Dickinson Blvd., 79735 (tel. 915/336-9737).

Fort Worth

Tourist Information: Convention and Visitors Bureau, Water Gardens Place, 100 East 15th St., Suite 400, 76102 (tel. 817/336-8791).
Help: Visitor Information Center, 123 E. Exchange, 76106 (tel. 817/624-4741).
Accommodations: Motel 6, 6401 Airport Freeway, Haltom City, 76117 (tel. 817/834-7136).
- Motel 6, 6600 South Freeway, 76134 (tel. 817/293-8595).
- Motel 6, 8701 I-20 West, 76116 (tel. 817/244-6060).
- Motel 6, 3271 I-35 West, 76106 (tel. 817/625-4359).
- Allstar Inn, 1236 Oakland Blvd., 76103 (tel. 817/834-7361).
- Allstar Inn, 3275 I-35 West, 76106 (tel. 817/625-8941).
- Budget Host—Caravan Motor Hotel, 2601 Jacksboro Hwy., 76114 (tel. 817/626-1951).

Gainesville

Accommodation: Budget Host—Caravan Motor Hotel, Jct. I-35 and U.S. 82, P.O. Box 856, 76240 (tel. 817/665-5555).

Galveston

Accommodation: Motel 6, 7404 Ave. J, RR 4, 77551 (tel. 409/740-3794).

Grand Prairie

Accommodation: Motel 6, 406 East Safari Blvd., 75050 (tel. 214/642-9424).

Greenville

Accommodation: Motel 6, 5109 I-30, 75401 (tel. 214/455-0515).

Harlingen

Accommodation: Motel 6, 224 South U.S. Expressway 77, 78550 (tel. 512/421-4200).

Houston

Houston—a city affected by economic problems recently—is recovering quickly and will soon become the booming modern-day metropolitan area that it used to be. The city continues to serve sightseers with its many day and night attractions and accommodations. Don't miss the Transco Tower Plaza in the Galleria area, 2700 Post Oak Blvd.; the Houston Arboretum and Nature Center on Memorial Drive (tel. 713/681-8433); the San Jacinto Battleground and Battleship Texas; the Astrodomain, comprised of Astroworld, Waterworld, and Astrodome; the Goodyear Blimp; the Lyndon B. Johnson Space Center (tel. 713/483-4321); the Downtown Pedestrian Tunnel System, full of underground shops, offices, and cafes; and the Houston Zoological Gardens in Hermann Park (tel. 713/523-5888).

An excellent guide to this big and aggresively modern city is "Texas Monthly's" *Guide to Houston,* by Felicia Coates and Harriet Howle ($3.95). "Texas Monthly" itself is a good guide to places to eat and things to do; look, too, at *Houston City Magazine* for the same kind of information. Two other useful guides are *Day Trips from Houston,* by Carol Barrington, Globe Pequot Press ($7.95), and *A Marmac Guide to Houston and Galveston,* by Dale Young, Pelican Publishing Co. ($7.95). For free maps and information about tours and sightseeing, stop at the Greater Houston Convention and Visitors Council, 3300 Main St., 77002 (tel. 713/523-5050). Their monthly "Houston Day and Night" brochure and "Houston Area Maps and Attractions" are quite useful. They also have two toll-free numbers: 800/392-7722, inside Texas; and 800/231-7799, outside Texas.

Other informational resources include the Arts and Entertainment sections of the *Houston Post* (especially Friday's "Weekend" section) and the *Houston Chronicle* (especially Sunday's "Zest Magazine" section), the magazines *Public News* and *Inner View,* which can be picked up on a university or college campus, and *Houston Key Magazine,* available in many downtown hotels. To find out about events, clubs, restaurants, etc., call "CONCERT" at 713/266-2378, from any touchtone phone. And be warned: Houston can be incredibly hot and steamy. Hot enough, in fact, to have necessitated air-conditioned tunnels connecting the downtown buildings.

Mid- to late-March is the time for the Houston International Festival—a period when Houston applauds itself with a melange of food, arts, music, crafts, and dance. If you're going to be on or around the campus of the University of Houston, you should probably stop at the offices of ACCESS, Room N-11, University Center (see "On Campus" for details). For up-to-the-minute information on Houston, contact Showtix, 400 Rush at Smith in Tranquility Park (tel. 713/227-9292).

Getting There: There's an airport limousine bus service from the Intercontinental Airport to the Downtown Air Terminal in the Hyatt Regency Hotel. The 25-mile ride costs $6; the same trip by taxi would be $21. Two bus routes from Hobby Airport, nos. 73 and 88, both 60¢, take about one hour.

● The Greyhound-Trailways Station is at 2121 Main St. (tel. 713/759-6500); and Amtrak's terminal is at 902 Washington St. (tel. 713/224-1577).

Getting Around: *"This is a very difficult city to get around in if you don't have a car."*

● For 15¢ you can ride any bus within the boundaries of a Shoppers Special Route, on Main Street from Franklin on the north to Pierre on the south. The regular fare on the Metro bus is 60¢; transfers are free. Buses run every 15 to 30 minutes. For information on public transportation, you can visit the Metro Ride Store on the corner of Capital and Franklin, downtown, or call 713/635-4000. But the best way, by far, to see Houston is by car. If you don't have your own, you can get a good rental deal at Budget Rent-a-Car, with offices located all over town. A Toyota or Datsun costs $35 a day with unlimited mileage. Because Houston is such a car-orientated town, there are loads of other car-rental places too.

Help: Crisis Hotline of Houston, 713/228-1505.

● Crisis Help Line, 713/488-7222.

● United Way, 713/527-0222.

On Campus: The University of Houston—University Park has temporary housing in campus dorms available during the summer for $250/month and $514/month. Call 713/749-2185.

On campus, the *Daily Cougar* newspaper is a good source of information on odd jobs, discount stores, rides, and what's going on—in addition to the board on campus in the University Center Underground. Through ACCESS (information/referral/off-campus housing), one can obtain social, cultural and educational information about Houston, and complimentary tickets for the annual Rodeo and Jones Hall Concerts. Contact the University of Houston—University Center, ACCESS, N-13, Houston, 77004 (tel. 713/749-3327).

Accommodations: YMCA, Ⓢ(10%), 1600 Louisiana St., 77002 (tel. 713/659-8501). Men only. $15 per night; $64 to $68 per week. Air-conditioned; color television in every room; telephone included. "We have a complete referral service here . . . any traveler coming here will find that he will get assistance when needed."

● Houston Hostel, 5530 Hillman, 77023 (tel. 713/926-3444). $5 for AYH and ISIC members or nonmembers in dorm beds.

● The Grant Motel, Ⓢ √ 🅱, 8200 South Main St., 77025 (tel. 713/668-8000). Near Rice University-Texas Medical Center area. $25 single; $29 double; $39 triple; $41 quad. "Quiet, clean rooms with extra-long beds."

● Days Inn, I-45N and Cavalcade, 100 West Cavalcade, 77009 (tel. 713/869-7121).

● Days Inn, I-45 at Wayside, 2200 South Wayside, 77023 (tel. 713/928-2800).

● Hampton Inn, 12727 Southwest Frwy., Stafford, 77477 (tel. 713/240-2300).

● Motel 6, 9638 Plainfield Rd., 77036 (tel. 713/778-0008).

● Super 8 Motel, 889 West Bay Area Blvd., Webster, 77598 (tel. 713/338-1526).

- Rodeway Inn, 5820 Katy Fwy. at Washington Avenue, 77007 (tel. 713/869-9211). $31 single; $36 double; $41 triple; $46 quad; $5 extra per person.

Bed and Breakfast Society of Houston, 921 Heights, 77008 (tel. 713/868-4654). $25 to $45 single; $35 to $50 double. Places travelers in private homes around Houston. Reservations recommended 3 to 4 days in advance.

- University Hilton Hotel, 4800 Calhoun Rd., 77004 (tel. 713/741-2447). $42 single; $52 double. Located on the University of Houston-University Park Campus.

- Manor House Motor Inn, 14833 Katy Frwy., I-10, 77094 (tel. 713/497-5000). $35 single; $40 double.

Where to Eat: The Original Ninfa's (there are three others), 2704 Navigation Rd. In the Port of Houston area near the bayou. Call 713/228-1175 for hours. "Just about the best Mexican food in Houston." The atmosphere is pure fiesta. Tacos al carbon, the specialty of the house, costs about $7.50 at dinnertime.

- Goode Company, 5107 Kirby Dr., in the Rice University area, (tel. 713/522-2530). Texas-style barbecue that you've got to try at least once while you're in Houston. Cost: $7.95/lb.

- Merida Restaurant, 2509 Navigation, just east of downtown (tel. 713/227-0260 or 225-0403). Very good Mexican food.

- Denny's, 10707 Katy Fwy., I-10 (tel. 713/468-4537). Open 24 hours—good for breakfast.

- Sizzler Family Steakhouse, 1703 Old Spanish Trail (tel. 713/795-0320). $6.99 steak and all-you-can-eat shrimp.

- Wok Bo, 10725 W. Bellfort, off US 59 (tel. 713/495-8971). Be ready to eat a lot of good Chinese food—more than 15 entrèes you can choose from and all you can eat for $3.99 (lunch) and $4.99 (dinner).

- The Old Spaghetti Warehouse, 901 Commerce St. at Travis, downtown (tel. 713/229-0009). Antiques, plants, and of course, spaghetti. A special spaghetti dinner with soup, salad, and a beverage costs $3.25.

- James Coney Island, 1142 Travis (tel. 713/652-3819). Chili, sandwiches, salads, and hot dogs. Conveniently located and usually open from 7 a.m. to 10 p.m. every day of the week. Two Coney Islands (hot dogs) and a beer are $3.25.

- Leo's Coffee Shop, 1203 Fannin, downtown (tel. 713/652-5955). Open 24 hours. American food, with nothing over $6. "The atmosphere is interesting—especially in the wee hours."

- Pancho's Mexican Buffet, 5311 Bissonnet (tel. 713/666-3531). Bellaire area. On the buffet you have your choice of enchiladas, tacos, guacamole, soup, chili rellenos, tamales, chalupas, rice, and beans—all for $3.99.

- Frenchy's Po Boy, 3919 Scott (tel. 713/748-2233). Fast food in the Creole style. Three pieces of chicken, fries, and "dirty" rice is $2.85 on the campus special—no wonder it's so popular with the students.

- Lyby's Cafeteria, 2730 Fondren Rd. (tel. 713/785-5240) and others all over Houston. In the heart of Bellaire. Nothing fancy, just clean and reliable.

What to See and Do: From May to October, the arts go outdoors to Miller Theater in Hermann Park near the Medical Center. Ballet, symphony, opera, plays—almost every night there's something to see and it's all free. Call 713/222-3576 for information.

- NASA's Lyndon B. Johnson Space Center, 20 miles south of Houston. Here you can see Mission Control, where space flights from Gemini to the

Space Shuttle *Columbia* have been monitored. Free walking tours are available Monday through Friday. Call 713/483-4321 for reservations.

● The Astrodome Sports Stadium claims to be the largest single attraction in the state of Texas. There are tours every day. Call 713/749-9500 for details.

● Rothko Chapel, 1411 Sul Ross. Fourteen of Mark Rothko's paintings hang in this ecumenical chapel in an interesting neighborhood southwest of downtown. For information, call 713/524-9839.

● Museums: The Museum of Fine Arts, 1001 Bissonnet (tel. 713/526-1361). Open Tuesday through Sunday, and the Contemporary Arts Museum, 5216 Montrose Blvd., (tel. 713/526-3129), follows the same schedule. Admission is free to both.

● Astro World, 9001 Kirby Dr. (tel. 713/779-1234). An amusement park with rides like the Sky Screamer and LRB, Water World—a recreation park with lots of water games for anyone who wants to cool off, and the Southern Star Amphitheater. For ticket information, call 713/795-0395.

● If you're lucky enough to be in Houston at the end of March you'll be able to enjoy the Houston Festival, a celebration of the city that goes on all around town.

● Other events include: Houston Livestock Show and Rodeo in the Astrodome (February/March); Houston International Festival in downtown parks (10 days in late March); Westheimer Colony Arts Festival—call 713/521-0133 (late April); Cinco de Mayo Festival (May 5); Juneteenth Blues Festival in Hermann Park—call 713/528-6740 (early summer); Texas Renaissance Festival in Plantersville, north of Houston (October).

At Night: For jazz and rock: Paradise Island Club, 4705 Main St. Open until 2 a.m. Tuesday through Sunday. This is a smoky and usually loud spot where you can hear progressive jazz and rock 'n' roll, but probably not each other.

● For comedy: Comedy Workshop, San Felipe at South Shepherd. Every night, for a $3 cover, you can see a comedy revue. Next door, at the Comic's Club Annex, you can hear stand-up comics. Call 713/524-7333.

● For dancing: Todd's, 5050 Richmond. Nice dance floor bar with free buffet from 6 p.m. to 9:30 p.m.

● Rox-Z, Gessner and Westpark. Loud top 40 music, but nice young crowd.

● The Ocean Club, 1885 St. James Place (tel. 713/963-9303). Trendy top 40 club with dance floors on 3 levels. Sophisticated young crowd.

● Gilley's Club, 4500 Spencer Hwy. "A real honky-tonk immortalized by the film *Urban Cowboy*."

● Cooter's, 5164 Richmond (tel. 713/961-7494). The crowd comes to dance, eat, drink, and meet others. Reputed to have the longest happy hour in Houston—from 3 to 9 p.m. every Monday through Friday. "A vibrant, warm club for eating, dancing, and socializing."

● For jazz: Corky's, 623 Hawthorne. A converted old wood-frame house where you can hear jazz from 6 p.m. to 2 a.m.

● Cody's, 3400 Montrose (tel. 713/522-9747). You can hear jazz Monday to Friday 4 p.m. to 2 a.m., Saturday 6 p.m. to 2 a.m.

● Rockefeller's, 3620 Washington Ave. (tel. 713/861-9365). The place to see the stars of the jazz world like Ramsey Lewis and Dave Brubeck. In a beautifully restored building about five minutes from downtown.

● Paraden Bar & Grill, 401 McGowen. A casual place to hear jazz and relax.

● For country and western music: Vagabond Club, 4815 North Freeway. Nonstop music that's mostly country and western.

- Bullwhip Country and Western Bar, 7011 S.W. Freeway (tel. 713/778-1200).
- For arts performances: Jones Hall, 615 Louisiana (tel. 713/224-4240). Where the Houston Symphony performs and the Society for the Performing Arts presents ballet.
- The Alley Theatre, 615 Texas Ave. (tel. 713/228-8421), is reputed to be one of the best regional theaters in the U.S. There are student discounts of up to 25%.
- Stages, 3201 Allen Parkway (tel. 713/52-STAGE).
- Delia Stewart Jazz Dance Company, 1202 Calumet (tel. 713/522-6375). Modern Dance Company that performs in various events around Houston.

Shopping: Anything you could possibly desire should be somewhere in the Galleria Shopping Center, 5015 Westheimer Rd., which is becoming a tourist attraction in itself. The complex is covered, so you'll never know what the weather is like outside, and inside you can eat a Big Mac, go to a movie, or look at Gucci's latest.

- Crown Books, 1219 Travis, downtown (tel. 713/655-1163). Discounted books.
- Bookstop, 2922 S. Shepherd (tel. 713/529-2345). Discount available with store discount card.
- Records: Sound Warehouse, 6520 Westheimer Rd. (tel. 713/977-7130) and Soundwaves, 9150 South Main (tel. 713/660-6181).
- Cactus Records and Tapes, Sharpstown Ctr. (tel. 713/921-8363).
- Camping equipment: Academy, 2030 Westheimer Rd. (tel. 713/526-0929).
- Gifts: Trading Fair II, 5515 South Loop E., and the Market Place, 10900 Old Katy Rd. Both markets with all kinds of merchandise to tempt you.

Huntsville

Accommodations: Motel 6, 1607 I-45, 77340 (tel. 409/291-6927).
- Super 8 Motel, 3211 Hwy. 45, 77340 (tel. 409/291-3303).

Irving

Accommodation: Allstar Inn, 510 South Loop 12, 75060 (tel. 214/445-1151).

Killeen

Accommodation: Red Carpet Inn, 605 North Gray St., 76540 (tel. 817/634-3151).

Kingsville

Accommodation: Motel 6, 101 North U.S. 77 Bypass, 78363 (tel 512/592-5106).

Laredo

Accommodations: Budget Host—The Mayan Inn, 3219 San Bernardo, 78040 (tel. 512/722-8181).
- Motel 6, 5310 San Bernardo Ave., 78041 (tel. 512/725-8187).

Longview

Accommodations: TraveLodge, 1507 East Marshall Ave., 75601 (tel. 214/758-3303).
- Motel 6, 110 West Access Rd., 75603 (tel. 214/758-5256).
- Imperial 400 Motor Inn, 1019 East Marshall St., 75601 (tel. 214/753-0276).

Lubbock

On Campus: People for Texas Tech University congregate at The Fast and Cool Club, 2408 4th St. (tel. 806/747-5573) or J. Patrick O'Malley's, 1211 University (tel. 806/762-2300). When they're hungry they go to Gardski's Loft, 2009 Broadway (tel. 806/744-2391) for great hamburgers, or Mesquite's, 2409 University.

Accommodation: Motel 6, 909 66th St., 79413 (tel. 806/745-5541).

Lufkin

Accommodation: Motel 6, 1110 South Timberland, 75901 (tel. 409/637-7850).

Marshall

Accommodation: Motel 6, Rte. 1, I-20 and U.S. 59, 75670 (tel. 214/935-4393).

McAllen

Accommodations: Motel 6, 700 U.S. 83 Expressway, 78501 (tel. 512/687-3700).
- Red Carpet Inn, U.S. 83 and Jackson Road, P.O. Box 908, 78501 (tel. 512/787-5921).
- Allstar Inn, 200 East Expressway 83, 78501 (tel. 915/783-1123).

Midland

Accommodation: Motel 6, 1000 South Midkiff, 79701 (tel. 915/697-3197).

North Richland Hills

Accommodation: Allstar Inn, 7804 Bedford Euless Rd., 76118 (tel. 817/485-3000).

Odessa

Accommodations: Motel 6, 2925 East Hwy. 80, 79761 (tel. 915/332-2600).
● Motel 6, 200 East I-20 Service Rd., 79766 (tel. 915/333-4025).

Orange

Accommodation: Motel 6, 4407 27th St., 77630 (tel. 409/883-4891).

Pecos

Accommodation: Motel 6, 3002 South Cedar, P.O. Box 960, 79772 (tel. 915/445-9034).

Pittsburg

Accommodation: Scottish Inn, 611 Greer Blvd., 75686 (tel. 214/856-6574).

Port Arthur

Accommodations: Imperial 400 Motor Inn, 2811 Memorial Blvd., 77640 (tel. 409/985-9316).
● Motel 6, 5201 East Parkway, 77619 (tel. 409/962-6611).

San Angelo

Accommodation: Motel 6, 311 North Bryant, 76903 (tel. 915/658-8061).

San Antonio

"This is a beautiful and charming city."

Tourist Information: San Antonio Convention and Visitors Bureau, P.O. Box 2277, 78298 (tel. 512/299-8123).
● Visitor Information Center, 317 Alamo Plaza (tel. 512/299-8155)
Help: Help Line, 512/227-4357.
Accommodations: Budget Host—Siesta Motel, 4441 Fredericksburg Rd., 78201 (tel. 512/733-7154).
● San Antonio International Hostel (AYH), Ⓢ √ ★, 621 Pierce St., P.O.

Box 8059, 78208 (tel. 512/223-9426). $8.50 for AYH members. Rooms: $16 to $36 single; $19 to $39 double; $8 for each additional person; $4 each additional child under 17 years.
- Hampton Inn, 4803 Manitou Dr., 78229 (tel. 512/734-3500).
- Motel 6, 9503 I-35 North, 78233 (tel. 512/650-4419).
- Motel 6, 138 North W.W. White Rd., 78219 (tel. 512/333-1850).
- Allstar Inn, 5522 North Panam, 78218 (tel. 512/661-8791).
- Drury Inn, 8300 I-35 North and Walzem Road, 78239 (tel. 512/654-1144).
- Regal 8 Inn, 4621 East Rittiman Rd., 78218 (tel. 512/653-8088).
- Super 8 Motel, 11027 I-35 North, 78233 (tel. 512/637-1033).

San Marcos

Accommodation: Motel 6, 1321 I-35 North, 78666 (tel. 512/396-8705).

Sherman

On Campus: Austin College is in Sherman. Sherman is a "dry" town but Denison nearby is "wet." You can meet students at the "Pouch Club"—it requires membership, although two guests are allowed and you could be one of them. "The Chefette" on West Houston has good, home-style cooking to satisfy your hunger pangs.

Accommodation: Super 8 Motel, 111 Hwy. 1417 East, 75090 (tel. 214/868-9325).

Snyder

Accommodation: TraveLodge, 1006 25th St., 79549 (tel. 915/573-9395).

Sweetwater

Accommodation: Motel 6, 510 N.W. Georgia, 79556 (tel. 915/235-4387).

Temple

Accommodations: Motel 6, 1100 North General Bruce Dr., 76501 (tel. 817/778-0272).
- Econo Lodge, 1001 North General Bruce Dr., 76501 (tel. 817/771-2234).

Texarkana

Accommodations: Motel 6, 1924 Hampton Rd., 75503 (tel. 214/793-1413).
- Scottish Inn, 4505 N. Stateline Ave., 75501 (tel. 214/793-5546).

Tyler

Accommodation: Motel 6, 3236 Brady Gentry Pkwy., 75702 (tel. 214/595-6691).

Victoria

Accommodation: Motel 6, 3716 Houston Hwy., 77901 (tel. 512/573-1273).

Van Horn

Accommodation: Friendship Regal Inn, Interstate 10 and West 20, 79855 (tel. 915/283-2992).

Waco

Accommodation: Motel 6, 1509 Hogan Lane, Bellmead, 76705 (tel. 817/799-4957).

Weslaco

Accommodation: Vali-HO Motel, 2100 East Bus. 83, 78596 (tel. 512/968-2173). $27 to $29 for one or two in one bed; $29 to $35 for two in two beds; $31 to $42 triple or quad.

Wichita Falls

Accommodations: Hampton Inn, 1317 Kenley Ave., 76305 (tel. 817/766-3300).
- Motel 6, 1812 Maurine St., 76305 (tel. 817/322-8817).

Utah

Brigham Young and his Mormon followers are the ones to thank for Utah. Brigham Young took one look, said "This is the place," and founded Salt Lake City in 1847. The Mormons have been major contributors to the culture and development of Utah ever since.

What to see in Utah? In Salt Lake City: Mormon Temple Square, Beehive House (where Brigham Young lived with several of his wives), Trolley Square, Kennecott Copper Mine, Pioneer Trail State Park, Hogle Zoo, and Capitol Hill. Not to be missed, too, are the natural wonders of the state: Arches National Park, Bryce Canyon National Park ("a helluva place to lose a cow" is what one of the first settlers is reputed to have said of these beautiful badlands), Canyonlands National Park, Capitol Reef National Park, and Zion National Park. Flaming Gorge and Glen Canyon National Recreation Area offer boating, fishing, and camping facilities. The Great Salt Lake, 70 miles long and 30 miles wide, is what is left of a lake that was once ten times that size. Sixteen world-class ski resorts, 7 within one hour's drive of Salt Lake City, complete the picture. "Utah has the greatest snow on earth."

Some Special Events: United States Film Festival in Park City (January); Reenactment of the driving of the Golden Spike at Promontory Point (May); Utah Arts Festival in Salt Lake City (June); Western Film Festival in Ogden (July); Utah Shakespearean Festival in Cedar City (July to mid-August); Festival of the American West in Logan (late July to August); Swiss Days in Midway, Tomato Days in Hooper, and Melon Days in Green River (September); Oktoberfest at Snowbird (October); and the Annual Lighting of Temple Square in Salt Lake City (November).

Tourist Information: Judging from the *1987 Travel Guide,* accommodations are especially reasonable, most falling well within our price guidelines. Information on this and much more is available from the Utah Travel Council, Council Hall, Capitol Hill, Salt Lake City, UT 84114.

N.B. A bed-and-breakfast reservation service for Utah is Bed & Breakfast Association of Utah, P.O. Box 16465, Salt Lake City, UT 84116. (tel. 801/532-7076).

Beaver

Accommodation: TraveLodge, 6 North Main St., 84713 (tel. 801/438-2409).

Bryce Canyon

Camping: Bryce Canyon National Park, 84717 (tel. 801/834-5322). Two campgrounds. North open year round; Sunset open mid-May to September. Horseback riding. $5 per campsite per night. $5 entrance fee per vehicle.

Cedar City

Accommodations: Comfort Inn, 150 N. 1100 West, 84720 (tel. 801/586-2082).
● Imperial 400 Motor Inn, 344 South Main St., 84720 (tel. 801/586-9416).

Green River

Accommodation: Motel 6, 946 East Main, 84525 (tel. 801/564-3436).

Kanab

Accommodation: Budget Host—K Motel, 330 South 100 East, P.O. Box 1301, 84741 (tel. 801/644-2611).

Moab

Camping: Canyonlands National Park, 84532 (tel. 801/259-7164). Campgrounds at Squaw Flat, Willow Flat, and Devils Garden. Open all year. No water at Willow Flat. No hook-ups.
● Arches National Park, c/o Canyonlands National Park, 84532 (tel. 801/259-8161). Campground at Devil's Garden (18 miles north of Visitor Center). Open year round; toilets available March to October. $5 per campsite per night. Free during the rest of the year, but there is no water. No wood or wood collecting. $5 entrance fee per carload and motorcycles; $2 per individual, bike, or commercial bus.
● Natural Bridges National Monument, c/o Canyonlands National Park, mailing address: Star Route, Blanding, UT 84511 (tel. 801/259-5174). Campground with 13 sites (four miles off Utah 95). Water available at Visitor Center. $3 entrance fee per vehicle. Camping is free.

Nephi

Accommodation: Super 8 Motel, I–15, Nephi Exit, 84648 (tel. 801/623-0888).

Odgen

Accommodations: Budget Host—Millstream Motel, 1450 Washington Blvd., 84404 (tel. 801/394-9425).
- Motel 6, 1455 Washington Blvd., 84404 (tel. 801/627-4560).
- Super 8 Motel, 1508 W. 2100 South, 84401 (tel. 801/731-7100).
- TraveLodge, 2110 Washington Blvd., 84401 (tel. 801/394-4563).

Price

Accommodation: Quality Inn, 641 W. Price River Dr., 84501 (tel. 801/637-7000).

Provo

On Campus: According to one student at Brigham Young University here, "This is a beautiful, clean college community close to the mountains, lakes, and big cities." While in the area, consider breakfast at Annie's Pantry, 150 South University (famous for scones); or lunch or dinner at the Brick Oven, 150 East 800 North; The Underground (steak and sea food), North University Avenue; Grand View Cafe (Chinese food), 66 North 500 West; Jimba's (burgers), 278 West Center; The Sensuous Sandwiche, 300 West Center; Los Hermanos (Mexican), 10 West Center; La France (French, of course), 463 North University Ave.; Bamboo Hut (Hawaiian), right next to Provo High on University.

The *Daily Universe* is the campus newspaper; ASBYU hotline is 801/378-3283. In the Wilkensen Center at the University, you'll find a ride/apartment board.

Accommodations: Motel 6, 1600 South University Dr., 84601 (tel. 801/375-5064).
- Budget Host—University Western Inn, 40 West 300 South, 84601 (tel. 801/373-0660).
- Super 8 Motel, 12th South & University Avenue, 84601 (tel. 801/375-8766).
- TraveLodge, 124 South University Ave., 84601 (tel. 801/373-1974).

St. George

Accommodations: Comfort Inn, 999 E. Skyline Dr., 84770 (tel. 801/628-4271).
- Motel 6, 205 North 1000 East St., 84770 (tel. 801/628-7979).
- Super 8 Motel, 915 South Bluff St., 84770 (tel. 801/628-4251).
- TraveLodge, 175 North 1000 East St., 84770 (tel. 801/673-4621).
- TraveLodge, 60 West St. George Blvd., 84770 (tel. 801/673-4666).

Salt Lake City

Tourist Information: Salt Lake Convention and Visitors Bureau, 180 South West Temple, 84101 (tel. 801/521-2822). According to someone at the tourist office: "Salt Lake is a friendly, clean city."

Accommodations: Avenues Residential Center (AYH-SA), 107 F St., 84103 (tel. 801/363-8137). $12.02 for AYH members. Advance reservations suggested December 1 to May 1 and 1st week of October.

● Carlton Hotel, Ⓢ√ ★ ⑤, 140 East South Temple St., 84111 (tel. 801/355-3418). Just 1 ½ blocks from bus station; 6 blocks from train station. $34.50 single; $39.50 twin; $44.50 triple or quad. "Older hotel, completely renovated, very clean and personable.

● Imperial 400 Motor Inn, 476 South State St., 84111 (tel. 801/533-9300).
● Motel 6, 176 West 6th South St., 84101 (tel. 801/531-1252).
● Motel 6, 1990 West North Temple St., 84116 (tel. 801/364-1053).
● Motel 6, 496 North Catalpa, 84047 (tel. 801/561-0058).
● Days Inn, 1900 West North Temple, 84116 (tel. 801/539-8538).
● Super 8 Motel, 616 South 200 West, 84101 (tel. 801/534-0808).

Springdale

Camping: Zion National Park, one mile north of Springdale on S.R. 9, 84767 (tel. 801/772-3256). Three campgrounds: Watchman, open year round; South, open April 15 to September 15. $6 per campsite per night for up to eight people. Lava Point is an undeveloped campground located 37 miles from the Park Visitor Center with six campsites available at no charge. Discount for Golden Age and Golden Access holders.

Vernal

Accommodation: Econo Lodge, 311 East Main St., 84078 (tel. 801/789-2000).

Wendover

Accommodations: Motel 6, 545 State Hwy., P.O. Box 190, 84083 (tel. 801/665-2267).
● Friendship Inn, 809 State Hwy., 84083 (tel. 801/665-2211).

Vermont

Known as the "Green Mountain State," Vermont has tried zealously and successfully to protect its natural beauty. Some would say it's the most attractive state east of the Mississippi.

Vermont is a state of small, picturesque villages. Its largest city, Burlington, has fewer than 50,000 inhabitants. The geography is characterized by a pleasant mix of mountain and valley, unmarked by intrusive billboards and commercial advertising. Its Long Trail is a mountain footpath extending the length of the state, with free shelters every 6 to 10 miles (10 to 20 kilometers).

As the state with the United States' first ski tow (in 1934), it has long been a leader in the field of winter sports. It has more than 20 major downhill ski areas and more than 50 cross-country ski touring centers. Ski-country accommodations range from austere dormitories to luxurious condominiums to dairy farms and bed-and-breakfasts.

In summer, many of the ski areas are available for hiking, swimming, and mountain climbing, and there are numerous opportunities for water sports on the many lakes that dot the state. Besides physical beauty, the state offers a great deal in the way of cultural attractions: summer theaters, music festivals (the one at Marlboro is the best known), outstanding language schools at Middlebury College and the School for International Training, and a host of arts and crafts fairs.

Another popular time of the year for tourists to visit Vermont is in late September and early October, when fall weather turns the green of the mountains into a bright blanket of red, orange, and yellow. But if you were to consult with the residents, you'd be told that late spring is equally colorful, when the apple blossoms turn the hillsides pink.

Because of its rather rugged winter climate, Vermont's people tend to be independent individualists. It is one of the few states that was once a republic; the founding fathers refused to join the original 13 colonies until it was proven that the experiment in federal government wasn't designed to concentrate too much power in one person. Life in Vermont today is an echo of those early days —the state is warmly hospitable to new ideas, to experimentalists, to people seeking freedom from urban pressures.

Chris Tree and Peter Jennison's book, *Vermont: An Explorer's Guide,* published by Countryman Press, is "top notch."

Some Special Events: Winter Carnival in Stowe, and Ice Harvest in Brookfield (January); Morgan Horse Sleigh Ride Festival in Shelburne (February); Bear Mt. Mogul Challenge in Killington (March); Maple Festival in St. Albans, and Maple Sugar Festival in St. Johnsbury (April); Balloon Festival in Quechee, and Strawberry Festival in East Montpelier (June); Vermont Fool's Fest in Montpelier, and Aquafest in Newport (July); Marlboro Music School and Festival (July and August); Antique and Classic Car meet in Stowe, and Bread and Puppet Theatre's Domestic Resurrection Circus in Glover (August); and Foliage Train Excursions in St. Johnsbury and Morrisville (September).

Tourist Information: Vermont Travel Division, 134 State St., Montpelier, VT 05602 (tel. 802/828-3236).

N.B. A bed-and-breakfast reservation service for Vermont is American B&B in New England, Box 983, St. Albans, VT 05478 (tel. 802/223-3443).

Bennington

On Campus: Bennington College, now the most expensive college in the country, is in this historic town in southwestern Vermont, with its famous battlefield and monument. We're told that the attitude toward young people on the road is "generally helpful, although there is a New England reserve." There are numerous family-run restaurants in the area where travelers can get an inexpensive meal—two possibilities are Northside Diner, 132 Northside Dr. (tel. 802/442-8919) and Geannelis Restaurant, 520 Main St. (tel. 802/442-9778). A good place to meet young people is the Villager on Main Street (tel. 802/447-0998) in North Bennington.

Brattleboro

Help: Hotline for Help, 17 Elliot St., 05301 (tel. 802/257-7989). General counseling and referrals. They suggested the Latchis Hotel on South Main Street, which is rundown but inexpensive, or the Holly Motel. Call them and they'll be happy to provide you with any information they can. Some places to go to meet local people are Common Ground Restaurant, Mole's Eye, Via Condotti, and the Tavern.

Accommodation: Susse Chalet Motor Lodge, I–91, Exit 3, on Rte. 5 North, 05301 (tel. 802/254-6007).

Burlington

On Campus: During the school year you'll find a high concentration of students at the Billings Student Center at the University of Vermont. While you're there you can pick up a copy of the student newspaper, the *Vermont Cynic,* to find out what's going on on campus and around town. Some of the favorite student haunts downtown include B. T. McGuire's on Church Street, NRB's and Finbar's on Main Street. For a reasonable-priced meal try Carbur's for a sandwich (they have a 25-page sandwich menu so be sure to have plenty of time for reading), 119 St. Paul St., or Deja Vu on Pearl Street, a popular student hangout at night. For good, inexpensive Italian food, there's Filomenas Pizza on Riverside Road. For great ice cream, it's Ben and Jerry's Homemade on Cherry Street. If you'd rather be outdoors, take a ferry ride across Lake Champlain at sunset or hike on the Long Trail of the Green Mountains.

Accommodation: Mrs. Farrell's Youth Hostel (AYH), 27 Arlington Court, 05446 (tel. 802/878-8222). $10 for AYH members. Advance reservations essential.

Craftsbury Common

Accommodation: The Craftsbury Center Hostel (AYH-SA), Ⓢ (10% for nonmembers), P.O. Box 31, 05827 (tel. 802/586-7767). $10 for AYH members; $16 per person double occupancy. Meals available at extra cost. Cross-country ski-touring center in the winter. "Longest snow season in New England."

Rochester

Accommodations: Schoolhouse Youth Hostel (AYH), ★ ($1), South Main Street, 05767 (tel. 802/767-9384). Open year round except April 15 to May 15. $6 to $9 per person per night, plus $1 linen charge. The hostel was built in 1827 as a church, was converted to a gym and school in 1940, and became a hostel in 1963. Near Killington and Sugarbush ski areas and adjacent to the Green Mountain National Forest.

● The New Homestead, South Main Street, 05767 (tel. 802/767-4751). Open year round—as a ski lodge only during winter. $20 single; $32 double. Price includes breakfast and linens. Advance reservations necessary.

● Liberty Hill Farm, Liberty Hill Road, 05767 (tel. 802/767-3926). $25 to $30 per person bed-and-breakfast. Less for children. A large historic farmhouse on an operating dairy farm. Family-style dinners and full breakfasts. Two week advance reservations preferred.

Shelburne

Accommodation: Econo Lodge, Rte. 7, Shelburne Road, 05482 (tel. 802/985-3334).

South Wallingford

Accommodation: Green Mountain Tea Room and Guest House, Rte. 7, 05773 (tel. 802/446-2611). Vermont Transit and Greyhound buses stop in front of Tea Room. $20 to $25 single; $30 to $45 double. Breakfast and luncheon served at reasonable prices, "and afternoon tea is most definitely served. We have thirty varieties." An old colonial house dating from 1792.

Stowe

Accommodation: Fiddler's Green Inn, Rt. 108, Mountain Road 05672 (tel 802/253-8124). Summer rates: $20 to $27 single; $12 to $13.50 per person double; $10 per person triple or quad. Winter rates: $39 to $55 single; $39 to $43 per person double; $31 per person triple; $29 per person quad. Winter rates include breakfast and dinner.

Underhill Center

Accommodation: Underhill Center Youth Hostel (AYH), Box 148, West Bolton Road, 05490 (tel. 802/899-2375). Open June 1 to September. $6 for AYH members; $8.50 for nonmembers. No cars or buses allowed at hostel; parking ½ mile away.

Warren

Accommodation: Old Homestead, Ⓢ√, P.O. Box 118, 05674 (tel. 802/496-3744). Open year round. $25 single; $20 per person double or triple. Advance reservations preferred.

West Hartford

Accommodation: Clifford's Guest Home, Pomfret Road, 05084 (tel. 802/295-3554). $15 single; $30 double, including breakfast. "A very lovely old farmhouse—pleasant rooms, comfortable and clean." No pets.

White River Junction

Accommodation: Susse Chalet Motor Lodge, jct. of I–91, I–89 on Rte. 5 (tel. 802/295-3051, or toll free 800/259-3051).

Woodford

Accommodation and Camping: Greenwood Lodge (AYH), Rte. 9, 05201 (tel. 802/442-2547); mailing address in July through Labor Day: P.O. Box 246, Bennington, 05201; off-season: Ed and Anna Shea, 197 Lyons Rd., Scarsdale, NY 10583 (tel. 914/472-2575). Open July through Labor Day and fall foliage weekends. $10 per person in dorms; $25 double; $12 per person on fall foliage weekends. Tent sites summer and fall foliage weekends: $8 for one or two persons; $1.50 for each additional person to five per site. Recreational facilities on premises. Eight miles from Bennington; three miles from Appalachian and Long Trail hiking. Advance reservations suggested.

Virginia

Virginia is physically and philosophically the gateway to the South. The state is rich with the echoes of history; Jamestown was the site of the first English settlement in North America, in 1607; a Virginian, Richard Henry Lee, introduced the motion to separate the 13 colonies from England in 1776; Thomas Jefferson was the guiding hand behind the Declaration of Independence; and no one has to be reminded that George Washington was from this state as well. Much of the agony of the Civil War took place in Virginia: it was at Appomattox that Robert E. Lee surrendered in 1865. To get a sense of Virginia's history—and the history of the entire U.S., in fact—you should plan a visit to Williamsburg, the beautifully reconstructed capital of 18th-century Virginia, George Washington's residence in Mount Vernon, Jefferson's Monticello in Charlottesville, and Yorktown, where the American Revolution ended with the British soldiers marking out to the tune of "The World Turned Upside Down." Somewhat less well known but still worth a visit are the Virginia Museum of Fine Arts in Richmond, with its fine collection of Fabergé jewelry made for Russia's last czar, and the Mariners' Museum in Newport News.

For the people who like the out-of-doors, Virginia has lots of excellent camping. Shenandoah National Park and the Blue Ridge Parkway stretch from western Virginia through to North Carolina and present campers with some exquisite spots to spend a night or two. The Skyline Drive, which winds through Shenandoah National Park, is a spectacular 105 miles of overlooks and trails that are a treat for city-worn tourists.

Virginia Beach, 28 miles of shoreline from Cape Henry to Virginia's Outer Banks, is a popular fair-weather retreat. And for the curious, there's Tangier Island in Chesapeake Bay, an unspoiled spot where some of the natives still speak "old English" and work as fishermen; there's a boat that connects the mainland with the island from Reedville, Virginia, at certain times of the year and from Crisfield, Maryland, all year.

Several books we recommend are *The Insider's Guide: Williamsburg, Virginia Beach, Norfolk, Hampton, and Yorklawn,* published by Insider's Publishing Group; *A Complete Traveler's Touring Guide: Virginia,* by George Scheer III, published by Burt Franklin and Co.; *The Great Weekend Escape Book: From Williamsburg to Catly Hunk Island,* by Michael Spring, published by E.P.

Dutton; *Fodor's Virginia,* published by Fodor's Travel Guides ($7.95); *Fodor's Chesapeake,* published by Fodor's Travel Guides ($7.95); *The Virginia One-Day Trip Book,* by Jane Ockershausen Smith, published by EPM Publications ($8.95); and *Virginia: Off the Beaten Path,* by Judy and Ed Colbert, published by Globe Pequot ($7.95).

Some Special Events: Stonewall Jackson's Birthday Celebration in Lexington (January); Revolutionary War Encampment and Skirmish in Alexandria (February); Outdoor Odyssey in Chesterfield (April); Pony Penning in Chincoteague (July); Old Fiddler's Contest in Galax (August); State Fair in Richmond (September); and Oyster Festival in Chincoteague (October).

Tourist Information: Virginia Division of Tourism, 202 North Ninth Street, Suite 500, Richmond, VA 23219 (tel. 804/786-2051).

Ashland

Accommodation: Econo Lodge, I–95 and Rte. 54 jct., P.O. Box 308, 23005 (tel. 804/798-9221).

Blacksburg

On Campus: Virginia Polytechnical Institute is in Blacksburg—a university town on a plateau between the Blue Ridge and the Appalachian Mountains. To eat inexpensively, go to Squires Student Center. At the University Mall, try the Chinese food at Hunan and don't leave without trying Gillie's Ice Cream. When you're in Blacksburg consider a tube ride down the New River, a hike to Cascades, a swim in Claytor Lake, or a car trip to Mabry Mill on the Blue Ridge Parkway.

Accommodation: Econo Lodge, 3333 South Main St., 24060 (tel. 703/951-4242).

Bluemont

Accommodation: Bears Den (AYH), Rte. 1, Box 288, 22012 (tel. 703/554-8708). $8 for AYH members. Bring own linen or rent at hostel. No sleeping bags.

Bristol

Accommodations: Econo Lodge, 912 Commonwealth Ave., 24201 (tel. 703/466-2112).
- Scottish Inn, 4795 Lee Hwy., 24201 (tel. 703/669-4148).
- Super 8 Motel, 2139 Lee Hwy., 24201 (tel. 703/466-8800).

Carmel Church

Accommodation: Days Inn, I–95 and Va. 207, P.O. Box 70, Ruther Glen, 22546 (tel. 804/448-2011).

Charlottesville

Accommodations: Econo Lodge, 2014 Holiday Dr., 22901 (tel. 804/295-3185).
- Econo Lodge, 400 Emmet St., 22903 (tel. 804/296-2104).
- Hampton Inn, P.O. Box 8260, Seminole Square, 22906 (tel. 804/978-7888).
- Knights Inn, U.S. 29 at U.S. 250 Bypass, 1300 Seminole Trail, 22906.
- Super 8 Motel, 390 Greenbrier Dr., 22906 (tel. 804/973-0888).

Chesapeake

Accommodations: Econo Lodge, 3244 Western Branch Blvd. (Rte. 17), 23321 (tel. 804/488-4963).
- Econo Lodge, 4725 West Military Hwy., 23321 (tel. 804/488-4963).
- Red Roof Inn, 724 Woodlake Dr., 23320 (tel. 804/523-0123).

Chester

Accommodation: Days Inn, I–95 and Va. 10, Exit 6 W., P.O. Box AN, 23831 (tel. 804/748-5871).

Christiansburg

Accommodations: Econo Lodge, 2430 Roanoke St. SE, 24073 (tel. 703/382-6161).
- Days Inn, I–81 and U.S. 11, Exit 37, P.O. Box 768, 24073 (tel. 703/382-0261).
- Hampton Inn, 50 Hampton Blvd., 24073 (tel. 703/382-2055).

Culpeper

Accommodations: Econo Lodge, U.S. 15 and U.S. 29 Bypass, P.O. Box 407, 22701 (tel. 703/825-5097).
- Super 8 Motel, 889 Willis Lane, 22701 (tel. 703/825-8088).

Danville

Accommodation: Econo Lodge, 1390 Piney Forest Rd., 24540 (tel. 804/797-4322).

Emporia

Accommodations: Days Inn, I–95 and U.S. 58, Exit 58 W., P.O. Box 1036, 23847 (tel. 804/634-9481).
- Hampton Inn, I–95 and U.S. Hwy. 58 West, Exit 3B, 23847 (tel. 804/634-9200).
- Quality Inn, I–95 and U.S. 301, Exit 2, P.O. Box 787, 23847 (tel. 804/634-4181).

• Quality Inn, I–95 and U.S. 301, Exit 6, Rte. 2, Box 226, 23847 (tel. 804/535-8535).

Farmville

Accommodation: Super 8 Motel, Hwy. 15 South, 23901 (tel. 804/392-8196).

Fredericksburg

Accommodations: Econo Lodge, I–95 and Rte. 3, P.O. Box 36, 22404 (tel. 703/786-8374).
• Econo Lodge, 5321 Jefferson Davis Hwy., 22401 (tel. 703/898-5440).
• Scottish Inn, P.O. Box 3645, College Station, 22401 (tel. 703/898-1000).
• Days Inn, Falmouth & Warrenton Exit, I–95 and U.S. 17 North, Rte. 12, Box 36, 22401 (tel. 703/373-5340).
• Hampton Inn, 2310 Plank Rd., I–95 and Rte. 3 East (tel. 703/371-0330).

Front Royal

Accommodation: Friendship Skyline Motel, 622 South Royal, 22630 (tel. 703/636-6739).

Gloucester Point

Accommodation: Friendship Gloucester Point Inn, Rte. 17 at York River Bridge, 23061 (tel. 804/642-3337).

Hampton

Accommodations: Red Roof Inn, 1925 Coliseum Dr., 23666 (tel. 804/838-1870).
• Econo Lodge, 1781 North King St., 23669 (tel. 804/723-0741).
• Econo Lodge, 2708 Mercury Blvd., 23666 (tel. 804/821-8976).
• Hampton Inn, 1813 West Mercury Blvd., 23666 (tel. 804/838-8484).

Harrisonburg

Accommodations: Econo Lodge, Rte. 33 and I–81, P.O. Box 1311, 22801 (tel. 703/433-2576).
• Eastern Mennonite College Residence Hall, College Ave., 22801 (tel. 703/433-2771, ext. 135). Open May 1 to August 17. $10 single; $16 double. Weekly rate: $70 single; $56 double. Advance reservations of two days necessary.
• Knights Inn, I–81 at U.S. 33, 10 Linda Lane, 22801 (tel. 703/433-6939).
• Red Carpet Inn, Rte. 11 South, P.O. Box 631, 22801 (tel. 703/434-6704).
• Super 8 Motel, I–81, Exit 62 (tel. toll free 800/843-1991).

Lexington

"This is a rural area, most of the people are farming or working in factories. There is a strong work ethic—Scottish-Irish Presbyterian roots; people don't relate too well to folks who don't settle down to work, raise crops and kids."

Accommodations: Econo Lodge, I-64 and U.S. 11, 24450 (tel. 703/463-7371).
● Days Inn, I-81 and U.S. 11, Exit 53, P.O. Box 1329, 24450 (tel. 703/463-9131).
● Super 8 Motel, Rte. 7, Box 99, 24450 (tel. toll free 800/843-1991).

Luray

Camping: Shenandoah National Park, Rte. 4, Box 292, 22835 (tel. 703/999-2229). There are four major campgrounds with a total of over 600 sites, plus backcountry camping. $9 per night at Big Meadows; $7 per night all other campground. Big Meadows open March to December; others open from April or May to October. You can make reservations through Ticketron for Big Meadows. Luray Caverns are nearby.

Lynchburg

Accommodations: YWCA, 626 Church St., 24504 (tel. 804/847-7751). Women only. $8.50 per person per night. Advance reservations suggested.
● Econo Lodge, 2400 Stadium Rd., 24501 (tel. 804/847-1045).

Martinsville

Accommodation: Econo Lodge, 800 South Virginia Ave., 24078 (tel. 703/647-3941).

Newport News

Accommodations: Econo Lodge, 11845 Jefferson Ave., 23606 (tel. 804/599-3237).
● Days Inn, 14747 Warwick Blvd., 23602 (tel. 804/874-0201).
● Friendship Fort Eustis, 16923 Warwick Blvd., 23606 (tel. 804/887-9122).
● Knights Inn, I-64 at U.S. 17, 797 J. Clyde-Morris Blvd., 23601 (tel. 804/595-6336).

Norfolk

Tourist Information: Norfolk Convention and Visitors Bureau, 236 E. Plume St., 23510 (tel. 804/441-5266).
Help: Family Service/Travelers Aid, Inc., 222 19th St. West, 23517 (tel. 804/622-7017).

Accommodations: YMCA, 312 West Bute St., 23510 (tel. 804/622-6328). Men and women. $19 to $21 single; $38 to $42 double. Fitness center available.
- Econo Lodge, 5819 Northhampton Blvd., Virginia Beach, 23452 (tel. 804/464-9306).
- Hampton Inn, 1450 N. Military Hwy., 23502 (tel. 804/466-7474).

Petersburg

Accommodations: Econo Lodge, 25 South Crater Rd., 23803 (tel. 804/861-4680).
- Econo Lodge, 16905 Parkdale Rd., 23805 (tel. 804/862-2717).
- Days Inn, 2310 Indian Hill Rd., Colonial Heights, 23834 (tel. 804/520-1010).

Pulaski

Accommodation: Red Carpet Inn, I–81, Exit 31, P.O. Box 1266, 24301 (tel. 703/980-2230).

Richmond

"A beautiful city representing four centuries of legend, history, and tradition."

Accommodations: Massad's House Hotel, ∨ ★, 11 North 4th St., 23219 (tel. 804/648-2893). Near bus station. $29 single; $36 double; $38 triple; $45 quad.
- Days Inn, 5500 Williamsburg Rd., Sandston, 23150 (tel. 804/222-2041).
- Econo Lodge, 5408 Williamsburg Rd., Sandston, 23150 (tel. 804/222-1020).
- Econo Lodge, 6523 Midlothian Turnpike, 23225 (tel. 804/276-8241).
- Econo Lodge, 2125 Willis Rd., 23237 (tel. 804/271-6031).
- Econo Lodge, 1501 Robin Hood Rd., 23220 (tel. 804/359-4011).
- Red Roof Inn, 4350 Commerce Rd., 23234 (tel. 804/271-7240).
- Red Roof Inn, 100 Grashamwood Place, Chippenham Parkway and Midlothian Turnpike, 23225 (tel. 804/745-0600).
- Motel 6, 5704 Williamsburg Rd., 23150 (tel. 804/222-7600).

Roanoke

Accommodations: TRUST, 404 Elm Ave. SW, 24016, about 1 mile from I-581 (tel. 703/344-1978). Provides emergency overnight housing and facilities for 24 hours. Men and women. No charge for services. Cooking facilities available. The people at TRUST invite you to stop by for information on Roanoke.
- Days Inn, I–581 and U.S. 460, P.O. Box 12325, 535 Orange Ave., 24024 (tel. 703/342-4551).
- Econo Lodge, 6621 Thirlane Rd. NW, 24019 (tel. 703/563-0853).
- Econo Lodge, 3816 Franklin Rd. SW, 24014 (tel. 703/774-1621).
- Econo Lodge, 308 Orange Ave. NW, 24016 (tel. 703/343-2413).

Salem

Accommodation: Econo Lodge, 1535 East Main St., 24153 (tel. 703/986-1000).

Skippers

Accommodation: Econo Lodge, I-95 and Hwy. 629, Exit 1, 23879 (tel. 804/634-6124).

South Hill

Accommodations: Econo Lodge, 623 East Atlantic St., 23970 (tel. 804/447-7116).
● Super 8 Motel, 922 E. Atlantic St., 23970 (tel. 804/447-7655).

Staunton

Accommodations: Econo Lodge, 1031 Richmond Rd., 24401 (tel. 703/885-5158).
● Days Inn, I-81 and Va. 654, Exit 55A, P.O. Box 2307, 24401 (tel. 703/337-3031).
● Master Host Inn, P.O. Box 149, 24401 (tel. 703/248-0888).
● Red Carpet Inn, U.S. 11 North, P.O. Box 1018, 24401 (tel. 703/248-1201).
● Augusta Motel, Rte. 1, Box 23, 24467 (tel. 703/248-8040). $22 to $25 single; $24 to $29 double; $3 for each additional person.
● Frederick House, 18 East Frederick St., 24401 (tel. 703/885-4220). $30 to $45 single; $30 to $50 double; $50 to $60 triple; $60 to $70 quad. Three historic houses located in historic downtown.

Suffolk

Accommodation: Econo Lodge, 1017 North Main St., 23434 (tel. 804/539-3451).

Triangle

Camping: Prince William Forest Park, 619 West, ¼ mile from I-95, P.O. Box 209, 22172 (tel. 703/221-7181). Group and individuals tent camping and trailers year round. Backcountry permit camping available mid-May to late September. $5 per family campsite per night; $10 per group campsite per night.

Urbanna

Accommodation: Sangraal-by-the-Sea (AYH-SA), Ⓢ √ ★ ⓑ, P.O. Box 187, 23175 (tel. 804/776-6500). Call the hostel for a pickup from bus or train station in Williamsburg or Saluda (call ahead). $8 for AYH members. Nonmembers: $15.50 single; $12.25 per person double; $10.50 per person triple or quad. Meals provided at extra cost. "Sangraal is a Swiss-style chateau lodge on the waterfront with canoeing, sailing, and hiking trails, and is near the historical areas of Williamsburg and Yorktown."

Verona

Accommodation: Scottish Inn, I–81, Exit 59, P.O. Box 586, 24482 (tel. 703/248-8981).

Virginia Beach

Accommodations: Red Roof Inn, 196 Ballard Ct., 23462 (tel. 804/490-0225).
● Budget Host—The Boardwalk Inn, 2604 Atlantic Ave., 23451 (tel. 804/425-5971).
● Angie's Guest Cottage (AYH-SA), 302 24th St., 23451 (tel. 804/428-4690). Open April to October 15. $10.80 summer, $7.85 winter for AYH members.

Waynesboro

Accommodations: Budget Host—West Lawn Motel, 2240 West Main St., 22980 (tel. 703/942-9551).
● Super 8 Motel, I–64, Exit 17 at U.S. 340, 22980 (tel. toll free 800/843-1991).

Williamsburg

Accommodations: Motel 6, 3030 Richmond Rd., 23185 (tel. 804/565-3433).
● Budget Host—Governor Spottswood Motel, 1508 Richmond Rd., 23185 (tel. 804/229-6444).

Winchester

Accommodations: Econo Lodge, 1507 Martinsburg Pike, 22601 (tel. 703/662-4700).
● Hampton Inn, 643 Milwood Ave., 22601 (tel. 703/667-8011).

Wytheville

Accommodations: Comfort Inn, Holston Road, P.O. Box 567, 24382 (tel. 703/228-4488).
● Econo Lodge, 1190 East Main St., 24382 (tel. 703/228-5517).
● Knights Inn, I–77/81 at U.S. 11, 2020 E. Main St., 24382 (tel. 703/228-7988).

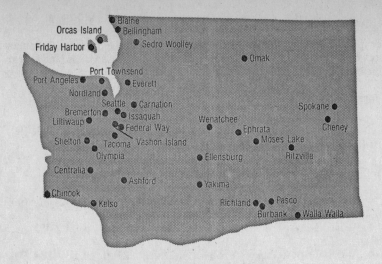

Washington

Let's start with the Olympic Peninsula, with its 8000-foot mountains, undying glaciers, and hot springs. Much of the peninsula is mesmerizing and powerful. The Olympic National Park is the principal sight and the world's only nontropical rain forest, in the Hoh River Valley. This is great country for *experienced* hikers and backpackers, but mountain treks should be done in groups with someone who knows the terrain and how to survive when lost.

The ocean beach at Kalaloch is part of the national park and has highway access; there is a lodge on the beach. To get around the peninsula by road on Hwy. 101 takes a full day at top speeds without stopping. To see anything and to enjoy the country requires a minimum of three days. For those going on to Canada, there is a ferry service several times daily from Port Angeles to Victoria, British Columbia. The peninsula is sometimes rainy, but towering, lush evergreens and carpet-like moss, broken only by glittering creeks and streams, engulf this hauntingly beautiful area. There's a summer arts and music festival in Port Townsend.

Southwest Washington is bordered by the Cascade Range on the east, the Pacific on the west, the Columbia River on the south, and the Olympic Peninsula on the north. The awesome force of nature can extract a terrible price and that's clear at Mount St. Helens, where you can still see the deep scars inflicted by the May 18, 1980 eruption. This region is the gateway to the Columbia Gorge National Scenic Area. The main shipping channel of this mighty river runs very near the river's banks along S.R. 4, which leads to the Long Beach Peninsula. A bridge from Puget Island leads to Cathlamet, a picturesque Scandinavian community with freshly whitewashed barns and herds of dairy cows. Farther west on S.R. 4 is Skamokawa, once called "Little Venice" because it was built around the many tributaries of Skamokawa Creek. The first oyster-harvesting community, settled in 1854, appropriately named Oysterville, is now a national historic district. Vancouver, the oldest continuous community in Washington, is now the state's sixth-largest city, boasting an active port.

The Puget Sound area extends from the Canadian border south to the state capital at Olympia along an inland sea over 100 miles in length and dotted with wooded islands and peninsulas, many of which are reachable via an extensive state ferry system. The sound is noted for its delicious salmon, oysters, clams, mussels, octopus, and other marine life. Although this area contains the bulk of the population of the state of Washington, one is never far from mountain and coastal scenery.

Bellingham, the state's seventh-largest city, is on a harbor with waterfront restaurants, fishing charters, and 1500 acres of developed park. Everett is home to the much-visited Boeing Tour Center, housed in the largest building by volume in the world. At Lynden, the Pioneer Museum displays antique farm equipment and chronicles local history. In Darrington, enjoy monthly bluegrass jam sessions, highlighted each year by a bluegrass festival, an event popular with locals in this region. "The Puyallup" is the largest fair in the Pacific Northwest, and the Tacoma Dome is the world's largest wood dome. Old-timers say Puyallup means "friendly people", and it sure fits. This lush valley in the shadow of Mount Rainier bursts into bloom each spring, and the annual Daffodil Parade makes its way through Tacoma, Puyallup, Sumner, and Orting.

Tacoma is undergoing a cultural renaissance. It is the state's third-largest city and is in the midst of a bold architectural and cultural rebirth. Stroll among Impressionist paintings and the Early American Collection at the Tacoma Art Museum. Wander through five floors of pioneer artifacts, Indian history, and nautical lore at the Washington State Historical Museum. Or examine exotic plants at the Seymour Conservatory, a historical conservatory in the Victorian style. Tacoma is one of the largest natural deep-water ports in the world. Walk or bike along the park-like waterfront as ships glide in from Dakar, Monrovia, Yokohama, Piraeus, and other points between.

Olympia is democracy in action. Just off Interstate 5 in Olympia, you'll see the neo-classical dome of Washington's Capitol Building. At 287 feet, it is the fifth-highest all-masonry-domed building in the world. While you're in the Olympia area, set aside some time to see the Crosby House, the Henderson House, the State Library, and the State Capital Museum in the Clarence J. Lord Mansion, with its exhibit of the Mount St. Helens' eruption, and displays on Northwest Native American culture and history.

Seattle and King County offer the vacationer almost everything—urban sophistication, cultural diversity, outdoor recreation, and some of the most magnificent scenery in the country. Get a bird's-eye view from the 605-foot Space Needle or ride a monorail high above city streets between downtown and the Seattle Center.

Some Special Events: Snofest in Omak (January); Rainier Snowbust at Snoqualmie (February); Whale Watching at Westport (March); Skagit Valley Tulip Festival in Mount Vernon, Anacortes, LaConner, Burlington, and Sedro Woolley (April); Lilac Week in Woodland (May); Salty Sea Days in Everett (June); Seafair in Seattle (July); International Kite Festival at Long Beach (August); Ellensburg Rodeo in Ellensburg (September); West Coast Oyster Shucking Championship and Washington State Seafood Festival in Shelton (October); Whitman Memorial Observance in Walla Walla (November); and Christmas Lighting Festival in Leavenworth (December).

Tourist Information: Travel Development Division, Department of Trade and Economic Development, 101 General Administration Building, Olympia WA 98504-0613. For a copy of a 172-page travel guide, please call toll free 800/

544-1800. For other information on traveling in Washington State, please call 206/586-2088 or 586-2102.

N.B. Two bed-and-breakfast reservation services for Washington are B&B Service (BABS), P.O. Box 5025, Bellingham, WA 98227 (tel. 206/733-8642); and RSVP Bed & Breakfast Reservations, P.O. Box 778, Ferndale, WA 98248 (tel. 206/384-6586).

Ashford

Accommodation: The Lodge Youth Hostel (AYH), P.O. Box 86, 38608 SR 706 East, 98304 (tel. 206/569-2312). $7 summer, $8 winter for AYH members.

Bellingham

"Bellingham is a fine town and has a lot of alternative-lifestyle people living in it. The south side of town is a traveler's dream, with restored buildings, easy-living people, and lots of color. People here are always helping each other and keeping up on the most recent information concerning politics, energy use, pollution, etc. There are a few places that house people for free, but the problem is that these houses are privately owned and do not advertise as places of refuge. Most people just stumble across them. If you come to Bellingham, walk our coastline. Although we haven't escaped pollution, there are some very fine places along the shore. Just follow the railroad tracks south of town."

Accommodations: Motel 6, 3701 Byron Ave., 98225 (tel. 206/671-4494).
● TraveLodge, 202 East Holly St., 98225 (tel. 206/734-1900).

Blaine

Accommodation: Birch Bay Hostel (AYH), former Blaine Air Force Base, Alderson Road, 98230 (tel. 206/371-2180). $5 for AYH members. Open May to October 15. By reservation only: October 16 to April 30.

Bremerton

Accommodation: Super 8 Motel, 5068 Kitsap Way, 98310 (tel. 206/377-8881).

Burbank

Accommodation: Burbank Home Hostel (AYH), 509 Maple St., Box 01, 99323 (tel. 509/547-3420). $9.95 for AYH members. Includes breakfast. Advance reservations necessary.

Carnation

Accommodation: Carnation Hostel (AYH), 6602 Tolt Rd. NE, 98014 (tel. 206/333-6175 or 333-4456). $4 for AYH members. The hostel is a 100-year old log cabin located on a 20-acre farm. "There are gardens, farm animals, and the Tolt River."

Centralia

Accommodation: Motel 6, 1310 Belmont Ave., 98531 (tel. 206/330-2057).

Cheney

Help: Rap-In, Eastern Washington University, 509/359-7979. Closed during university vacations. Open 6 p.m. to 10 p.m. every day.

Accommodation: Eastern Washington University Dormitories, Ⓢ★, Louise Anderson Hall, 99004 (tel. 509/359-7022). Open year round but space is limited during fall, winter, and spring. $11.40 single, $9.40 per person, double. Student rate: $7 per person, double.

Chinook

Accommodation: Fort Columbia Hostel (AYH), Fort Columbia State Park, P.O. Box 224, 98614 (tel. 206/777-8755). Open June to November 1 (5 p.m. to 9 p.m.) $5 for AYH members.

Ellensburg

Accommodation: Super 8 Motel, 1500 Canyon Rd., 98926 (tel. 509/962-6888).

Ephrata

Accommodation: TraveLodge, 31 South Basin St. SW, 98823 (tel. 509/754-4651).

Everett

Accommodations: Allstar Inn, 224 128th St. SW, 98204 (tel. 206/353-8120).
● Motel 6, 10006 Evergreen Way, 98204 (tel. 206/347-2060).

Federal Way

Accommodation: Super 8 Motel, 1688 S. 348th St., 98063 (tel. 206/838-8808).

Friday Harbor

Accommodation: Elite Hotel (AYH-SA), P.O. Box 1551, 98250 (tel. 206/378-5555). Friday Harbor is on San Juan Island, and the Elite is 1½ blocks from the ferry landing. $7.50 for AYH members in dorms; $25 for a single or double.

Bring a sleeping bag, or linens available at extra cost. The hotel has a cafe, sauna, and hot tubs. Advance reservations of three weeks necessary in summer.

Issaquah

Accommodation: Motel 6, 1885 15th Pl. NW, 98027 (tel. 206/392-8405).

Kelso

Accommodation: Motel 6, 106 Minor Rd., 98626 (tel. 206/425-3229).

Lilliwaup

Accommodation: Mike's Beach Resort, Rte. 1, Box 95, 98555 (tel. 206/877-5324). Located on Hood Canal. Open May 15 to October 1. $3.75 for AYH members; nonmembers pay higher rates.

Moses Lake

Accommodations: Motel 6, 2822 Wapato Dr., 98837 (tel. 509/766-0250).
- Imperial 400 Motor Inn, 905 West Broadway, 98837 (tel. 509/767-8626).
- Super 8 Motel, 449 Melva Lane, 98837 (tel. 509/765-8886).
- TraveLodge, 316 South Pioneer Way, 98837 (tel. 509/765-8631).

Nordland

Accommodation: Fort Flagler State Park Hostel (AYH), 98358 (tel. 206/385-1288). Men, women, and children. $4.50 for AYH members; $6.50 for nonmembers. In winter advance reservations of one week necessary.

Olympia

Accommodations: Motel 6, 400 West Lee St., Tumwater, 98501 (tel. 206/754-7320).
- Super 8 Motel, 4615 Martin Way, Lacey, 98503 (tel. 206/459-8888).

Omak

Accommodation: TraveLodge, 121 North Main St., 98841 (tel 509/826-0400).

Orcas Island

Accommodation: Doe Bay Village (AYH-SA), Star Route, Box 86, Olga,

98279 (tel. 206/376-2291 or 376-4755). $9.50 for AYH members. Advance reservations necessary July 2 to September 8.

Pasco

Accommodation: Motel 6, 1520 North Oregon St., 99301 (tel. 509/546-2010).

Port Angeles

Accommodations: Budget Host—Aircrest Motel, 1006 E. Front St., 98362 (tel. 206/452-9255).
- Super 8 Motel, 2104 E. 1st St., 98362 (tel. 206/452-8401).

Port Townsend

Accommodation: Fort Worden Youth Hostel (AYH), 98368 (tel. 206/385-0655). Open year round, except December 15 to January 3 and Thanksgiving Day. $5 for AYH members; $7 for nonmembers. Buy food on Water Street before coming to hostel.

"Hostels like the one in Port Townsend were fantastic—that place is a home away from home."

Richland

Accommodation: Imperial 400 Motor Inn, 515 George Washington Way, 99352 (tel. 509/946-6117).

Ritzville

Accommodation: Comfort Inn, 1405 Smitty's Blvd., 99169 (tel. 509/659-1007).

Seattle

Built on seven hills (remind you of another famous city?) between the Olympic and Cascade Mountain ranges, and right alongside the shores of Puget Sound and several freshwater lakes, Seattle is an appealing town. From the Observation Deck of the Space Needle, in Seattle Center (the park that was the site of the 1962 World's Fair), you can get a good look at it all: downtown, the Pike Place Market, the Waterfront, Pioneer Square, Fisherman's Terminal, Woodland Park and Zoo, Capitol Hill, Seattle University, the University of Washington, and 14,000-foot-high Mount Rainier.

Anyone who's going to spend more than just a day or two in the "Emerald City" should probably take a look at some of these guidebooks:

Seattle Best Places, edited by David Brewster, Sasquatch Books, Seattle ($8.95); *The Poor Man's Gourmet Guide to Seattle Restaurants,* by Bob Chieges and David Tatelman, Homestead Book Company, Seattle, 1986 ($2.95); *Seattle Rainy Day Guide,* by Clifford Burke, Solstice Press, Chronicle Books, San Francisco ($6.95); *Seattle, Past to Present,* by Roger Sale, University of Washington Press, Seattle ($9.95); *Footsore: Walks and Hikes Around Puget Sound,* by Harvey Manning, Mountaineers Press, Seattle (four volumes at $9.95 each); *Seattle Eats,* by Carol Brown, Sasquatch Books, 1985 ($6.95); and *The Seattle Guidebook,* by Archie Satterfield, Pacific Search Press, Seattle, 1986 ($9.95).

To find out what's happening, check any of the following newspapers: *The Weekly, The Rocket* (for music news), the *Seattle Times,* the *Post Intelligencer Daily,* and/or the *Clinton Street Quarterly.* At the University of Washington, there's an information center at 4014 University Way NE (tel. 206/543-9198).

Getting There: The airport, Sea-Tac International (the Tac is for neighboring Tacoma), is about 15 miles from downtown Seattle. By taxi, the trip costs $25. For a more reasonable price, try the Greyline Downtown Airporter bus, which costs $5 one way or $9 round trip to and from the main hotels downtown (tel. 206/624-5077). For those going north out of town, the Everett Airporter (a van, not a bus), which costs $7 one way or $12 round trip (tel. 206/743-3344), will take you to the University Plaza Hotel which is just off I-5 located about 6 blocks directly west of the University of Washington. For the same price they will continue on to "Northgate" (one of Seattle's main shopping malls), and let you off at the Ramada Inn, or you can go as far north as Everett for $11. The biggest bargain of all is the Metro bus 174 that costs $1.

● The Greyhound bus station is at 8th and 811 Stewart Streets (tel. 206/624-3456). The Trailways bus terminal is at 6th and Westlake (tel. 206/624-5955). The train station is at 3rd and Jackson Streets. All are served by Metro bus. There are Metro information booths at each station, where you can pick up maps and bus schedules and directions to where you're heading.

Getting Around: To get into a taxi costs about $1 and it's $1 for every mile you ride, although fares vary. You can flag a taxi but that's tricky; it's best to call ahead one of the following: Farwest (tel. 206/622-1717); Yellow Cab, the cheapest (tel. 206/622-6500); or Grey Top (tel. 206/622-4949).

● To rent a car in Seattle you can, of course, seek out the standard brands—Avis, Hertz, etc.—but for something less expensive, try Yesterday's Rent a Car (tel. 206/789-5305), in Ballard, where it costs $13.95 for a big, damaged Chevy Impala or $2 more for something in somewhat better shape.

● The monorail links downtown Seattle and Seattle Center; a ride costs 35¢. The buses run often and cost 65¢ for a one-zone ride and $1 for one that covers two zones (55¢ and 85¢ off-peak and on weekends). Zone 1 covers the entire city; Zone 2, the periphery and surrounding King County. For bus information, call 206/447-4800. If you have a bike and you want to take it on the bus with you, call the Bicycle Hot Line at 206/522-BIKE, and find out how. Another rather unique feature of Seattle Metro Transit, called Magic Carpet, lets you ride for free in the downtown core area. The driver will explain how far you can travel without paying a fare. This certainly simplifies visits to the Pioneer Square and Pike Place Market areas, theaters, movies, shopping, and sports events at the Kingdome.

Tourist Information: For maps and answers to tourist questions of any kind, stop at the Convention and Visitors Bureau at 666 Stewart St. (open Monday to Friday, 8:30 a.m. to 5 p.m.) or at Sea-Tac International Airport, carousel 10, baggage claim area, open daily 9:30 a.m. to 7:30 p.m. (tel. 296/433-5218).

Help: Travelers Aid, 909 Fourth Ave., 98104 (tel. 206/447-3888). Hours: 8:30 a.m. to 9 p.m. Monday through Friday, 10 a.m. to 1 p.m. Saturday.

● Crisis Clinic (for emotional crises), 1530 Eastlake Ave. East (tel. 206/447-3222). Information and referrals. Hours: 9 a.m. to 5 p.m. Monday to Friday.

Accommodations: Occasionally there's space in the University of Washington dormitories; for groups only, call 206/543-7636.

● YMCA, Downtown Branch, 909 Fourth Ave., 98104 (tel. 206/382-5000). $10.24 for AYH members. Sleeping bag required.

● YWCA, 1118 Fifth Ave., 98101 (tel. 206/447-4888). Women only. $21 to $26 single; $32 to $38 double; $6 per night for additional cots. Exercise equipment, and a pool in the building; a deli and coffeeshop for postexercise hunger. Advance reservations of two weeks suggested.

● College Inn Guest House, 4000 University Way NE, 98105 (tel. 206/633-4441). A restored old inn with rooms without bath, as they were in the 1900s, but with period furnishings. Young and friendly management. College Inn Cafe and Pub downstairs are both student handouts with moderately priced food and drink. $32 to $35 single; $38 to $45 double; $49 triple. Price includes a continental breakfast.

● Allstar Inn, 16500 Pacific Hwy. South, at Sea-Tac Airport, 98188 (tel. 206/246-4101).

● Commodore Hotel, 2013 2nd Ave., 98121 (tel. 206/448-8868). $19 to $25 single; $24 to $29 double; $8 per night dorm room.

● Imperial 400 Motor Inn, 17108 Pacific Hwy. South, 98188 (tel. 206/244-1230).

● Vance Downtown Hotel, 620 Stewart St., 98101 (tel. toll free 800/426-0670). $38 single; $44 double; $60 quad. Children under 18 stay free.

● Kennedy Hotel, 1100 5th Ave., 98101 (tel. 206/623-6175). In the downtown area. $34.95 single; $36.95 twin; $38 double; $5 for each extra person.

● Pacific Hotel, Fourth and Marion Streets (tel. 206/622-3985). $26 single ($17 without bath); $28 double ($23 without bath). Children under 12 stay free.

Where to Eat: Pike Place Market has a number of eateries, ranging from what many people consider Seattle's best restaurant—Labuznik, 1924 First Ave. (tel. 206/441-8899), with Central European food that's expensive—to ethnic places serving moderately priced French food—Le Bistro, 93A Pike St. (tel. 206/682-3049); inexpensive Greek food—Athenian Inn, Pike Pl. (tel. 206/624-7166); and not very expensive Bolivian food, Copacabana, Pike Pl. (tel. 206/622-6359). We've been told that the saltenas, deep-fried meat pastries, are especially good in this small but cozy restaurant, and one friend urges that you "try the shrimp soup."

● Julia's 14 Carrot Cafe, 2305 Eastlake Ave. East (tel. 206/324-1442). Open 7 a.m. to 2 p.m. Monday; 7 a.m. to 10 p.m. Tuesday to Saturday; 8 a.m. to 3 p.m. Sunday. Great breakfasts, $3 to $6; dinner $6 to $9. Casual atmosphere and renowned for vegetarian specialties.

● Tlaquepaque Bar/Restaurant, 1122 Post Ave., 98101 (tel. 206/467-8226). Open 11:30 a.m. to 10:30 p.m. Monday to Thursday; 11:30 a.m. to 11:30 p.m. Friday and Saturday; 3 p.m. to 10 p.m. Sunday. Mexican food, $5 to $10. A fun and busy atmosphere.

● Ivar's Salmon House, 401 N.E. Northlake Way, in the university district (tel. 206/632-0767). You can get a classic meal of alder-smoked salmon, Indian style, with cole slaw and cornbread for $5.25 at lunch; expect to pay approximately $8 to $9 for dinner. There is also a takeout stand on Northlake Way near the restaurant entrance, and you can take your salmon ($4.25), or fish and chips ($2.09), down to the floating pier in front of the restaurant.

● Last Exit on Brooklyn, 3930 Brooklyn Ave. NE (tel. 206/545-9873). Good coffee, sandwiches, chess, and conversation.

● Woerne's European Cafe, 4108 University Way NE (tel. 206/632-7893). German food and pastries.

● Sunlight Cafe, 6403 Roosevelt Way NE (tel. 206/522-9060). University district. Vegetarian dinners, weekend brunches, and an expresso bar in the morning. Soup, salad, and an entree for only $5.95. "This is a good place in the morning—people travel from all over for sesame waffles with all kinds of toppings, fresh orange juice, and good coffee with free refills. Laid-back and very friendly."

● Rama House, 2228 Second Ave. (tel. 206/624-2931). Thai food downtown. Inexpensive and excellent quality. Like things hot? Try the items on the menu with the four stars-wow!

● Market Cafe, 1523 1st Ave. (tel. 206/624-2598). Near Pike Place Market, on the waterfront. Simple food that's filling. The best blueberry pancakes around. It's a crowded, cheerful kind of place where the clientele ranges from local business types to the down and out.

● Taqueria Mexico, 4226 University Way, NE (tel. 206/633-5256). Inexpensive, authentic Mexican food in the university district. The tortillas are made right on the spot.

● Across the Street Cafe, 3423 Fremont North (tel. 206/632-2119). American-style food, three-egg omelettes, hash browns, and homemade muffin and coffee for $3.95. A homey, neighborhood favorite with the best cinnamon rolls in town.

● Musashi's, 1400 North 45th (tel. 206/633-0212). A neighborhood secret with a devoted following. Only eight tables and what one friend considers "the best sushi in town."

What to See and Do: You'll have to visit the Seattle Center, four blocks from Pier 70, the site of the 1962 World's Fair, which has been transformed into a park that offers performing arts, museums, the Pacific Science Center, shops, an amusement park, and the Space Needle.

● Hotlines include: "What's Going On . . ." Phone Line, 206/547-9890. For lists music and comedy events; Arts Hotline, 206/447-ARTS; Jazz Hotline, 206/624-5277.

● The months of July and August are full of events dealing with "Sea Fair." The main celebration centers around the Hydroplane races on lake Washington and the Torchlight Parade. Other Seattle events include Bumbershoot at the Seattle Center (September), Seattle Marathon (March), University District Street Fair (May), and Folklife Festival (May).

● The waterfront along Alaskan Way is another must-see. Here you'll find shops, restaurants, harbor tours, an aquarium, and a fine park.

● Pioneer Square, two blocks from the waterfront, Seattle's birthplace, has been restored to the splendor of 1889, the year that the Seattle fire struck. Leaded windows, wrought iron, restored brick and stone storefronts, and two cobblestone plazas are all wonderful reminders of Seattle's Klondike Gold Rush

Days. After the fire of 1889, the streets of Pioneer Square were raised. The original sidewalk level remained beneath, leaving shopfronts in large caverns that were forgotten over the years. Now it's possible to take an underground tour of the area. Call 206/682-4646 for information.

- Ballard Locks. Take bus 17 on 4th or bus 43 from downtown. Watch everyone indulge in Seattle's favorite pastime—boating. Locks open and close and water levels rise and fall. Quite a parade of yachts line up, but better even than watching boats is watching the migrating salmon as they leap up the fish ladders on their long trip home. There are underwater observation points as well as above-water viewing. Different species travel in different seasons, so your chances of seeing salmon when you're there are pretty good.

- Discovery Park. Take bus 33 from 4th and Union for nature walks and splendid views of Puget Sound.

- Seattle Art Museum, in Volunteer Park (tel. 206/625-8900). In a beautiful setting overlooking Puget Sound. Special exhibits and permanent collection. Bus 10 on Pike. Admission: $2 adults; $1 senior citizens and students; under 6 free. Open Tuesday to Friday, 10 a.m. to 5 p.m.; Thursday, 10 a.m. to 9 p.m.; free Saturday, 10 a.m. to 5 p.m., and Sunday, noon to 5 p.m.

At Night: For theater: If you like theater, Seattle is a goldmine of small and large companies that often perform material which has never, or not yet been to Broadway. Try particularly the Seattle Rep (tel. 206/443-2210); A.C.T., the Intiman Theater (tel. 206/624-2992); the Empty Space (tel. 206/587-3737); the Bathhouse Theater (tel. 206/524-9108); and the many small theaters around Pioneer Square. Many of these theaters offer student discounts or reduced-price last-minute tickets.

- For classical music: The Seattle Symphony performs at the Opera House in Seattle Center (tel. 206/443-4740). There are also many chamber music, vocal recitals, and University of Washington musical events all through the year. Check the newspapers.

- For rock music: People who like rhythm and blues and rock congregate at the Central Tavern and Cafe, 207 1st St. South near Pioneer Square (tel. 206/622-0209). The crowd stands around the bar or sits, but either way they obviously enjoy themselves.

- For jazz: Jazz Alley, 2033 6th and Lenora (tel. 206/441-9729); Old Timers Cafe, 620 1st (tel. 206/623-9800). Small and casual.

- For dance: There is lots of dance in Seattle, both from touring companies and resident troupes. The Pacific Northwest Ballet (tel. 206/447-4655) is functioning as of this writing. Check newspapers for current dance events.

- Be sure to check the University of Washington *Daily* for university events: concerts, plays, film series, lectures, visiting celebrities, etc., and refer to our arts hotline in our Seattle introduction.

- For dancing: Pier 70 Restaurant and Chowder House at Alaskan Way and Broad (tel. 206/728-7071). There's a big terrace dance floor right on the waterfront, which attracts a large singles crowd because of its live music and the chance to dance. Expect a cover charge.

- Tug's Belltown Tavern, 2207 1st Ave. (tel. 206/623-2813). No cover before 11 p.m., $1.50 to $2.50 after that. Funky danceteria with new wave, rock, reggae, and beyond. For serious dancing.

- Doc Maynards, 610 1st Ave. (tel. 206/682-4649). A younger crowd—very casual. Open for breakfast and lunch. Dancing from 8 p.m. to 2 a.m.

● Murphy's, 2110 N. 45th St. (tel. 206/634-2110). A neighborhood favorite Irish pub complete with dart board. Traditional Irish music every night and lots of varieties of beer.

● To hear folk music: Kells, 1916 Post Alley (tel. 206/682-1397). Irish atmosphere, good food; The Backstage, 2208 N.W. Market St. (tel. 206/789-6953). Located in the Scandinavian part of town. Type of music varies. Evening performances $5 to $10.

● For films: Seattle is a great movie town—maybe because of the notoriously wet weather. There are many wonderful renovated theaters with a wide selection of mainstream to avant-garde films. The city has its own international film festival every May where many foreign films debut. Two theaters are The Varsity in the University district, 4329 University Way, NE (tel. 206/632-3131), and the Neptune, 1303 N.E. 45th St. (tel. 206/633-5545), located near the University of Washington. Take any bus (the 71, 72, or 73) on 3rd Avenue to the University area.

Shopping: Pike Place Market, 1st and Pike, downtown. A series of roofed-over and open-air stalls where truck farmers and hawkers sell their wares—produce, flowers, antiques, crafts, art, etc. Open Monday to Saturday, 9 a.m. to 6 p.m.

● People in the Northwest love the out-of-doors. They hike, they ski, and they climb mountains with a vengeance. If you'd like to do the same, you might want to stop at Recreational Equipment, Inc., 1525 11th Ave. (tel. 206/323-8333), to take a look at the tents, packs, boots, etc. If you don't want to buy, you can rent here instead.

● University Book Store, 4326 University Way NE (tel. 206/634-3400). Over 60,000 books to choose from.

● The Elliott Bay Book Company, 1st South and South Main in Pioneer Square (tel. 206/624-6600). Lots more books.

● Shorey's, 110 Union and 119 South Jackson (tel. 206/624-0221). Books in Pioneer Square.

● Peaches, 811 N.E. 45th St. (tel. 206/633-2990). All kinds of records in the university district.

● Wide World of Music, 215 Pike. Records downtown.

● Northwest Native, 815 East Thomas (tel. 206/322-0090). A good place for one-of-a-kind souvenir T-shirts.

Sedro Woolley

Camping: North Cascades National Park, 98284 (tel. 206/856-5700). Hike-in campgrounds open from May to October 15. No vehicle access. Free permit required.

● Ross Lake National Recreation Area, c/o North Cascades National Park, 98284. Five campgrounds accessible by car; one closed Labor Day to June, one closed November to May, one closed November to April, two open all year (snow may limit access). Twenty campgrounds are accessible by boat only or by boat and trail and are open June to November. Colonial Creek and Newhalem Creek Campgrounds $5 per site; Goodell Creek Campground $3 per site; all others no charge.

● Lake Chelan National Recreation Area, c/o North Cascades National

Park, 98284. Forty-six campgrounds are accessible by boat and trail. Boat launching at Chelan. Open April to November. No fee.

Shelton

Accommodation: Super 8 Motel, 6 Northview Circle, 98584 (tel. 206/426-1654).

Spokane

Tourist Information: Spokane Convention and Visitors Bureau, West 301 Main, 99201 (tel. 509/747-3230).

On Campus: On the Gonzaga University campus, near Crosby Library, you'll find a bulletin board with rides and apartments listed. For food, try the Chef Restaurant, North 1329 Hamilton. Two places to go to meet students are Bulldog, 1300 block on Hamilton, and the Forum, 1400 block on Hamilton.

Accommodations: Motel 6, 1508 South Rustle St., 99204 (tel. 509/459-6120).
- Days Inn, 1919 North Huntchinson Rd., 99212 (tel. 509/926-5399).
- Super 8 Motel, 2020 Argonne, 99212 (tel. 509/928-4888).

Tacoma

Accommodations: Motel 6, 5201 20th St. East, Fife, 98424 (tel. 206/922-1270).
- Allstar Inn, 5817 20th St. East, Fife, 98424 (tel. 206/992-1680).

Vashon Island

Accommodation: Vashon Hostel (AYH), c/o Judy Mulhair, Rte. 5, Box 349, 98070 (tel. 206/463-2592). Open May 1 to October 31. $5 for AYH members; $8 for nonmembers. Advance reservations necessary.

Walla Walla

Accommodation: Imperial 400 Motor Inn, 305 North Second Ave., 99362 (tel. 509/529-4410).

Wenatchee

Accommodation: Imperial 400 Motor Inn, 700 North Wenatchee Ave., 98801 (tel. 509/663-8133).

Yakima

Accommodations: Motel 6, 1104 North 1st St., 98901 (tel. 509/454-0080).
- Imperial 400 Motor Inn, 510 North 1st St., 98901 (tel. 509/457-6155).
- Super 8 Motel, 2605 Rudkin Rd., Union Gap, 98903 (tel. 509/248-8880).

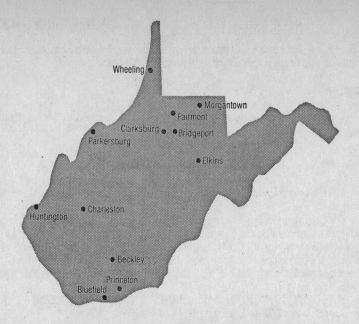

West Virginia

West Virginia has a great deal of natural beauty. The eastern part of the state has the highest mountains, several caverns, and glades. The western part, although more urbanized, has its share of rural scenery. West Virginia has 36 state parks and forests, many with camping facilities.

One of the most popular of the state's tourist attractions is Harpers Ferry National Historic Park, where the Shenandoah and Potomac Rivers meet. In the mid-19th century, this thriving town fell victim to the Civil War. Remains of the arsenal, some restored buildings, and special exhibits are on view in summer.

For outdoors excitement in West Virginia do your research in *Wildwater West Virginia, Volume I: The Northern Streams* and *Volume II: The Southern Streams,* by Paul Davidson et. al. (Menasha Ridge Press, $9.95); *Hiking the Mountain State: The Trails of West Virginia,* by Allen de Hart (Appalachian Mountain Club Press, $12.95); and *Adventure Vacations in the Mid-Atlantic States,* by Carolyn Mulford and Betty C. Ford (EPM Publications, $9.95). For guides with West Virginia accommodations and sights see our "Some Books to Read" section on page 19.

Some Special Events: Jazz Festival in Charleston, and Heritage Days in Parkersburg (April); Antique Steam and Gas Engine Show in Point Pleasant, and Vandalia Gathering in Charleston (May); Mountain Heritage Arts and Crafts Festival in Harpers Ferry, and Regatta Festival in Sutton (June); Mountain State Art and Crafts Fair in Ripley, and Pioneer Days in Marlington (July); Augusta Festival in Elkins, Water Festival in Hinton, and Appalachian Arts and Crafts Festival in Beckley (August); Italian Heritage Festival in Clarksburg, and

Harvest Moon Festival in Parkersburg (September); Mountain State Forest Festival in Elkins (October).

Tourist Information: Travel West Virginia, State Capitol Complex, Charleston, WV 25305 (tel. toll free 800/CALLWVA).

For a list of West Virginia bed-and-breakfast inns, write to the above address.

Beckley

Accommodations: Days Inn, 102 Harper Park Dr., 25801 (tel. 304/255-5291).

● Super 8 Motel, 2014 Harper Rd., 25801 (tel. toll free 800/843-1991).

Bluefield

Accommodation: Econo Lodge, 3400 Cumberland Rd., 24701 (tel. 304/327-8171).

Bridgeport

Accommodation: Econo Lodge, Rte. 2, Box 168, 26330 (tel. 304/842-7381).

Charleston

Accommodations: Red Roof Inn, 6305 MacCorkle Ave., Kanawha City, 25304 (tel. 304/925-6953).

● Red Roof Inn, 4006 MacCorkle Ave. SW, South Charleston, 25309 (tel. 304/744-1500).

● Red Roof Inn, P.O. Box 468, Putnam Village Shopping Center, Hurricane, 25526 (tel. 304/757-6392).

● Knights Inn, I–77 at 6401 MacCorkle Ave. SE, 25304 (tel. 304/925-0451).

● Knights Inn, I-64 at Cross Lanes, 330 Goff Mountain Rd., Cross Lanes, 25313 (tel. 304/776-5911).

Clarksburg

Accommodations: Red Carpet Inn, 112 Tolley Dr., 26301 (tel. 304/842-7371).

● Knights Inn, I-79 at U.S. 50, 1235 W. Main St., Bridgeport, 26330 (tel. 304/842-7115).

Elkins

Accommodation: Econo Lodge, 4533 East, Rte. 1, Box 15, 26241 (tel. 304/636-5311).

Fairmont

Accommodation: Red Roof Inn, Rte. 1, I-79 at U.S. 250, Exit 132, Box 602, 26554 (tel. 304/366-6800).

Huntington

Accommodation: Red Roof Inn, 5190 U.S. Rte. 60 East, 25705 (tel. 304/733-3737).

Morgantown

Accommodation: Econo Lodge, 15 Commerce St., 26505 (tel. 304/296-8774).

Parkersburg

Accommodations: Red Roof Inn, 3714 East 7th St., 26101 (tel. 304/485-1741).
● Days Inn, I-77 and W. Va. 31, Exit 185, Williamstown, 26187 (tel. 304/375-3730).

Princeton

Accommodations: Econo Lodge, 901 Oakvale Rd., 24740 (tel. 304/487-6161).
● Scottish Inn, 1009 Oakvale Rd., 24740 (tel. 304/425-8116).

Wheeling

Accommodation: YWCA, ♿, 1100 Chapline St., 26003 (tel. 304/232-0511). Women only. $11.50. Weekly rates: $49.10. Advance reservations of one week necessary.

Wisconsin

Wisconsin is an Indian word meaning "gathering of the waters." Over 14,000 lakes gather statewide offering visitors exciting water recreation, fishing, and relaxation year round. Lakes Superior and Michigan bound the state to the northwest and east with the Mississippi River punctuating bluffs and lowlands to the west. The northern half of the state hosts lush forests and dramatic waterfalls contrasting the gently rolling hills and valleys to the south. Wisconsin summers are moderate followed by brilliantly colorful falls, crisp white winters , and lush springs that bring out thousands of acres of cherry and apple blossoms.

The rich prairie land in the southern part of the state attracted settlers in droves in the mid-1800s and eventually large numbers of immigrants—Germans, Poles, and Scandinavians—came to join them.

Some of the things to see in Wisconsin include Apostle Islands National Lakeshore, where Longfellow's Hiawatha lived by the "Shining Big Sea Water" of Lake Superior; Wisconsin Dells, a stretch of the Wisconsin River that has many man-made attractions including a water show and an amusement park.

Since much of Wisconsin's economy depends on pulp and paper products, it would be interesting to pay a visit to the U.S. Forest Products Laboratory in Madison. Operated by the U.S. Forest Service and the University of Wisconsin, the laboratory is always experimenting with ways to use wood and wood products and to conserve the state's resources. Madison is also the home of the University of Wisconsin system, which has campuses in several other cities.

Two other products closely associated with Wisconsin are cheese and beer, so if you have enough time, consider a tour of a cheese plant or a brewery.

Some Special Events: Maifest in Jacksonport (May); International Picnic in Green Bay, and Sawdust City Days in Eau Claire (June); King Richards Renaissance Faire in Kenosha (July); State Fair in Milwaukee's suburb of West Allis (August); U.S. Watermelon Seed-Spitting Championship in Pardeeville (September); Fall Festival in Sister Bay, and Harvest Festival and Grape Stomping Contest in Prairie du Sac (October).

Tourist Information: Wisconsin Division of Tourism, 123 West Washington Ave., P.O. Box 7606, Madison, WI 53707 (tel. 608/266-1018, toll free 800/ESCAPES). Available from the tourist office is *Wisconsin Auto Tour Escapes,* which details 21 routes around the state and includes an "Attractions Guide".

N.B. For additional accommodations, you can order the *Bed and Breakfast Guide* by Carol Jean Buelow for $3 from 458 Glenway St., Madison, WI 53711. A bed-and-breakfast reservation service for Wisconsin is B&B Guest Homes, Rte. 2, Algoma, WI 54201 (tel. 414/743-9742).

Adams

Accommodation: Oakcrest Motel, 324 North Main St., Box 146, 53910 (tel. 608/339-3369). $18 single. Advance reservations of one week necessary during summer.

Appleton

Accommodations: Quality Assured Inn, √, 2000 Holly Rd., P.O. Box 206, 54912 (tel. 414/734-9872). $19.95 single; $24.95 double; $29.95 triple; $34.95 quad. Extra charge for linen. Good recreational facilities; outdoor pool.
- Budgetel Inn, 3920 W. College Ave., 54914 (tel. 414/734-6070).
- Exel Inn, 210 North Westhill St., 54914 (tel. 414/733-5551).
- Super 8 Motel, 3624 West College Ave., 54914 (tel. 414/731-0880).

Ashland

Accommodations: Friendship Ashland Motel, 2300 West Lake Shore Dr., 54806 (tel. 715/682-5503).
- Super 8 Motel, 1610 Front St., P.O. Box 69, 54806 (tel. 715/682-9377).

Beloit

On Campus: You'll meet students and find out about rides and apartments in the Campus Center of Beloit College. If you're hungry while you're in the neighborhood of the campus, try DK's snack bar in the Campus Center, Domenico's for pizza, on the main downtown street (534 East Grand Ave.); Ron's for good diner food; and Danbe's 615, 615 Broad, for sandwiches and full dinners. At night you'll find good company by going to Goody's Bar or The Korner House

Accommodation: Super 8 Motel, 3002 Milwaukee Rd., 53511 (tel. 608/365-8680).

Cable

Accommodation: Ches Perry Youth Hostel (AYH), Box 164, 54821 (tel. 715/798-3367). Open ski season, from Thanksgiving to the end of March. $4.75 for AYH members. Advance reservations necessary April to November. Write to AYH, 3712 North Clark St., Chicago, IL 60613.

Dodgeville

Accommodations: Spring Valley Trails (AYH-SA), ★ 🏷, RR 2, Box 170, 53533 (tel. 608/935-5725). Open year round. $6. Recreational facilities and campground available.
● Folklore Village Farm (AYH), Rte. 3, 53533 (tel. 608/924-3725). $3.50 per night in bunkhouse, summer; $4.50 winter; $7.50 per night in farmhouse. Closed December 25. Advance reservations necessary.

Eau Claire

On Campus: Here is the home of the University of Wisconsin—Eau Claire. If you need anything while you're here, put a notice up in the university union, Davies Center. To meet students, go to any of the places on Water Street like the Old Home Tavern, the Joynt, Shenannigan's. At Old Country Buffet, you can have an all-you-can-eat feast for $5. To find a place to stay, stop at the Lobby Shoppe information desk or the housing office at Towers 112.

For information on campus accommodations, contact the Housing Office (tel. 715/836-3674).

For a tour of the campus, go to the Admissions Office, 115 Schofield, at 11 a.m. or 2 p.m. weekdays, 11 a.m. on Saturday. Chippewa Valley Museum is outstanding for a regional museum. Water Street is an interesting old business section near campus with lots of bars, and Putnam Park is a good place for a hike.

Accommodations: Exel Inn, 2305 Craig Rd., 54701 (tel. 715/834-3193).
● Super 8 Motel, 6260 Texaco Rd., 54703 (tel. 715/874-6868).

Fond du Lac

Accommodations: Motel 6, 738 West Johnson St., 54935 (tel. 414/923-0678).
● Days Inn, 107 North Pioneer Rd., 54935 (tel. 414/923-6790).

Green Bay

"Green Bay is a provincial town, big on bowling and football."

Help: Green Bay Area New Community Clinic, 414/437-9773.
- Crisis Line, 414/432-8832.
Accommodations: YMCA, ♿, 235 North Jefferson St., 54301 (tel. 414/435-5361). Men only. $15 single. Weekly rate: $46 first three weeks. Six blocks from bus station.
- Motel 6, 1614 Shawano Ave., 54303 (tel. 414/494-6730).
- Exel Inn, 2870 Ramada Way, 54304 (tel. 414/499-3599).
- Imperial 400 Motor Inn, 119 North Monroe, 54301 (tel. 414/437-0525).
- Super 8 Motel, 2868 Oneida St., 54304 (tel. 414/494-2042).

Hudson

Accommodation: Super 8 Motel, 808, Exit 2 Dr., 54016 (tel. 715/386-8800).

Janesville

Accommodations: Motel 6, 2422 Fulton St., 53545 (tel. 608/756-1742).
- Super 8 Motel, 3430 Milton Ave., 53545 (tel. 608/756-2040).

Kenosha

Accommodations: Budgetel Inn, 7540 118th Ave., 53142 (tel. 414/857-7911).
- Super 8 Motel, 7601 118th Ave., 53142 (tel. 414/857-7963).

La Crosse

Help: First Call for Help, 608/782-8010.
On Campus: Here is the home of the University of Wisconsin—La Crosse. The town is located on the banks of the Mississippi River and is surrounded by rolling bluffs. Travelers can call University Information, 608/785-8900 or the La Crosse Area Convention and Visitors Bureau, 608/782-2366.
Accommodations: Exel Inn, 2150 Rose St., 54603 (tel. 608/781-0400).
- Bluff View Inn, 3715 Mormon Coulee Rd., 54601 (tel. 608/788-0600). $26 for one; $32 for two in one bed; $39 for two in two beds.
- Hampton Inn, 2110 Rose St., 54603 (tel. 608/781-5100).
- Night Saver Inn, 1906 Rose St., 54601 (tel. 608/781-0200). $26.50 for one; $33.75 double.
- Super 8 Motel, 1625 Rose St., 54603 (tel. 608/781-8880).

Madison

"A big small town with lovely scenery and lakes; lots of activities both in and out of doors for all ages."

Help: Dane County Mental Health/Crisis Intervention, 608/251-2341 or 251-2345.

● Madison Community Health Center, 1133 Williamson St., 53703 (tel. 608/255-0704). Provides low-cost health care.

● Women's Transit Authority, 608/263-1700. Evening transport service, 8 p.m. to 2 a.m.

On Campus: A friend at the University of Wisconsin in Madison (the largest U. of W.) gave us five telephone numbers for travelers to use if they need advice or help: Wisconsin Union Main Desk, 608/262-1331; Campus Assistance Center, 608/263-2400; Counseling Center, 608/262-1744; Visitors Information Booth, 608/262-3318; and the Union Travel Center, second floor, Memorial Building, 608/262-6200. To meet students, have an inexpensive meal, check the ride boards, stop at the Memorial Union to taste Babcock's ice cream, 800 Langdon St., or Union South, corner of Randall Avenue and Johnson Street. According to one Madisonian, his city is "a great place to visit or go to school. It welcomes young people and student travelers."

Some good places in Madison for an inexpensive, filling meal are Shanghai Minnie's, 608 University Ave.; Husnu's, 547 State; Amy's Cafe, 414 West Gilman, for veggie sandwiches; and Lakefront Cafeteria, 800 Lanedon St., for good cafeteria fare.

What to do in Madison? Visit the State Capitol, visit the university, bike or hike through the arboretum, walk down State Street and see the State Street Mall. In spring, summer, and fall, visit the Saturday Farmer's Market on Capitol Square.

For up-to-date information on many entertainment events, pick up an *Isthmus* newspaper at any State Street store. It comes out every Thursday.

Accommodations: University YMCA (AYH-SA), 306 North Brooks St., 53715 (tel. 608/257-2534). AYH space available May 15 to August 15 only. Weekly and monthly rentals available all year. Men and women; no small children. Near bus station and recreational facilities. $8 for AYH members. Located on the University of Wisconsin, Madison campus.

● Friendship Aloha Inn, 3177 East Washington Ave., 53704 (tel. 608/249-7667).

● Red Roof Inn, 4830 Hayes Rd., 53704 (tel. 608/241-1787).

● Exel Inn, 4202 East Towne Blvd., 53704 (tel. 608/241-3861).

● Motel 6, 6402 East Broadway, 53704 (tel. 608/221-0415).

● Regal 8 Inn, 1754 Thierer Rd., 53704 (tel. 608/241-8101).

Manitowoc

Accommodations: Budgetel Inn, 908 Washington St., 54220 (tel. 414/682-8271).

● Days Inn, 4004 Calumet Ave., 54220 (tel 414/684-7841).

Marinette

Accommodation: Super 8 Motel, 1508 Marinette Ave., 54143 (tel 715/735-7887)

Marshfield

Accommodation: Friendship Motel Downtown, 750 South Central Ave., 54449 (tel. 715/387-1111).

Milwaukee

Tourist Information: Greater Milwaukee Convention and Visitors Bureau, Inc., 756 North Milwaukee St., 53202 (tel. 414/273-3950).

Help: Advocates/Travelers Aid, 3517 West Burleigh St., 53210 (tel. 414/873-1521).

On Campus: The University of Wisconsin has a campus in Milwaukee, located a few blocks from Lake Michigan. The UWM Student Union on Kenwood Blvd. has a bulletin board where apartments, rides, etc., are listed. For a good and inexpensive meal in the area, you could try Kalt's on Oakland Avenue (restaurant and bar); or William Ho's, on North Oakland Avenue (for Chinese food). Some good places to meet students are the Union Snack Bar, Gasthaus, and Brubaker's.

Accommodations: Budgetel Inn, 20391 W. Bluemound Rd., 53186 (tel. 414/782-9100).
- Motel 6, 5037 South Howell Ave., 53207 (tel. 414/482-4414).
- Exel Inn, 5485 North Port Washington Rd., 53217 (tel. 414/961-7272).
- Exel Inn, 1201 West College Ave., 53221 (tel. 414/764-1776).
- Exel Inn, 115 North Mayfair Rd., Wauwatosa, 53226 (tel. 414/257-0140).
- Red Roof Inn, 6360 South 13th St., Oak Creek, 53154 (tel. 414/764-3500).
- Super 8 Motel, N. 96 W. 17490 County Line Rd., Germantown, 53022 (tel. 414/255-0880).

Oshkosh

Accommodations: Budgetel Inn, 1950 Omro Rd., 54901 (tel. 414/233-4190).
- Motel 6, 1015 South Washburn St., 54901 (tel. 414/235-0265).

Rice Lake

Accommodation: Red Carpet Inn, 2401 S. Main, 54868 (tel. 715/234-6956).

Sheboygan

Accommodations: Budgetel Inn, 2932 Kohler Memorial Dr , 53081 (tel 414/457-2321).
- Super 8 Motel, 3402 Wilgus Rd., 53081 (tel. 414/458-8080).

Stevens Point

Accommodation: Super 8 Motel, 247 N Division St., 54481 (tel 715/341-8888)

Superior

Accommodation: Super 8 Motel, 4901 E. 2nd, 54880 (tel. 715/398-7686).

Tomah

Accommodations: Budget Host—Daybreak Motel, Hwy. 12 and 16 East, 54660 (tel. 608/372-5946).
- Super 8 Motel, I-94 and Hwy. 21, Exit 143, P.O. Box 48, 54660 (tel. 608/372-3901).

Turtle Lake

Accommodation: Sugarbush Lodge, Rte. 2, 54889 (tel. 715/986-2484). $10 per person; $50 per person weekly rate. Lodge is on a 950-acre recreational and educational center with hiking, canoeing, and skiing. "An excellent place for peace and quiet." Advance reservations necessary December 1 to March 15. Bring own blankets, sleeping bags, etc.

Wausau

Accommodations: Budgetel Inn, 1910 Stewart Ave., 54401 (tel. 715/842-0421).
- Exel Inn, 116 South 17th Ave., 54401 (tel. 715/842-0641).

Wisconsin Dells

Accommodation: Super 8 Motel, Hwy. 13 and I-90-94, P.O. Box 467, 53965 (tel. 608/254-6464).

Wisconsin Rapids

Accommodation: Super 8 Motel, 3410 8th St. South, 54494 (tel. 715/423-8080).

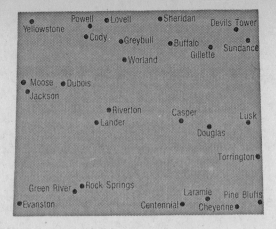

Wyoming

Wyoming is blessed with a great number of tourist attractions and just about all of them are natural. Yellowstone National Park, our oldest national park with over two million acres, was set aside in 1872 and is preserved to this day in all its beauty. The geyser Old Faithful still spouts. And now 300 miles of paved roads connect the park's various features and its campsites. And then there's Grand Teton National Park—another beautiful place to fish, hike, or camp. Wyoming can also claim two national monuments—Devil's Tower (the oldest, designated by Teddy Roosevelt) and Fossil Butte. There are seven national forests in Wyoming, including Shoshone—the nation's first. Two regions are designated national recreation areas—Big Horn Canyon and Flaming Gorge. And there are historic spots to visit all along the Oregon Trail, the first road west, which crosses Wyoming from Fort Laramie to Fort Bridger. It seems to be no exaggeration for Wyoming to claim the title of the "First State in Outdoor America." Stay in a dude ranch or lodge, hike or horseback ride into the mountain, raft a stretch of world-class white water, share the pioneer heritage of this scenic state at one on the many summer rodeos.

The Wyoming Travel Commission (address below) offers a variety of travel publications including *Self-Guided Tours,* a series of four brochures giving drive-yourself itineraries; *Vacation Guide, Find Yourself in Wyoming, Wyoming Travel Tips,* and *Family Water Sports.* All are free.

Some Special Events: Wyoming State Winter Fair in Lander (January); Winter Festival in Pinedale (February); Old Time Fiddle Contest in Shoshone (May); Woodchoppers Jamboree in Encampment, and Shoshone Indian Days, Pow Wow and Rodeo in Fort Washakie (June); Jubilee Days Rodeo in Laramie, and Frontier Days in Cheyenne, the world's largest outdoor rodeo that lasts for nine days (July); Gift of the Waters Pageant (commemorating the deeding of the hot springs from the Shoshone Indians to the people of Wyoming) in Thermopolis (August).

Tourist Information: Wyoming Travel Commission, I-25 at College Drive, Cheyenne, WY 82002 (tel. 307/777-7777 or toll free 800/225-5996).

N.B. A bed-and-breakfast reservation service for Wyoming is B&B Rocky Mountains, P.O. Box 804, Colorado Springs, CO 80901 (tel. 303/630-3433).

Buffalo

Accommodations: Budget Host—Wyoming Motel, Clearmont Rte. (Box 11), 82834 (tel. 307/684-5505).
● Friendship Z-Bar Motel, 626 Fort St., 82834 (tel. 307/684-5535).
● Super 8 Motel, Clearmont Rte., Box 10, 82834 (tel. 307/684-2531).

Casper

Accommodations: Motel 6, 1150 Wilkins Circle, 82601 (tel. 307/234-3903).
● Days Inn, 400 Frontier Ave., 82061 (tel. 307/235-6668).
● Imperial 400 Motor Inn, 440 East "A" St., 82601 (tel. 307/234-3501).
● Super 8 Motel, 3838 CY Ave., 82604 (tel. 307/266-3480).

Centennial

Accommodation: Budget Host—The Old Corral Motor Hotel, Hwy. 130 (Box 217), 82055 (tel. 307/745-5918).

Cheyenne

Accommodations: Motel 6, 1735 Westland Rd., 82001 (tel. 307/635-6806).
● Budget Host—Home Ranch Motel, 2414 East Lincolnway, 82001 (tel. 307/634-3575).
● Friendship Fleetwood Motel, 3800 East Lincolnway, 82001 (tel. 307/638-8908).
● Super 8 Motel, 1900 W. Lincolnway, 82001 (tel. 307/635-8741).

Cody

Cody is far more than the last town before the scenic 50-plus-mile drive to the east entrance of Yellowstone National Park. It has many attractions of its own, including fine museums, frequent special events, and sports opportunities from riding to rafting. Cody is full of history of the American West—the countryside, and even some buildings in town, remain much the same as they were when the trappers and Indians were its only inhabitants. Nearby Shoshone National Forest, where the national ecological movement originated, offers opportunities for camping in its ten campgrounds. Campgrounds are available right in Cody, too.

"I urge you to stop and take a look. Consider staying at a ranch for a few days. You'll come away with an unforgettable experience of the west, still much the way it was 100 years ago."

Tourist Information: Cody Country Chamber of Commerce, 836 Sheridan Ave., P.O. Box 2777, 82414 (tel. 307/587-2297).

Accommodations: 7K's Motel and RV Park, 232 West Yellowstone Ave., 82414 (tel. 307/587-2532 or 587-5890). Open May through October. $24 single; $28 double; $42 quad. Advance reservations of ten days necessary in July and August.

● The Lockhart Bed and Breakfast Inn and Motel, 109 W. Yellowstone, 82414 (tel. 307/587-6074). $35 to $65 per room at the B&B Inn; $20 to $40 per room at the motel (no breakfast).

● Budget Host—High Country Motor Inn, 405 Yellowstone Ave., 82414 (tel. 307/587-5960).

● Super 8 Motel, 730 Yellowstone Rd., 82414 (tel. 307/527-6214).

● Trail Inn, 2750 Northfork Hwy. (tel. 307/587-3741). $28.50 to $52 per night.

● Wise Choice Inn, 2901 Northfork Rd. (tel. 307/587-5004). $27 to $50 per night.

Devils Tower

Camping: Devils Tower National Monument, 82714 (tel. 307/467-5370). Campground at Belle Fourche River open May through September. $6 per campsite.

Douglas

Accommodations: Akers Acres, Range Rider Reservations, 951 Missouri Valley Rd., 82633 (tel. 307/856-3064). Twelve miles from Douglas. $25 single; $35 double; $15 for children under 12. Breakfast included.

● Super 8 Motel, 314 Russell Ave., 82633 (tel. 307/358-6800).

Dubois

Accommodations: Branding Iron Motel, Ⓢ √ ★, 401 West Ramshorn, 82513 (tel. 307/455-2893, or toll free 800/341-8000). $22 to $25 single; $25 to $29 double; $31 triple; $33 quad. Lower rates apply in winter.

● Budget Host—Black Bear Country Inn, 505 West Ramshorn, P.O. Box 595, 82513 (tel. 307/455-2344 or 455-2626).

Evanston

Accommodations: Friendship Classic Lodge, 202 Hwy. 30 East, 82930 (tel. 307/789-6830).

● Super 8 Motel, 70 Hwy. 30 East, 82930 (tel. 307/789-7510).

Gillette

Accommodations: Econo Lodge, 910 E. Box Elder Rd., 82716 (tel. 307/682-3999).

● Super 8 Motel, 208 S. Decker Court, 82716 (tel. 307/682-8078).

Green River

Accommodation: Super 8 Motel, 280 W. Flaming Gorge, 82935 (tel. 307/875-9330).

Greybull

Accommodation: Antler Motel, 1116 North 6th, 82426 (tel. 307/765-4404). $25 for one or two in one bed; $30 to $35 for two in two beds.

Jackson

Accommodations: Motel 6, 1370 West Broadway, 83001 (tel. 307/733-1620).
● Super 8 Motel, 1520 S. Hwy. 89, 83001 (tel. 307/733-6833).

Lander

Accommodation: Silver Spur Motel, Ⓢ √ ★, 340 North 10th, 82520 (tel. 307/332-5189). $24 for one; $28 double; $34 triple; $38 quad. Advance reservations suggested during summer months.

Laramie

"This is a small town with a friendly atmosphere; close to mountain ranges and good skiing."

On Campus: The University of Wyoming is in Laramie. In the Student Union, you'll find a ride board and in the campus paper, *The Branding Iron,* you'll find out what's happening on campus.
Accommodations: Motel 6, 621 Plaza Lane, 82070 (tel. 307/742-2307).
● Budget Host—Camelot Motel, 523 Adams, 82070 (tel. 307/721-8860).
● Super 8 Motel, I-80 at Curtis Street Exit, P.O. Box 1284, 82070 (tel. 307/745-8901).

Lovell

Accommodation: Super 8 Motel, 595 E. Main, 82431 (tel. 307/548-2725).

Lusk

Accommodation: Budget Host—Trail Motel, 305 W. 8th St., Box 1087, 82225 (tel. 307/334-2530).

Moose

Camping: Grand Teton National Park, P.O. Drawer 170, 83012 (tel. 307/

733-2880). Five campgrounds. Open May to mid-October. $7 per campsite per night.

● John D. Rockefeller, Jr., Memorial Parkway, c/o Grand Teton National Park, P.O. Drawer 170, 83012 (tel. 307/733-2880). Open mid-June to September. $7 per campsite per night.

Pine Bluffs

Accommodation: Friendship Travelyn Motel, I-80 at 7th Street, 515 W. 7th St., 82082 (tel. 307/245-3226).

Powell

Accommodation: Super 8 Motel, 845 E. Coulter, 82435 (tel. 307/754-7231).

Riverton

Accommodations: Cottonwood Ranch, 951 Missouri Valley Rd., 82501 (tel. 307/856-3064). $20 single; $25 to $30 double; $40 triple or quad. Breakfast included.

● Super 8 Motel, 1040 N. Federal, 82501 (tel. 307/856-8108).

Rock Springs

Accommodations: Motel 6, 2615 Commercial Way, 82901 (tel. 307/362-1850).

● Budget Host—Springs Motel, 1525 9th St., Box 1596, 82901 (tel. 307/362-6683).

Sheridan

Accommodation: Super 8 Motel, 2435 N. Main St., 82801 (tel. 307/672-9725).

Sundance

Accommodation: Budget Host—Arrowhead Motel, Box 191, 214 Cleveland, 82729 (tel. 307/283-3307).

Torrington

Accommodation: Super 8 Motel, 1548 S. Main, 82240 (tel. 307/532-7118).

Worland

Accommodation: Super 8 Motel, 2500 Big Horn Ave., 82401 (tel. 307/347-9236).

Yellowstone

Accommodations: TW Recreational Services, Inc., 82190 (tel. 307/344-7311). There are cabins operated by TW Services throughout the park that are reasonably priced. TW Services handles general reservations for all accommodations in Yellowstone Park.

● Lake Yellowstone, open mid-June to late September. Cabins: $43 to $55 with bath for one or two; $5 for each additional person. Children under 11 stay free.

● Old Faithful Inn, open May 6 to October 14. See above listing for rates.

● Old Faithful Snow Lodge and Cabins, open May to November and mid-December to mid-March. See Lake Yellowstone listing for rates. Hotel rooms and cabins without baths available.

● Mammoth Hot Springs Hotel and Cabins, open late May to mid-September; and mid-December to mid-March. See above listing for rates.

● Reservations at all of the above are highly recommended. Write to TW Recreational Services or call the above number for a detailed brochure.

Camping: Yellowstone National Park, 🔩, 82190 (tel. 307/344-7381). Twelve campgrounds open May or June through September or October, except Mammoth Campground which is open year round. Bridge Bay, three miles south of Lake Village, and Grant Village, two miles south of West Thumb Junction, are the largest with over 400 sites each. $5 or $6 per campsite per night.

NOW!
ARTHUR FROMMER LAUNCHES HIS SECOND TRAVEL REVOLUTION with

The New World of Travel

The hottest news and latest trends in travel today—heretofore the closely guarded secrets of the travel trade—are revealed in this new sourcebook by the dean of American travel. Here, collected in one book that is updated every year, are the most exciting, challenging, and money-saving ideas in travel today.

You'll find out about hundreds of alternative new modes of travel—and the many organizations that sponsor them—that will lead you to vacations that cater to your mind, your spirit, and your sense of thrift.

Learn how to fly for free as an air courier; travel for free as a tour escort; live for free on a hospitality exchange; add earnings as a part-time travel agent; pay less for air tickets, cruises, and hotels; enhance your life through cooperative camping, political tours, and adventure trips; change your life at utopian communities, low-cost spas, and yoga retreats; pursue low-cost studies and language training; travel comfortably while single or over 60; sail on passenger freighters; and vacation in the cheapest places on earth.

And in every yearly edition, Arthur Frommer spotlights the 10 GREAT-EST TRAVEL VALUES for the coming year. 384 pages, large-format with many, many illustrations. All for $12.95!

ORDER NOW
TURN TO THE LAST PAGE OF THIS BOOK FOR ORDER FORM.

NOW, SAVE MONEY ON ALL YOUR TRAVELS!
Join Arthur Frommer's $35-A-Day Travel Club™

Saving money while traveling is never a simple matter, which is why, over 26 years ago, the **$35-A-Day Travel Club** was formed. Actually, the idea came from readers of the Arthur Frommer Publications who felt that such an organization could bring financial benefits, continuing travel information, and a sense of community to economy-minded travelers all over the world.

In keeping with the money-saving concept, the annual membership fee is low—$18 (U.S. residents) or $20 U.S. (Canadian, Mexican, and foreign residents)—and is immediately exceeded by the value of your benefits which include:

(1) The latest edition of any TWO of the books listed on the following pages.

(2) An annual subscription to an 8-page quarterly newspaper *The Wonderful World of Budget Travel* which keeps you up-to-date on fastbreaking developments in low-cost travel in all parts of the world—bringing you the kind of information you'd have to pay over $35 a year to obtain elsewhere. This consumer-conscious publication also includes the following columns:

Hospitality Exchange—members all over the world who are willing to provide hospitality to other members as they pass through their home cities.

Share-a-Trip—requests from members for travel companions who can share costs and help avoid the burdensome single supplement.

Readers Ask ... Readers Reply—travel questions from members to which other members reply with authentic firsthand information.

(3) A copy of *Arthur Frommer's Guide to New York*.

(4) Your personal membership card which entitles you to purchase through the Club all Arthur Frommer Publications for a third to a half off their regular retail prices during the term of your membership.

So why not join this hardy band of international budgeteers NOW and participate in its exchange of information and hospitality? Simply send $18 (U.S. residents) or $20 U.S. (Canadian, Mexican, and other foreign residents) along with your name and address to: $35-A-Day Travel Club, Inc., Gulf + Western Building, One Gulf + Western Plaza, New York, NY 10023. Remember to specify which *two* of the books in section (1) above you wish to receive in your initial package of member's benefits. Or tear out the next page, check off any two of the books listed on either side, and send it to us with your membership fee.

Date_____

FROMMER BOOKS
PRENTICE HALL PRESS
ONE GULF + WESTERN PLAZA
NEW YORK, NY 10023

Friends:

Please send me the books checked below:

FROMMER'S $-A-DAY GUIDES™

(In-depth guides to sightseeing and low-cost tourist accommodations and facilities.)

☐ Europe on $30 a Day $13.95
☐ Australia on $30 a Day $11.95
☐ Eastern Europe on $25 a Day $10.95
☐ England on $40 a Day $11.95
☐ Greece on $30 a Day. $11.95
☐ Hawaii on $50 a Day $11.95
☐ India on $25 a Day $10.95
☐ Ireland on $30 a Day. $10.95
☐ Israel on $30 & $35 a Day $11.95
☐ Mexico (plus Belize & Guatemala)
on $20 a Day. $10.95

☐ New Zealand on $40 a Day $11.95
☐ New York on $50 a Day. $10.95
☐ Scandinavia on $50 a Day. $10.95
☐ Scotland and Wales on $40 a Day. $11.95
☐ South America on $30 a Day $10.95
☐ Spain and Morocco (plus the Canary
Is.) on $40 a Day $10.95
☐ Turkey on $25 a Day $10.95
☐ Washington, D.C., & Historic Va. on
$40 a Day $11.95

FROMMER'S DOLLARWISE GUIDES™

(Guides to sightseeing and tourist accommodations and facilities from budget to deluxe, with emphasis on the medium-priced.)

☐ Alaska $12.95
☐ Austria & Hungary $11.95
☐ Belgium, Holland, Luxembourg $11.95
☐ Egypt. $11.95
☐ England & Scotland $11.95
☐ France $11.95
☐ Germany $12.95
☐ Italy. $11.95
☐ Japan & Hong Kong $13.95
☐ Portugal, Madeira, & the Azores $12.95
☐ South Pacific. $12.95
☐ Switzerland & Liechtenstein $12.95
☐ Bermuda & The Bahamas. $11.95
☐ Canada $12.95
☐ Caribbean $13.95

☐ Cruises (incl. Alaska, Carib, Mex,
Hawaii, Panama, Canada, & US) $12.95
☐ California & Las Vegas $11.95
☐ Florida $11.95
☐ Mid-Atlantic States $12.95
☐ New England. $12.95
☐ New York State $12.95
☐ Northwest $11.95
☐ Skiing in Europe $12.95
☐ Skiing USA—East $11.95
☐ Skiing USA—West $11.95
☐ Southeast & New Orleans. $11.95
☐ Southwest. $11.95
☐ Texas $11.95

FROMMER'S TOURING GUIDES™

(Color illustrated guides that include walking tours, cultural & historic sites, and other vital travel information.)

☐ Egypt. $8.95
☐ Florence $8.95
☐ London $8.95

☐ Paris $8.95
☐ Venice $8.95

TURN PAGE FOR ADDITIONAL BOOKS AND ORDER FORM.

THE ARTHUR FROMMER GUIDES™

(Pocket-size guides to sightseeing and tourist accommodations and facilities in all price ranges.)

☐ Amsterdam/Holland	$5.95	☐ Mexico City/Acapulco	$5.95
☐ Athens	$5.95	☐ Minneapolis/St. Paul	$5.95
☐ Atlantic City/Cape May	$5.95	☐ Montreal/Quebec City	$5.95
☐ Boston	$5.95	☐ New Orleans	$5.95
☐ Cancún/Cozumel/Yucatán	$5.95	☐ New York	$5.95
☐ Dublin/Ireland	$5.95	☐ Orlando/Disney World/EPCOT	$5.95
☐ Hawaii	$5.95	☐ Paris	$5.95
☐ Las Vegas	$5.95	☐ Philadelphia	$5.95
☐ Lisbon/Madrid/Costa del Sol	$5.95	☐ Rome	$5.95
☐ London	$5.95	☐ San Francisco	$5.95
☐ Los Angeles	$5.95	☐ Washington, D.C.	$5.95

SPECIAL EDITIONS

☐ A Shopper's Guide to the Caribbean	$12.95	☐ Motorist's Phrase Book (Fr/Ger/Sp)	$4.95
☐ Bed & Breakfast—N. America	$8.95	☐ Swap and Go (Home Exchanging)	$10.95
☐ Guide to Honeymoon Destinations (US, Canada, Mexico, & Carib)	$12.95	☐ The Candy Apple (NY for Kids)	$11.95
		☐ Travel Diary and Record Book	$5.95
☐ Beat the High Cost of Travel	$6.95	☐ Where to Stay USA (Lodging from $3 to $30 a night)	$10.95
☐ Marilyn Wood's Wonderful Weekends (NY, Conn, Mass, RI, Vt, NH, NJ, Del, Pa)	$11.95		

☐ Arthur Frommer's New World of Travel (Annual sourcebook previewing: new travel trends, new modes of travel, and the latest cost-cutting strategies for savvy travelers) $12.95

SERIOUS SHOPPER'S GUIDES

(Illustrated guides listing hundreds of stores, conveniently organized alphabetically by category.)

☐ Italy	$15.95	☐ Los Angeles	$14.95
☐ London	$15.95	☐ Paris	$15.95

ORDER NOW!

In U.S. include $1.50 shipping UPS for 1st book; 50¢ ea. add'l book. Outside U.S. $2 and 50¢, respectively.

Enclosed is my check or money order for $_____

NAME _____

ADDRESS _____

CITY _____ STATE _____ ZIP _____